Information Technology Law in Italy

Information Technology Law in Italy

Giovanni Ziccardi

This book was originally published as a monograph in the International Encyclopaedia of Laws/Privacy and Technology Law.

Founding Editor: Roger Blanpain
General Editor: Frank Hendrickx
Volume Editors: Jos Dumortier, Pieter Gryffroy, Ruben Roex & Yung Shin Van Der Sype

Wolters Kluwer

Published by:
Kluwer Law International B.V.
PO Box 316
2400 AH Alphen aan den Rijn
The Netherlands
E-mail: lrs-sales@wolterskluwer.com
Website: www.wolterskluwer.com/en/solutions/kluwerlawinternational

Sold and distributed by:
Wolters Kluwer Legal & Regulatory U.S.
920 Links Avenue
Landisville, PA 17538
United States of America
E-mail: customer.service@wolterskluwer.com

ISBN 978-94-035-2879-3

e-Book: ISBN 978-94-035-2889-2
web-PDF: ISBN 978-94-035-2899-1

The Author

Giovanni Ziccardi**,** Full Professor of 'Philosophy of Law', 'Legal Informatics' and 'Smart Cities, Artificial Intelligence and Digital Transformation Law' at the Faculty of Law, University of Milan. Former Jean Monnet Chair on 'European Citizens Data Governance and Cybersecurity'. Director of the *Information Society Law Research Center* (ISLC) of the University of Milan (http://islc.unimi.it) and Founder and Director of the postgraduate courses on 'Computer Crimes and Digital Investigation' and 'Coding for Lawyers, Smart Contracts, Legal Tech and Legal Design' at the University of Milan. Member of the Security and Data Protection Committee and of the Ethical Committee of the University of Milan. Member of the Board of Centrico S.p.A.

Giovanni Ziccardi is a graduate of Modena University and holds a PhD in 'Legal Informatics' from the University of Bologna. Lawyer, he is the Founder and Chairman of the 'Italian Cyberspace Law Conference', one of the most important European Conferences concerning cyberspace law. He is the editor-in-chief of the International Scientific Review 'Ciberspazio e Diritto – Rivista Internazionale di Informatica Giuridica' ('Cyberspace and Law – Legal Informatics International Review'), Mucchi Editore, Modena. Before teaching law at the University of Milan, Professor Ziccardi spent seven years conducting research at the Research Centre of History of Law, Philosophy and Sociology of Law and Computer Science and Law (CIRSFID) at the University of Bologna. The research was developed under the supervision of Professor Enrico Pattaro, Director of the Centre.

He is admitted to practise before the Italian Courts.

This monograph has been reviewed by the Author and is up-to-date as of 30 August 2024. The following authors contributed to the creation and review of this monograph: Arianna Arini, Simone Bonavita, Luigi Cristiano, Giulia Escurolle, Maria Antonella Incardona, Paulina Kowalicka, Maria Grazia Peluso, Pierluigi Perri, Giulia Pesci, Lorenzo Piatti, Desideria Giulia Pollak, Alessandra Salluce, Samanta Stanco, Elisabetta Stringhi, Gabriele Suffia, Angela Zampetti.

The Author

Table of Contents

List of Abbreviations

AGCM	*Autorità Garante dell Concorrenza e del Mercato*
AGCOM	*Autorità per le Garanzie nelle Comunicazioni* (National Regulatory Agency)
AgID	*Agency for Digital Italy*
AIPA	*Autorità per l'Informatica nella Pubblica Amministrazione* (Agency for Information Technology in the Public Administration)
ASSINFORM	The Italian Association of Producers of ICT Technologies and Services
BIOS	Basic Input-Output Software
CART	Computer Analysis and Response Team ccTLD County Code Top-Level Domain
CICR	*Comitato Interministeriale per il Credito ed il Risparmio* (Interministerial Committee for Credit and Savings)
CNIPA	*Centro Nazionale per l'Informatica nella Pubblica Amministrazione* (The National Center for Information Technology in Public Administration)
CNS	*Carta Nazionale dei Servizi* (National Services Card)
CONSIP Spa	*Concessionaria servizi informativi pubblici* (Concessionaire of Public Informational Services)
Corecom	*Comitato Regionale per le Comunicazioni*
CRL	*Lista dei Certificati Revocati*
CSL	*Lista dei Certificati Sospesi*
CVCN	*Center for National Evaluation and Certification*
D.P.R.	Decree of the President of the Republic
DBAN	DataBase of Assigned Names
DESI	Digital Economy and Society Index
DIT	Department of Innovations and Technology
DNS	Domain Name System

List of Abbreviations

DOI® technology	Digital Object Identifier System
DRS	Dispute Resolving Services
DSS	Dynamic Spectrum Sharing
EEC	European Economic Community
eIDAS	Electronic Identification and Trust Services
ENAC	Italian Civil Aviation Authority
EURATOM	European Atomic Energy Community
FTTH	Fibre to the Home
FWA	Fixed Wireless Access
GATT	General Agreement on Tariffs and Trade
ICT	Information and Communication Technologies
IDS	Intrusion Detection Systems
ISP	Internet Service Provider
ISS	Information Society Services
ISTAT	Italian National Institute of Statistics
IT-NIC	Italian Naming Authority
LAR	Letter of Assumption of Responsibility
LEFT	Legal Electronic Forensics Team
MD5	Message Digest 5
mEDRA	Multilingual European DOI Registration Agency
MHP	Multimedia Home Platform
NATO	North Atlantic Treaty Organization
OECD	The Organization for Economic Cooperation and Development
PCS	Public Connectivity System
PGP	Pretty Good Privacy
PNRR	National Recovery and Resilience Plan
PT	Post and Telegraph Administration
RUPA	Unitary Informational Network for the Public Administration
SHA1	Secure Hash Algorithm 1
SIA	*Società Italiana per l'Automazione* (Italian Society for Automatization)
SISDE	The Civilian Intelligence Service
SISMI	The Military Intelligence Service
SMS	Short Message Service
TCP/IP	Transfer Control Protocol/Internet Protocol
TIF	*Testo Unico sull'Intermediazione Finanziaria* (Consolidation on Financial Intermediation)
TRIPS	The Agreement on Trade-Related Aspects of Intellectual Property Rights

TUB	*Testo Unico Bancario* (Consolidation on Banking)
UCB	*Ufficio centrale dei brevetti* (Central Patent Office)
UCC	Universal Copyright Convention
UIC	*Ufficio Italiano Cambi*
UMTS	Universal Mobile Telecommunications System
WCT	WIPO Copyright Treaty
WIPO	Word Intellectual Property Organization
WPPT	WIPO Performances and Phonograms Treaty
WTO	World Trade Organization

List of Abbreviations

Preface

After four editions of this work, which have been constantly updated, it became apparent that there was a need to *completely rewrite* the volume due to various factors that have occurred over the past five years in Italy.

Apart from the pandemic and the economic crisis, which have greatly affected the digital world, never before have both the European Union and national legislators taken the decision to regulate the digital world with increasing frequency as in recent years, especially in the field of cyber and national security, artificial intelligence, cybercrimes, data protection, digital investigations, copyright, digital services and e-commerce, smart contracts and digitalization of the Public Administration.

There are now dozens of regulations already issued, and in the pipeline, and they are destined to grow with increasing frequency as all laws are becoming 'digital-oriented'. Even in Italy, regulatory measures and court rulings have had an incredible peak in recent years, which has led us to completely revise the work you are about to read and include, for the first time, also the most important judge decisions ('case law') related to ICT law.

The work was carried out at the Department of Legal Sciences 'Cesare Beccaria' of the University of Milan, at the Information Society Law Center (ISLC) and was written by Giovanni Ziccardi.

The case law cited in the volume is taken from the Italian legal database 'De Jure', Giuffrè Francis Lefevbre.

The following authors contributed to the creation and the review of this monograph: Arianna Arini, Simone Bonavita, Luigi Cristiano, Giulia Escurolle, Maria Antonella Incardona, Paulina Kowalicka, Maria Grazia Peluso, Pierluigi Perri, Giulia Pesci, Lorenzo Piatti, Desideria Giulia Pollak, Alessandra Salluce, Samanta Stanco, Elisabetta Stringhi, Gabriele Suffia, Angela Zampetti.

Milan, Italy, August 2024

General Introduction

Chapter 1. General Background of the Country

§1. The Geography and Territory of Italy

1. Italy is a state in southern Europe. Its capital is Rome ('Roma'). It borders France to the west, Switzerland and Austria to the north, Slovenia to the east, and San Marino and Vatican City in the centre. Its territory also includes Sardinia and Sicily, two large islands, as well as several smaller islands.[1]

The total surface area of Italy amounts to 302,073 square kilometres and, due to its conformation, the country is characterized by a predominantly hilly territory (41.6% of the total surface area), followed by mountainous (35%) and lowland (23.2%). Many municipalities extend territorially from mountain to hill or from hill to plain, sometimes covering all three altitude zones.

2. The peninsula is washed by the Adriatic Sea to the east, the Ionian Sea to the southeast, the Tyrrhenian Sea to the west and the Ligurian Sea to the northwest. The main mountain ranges are the Alps (*Mont Blanc*, at 4,810 m, is the highest mountain in Europe) and the Apennines, which run the length of the peninsula from Liguria to Sicily. South of the Alps lies the *Po Valley* ('Pianura Padana'), a large alluvial expanse formed by the river Po and its tributaries. There are numerous volcanoes on the peninsula: the most famous are *Vesuvio*, near Naples, and *Etna*, near Catania, which at 3,323 m is the highest volcano in Europe.[2]

3. The independent countries of San Marino and Vatican City are enclaves within Italian territory. The State of Vatican City was born with the *Lateran Treaty*, concluded between the Holy See and Italy on 11 February 1929 and ratified on 7 June 1929. Its personality as a sovereign body of public international law, distinct from the Holy See, is universally recognized.

1. For a first illustration of the conformation of the Italian territory, *see* https://www.turismo.it/italia/scheda/italia/territorio/.
2. *See*, again, https://www.turismo.it/italia/scheda/italia/territorio/.

§2. The Population

4. ISTAT, the *Italian National Statistics Institute*, is considered an official and authoritative source for all data concerning Italy and its citizens.[3] Every year, it publishes several reports that help to draw a picture as accurate as possible of many aspects of the Italian State. The data below are taken from the most recent studies made public by ISTAT, and available on its website.[4]

In 2023, according to ISTAT, there were 58,851,000 citizens resident in Italy. This is 179,000 fewer than at the beginning of the previous year.

The ISTAT Report of 2023[5] describes a demographic situation characterized by a *progressive decline* in births that, for the first time since the unification of Italy, in 2022 fell below 400,000 units, against 713,000 deaths. Births decreased by 1.1% compared to 2021 and the fertility rate in 2022 marked a return to 2020 levels, with an average of 1.24 children per woman, remaining below the pre-COVID-19 period (in 2019 the fertility rate was 1.27).

5. Today, life expectancy at birth is 80.5 years for men and 84.8 for women. The over-65 year olds account for almost a quarter of the total population. Residents between 15 and 64 years of age drop to 63.4% and children and young people up to 14 years of age to 12.5%.

On 1 January 2023, the number of over 100-year-olds reached an all-time high with 22,000 people, more than 2,000 more than the previous year. Eighty per cent of the very old are women. The prediction is that in 2041 the number of over-80 year olds will exceed 6 million and the number of over-90 year olds will be around 1.4 million.

This is a demographic situation that, according to ISTAT, puts the sustainability of the country's system at risk.

6. Between 2004 and 2022, the employment rate among 15–34-year-olds decreased by 8.6% and now stands at 43.7%. For those aged 50–64, on the other hand, it increased by 19.2%. Skilled employment is growing slowly compared to the European average and now accounts for only 36% of the total against 47% in Germany and 49% in France. In Europe, Italy ranks second only to Bulgaria for the high average age of the employed.

§3. The Current Political Situation

7. In the general political elections of 2022, the lowest turnout ever was recorded: not even 64% of the eligible voters went to the polls. For the first time, the law on the reduction of the number of Members of Parliament, confirmed by the

---

3. To consult the part of the ISTAT website containing its main studies *see* https://www.istat.it/it/archivio/137001#.
4. *See*, again, https://www.istat.it.
5. *See*, again, https://www.istat.it.

constitutional referendum of 2020, was used (reducing elected Deputies from 630 to 400 and elected Senators from 315 to 200).

The centre-right coalition won with about 44% of the votes, having an absolute majority in Parliament. *Fratelli d'Italia* established itself as the first party with about 26% of the votes. The centre-left coalition, including the *Democratic Party*, obtained a total of around 26% of the votes, with the *Democratic Party* itself receiving around 19%.

On 21 October 2022, President of the Republic Sergio Mattarella entrusted *Fratelli d'Italia* President Giorgia Meloni with the task of forming a new government, which she accepted.

Meloni took office as prime minister the following day, becoming the first woman to hold this position in the history of the Republic.

§4. The Ancient Age

8. The history of Italy is characterized by a strong fluctuation: in some periods, Italy was one of the great centres of political, cultural, and civil development of the planet, and in others one of the peripheries. The high points are to be found in the Greek[6] and Roman Ages,[7] when Italy, first Republican and then Imperial (3rd century B.C.–4th century A.D.) was the greatest power in the Western world, and in the *Renaissance* (15th–16th centuries), when the country, although divided into regional states incapable of preserving their political independence, was the seat of a splendid civilization. Italy recovered its political unity – lost in 476 A.D. following the collapse of the Western Roman Empire – only in 1860–1861, with the formation of the National State following the *Risorgimento.*[8]

9. Italy took on its own physiognomy in the *Bronze Age* when defined regional structures with common cultural traits emerged between the 12th and 10th centuries

6. For a complete overview of the Greeks influence in Italy *see*, *generally*, D. Musti, 'Storia Greca. Linee di sviluppo dall'età micenea all'età romana' (Laterza, Roma-Bari, 1989); C. Bearzot, 'Manuale di storia greca' (Il Mulino, Bologna, 2005); M. Corsaro, L. Gallo, 'Storia greca' (Le Monnier, Firenze, 2010). For an overview of the political aspects of the institutions of ancient Greece, and their influences on Italian primitive forms of government (especially: democracy) *see*, *generally*, P. Cartledge, 'Il pensiero politico in pratica. Grecia antica (secoli VII a.C.–II d.C.)' (Carocci Editore, Firenze, 2011); S. Gastaldi, 'Introduzione alla storia del pensiero politico antico' (Laterza, Roma–Bari, 2008); D. Musti, 'Demokratìa. Origini di un'idea' (Laterza, Roma–Bari, 1995).
7. For an overview of the Roman mythology concerning the Rome foundation, *see* T. Mommsen, 'Storia di Roma dalle origini alla Repubblica' (Gherardo Casini Editore, Roma, 2001). For an overview of old Roman history, *see* P. Brown, 'Il mondo tardoantico da Marco Aurelio a Maometto' (Einaudi, Torino, 1974); G. Geraci, A. Marcone, 'Storia romana' (Le Monnier, Firenze, 2011); H. H. Scullard, 'Storia del mondo romano' (BUR, Milano, 1992); G. Giannelli, 'Trattato di storia romana' (Patron, Bologna, 1975); S. Mazzarino, 'L'impero romano' (Laterza, Bari-Roma, 1986). For an overview of economics, political and religious aspects of ancient Rome *see*, *generally*, C. Nicolet, 'Strutture dell'Italia romana (Jouvence, Roma, 1984); F. Jacques, J. Scheid, 'Roma e il suo impero. Istituzioni, economia, religione' (Laterza, Bari–Roma, 2008); F. Rohr Vio, 'Le voci del dissenso. Ottaviano Augusto e i suoi oppositori' (Il Poligrafo, Padova, 2000).
8. *See* M. Salvadori 'Italia, storia di', Enciclopedia dei ragazzi Treccani (2005), https://www.treccani.it/enciclopedia/storia-di-italia_%28Enciclopedia-dei-ragazzi%29/.

B.C. In the 9th century, at the height of the *Iron Age*, the Villanovan culture developed, which saw the establishment of urban centres differentiated from the countryside. About a century later, the *Etruscan* civilization began, which spread from central Italy to Campania, and had its heyday between the 7th and 6th centuries. In the 5th–4th centuries, Celtic tribes of Gallic origin settled in the Po Valley. From the 8th century onwards, colonies began to be established in Sicily and other parts of southern Italy by the Greeks, who brought their great culture there. [9]

10. Founded in 754 or 753, between the 4th and 3rd centuries, Rome, having established its hegemony over peninsular Italy, ascended to the role of *dominant power* in the Western world, definitively consolidated by the conquests of Marius, Sulla, Pompeus, and Caesar in the 1st century B.C. At this time, the republican institutions gradually entered a crisis, opening the door to the advent of the empire by Octavian Augustus (27 B.C.–14 A.D.). Italy held its supremacy for about three centuries until Constantine around 330 A.D. moved the capital to Constantinople. The decline of Italy created the conditions for barbarian invasions in the 5th century. Rome was conquered several times, and in 476 the king of the Heruli, Odoacer, deposed Romulus Augustulus, the last Western Roman emperor. [10]

§5. The Middle Age

11. In the Middle Ages, between the end of the Roman Empire and the beginning of the Modern Age, Italy first experienced a long period of domination by the *Barbarians* on the one hand and the *Byzantines* on the other, and a profound retreat of city life, cultural impoverishment, demographic and economic regression; then, from the 11th century onwards, a process of strong recovery began, which in the Centre-North saw the free communes (communes, civilization) as protagonists.

In the Middle Ages, a powerful factor for cultural and religious unity was the *Church*. After Italy fell into the hands of the Barbarians, a decisive imprint was left by the Ostrogoth king Theodoric (489–526), who, by initiating the Roman-Barbarian kingdoms, entrusted political and military power to the rulers and administrative functions to the Italics. The intention of the Byzantines (the Eastern Romans) to reconquer Italy during a long and devastating war (535–553) had the effect of bringing about the end of the political unity of the peninsula, divided into a part subject to the Barbarians and another dominated by Byzantium. [11]

12. In 569, the Goths were succeeded by the Lombards, who settled in northern Italy and chose Pavia as their capital. Major events took place during the Longobard domination. On the one hand, the establishment of *Venice* as a politically autonomous centre, which arose because of populations fleeing the new invaders

9. *See* M. Salvadori 'Italia, storia di', Enciclopedia dei ragazzi Treccani (2005), https://www.treccani.it/enciclopedia/storia-di-italia_%28Enciclopedia-dei-ragazzi%29/.
10. *See* M. Salvadori 'Italia, storia di', Enciclopedia dei ragazzi Treccani (2005), https://www.treccani.it/enciclopedia/storia-di-italia_%28Enciclopedia-dei-ragazzi%29/.
11. *See* M. Salvadori 'Italia, storia di', Enciclopedia dei ragazzi Treccani (2005), https://www.treccani.it/enciclopedia/storia-di-italia_%28Enciclopedia-dei-ragazzi%29/.

and entrusting themselves in the second half of the 8th century to the rule of their own doges. On the other, the formation of the first nucleus of what was to become the *Church State*, following the donation of Sutri to the Pope by King Liutprand in 728. Lombard domination was ended in 774 by the Frankish king Charlemagne, who, having himself crowned *Emperor of the Holy Roman Empire* in 800, incorporated into it the territories that had been Lombard, except for Italy subject to the Byzantines and Sicily, which was conquered in 827 by the Arabs. [12]

13. In the course of the 10th century the break-up of the Holy Roman Empire led to the emergence of multiple centres of power in the hands of feudal lords, some of them very powerful, who were finally brought under Germanic sovereignty by Otto I, in 962 crowned emperor of the new *Germanic Holy Roman Empire* by Pope John XII. A drastic change in the physiognomy of Italy was brought about in the 11th century by the rise in the north-central part of the Communes – the reborn cities that formed themselves into de facto autonomous centres of power – and by the rule of the Normans in southern Italy, who put an end to the power of the Byzantines and the Arabs.[13]

14. The late Middle Ages witnessed a vigorous cultural and socio-economic revival: there was a sharp increase in manufacturing production, the cities repopulated, and the countryside saw a strong revival of cultivation. The dynamic element of this renewal was first and foremost the communes. The German emperors' intention to crush their autonomy failed when Frederick Barbarossa was defeated in 1176 by the *Lombard League* at Legnano. Southern Italy also experienced a phase of great revival in the first half of the 13th century during the reign of Frederick II of Swabia; but the kingdom was lost by his son Manfred, who had to cede it in 1266 to the Angevins, who however lost Sicily, which passed to the Aragonese in 1302.[14]

15. The Middle Ages slowly moved into a new epoch between the last decades of the 13th century and the 14th because of increasing social development and the crisis of the municipal civilization, which saw the free communes cede to the power of seignories that took control and which in the 15th century gave rise to principalities. Great in the 13th and 14th centuries was the political and commercial influence of the *Maritime Republics* of Genoa, Pisa, Venice, and Amalfi, which clashed in a struggle for supremacy that finally ended in favour of Venice. In the Middle Ages, the consequences of the conflicts, which became bitter at times, between the papacy, which asserted its right to legitimize political power, and the empire and later the new national monarchies, which were increasingly firm in claiming their autonomy, which was increasingly affirmed over time, were profound in Italy as well.[15]

---

12. *See* M. Salvadori 'Italia, storia di', Enciclopedia dei ragazzi Treccani (2005), https://www.treccani.it/enciclopedia/storia-di-italia_%28Enciclopedia-dei-ragazzi%29/.
13. *See* M. Salvadori 'Italia, storia di', Enciclopedia dei ragazzi Treccani (2005), https://www.treccani.it/enciclopedia/storia-di-italia_%28Enciclopedia-dei-ragazzi%29/.
14. *See* M. Salvadori 'Italia, storia di', Enciclopedia dei ragazzi Treccani (2005), https://www.treccani.it/enciclopedia/storia-di-italia_%28Enciclopedia-dei-ragazzi%29/.
15. *See* M. Salvadori 'Italia, storia di', Enciclopedia dei ragazzi Treccani (2005), https://www.treccani.it/enciclopedia/storia-di-italia_%28Enciclopedia-dei-ragazzi%29/.

16. In the 15th century, a system of regional states was consolidated, the largest of which were Venice, Milan (with the Visconti and Sforza families) Florence, (with the Medici) the Papal States and Naples. In the 15th century, thanks to considerable economic development and the blossoming of Renaissance culture, Italy became in many ways the *major centre* of European civilization, but it showed a very serious political and military weakness in the face of the expansionism of the great national monarchies of France and Spain.[16]

17. Between 1494 and 1559, Italy was a battleground between the French and the Spanish, with the regional States having no other destiny than to side with one or the other. Finally, peace was reached in 1559 with the *Treaty of Cateau-Cambrésis* and the establishment of Spanish rule from Milan to Sicily, while the French maintained strong positions in Piedmont. Only Venice preserved its independence. The dominance of Catholic Spain provided decisive support for the Catholic Church in its efforts to prevent the Reformation from penetrating Italy, whose influence was reduced to marginal niches. Thus Italy, the seat of the papacy, was able to erect itself as a bastion of the Counter-Reformation.[17]

18. The triumphant Counter-Reformation spirit, hostile to all forms of intellectual and religious freedom, led in the second half of the 16th century and in the 17th century to a growing cultural decadence, despite peaks of excellence such as that represented by *Galileo Galilei*. At the same time, the relative loss of importance of Mediterranean trade currents following the effects of the discovery of *America* (1492) marked the beginning of a negative economic cycle, which expressed itself in the contraction of industrial activities and the expansion of agricultural activities. Particularly pronounced was the decline in Southern Italy, where very backwards agrarian structures became established.[18]

19. After a series of great European wars at the turn of the 17th and 18th centuries, in which Louis XIV's France was the protagonist, in 1714 with the Peace of Rastatt Austria replaced Spain as the hegemonic power on the Peninsula. A significant event was the erection of the Duchy of Savoy as a Kingdom. Another important turning point was the Treaty of Aachen in 1748, which sanctioned the transfer of the Kingdom of Naples to the Bourbons of Spain.[19]

---

16. *See* M. Salvadori 'Italia, storia di', Enciclopedia dei ragazzi Treccani (2005), https://www.treccani.it/enciclopedia/storia-di-italia_%28Enciclopedia-dei-ragazzi%29/.
17. For an overview of the modern history of Italy, *see* C. Capra, 'Storia moderna (1492-1848) (Le Monnier, Firenze, 2004); P. Prodi, 'Introduzione allo studio della storia moderna' (Il Mulino, Bologna, 2005).
18. *See* M. Salvadori 'Italia, storia di', Enciclopedia dei ragazzi Treccani (2005), https://www.treccani.it/enciclopedia/storia-di-italia_%28Enciclopedia-dei-ragazzi%29/.
19. *See* M. Salvadori 'Italia, storia di', Enciclopedia dei ragazzi Treccani (2005), https://www.treccani.it/enciclopedia/storia-di-italia_%28Enciclopedia-dei-ragazzi%29/.

§6. The Enlightenment Culture

20. The 18th century was the century in which the *Enlightenment* culture, which appealed to the enlightenment of *reason* as a guide to human action, and that of the enlightened sovereigns, intended to promote a course of reform, developed in Europe. Although in a secondary position compared to the great European states, Italy participated in both innovative currents. The Italian *Enlightenment*, with personalities such as *Cesare Beccaria*, had its major centres in Milan and Naples, and political reformism in the Lombardy of Maria Theresa and Joseph II, in the Tuscany of Peter Leopold and in the Kingdom of Naples of Charles VII and Ferdinand IV.[20]

21. The *French Revolution* also deeply affected Italy, which, devastated by Napoleon's conquests that began in 1796, became firmly part of the French Empire during his reign. During the Napoleonic period, the country underwent significant economic and social reforms, and the seeds of a nascent *national sentiment* were sown. After the collapse of the Napoleonic Empire, the age of *Restoration* began, in effect only partially due to the impossibility of cancelling many of the reforms introduced: as a consequence of the decisions of the Congress of Vienna (1814–1815) the old regimes ousted by the French were restored and power returned to the previous dynasties within the framework of a renewed hegemony of Austria, which directly incorporated Lombardy-Veneto. The only Italian state that retained relative autonomy was the Kingdom of Sardinia, which returned to the Savoy.[21]

§7. The Advent of the Kingdom of Italy

22. Between the Restoration and 1860, Italy experienced the political and civil renewal movement – whose origins can be traced back to the period of French domination – known as the *Risorgimento*, which culminated in the formation of the unitary state. Italian unity was mainly the result of the initiative of Savoy's Piedmont, which initially aspired to establish a kingdom in Upper Italy, and the most prominent representative of the democratic movement was Giuseppe Mazzini, who aimed to establish a united and republican Italy.[22] After a series of unsuccessful uprisings in 1820–1821 and 1830–1831, in 1848–1849 Carlo Alberto's Piedmont, first supported and then abandoned by the other Italian states, went to war against

20. *See* M. Salvadori 'Italia, storia di', Enciclopedia dei ragazzi Treccani (2005), https://www.treccani.it/enciclopedia/storia-di-italia_%28Enciclopedia-dei-ragazzi%29/.
21. *See* M. Salvadori 'Italia, storia di', Enciclopedia dei ragazzi Treccani (2005), https://www.treccani.it/enciclopedia/storia-di-italia_%28Enciclopedia-dei-ragazzi%29/.
22. *See, generally*, A.M. Banti, 'Il Risorgimento Italiano' (Laterza, Bari-Roma, 2011); G. Pécout, 'Il lungo Risorgimento. La nascita dell'Italia contemporanea (1770-1922)' (Bruno Mondadori, Milano, 2004); A. Gramsci, 'Il Risorgimento' (Editori Riuniti, Roma, 2000).

Austria, but was defeated (First War of Independence); meanwhile, the republican and democratic movement emerged strongly in armed struggles against the Austrians in Milan, Venice and Rome.[23]

23. In 1831, Mazzini founded *Giovane Italia*, a grouping aimed at achieving the unity of the country and the republic through popular insurrection. In 1852, in Piedmont, the only Italian state to retain a liberal constitution after 1848, Count Camillo Benso di Cavour became prime minister during the reign of Victor Emmanuel II, who initiated a profound process of economic and social modernization. Cavour,[24] having obtained the alliance of the French Emperor Napoleon III, moved Piedmont against Austria in 1859, which was defeated (Second War of Independence). In 1860, Giuseppe Garibaldi,[25] with a small army of irregulars (Expedition of the Thousand), gradually increasing in size, overthrew the Bourbon kingdom of the *Two Sicilies*, inducing Cavour to make the goal of Italian unity his own.[26] A series of plebiscites sanctioned the unification of the various regions to Piedmont.[27]

24. On 17 March 1861, Victor Emmanuel II was proclaimed king of Italy. In 1866 following the war that saw Italy allied with Prussia (*Third War of Independence*), Veneto was annexed. In 1870, it was the turn of Rome. The national government was ruled until 1876 by the liberal right. The political and administrative unification of a country marked by great differences was very difficult, first because of the outbreak of brigandage, an expression of widespread social unease, in the southern regions, where the 'southern question' emerged in all its extent. The economic conditions of an overall still backward country were very precarious.[28]

25. A very serious problem was that the Church, which regarded the Italian state as a usurper for destroying the temporal power of the Popes, forced Catholics not to vote and not to participate in political life. But the results were overall positive. In 1876 the government was taken over by the liberal left, which expanded suffrage; in 1883 it formed an alliance with Germany and Austria (*Triple Alliance*), which guaranteed Italian unity; it introduced measures to protect Italy's weak industry; it

23. *See* M. Salvadori 'Italia, storia di', Enciclopedia dei ragazzi Treccani (2005), https://www.treccani.it/enciclopedia/storia-di-italia_%28Enciclopedia-dei-ragazzi%29/.
24. Concerning the Cavour politics, *see, generally*, L. Cafagna, 'Cavour' (Il Mulino, Bologna, 1999); R. Romeo, 'Cavour e il suo tempo', I-III (Laterza, Roma–Bari, 1969-1984).
25. Concerning the *Expedition of the Thousand, see, generally*, I. Nievo, 'Diario della spedizione dei Mille' (Mursia, Milano, 2010); D. Mack Smith, 'Garibaldi. Una grande vita in breve' (Laterza, Roma–Bari, 1982).
26. *See* M. Salvadori 'Italia, storia di', Enciclopedia dei ragazzi Treccani (2005), https://www.treccani.it/enciclopedia/storia-di-italia_%28Enciclopedia-dei-ragazzi%29/.
27. Concerning the unification of Italy, *see* A. Di Michele, 'Storia dell'Italia repubblicana (1948–2008)' (Milano, Garzanti, 2008); A. Capone, 'Destra e Sinistra da Cavour a Crispi' (TEA, Milano, 1996); M. Isnenghi, 'I luoghi della memoria. Personaggi e date dell'Italia unita' (Laterza, Bari-Roma, 2010); P. Ginsborg, 'Storia d'Italia dal dopoguerra a oggi' (Einaudi, Torino, 2006); A. Lepre, C. Petraccone, 'Storia d'Italia dall'Unità a oggi' (Il Mulino, Bologna, 2008).
28. *See* M. Salvadori 'Italia, storia di', Enciclopedia dei ragazzi Treccani (2005), https://www.treccani.it/enciclopedia/storia-di-italia_%28Enciclopedia-dei-ragazzi%29/.

began a colonial expansion first in Eritrea and then in Ethiopia, but suffered a disastrous defeat at Adua in 1896, during the government of Francesco Crispi.[29]

26. Meanwhile, the working masses began to organize under the leadership of anarchist and socialist groups and trade union organizations took root. In 1892, the *Socialist Party* arose, with the aim of establishing a society based on *collective property*. Social conflicts were numerous and acute. At the beginning of the 1890s, the *Fasci Siciliani* movement met with harsh repression. In 1898, hunger riots broke out in Milan, which were suppressed in blood. Then the government of General Pelloux planned the introduction of reactionary laws with the support of King Umberto I, who was however assassinated in 1900 by an anarchist and succeeded by Victor Emmanuel III.

§8. The 20th Century and the World Wars

27. The reactionary policy was rejected by the liberal left, which came into government in 1901 and of which the greatest exponent was *Giovanni Giolitti*, who ruled the country almost uninterruptedly from 1903 to 1914, during what has been called the *Giolittian Age*.

Giolitti promoted the development of industry in the North; he supported the right of workers not only to organize but also to strike, as long as it was for economic and not political reasons; he introduced universal male suffrage in 1912; and he favoured the inclusion of moderate Catholics in political life.[30]

Nevertheless, the social and political conflicts remained acute, fuelled by the revolutionary socialists, opposed by the reformist socialists, who were in favour of agreements with the bourgeoisie sensitive to the workers' demands for upward mobility. In 1911–1912 Giolitti led Italy to war with Turkey, from which Libya was taken and became an Italian colony. At the outbreak of the First World War in 1914, aware of the country's weaknesses, Giolitti tried in vain to prevent its entry into the conflict. The intervention became a reality on 24 May 1915 with the opposition of the socialist and Catholic masses and part of the ruling class itself but with the support of the interventionist groups and the monarchy. Italy therefore entered the war first against Austria and then Germany, alongside France, Great Britain, and Russia, who promised lavish territorial compensation.[31]

28. The war was a severe test for Italian society. After very critical moments, Italy finally achieved a decisive victory at *Vittorio Veneto* in October 1918. The post-war period opened a phase of deep economic and political crisis. Italy obtained Venezia Giulia, Istria, Trentino, and South Tyrol, but not the territories of Dalmatia and the colonial compensation promised by the Allies. The socialists and then the

29. *See* M. Salvadori 'Italia, storia di', Enciclopedia dei ragazzi Treccani (2005), https://www.treccani.it/enciclopedia/storia-di-italia_%28Enciclopedia-dei-ragazzi%29/.
30. *See* M. Salvadori 'Italia, storia di', Enciclopedia dei ragazzi Treccani (2005), https://www.treccani.it/enciclopedia/storia-di-italia_%28Enciclopedia-dei-ragazzi%29/.
31. *See* M. Salvadori 'Italia, storia di', Enciclopedia dei ragazzi Treccani (2005), https://www.treccani.it/enciclopedia/storia-di-italia_%28Enciclopedia-dei-ragazzi%29/.

communists – the latter formed into a party in 1921 – inflamed by the Bolshevik Revolution of October 1917, put the war on trial and proclaimed that the time had come to overthrow capitalism. The elections of 1919 were a great success for the socialists and for the Catholics who organized themselves into an autonomous party for the first time – the *People's Party* – and marked the organic crisis of the liberal ruling class, which despite a position of serious weakness remained in government until 1922.[32]

29. In 1919, *Fascism* was born, founded by the former socialist Benito Mussolini, who took on the socialists and communists in the first place, in a framework of violence in which the fascist squads, also supported by the military, eventually prevailed.[33] In October 1922 Mussolini went into government with the support of the Liberals and Populars, many of whom considered Fascism a passing phenomenon. But the Duce of Fascism, with the support of the monarchy, the Church and a large part of the bourgeoisie, destroyed the liberal state between 1924 and 1926 and created an *authoritarian state*. The Fascist regime wanted to become *totalitarian*, i.e., to dominate the entirety of the country's life, but the monarchy and the Church continued to limit it. In 1929, the State and the Church signed the *Lateran Pacts*, which ended the conflict that had arisen in 1870 when Rome was taken by Piedmontese troops.

30. Fascism subjected Italian society, in particular, the working masses, to its *dictatorship*, repressed anti-fascist movements, and responded to the economic crisis of 1929 with strong state intervention. It had the ambition to make Italy a great military power. In 1935–1936, Italy went to war against Ethiopia, which was reduced to an Italian colony. In 1936–1939, it was instrumental in General Franco's victory in the Spanish Civil War. Between 1936 and 1939 it tied its fate to that of Nazi Germany. In 1938, racial laws were introduced against the Jews.[34]

31. When Germany started the Second World War in 1939, Italy first kept out of it; then on 10 June 1940, counting on the German victory, it entered the conflict. However, the military situation gradually deteriorated, leading to the collapse of the regime in July 1943 and the *armistice* with the Anglo-Americans in September, who had started the invasion of the country. After the armistice, in north-central Italy, which had been occupied by the Germans, a neo-fascist regime was created with the formation of the *Italian Social Republic*, and the Resistance movement led by the partisans against Nazis and Fascists took vigour; while in southern Italy, occupied by

32. *See* M. Salvadori 'Italia, storia di', Enciclopedia dei ragazzi Treccani (2005), https://www.treccani.it/enciclopedia/storia-di-italia_%28Enciclopedia-dei-ragazzi%29/.
33. *See* M. Salvadori 'Italia, storia di', Enciclopedia dei ragazzi Treccani (2005), https://www.treccani.it/enciclopedia/storia-di-italia_%28Enciclopedia-dei-ragazzi%29/.
34. *See* M. Salvadori 'Italia, storia di', Enciclopedia dei ragazzi Treccani (2005), https://www.treccani.it/enciclopedia/storia-di-italia_%28Enciclopedia-dei-ragazzi%29/.

the Anglo-Americans and where the king had taken refuge, a government was formed supported by the resurgent anti-fascist parties. In April 1945, Italy was liberated and Mussolini was executed.[35]

32. The economic reconstruction of the country was fairly rapid, also thanks to American aid. In 1946, an institutional referendum led to the birth of the Republic and in 1948 a new Constitution came into force. The major parties emerged as the Christian Democrats, the Socialist Party and the Communist Party, whose leaders were respectively Alcide De Gasperi, Pietro Nenni and Palmiro Togliatti. In 1947, De Gasperi put an end to the anti-fascist unity governments that had led the country after the liberation. Following the great electoral victory achieved in the 1948 elections, which marked the defeat of the pro-Soviet social communists, the Christian Democrats, imprinting a moderate line on national politics, led various governments based on centre coalitions until 1962 and in foreign policy consolidated the alliance with the United States.[36]

33. Italy was a founding member of NATO, the European Economic Community (EEC), the Council of Europe and the OECD, joined the Economic and Monetary Union in 1999, adheres to the *Schengen Treaty*, is a member of the G7, G8, G20 and participates in the NATO nuclear sharing project.

On 14 December 1955, Italy became part of the *United Nations* by the unanimous vote of the Security Council and of the General Assembly. The long effort by Italian diplomacy, spanning a decade, to gain the country's entry into the international body was concluded. This effort, aimed at sharing ideals and principles, ends subjection to the peace treaty and redefines the position of the former enemy.

Italy was also one of the *protagonists*, together with the other founding Countries of the *European Community*, in the project to build a Europe without borders and customs barriers. In many cases, Italy has hosted key events for the community history.

Since the autumn of 1941, Altiero Spinelli and Ernesto Rossi – then confined to the island of Ventotene – fixed principles in the Manifesto for *European Federalism*. In 1955, a conference was held in Messina which laid the foundations of the *Treaty of Rome*. In 1957 in Rome, representatives of the six founding Countries signed the two Treaties establishing the European Economic Community and the European Atomic Energy Community (EURATOM). Both Treaties entered into force in January 1958, after ratification by the respective six Parliaments.[37]

35. *See* M. Salvadori 'Italia, storia di', Enciclopedia dei ragazzi Treccani (2005), https://www.treccani.it/enciclopedia/storia-di-italia_%28Enciclopedia-dei-ragazzi%29/.
36. *See* M. Salvadori 'Italia, storia di', Enciclopedia dei ragazzi Treccani (2005), https://www.treccani.it/enciclopedia/storia-di-italia_%28Enciclopedia-dei-ragazzi%29/.
37. *See, generally*, L. Tosi, 'L'Italia e le organizzazioni internazionali. Diplomazia multilaterale nel Novecento' (CEDAM, Padova, 1999); A. Villani, 'L'Italia e l'Onu negli anni della coesistenza competitiva (1955-1968)' (CEDAM, Padova, 2007); B. Baldi, 'Regioni e federalismo. L'Italia e l'Europa' (Clueb, Bologna, 2006).

34. The 1950s saw an impetuous development, particularly in industry, to the extent that one could speak of an 'economic miracle'. In 1957, Italy joined the *European Common Market*, which laid the foundations for European integration. In 1962 centrism came to an end and the phase of centre-left governments began, i.e., based on the centre parties and the Socialist Party, which had broken its alliance with the Communist Party since 1956, the year of the revelation of Stalin's crimes and the Soviet invasion of Hungary. The centre-left's ambitions to initiate a strong reformist process were for the most part disappointing.

35. A wave of political and social protests, supported by masses of students and workers, began in 1967 and spread over the following year (*Sixty-Eight*). Important reforms were the launch in 1970 of the regional system and the law that introduced divorce. The protest paved the way for the emergence of extreme right-wing organizations, aiming to introduce an authoritarian regime, and extreme left-wing organizations, intent on sparking a proletarian revolution, some of which turned to terrorist methods.

36. *Terrorism* from the extreme right and extreme left bloodied the country for years and reached its climax with the assassination of Christian Democrat statesman Aldo Moro in 1978 by the Red Brigades. The centre-left, which had entered a crisis in the mid-1970s, was given a new impetus at the end of the decade by the Socialist Party leader Bettino Craxi who, presenting himself as a proponent of modern left-wing reformism, strengthened the alliance with the Christian Democrats and led the government between 1983 and 1987.

37. In the 1980s and the 1990s, the Sicilian judges Giovanni Falcone and Paolo Borsellino, aided by courageous men of the police forces, managed to stop the activities of many members of mafia gangs. But, on 23 May 1992, Falcone's car was blown up on the highway that connects Palermo to Trapani. On July 19 of the same year, a car bomb exploded under Paolo Borsellino's mother's house, while Paolo was there. The judge died with his five bodyguards.

38. At the beginning of the 1990s, the political system that had emerged after the war came to an end (to the extent that one could even speak of the end of the 'First Republic') as a result of the combined effects of the collapse of Soviet communism and the action of the judiciary (Operation *Clean Hands*) directed against widespread *public corruption*, in which numerous exponents of the government parties and the business world, in particular, were involved.

39. The collapse of the Communist regimes led the Communist Party to disband in 1991, giving rise to the Democratic Party of the Left. In 1993–1994, the Socialist Party and the Christian Democrats also dissolved, while the Northern League emerged in northern Italy, a political formation that, after waving the banner of Padania's secession from the rest of the country, set itself the goal of transforming the state in a federal sense.

40. In 1993, entrepreneur Silvio Berlusconi gave birth to *Forza Italia*, a party aimed at gathering moderate consensus around it; in 1994, *Alleanza Nazionale*, a right-wing party that absorbed the Italian Social Movement, the neo-fascist party that arose after the war, was formed. The introduction of a majority electoral system in 1993 led to the formation of *two poles*, one of the centre-right and the other of the centre-left, in strong conflict. The centre-right won the elections in 1994, and the centre-left in 1996. In 2001 and in 2022, the centre-right returned to power.

41. An important moment for Italy was the entry into the single European currency (Euro), which replaced the traditional national currencies in various EU countries as of 2002.

§9. The Italian Constitution

42. On 27 December 1947, the text of the Italian Constitution was signed by the Provisional Head of State and came into force on 1 January 1948 with its 139 articles.[38]

The Italian Constitution is at the top of the hierarchy of sources of the Republic's legal system.

Recognized as a rigid, long, voted, compromising, secular, and democratic constitution, it consists of 139 articles and 18 transitional and final provisions.

It represents the main source of law of the Italian Republic, from which all other legal norms of the State system *depend hierarchically*.

The process that consolidates the principles of the Constitution, concretizing them in ordinary law, is called 'implementation of the Constitution'. This process has lasted decades, and some believe it is not yet complete.

43. The text of the Constitution was born after the fall of fascism and the end of World War II, and its history is intertwined with the birth of the Italian Republic.

The provisional government of the time asked Italians, on 2 June 1946, to choose whether to keep Italy a *Monarchy* or make it a *Republic*. 54% of the final votes (more than twelve million) were in favour of the republican state. On the same date, the election of the Constituent Assembly was also held and the constitutional draft was presented in February 1947, when the debate in the Chamber began, lasting for almost a year.

44. The Italian Constitution was approved by the Constituent Assembly on 22 December 1947, with 458 votes in favour, 62 against and no abstentions, out of a total of 520 voters. It was then promulgated by the Provisional Head of State Enrico De Nicola on the following 27 December and came into force on 1 January 1948.

---

38. For an easy introduction to the Italian Constitution *see*: A. Maritati, *Conoscere la Costituzione italiana. Un percorso guidato*, Laterza, 2019; S. Loffredi, *La Costituzione degli animali. La nascita della Costituzione italiana spiegata ai bambini*, Piemme, 2020; A. Barbera, *La Costituzione della Repubblica italiana*, Giuffrè, 2016; V. Cocozza, *Percorsi ricostruttivi per la lettura della Costituzione italiana*, Giappichelli, 2016.

It consists of 139 articles and their paragraphs, plus 18 transitional and final provisions, divided into *four sections*:

i. fundamental principles (Articles 1–12);
ii. part one: rights and duties of citizens (Articles 13–54);
iii. part two: order of the republic (Articles 55–139), and
iv. transitional and final provisions (Provisions I-XVIII).

§10. The Fundamental Principles of the Italian Constitution

45. The fundamental principles are those of democracy, labour, freedom, equality and pluralism. Specifically: democracy (Article 1, paragraph 1), sovereignty of the people (Article 1, paragraph 2), inviolability of rights (Article 2), formal equality and substantive equality (Article 3), right to work (Article (4), recognition of local autonomy (Article 5), protection of linguistic minorities (Article 6), religious freedom (Article 8), development of culture, environmental protection and the historical and artistic heritage (Article 9), recognition of international cooperation (Article 10), repudiation of war as an instrument of offence (Article 11) and structure of the Italian flag (Article 12).

46. The first part of the Constitution focuses on the *rights and duties* of the citizen. Rights are recognized and protected not only with reference to each individual, but also within the *social formations* in which they are active (family, local community, parties, trade unions, associations, and others).

In addition to rights, the *duties* of citizens are also listed. These include the right duty to work, consisting of carrying out an activity that is useful to society, loyalty to the Republic, payment of taxes, the duty of parents to care for their children, and the duty to vote and to defend the homeland.

47. The second part of the Constitution includes the Ordering of the Republic and describes the characteristics of its guarantor identified in the *President of the Republic*, the legislative power, the executive power, the judiciary and local authorities and the institutions guaranteeing the Constitution itself.

The first title concerns legislative power and is divided into *two sections*:

i. Parliament and
ii. the formation of laws.

For the structure of the Parliament of the Italian Republic, the Constitution has provided for a form of perfect bicameralism consisting of *two chambers*:

i. the Chamber of Deputies, and
ii. the Senate of the Republic (Article 55(1)).

The second title, from Articles 83 to 91, concerns the election procedures, powers and responsibilities of the *President* of the Italian Republic, whom the Italian legal system identifies as the Head of State, guarantor of the balance of powers and representative of national unity.

The third title, from Articles 92 to 100, concerns the *executive power* and is divided into three sections:

i. the Council of Ministers;
ii. the Public Administration, and
iii. auxiliary bodies. The Council of Ministers is a collegial body that constitutes the Government of the Republic and consists of the President of the Council of Ministers and the ministers.

The fourth title, Articles 101 to 113, concerns the *judiciary* and is divided into two sections:

i. judicial order, and
ii. rules on jurisdiction.

48. The fifth title, Articles 114 to 133, concerns the rules on *local governments*. This part is very articulate and has undergone a thorough revision. It was originally divided into regions, provinces and municipalities to which metropolitan cities have been added since 2001. Among the regions, according to Article 116, Friuli-Venezia Giulia, Sardinia, Sicily, Trentino-Alto Adige/Südtirol and Valle d'Aosta/Vallée d'Aoste enjoy special forms of autonomy guaranteed by their special statutes.

The sixth title, from Articles 134 to 139, concerns the guarantees put in place to preserve the Constitution and is divided into two sections:

i. The Constitutional Court and
ii. Revision of the Constitution – Constitutional Laws.

§11. Principles of State and Government at the Heart of the Constitution

49. In terms of the form of state, Italy is a *democratic republic*, because, in this form, sovereignty belongs to the people, i.e., to all citizens. But the people, according to Article 1, do not exercise their sovereignty unconditionally, but rather 'in the forms and within the limits of the constitution'. Above everything else – even the people – there is therefore the Constitution. Consequently, it is not configured as a 'majoritarian democracy' – where the majority is allowed to do anything, even change the constitution at will – but as a 'constitutional democracy', in which the majority, responsible for governing the country, must, in exercising its powers, first and foremost respect the principles and rules laid down in the constitution.

50. At the centre of the system is the human person (the individual, even before the citizen) with their inviolable rights and mandatory duties of political, economic and social solidarity (Article 2).

51. Among the founding values of the Republic, the first position is assigned to the *principle of equality* affirmed in Article 3. This principle is understood both in a formal sense (as equality before the law) and in a substantive sense (as equality in opportunities and starting points). The latter profile requires the Republic to actively intervene to 'remove economic and social obstacles, which, by limiting freedom and equality, prevent the full development of the human person and the effective participation of all workers in the political, economic and social organisation of the country'.

52. At the basis of the 'economic constitution' there is *work*, recognized in Article 1 as the foundation of the Republic. Hence the recognition, in Article 4, of a 'right to work' attributed to all citizens and correlated with the state's obligation to *promote*, through an economic policy aimed at maximizing employment, the conditions capable of making this right 'effective'.

53. Finally, on a territorial level, the Republic is configured as a regional state inspired by the principles of *autonomy* and *decentralization* (Article 5), principles that become operative not only through the administrative powers but also through the political ones assigned to the Regions (which have their own legislative power) and other local authorities.

54. Still, within the sphere of fundamental principles, other founding values are identified in the secularity of the State (Articles 7 and 8), the promotion of culture and research (Article 9), the repudiation of war, and the possible renunciation of portions of State-sovereignty in favour of supranational systems aimed at guaranteeing peace and justice among nations (Articles 10 and 11).

§12. The Form of the State

55. Italy is characterized by a democratic, constitutional, social, and pluralistic form of State. Italy is a democratic State because the main constitutional bodies of the State and territorial authorities are elected according to the rules of representative democracy.

Italy is a State *under the rule of law* as Italian citizens are granted civil rights that can be protected by an independent judiciary and the State is obliged to observe the laws no less than citizens; Italy is a welfare State since compulsory forms of assistance and social security are provided.

Italy is a State with a pluralistic structure due to the presence of numerous territorial autonomies that, within the limits of their competences, can also express a political orientation that differs from that of the central State.

§13. The Italian Form of Government

56. The Italian State is a *parliamentary republic*. Parliament, holder of legislative power, plays a central role, the Government being an expression of the parliamentary majority. The Prime Minister is the head of executive power and chooses the members of the government, while the President of the Republic essentially acts as the *guarantor* of the democratic order.

57. The peculiarity of the parliamentary form of government is that the government, holder of executive power, depends on Parliament and specifically on those political parties that manage to reach agreement in Parliament to form a majority. The parliamentary majority, with the cooperation of the President of the Republic, assumes responsibility for the formation of the government and, through the vote of confidence, assumes political responsibility for government action.

58. In fact, the Government only acquires full powers once it has obtained the confidence of both branches of Parliament and, very importantly, this relationship of confidence can be revoked at any time. If the relationship of trust established between Parliament and the Government is broken, the Prime Minister is obliged to resign from the Government they preside over and submit their resignation in the hands of the President of the Republic.

§14. The Italian Electoral System

59. The Constitution establishes a fixed number of elected seats for the Chamber of Deputies and the Senate. Prior to Constitutional Law No. 1 of 19 October 2020,[39] parliamentary elections resulted in 630 deputies and 320 senators. With the 2020 constitutional reform, the number of deputies was reduced to 400 and the number of senators to 200. The first general election to elect the Parliament with a reduced composition was on 25 September 2022.

60. Electoral constituencies are divisions of the Italian territory, each of which is entitled to express a certain number of seats. There are uninominal constituencies, which express only one Member of Parliament, and plurinominal constituencies, which express more than one Member of Parliament.

61. Another change, effective as of 2021 (Constitutional Law 1/2021,[40] which amended Article 58 of the Constitution), is that anyone over the age of 18 may vote, whereas in the past it was necessary to be at least 25 years old to vote for members of the Senate.

---

39. *See* the full official text, in Italian, at https://www.gazzettaufficiale.it/eli/id/2020/10/21/20G00151/sg.
40. *See* the full official text, in Italian, at https://www.normattiva.it/uri-res/N2Ls?urn:nir:stato:legge.costituzionale:2021-10-18;1.

62. The votes cast by voters are recorded as percentages. The method by which voting percentages are transformed into the allocation of electoral seats is contained in the electoral law and may consist of a majority, proportional or mixed method.

§15. The Legislative Process

63. The Constitution states that the legislative function is exercised collectively by the two chambers (Article 70). This means that for a bill to become law, it must be approved in the identical text by the Chamber and Senate.

64. The law formation process (the so-called *iter*) is therefore divided into successive stages: the presentation of the bill (legislative initiative), approval by the Chamber to which it was first presented, the transmission of the text to the other Chamber and its approval in the same wording or with amendments. If it is amended, the draft passes from one Chamber to the other, until it is approved by both in the identical wording (this is the so-called *navette*); promulgation by the President of the Republic (who may refer the law back to the Chambers for reconsideration) and publication in the Official Gazette.

65. The Legislative initiative consists of the submission to one of the two chambers of a *bill*, consisting of one or more articles and preceded by an explanatory report. It is the responsibility of the Government, individual deputies, senators (each in the Chamber to which they belong), the people (50,000 electors), the *National Economic and Labour Council* and the *Regional Councils*.

66. In the House, texts submitted by the government are referred to as *bills*, while all others are referred to as *proposals*. When referring indifferently to all legislative initiatives, they are referred to in everyday language as bills. Once introduced, draft bills are announced to the Assembly, printed, and distributed as quickly as possible. They are then assigned to the standing committee responsible for the subject matter of the bill.

67. Concerning the examination and approval by the Chamber, the ordinary procedure consists of *two stages*: examination by the Standing Committee, which is responsible for carrying out a preliminary investigation and assessment and preparing a text for discussion in the Assembly (therefore called the Referral Committee); discussion and deliberation by the Assembly.

68. In its preparatory work, the Commission may decide to deal with two or more drafts together (known as a *combination*) to submit a single report and a single text to the Assembly. To this end, it may choose one of the projects as the basic text for discussion or it may proceed – possibly by instructing a select committee – to draft a unified text of the various projects.

69. During the examination, the Commission obtains the opinions of other commissions that meet in consultative sessions to make *comments* and *suggestions* on the parts of the draft under their jurisdiction.

The members of the Commission outline the positions of the various political parties on the content of the measure and submit proposals for changes (amendments) on which the Commission deliberates. The opinions and data deemed necessary are acquired, also through hearings of non-parliamentarians, and the Government participates in the preliminary investigation and drafting of the text.

At the end of its work, the Commission appoints a *rapporteur* to prepare the report for the Assembly, which contains the text prepared by the Commission and to which minority reports may be added. The debate in the plenary is followed by a Committee of Nine, comprising the rapporteurs and representatives of the groups of the Commission that carried out the referral examination.

70. The debate in the House starts with an illustration by the rapporteur, an intervention by the government representative and those of the Members who speak on the general lines of the measure, expressing the position of the groups.

The individual articles of the draft are then examined, voting on the amendments tabled to the text prepared by the Commission.

In the final stage, after the examination of any agendas (which are documents addressing the Government on how the future law is to be implemented) and after the explanations of vote on the measure, the bill *as a whole* is approved.

71. Alongside the ordinary procedure (which must be followed compulsorily for certain types of law) there are *two abbreviated procedures*: the first (approval in committee in legislative session) involves the procedure being concluded entirely within a committee: it provides for the preliminary examination and final approval of the bill together, with the same formalities as those laid down for the Chamber; the second, of very limited use in the Chamber, is called *in sede redigente* and entails the approval in the Chamber of a bill whose articles are formulated in the Commission, without the Chamber being able to amend the text.

72. A project approved by the Senate is examined according to the same procedure followed for those who begin their journey in the House.

The message from the President of the other branch of Parliament will therefore be printed in the same way as for other projects: assigned to the Commission in legislative or referential session, the project will follow all the stages of the ordinary or legislative procedure.

If, however, it is a draft that has already been approved by the Chamber and that returns to *Montecitorio* because the Senate has made amendments to it, the examination in the Chamber will only concern the amended parts. In our system of perfect bicameralism, the shuttle between the Chamber and the Senate continues until the two branches of Parliament agree to approve a perfectly identical text.

73. Promulgation is the act by which the Head of State certifies that a certain text has been approved as a law and orders its publication and observance.

Promulgation must take place within a maximum of one month from the final approval of the law. But the President of the Republic may refer the law back to the Chamber of Deputies, with a reasoned message, to request a new deliberation. The presidential referral reopens the legislative procedure, and if the law is approved again, it must be promulgated.

74. Immediately after promulgation, the law is *published.* The publication of the law is done by the Minister of Justice and technically consists of the insertion of the text in the Official Compendium of Legislative Acts of the Italian Republic and its publication in the Official Gazette of the Italian Republic.

75. The law comes into force – and thus becomes binding on all – on the fifteenth day after its publication in the Official Gazette (*vacatio legis*) unless the law itself prescribes a shorter or longer period. The date of the law is that of the decree of promulgation, and the number of its insertion in the Official Compendium.

§16. THE ITALIAN JUDICIAL SYSTEM

76. The judicial system can be understood as the set of state bodies called upon to what in technical terms is called *ius dicere*, i.e., to take a decision on a given dispute according to the rules of law.

Depending on their organizational set-up and the type of matter they are called upon to adjudicate on, these bodies constitute *constitutional*, *ordinary* or *special* courts.

77. By ordinary judiciary is meant that which is established and regulated by the judicial system, and by special jurisdiction is meant that which deals exclusively with certain matters. To ensure the uniform application of the law, the Constitution, in Article 102, delegates the application of the law to the ordinary courts alone, and also prohibits the establishment of *special courts*, with the exception of those specifically mentioned in Article 103 Const.

78. Constitutional jurisdiction is vested in the *Constitutional Court*, a constitutional body composed of *fifteen judges* (chosen among highly qualified jurists), one-third of whom are appointed by the President of the Republic, one-third by the Parliament in common session and one-third by the supreme ordinary and administrative courts (Article 135 of the Constitution). The composition of the body is functional to guarantee the *independence* and *impartiality* of the judges themselves, as well as a composition of the Court that reflects a plurality of knowledge and experience as well as political orientations.

79. The Constitutional Court adjudicates (Article 134 Const.):

i. on disputes relating to the constitutional legitimacy of laws and acts, having the force of law, of the State and the Regions;

ii. on conflicts of attribution between the powers of the State and those between the State and the Regions and between the Regions;
iii. on charges brought against the President of the Republic, in accordance with the Constitution (*see* Article 90 Const.).

80. The case concerning the review of the constitutionality of laws may be brought principally by specifically authorized subjects (State, Regions, Autonomous Provinces) or (and this is the so-called *incidental judgment*) by each judge, who, in the course of a trial, doubts the conformity with the Constitution of the law that he or she would be called upon to apply to the individual case (this is the so-called *diffuse review*). In this case, also to avoid the proliferation of appeals, the question of constitutional legitimacy must be relevant to the decision of the trial and not manifestly unfounded. The individual judge, therefore, cannot disapply a rule that he or she considers contrary to the Constitution, having to raise the question before the Constitutional Court.

81. Judgment in conflicts of attribution, in turn, relates to cases in which a state power, through an act of its own, 'invades' the attributions of another State power, attributions fixed by a constitutional norm.

82. Finally, the judgment on the charges against the President of the Republic takes the form of judging the latter for the crimes of high treason or attack on the Constitution, following an indictment by the Parliament in session.

83. The special jurisdictions provided for by the Constitution are the *administrative*, *accounting*, and *military* jurisdictions. The *administrative jurisdiction* (delegated to the Council of State in second instance and to the Regional Administrative Courts in first instance) deals with disputes concerning legitimate interests (and, in some cases, subjective rights) in relations involving the public administration, judging the legitimacy of administrative acts. The autonomous governing body is the Presidency Council of Administrative Justice. The *accounting jurisdiction* (delegated to the Corte dei Conti and its regional sections) has as its object the preventive control of legitimacy over numerous acts of the Government and other public bodies, the subsequent control over the management of the budget and assets of public administrations, the subject of public accounting, as well as the liability of employees and officials of the State or other public bodies. The autonomous governing body is the Presidency Council of the Court of Auditors. *Military jurisdiction* is competent for military offences committed by members of the armed forces. The autonomous governing body is the Council of Military Judiciary.

84. Ordinary jurisdiction, as mentioned, is exercised by ordinary magistrates, who are considered such because they are established and regulated by the rules of judicial organization (Article 102 of the Constitution; Articles 1 and 4 Royal Decree No. 12 of 30 January 1941). The exercise of ordinary judicial functions is assisted by guarantees, provided for in the Constitution: autonomy from any other power of the State, submission to the law alone, internal independence (from any hierarchical constraint, that is) and external independence (from any external conditioning), provision for the natural judge pre-established by law, immovability.

In addition to these guarantees, the power to decide on the careers, transfers, appointments, disciplinary judgments of magistrates and, more generally, any other measure concerning the status of magistrates is delegated to the *Superior Council of the Magistracy*, an organ of constitutional relevance autonomous from any other power of the State.

85. As mentioned, the ordinary judiciary is such because it is identified by the so-called rules of judicial organization, i.e., by the set of legal texts that regulate its organization and functions.

86. The constitutional rules are Articles 101 to 113 of the Constitution, which set out the guarantees for the judiciary (autonomy, independence, etc.) and the guarantees relating to judgments (due process in contradictory between the parties, on equal terms, before a third and impartial judge; reasonable duration of the trial itself; obligation to state reasons for measures; appealability to the Supreme Court of Cassation of all judgments and measures on personal liberty).

87. Ordinary jurisdiction is distinguished into *civil* and *criminal*, depending on the subject matter on which the judge is called upon to decide.

Civil jurisdiction has as its object the resolution of a dispute concerning the protection of rights or, in any case, the application of a law (e.g., the civil court may deal with property, family law, obligations and contracts, personal rights).

Criminal jurisdiction has as its object the decision on the violation of criminal rules and, therefore, on the merits of the criminal action brought by the public prosecutor against a certain person, who these rules are alleged (subject, of course, to the presumption of innocence) to have violated.

88. Functions in the criminal field are distinguished into *adjudicative* and *prosecutorial*, the former obviously belonging to those who make the decision, the latter to the magistrates (the so-called public prosecutor's office) who conduct the investigation. At the end of the investigations, the latter exercise the prosecution or ask for the case to be dismissed, support the prosecution at trial, and perform prosecutorial functions in the subsequent levels of judgment (through the power to appeal sentences and to make requests to these bodies).

89. At first instance jurisdiction, both civil and criminal, is exercised by the following bodies:

i. Justice of the Peace, an honorary monocratic body.
ii. Ordinary Court, which judges in a monocratic or collegiate composition, depending on the type of dispute.
iii. Juvenile court, judging in a collegial composition supplemented by experts.
iv. Supervisory Court, which judges in a monocratic or collegial composition (supplemented by experts).

At first instance, the prosecution functions are exercised by:

i. Public prosecutor's office at the ordinary court (also for offences within the jurisdiction of the justice of the peace).
ii. Public prosecutor's office at the juvenile court.
iii. Public Prosecutor's Office at the Court of Appeal, for proceedings before the Surveillance Court.

In the second instance, jurisdiction is exercised by the following offices:

i. Court of Appeal, for appeals against decisions of the ordinary court and the Juvenile Court.

Ordinary Court, for appeals against decisions of the justice of the peace (as well as for appeals against measures on personal liberty).

ii. Supervisory Court, for appeals against decisions of the supervisory magistrate.

In the second instance, the prosecution functions are exercised by the public prosecutor's office at the court of appeal.

90. Jurisdiction of legitimacy is exercised by the Supreme Court of Cassation; in proceedings before the Court, the accuse functions are exercised by the Public Prosecutor's Office at the Court of Cassation. Lastly, the National Anti-Mafia and Anti-Terrorism Directorate must also be included among the bodies, which exercise national coordination functions. A further macro-distinction within ordinary jurisdiction is between 'togati' judges (who perform judicial functions professionally and are therefore hired on a permanent basis following a public competition) and 'honorary' judges.

91. The functions performed by honorary magistrates are those of:

i. justice of the peace, who is assigned jurisdiction in the civil and criminal sectors, respectively on cases of reduced value or for offences of reduced gravity;
ii. honorary court judge (the so-called g.o.t.), who performs judging functions at first instance in ordinary courts;
iii. honorary deputy public prosecutor (v.p.o.), who performs prosecuting functions at first instance in public prosecutors' offices;
iv. expert of the juvenile court, who forms the panels of that body;
v. expert of the juvenile court of appeal, who forms the panels of the court of appeal in juvenile proceedings;
vi. court of appeal auxiliary judge, who performs judicial functions at the courts of appeal;
vii. expert member of the supervisory court, who forms the panels of that court;

viii. expert member of the specialized agrarian sections at ordinary courts of first instance;
ix. expert member of the regional courts of public waters and expert member of the High Court of Public Waters.

As provided for in the Constitution, the direct participation of the people in the administration of justice finds its highest point in the composition of the Assize and Appeal Courts, whose panels are supplemented – for individual trials – by popular judges.

92. By *tabular system* is meant that a set of rules, fixed in general by the SCM and in concrete terms by the individual heads of offices, on the basis of which the allocation of judges to the sections into which offices and panels are divided is decided, as well as the rules by which the allocation of trials and cases to individual judges is decided. These rules – pursuant to Article 7-*bis* of Royal Decree No. 12 of 1941 – are predetermined in the circular on the formation of the tables issued every three years by the Superior Council and in the so-called tables of organization, adopted by each judicial office, which contain all the criteria described above, implementing the general rules established by the circular.

This system is of fundamental importance in order to implement the constitutional principles of the natural judge pre-established by law and the independence and impartiality of the judge.

In fact, the establishment of certain and general rules, determined upstream, allows, on the one hand, to be able to identify – in an almost automatic manner – *ex ante* (and not ad hoc after the commission of the offence or the establishment of a civil dispute) the judge who will be called upon to judge on a given case and on the other hand prevents the possibility of 'external' interventions aimed at affecting the identification of the judge himself.

§17. Conclusions: The Seven Peculiarities of the Italian Constitution

93. (1) *Foundational principles of democracy and anti-Fascism and reaction to Fascism.* The Italian Constitution was drafted in the aftermath of World War II and the fall of Mussolini's fascist regime. As a result, it strongly emphasizes democratic principles, individual rights, and the rejection of totalitarianism. The Constitution begins with an explicit declaration that Italy is a democratic republic founded on labour (Article 1). The Constitution contains provisions that explicitly ban the reorganization of the fascist party (Article 12 of the Transitional and Final Provisions), reflecting its roots in the resistance to fascism.

94. (2) *Emphasis on social rights, economic democracy and social State.* The Italian Constitution enshrines a strong commitment to social rights, more so than many other Western constitutions. It includes a wide range of social and economic rights, such as the right to work (Article 4), health (Article 32), education (Article 34), and social security (Article 38). The Constitution also provides for the regulation of private economic initiatives to ensure that it does not conflict with social utility or harm security, liberty, and human dignity (Article 41). This reflects a broader European tradition of integrating social welfare with economic policy, differing from more market-oriented constitutions like that of the United States.

95. (3) *A strong Constitutional Court and judicial review.* The Italian Constitution establishes a Constitutional Court ('Corte Costituzionale'), which has the power to review and invalidate laws that are in conflict with the Constitution. This court is one of the first of its kind in Europe, and it plays a crucial role in safeguarding the Constitution. The decisions of the Constitutional Court are binding on all other courts, emphasizing the supreme authority of the Constitution in the Italian legal system.

96. (4) *Rigidity and amendments: a rigid Constitution.* The Italian Constitution is considered 'rigid', meaning that it cannot be amended by ordinary legislative procedures. Amendments require a more complex process, including a double reading in both houses of Parliament and, if not passed by a two-thirds majority, a popular referendum (Article 138). This contrasts with the flexibility of some constitutions, like the UK's unwritten constitution or the relative ease of amending the U.S. Constitution.

Certain fundamental principles, particularly those enshrined in the first 12 articles, are considered inviolable and cannot be amended, ensuring the stability of the Republic's foundational values.

97. (5) *Balanced parliamentary system and a bicameral Parliament.* Italy's Parliament is bicameral, consisting of the Chamber of Deputies and the Senate, with both houses having equal powers (perfect bicameralism). This system differs from other countries like the UK, where the House of Commons holds more power, or the U.S., where the Senate and House have distinct roles. The Italian system includes multiple checks and balances, reflecting a desire to avoid concentration of power, influenced by the experiences under fascism. This includes the President of the Republic, who has a balanced, mostly ceremonial role but with important powers, such as the ability to dissolve Parliament and appoint the Prime Minister.

98. (6) *Regional Autonomy and Regions with special statutes.* The Italian Constitution grants a significant degree of autonomy to its regions, particularly those with special statutes, such as Sicily, Sardinia, Trentino-Alto Adige/Südtirol, Aosta Valley, and Friuli Venezia Giulia. These regions have greater legislative powers and financial autonomy due to their unique cultural, historical, or geographical circumstances (Articles 116–117). The Constitution allows for the devolution of powers to regions in various areas, a feature more pronounced than in many other European countries with unitary systems.

99. (7) *Promotion of International peace and justice.* The Italian Constitution explicitly promotes international peace and justice, committing Italy to renounce war as a means of resolving international disputes and to adhere to international agreements that secure peace and justice among nations (Article 11). This reflects the post-war consensus and Italy's commitment to multilateralism.

100. In summary, the Italian Constitution is distinctive for its emphasis on anti-fascism, social rights, and economic democracy, its rigid amendment procedures, the strong role of the Constitutional Court, and its balanced parliamentary system. It also grants significant autonomy to regions and emphasizes Italy's commitment to international peace, making it a unique document among the world's major constitutions.

Chapter 2. Telecommunications Infrastructure

§1. A Brief Introduction to the Italian ICT Infrastructure

101. As of 2024, Italy's telecommunications infrastructure is relatively advanced, but it exhibits notable regional disparities.

The country has made significant progress in recent years, particularly with the deployment of 5G networks and the expansion of high-speed broadband services. However, challenges remain in ensuring uniform access across all regions, particularly in rural and less densely populated areas.

Italy has been expanding its fibre optic network to improve broadband connectivity.

102. The government's BUL (*Ultra-Broadband*) Plan[41] aims to provide high-speed Internet access across the country, focusing on underserved areas. Major telecom operators, including TIM, Fastweb, and Open Fiber, are key players in this expansion.

While urban areas, especially in the north, enjoy high-speed fibre connectivity, rural and southern regions still face slower Internet speeds and less reliable service.

Italy is one of the leading European countries in 5G deployment, with major cities and industrial areas already covered. Telecom operators such as TIM, Vodafone, and Wind Tre are actively rolling out 5G services, with the technology expected to enable advancements in IoT, smart cities, and other innovative applications.

Although 5G coverage is growing, there are challenges related to infrastructure deployment in less densely populated areas. Regulatory hurdles and local opposition to the installation of 5G antennas in some regions also present obstacles.

103. Italy has a well-established mobile network, with extensive 4G/LTE coverage across the country. This has laid a strong foundation for the transition to 5G, though again, coverage is more robust in urban areas compared to rural ones.

The focus remains on enhancing network capacity and coverage, especially as data consumption continues to rise with increasing smartphone and mobile Internet usage.

As part of the broader EU *Recovery and Resilience Facility*, *Digital Italy Plan* includes significant investments in digital infrastructure, aiming to boost broadband access and further 5G deployment, particularly in underserved areas.

The Italian government is working closely with private telecom companies to accelerate infrastructure development, leveraging both public funds and private investment.

Despite progress, Italy still faces challenges in ensuring comprehensive and equitable telecommunications infrastructure across the country. Rural and remote areas lag behind in terms of both broadband and mobile network access.

The telecom sector also navigates complex regulatory frameworks, which can slow down infrastructure deployment.

---

41. *See* at https://bandaultralarga.italia.it.

104. The lockdown, in fact, has inevitably generated a disruptive impact on Italian telecommunications networks, with the exponential *increase* in traffic caused by data-intensive services (videogame platforms, streaming portals, distance learning, video calls), which have put a strain on a system that, fortunately, has held up.

AGCOM's data[42] indicate an increase in data flow on the fixed network that almost doubled compared to 2019 in March 2023 (+90%) and April (+80%), also showing a growth over previous years of more than 30% throughout the summer period. To a lesser extent, the increase also affected the mobile networks, which saw a peak growth of 79% in March and 78.9% in April, although a strong increase (over 50%) had already been recorded in the months preceding the lockdown, thus independent of exogenous factors.

Despite the traffic explosion, the system held up well. In detail, an analysis carried out by MedUX estimated a drop in download speed on the fixed network during peak hours (h20-21) of only 10% nationwide.[43]

105. The future scenario of telecommunications networks in Italy will be linked to the way in which the funds made available through the *Next Generation EU* will be allocated, and which will flow into the *National Recovery and Resilience Plan.* In detail, the mission has been divided into *three main axes*:

i. digitization, innovation and security in Public Administration (EUR 10.1 billion);
ii. innovation, competitiveness, digitization 4.0 and internationalization (EUR 35.5 billion), and
iii. culture and tourism (EUR 3.1 billion).[44]

§2. THE NATIONAL STRATEGY FOR ULTRA BROADBAND

106. Approved to foster fibre coverage of areas of market failure, the *National Strategy for Ultralarge Bandwidth* has so far mobilized about 12 billion in public and private investments. The latest *Project Progress Report* released by *Infratel* (dated 30 November 2020)[45] shows a positive scenario both from the planning point of view (with over 8,300 fibre projects delivered out of about 8,900 planned and almost 7,000 delivered out of 7,100 for Fixed Wireless Access), and in terms of authorization (with 7,700 approvals for Fibre to the Home – FTTH and 6,500 for FWA).

107. As far as executive planning is concerned, as of 30 November 2020, almost 4,200 fibre projects and 1,650 FWA projects had been delivered, translated into

42. *See* https://www.agcom.it/pubblicazioni/relazioni-annuali/relazione-annuale-2024-sullattivita-svolta-e-sui-programmi-di.
43. *See* https://medux.com/reports.
44. For a story about the evolution of telecommunications (and law) in Italy *see* V. Franceschelli, 'Convergenza' (Giuffrè, Milano, 2009). *See, also*, F. Bassan, 'Diritto delle comunicazioni elettroniche' (Giuffrè, Milano, 2010).
45. *See* https://www.infratelitalia.it.

5,128 open sites (3,600 FTTH and 1,528 FWA) and 3,126 completed plants (1,712 FTTH and 1,414 FWA). According to the Report, the total value of the execution orders amounts to approximately EUR 1.4 billion, of which EUR 796 million is already in progress (about 58%).

§3. The Single Network Project and 5G

108. The evolution of ultra-broadband coverage is closely linked to the *Rete Unica* project. After Tim's spin-off of its passive infrastructures of the secondary access network (from the street cabinet to the users' premises), both copper and fibre, entrusted to the newco *Fibercop* (in the meantime, an AGCM investigation has begun), Enel's board of directors approved the mandate to sell its 50% of *Open Fiber* (more precisely, between 40% and 50%) to the Australian fund *Macquarie*.

109. The roll-out of 5G networks in 2020 has suffered a series of slowdowns, mainly due to the pandemic crisis and partly to the wave of fake news that triggered opposition from many local administrations. Italy, moreover, is one of the first countries in the EU to have launched commercial 5G service (in June 2019, together with Spain) and is in third place, after Spain and Germany, in terms of the number of trials, although these will be strongly declining in 2019–2020. The commercial 5G service started in 13 cities (Rome, Milan and surrounding areas, Naples, Bologna, Turin, Florence, Genoa, Brescia, Sanremo, Ferrara, Livigno, Cortina, Selva di Val Gardena) and is expected to cover most major urban centres over the next years.

110. In the security sphere, the process of composing the regulatory framework to guarantee 5G networks is proving to be rather complex.

Law No. 133 of 2019[46] established the *national cybersecurity perimeter*, opening a fractioned implementation path with diversified timeframes through four decrees (DPCM) and a regulation aimed at establishing, among other things, the modalities, and procedural criteria for identifying the entities included in the perimeter.

111. The first DPCM (of 30 July 2020),[47] intervened on four fundamental points:

i. the definition of the modalities for identifying the subjects to be included;
ii. the declination of the criteria by which the identified subjects prepare and update the list of IT networks, infrastructures and services;
iii. the attribution to the National Assessment and Certification Centre (CVCN) of the power to carry out verifications and impose conditions and tests of hardware and software; and
iv. the establishment of an inter-ministerial table with support functions.

---

46. *See* https://www.normattiva.it/uri-res/N2Ls?urn:nir:stato:legge:2019-11-18;133.
47. *See* at https://www.gazzettaufficiale.it/eli/id/2020/10/21/20G00150/sg.

112. The topic of *cybersecurity* was also taken up by the government in the PNRR. In particular, the document highlights the desire to establish a 'cybersecurity development and research centre' that would operate through the establishment of public-private partnerships in which national champions in the sector and universities would be involved. The centre should be the natural Italian interlocutor for the *European Centre for Industrial, Technological and Research Development on Cybersecurity* (currently being set up) and the related network of national coordination centres.

§4. Telecommunications Networks as a Tool for Economic Development

113. In Italy too, telecommunications networks are seen as one of the main drivers of an area's economic and social development. These, in fact, are the main enabling factors for innovation and scientific research: enabling the use of new technologies – such as artificial intelligence, cloud computing and IoT – and removing physical barriers to individuals' access to services and information. Network development is also a fundamental prerequisite in the creation of smart cities, contributing significantly to social and environmental sustainability.

114. Italy has launched, starting in 2018 but with greater momentum from 2020, a process of simplifying the authorization procedures for telecommunications infrastructures in order to facilitate the deployment of networks, meet the objectives set by the PNRR and the *Italy 1Giga* and *Italy 5G Plans*, and recover a leading role at European level.

With regard to the provision of digital public services by Italian local authorities, data from the *Survey on the Digital Maturity of Capital Municipalities* conducted by FPA[48] show a positive trend in the usability of services provided online.

In 2023, 86% of capital municipalities have at least a medium-high level of digital service maturity, while only 2% is at the lowest level of maturity. The gap between the northern and southern areas is also narrowing.

115. According to the latest data published by AgID on innovative procurement,[49] 112 'innovative challenges' were identified from 2012 to 2022, totalling more than EUR 1.3 billion. Innovative procedures were mainly used in the areas of health, food and quality of life (38%), digital agenda, smart communities and smart mobility systems (27%), smart and sustainable industry, energy and environment (21%).

116. The government intends to update the *Transition 4.0* plan into Transition 5.0, attempting to create a link between digital and green transition, so that *RePowerEU* funds can be used. Such a reform would be desirable soon, as also suggested

---

48. *See* at https://www.astrid-online.it/static/upload/fpa-/fpa-indagine-maturita-digitale-dei-comuni-2023-def.pdf.
49. *See* at https://www.agid.gov.it/it/ambiti-intervento/appalti-innovativi.

by the OECD, which, in its latest *Economic Outlook* (June 2023),[50] noted widespread delays in the spending of the National Recovery Plans, explicitly highlighting the need for spending projects on infrastructure that can facilitate the digital transition along with the green transition.

§5. Infrastructure Coverage and Connectivity Data

117. On the fixed telecommunications side, according to the mapping conducted by *Infratel* in 2021, the share of households covered at least 30 Mbps in 2021 stands at 64.1% nationwide. In detail, 22.8% of Italian civic centres are covered with technology capable of guaranteeing connectivity between 30 Mbps and 100 Mbps; 23.8% are equipped with a connection speed between 100 and 300 Mbps; and, finally, 17.5% of civic centres can count on connectivity above 300 Mbps.

118. Focusing the analysis at the local level, significant territorial differences emerge. Regarding the rate of households covered at a connection speed of at least 30 Mbps, the data show that four southern regions excel, namely Apulia (88.5%), Sicily (75.5%), Calabria (75.2%) and Sardinia (69.1%). Analysing only the households covered with technologies providing connection speeds between 300 Mbps and 1 Gbps, the most covered regions are those in the centre and north. Regarding the state of mobile telecommunications networks, the latest *Infratel* surveys (2021) show that 2.4% of the national territory is still completely uncovered.

119. Regarding the state of the country's 5G network coverage, on the other hand, an analysis carried out by EY and updated in September 2021 indicated that 95% of the Italian population and more than 7,500 Italian municipalities had been reached. This value is confirmed by DESI 2022, according to which Italy ranks first in Europe for 5G coverage as a percentage of households with 99.7%. The achievement of this share was also made possible using *Dynamic Spectrum Sharing* (DSS) technology, while standalone 5G coverage of the national territory stands at 7.3%.[51]

§6. Strategic Plans for the Future

120. With the *Italia a 1 Giga* Plan, the aim is to guarantee connectivity to the civic centres in need of public intervention, which represent 20.9% of those in Italy. According to the data reported on *Infratel*'s portal dedicated to the progress of the plans connected to the PNRR 'connetti.italia.it', as of 30 June 2023, the number of civic centres reached thanks to *Italia a 1 Giga* is 123,469, i.e., 2.79% of the total planned, while a further 9.75% (430,400 civic centres) are in the process of being worked on.

---

50. *See* at https://www.oecd-ilibrary.org/economics/oecd-economic-outlook/volume-2023/issue-1_ce18 8438-en#:~:text=Economic%20growth%20will%20remain%20robust,inflation%20of%20household s'%20purchasing%20power.
51. *See* https://openfiber.it/en/open-fiber-world/news/ey-survey-connectivity/.

121. The *Italia 5G Plan*, on the other hand, in line with the provisions of the PNRR, aims to incentivize the construction of 5G mobile network infrastructures in areas of market failure throughout the country, with an overall endowment of EUR 2.02 billion earmarked for two distinct but complementary lines of action: the first envisages the construction of a fibre optic backhauling network for the *Radio Base Stations* (SRBs) that, according to the mapping carried out by *Infratel Italia* in 2022, would still be without relocation in 2026; the second of complete *ex-novo* network infrastructures, with a capacity of at least 150 Mbps downlink and 30 Mbps uplink, in the areas of the country that would be without infrastructures capable of offering connectivity at least 30 Mbps in 2026.

122. An analysis of the data available on the *connetti.italia.it* portal shows that, regarding the first line of intervention, 5.69% of the 11,098 planned sites have already been relocated, while a further 9.87% are in the process of being relocated. As far as the second line of intervention is concerned – the Italy 5G Densification Plan – the 'state of progress' of the first milestone has just been closed as of 30 June 2023. Despite the complexities involved in the construction of new infrastructure and the slowness in obtaining permits for obstacles on the part of some local authorities, activity nevertheless appears to be on track. Of the 1,385 planned interventions, 11% are currently being worked on.

§7. The Need for a Simplification of Procedures

123. Decree-Law No. 76 converted by Law No. 120/2020 ('Simplification Decree') provided for the assimilation of high-speed fibre optic electronic communication networks to primary urbanization works. It definitively clarified the inapplicability of building and urban planning regulations to the installation of such networks. The Decree also extended the application of the reduced term of eight days for the issue of authorization in the case of opening holes, opening manholes for the laying of cables or pipes laying aerial cables or pipes on existing infrastructures and connecting users. The provision also applies to authorizations for the execution of crossings and parallels on ports, interports, water, maritime and forest areas and other immovable property belonging to the State, regions, local authorities and other public bodies, including railway and motorway grounds, and has affected the *Fibre Decree* by enabling the use of micro-trenching in urban and extra-urban areas and limiting the production of documents to be submitted by operators.

124. The same decree then intervened on the authorization procedures for mobile networks, regulating the siting of temporary mobile telecommunications installations and non-substantial variations to installations already provided with a license (including modifications relating to the radioelectric profile, which entail increases in height of no more than 1 meter and increases in the surface area of the outline of the building of no more than 1.5 square meters).

Finally, it has expressly forbidden municipalities to introduce limitations on the location in general areas of the territory of radio base stations for electronic communications networks of any type and to affect, even indirectly or by means of contingent and urgent measures, the limits of exposure to electric, magnetic and electromagnetic fields, the warning values and quality objectives, which are reserved, by law, to the State.

125. Subsequently, Law Decree No. 77/21 (converted into Law No. 108/21) ('Simplification-*bis* Decree') once again dealt with the authorization procedures for fixed and mobile networks, introducing important innovations among which the obligation for the person in charge of the procedure to convene a *Services Conference* in the event that the installation of the infrastructure is subject to the acquisition of one or more measures, determinations, opinions, understandings, concerts, *nulla osta* or other concession acts, etc., within five days from the submission of an application, and the formation of a silence assent after ninety days from the submission of an authorization application.

126. In addition to this, there are important simplifications for projects that have already been implemented and that require variations during construction of up to 10% of the infrastructure and ancillary elements (notification of the variation to the proceeding administration that received the original application and to all the administrations and entities involved, with at least fifteen days' notice, enclosing cartographic documentation of the work that gives an account of the changes and the possibility for the operator to commence work if, within fifteen days of the date of notification of the variation, the parties and entities involved have not communicated a negative decision).

127. With regard to furniture, the decree under review provides that until 31 December 2026, certain alterations that do not entail increases in heights exceeding 1.5 meters and increases in the outline area exceeding 1.5 square meters are to be carried out subject to the commencement of works notice to the municipal administration, accompanied by a self-certification describing the interventions and the technical characteristics of the plants (with the possibility of activating the plants after thirty days) and without the need to apply for authorizations pursuant to Legislative Decree No. 42/04.

128. On this simplification process, Legislative Decree No. 207/2021 was grafted, with which Directive 2018/1972 establishing the European Electronic Communications Code was implemented, and, most recently, Law Decree No. 13 of 24 February 2023, converted into Law No. 41/2023, which affected several important persisting criticalities in terms of application. The former, in particular, on the one hand, introduced important innovations with respect to the fulfilments and clearances falling within the competence of the Civil Engineers and ENAC/ENAV, setting certain deadlines for the latter to issue the relevant clearances; on the other hand, it sanctioned the prohibition to impose additional charges or fees (without prejudice to the application of the fee provided for by Article 1, paragraph 816, of Law No. 160 of 27 December 2019).

129. Decree-Law No. 13/2023, on the other hand, provided for the reduction of the term from ninety to sixty days for the formation of the silence of consent relating to authorization requests for electronic telecommunications infrastructures, set peremptory terms for the adoption of road regulation measures, provided for the sending of documentation in digital format and via PEC, provided for specific forms of simplification for interventions of no relevance, also with regard to seismic authorization (microcells, indoor and tunnel roofing systems and infrastructures consisting of poles less than or equal to 4 meters in height and weighing no more than 6.00 KN), as well as for the construction of high-speed electronic communication infrastructures in areas encumbered by civic uses, and required that, in order to be able to take part in service conferences, agencies must meet the simultaneous requirements of involvement in the proceedings and being affected by the installation, including agencies responsible for monitoring exposure to electric, magnetic and electromagnetic fields.

130. The same decree also recognized the possibility, for the operators to benefit from the extension set forth in Article 1, paragraph 11, of Law Decree No. 228/2021, converted into Law No. 15 of 25 February 2022, to request the maintenance of the rights of use of the frequencies in the 24.5–26.5 GHz band until 31 December 2026, subject to the submission of a specific request to be made by 31 July 2023. Lastly, the same decree established that the *Special Superintendency* for the NRP is competent to adopt the final measures relating to the protection functions, replacing the *Archaeological, Fine Arts and Landscape Superintendencies.*

131. The annual law on the market and competition, the last of which, relating to 2021, which came into force on 27 August 2022, was also dedicated to the development of digital infrastructures and electronic communications services, providing – on the one hand – for obligations on the part of operators of physical infrastructures to guarantee the use of such infrastructures in the event of a request by a telecommunications operator for the laying of fibre optic cables (Article 22) and – on the other hand – prescribing a duty of cooperation in the adoption of any useful initiative for the coordination with other network operators, aimed at rationalizing the interventions dedicated to the implementation of fibre access networks (Article 23).

§8. The Centrality of Smart Cities and Smart Communities

132. On 29 September 2022, as part of the *Digital Europe Programme*, the call for proposals 'Data Space for Smart Communities' worth EUR 18 million was published, with the aim of identifying 10–12 pilot projects. In the national context, the start of the Italian debate on intelligent communities dates back to CIPE Resolution No. 150 of 21 December 2000, concerning the 'National Research Programme' for the years 2001–2003, which included *six major projects*, including one entitled 'Development of enabling platforms – intelligent communities'. This is a particularly important issue that led to the adoption of Directorial Decree No. 391 of 5 July 2012, with which the Ministry of Education, Universities and Research published a notice for the presentation of project ideas for smart cities and communities and social innovation, making available to the projects FAR resources totalling EUR 655.5 million, of which 170 in the form of a contribution to expenditure and 485.5 in the form of subsidized credit.

133. With the adoption, in 2012, of the *Italian Digital Agenda* and the establishment of AgID, smart communities have taken on a central role that has found expression in the 2019–2021 *Three-Year Plan* as well as in the 2021–2023 Update, which devotes ample space to the *Smarter Italy* programme. The latter consists of 11 urban centres, the 'Smart Cities', and 12 small centres that make up the 'Villages of the Future'. Within the framework of this programme, the first call for tenders was published in May 2022 for 'Innovative solutions for decision support with predictive/adaptive functions for Smart Mobility' – amounting to EUR 8.5 million, while on 14 September, the second call for tenders was published, once again dedicated to Smart Mobility and in particular to the design of 'Innovative solutions for improving freight mobility' for a total contract value of approximately EUR 7.3 million.

134. With the adoption of the new national ultra-wideband strategy (published on 27 May 2021), Italy's ambitions have been further strengthened, with fixed network connection speeds of at least 1 Gbit/s throughout the country by 2026, a full four years ahead of the EU timetable.

135. The implementation of the 2015 *Ultralarge Bandwidth Plan* was entrusted to *Infratel*, with the objective of providing 7,700 municipalities with a fibre connection, in addition to the municipalities to be covered with a mixed fibre-wireless (FWA) connection, with performance up to 100 Mbps. The municipalities to be covered were divided into three different tenders, divided into regional (or Autonomous Provinces) lots:

i. the first tender included 5 lots in 3,031 municipalities in Abruzzo, Molise, Emilia-Romagna, Lombardy, Tuscany and Veneto;
ii. the second tender included 6 lots covering 3,712 municipalities in 10 regions (Basilicata, Campania, Friuli-Venezia Giulia, Lazio, Liguria, Marche, Piedmont, Sicily, Umbria and Valle d'Aosta) and the Autonomous Province of Trento;
iii. the third call, addressed to Sardinia, Apulia and Calabria, was awarded on 18 December 2018 and provides for the connection of more than 317 thousand real estate units in 959 municipalities.

136. As of 20 April 2023, there were 9,907 approved projects out of 11,188 planned in Fiber to the Home and 6,823 approved projects out of 7,116 planned in Fixed Wireless Access. At the construction level, 9,281 execution orders were issued for fibre infrastructures, of which 6,781 were closed, i.e., with CUIR (Communication of Completion of Network Installation), against 4,698 positive tests. For FWA sites, 3,093 orders were issued, of which more than 2,955 with CUIR and 1,203 sites already positively tested. The economic progress of the project at the national level has currently reached about 82% in terms of work status with EUR 2.3 billion deployed on over EUR 2.55 billion of works ordered from *Open Fiber*.

The economic progress of the project at the national level has currently reached about 82% in terms of the state of execution of the works with EUR 2.3 billion employed on over EUR 2.55 billion of works ordered.

Chapter 3. The Information and Communications Technology Market

§1. An Introduction to the ICT Market and Spending in Italy

137. The Information and Communication Technology (ICT) market in Italy is a dynamic and growing sector, though it faces certain challenges. The market plays a crucial role in the country's digital transformation, contributing significantly to the economy and the modernization of various industries.

The ICT sector in Italy has been expanding steadily, driven by increased demand for digital solutions across public and private sectors. Investments in cloud computing, cybersecurity, data analytics, and artificial intelligence are particularly strong.

The market includes both large multinational companies and a significant number of small and medium-sized enterprises (SMEs) that are innovative and specialized in niche areas.

138. The Italian government has been actively promoting digital transformation through initiatives like the *Digital Italy 2026* plan, which is part of the broader EU *Recovery and Resilience Facility*. This plan aims to modernize infrastructure, enhance digital skills, and foster innovation in the ICT sector.

Public and private sectors are increasingly adopting digital solutions to improve efficiency and competitiveness. This includes investments in smart cities, *Industry 4.0*, and e-government services.

Italy has made significant progress in deploying 5G networks, with major telecom operators rolling out services in urban areas. The expansion of 5G is expected to boost the ICT market by enabling new technologies such as the *Internet of Things* (IoT) and advanced mobile applications.

However, rural and less densely populated areas still face challenges in terms of connectivity and digital infrastructure.

139. The ICT market in Italy faces several challenges, including regional disparities in digital infrastructure, a shortage of digital skills, and the need for further investment in research and development.

There is also a need to address cybersecurity concerns as digital adoption increases across sectors.

The ongoing digital transformation presents, at the same time, significant opportunities for growth in the ICT market. Sectors such as fintech, healthtech, and e-commerce are expected to drive demand for ICT services and solutions.

140. According to the *IDC Worldwide ICT Spending Guide: Enterprise and SMB by Industry*,[52] ICT spending in Italy will reach USD 84.2 billion in value per

52. *See* at https://www.idc.com/getdoc.jsp?containerId=IDC_P33207.

year, rising to USD 96.4 billion in 2026 and growing at a CAGR of 4.9% over the period 2021–2026 (lower than the European average of 5.4%).[53]

Insurance, professional services and banking will drive ICT spending in the long run. Although Italian inflation unexpectedly increased, driven by energy price increases, technology spending will continue to outpace GDP growth.

As far as technology sectors are concerned, *software* will be the fastest-growing sector in Italy, with a five-year CAGR of 11.4%. Software spending will be driven mainly by the adoption of enterprise resource management (ERM) and content management applications, but also by the rapid growth of artificial intelligence platforms.

The consumer sector will remain the main source of ICT spending in Italy, but in the B2B segment, the banking sector will invest the most.

The 2022 and 2023 results offer an opportunity to accelerate digital transformation and the banking system will also play a key role in the implementation of the *National Recovery and Resilience Plan*, as it will help local administrations migrate their data to secure and efficient cloud systems, and provide support in the management of cash and treasury services through new digital systems.

141. Despite the difficulties encountered by OpenAI for ChatGPT in Italy, AI platforms will continue to grow rapidly in the country, with a five-year CAGR of 42.8%.

Healthcare will accelerate investment in AI platforms in the long term, partly due to the NRP. The sector aims to drastically improve diagnoses and enable more accurate and personalized treatments. The *National Recovery and Resilience Plan* will enable technological modernization and digitization-oriented interventions in healthcare facilities – in terms of processes, infrastructure and IT assets – and encourage the adoption of telemedicine tools.

Other growth areas for ICT investments in Italy will include infrastructure as a service (IaaS). IaaS will be a reference technology model for Italian companies, with a CAGR of 24.8% over the period considered by IDC, as with-it companies will be able to avoid the costs associated with maintaining physical servers and hardware.[54]

§2. The Latest Assintel Report and the Italian Market in 2023

142. In the Assintel-IDC report,[55] software (+11.8%) and IT Services (+5.2%) are doing well, hardware (-1.5%) and TLC (-0.8%) are slowing down, and small companies continue to suffer from a lack of resources and skills.

The Italian ICT market continues to grow and in 2023 its value reached EUR 39 billion, +4.8% compared to the previous year.

53. *See* at https://www.anitec-assinform.it/media/comunicati-stampa/nel-2023-il-mercato-digitale-italiano-e-cresciuto-piu-del-pil.kl.

54. *See, also*, S. Casini, *Il mercato del Digitale in Italia ha di fronte un triennio con un grande potenziale di crescita*, at https://www.innovationpost.it/attualita/il-mercato-del-digitale-in-italia-ha-di-fronte-un-triennio-con-un-grande-potenziale-di-crescita/.

55. *See* at https://www.assintel.it/osservatori-2/assintel-report/assintel-report-2023/.

However, it is a two-speed sector, with information technology growing at +5.8% (+8.4% forecast for 2024) and the telecommunications segment dropping instead by 0.8%. These are some of the figures of the *Assintel Report* 2023, the research conducted by Assintel (Confcommercio's National Association of ICT and Digital Companies) together with the research companies IDC Italia and Istituto Ixé, with the sponsorship of Grenke, Intesa Sanpaolo, TIM and Open Gate Italia.

143. In the coming year, 8 out of 10 enterprises will confirm their investments in digitalization and 29% will increase them, while 8.5% are in a complete digital fast (130,000 enterprises, mainly small ones).

The main obstacles to digitization are confirmed to be low financial availability (31%) and lack of digital culture and skills (32.4%), problems felt particularly in the micro and small enterprise segment.

On a macroeconomic level, according to IDC data, the growth of the IT sector is driven by software (+11.8%) and IT Services (+5.2%), while hardware is slowing down (-1.5%).

144. Going into the details of the report, which surveyed 1,000 companies and public administrations, it emerges that the three most prevalent technologies are collaboration (personal computers and smartphones) present in 79.1% of companies, connectivity (ultra-broadband and Wi-Fi) with 73.3%, and cybersecurity (65.1%).

About half have already adopted corporate website solutions, especially e-commerce (53.9%) and management and back-office solutions (47%).

Fewer than 10%, on the other hand, invest or are planning to invest in emerging technologies such as artificial intelligence (7%) and blockchain/NFT (2.8%), although the macroeconomic growth rates of all these remain in double digits.

Speaking of the future, 29% of companies say they will increase their investments in digital in 2024, an improvement of 7 points compared to 2023.

This confirms the very clear gap between large enterprises, almost all of which (93.8%) will continue to invest in technology by upgrading and modernizing their equipment set, and micro enterprises (25.8%) and small enterprises (38.7%), which clearly have fewer investment opportunities. The report also shows that B2B companies invest more than B2C companies and those where the average age of the decision-maker is under 44.

145. Budget growth in 2023 over 2022 compared with intentions over 2024 shows a substantial disappearance of differences, with all sectors having around 30% of companies planning budget increases. Trade will have the strongest growth, rising from 16% to 30% of companies. Industry will grow from 22% to 27%. Services from 22% to 29%. The public sector will fall from 36% to 30%.

146. If we get into the specifics of the technologies on which investments will focus the most, we see that: commerce will focus on customer management (17%) and web/e-commerce solutions (14%), industry on IT infrastructure (11%) and management (10%), the services on web/e-commerce (13%) and cloud (11%)

147. A differentiated picture also emerges geographically.

In 2023, companies in the Northeast are the most likely to increase their budgets (25%), followed by those in the South and Islands (22%), the Centre (21%) and finally the North West (19%). In the context of the improvement expected by 2024, companies in the Northwest will remain more conservative, while the other areas of the country will grow more: first of all those in Central Italy (36%), followed by those in the South and Islands and the North East (31%).

148. The Information and Communication Technologies (ICT) asset – which IDC estimates will reach an expenditure value of almost EUR 39 billion by the end of 2023 – is perceived as indispensable to compete in the market, with more than 90% of Italian companies reporting the use of some digital technology: from the massive diffusion of basic tools, such as computers, smartphones and network connections – to the complex digitization of production processes in manufacturing companies, as well as communication and marketing activities.

149. But there is also a nucleus of companies that is still totally refractory to digitalization, which remains limited in percentage terms (8.5%) and which in absolute terms accounts for about 130,000 companies, predominantly small and very small.

An articulated picture where the penetration of the most advanced and specialized tools remains selective.

150. In particular, familiarity with emerging technologies is still low, with respect to which only relatively small shares of enterprises are developing projects.

While virtual/augmented reality, robotics and artificial intelligence are beginning to spread to a core of almost a tenth of enterprises, blockchain and NFT technologies are only dealt with by very small vanguards of companies (3%), while a slightly higher familiarity characterizes Internet of Things projects (14%), objects with sensors, software and other integrated technologies for the purpose of connecting and exchanging data with other devices and systems on the Internet.

151. Communication and marketing are the processes most affected by digitization. Companies' innovation processes are mainly driven by the need to enhance communication and marketing activities, which is a priority theme for 31%, then by improving customer management (22%), followed by sustainability-related aspects (16%) and corporate reorganization (15%). Clearly, the needs are very differentiated according to the types of companies, but in any case, they focus first on the aspects most directly related to business development and the improvement of company performance.

152. The issues of sustainability and environmental impact reduction also represent rather relevant areas of innovation, especially for large companies that devote a great deal of attention to these aspects. Under these pushes, companies declare their intention to continue the digitization process, mainly by confirming the budgets allocated to ICT technologies and services or, even, as recorded for at least a quarter of the companies, by increasing them.

153. Obstacles include a lack of skills. Among the main obstacles to digitization identified by companies, alongside financial availability, by definition binding and reported by 31%, there are other aspects relating to culture and skills that hinder investment, such as the level of internal skills (16.7%), as well as the corporate culture, little oriented towards innovation and change (15%), and a management reluctant to innovate (4.6%).

On these two fronts, skills and culture, the survey returns a very articulated picture: just over a fifth of the companies (22%) report an optimal situation on both dimensions, while the remaining companies complain of shortcomings, either on the skills front (38%) or on the innovative culture front (16%) or on both (22%), evidently influencing the propensity to consolidate and invest in digitalization.

Chapter 4. Electronic Commerce: Facts and Figures

§1. The State of E-commerce in Italy

154. E-commerce in Italy is a rapidly growing sector, with significant progress in recent years. The COVID-19 pandemic accelerated the adoption of online shopping, and this trend has continued, with more Italian consumers and businesses embracing digital commerce.

E-commerce sales have been consistently rising, with strong growth in sectors like fashion, electronics, and food & groceries. Both local and international e-commerce platforms, such as *Amazon*, *Zalando*, and Italian-based companies like *Yoox* and *ePRICE*, are popular among Italian consumers.

Mobile shopping is increasingly prevalent, with a growing number of consumers using smartphones and tablets to make purchases. Mobile-friendly websites and apps are essential for businesses to capture this market segment.

Many Italian retailers are adopting omnichannel strategies, integrating online and offline experiences to meet consumer demands. This includes offering services like click-and-collect, where customers can order online and pick up in-store.

The use of digital payment methods, including credit/debit cards, *PayPal*, and emerging options like digital wallets, is widespread. The *PagoPA* platform is also increasingly used for various transactions, particularly for public services.

155. Despite the growth, challenges remain. Italy has relatively lower Internet penetration and digital literacy compared to other European countries, which can limit e-commerce's reach.

Additionally, logistical issues, such as delivery infrastructure in more remote areas, and concerns over cybersecurity, are areas needing improvement.

The Italian government and businesses continue to invest in digital infrastructure and initiatives to support e-commerce growth. The trend is expected to continue upward, driven by ongoing digital transformation efforts and the evolving preferences of Italian consumers.

156. Providing a snapshot of Italy's digital commerce is a complex task.

First, we must consider the new purchasing habits of consumers, for whom, especially in the case of *Generation Z*, the boundary between online and offline no longer makes sense.[56]

The other side of the market is made up of businesses, which are faced with an unstable economic situation, also due to geopolitical factors, and the urgency of

56. *See* V. Piccolo, 'Il boom dell'e-commerce in Italia: nel 2023 il giro d'affari supera gli 80 miliardi di euro', at https://www.milanofinanza.it/news/il-boom-dell-ecommerce-in-italia-nel-2023-il-giro-d-affari-supera-gli-80-miliardi-di-euro-202404101815283856. *See, also*, R. Liscia, 'eCommerce in Italia, motore di crescita: dati e prospettive', at https://www.agendadigitale.eu/mercati-digitali/ecommerce/ecommerce-in-italia-motore-di-crescita-dati-e-prospettive/.

acquiring those digital and technological *skills* that are essential to remain competitive in the market.[57]

In 2023, B2C online purchases grew by 13% and reached a value of EUR 54 billion. Online penetration of total retail purchases is 12%, stable compared to 2022.

This was reported by the *Foundation for Digital Sustainability*[58] in its 2023 *E-Commerce Report.* [59] 63% of the surveyed sample say they use e-commerce sites and applications, with the largest share (41%) saying they use them regularly.

157. In 2023, online purchases by Italians grew by 13%. Products increased by 8% compared to 2022; services reached 18.8 billion (+22%). Among products, after the general slowdown in growth in 2022, clothing, beauty and IT are the most dynamic sectors today (with increases of around 10%), while the progression of food & grocery is slowing down (+1% compared to twelve months before).

Among services, growth continues in tourism and transport (+27% compared to 2022) and event ticketing. Online penetration of total retail purchases is 12%, stable compared to 2022.

§2. The Profile of Buyers

158. The profile of online shoppers was revealed by a *Netcomm NetRetail* survey[60] that starts from one point: the number of online shoppers. Although they were not expected to grow in 2023, having stabilized at around 33 million, the growth trend of the last 10 years leads one to interpret this figure more as a reabsorption of the pandemic boom than as a halt in the digitalization of consumers in Italy.

Furthermore, in the last three years, the growth of *habitual online shoppers* (people who buy on average at least once a month) has been 5.5 times that of *sporadic shoppers* (people who declare less than three purchases in a quarter): 'habituals' have reached 24.4 million in 2023, testifying to the fact that e-commerce has now entered the purchasing habits of Italian consumers.

159. While in the early stages of the advent of e-commerce, the average age of shoppers was 36 years old, it has now *risen* considerably (46 years on average) and the share of shoppers in large urban centres has decreased: in short, the profile of online shoppers is gradually approaching that of the entire population.

Also, according to the *Netcomm NetRetail* survey, the Italians' shopping experience is increasingly *omnichannel*: digital is also becoming a resource for guiding the purchase decision, even if it then ends up in a physical shop.

---

57. For a map of e-commerce in Italy in 2024 *see* F. Meta, 'E-commerce, la prima mappa del business: 88mila le aziende italiane che vendono online', at https://www.corrierecomunicazioni.it/digital-economy/ecommerce/e-commerce-la-prima-mappa-del-business-88mila-le-aziende-italiane-che-vendono-online/.
58. *See* at https://sostenibilitadigitale.it.
59. *See* https://sostenibilitadigitale.it/ricerca/sustainable-commerce-cosa-pensano-gli-italiani-del-rapporto-tra-digitale-sostenibilita-e-retail/.
60. *See* at https://www.consorzionetcomm.it/download/netretail-2024-gli-acquisti-digitali-degli-italiani-full-report/.

In fact, in 40% of cases, Italian consumers inform themselves online before buying in shop, mainly by consulting the website of an online retailer or the product/service, using a search engine or a comparator (of offers or features) and suggestions found via social networks (comments and ratings).

160. The incidence of e-commerce on total retail (online + offline) increased to 13% (it was 12% in 2022). In services, the tourism and transport sectors are driving growth (+30%). In products, the most dynamic sectors, with growth rates in line with or above average, are beauty (+11%), computers and consumer electronics (+8%) and publishing (+8%).

On the one hand, services are experiencing a 'second youth', mainly thanks to the very positive performance of the tourism and transport sectors, and the value of online purchases reaches EUR 19.2 billion (+25%). On the other hand, product e-commerce reaches EUR 35 billion (+8%), a more controlled growth than in previous years and largely linked to inflation.

161. Online B2C e-commerce in Italy continues to grow, albeit more slowly than in recent years, and has now assumed such relevance as to be considered central and indispensable for the evolution of retail.

However, inflation, regulatory changes, and the growing attention of public opinion and institutions to the protection of the individual, as a consumer and as a worker, make it necessary to continuously transform the e-commerce value chain.

Today, the challenge for merchants is particularly oriented towards flexibility (to counteract contextual uncertainty and to respond quickly to changes in monetary policies and consumer habits) and sustainability (to ensure compliance with social principles and environmental protection).

162. After a marked acceleration in the last three years, the number of Italian digital consumers has stabilized at *33 million.*

This is a very demanding portion of customers, who no longer make a distinction between online and offline but demand an increasingly personalized offer from digital shops as much as from more traditional shops.

While Italian consumers are grappling with the dynamics of inflation and economic uncertainty – especially in the food and durable goods sectors – it is worth remembering that the dynamics of recession do not directly impact those consumers of luxury and high-end goods in sectors such as fashion, design, food, automotive and cosmetics, which represent a flagship for Italy on an international level.

§3. Innovative Approaches and Environmental Sustainability

163. Retailers and e-commerce merchants, in Italy and abroad, are open to experimenting with frontier technologies capable of improving consumer relationship activities and optimizing back-end processes.

Some examples are the use of artificial intelligence to personalize the customer experience during browsing, choice and online purchase, *virtual try-on* to allow shoppers to virtually test a product experience through the use of cameras, or *extended reality* to simulate the 'physicality' of a shop visit also through digital channels, to improve consumer relationship activities and to optimize back-end processes.

There is also a growing focus on the development of social and environmental sustainability initiatives.

The first area includes corporate welfare actions, projects to support local communities or humanitarian initiatives, and activities to support diversity and inclusion. In the second, there are projects mainly in logistics, such as the adoption of recycled packaging for shipments, the use of electric vehicles for last-mile deliveries, and the expansion of the PUDO (Pick Up/Drop Off) network.

Finally, business models are emerging that propose a more conscious style of consumption, such as the second-hand market which, especially in the clothing and furnishing and home living sectors, is changing the relationship between brands and consumers both offline and online.

The most frequently purchased goods in 2023 are those in the fashion sector and those in the consumer electronics sector.

Nevertheless, in this context, all goods categories experienced a spending contraction, except for the food and tourism sectors.

The spending contraction was due to the too-abrupt growth during the lockdown, but also to the energy crisis and the war in Ukraine. Factors that led to a temporary increase in transport costs.

Chapter 5. E-Government

§1. E-Government in Italy in Summary

164. Italy has made significant strides in e-government, although challenges remain.

The Italian government has been investing in digital transformation to improve public services, transparency, and efficiency. Key initiatives include the *Digital Italy Agency* (AgID),[61] which coordinates the implementation of digital policies, and the *Italia Digitale 2026* plan,[62] part of the EU's *Recovery and Resilience Facility*, aiming to accelerate digitalization in Public Administration.

165. The government has implemented several digital services, such as SPID (*Public Digital Identity System*),[63] which allows citizens to access various public services online securely. The *PagoPA* platform[64] facilitates digital payments to public administrations, while ANPR (*National Resident Population Register*)[65] centralizes citizen data for easier access and management by different government agencies.

Despite these advancements, Italy faces challenges, including *digital literacy gaps* among the population, *regional disparities* in digital infrastructure, and the need for further *modernization* of public sector IT systems.

§2. Italy in the European Framework

166. Italy is still below the European average in the efficiency of digital public services: this is the finding of the *eGovernment Benchmark Report 2023*,[66] the European Commission document that monitors the state of digitalization of digital public services in the group of EU27+ countries (all EU Member States plus Albania, Iceland, North Macedonia, Montenegro, Norway, Serbia, Switzerland and Turkey), drawn up by a working group coordinated by Capgemini[67] in which the Politecnico di Milano[68] has been participating for eight years.

167. Out of a total score set at 100, the average performance of digital public services in Europe is 70 points, with the strong contribution of Malta, the first country with 91 points, Estonia (92), and other states showing advanced levels such as Luxembourg (89), Iceland (88), Finland (86), the Netherlands (85), Lithuania (85),

61. *See* at https://www.agid.gov.it/it.
62. *See* at https://innovazione.gov.it/italia-digitale-2026/.
63. *See* at https://www.spid.gov.it.
64. *See* https://www.pagopa.gov.it.
65. *See* https://www.anagrafenazionale.interno.it.
66. *See* the full text at https://digital-strategy.ec.europa.eu/en/library/egovernment-benchmark-2023.
67. *See* https://www.capgemini.com/it-it/.
68. *See* https://www.polimi.it.

Denmark (85), Latvia (82), Turkey (81) and Norway (80). Italy, despite improvements in recent years, scores *61 points*, far from the best group.[69]

168. The *eGovernment Benchmark Report* evaluates online public services through 14 indicators organized in 4 dimensions:

i. the centrality of the end-user in the service design;
ii. the transparency of information with respect to service delivery;
iii. key technological factors for service deployment, and
iv. the availability of cross-border services. The study employs the mystery shopping methodology: in 2021 and 2022, simulators of service use (shoppers) consulted more than 15,000 public administration websites, testing the user journey of the services offered.

According to the Report, to achieve 100% digitization of basic public services by 2030, as prescribed by the *Digital Compass*,[70] European territories must take three actions.

169. First, they must close the gap between domestic and cross-border users by overcoming language barriers and enabling authentication through digital identity which, although established and distributed on a national basis, respects the common European eIDAS standard.

Second, they must reduce the gap between citizens and businesses, which already enjoy more mature digital services, while as many as 1 in 5 European citizens do not interact online with their public administration.

Finally, it is necessary to close the gap between institutional levels: it is mainly central administrations that deliver services digitally, followed by the regional and to a lesser extent the local level.

§3. The Evolution of the Legislative Framework

170. Beginning in the mid-1990s, ICT assumed considerable importance in economic growth both at the European and national level, and consequently in Italy the need arose to develop *legislative and planning interventions* aimed at supporting the process of transition to digital technology in administrative procedures, in the functioning and organization of the Public Administration, both central and local, and in the provision of services to citizens and businesses.

69. For an introduction to the e-government framework in Italy, *see*: W. D'Avanzo, 'E-government e società del controllo. Il lato oscuro del mondo digitale', Rubbettino, Soveria Mannelli, 2023; L. Tivelli e S. Masini, 'Un nuovo modo di governare, Fazi, 2002; A. Rocchi, Nuovi modelli organizzativi nella pubblica amministrazione', Rubbettino, Soveria Mannelli, 2015; M. Iaselli, 'L'e-procurement', Liguori, Napoli, 2005.

70. *See* https://commission.europa.eu/strategy-and-policy/priorities-2019-2024/europe-fit-digital-age/europes-digital-decade-digital-targets-2030_it.

In this context, over the last thirty years, the legislature has recognized it as a primary need for national economic growth also in relation to the challenges and objectives set at the European level.[71]

171. In the historical reconstruction of the long and complex process of defining the regulatory framework of the digital transition in Italy, the main stages that led to the genesis and evolution of the two main enabling steps such as the *Digital Administration Code* (CAD, hereinafter also 'Code') and the *Italian Digital Agenda* (ADI) will be retraced.

An initial phase of standardization, which anticipated a series of provisions and guidelines that were subsequently taken up and rationalized, ran from the mid-1990s to 2006 when the first version of the CAD came into force.

172. In particular, in 1993, with Legislative Decree No. 39,[72] the first regulations on the subject of automated information systems of public administrations were introduced in order to regulate the design, development and management of information systems with the aim of improving services, transparency and cost containment of administrative action and the strengthening of cognitive supports for decision-making.

The decree provides that the administrative acts adopted by the PA are to be prepared through automated digital systems and establishes the *Authority for Information Technology in Public Administration* (AIPA), regulating in Article 7 its tasks of guiding, coordinating, promoting, and controlling the transition process of administrations to digital.

173. The AIPA authority was later succeeded by the Centro Nazionale per l'Informatica nella Pubblica Amministrazione (CNIPA) in 2003, followed by DigitPA in 2009 and finally the *Agenzia per l'Italia digitale* (AgID) in 2012.

174. Legislative Decree No. 39 of 1993 highlights a key issue, subsequently taken up and developed by the legislator, which concerns the integration and interconnection between the information systems of public administrations and compliance with shared standards, aspects that are also defined in harmony with EU regulations.

---

71. *See* the correct temporal reconstruction by F. Cafiero and A. Lisi, 16 Mar. 2022, 'Codice dell'amministrazione digitale, cos'è e quali sono i punti principali da conoscere', at https://www.agendadigitale.eu/documenti/codice-dellamministrazione-digitale-cose-e-quali-sono-i-punti-principali-da-conoscere/. *See, also*, G. Manca, 'Breve storia della PA digitale: la genesi e l'evoluzione del Codice dell'Amministrazione Digitale', 6 Jul. 2020, at https://www.agendadigitale.eu/cittadinanza-digitale/breve-storia-della-pa-digitale-la-genesi-e-levoluzione-del-codice-dellamministrazione-digitale/.
72. *See* the full official text (in Italian) at https://www.normattiva.it/uri-res/N2Ls?urn:nir:stato:decreto.legislativo:1993-02-12;39.

175. The following years also saw the enactment of: Law 127/1997,[73] containing measures for streamlining administrative activity and decision-making and control procedures, including the introduction of the *Electronic Identity Card* (CIE); Presidential Decree 513/1997,[74] regulating the criteria and procedures for the formation, filing and transmission of documents by computer and telematic means and, in Chapter II, containing important references to the regulation of digital signatures; Presidential Decree 428/1998,[75] containing rules for the management of computerized protocol and document flows by public administrations; Presidential Decree 445/2000,[76] which brings together in a single text all the legislative and regulatory provisions on administrative documentation, both digital and traditional paper-based.

176. In June 2000, in line with the Europe 2002 initiative and after several years of sporadic and non-continuous initiatives, Italy endowed itself with the *Action Plan for the Information Society*, which considers the digital transition a strategic priority and identifies the following four areas of intervention: (i) human capital (training, education, research, development), (ii) e-Government (online services of the Public Administration), (iii) e-Commerce (coordination, rules and procedures), (iv) infrastructures, competition and access.

177. Also in June 2000, the Council of Ministers, on the initiative of the Minister of Public Administration *Franco Bassanini*, approved the e-government action plan, which placed great emphasis on actions aimed at digitalizing the services provided to citizens and businesses and at allowing users telematic access to public administration services and information.

The basic idea is to implement a process of technological innovation whose protagonists are the local administrations that in a decentralized and federal model of the State represent the front-office of the administrative system, in more direct contact with citizens, while the central administrations play the back-office role.

It was soon realized that the realization of this process requires a cooperative implementation and a shared transversal vision between States, regions and local authorities.

178. In 2002, following the adoption of the new European e-Europe 2005 strategy, Italy approved the *Government's Guidelines* document for the development of the Information Society in the legislature (2002–2006) containing the following three lines of action:

---

73. *See* the full official text (in Italian) at https://www.normattiva.it/uri-res/N2Ls?urn:nir:stato:legge:1997-05-15;127!vig=.
74. *See* the full official text (in Italian) at https://www.normattiva.it/uri-res/N2Ls?urn:nir:presidente.repubblica:decreto:1997-11-10;513.
75. *See* the full official text (in Italian) at https://www.normattiva.it/uri-res/N2Ls?urn:nir:presidente.repubblica:decreto:1998-10-20;428.
76. *See* the full official text (in Italian) at https://www.normattiva.it/uri-res/N2Ls?urn:nir:presidente.repubblica:decreto:2000-12-28;445.

i. to improve the efficiency and effectiveness of the PA by leveraging technological innovation;
ii. to stimulate the development of the country system by disseminating new technologies;
iii. to guarantee Italy a leading role in the elaboration of European policies and in the promotion of international cooperation on technological innovation.

179. After a first decade of regulatory interventions, a strong awareness was acquired in our country of the need for a strategic and less fragmented vision of the PA's development plans towards digital and, in this new context, the first version of the *Digital Administration Code* was issued with Legislative Decree No 82 of 7 March 2005, which came into force on 1 January 2006.[77]

180. The CAD represents an important step in this regard as it organizes in a *single regulatory text* all the provisions on the digital activities of administrations and introduces the possibility for citizens to relate to administrations through information and communication technologies.

It also deals, in an organic and in-depth manner, with the use of IT tools in the management of administrative activities and in organizational and procedural aspects with particular attention to relations with citizens and businesses.

181. Only three months after its entry into force, the CAD was amended for the first time by Legislative Decree 159/2006[78]: among the most important additions, it is worth mentioning the transposition into the code of the entire text of Legislative Decree 42/2005[79] (which was repealed at the same time) on the regulation of the *Public Connectivity System* (SPC) and the *International Network of Public Administrations.*

182. The *second regulatory phase* ran from 2008 to 2012 and saw first a number of specific interventions to implement the provisions of the CAD, then the amendment of the Code in terms of simplifying the text and updating it to rapid ICT developments, and finally the definition, first at European level and then at national level, of a *Digital Agenda*, which constitutes a fundamental step in the PA's transition process to digital.

183. In the course of 2008, the legislator promoted interventions aimed at implementing some of the provisions of the CAD, such as the digitalization of administrative documents and the use of *Certified Electronic Mail* (PEC) as a tool for communications: with Decree Law 112/2008, converted with amendments by Law

77. *See* the full official text (in Italian) at https://www.normattiva.it/uri-res/N2Ls?urn:nir:stato:decreto.legislativo:2005-03-07;82.
78. *See* the full official text (in Italian) at https://www.normattiva.it/uri-res/N2Ls?urn:nir:stato:decreto.legislativo:2006-04-04;159.
79. *See* the full official text (in Italian) at https://www.gazzettaufficiale.it/eli/id/2005/03/30/005G0066/sg.

133 of 6 August 2008,[80] administrations are obliged to provide for a 50% reduction, compared to the previous year, of the expenses related to the printing of reports and any other type of publication required by laws and regulations. This law constitutes an incentive for administrations to *dematerialize* and transition to digital documents with the simultaneous elimination of paper; Decree Law No. 185/2008, converted by Law No. 2 of 28 January 2009,[81] introduced the obligation for companies, professionals and administrations to set up a *Certified Electronic Mailbox* in order to speed up communications between the PA and citizens and businesses.

184. However, in this historical period, characterized by political instability, a unified strategy at the national level of the digitization process of public administrations is lacking and the need to set up a *control room* at the central level for the revision and rethinking of the national technical structures in charge of implementing the digital transition plans is becoming felt.

185. It was in this context that in December 2008 the Minister for Public Administration and Innovation presented the 2012 *E-government Plan*, which started from the realization of the need to rationalize the numerous digital initiatives that in previous years had involved a multiplicity of both central and peripheral administrations and had entailed huge costs and initiatives that were often uncoordinated, with waste and duplication.

186. In 2009, with Law 69,[82] a number of regulations were introduced with the aim of speeding up the process of digitization of administrations, and among these the delegation of power to the Government to adopt one or more legislative decrees to amend the CAD also in order to bring it into line, four years after it was first issued, with the rapid developments that have taken place in the ICT sphere.

The delegation of powers provides for the introduction of sanctions for administrations that do not comply with the provisions of the code and for the simplification of the code in order to encourage the adoption and use of technologies by the Public Administration, citizens and businesses.

187. In accordance with and in implementation of this proxy, a reform of the CAD was issued in 2010 with Legislative Decree No. 235 of 30 December 2010.[83]

This decree is defined as the *second pillar* on which the process of renewal and modernization of the public administration initiated with the approval of Legislative

80. *See* the full official text (in Italian) at https://www.normattiva.it/uri-res/N2Ls?urn:nir:stato:legge:2008-08-06;133.
81. *See* the full official text (in Italian) at https://www.normattiva.it/uri-res/N2Ls?urn:nir:stato:legge:2009-01-28;2.
82. *See* the full official text (in Italian) at https://www.normattiva.it/uri-res/N2Ls?urn:nir:stato:legge:2009-06-18;69!vig.
83. *See* the full official text (in Italian) at https://www.gazzettaufficiale.it/eli/id/2011/01/10/011G0002/sg.

Decree No. 150/2009[84] is based, which introduces the principles of meritocracy, reward, transparency, and empowerment of Public Administration managers.

188. During this period, an important step at the European level on the subject of e-Government was the establishment, in May 2010, of the *Digital Agenda for Europe*, which constitutes one of the seven pillars of the Europe 2020 Strategy, that is, one of the seven 'flagship initiatives' aimed at achieving the objectives of relaunching the EU economy and growth up to 2020.[85]

This initiative gave rise to the need to set up an Italian Digital Agenda (ADI)[86] with the aim of creating a *national strategy* based on the principles outlined at the European level and adapting them to national priorities and needs.

In March 2012, therefore, the *Cabina di Regia per l'Agenda Digitale Italiana* (Steering Committee for the Italian Digital Agenda) was set up, which, by the end of June 2012, set itself the goal of preparing a series of regulatory interventions that would form the basis, together with operational projects, for the strategy of this Agenda.

189. In June 2012, the *Agenzia per l'Italia Digitale* (Agency for Digital Italy) was also established, which is responsible for the realization of the objectives of the Italian Digital Agenda, in consistency with the guidelines drawn up by the Steering Committee and with the European Digital Agenda.

AgID performs the functions of coordination, direction and regulation previously entrusted to DigitPA, contributing to the widespread use of information and communication technologies, and promoting innovation and economic growth: the aim is to leverage the potential of ICT technologies to foster innovation, progress and economic growth, with the development of the single digital market as its main objective.

190. In October 2012, the Italian government approved Decree-Law No. 179 *Crescita 2.0*,[87] converted into law on 17 December 2012, No. 221,[88] within which the first part is dedicated precisely to the issues of the *Digital Agenda*.

191. The third regulatory phase runs from 2016, when the European Electronic IDentification Authentication and Signature (eIDAS) Regulation was issued, to the present day.[89]

---

84. *See* the full official text (in Italian) at https://www.normattiva.it/uri-res/N2Ls?urn:nir:stato:decreto.legislativo:2009-10-27;150!vig=.
85. *See* https://www.europarl.europa.eu/factsheets/en/sheet/64/digital-agenda-for-europe.
86. *See* https://www.funzionepubblica.gov.it/digitalizzazione/agenda-digitale.
87. *See* the full official text (in Italian) at https://www.normattiva.it/uri-res/N2Ls?urn:nir:stato:decreto.legge:2012-10-18;179.
88. *See* the full official text (in Italian) at https://www.gazzettaufficiale.it/eli/id/2012/12/18/012G0244/sg.
89. *See*, on the European Union website, at https://digital-strategy.ec.europa.eu/en/policies/eidas-regulation.

192. A nodal step in the standardization process at the European level, particularly with regard to electronic identification tools, is in fact the enactment of EU Regulation No. 910/2014 on digital identity known as the eIDAS Regulation.

Entered into force in July 2016, this regulation provides a common regulatory basis for secure electronic interactions between citizens, businesses and public administrations and enhances the security and effectiveness of electronic services and e-business and e-commerce transactions in the European Union.

Also, in order to comply with the provisions of the eIDAS Regulation, the CAD is further amended and supplemented by Legislative Decree No. 179 of 26 August 2016.[90]

The decree introduces the concept of *digital first*, reformulates many articles on IT documents and electronic signatures, and redefines the role of AgID, recognizing it as a function of coordinating the activity of implementing the European guidelines relating to the digital transition.

In particular, AgID is given the following tasks:

i. to issue rules, standards and technical guides on the Digital Agenda, digitalization of public administration, IT security, interoperability and application cooperation between public and EU IT systems supervising the activities carried out by trust service providers, Certified Electronic Mail operators, accredited registrars and public and private entities involved in the Public Digital Identity System (SPID);
ii. drafting the Three-Year Plan for Information Technology in Public Administration – setting out the objectives and main measures for the development and management of the information systems of public administrations – and verifying their implementation.

193. A subsequent reform of the CAD is implemented with Legislative Decree No. 217 of 13 December 2017,[91] which assigns AgID the task of drawing up special *Guidelines*, which replace the previous technical rules of less rapid adoption and not well adapted to the times of technological evolution but also to the consequent normative evolution at European level.

With this regulatory intervention, the CAD is further rationalized and also simplified in terms of language.

The first part of the CAD is given the nature of a *Charter of Digital Citizenship* in that it contains the fundamental rights of citizens and businesses in the area of digital administration.

194. Other recent changes to the CAD are introduced with the Decree-Law No. 76 of 16 July 2020, the so-called Simplification Decree[92] converted with amendments

90. *See* the full official text (in Italian) at https://www.gazzettaufficiale.it/eli/id/2016/09/13/16G00192/sg.
91. *See* the full official text (in Italian) at https://www.normattiva.it/uri-res/N2Ls?urn:nir:stato:decreto.legge:2017-13-12;217.
92. *See* the full official text (in Italian) at https://www.gazzettaufficiale.it/eli/id/2020/07/16/20G00096/sg.

into Law No. 12/2020,[93] which intervenes on many articles with the aim of *speeding up* the digital transition of the Italian Public Administration.

The most important innovations are those contained in Chapter I of Title III of the Decree, which is dedicated to *Digital Citizenship* and access to the digital services of the public administration and concerns the concepts of digital identity, digital domicile and access to digital services.

Important is, also, the '*bis*' Simplification Decree (Decree-Law No. 77 of 31 May 2021[94] converted into Law No. 108 of 29 July 2021[95]), which in Article 41 supplements the CAD by introducing Article 18-*bis* entitled 'Violation of digital transition obligations'.

The provision confers on AgID the power to supervise, verify, control, and monitor compliance not only with the provisions of the CAD but also with any other rule on the subject of technological innovation and digitalization of public administration, including those contained in the Guidelines and in the three-year plan for information technology in public administration.

The discipline of sanctions in the event of violation of obligations related to digital transformation is strengthened, in order to ensure the implementation of the Italian and European Digital Agenda as well as the digitization of citizens, public administrations and businesses.

In the case of violations, the Agency may proceed ex officio or upon notification by the *Digital Ombudsman*. If it finds that there has been a violation of the obligations set out in the rules expressly indicated in paragraph 5 of the new Article 18-*bis*, it may proceed with the notification and, if the violations are ascertained at the end of the procedure, it may impose an administrative pecuniary sanction in proportion to the seriousness of the violation ascertained.

93. *See* the full official text (in Italian) at https://www.normattiva.it/uri-res/N2Ls?urn:nir:stato:legge:2020-09-11;120.

94. *See* the full official text (in Italian) at https://www.gazzettaufficiale.it/eli/id/2021/05/31/21G00087/sg.

95. *See* the full official text (in Italian) at https://www.normattiva.it/uri-res/N2Ls?urn:nir:stato:legge:2021-07-29;108.

Part I. Digital Market Regulation

Chapter 1. Legal Status of Standards and Technical Specifications

§1. Introduction

195. The *Agency for Digital Italy* (AGID) has drawn up a document, attached to the guidelines on the formation, management and storage of computerized documents, which has highlighted, and neatly broken down, the *main standards* and *technical specifications* that must also be taken into account in the Italian legal framework.[96]

It is not an exhaustive list, but divides the reference standards into three main areas:

i. standards and technical specifications for document management;
ii. those for digital preservation and
iii. those for IT security.

§2. Standards and Technical Specifications for Document Management

196. The first standard cited is UNI ISO 15489-1, an international standard that provides guidelines for *records management*. It is designed to help organizations ensure that their records are accurate, reliable, and accessible and that they support business activities, legal requirements, and stakeholder needs. The standard is widely recognized as a benchmark for best practices in records management, and it is applicable to all types of organizations, regardless of size, industry, or geographic location.

The goal is to ensure that records are managed in a systematic, efficient, and reliable manner, following several records management principles (accountability, transparency, integrity, protection, compliance, availability, retention and disposition).

Compliance with legal, regulatory, and organizational requirements is a key focus, ensuring that records are managed in accordance with applicable laws and regulations.

96. *See* the full document at https://www.agid.gov.it/sites/agid/files/2024-05/linee_guida_tecnologie_e_standard_sicurezza_interoperabilit_api_sistemi_informatici.pdf.

197. The second standard is UNI ISO 15489-2, a complementary part of the ISO 15489 standard, providing more detailed guidance on the implementation of the principles and requirements outlined in UNI ISO 15489-1.

While ISO 15489-1 focuses on the general framework and principles of records management, ISO 15489-2 offers *practical advice* and techniques to help organizations establish and maintain an effective records management system and how to apply the principles of ISO 15489-1 in practice (identifying the records to be managed, understanding their lifecycle, and integrating records management into existing business processes).

198. The standard ISO/TS 23081-1 is a technical specification that provides the foundational principles and framework for managing *metadata* in the context of records management. It is part of the ISO 23081 series, which focuses on metadata used to identify, describe, and manage records throughout their lifecycle.

This technical specification is crucial for organizations seeking to ensure that their records are properly described and accessible over time, especially in digital environments.

The four key principles are:

i. *purpose-driven* (metadata should be created and managed with a clear purpose, aligned with organizational needs and records management objectives);
ii. *interoperability* (metadata should be structured in a way that facilitates interoperability across different systems and platforms);
iii. *sustainability* (metadata must be managed in a manner that ensures its long-term usability, even as technologies change), and
iv. *accountability* (organizations should ensure that metadata management practices are accountable and transparent, with clear responsibilities assigned).

199. ISO/TS 23081-2 is a technical specification that builds upon the principles outlined in ISO/TS 23081-1 by addressing the conceptual and practical issues involved in implementing metadata for records management.

It provides detailed guidance on how to develop and manage metadata in a way that supports the identification, management, and accessibility of records throughout their lifecycle.

This part of the ISO 23081 series is essential for organizations looking to *effectively* implement metadata strategies within their records management systems and to discuss different models and structures for metadata, providing guidance on how to design and implement metadata schemas that meet organizational needs.

It also introduces the concept of *metadata models*, which define the relationships between different metadata elements and how they support records management processes.

200. ISO 16175-1 is the first part of a *three-part series* of technical specifications that provides guidance on the functional requirements for records management in *electronic office* environments.

The series is designed to help organizations ensure that their electronic records management systems (ERMS) meet the necessary functional requirements to manage records effectively, ensuring their *integrity* (protecting records from unauthorized alteration or destruction), *authenticity* (maintaining the authenticity of records, ensuring they are what they purport to be), *reliability* (ensuring that records are reliable and trustworthy over time), and *usability* over time (ensuring records are accessible and usable when needed).

201. ISO 16175-2 is the second part of the ISO/TS 16175 series. This technical specification is designed to help organizations specify, evaluate, and implement digital systems that manage records effectively, ensuring their integrity, authenticity, and accessibility over time.

It describes *core functions* like capture, registration, classification, access and retrieval, retention and disposition, security and access control, audit trails, search and reporting, version control, backup and recovery, digital preservation and workflow management.

202. ISO 16175-3 is the third part of the ISO/TS 16175 series which focuses on the functional requirements for records management within *business systems*.

Unlike traditional records management systems that are specifically designed to manage records, *business systems* are operational systems used to perform routine business functions (e.g., financial systems, HR systems, customer relationship management systems) that may also create and manage records. This standard provides guidance on ensuring that records within these business systems are managed effectively to maintain their integrity, authenticity, reliability, and usability.

203. ISO 15836, also known as *The Dublin Core Metadata Element Set*, is an international standard that specifies a simple and standardized set of metadata elements used to describe a wide range of resources, particularly in the context of digital resources.

The Dublin Core is widely used in various information management and digital archiving applications to facilitate the discovery, sharing, and interoperability of resources across different systems and platforms. Its purpose is to create a basic, yet flexible, metadata schema designed to facilitate the discovery and management of resources. It is named after the *Dublin Core Metadata Initiative* (DCMI), which developed the schema.

The standard specifies 15 core metadata elements that can be used to describe resources. Each element is optional and repeatable, providing flexibility in application. One of the key strengths of the Dublin Core is its ability to promote *interoperability* between different systems and organizations, facilitating the exchange and integration of information across various platforms.

204. ISO 9001 is an internationally recognized standard that specifies the requirements for a *quality management system* (QMS). It is designed to help organizations ensure that they meet the needs of customers and other stakeholders while complying with statutory and regulatory requirements related to a product or service. ISO 9001 is part of the ISO 9000 family of standards and is the only standard in the family that can be certified.

ISO 9001 introduces a *risk-based approach* to quality management, requiring organizations to identify and address risks and opportunities that could impact their QMS.

205. ISO 30300:2011 is a part of the ISO 30300 series, which focuses on management systems for records. This specific standard provides the foundational concepts, principles, and vocabulary related to the management systems for records (MSR). It is designed to help organizations understand and implement records management systems that support their business needs, legal obligations, and stakeholder requirements.

It emphasizes that records management is not just about keeping records but about ensuring that they are reliable, usable, and maintained appropriately throughout their lifecycle.

The principles of transparency, accountability, integrity, protection, and systematic management are central to the effective management of records and are emphasized throughout the standard.

206. ISO 30301:2011 is part of the ISO 30300 series, which provides a framework for establishing, implementing, maintaining, and improving a records management system within an organization.

The standard highlights the crucial role of top management in establishing, maintaining, and improving the MSR, ensuring that it is integrated into the organization's operations and that adequate resources are provided.

Organizations are required to address risks and opportunities related to records management, ensuring that the MSR is resilient and capable of adapting to changes in the internal and external environment.

207. ISO 30302:2015 is designed to help organizations effectively establish, implement, maintain, and improve their records management systems, ensuring they meet their business objectives, legal requirements, and stakeholder expectations.

ISO 30302:2015 includes annexes that provide additional guidance and examples to support the implementation process.

These annexes may include sample templates, checklists, and case studies to help organizations apply the guidelines in practical scenarios. The inclusion of annexes and additional resources makes the standard highly practical.

208. ISO/TR 23081-3 is a technical report that provides a self-assessment method for organizations to evaluate their metadata practices in records management. It is part of the ISO 23081 series, which focuses on metadata for records. This part specifically helps organizations assess how well they are implementing the principles and guidelines set out in the earlier parts of the ISO 23081 series (ISO 23081-1 and ISO 23081-2).

209. The MoReq 2001 (*Model Requirements for the Management of Electronic Records*) is a set of functional requirements and guidelines designed to provide a standardized approach to electronic records management (ERM) within organizations. Developed under the auspices of the European Commission, MoReq 2001 is intended to help organizations ensure that their electronic records management systems (ERMS) meet both operational and regulatory needs.

210. The MoReq 2 Specification 2008 is an enhanced version of the original MoReq, released in 2008. MoReq2 builds on the foundation of MoReq 2001, offering more comprehensive and flexible specifications to accommodate the evolving needs of records management in increasingly complex digital environments.

One of the significant additions in MoReq2 is the introduction of a *testing and certification framework*. The specification includes a detailed test framework that vendors can use to demonstrate that their ERMS products meet the requirements outlined in MoReq2.

This testing framework is intended to provide assurance to organizations that the systems they procure are compliant with the MoReq2 specifications.

211. The MoReq2010, also known as MoReq2 Revised, is a significant update and expansion of the MoReq2 (2008) standard. It aims to provide a comprehensive and modular framework, addressing the increasingly complex requirements of digital *recordkeeping* in various organizational contexts. MoReq 2010 is designed to be more flexible and adaptable, allowing for implementation across different industries and jurisdictions.

One of the most significant innovations in MoReq 2010 is its *modular structure*. The core module provides essential requirements for electronic records management, while additional modules can be selected based on specific needs.

This modular approach allows organizations to implement only the modules relevant to their business processes, making the standard highly adaptable.

§3. Standards and Technical Specifications for Digital Preservation

212. UNI 11386, often referred to as the SinCRO standard, is an Italian technical standard that outlines the requirements and guidelines for the creation, management, and preservation of *electronic documents*.

The standard is particularly relevant for organizations operating in Italy, providing a framework to ensure that electronic documents are managed in a way that maintains their integrity, authenticity, reliability, and usability over time.

UNI 11386 is applicable to any organization that handles electronic documents, whether in public administration or private sectors and provides guidelines for ensuring these documents are legally valid and can be preserved over time.

The standard provides detailed requirements for the creation of electronic documents, emphasizing the need for standardized formats that ensure long-term accessibility and usability. It specifies the types of metadata that must be associated with electronic documents to support their management and preservation. These metadata include information such as the document's creation date, author, format, and any relevant classification data.

UNI 11386 outlines the processes for managing electronic documents throughout their lifecycle, from creation to final disposition. The standard emphasizes the importance of a *structured approach* to document management, including the use of classification schemes, file plans, and metadata to organize and retrieve documents efficiently. It also provides guidelines for *version control*, ensuring that changes to documents are tracked and that the correct versions are maintained and accessible.

The preservation of electronic documents is a key focus of UNI 11386. The standard provides guidelines on how to ensure that electronic documents remain accessible, readable, and usable over the long term. It addresses the technical aspects of document preservation, including the use of preservation formats, migration strategies, and the need for regular audits to verify the integrity of preserved documents. The standard also highlights the importance of digital signatures and other security measures to maintain the authenticity and integrity of electronic documents during the preservation process.

UNI 11386 includes specific requirements to ensure that electronic document management and preservation practices comply with Italian legal and regulatory frameworks.

The standard provides guidance on how to meet the *legal requirements* for document authenticity, integrity, and reliability, which are essential for ensuring that electronic documents can be used as evidence in legal and administrative proceedings.

It also discusses the importance of complying with data protection regulations, particularly concerning the management of personal data within electronic documents.

The standard places significant emphasis on the role of metadata in the management and preservation of electronic documents. It specifies the types of metadata that should be captured and managed, including administrative, descriptive, and technical metadata. This metadata is crucial for supporting document retrieval, ensuring document integrity, and facilitating long-term preservation.

213. ISO 14721, also known as the *OAIS Reference Model*, is a widely recognized standard that provides a framework for the long-term preservation of digital information. The OAIS model was originally developed by the *Consultative Committee for Space Data Systems* (CCSDS) and was later adopted as an ISO standard. It is used by organizations around the world to design and implement digital archives that ensure the preservation, accessibility, and usability of digital information over time.

OAIS is designed to serve as a conceptual framework for understanding and applying the functions necessary for the preservation of digital information. The model provides *terminology* and *concepts* that help standardize the processes and structures used in digital archiving.

The standard outlines the functional components of an OAIS, which are grouped into six major functions:

i. *ingest* (the processes involved in acquiring and receiving information from producers – content creators and preparing it for archival storage);
ii. *archival storage* (the functions related to the storage, maintenance, and retrieval of digital information over time, including data integrity checks and backup processes);
iii. *data management* (the activities required to manage the metadata that describes the archived information, ensuring it can be searched, retrieved, and understood);
iv. *administration* (the functions necessary to manage the overall operation of the archive, including policies, system monitoring, and user access management);
v. *preservation planning* (the processes involved in monitoring the environment and technology to anticipate and respond to changes that could impact the long-term accessibility of the archived information), and
vi. *access* (the functions that support the identification, retrieval, and delivery of archived information to users, ensuring it remains accessible and usable).

§4. Standards for Reliability and Certification

214. ISO 16363, also known as the *Audit and Certification of Trustworthy Digital Repositories*, is an international standard that provides a comprehensive framework for assessing the trustworthiness of digital repositories.

The standard outlines the criteria and processes required to audit and certify digital repositories, ensuring that they can reliably preserve digital information over the long term. It is particularly relevant for organizations involved in the preservation of digital assets, such as archives, libraries, and research institutions.

215. ISO 16919 is an international standard that outlines the requirements for organizations that conduct audits and provide certification for digital repositories seeking to be recognized as trustworthy.

This standard is closely related to ISO 16363, which provides the criteria for auditing and certifying trustworthy digital repositories.

ISO 16919 ensures that the bodies performing these audits and certifications operate with the highest level of integrity, competence, and consistency.

216. ISO 17068 is an international standard that provides guidelines for the establishment, management, and operation of a trusted third party (TTP) repository for digital records.

The standard outlines the requirements and best practices for ensuring that digital records are stored, managed, and preserved securely and reliably by a third-party service provider.

This standard is particularly relevant for organizations that outsource the management of their digital records to external providers.

ISO 17068 emphasizes the need for trust between the client organization and the TTP repository. The repository must operate transparently and be accountable for the management and preservation of the client's digital records.

The standard outlines strict security and confidentiality requirements to protect digital records from unauthorized access, modification, and loss. This includes implementing robust access controls, encryption, and secure storage practices.

ISO 17068 ensures that TTP repositories comply with all relevant legal and regulatory requirements, including those related to data protection, privacy, and intellectual property.

§5. Standards and Technical Specifications for Information Security

217. The ISO/IEC 27001 is an internationally recognized standard for information security management systems (ISMS).

It provides a systematic approach to managing sensitive company information so that it remains secure.

This standard includes people, processes, and IT systems by applying a risk management process.

ISO/IEC 27001 is part of the ISO/IEC 27000 family of standards, which are designed to help organizations manage the security of assets such as financial information, intellectual property, employee details, and information entrusted by third parties.

ISO/IEC 27001 places significant emphasis on risk management, requiring organizations to identify, assess, and treat information security risks. The risk-based approach ensures that the ISMS is tailored to the specific needs and vulnerabilities of the organization.

ISO/IEC 27001 mandates the establishment of processes for detecting, responding to, and recovering from information security incidents, ensuring that organizations can manage and mitigate the impact of security breaches.

218. ISO/IEC 27017 is a security standard that provides guidelines for information security controls specifically designed for cloud services.

It is an extension of the ISO/IEC 27002 standard, which offers best practices for information security management.

ISO/IEC 27017 addresses both cloud service providers (CSPs) and cloud service customers (CSCs), providing recommendations to help them manage and secure cloud environments effectively.

The core of ISO/IEC 27017 consists of cloud-specific adaptations of the information security controls outlined in ISO/IEC 27002. These controls are tailored to address the risks and challenges associated with cloud environments.

The standard highlights the importance of clearly defining the division of security responsibilities between cloud service providers and customers. Understanding and formalizing these responsibilities is critical for ensuring comprehensive security coverage.

ISO/IEC 27017 provides specific guidance on securing virtualized environments, which are common in cloud computing. This includes ensuring proper segregation of resources and maintaining the security of virtual machines.

ISO/IEC 27017 advises on managing data location and the legal implications of storing and processing data in different jurisdictions. This is particularly important for organizations operating in multiple regions with varying legal requirements.

The standard emphasizes the importance of managing cloud service contracts and service level agreements (SLAs) to ensure that security requirements are clearly defined and met by the cloud service provider.

219. ISO/IEC 27018 is a security standard that focuses specifically on protecting personal data in cloud computing environments. It is an extension of ISO/IEC 27001 and ISO/IEC 27002, providing additional controls and guidelines tailored to cloud service providers (CSPs) that process personally identifiable information (PII). The standard is designed to help CSPs implement measures that protect PII and ensure compliance with applicable privacy regulations.

The standard applies to any public cloud service provider that processes PII on behalf of customers. It is relevant for all types of cloud services, including Infrastructure as a Service (IaaS), Platform as a Service (PaaS), and Software as a Service (SaaS).

The primary focus is on helping cloud service providers ensure that their data processing activities comply with applicable privacy laws and regulations.

ISO/IEC 27018 emphasizes the importance of obtaining explicit consent from data subjects before processing their PII. Cloud service providers must ensure that data subjects are informed about how their data will be used and that they have given clear consent.

The standard requires that PII be collected and processed only for specified, explicit, and legitimate purposes. CSPs must ensure that PII is not used in ways that are incompatible with the purposes for which it was originally collected.

ISO/IEC 27018 promotes the principle of data minimization, where only the minimum amount of PII necessary for the specified purposes is collected and processed.

The standard mandates that PII be used and retained only for as long as necessary to fulfil the purposes for which it was collected. It also includes guidelines on how PII can be disclosed to third parties, ensuring that such disclosures are lawful and subject to appropriate safeguards.

Cloud service providers must be transparent about their data processing activities, including how PII is collected, processed, stored, and shared. This involves providing clear and accessible information to data subjects and customers about data handling practices.

ISO/IEC 27018 includes provisions to support the rights of data subjects, such as the right to access, correct, and delete their PII. Cloud service providers must have processes in place to respond to data subjects' requests in a timely and effective manner.

The standard includes guidelines for managing and reporting data breaches involving PII. Cloud service providers must have procedures in place to detect, respond to, and report breaches to affected parties and relevant authorities promptly.

220. ETSI TS 101 533-1 V1.2.1 is a technical specification developed by the European Telecommunications Standards Institute (ETSI). It provides general system requirements for the management of Secure Elements (SEs) in smart cards and other secure devices. Secure Elements are tamper-resistant platforms that can securely host applications and store sensitive data, such as cryptographic keys and personal information.

221. ETSI TR 101 533-2 V1.2.1 is the second part of the technical specification focused on the remote management of Secure Elements (SEs). This document builds on the general system requirements outlined in Part 1 and provides detailed requirements for the secure remote management of SEs, particularly in the context of over-the-air (OTA) updates and remote provisioning.

The document emphasizes the need for secure channels and protocols to prevent unauthorized access or tampering during remote provisioning and updates.

§6. Minimum ICT Security Measures in the Public Administration

222. Public Administrations are required to comply with the minimum ICT security measures issued by AgID in Circular No. 2/2017 of 18 April 2017.

The circular is part of the broader effort to enhance cybersecurity and ensure the protection of digital assets and data within public sector entities. These measures are mandatory and serve as a baseline for securing ICT infrastructures across public administrations.

The circular applies to all public administrations in Italy, including central and local government bodies, agencies, and other public sector entities. It sets out mandatory security measures that these organizations must implement to protect their ICT systems and data.

The goal is to standardize cybersecurity practices across the public sector, ensuring that all entities adhere to a common set of minimum security requirements.

223. Public Administrations are required to adopt a risk management approach to cybersecurity. This involves identifying, assessing, and mitigating risks to their ICT infrastructure and information assets.

The circular emphasizes the need for regular risk assessments to identify potential threats and vulnerabilities. These assessments should inform the implementation of appropriate security controls to mitigate identified risks.

224. The circular mandates the establishment of a formal security governance framework within Public Administrations. This includes defining roles and responsibilities for cybersecurity within the organization, appointing a Chief Information Security Officer (CISO), and ensuring that senior management is involved in cybersecurity decision-making.

Security governance also involves the development and implementation of security policies, procedures, and guidelines that are aligned with the organization's overall strategic objectives.

225. The circular specifies a set of technical and organizational measures that Public Administrations must implement to secure their ICT systems. These measures are grouped into different categories, including:

1. *Access Control.* Implementing strong authentication and authorization mechanisms to ensure that only authorized users have access to ICT systems and data.
2. *Data Protection.* Ensuring the confidentiality, integrity, and availability of data through encryption, backup, and secure data storage practices.
3. *Network Security.* Protecting network infrastructure through the use of firewalls, intrusion detection/prevention systems (IDS/IPS), and secure network configurations.
4. *System Security.* Ensuring that all ICT systems are regularly updated with the latest security patches and protected against malware and other threats.
5. *Incident Management.* Establishing processes for detecting, responding to, and recovering from cybersecurity incidents, including the reporting of incidents to relevant authorities.

226. The circular emphasizes the importance of cybersecurity awareness and training for all employees within public administrations. Staff members should be regularly trained on security best practices, the importance of data protection, and how to recognize and respond to potential security threats.

Public administrations are required to conduct regular awareness programs and provide training that is tailored to the roles and responsibilities of their employees.

227. Continuous monitoring of ICT systems is required to detect and respond to security incidents in a timely manner. The circular mandates the implementation of monitoring tools and processes that allow for the real-time detection of suspicious activities.

In addition, Public Administrations must conduct regular audits and security assessments to ensure that the minimum security measures are being effectively implemented and adhered to.

228. Public administrations are required to document their compliance with the minimum security measures outlined in the circular. This includes maintaining records of risk assessments, security policies, incident reports, and audit findings.

The circular also mandates regular reporting to AgID or other relevant authorities on the implementation of these security measures, including any significant security incidents and the steps taken to address them.

229. The circular requires Public Administrations to have a well-defined incident response plan in place. This plan should outline the steps to be taken in the event of a cybersecurity incident, including containment, eradication, recovery, and post-incident analysis.

Public administrations must also ensure that they have adequate resources and procedures in place for the rapid recovery of ICT services following an incident, minimizing downtime and the impact on operations.

Chapter 2. Legal Status of Standard Terms and Conditions

§1. The Italian Legal Framework

230. In the Italian legal framework, the legal status of terms and conditions and general contractual clauses is governed by various provisions of the *Italian Civil Code*, particularly within the context of *contracts*.

231. General contractual clauses are considered binding and enforceable for the contracting parties provided they meet certain requirements under Italian law.[97]

These are the most important principles:

i. *freedom of contract* (Article 1322 of the Italian Civil Code). Parties are generally free to determine the content of their contract, including the inclusion of general clauses, provided that the terms do not violate mandatory legal provisions or public order;
ii. *transparency and good faith* (Article 1375 Italian Civil Code.). The interpretation and application of general clauses must adhere to principles of good faith and fairness. Clauses that are unclear or ambiguous may be interpreted against the party that drafted them (Article 1370 Italian Civil Code);
iii. *Unfair Clauses* (Article 1341 and Article 1342 Italian Civil Code). Certain clauses, particularly those that limit the liability of one party, impose significant obligations on the other party, or provide for automatic renewal of the contract, must be specifically approved in writing by the non-drafting party. If such approval is not obtained, these clauses may be deemed null and void.

232. Terms and conditions, often used in consumer contracts or standardized agreements, are subject to additional scrutiny:

i. *incorporation and awareness* (Article 1341 Italian Civil Code). Terms and conditions are binding only if the party accepting them is aware of them or could reasonably be expected to have known about them. They must be provided in a clear and understandable manner;
ii. *unfair terms* (Legislative Decree 206/2005). For contracts between businesses and consumers, the Italian Consumer Code ('Codice del Consumo') applies. It regulates unfair terms and provides that any clause creating a significant imbalance in the rights and obligations of the parties to the detriment of the consumer is considered unfair and, therefore, void. Article 33 (Italian Consumer Code) provides a presumption of vexatiousness of certain clauses unless then proven otherwise. Article 36, c. II, (Italian Consumer Code) provides a list of clauses that are always considered unfair and void even if they are negotiated between the parties. The remainder of the contract remains in effect, provided it can continue without the unfair terms;

---

97. *See* S. Patti, 'Le condizioni generali di contratto' (Cedam, Padova, 1996); L. Nissolino, 'Le clausole abusive nei contratti', 'Il Sole 24 Ore', 2004.

iii. *mandatory provisions.* Any clause that contradicts mandatory provisions of law or public policy will be considered null and void (Article 1418 Italian Civil Code). Courts in Italy have the authority to interpret contracts and their clauses. If a dispute arises, courts will consider the entire contract, including general clauses and terms and conditions, to determine the intent of the parties and the fairness of the terms;
iv. *void and voidable clauses* (Articles 1418 et seq. Italian Civil Code). Clauses that contravene specific legal requirements can be declared void or voidable by the courts;
v. *interpretation against the drafter* (Article 1370 Italian Civil Code). If a clause is ambiguous, it will be interpreted in favour of the party that did not draft it, especially in the case of pre-formulated standard contracts.

233. General terms and conditions are a set of clauses that are not included in the document but are nevertheless part of the negotiation content.

General terms and conditions prepared by one of the contracting parties are effective against the other if at the time of conclusion of the contract the latter knew or ought to have known of them using ordinary diligence: so states Article 1341 Italian Civil Code.

234. Both the case envisaged by Article 1341 Italian Civil Code and that envisaged by Article 1342 Italian Civil Codefall within the phenomenon of *contracts by adhesion*, i.e., those contracts that a party prepares in a uniform manner in order to regulate a potentially infinite series of relationships to which it will become a party.

Article 1342 Italian Civil Code, however, also includes the case of parties who enter into a contract using a form prepared by others.

Articles 1341 Italian Civil Code and 1342 Italian Civil Code thus do not refer to a type of contract but to a mode of formation of certain contracts. The phenomenon is also known as mass or standardized, contracts (hence the name standard contracts, or also contracts by adhesion).

235. The rule (Article 1341, c. I, Italian Civil Code) says that when one of the contracting parties has prepared general terms and conditions, they are incorporated in the individual contract if the other party has known them or ought to have known them with ordinary diligence.

In essence, the rule imposes two duties on both parties:

i. on the adhering party, it imposes to ascertain the general terms and conditions of the contract practised by the contractor;
ii. it imposes on the latter to make them knowable, i.e., to make them available to the customer and to formulate them in an intelligible text.

If the contracting party did not know the clauses despite using ordinary diligence, they would be null and void.

236. The following clauses (considered vexatious) must be approved in writing (Article 1341, c. II, Italian Civil Code):

i. clauses limiting liability, clauses limiting the right to withdraw from the contract or to suspend its performance, forfeiture clauses;
ii. clauses limiting the right to raise objections;
iii. clauses restricting freedom of contract in relations with third parties;
iv. clauses tacitly extending or renewing the contract;
v. arbitration clauses;
vi. clauses derogating from territorial jurisdiction.

A reference to the *numbers* and a brief description, such as the titling of the clause, of the vexatious clauses and their unitary approval also constitutes approval.

§2. The Main Case Law

237. In a decision of T.A.R. (Administrative Regional Tribunal) in Rome (Lazio), section I, 1 June 2023, decision No. 9344, stated that it constitutes *misconduct* to publish online the general terms and conditions of the contract *only in English*, even in the 'online shop' section, thus preventing a clear and immediate understanding of the contractual discipline by Italian consumers, in violation of Article 22 of the Consumer Code.

In this regard, Article 9 of the same Code, entitled 'Indications in the Italian language', provides that 'all information intended for consumers and users must be provided at least in Italian'.

Such conduct makes the real content and terms of the offer or product not clearly perceptible, thereby misleading the consumer and influencing him to take economic actions that he would not otherwise have taken.

238. In the decision of Court ('Tribunale') of Rome, on 9 February 2022, concerning a *dead husband*, it was stated legitimate the wife's request for access to retrieve personal data from man's accounts was.

The 'family reasons deserving protection' pursuant to Article 2-*terdecies* of Legislative Decree No. 196/2003 prevail over the content rights non-transferability clause stipulated by the Internet service provider with the then deceased user who subscribed to the general conditions.

The exercise of the right of access to the personal data of the deceased under Article 2-*terdecies*, paragraph 1, of Legislative Decree No. 196/2003, kept within an *iCloud* account made available by a provider of an information society service under a distance contract, must be allowed to heirs who can prove that they have family reasons worthy of protection and, therefore, cannot be made subject to the recurrence of further requirements, provided for by the contract underlying the use of the account but extraneous to the legislation on access to personal data.

In the present case, the family reasons deserving protection had been identified and alleged by the appellant widow in her wish to transmit the memory of her father to her two young daughters, aged three and five, on account of the significant emotional content of the photos and videos stored in her father's *iCloud* account.

239. According to Court of Cassation, Civil section II, 21 June 2024, No. 17157, in relation to a *database licence agreement*, was stated that a database licence agreement is not subject to formal requirements and, therefore, proof of its conclusion may also be furnished by presumptions as to the actual performance of the services covered by the agreement.

Chapter 3. International Private Law Applied to the Online Environment

240. In Italy, the legislation regulating private international law (DIP) is enshrined in Law No. 218/1995. It is an outdated regulation and today of residual application, in favour of the application of both international conventions and regulations of European derivation, which are applied on a primary basis.[98]

241. As is well known, the rules of private international law are so-called *conflict rules*. They are called upon to regulate certain cases when they present elements of internationality; it is evident that in these cases it is necessary to determine not only the applicable law but also the competent judge to regulate the specific case.

242. The Italian legislature, with Law No. 218/1995, has regulated certain specific matters that are more likely to have elements of internationality, specifically: the capacity and rights of persons; legal persons; family relations; adoptions; protection of incapacitated persons and maintenance obligations; successions; rights in rem; contractual and non-contractual obligations.

243. Therefore, the online environment is not expressly regulated in Italy; it will then be necessary to verify on a case-by-case basis the applicability, once the presence of specific international conventions and European Regulations has been excluded, of the DIP rules to a given case, such as in the case of contracts concluded in the digital environment where the need to identify the applicable law or the competent judge arises.

---

98. *See* F. Mosconi, C. Campiglio, 'Diritto internazionale privato e processuale' (Utet, Milano, 2022); S. Armellini, B. Barel, 'Diritto internazionale privato' (Giuffrè, Milano, 2022); D. Carreau, F. Marrella, 'Diritto internazionale' (Giuffrè, Milano, 2023); A. Gioia, 'Diritto internazionale' (Giuffrè, Milano, 2022); A. Tanzi, 'Introduzione al Diritto Internazionale Contemporaneo' (Cedam, Padova, 2023).

Chapter 4. Competition Law Applied to the Digital Market

§1. The Role of the Italian Authority

244. The Italian Competition Authority is an administrative independent Authority, established by Law No. 287 of 10 October 1990 ('The Competition and Fair Trading Act'), which introduced *antitrust rules* in Italy.

Subsequent laws endowed it with additional powers, the most important of which concern the repression of unfair commercial practices, misleading and unlawful comparative advertising and the application of conflict of interests laws to government office holders.

Being an independent Authority it has the status of a *public agency* whose decisions are taken on the basis of the Act without any possibility of interference by the Government.

245. The Authority's independence is reinforced by the appointment procedures and prerequisites of its Chairman and three Members.

They remain in office for a seven-year non-renewable term and are jointly appointed by the Presidents of the Chamber of Deputies and Senate.

The prerequisites for the Chairman include a reputation for independence and service in other high-level institutional positions.

The Members are selected among the magistrates of the State Council, the Court of Auditors and the Court of Appeals, full university professors of economics or jurisprudence and outstanding personalities from the economic sector with impeccable reputations.[99]

§2. Competition Law in the Digital Market in Italy

246. Italy's approach to competition law in the digital market is framed within both national legislation and European Union (EU) competition law.

The digital market, with its unique characteristics such as network effects, big data, and platform dominance, presents specific challenges that Italian authorities and courts address through a combination of existing laws and new regulatory frameworks.

247. Key norms governing competition in the digital market are the Italian Antitrust Law (Law No. 287/1990). It is the foundation of Italy's competition law, which establishes rules against anti-competitive agreements, abuses of dominant positions, and mergers that could significantly impede competition. This law is applied across all sectors, including digital markets.

In particular, Article 2 prohibits anti-competitive agreements (similar to Article 101 of the Treaty on the Functioning of the European Union), Article 3 prohibits

99. *See* https://en.agcm.it/en/about-us/.

the abuse of a dominant position (similar to Article 102 of the Treaty on the Functioning of the European Union), Article 6 concerns the control of concentrations (mergers and acquisitions) that might create or strengthen a dominant position in a way that significantly impedes competition.[100]

248. Given that Italy is a member of the European Union, EU competition law, particularly Articles 101 and 102 of the Treaty on the Functioning of the European Union (TFEU), also applies. These provisions deal with anti-competitive agreements and abuses of dominant positions at the EU level.

The *Digital Markets Act* (DMA), adopted by the EU in 2022, also plays a significant role in regulating large digital platforms (referred to as 'gatekeepers'). This regulation directly affects how competition law is applied in Italy to digital markets.

249. The Italian Consumer Code (Legislative Decree No. 206/2005) is relevant when digital market practices intersect with *consumer rights*.

It includes provisions against unfair commercial practices, which can often overlap with competition law issues in digital markets. A commercial practice is unfair when, contrary to the principle of professional diligence, it distorts or is likely to distort to an appreciable extent the economic behaviour of the average consumer it reaches or to whom it is directed.

The Consumer Code distinguishes between misleading and aggressive commercial practices. The former (Articles 21–23 of the Consumer Code) are likely to mislead the average consumer by distorting his or her decision-making process. If the company acts with harassment, coercion or other forms of undue influence, its behaviour is considered aggressive (Articles 24–26 of the Consumer Code).[101]

250. The Italian Competition Authority (AGCM) often cooperates with other regulatory bodies such as the Communications Regulatory Authority (AGCOM) and the Data Protection Authority ('Garante per la protezione dei dati personali') to address competition issues in the digital market.

§3. Competition Law and the Digital Sector

251. Several areas of intervention concerned in the last years in the digital sector.

Two investigations, in 2023, addressed the issue of *personal data.*

> The first proceeding has led to the adoption of commitments aimed at removing the obstacles posed by Google to sharing data with other platforms at the

---

100. *See* M. Lamicela, 'Pratiche commerciali scorrette e rimedi: nuove strategie di private enforcement tra restituzioni e risarcimento' (Giappichelli, Torino, 2024).

101. *See* G. De Cristofaro (ed.), 'Pratiche commerciali scorrette e codice del consumo: il recepimento della direttiva 2005/29/Ce nel diritto italiano (decreti legislativi nn. 145 e 146 del 2 agosto 2007)' (Giappichelli, Torino, 2008).

request of users. The second, ongoing, is examining the apparently discriminatory ways in which Apple acquires users' consent to the tracking of their browsing data through downloaded applications.

252. The Authority intervened also by taking precautionary measures to ensure the proper conduct of negotiations between META and SIAE to define the remuneration of *Italian artists* for music content made available on the platform's social networks.

For the first time, the Authority used the presumption of economic dependence related to the use of intermediation services provided by a digital platform.

The innovative approach consisted in deeming SIAE's economic dependence on META to exist, irrespective of the fact that SIAE is the main collecting society active in Italy and that it does not develop a significant part of its turnover with META, valuing, on the contrary, the indispensability of access to the platform in order to reach users.

This approach, which was shared by the Lazio Regional Administrative Court in the judgment that upheld the precautionary measure, is based on the conviction that, in order to fully grasp the internal dynamics of digital ecosystems, the abuse of economic dependence cannot but take on different connotations and hermeneutical criteria compared to traditional economic sectors.

253. On the other hand, the Authority's interventions have sought to remedy the intrinsic fragility of *consumers in the digital world*, which stems from information and negotiation asymmetries.

Indeed, the development of digital platforms has led to the emergence of new marketing models, characterized by unprecedented forms of interaction between consumers and businesses.

254. The sharing of one's consumption experiences on social networks and in dedicated virtual spaces, which is part of the broader phenomenon of *feedback* and content generation by users, has proved likely to significantly orient purchase choices. Companies' promotional strategies have therefore adapted to the new context, making the most of consumer reviews in the marketing of products or services, or exploiting the visibility of *influencers*, who are able to reach a large number of potential buyers with their messages.

In this regard, the proceedings aimed at repressing misconduct in relation to online reviews and the investigations conducted in the field of influencer marketing are worth mentioning.

The latter have highlighted, *inter alia*, how consumer behaviour can be unduly prejudiced by communication based on an ambiguous mixture of sponsorship and *charitable initiatives*, leading them to believe – contrary to the truth – that they are contributing to the charitable initiative through the purchase of the product.

255. This profile was the focus of the proceedings closed against the companies Balocco S.p.A. Industria Dolciaria, Fenice S.r.l. and TBS Crew S.r.l. – the last two companies referable to the influencer Chiara Ferragni – concerning the initiative 'Pandoro Pink Christmas'.[102]

At the end of the investigation, the Authority ascertained that the donation advertised as being linked to the sales of the 'Pandoro Pink Christmas' had been made by Balocco alone several months before the launch of the product on the market, for a fixed amount, therefore without any relation to the quantities of the product sold, and without any direct participation of the influencer involved in the charitable initiative.

256. In another respect, the Authority intervened to ensure compliance with the diligence obligations incumbent on digital platforms offering services to consumers in the absence of a monetary consideration.

In these cases, it must be avoided that the adoption of aggressive practices aimed at extending the time for consumers to use the service, also by means of *algorithmic profiling techniques*, determines a more intense prejudice for the most vulnerable categories of users.

For example, the Authority sanctioned *TikTok* in relation to certain dangerous content conveyed to the user segments most exposed in terms of safety, i.e., minors, through a recommendation system based on profiling and aimed at increasing interactions and time spent online.

257. In addition, the more traditional enforcement activities in online commerce continued, aimed at repressing the non-delivery of products, the failure to refund the amount paid for order cancellation or the exercise of the right of withdrawal, as well as the charging to consumers of an additional commission in relation to the chosen payment instrument (the so-called credit card surcharge).

258. The particular vulnerability of certain categories of users in relation to digitalization processes inspired the Authority's precautionary intervention concerning the way in which a leading banking institution had *migrated* hundreds of thousands of account holders to a digital bank of the same group, without having obtained their prior consent, with substantial changes to the services contractually provided for.

Faced with more than 5,000 reports received, the Authority ordered that consumers be provided with full information and be given a reasonable deadline to give their express consent to the transfer.

259. The Internet allows users to purchase goods and services directly from producers, typically through apps or websites.

The resulting *disintermediation processes* can have an impact not only on distribution chains but also on the functioning of markets.

For example, in the airline sector, a new proceeding is examining the consequences of obstacles that the main carrier operating in Italy places in the way of the

102. *See* https://www.bbc.com/news/world-europe-67759633.

purchase of airline tickets through traditional and online agencies, by asking consumers who have not purchased their tickets through the company's website to go through a lengthy and complex digital recognition procedure.

Potentially restrictive conducts in ticketing were also addressed in the railway sector: the Authority made binding commitments allowing all operators concerned to sell a combined ticket for journeys comprising regional routes (operated exclusively by the dominant operator) and routes covered by competing high-speed services.

§4. Competition Rules and Digital Platforms

260. The application of antitrust rules to *digital platforms* is a topic of keen interest for competition authorities.

In fact, the digital platform sector is the one that has recorded one of the highest growth rates in recent years in terms of turnover and profits, bringing significant benefits, consisting of an increase in the services offered, more advantageous prices for users and wider sales opportunities for companies.

In this context, competition authorities have focused their attention on larger platforms in order to prevent their growing role in the digital economy from compromising the development of new services by third parties and/or reducing the benefits for users.

261. This is mainly also the rationale behind the *Digital Markets Act* – DMA (EU Regulation 2022/1925), which, as explained in the same title, aims to ensure 'fair and contestable markets in the digital sector'. The DMA, in a nutshell, establishes that digital platforms that exceed certain quantitative and qualitative thresholds (known as *gatekeepers*) are subject to – among others – specific obligations to refrain from discriminatory conduct, as well as to open parts of their system to competitors for services identified as core platforms services.

In this way, the DMA aims, on the one hand, to ensure that users continue to enjoy the substantial benefits of platform activities, and, on the other hand, that the individual service markets that make up the gatekeepers' ecosystems remain contestable so that other companies can exert a competitive incentive and provide innovative services.

262. Within this framework, the Italian Authority's interventions during 2023 focused on specific services offered by the main digital platforms, with the aim of fostering competition and/or guaranteeing their full use by users.

263. A first intervention, aimed at achieving both objectives, concerned an investigation launched in 2022 against Google for allegedly infringing Article 102 TFEU and relating to the platform's conduct with regard to *data portability*. The investigation was closed by the Authority by making mandatory the commitments proposed by the company with which the automation of data export from Google to other entities was ensured, such as allowing users to benefit from the right to data portability guaranteed by Article 20 of the General Data Protection Regulation

(GDPR), as well as the possibility for them to obtain the *maximum economic value* of such data from companies specialized in this type of service. At the same time, operators interested in the data available to *Google* were given the opportunity to access them pending the company's release of a direct portability solution by the first quarter of 2024.

264. A preliminary investigation procedure, opened in May 2023 against *Apple* for alleged abuse of a dominant position in violation of Article 102 of the TFEU, intends to verify, on the other hand, whether Apple's apparently discriminatory conduct could damage subjects, such as *app developers* or social networks, that finance their business through the collection of user data for advertising purposes.

In fact, according to the so-called ATT ('App Tracking Transparency') Policy, Apple, for the acquisition of consent – for privacy protection purposes – to the tracking of one's own Internet 'surfing' data, presents users with a different 'pop-up window' (prompt) depending on whether they are third-party apps or apps developed directly by Apple: this may lead to a different reaction by users to the request for consent to the use of their data, with effects on the activities of third parties.

265. Digital platforms have also become a key channel for *disseminating* artistic and musical content to the public. Even if, from the point of view of the platforms, such content is functional to the provision of an overall service (e.g., social networks), it is nevertheless necessary that the subjects linked to the provision of individual services – such as e.g., those who produce such content – are guaranteed all the rights recognized by the law. This is the subject of the investigation opened by the Authority in April 2023 against Meta for alleged abuse of economic dependence, in violation of Article 9 of Law 192/1998.

266. The investigation started from the abrupt interruption of negotiations between SIAE, which negotiates with Meta the remuneration of the artists it represents for the music content made available on the social networks *Facebook* and *Instagram*, and Meta, which manages it.

The latter, following the failure to agree on the information to be provided to SIAE to negotiate the amount of remuneration to be paid to music artists, had removed the content of the artists represented by SIAE.

Through the adoption of precautionary measures, the Authority ordered Meta to promptly restore the removed content, to immediately resume negotiations with SIAE in accordance with canons of good faith and fairness, and to provide all necessary information to enable SIAE to rebalance its commercial relationship with Meta.

§5. The 2023 Google Case

267. In July 2023, the Authority (AGCM) concluded with the acceptance of commitments an investigation proceeding, initiated against Alphabet Inc., Google LLC, Google Ireland Limited and Google Italy S.r.l., aimed at ascertaining possible violations of Article 102 of the TFEU, consisting of obstacles to the identification of adequate interoperability mechanisms, capable of making user data on the Google platform available to alternative platforms.[103]

268. At the time of the opening of the procedure, the Authority, following a report by the operator Hoda, contested the circumstance that the only service that Google made available to its users to request and obtain a copy of their personal data, called Takeout, was extremely articulated and complex, to the extent that it could:

i. prevent, de facto, the exercise of the right to data portability established by Article 20(2) of the GDPR, to the detriment of final consumers, who were thus deprived of the possibility of benefiting from the exploitation of their personal data;
ii. limit the possibility of alternative operators to Google to develop innovative ways of using personal data, so as to harm competition.

In particular, the complainant had represented the negative effects of Google's conduct on its own initiative aimed at developing, through the Weople platform, an innovative commercial activity, consisting of exploiting personal data with the owner's authorization in as yet unexplored product prospects, with particular reference to the national geographical context.

269. The relevant markets for the purposes of assessing the case were identified in thc set of activities that allow Google to accumulate, store and process end-users' data.

In order to remedy the critical competition issues that emerged during the opening of the case, Google submitted – pursuant to Article 14-*ter*, paragraph 1, of Law 287/1990 – and supplemented it at the end of the market test – a package of three commitments, two of which envisaged additional solutions to the Takeout service, aimed at facilitating the export of data to third-party operators, while the third offered the possibility to start testing, before the official release ('early adopter programme'), a new solution for direct data portability from service to service, which Google would make available to third-party operators authorized by the end user. Google undertook to complete the development of the commitments in a precise timeframe and to appoint a trustee to monitor compliance.

270. The Authority considered the commitments submitted by Google as suitable to remove the competition concerns highlighted in the opening decision. In fact, by guaranteeing a significant automation of the procedure available for the export of data, they appeared suitable to allow users to exercise the right recognized

103. *See* https://www.agcm.it/dotcmsCustom/getDominoAttach?urlStr=192.168.14.10:8080/41256297003874BD/0/42A8996C723B26AAC12589FD003925C3/$File/p30736.pdf.

by Article 20 of the GDPR; moreover, they provided for an interoperability mechanism capable of making the data available in Google's platform accessible to third-party platforms. This mechanism would have been available to users and third-party operators until the release by Google of a direct service-to-service portability solution, which, according to the operator, would take place in the first quarter of 2024.

The implementation of the third commitment would then have allowed third-party operators interested in Google's data to start testing the aforementioned direct portability solution with regard to certain services (notably Google Search and YouTube) in advance of its actual release.

Therefore, the Authority decided to make these commitments binding and to close the proceedings without finding an infringement.

§6. The Case META/SIAE

271. In the course of 2023, the Lazio Regional Administrative Court examined for the first time – in judgment No. 16069 of 30 October 2023 – a case of abuse of economic dependence carried out through digital platforms, providing important indications as to the interpretation to be given to the presumption introduced by Article 33 of the Annual Law on the Market and Competition 2021 within Article 9 of Law No. 192/1998.

272. In rejecting the individual objections put forward by Meta against the precautionary measure adopted by the Authority on 20 April 2023, the administrative judge first found that the provision 'shows the legislator's intention to provide a stronger protection to those who interface commercially with digital platforms, given the notorious market power of the latter, as well as the obvious inadequacy of the pre-existing means of protection: the regulatory instrument used is that of the (relative) presumption of economic dependence on the platform'.

273. The same then clarified how, for the purposes of the operation of the aforementioned presumption, the 'decisive role [of a digital platform] in reaching end users or suppliers, also in terms of network effects or data availability' must be considered. In particular, the TAR pointed out that Meta operates two digital platforms, Facebook and Instagram, qualifiable as social networks, which allow it to reach a huge audience of consumers.

274. In view of this intermediation capacity, Meta's role appeared 'decisive' in enabling the connection between its users and the works protected by SIAE. On this point, the court stated that, in the case at issue, the economic dependence is strictly related to the possibility of making protected musical works known, while it considered as secondary the circumstance that only a minimal fraction of SIAE's turnover was derived from its relations with the applicant.

275. This statement by the administrative judge appears to be of considerable importance insofar as it confirms the interpretation put forward by the Authority at the basis of the measure, releasing the assessment of the condition of economic dependence from the entity of the turnover deriving from the commercial transactions subject to assessment. Similarly, the court found that SIAE's dominant position in the market for user licences was not relevant, as this element did not affect the relationship between the parties in any way, given the absence of satisfactory alternatives to the commercial relationship with Meta.

276. As to the existence of the abuse, the administrative law judge found that the arbitrary interruption of commercial relations is not to be understood only in the absolute sense as a refusal to enter into a contract, but also covers conduct that leads to a clear stalemate or at least an abrupt halt in negotiations, with the possibility of subsequent reactivation in order to reach an agreement. Moreover, the dominant undertaking (Meta) is precluded from (substantially) unilaterally imposing its will by withdrawing from the negotiations if the latter is not accepted. Lastly, the court considered the effects on competition to be clear, in that, given the decisive role of the plaintiff company's platforms in the distribution of digital content, there may be a serious risk that SIAE will be abandoned by authors in favour of management entities that have entered into an agreement with Meta, most likely on less favourable terms.

277. An examination of the judgment shows how, with specific regard to the digital transactions sector, the intermediation capacity of the platform is in fact the decisive criterion for the definition of the presumption of economic dependence, even irrespective of elements such as the turnover actually realized in the context of the commercial relationships subject to assessment or the important position of the person using the services. The judgment, therefore, confirms the interpretation of the new legislation provided by the Authority, where it held that an effective protection of companies that use the intermediation services provided by a platform essentially revolves around the need to subject the most important operators in the digital market to a special liability regime. In ruling No. 5827 of 2024, the Council of State (the highest administrative jurisprudential body) reversed the 16069/2023 ruling. The judges found that the AGCM's decision had an incorrect premise; the subject of the negotiation was not the licensing of the dissemination to end-users of music content through social platforms, but only the collection of SIAE-protected content in the *Audio Library*. Meta's platforms thus merely make the *Audio Library* archive available to users. The Council of State did not see Meta's role as an intermediary function. However, the Council of State pointed out that it did not definitively ascertain the actual existence of a dominant position of Meta in the specific reference market (and the related abusive conduct), as well as the consequent condition of SIAE's economic dependence, as they will be assessed by the final AGCM ruling, which will be adopted at the outcome of the main proceedings.

§7. Competition and Digital Services

278. In the field of digital services, the Authority has concluded, by accepting commitments, a proceeding against the company HIYA Inc. concerning the alleged vexatiousness of certain contractual clauses in the 'Hiya Terms of Service for Consumer Services' relating to the provision of an app service that allows the identification of calls and the blocking of unwanted numbers. The proceedings constitute the first case of the closure of an investigation into unfair terms through the acceptance of undertakings, an institution applicable to this discipline by virtue of the reference to Article 27 of the Consumer Code contained in the new Article 37-*bis* of the Consumer Code.[104]

279. On the merits, the commitments submitted by the professional provided for the immediate amendment of the terms and conditions of use of the app HIYA, published within the app available for smartphones and accessible directly from the homepage of the website, through a special link, as well as the amendment of the content of the terms of service through the elimination of a series of clauses and the reformulation of the clauses under dispute.

280. The Authority considered the commitments to be suitable to guarantee users easy access to the provisions governing the use of the HIYA app, in line with the canon of clarity referred to in Article 35, paragraph 1, of the Consumer Code, and to overcome the findings of alleged vexatiousness set out in the opening. It was also considered in line with the objectives of economic efficiency and effectiveness of administrative action, the speed of implementation of the contractual changes, which also allowed for early and immediate feedback on the actual compliance of the professional.

281. The Authority intervened in the sector of the offer of services aimed at increasing the popularity of individual or corporate social profiles and concluded a structured proceeding against the company SWL Web Marketing SL concerning the sale of non-genuine reviews, which can be purchased on the website at marketing-seo.it.

282. The investigation was conducted pursuant to Articles 20 and 21 of the Consumer Code, prior to the implementation at the national level of Directive 2019/2161/EU (so-called Omnibus Directive), which introduced specific hypotheses of misleading practices aimed at combating the phenomenon of false reviews.

The proceedings established the existence of an unfair commercial practice consisting in the sale by the aforementioned company of non-authentic reviews, in that they were artificially generated in order to promote the visibility, products or services of those who purchased them, with the effect of altering users' consumption choices. The Authority imposed an administrative fine of EUR 10,000 on the company.

104. *See* https://www.agcm.it/dotcmsCustom/tc/2029/1/getDominoAttach?urlStr=192.168.14.10:8080/C12560D000291394/0/053E11EDCEA19DE3C1258A9E0059E0FE/$File/p31020.pdf.

§8. Online Sales of Products, Influencers, Challenges

283. In the sector of online sales of IT products, the Authority continued its intervention to crack down on the practice of applying the credit card surcharge, in violation of Article 62 of the Consumer Code. The Authority concluded with acceptance of commitments a proceeding initiated against the company De Pretto Eventi Store S.r.l.s., which applied to consumers, for purchases made on its website buy-digital.it, an additional commission of 1.9% compared to the cost of the goods in case of payment through 'credit and debit cards or innovative payment systems'. To resolve these critical issues, the trader has undertaken not to apply in the future any credit card surcharge (already promptly removed from the website) nor any other price surcharge linked to the use of a certain payment instrument and to return to consumers the sums collected from the application of the credit card surcharge in a reasonable timeframe.

284. The trader also undertook to publish for twelve months on the homepage of the website a specific notice aimed at informing consumers about their right to obtain a refund of the amount paid as a 'Payment Fee'. The Authority considered the proposed commitments to be suitable to remove the critical issues raised at the time of the opening of the proceedings and concluded the proceedings by ordering them to be mandatory, without finding an infringement pursuant to Article 27(7) of the Consumer Code.

285. In November 2023, the Authority initiated preliminary proceedings against the influencer Asia Valente, in her professional capacity, and the company Meta. The conduct object of the proceedings concerns the influencing market and the alleged presence of inauthentic interactions within the Instagram platform.

286. More precisely, the proceedings concern the publication by Asia Valente, on her Instagram profile, of photos and videos of restaurants, spas, hotels and other tourist facilities, with which she appears to have commercial relations, from which it does not seem to emerge the use of any wording highlighting the promotional nature of these contents, in alleged violation of Articles 20, 22, paragraph 2, and 23, paragraph 1, letter aa), of the Consumer Code, as likely to configure a case of hidden advertising.

287. The complaint against Asia Valente also concerns the alleged use of a high percentage of fake followers, on her Instagram profile, which could be susceptible to alter the perception of the popularity of the influencer, being a false appreciation capable of influencing the decision-making process of purchasing products and services promoted on the Instagram platform. Such conduct would seem capable of constituting, for Asia Valente, a breach of Articles 20, 23, paragraph 1, lett. bb-*quater*) of the Consumer Code, as well as a breach of Article 3, paragraph 1, letters a) and c), of Legislative Decree 145/2007. Meta, on the other hand, is accused of allegedly failing to adopt appropriate measures to maintain compliance with the provisions dictated by the policy lines, provided by the platform itself, concerning, more specifically, the publication of advertising content and the 'non-artificial' collection of followers.

288. The Authority has opened an investigation against the companies responsible for the TikTok platform with reference to the presence of videos of young people adopting self-harming behaviours with particular reference to the challenge that has gone viral of the so-called French scar. The Authority, in particular, contested to the companies the possible unfairness of a commercial practice that would consist, on the one hand, in the alleged failure to set up appropriate monitoring systems on the content published by third parties for lack of professional diligence expected by the platform in the presence of users of the service particularly vulnerable such as minors, in possible violation of Article 20 paragraphs 1 and 3 of the Consumer Code; on the other hand, in the alleged failure to apply its own Guidelines contemplating the removal of dangerous content relating to challenges, suicide, self-harm and unhealthy nutrition in possible violation of Article 21, paragraph 2 letter b) of the Consumer Code, as well as of Article 21 paragraph 4 of the Consumer Code as they are likely to reach adolescents and threaten their physical and psychological safety. It was also contested the alleged exploitation of artificial intelligence techniques capable of generating undue conditioning in users, in possible violation of Article 25(1)(c) of the Consumer Code. The reference is, in particular, to the algorithm underlying the operation of the platform which, using users' data, reproposes content similar to that already displayed and interacted with through the like function.

§9. Online Trading

289. In the area of online trading, the Authority has concluded two investigative proceedings, affirming the principle that, given the characteristics of the sector, in which consumers assume the risks connected to unforeseen events that can impact the value of investments made, the transparency and completeness of information on the economic conditions of the services offered is particularly important.

290. In assessing the conduct of the professionals concerned, account was also taken of the fact that this sector is of interest to large numbers of consumers, given that online trading currently allows people to invest even from home using their own computers and, therefore, the intermediation of a reliable third party becomes a crucial element for those operating in this way.

291. The Authority, in particular, conducted proceedings against the company FlatexDEGIRO Bank AG concerning two unfair commercial practices put in place in relation to the offer of financial instruments and investment services consisting of: (i) providing consumers with insufficiently transparent and misleading information such as not to allow them to understand the actual economic characteristics of the products/services offered, in breach of Articles 20, 21 and 22 of the Consumer

Code; (ii) in having induced the customer to unwittingly make – through the presence of an automatic pre-selection – a choice for the conversion into dollars of the sums deposited on the investment account, so-called Autofix, which was more onerous than the 'manual' alternative, in breach of Articles 20, 24 and 25 of the Consumer Code.

292. In particular, the investigation has allowed the Authority to ascertain, in relation to the first practice, the promotion by the professional, through various communication channels (website degiro.it, radio and television campaigns, social media), of its financial services, using claims designed to emphasize, contrary to the truth, the absence of commissions subsequently required to carry out the trading activity; with respect to the second practice, the provision in the case of investments in foreign currency, of an automatic mode of currency conversion, as a default setting, capable of inducing the client to make, in an unconscious manner, a choice that could be less advantageous than the manual conversion mode in that it was subject to the payment of additional charges. At the end of the investigation, a total administrative fine of EUR 4 million was imposed (EUR 1.5 million in relation to the first file, EUR 2.5 million in relation to the first case and EUR 2.5 million in relation to the second case).

293. In the same vein, the preliminary investigation procedure concluded with the establishment of the unfair commercial practice implemented by the company eToro Europe Ltd, in violation of Articles 20, 21 and 22 of the Consumer Code.

The investigation allowed the Authority to establish that the trader engaged in a misleading commercial practice, similar to the one contested to FlatexDEGIRO Bank, for not having adequately and immediately informed the user about the economic conditions and technical characteristics of the financial products/services offered on its website eToro.com/en.

294. In particular, the company let the user understand that he/she could trade in shares with zero commissions, without highlighting the presence of other costs of various kinds, risks of further disbursements linked to variations in exchange rates, as well as the existence of operational constraints and limitations on the rights of the customer acquiring shares, with particular reference to the impossibility of transferring the shares to other intermediaries.

The Authority therefore prohibited the further dissemination of this practice and imposed a fine of EUR 1.3 million on the company.

§10. The E-Commerce Sector

295. In the e-commerce sector, the Authority's activities have focused, first, on the repression of certain unlawful conducts carried out by some operators in the marketing of products of consumer electronics and household appliances carried out through their respective corporate websites.

296. Specifically, at the conclusion of an investigation against the companies Tomorrowland S.r.l., Pet Clan S.r.l. and their sole shareholder and director, the Authority ascertained the existence of multiple forms of conduct constituting distinct unfair commercial practices carried out, respectively, in the pre-purchase phase and in the post-purchase phase.

297. The practices consisted, in particular, of the non-delivery of the products sold, the failure or inadequate provision of after-sales service as well as the adoption of conduct aimed at hindering the exercise of consumers' rights of withdrawal and reimbursement, in breach of Articles 20, 21, 22, 24 and 25, 49(1)(b), (c) and (d), and 61 of the Consumer Code. Each of the two companies and their sole shareholder and director were jointly and severally fined EUR 100,000 and EUR 50,000 respectively.

298. Also in the e-commerce sector, the Authority intervened, in the pre-investigation phase, by transmitting Registrars of domains an invitation to close down some online sales sites for electronics and household appliances and, among these, the sites bompiano.net and Sopremito.com and Padronte.com through which companies that turned out to be 'non-existent' were deceiving consumers by reassuring them about the seriousness of the sites and inducing them to buy and pay for products (at heavily discounted prices), which were then not delivered. Following the Authority's intervention, the sites were permanently closed down.

299. The Authority concluded with acceptance of commitments to an investigation procedure against the company Le Style de Paris S.r.l.s., active in the online trade of clothing and accessories. The proceedings concerned the alleged impropriety of the promotion and sales methods practised and, in particular, the failure to respect delivery times, the failure to deliver the products ordered and paid for, the failure to reimburse the amount paid for the cancellation of the order or the exercise of the right of withdrawal and the failure and/or inadequate provision of after-sales service.

300. The trader submitted commitments consisting of providing consumers with more precise and clear information about the actual availability of the products at the time of the order and modifying the payment procedure in order not to charge consumers the price of the goods before the order has been processed; to strengthen its after-sales service as well as its complaint management; and to bring the website in line with current legislation by providing for the possibility of resolving any disputes through 'Alternative Dispute Resolution' procedures. The Authority considered the commitments suitable to remedy the possible illegitimacy profiles of the contested practice and concluded the proceedings by ordering their mandatory application without finding an infringement, pursuant to Article 27, paragraph 7, of the Consumer Code.

301. The Authority concluded a proceeding against the company Payiu Italia S.r.l., owner of the platform of the same name, with the establishment of an unfair commercial practice carried out through the adoption of misleading and aggressive conduct aimed at hindering the use of monthly credits purchased online by consumers in the form of subscriptions that were supposed to allow the purchase of consumer goods for a value equal to three times the amount initially paid, failing to refund the amount paid by users. After the adoption of precautionary measures, the investigation concluded with the establishment of the consumer offence in violation of Articles 20, 21, 22, 24 and 25 of the Consumer Code and the imposition of a fine of EUR 770,000 jointly and severally on the company and its sole managing partner.

§11. Competition Law and Online Reviews

302. Online reviews are very useful for professionals to promote and increase sales of products or services and, more generally, to improve their reputation with current and potential customers. Their dissemination has, in fact, a significant impact on consumers' commercial decisions, since the reviews of other customers who have already used the service and/or bought the advertised product can guide their choices.

In this regard, Directive 19/2161/EC and the Legislative Decree 26/2023 transposing it, recognized the serious unfairness of the dissemination of non-authentic reviews, introducing the new case of the misleading practice of 'sending, or instructing another legal or natural person to send, false consumer reviews or false appreciations or providing false information about consumer reviews or appreciations on social media, in order to promote products' (cf. Article 23(bb-*quater*) of the Consumer Code).

303. In this context, the Authority closed proceedings during the year against Facile Ristrutturare S.p.A. and Renovars S.p.A. and considered incorrect the online dissemination of non-authentic reviews, also by some Facile Ristrutturare's collaborators – in relation to whom the professional did not put in place appropriate measures and controls to prevent this phenomenon – as it was likely to mislead consumers both on the quality, timing and convenience of the advertised residential property renovation services, and on the qualifications, skills and awards attributed by customers to Facile Ristrutturare's services, in breach of Articles 20, 21(1)(b) and (f), and 22 of the Consumer Code.

304. The proceedings also concerned the application by Facile Ristrutturare of a hidden cost to consumers in the case of VAT at a reduced rate of 10%, instead of 22%, where the finishing materials for renovations were purchased by them through Facile Ristrutturare and from its partner suppliers. As a result of the established infringements, the Authority imposed a total fine of EUR 4.5 million on the professionals.

§12. The Pandoro Case

305. Commercial communications that combine sponsorship activities by so-called influencers with charitable activities are the subject of great attention due to their relevance and problematic nature, particularly in the context of the current digitalization of society and the economy. They, in fact, can significantly affect consumers' economic choices, leveraging their particular ethical sensitivity for charitable initiatives, especially if addressed to children or young people suffering from serious diseases or disabilities and on special occasions.

306. The unfairness of the aforesaid commercial communications or advertising campaigns emerges, in particular, where the intermingling of sponsorship and charitable initiatives – amplified by the role by definition played by the so-called influencers – is such as to mislead consumers by giving them the impression that they can directly contribute to the charitable initiative through the purchase of the advertised product. This – highly problematic – profile was at the centre of the proceedings closed against the companies Balocco S.p.A. Industria Dolciaria, Fenice S.r.l. and TBS Crew S.r.l. – the last two companies refer to the influencer Chiara Ferragni – concerning the initiative 'Pandoro Pink Christmas'.

307. At the outcome of the investigation, the modalities adopted to advertise the aforementioned Pandoro by the companies involved were found to be capable of integrating the extremes of an unfair commercial practice capable of misleading consumers as to the charity linked to the product. In fact, the Authority ascertained that the donation advertised as being linked to sales of the 'Pandoro Pink Christmas' had been made months before the product was launched on the market, for an amount that bore no relation to the quantities of the product sold and without any participation of the influencer in the charity initiative. The Authority imposed on the company Balocco S.p.A. Industria Dolciaria a fine of EUR 420,000, to the company Fenice S.r.l. a fine of EUR 400,000 and to the company TBS Crew S.r.l. a fine of EUR 675,000.

§13. Unfair Commercial Practices

308. The relationship between the rules on unfair commercial practices and the sectoral provisions has been at the centre, over the years, of an extensive legal debate and has been the basis of the various theses developed by jurisprudence to resolve the question of the breadth of the Authority's enforcement versus the administrative activities of the sectoral authorities.[105]

---

105. *See* M. De Benedetto, 'L'autorità garante della concorrenza e del mercato: organizzazione, poteri, funzioni' (Il Mulino, Bologna, 2000).

309. In the course of 2023, the jurisprudence on the merits returned to the subject, confirming the principles under which the applicability of the rules on unfair commercial practices in regulated sectors, established by the Court of Justice on 13 September 2018, must be recognized.

310. In particular, in its judgment No. 61 of 2 January 2023, the Lazio Regional Administrative Court confirmed the prevalence of the sectoral discipline only if an irremediable 'contrast' can be identified with that on unfair commercial practices. Such 'contrast' must go beyond mere dissimilarity or mere difference between the provisions to which it refers, highlighting a divergence that cannot be overcome by means of an inclusive formula that allows for the coexistence of both realities, without the need to distort them. Therefore, it only exists when provisions of strict EU derivation (i.e., of European rank), regulating specific aspects of unfair commercial practices, impose on traders, without any room for manoeuvre, obligations that are 'incompatible' with those laid down in Directive 2005/29/EC, giving rise to an irreconcilable divergence.

311. The principles were recalled in another ruling by the Regional Administrative Court of Lazio, which, in Judgment No. 2453 of 13 February 2023, reaffirmed the complementarity between the sectoral regulations on labelling and food supplements and the regulations on consumer protection. In particular, the court pointed out that the AGCM's competence to assess the unfairness of a commercial practice also exists in light of the general criteria and specific requirements of Regulation (EC) 1924/2006.

§14. The Influencer Marketing Sector

312. The 2023 annual sweep focused on the influencer marketing sector. In November 2023, the Italian Authority investigated nineteen influencers, established in Italy and active, primarily, on the social media platform Instagram.

313. Some software developed by the European Commission in the 'e-LAB' environment and, in particular, the smartphone simulator called 'BlueStacks 5' and the image and video capture tool called 'ShareX' were used to screen the relevant accounts.

314. Subsequently, the special questionnaires prepared by the EU Commission were filled in to monitor the various potential infringements on the subject of 'hidden advertising' in relation to the failure to use specific indicators – such as, for example, the #hashtag symbol followed by the words 'advertising' (or at least its abbreviation 'ADV'), 'publicity', 'sponsored' and other similar wording, which must always be followed by the name of the brand being promoted – essential to inform consumers of the real promotional nature of posts, images, stories, reels, videos, etc., which are the subject of a 'commissioned' relationship. the subject of a 'commissioning' relationship between influencer and sponsoring company, or the supply of products and services to the influencers free of charge with the constraint that they proceed to disseminate specific advertising messages.

315. At the end of the sweep on Instagram, it emerged as a first result that none of the monitored influencers appeared to have systematically and efficiently used suitable indicators to highlight the commercial nature of the activity carried out on the platform, with the possibility, therefore, of having to proceed to further investigative enquiries.

§15. The 2022 Investigation Against Google

316. In 2022, the Authority opened an investigation against Google aimed at verifying whether the platform's approach to data portability could constitute an abuse of a dominant position in violation of Article 102 TFEU. Google, in fact, holds a dominant position in several markets that allow for the acquisition of large amounts of data through the services it provides (Gmail, Google Maps, Android) and – as reported by an operator active in Italy that has developed an APP for the exploitation of user data – would have hindered interoperability in the sharing of data with other platforms.

317. As noted by the Authority itself in the IC53-Big Data survey, conducted jointly with the Communications Authority and the Garante per la protezione dei dati personali, the institution of data portability, governed by Article 20 of Regulation (EU) 2016/679 (GDPR), in reducing the costs of user switching from one platform to another, has an undoubted competitive value insofar as it contributes to lowering the barriers to entry in the markets of the digital sector that are rooted in the availability of data, as well as to reducing the network effects inherent in the activity of platforms.

318. The advisability of protecting this aspect in view of its pro-competitive value was also shared by the European legislator in the context of the EU Regulation on fair and contestable markets (Digital Market Act – DMA) adopted in July 2022. The DMA, in fact, in the general perspective of ensuring contestability and fairness for markets in the digital sector through a series of obligations aimed at regulating *ex ante* the conduct of gatekeepers providing digital platform services, has provided, *inter alia*, that the latter are obliged to ensure the effective portability of data.

319. In this sense, Article 6(9) of the DMA provides that 'the gatekeeper shall provide, upon request and free of charge, to end-users and third parties authorised by an end-user the effective portability of data provided by the end-user or generated through the end-user's activity in the context of the use of the relevant basic platform service, including by providing, free of charge, tools to facilitate the effective exercise of such data portability, as well as by providing continuous and real-time access to such data'. This requirement stems precisely from the observation that the absence of, or reduced access to, certain key inputs in the digital economy, such as data, represents a very high barrier capable of reducing the contestability of digital markets and depressing the potential for innovation that can take place in them (*see* DMA – recital 3).

320. Placing itself at the intersection between the traditional level of antitrust enforcement and that of regulation, of European scope, soon to be implemented, the Authority's intervention against Google offers an opportunity to explore the positive synergetic effects existing between the two orders of intervention. Moreover, the timeliness with which the Authority has intervened, in advance of the actual implementation of the DMA, together with the consideration that the measure initiating the preliminary investigation has reserved for the peculiarities of the national context and the local specificities of the conduct assumed by the dominant undertaking, suggest that the National Competition Authority is adequately equipped to play an active role in the application of the DMA, in the envisaged forms of collaboration with the Commission, according to the regulatory architecture that will be defined in the coming months in implementation of Articles 37 and 38 of the DMA.

§16. An Interesting Investigation on the Payment Sector

321. In the course of 2022, the Authority intervened in the payments sector, addressing for the first time in its preliminary investigation the competitive repercussions of the digital transformation that is sweeping the sector. Reference is made in particular to case A548 – Bancomat/Mandato Mastercard in which the interaction between the rules of the payment circuits and the technological constraints posed by the operating systems of mobile devices was the subject of preliminary investigation.

322. The preliminary investigation hypothesis concerned a possible abuse of a dominant position by the Mastercard circuit, which allegedly changed its rules on the acceptance of cards at merchants to preclude the competing circuit, Bancomat, from accessing mobile devices, primarily Apple and Samsung. The case was later resolved with the Authority's acceptance of the commitments proposed by Mastercard and, therefore, there was no ruling on the lawfulness of the conduct under investigation. Nevertheless, some general considerations can be drawn from the affair.

323. The use of payment cards through mobile devices (smartphones, mainly, but also smartwatches, tablets and potentially any portable electronic device) is already of great importance due to the absolute size of the phenomenon and the significant growth rates. In this transitional phase, therefore, all those mechanisms of card operation that can change the way cards are used and, therefore, advantage or disadvantage certain operators, assume particular competitive importance.

324. One thinks, for example, of payment cards carrying more than one circuit/brand: the technological choice of either registering them in the electronic wallet as a single card, with the possibility of being used on two different circuits or registering them as two separate cards, has repercussions on the competitive capacity of each circuit. As for the acceptance side, the way in which poses (i.e., card acceptance points) operate has obvious consequences on the use of one circuit or another. This is of course true for merchants' pos, the operation of which is carried out by shop staff, but it is even more true for unattended card acceptance points, for which *ex ante* regulation has important competitive consequences (think, for example, of underground turnstiles).

325. And, therefore, where the circuit and technological rules concretely favour the consumer in the choice of the circuit to be used, the subjects that offer better conditions to the cardholder will be advantaged (e.g., those that adopt cashback programmes). On the other hand, in the event that the rules favour the choice of the merchant (without prejudice to the right guaranteed to the consumer by the rules in force to choose otherwise), the following will advantage those with the best conditions in the area of card acceptance (e.g., those with the lowest merchant fees). The rules of operation should therefore be neutral as far as possible, within the framework of the behaviour permitted by the industry regulations.

326. Compliance with this regulation does not, however, guarantee the adoption of conduct that is respectful of the discipline of competition, the examination of which, of course, takes place according to the usual elements necessary for the assessment of antitrust cases (such as the overall characteristics of the market, the possible presence of positions of dominance, the existence of agreements or other forms of collaboration between operators, vertical relations, etc.).

327. For example, in the aforementioned case A548, the Authority, on the assumption that Mastercard held a dominant position in the Italian debit card market, hypothesized that its decision to impose that pos be regulated so that for each transaction the circuit had to be chosen on a case-by-case basis, resulted in the impossibility for Bancomat to access e-wallets (given the choice of technological operators to admit to their wallets only situations in which the transaction was carried out with a single action). This was therefore a situation in which, while complying with sector regulations, the interaction of the circuit rules with those of the technological operators could produce a restriction of competition. The reason why the Authority hypothesized an unlawful act against Mastercard, and not against the technological operators, is to be found in the context in which the case took place, in which the conduct of the technological operators was already known and uniform at a global level, whereas Mastercard's conduct, limited to the Italian territory and intervened with specific timing, appeared, in theory, specifically aimed at harming its competitor.

In contrast, at the European Union level, in an only apparently similar situation, the Commission is investigating Apple for an infringement consisting of preventing access to a component of the smartphone essential for payments (the so-called NFC), preventing or severely limiting the possibility of competing operators to develop e-wallets in the Apple environment, thus affecting other technological operators, as well as the licensees of the circuits that often develop their own wallets and, ultimately, the circuits themselves.

328. Ultimately, therefore, without prejudice to the necessary compliance with the sector's regulations, the adoption of conduct that is legitimate from a regulatory point of view does not exclude the circumstance that significant consequences may be produced on competition and, possibly, that antitrust offences may be committed, on which the Authority has been vigilant, and has obtained a prompt resolution of its competitive concerns by means of the commitments presented by the party without the need to take over the restriction.

§17. Investigations on the Performance of Internet Navigation Services

329. The Authority carried out intensive verification of the information provided by connectivity providers on the performance of Internet navigation services.

In a context in which the demand for digital services continues to grow both quantitatively (volumes of data exchanged) and qualitatively (use of increasingly sophisticated services requiring ever higher connection speeds), information on the performance of online surfing and, more generally, on the characteristics of services, assume an increasingly central character in orienting users' choices of their network access providers.

330. In this context, the Authority conducted a proceeding concerning the promotion by Telecom Italia S.p.A. of three fixed telephony offers (Premium, Executive and Magnifica) as a result of which it emerged that there was misleading information and omissions of information within the meaning of Articles 21(1)(b) and (d) and 22(2) of the Consumer Code. Telecom, in fact, had not immediately disclosed the consumer costs of telephone calls, the costs of deactivation and withdrawal before 24 months and, in the case of the Magnifica offer, which guaranteed particularly high surfing speeds (up to 10 Gigabit/s), the limitations on usability, the loss of the fixed number in the event of a switch to another operator or to another Telecom offer, and the possible inefficiencies deriving from its experimental nature. At the end of the investigation, Telecom was fined a fine of EUR 1 million.

331. In another proceeding, an unfair commercial practice was established by Iliad Italia S.p.A. with reference to promotional communications relating to mobile telephony offers with 5G technology included, which were found to be inadequate to make consumers understand that in order to take advantage of the offers in question, geographical coverage of Iliad's specific 5G network was necessary, and that the possession of a device, even one enabled in general to 5G, could not ensure compatibility with Iliad's 5G network where this was not included in smartphones enabled to surf on the operator's specific network. At the conclusion of the investigation, an administrative fine of EUR 1.2 million was imposed on Iliad.

332. The Authority also intervened with another six moral suasion initiatives against six operators, concerning the way in which they publicize offers to surf the Internet through the fibre, which guarantees the achievement of particularly high maximum speeds (up to 2.5 Gigabit/s). The offers did not adequately specify that the maximum speed was to be understood as the sum of the speeds of several devices connected to the different router ports and/or connected via Wi-Fi, or, in the case of a Wi-Fi connection, only achievable through latest-generation enabled devices. As a result of these interventions, all operators changed the graphics and supplemented the content of the information on surfing speed with the above-mentioned clarifications.

§18. An Investigation on TikTok

333. The Authority concluded with acceptance of commitments an initial preliminary investigation procedure initiated against TikTok Technology Limited concerning the way in which the services offered by the company were presented in relation to in-app purchases made through virtual currencies on the platform. The 'live stream' function of TikTok allows users who are at least 16 years old and who meet certain criteria defined by the company, to broadcast their videos live (so-called creator or live streamer). Other users can follow the live stream content in real time and those over 16 can express their appreciation by sending the creators 'virtual gifts'.

334. The sending of the virtual gift presupposes the availability on one's account of 'virtual coins' that the local user purchases on the platform. The professional, at a later stage, on the basis of the degree of popularity of the content resulting from the assigned gifts, grants the creator a prize in the form of 'diamonds' that the recipients, in turn, can transform into monetary compensation according to the calculation criteria defined by the platform. In this context, the Authority had hypothesized the adoption by TikTok of a misleading commercial practice in violation of Articles 20, 21 and 22 of the Consumer Code in that it had not provided the essential information elements for an immediate and clear perception of the economic conditions relating to the use of the virtual objects and of the actual consequences in terms of earnings that the user's choices have for the recipients of the virtual gifts.

335. In the course of the proceedings, TikTok submitted undertakings, committing itself, in particular:

i. to increase the level of transparency of the economic conditions relating to the use of virtual objects, by providing the consumer, both when purchasing virtual coins and when using those coins to purchase a virtual gift, information about the cost of the coin package, the euro value of each virtual coin, the history of purchases and gifts made, and the fees applicable to transactions;
ii. separating the conditions relating to the virtual elements dedicated to users who benefit from the content (the so-called *Coins Policy*) and the conditions

concerning the objects and the rewards destined to the creators of the contents (so-called Reward Policy), specifying in the latter the nature and the methods of obtaining the so-called diamonds and the relative conversion rate into money;

iii. to strengthen the precautions concerning the control of the age of the users and to reorganize the measures aimed at inhibiting the access of minors to the functions connected to the use of money. The Authority, deeming the commitments presented suitable to remove the criticalities highlighted, decided to make them binding on the company pursuant to Article 27, paragraph 7, of the Consumer Code and to make them binding on the company pursuant to Article 27, paragraph 7, of the Consumer Code and to close the proceedings without finding an infringement.

336. In the same sector, the Authority opened a second proceeding against TikTok concerning a hypothesis of non-transparent advertising spread on the platform and aimed at advertising Crystal Drops eye drops.

337. The investigation also involved the U.S. company Crystal Drops.Co., manufacturer of the drops, on account of the commercial return of the aforementioned advertising message, as well as on account of the potential misleading nature of a second commercial communication, concerning the same product, disseminated by the company on the website changeicolor.com, and of the possible violation, within the scope of the same communication, of Article 49, paragraph 1, letters b) and c), of the Consumer Code, in consideration of the manner in which the identity and address of the professional and the absence of the telephone number through which to contact him were indicated.

338. The Authority concluded the proceedings against the company Crystal Drops, which did not participate in the proceedings, ascertaining the nature of hidden advertising of the video broadcast on the TikTok platform and the deceptiveness and unlawfulness of the commercial communication disseminated on the website changeicolor.com with the imposition of a total fine of EUR 45,000. On the other hand, the commitments presented by TikTok, which undertook to adopt measures to prevent and combat surreptitious advertising aimed at precluding the misuse of the platform.

339. The commitments presented by TikTok in the aforementioned proceedings took into account the measures shared as a result of the action coordinated by the European Commission concluded in June 2022 aimed at increasing the level of transparency of the economic conditions relating to the use of virtual objects and at preventing hidden advertising.

§19. Big Platforms and the Sales of Goods and Services

340. In the course of 2021, the Authority completed significant proceedings in the digital markets, against some of the largest online platforms primarily active in the intermediation for the sale of goods or services.

In particular, the cases against Amazon and Google were concluded, with a finding of infringement, the imposition of sanctions and behavioural measures.

341. These markets are characterized by a high rate of innovation, significant network and lock-in effects, and the centrality of competitor and consumer data. These characteristics have favoured the attainment, by some groups, of economic dimensions and a ramified presence in the Italian industrial fabric such as to assume – in some cases – the nature of gatekeepers, capable of controlling access to markets by competitors and consumers.

342. The commercial strategies implemented by these groups are articulated, often marked by self-preferencing and able to leverage on the possession of an unparalleled amount of information on partners and consumers and on the nature of 'ecosystems', denoted by a pervasive offer of goods and services in multiple interconnected markets. By virtue of the peculiarities of digital markets, the effects of such strategies can occur and amplify very quickly and risk leading to the exit of nascent players or highly innovative companies. In this context, a static analysis of the degree of efficiency achieved – or attainable – by different players may fail to capture the net effect on consumer welfare in dynamic terms.[106]

343. In the cases that involved Google and Amazon, the Authority – having ascertained the position of absolute dominance of these companies and the restrictive nature of the conduct – deemed it necessary, in a perspective of protection of dynamic competition, to flank the sanction with the imposition of corrective measures, in order to guarantee maximum and immediate effectiveness to the investigative intervention and to favour the re-establishment of conditions of free competition in time to prevent the irreparable deterioration of the competitive process and to guarantee the contestability of the markets concerned.

344. A second aspect that becomes important arises from the supranational nature of the corporate groups involved and the adoption in many European markets of the conduct under investigation: the peculiarities of national markets and the local specificities of the conducts engaged in by companies may require that the protection of competitive processes be pursued by the authorities closest to the markets concerned, capable of guaranteeing effective and timely action to protect consumer welfare, and therefore justify the decentralized application of competition law by the best-positioned national authority, in a flexible model of allocation of competences.

---

106. *See* G. Colangelo, 'Big Data, piattaforme digitali e antitrust', in 'Mercato, concorrenza, regole', vol. 54 (3), 2016, pp. 425-460; U. Minneci, G. Greco, L. Ammannati, A. Canepa, 'Algoritmi, Big Data, Piattaforme Digitali – E-Book: La regolazione dei mercati in trasformazione' (Giappichelli, Torino, 2021).

345. At the same time, the uniform application of European competition law and the consistency of the actions of the various national authorities make constant and effective coordination with the European Commission and the other authorities within the ECN indispensable.

§20. THE TICKETONE CASE

346. In December 2020, the Authority found an infringement of Article 102 TFEU by the Eventim-TicketOne corporate group, for having abused its dominant position in the Italian market for the sale of tickets for live light music events.

347. The Authority's intervention concerns a particularly complex case, since the abuse of a dominant position was carried out through a unitary strategy articulated in a heterogeneous series of conducts, also of a signalling nature (consisting of boycott and retaliation actions) and of pre-emption, which not only saw the involvement of the German parent company and TicketOne S.p.A., as the company of the group active in the relevant market of the sale of tickets for live music events but also that of the national promoters acquired by the Eventim-TicketOne group in the period 2017-2018.

348. Only a combined reading of the various conducts engaged in by the Eventim-TicketOne group makes it possible to appreciate the exclusionary and competition-restricting scope of the single strategy implemented by the dominant undertaking. The conduct under investigation was all aimed, as a whole, at foreclosing the relevant market to competing ticketing operators, preventing them from selling, by any means and through any channel, a particularly high proportion of tickets for live light music events. In particular, the overall blocking effect produced by the abusive strategy of the Eventim-TicketOne group was more than 50% of the available tickets, in terms of volume and value.

349. The abuse of dominant position ascertained by the Authority is also characterized by structural aspects.

In particular, the Eventim-TicketOne group carried out, in the period 2017-2018 (i.e., after the expiry of the so-called Panischi agreements, by virtue of which, *inter alia*, TicketOne S.p.A. had enjoyed, for a fifteen-year period, the exclusive right to sell online all the tickets of the main national promoters), four transactions for the acquisition of some of the main production companies of live pop music events. In particular, the Authority considered these operations – which formally do not exceed the turnover thresholds provided for by the national merger control legislation – to be part of the overall abusive strategy of the Eventim- TicketOne group, insofar as they were aimed at making captive (i.e., intra-group) the exclusive relationships with the production companies subject to acquisition and by that means, to bind to the group the entire promotion activity carried out by some of the main promoters who are natural persons active in Italy, in a manner and for a duration prohibited by antitrust law, given the dominant position held in the relevant market.

350. Moreover, the abuse of the dominant position of the Eventim-TicketOne group, although its exclusionary effect was limited to the market for the sale of tickets for live light music events, also affected parties active at various other stages of the chain of production, organization and distribution of that type of event. On the one hand, the counterparties to the exclusive contracts entered into by the dominant undertaking were both ticketing operators and promoters of live light music events and, on the other hand, local promoters were also, in various capacities, involved in the implementation of the restrictive conduct, both by imposing the right of exclusivity in the event of the transfer of the rights to organize individual events and by being the recipients of a heterogeneous series of retaliatory and boycott conduct aimed at protecting the exclusivity of the Eventim-TicketOne group on the sale of tickets.

351. In view of the seriousness of the infringement, the Authority has imposed on the companies of the Eventim-TicketOne group a fine jointly and severally amounting to almost EUR 11 million and has also imposed specific behavioural obligations on them with the aim of allowing, through the removal of the obstacles to competition caused by the implementation of the abusive strategy, a greater opening up of the market and the establishment of physiological competitive dynamics.

§21. Free Access to Social Network Services

352. In 2020, the Lazio Regional Administrative Court adopted two rulings of particular interest concerning apparently free access to social network services (Lazio Regional Administrative Court, 10 January 2020, Nos 260, 261, PS/11112). The case dealt with is that of Facebook, the social network that has become, in the space of just a few years, of widespread diffusion on a worldwide scale.

353. One of the most successful elements of the platform is certainly to be found in the 'free' nature of the service for sharing multimedia content among members and the ease of access by even the most technologically unfamiliar users since, in order to subscribe to this online platform – a fact common to substantially all social networks – it is sufficient to initially enter a few necessary personal data such as one's name (or pseudonym), e-mail address, place and date of birth.

354. According to administrative case law, failing to inform consumers of the economic value from which the company benefits as a result of their membership in the social network constitutes an unfair commercial practice because it is aimed to mislead consumers preventing them from making an informed choice.

355. The personal data entered, however, are also others, since the 'diffusive power' of social platforms lies precisely in the ability to share information, images, videos, thoughts, etc., and in the interaction between the user and the platform itself.

The user, even by simply using the social network, continuously enters information about his profile, his tastes, his economic, political, religious and philosophical thoughts, and receives a lot of advertising (or 'sponsored') messages, advertisements, invitations to share particular 'pages' or content, etc. Such a mechanism serves to collect as much data as possible from users, to trace profiles to be passed on to third parties and/or to deliver targeted advertising messages.

356. The personal data entered by the user for the registration and use of online platforms thus represent the 'price' paid by the consumer for the service used, even if it is apparently free.[107]

357. The phenomenon of the 'patrimonialization' of personal data, which characterizes the new economies of digital markets, requires operators to respect, in the relevant commercial transactions, those obligations of clarity, completeness and non-misleading information provided for by consumer protection legislation. The user must be made aware of the exchange of services that underlies adherence to a contract for the use of a service, such as that of using a social network, and that the user's service is essentially the mass of data entered through registration and use.[108]

358. Together with the protection of personal data – as the expression of an individual's personality right subject to specific and unwaivable forms of protection, including the right to revoke consent, access, rectification, and oblivion – there is, therefore, a different field of protection of the data themselves, understood as the possible object of a sale and purchase, carried out both between market operators and between them and interested parties such as consumers.

359. The two levels of protection coexist in a complementary dimension, given that the discipline dictated by the European and national regulations on privacy concerns measures functional to the protection of personal data, understood as a fundamental right of the personality, while the consumer discipline imposes specific obligations of information so that the user makes an informed decision on the economic value of his personal data and the use that the online platform can make of it.

360. The gratuitousness of the social network service claimed suggests the absence of a counter-performance required of the consumer in exchange for the use of the service itself, but this is grounded only in the common meaning given by the average consumer, i.e., the absence of the giving of a sum of money. The use of the expression 'free' of the service does not allow the average consumer to understand that the trader will use the user's data for remunerative purposes, pursuing a commercial intent.[109]

---

107. *See* M. Hindman, 'The internet trap : how the digital economy builds monopolies and undermines democracy' (Princeton University Press, Princeton, 2018).
108. *See* V. Cuffaro, R. D'Orazio, V. Ricciuto, 'I dati personali nel diritto europeo' (Giappichelli, Torino, 2019).
109. *See* V. Ricciuto, 'Lo scambio di dati con i contenuti e i servizi digitali: una nuova modalità di contrarre?', in 'European Journal of Privacy Law & Technologies', fasc. 1, 2023, pp. 20-33.

361. On the basis of what has already been affirmed by the Authority (PS/10601 of 11 May 2017, in Boll. 18/2017), the Lazio Regional Administrative Court reiterated that the information assets constituted by users' data, as well as the profiling of those users for commercial use and for marketing purposes, acquires, precisely because of such use, an economic value capable, therefore, of configuring the existence of a consumer relationship between the professional and the user. Omitting to inform about the economic value from which the company benefits as a consequence of its registration to the social network constitutes, therefore, an unfair commercial practice because it is aimed at misleading the consumer and preventing the formation of an informed choice.

§22. The Fact-Finding Investigation on Big Data of 2019

362. In December 2019, the Authority, together with the Communications Guarantee Authority and the Personal Data Protection Authority, completed its fact-finding investigation on Big Data.

It follows the publication, in 2018, of the results of the 'Analysis of the propensity of online users to allow their data to be used for the provision of services'[110] and the adoption, in July 2019, of the Guidelines and Policy Recommendations on Big Data.[111]

363. The fact-finding investigation on Big Data is the first investigation conducted jointly by three Authorities, in the awareness that, in this matter, the profiles of their respective competences – privacy, consumer protection, competition and pluralism – are constantly intertwining. The survey highlighted that without an interdisciplinary approach, the challenges posed by the digital economy are difficult to tackle and that the tools available to the different Authorities are complementary and can be applied synergistically.

364. The investigation led to the awareness of some systematic elements in the relations between disciplines:

i. alongside the protection of privacy as a fundamental right, there is the need to avoid regulation that hampers dynamic competition;
ii. *ex ante* regulatory interventions, while appropriate insofar as they are aimed at mitigating the market power of digital platforms, must not hinder the development of innovative markets;
iii. competition in the so-called price-free markets cannot be examined only through lenses that are appropriate for the various traditional markets, where price and quantity – albeit always to a lesser extent – continue to play a central role.

---

110. *See* https://www.agcm.it/dotcmsdoc/allegati-news/IC_Big%20data_imp.pdf.
111. *See* https://www.garanteprivacy.it/home/docweb/-/docweb-display/docweb/9123073.

365. From the point of view of the Authority's competences, the investigation has revealed the existence in the Big Data sector of conduct that is potentially relevant for the purposes of competition and consumer protection enforcement. In the 'priceless markets', where some operators hold considerable market power, the ways in which individual data are collected may be vexatious in violation of the Consumer Code. In other cases, they may even constitute abusive conduct in violation of antitrust regulations.

366. Where the essential facility is data, a refusal to grant third parties access to such data has antitrust relevance if and to the extent that it is likely to reduce competition in a complementary/downstream market. On the other hand, the particular caution that even case law imposes when examining refusal-to-contract conduct in this field is justified by the need to protect both competition in the provision of services realized through the use of Big Data, and competition in the activities of collecting and analysing such data, which can bring benefits to consumers in the form of innovative services, often at zero monetary prices.

367. The relationship between a possible obligation to provide data and the GDPR (General Data Protection Regulation) must also be considered. More generally, data analysis and processing activities (analytics, cloud computing, data storage) may favour the implementation of potentially more widespread exclusionary conducts. The ability and incentives of firms to engage in restrictive conduct are moreover influenced by the high degree of vertical and conglomerate integration that characterizes the digital ecosystem. For instance, two particularly delicate situations can be identified.

368. The first is the one where a dominant operator provides companies (and/or consumers) with a plurality of complementary services, being able, for instance, to engage in tying practices capable of protecting or extending its dominant position.

The second is typical of vertical integration, in which the dominant operator provides a service to a third company, with which it competes at a different level of the chain, a situation that could favour the emergence of discriminatory conduct of an exclusionary nature.

369. Finally, the AGCM noted that the use of Big Data may also have an impact on price levels through the use of pricing algorithms.

Chapter 5. Regulation of the Electronic Communications Market

§1. Introduction

370. Electronic communications markets susceptible to *ex ante* regulation are identified by the European Commission.

The latter, according to Article 64 of Directive (EU) 2018/1972 of the European Parliament and of the Council of 11 December 2018, establishing the European Electronic Communications Code (ECC), is required to periodically review the list of such markets, updating the so-called Recommendation on relevant markets for electronic communications services and products susceptible to *ex ante* regulation.

371. To date, the European Commission has published four Recommendations. The first, dating back to 2003, identified eighteen markets as susceptible to *ex ante* regulation; the subsequent one of 2007, noting the evolution of markets towards fully competitive conditions, in particular retail markets, reduced the number of relevant markets from eighteen to seven. The Recommendation (No. 2014/710/EU), published on 9 October 2014, the third on the subject, further reduced the number of markets subject to regulation, excluding from the list the only retail market that had remained in the previous Recommendation and redefining, at the same time, some wholesale markets to take into account industry trends and technological developments.

372. In particular, Recommendation 2014/710/EU identified four wholesale markets susceptible to *ex ante* regulation, keeping the markets for fixed and mobile call termination services (interconnection services, markets 1 and 2) and reshaping the markets for fixed network access services through the identification of three relevant markets (market 3a for wholesale local access services at a fixed location, market 3b for wholesale central access services at a fixed location for consumer products and market 4 for wholesale high-quality access services at a fixed location, corresponding to terminating segments of leased lines).

373. Finally, the latest Recommendation (No. 2020/2245) of 18 December 2020, which is currently in force, identified only two relevant product and service markets of the electronic communications sector whose characteristics are such as to justify the imposition of *ex ante* regulatory obligations: market 1 for wholesale local access services at a fixed location (corresponding to market 3a of the previous Recommendation) and market 2 for wholesale dedicated capacity services (corresponding to market 4 of the previous Recommendation).

374. Under the CCEE, National Regulatory Authorities (NRAs) are required to periodically analyse the markets identified in the Recommendation as susceptible to *ex ante* regulation and, where special circumstances apply, may also identify relevant markets that differ from those identified in the Recommendation. NRAs are in any case required to analyse markets that are not identified in the Recommendation if they are regulated in their territory on the basis of previous market analyses.

375. Pursuant to Legislative Decree No. 207 of 8 November 2021, which transposed the CCEE (the Code) into national law, the Communications Guarantee Authority therefore periodically conducts market analyses aimed at identifying the relevant markets corresponding to the national situation, ascertaining whether there are undertakings with SMP and thus determining whether the imposition of *ex ante* regulatory obligations is justified in those markets.

In defining regulatory obligations, the Authority also applies the provisions of the Code which relate to specific cases, such as the wholesale-only SMP operator and commitments on co-investment in VHC networks, cooperation agreements and non-discriminatory access.

376. In Italy, The Electronic Communications Code – Legislative Decree 259/2003 – marks a necessary milestone in the system's structure, the convergence, also on a regulatory level, of the telecommunications, media and information technology sector, harmonizing all transmission networks and related services in a single regulatory framework.

With Legislative Decree No. 70 of 28 May 2012, Italy transposed European Directive 2009/140/EC, making substantial changes to the Electronic Communications Code.

§2. Interconnection Services

377. In order for subscribers of the various fixed network and mobile network operators to be able to communicate with each other, the networks must be *interconnected*, i.e., linked so that they can exchange traffic.

The Authority encourages and ensures appropriate forms of interconnection and interoperability of services, exercising its powers in such a way as to promote economic efficiency and sustainable competition and to bring the maximum benefit to end-users.

The Authority may impose on operators controlling access to end-users, in justified cases, and where not already provided for, the obligation to interconnect their networks, to the extent necessary to ensure end-to-end interconnection and to assess the intermediate services already made available.

378. When imposing obligations on an operator to grant access to its network facilities, and where this is necessary to ensure normal operation of the network, the Authority may lay down the technical or operational conditions to be met by the service provider or beneficiaries of access, in accordance with European law.

Interconnection is mainly carried out using IP technology, both on fixed and mobile networks. The Authority, in order to encourage the transition to IP interconnection and to create the prerequisites for it, has approved a number of regulatory measures relating to IP interconnection and interoperability for the provision of VoIP services on fixed networks (Resolution No. 128/11/CIR) and on mobile networks (Resolution No. 335/20/CIR).

379. In order to achieve interconnection between networks, operators must conclude interconnection contracts concerning the provision of one or more of the following services:

i. the origination (or sourcing) service of landline calls, which allows an operator to collect voice telephony traffic generated by users not directly on its network;
ii. the fixed-line termination service, which allows fixed-line and mobile operators to terminate calls originated by their customers on the fixed-line network to which the recipient of the call is subscribed;
iii. the transit service, which allows two operators not directly interconnected to exchange traffic with each other;
iv. the mobile call origination (or origination) service, which allows a virtual network operator (MVNO) to collect calls originated by its customers on the host MNO's network;
v. mobile call termination service, which allows fixed-line and mobile operators to terminate calls originated by their customers on the mobile network to which the call recipient is subscribed.

380. Notified operators are obliged to offer the above-mentioned services in compliance with the regulations in force, established by the Authority as part of the so-called market analysis.

381. Mobile collection services have never been regulated, since the market has a sufficiently large number of competing MNO operators.

Fixed-network and transit collection services are no longer subject to *ex-ante* regulation. First of all, at the EU level, the European Commission has considered that both markets no longer present characteristics that justify regulation, unless specific national circumstances apply. Indeed, they are not included in the list of markets susceptible to regulation identified by the European Commission and listed in Recommendation (EU) 2020/2245.

382. The Authority analysed them in accordance with the European Commission's indications that they were regulated, subjecting them to the so-called triple test in order to verify whether the competitive conditions justified the imposition of regulatory obligations. The Authority found that both markets no longer presented high and non-transitory barriers to entry; therefore, it removed, respectively Resolution No. 425/16/CONS, for the transit market, and Resolution No. 13/22/CONS for the collection market, the regulatory obligations previously imposed on Telecom Italia, an operator previously notified as having SMP in the collection and transit markets.

383. As a result of the aforementioned resolutions, Telecom Italia is not subject to any regulatory obligation in the supply of the services in question, being able to define the technical and economic conditions of supply in the context of commercial negotiations.

384. On the basis of the provisions of Article 75 of the new European Electronic Communications Code, established by Directive (EU) 2018/1972 of the European Parliament and of the Council, the European Commission adopted Delegated Regulation (EU) 2021/654, which defined a single maximum termination rate for voice calls on mobile networks at Union level and a single maximum termination rate for voice calls on fixed networks at Union level ('single Union-wide termination rates' or 'eurorate'), imposed on each provider of voice calls on mobile or fixed networks in each Member State, respectively.

385. Single Union-wide termination rates are based on the efficient costs of providing the service. For this purpose, the European Commission developed two models (one for fixed and another for mobile termination) of pure bottom-up long-run incremental costs (BU-LRIC), in cooperation with Axon Partners Group SA, in order to determine the efficient costs of both services. The single termination rate also includes the cost of interconnection kits.

386. In this way, the Commission intended to solve the most important competitive problem in the voice call termination markets.

As stated in the Commission's Recommendation No. 2020/2245 on Relevant Markets, in fact, the application of efficient tariffs limits the ability of operators to set excessive termination rates, which has posed 'the most serious threat to competition in these markets'. Moreover, strictly cost-oriented tariffs 'should be similar to those in competitive markets'.

387. For the reasons set out above, by defining single termination rates, the Commission removed the markets for voice call termination on fixed and mobile networks from the list of markets susceptible to *ex-ante* regulation published in the 2020 Recommendation, considering that these markets 'would no longer pass the three-criteria test at Union level'.

388. However, the Commission envisages that regulation of certain aspects of termination markets may still be justified in some Member States by specific circumstances, where it is found that, despite the imposition of eurorate, termination markets do not tend towards competition in the foreseeable future or continue to present competition problems. Such circumstances may be, for example, the refusal to interconnect received from certain operators or problems encountered by some operators in terminating their calls to other operators' networks. In these circumstances, the Authority could impose 'SMP-based obligations other than price controls if the three criteria test is met, or by using other appropriate regulatory means, i.e., Article 61(2) of the code, if the conditions specified therein are met'.

389. The maximum termination rates set by the European Commission apply to calls originating from Union numbers. However, as stipulated in Article 1(4) of the Delegated Regulation, the eurorate also applies to calls originating from numbers in countries outside the Union, if the third-country operators charge termination rates equal to or lower than the eurorate for calls originating from Union numbers on their own numbers, or if the Commission 'determines that, on the basis of information provided by a third country, termination rates for voice calls made from Union numbers to numbers in that third country are regulated in accordance with principles equivalent' to those used for the definition of eurorate.

390. Finally, Article 75 of the CCEE Directive states that 'national regulatory authorities shall closely monitor and ensure compliance with the application of Union-wide voice call termination rates by providers of voice call termination services'.

Despite the introduction of eurorate, the fixed and mobile voice call termination markets are currently subject to *ex ante* regulation.[112]

§3. Networks

391. The Authority performs regulatory, supervisory and sanctioning functions with regard to:

i. wholesale services relating to interconnection and access in electronic communications networks;
ii. management of scarce resources: numbering plans and frequency plans;
iii. retail telephony and data services and regulatory accounting;
iv. commissioning and financing of universal service for electronic communications services.

392. As far as regulatory functions are concerned, the Authority carries out a series of so-called horizontal regulation interventions, i.e., aimed at all electronic communication companies regardless of their market situation and whether or not they have 'significant market power' (SMP) in one or more electronic communication markets.

393. Examples of horizontal regulation are the definition of obligations relating to number portability in both the mobile (Mobile Number Portability, MNP) and fixed network (Number Portability, NP) spheres, procedures for switching users to the fixed network (activations and migrations), and plans for scarce resources (numbering and frequencies).

394. Supervisory activities are aimed at verifying compliance by electronic communication operators with the obligations imposed by regulation, regardless of whether they derive from horizontal regulation or from regulation adopted with regard to SMP operators only. In this context, supervision of measures to ensure non-discrimination (so-called equivalence) in the provision of regulated services is important.

112. *See* M. Sebastiani, 'L'evoluzione dei mercati e la sorte della regolazione dell'accesso nei settori a rete', in 'Economia dei Servizi', fasc. 3, 2010, pp. 471-496; D. Sorace, 'La desiderabile indipendenza della regolazione dei servizi di interesse economico generale', in 'Mercato, Concorrenza, Regole', fasc. 2, 2003, pp. 337-354.

The supervisory function also includes the activity of resolving disputes between electronic communication operators, in accordance with Article 23 of the Electronic Communications Code.

395. Lastly, the sanctioning function is carried out against operators whose failure to comply with the regulatory obligations imposed was ascertained during the supervisory phase.

The sanctioning function also includes the conduct of the sanctioning proceedings in which the operators avail themselves of the faculty, provided for by Decree-Law No. 223 of 4 July 2006, to make commitments, of a pre-eminently behavioural nature, in order to remedy the objections raised in the course of the sanctioning proceedings and to restore and improve the correct market conditions, negatively affected by the regulatory violations ascertained.[113]

§4. Media

396. The European Union has recognized the central role of independent national authorities in the audiovisual media services sector.

The competences of the Authority on audiovisual media services concern the regulatory, supervisory and sanctioning functions in the field of television broadcasting originally attributed to it by Law No. 249 of 31 July 1997 and subsequently extended by Law No. 28 of 22 February 2000, with regard to *par condicio* and by Legislative Decree No. 9 of 9 January 2008, with regard to sports audiovisual rights and the right to report.[114]

397. The main provisions have been gathered in the 'Testo Unico dei servizi di media audiovisivi' (TUSMA), Legislative Decree No. 208 of 8 November 2021, implementing Directive (EU) 2018/1808 of the European Parliament and of the Council of 14 November 2018 on the single text for the provision of audiovisual media services in view of changing market realities', as amended by Legislative Decree No. 50, on 'Supplementary and corrective provisions to Legislative Decree No 208 of 8 November 2021', on the single text for the provision of audiovisual media services in view of changing market realities, implementing Directive (EU) 2018/1808 amending Directive 2010/13/EU'.

398. These competences are articulated as follows: (i) authorization and regulatory discipline relating to access to content and multimedia platforms; (ii) protection of pluralism and competition in the media, and in particular the investigative functions under Title VI of the TUSMA; (iii) prominence of audiovisual and radio

113. *See* C.E. Cazzato, S. De Luca, 'Zero rating: tra regolazione e concorrenza. Una prima analisi', in 'Mercato, Concorrenza, Regole', Vol. 57 (3), 2017, pp. 527-546; P. Lupi, A. Perrucci, 'Quanti giorni in un mese?', in 'Mercato, Concorrenza, Regole', Vol. 59 (2), 2018, pp. 247-268.

114. *See* G.B. Ramello, F. Silva, A. Nicita (eds), 'La nuova televisione: Economia, mercato, regole' (Il Mulino, Bologna, 2009); F. Bassan, E. Tosi (eds), 'Diritto degli audiovisivi: commento a nuovo Testo Unico dei servizi di media audiovisivi e radiofonici come modificato dal D. lgs. 15 marzo 2010, n. 44' (Giuffrè, Milano, 2012).

media services of general interest influencers; (iv) obligations concerning European works and independent producers European quotas; (v) publishing; (vi) public service broadcasting and verification of public service concessionaire obligations; (vii) sports rights; (viii) protection and guarantee of rights; (ix) protection of minors; (x) propaganda, advertising, information, political communication and supervision for equal access to the media, *par condicio* respect for the fundamental rights of the individual in the communications sector, in particular, with specific competences relating to combating hate speech within the audiovisual media services system and video-sharing platform services; (xi) consumer and user protection surveys; (xii) verification of compliance with the rules on the right of reply; (xiii) advertising, including institutional advertising.

399. In this perspective, is fundamental the work of rationalizing and updating sector legislation through the creation of single regulatory texts.

An example of this is the outline of the new regulation on contracts between operators and users, recently put out for public consultation (Resolution No. 89/23/CONS), which covers all the main topics of interest to consumers, as well as the single text on mobile service quality indicators, which rationalizes and unifies the entire regulations on the quality of supply and service charters (Resolution No. 23/23/CONS).

In addition, there is public consultation on the quality of customer contact services in the electronic communications sector and audiovisual media services (Resolution No. 436/22/CONS), which aims to update the discipline dating back to 2009.

400. The services MisuraInternet and Broadband Map services have been updated direct, immediate and free knowledge of the cost and quality of the network connection.

The platform for digital dispute resolution, Concilia disputes, ConciliaWeb, has become a model used both in other areas, by AGCOM and other authorities.

401. In order to protect minors, AGCOM, with effective cooperation with the CNU, has approved the guidelines for parental control services (SCP) that must be used by electronic communications operators to block domains and sites offering illegal and harmful content.

402. With Resolution No. 255/24/CONS of 10 July 2024, the Communications Regulator intervened to modernize the regulations on customer care services in the electronic communications sector.

The new discipline aims to guarantee (a) maximum accessibility to the customer care service, provided through the traditional telephone channel (which remains mandatory), in addition to the digital contact mode that operators can make available to their customers; (b) the transparency and traceability of complaint handling procedures; (c) the quality of customer service.

403. The new regulation, in building on the previous regulatory framework defined by Resolution No. 79/09/CSP, takes into account the provisions of the new

Electronic Communications Code and the complex and changed market context, and makes use of an in-depth regulatory impact analysis, which has highlighted, in particular, a growth trend in the digital contact mode for customer assistance, which has risen from approximately 45% in 2020 to over 55% of total customer assistance requests by 2022.

For this reason, the new regulation establishes, for the first time, Guidelines on the provision and management of digital support channels, which were not provided for in the current regulatory framework.

404. The impact analysis showed that the average duration of telephone assistance contacts received by electronic communication operators in recent years has ranged from a minimum of about 270 seconds (consumer customers on mobile networks) to a maximum of about 410 seconds (consumer customers from fixed locations).

405. Telephone contacts take place in 97% of cases in the time slot between 8:30 and 21:30, while 88% of them are distributed between Monday and Friday.

The average response time to telephone contacts, which includes the operator's response time and the minimum Interactive Voice Response (IVR) time to access the 'operator' choice, after a peak of 144 seconds in 2021, settled in 2022 at 2020 values, with a slight decrease from 135 seconds to 132 seconds.

The rate of calls to the operator served within 20 seconds averaged 51% over the three-year period 2020–2022, albeit with considerable variance in the values experienced by the various operators.

406. In this context, the new framework establishes the following provisions: free customer care services, confirming the current regulatory framework; The telephone customer care service with a human operator is provided, for electronic communications services, at least on weekdays between 8.30 am and 9.30 pm (until 7.30 pm for business customer care numbers); The options in the IVR tree for talking to an attendant are explicit, transparent and comprehensible, enabling the user to obtain assistance from an attendant and to file a complaint in the shortest possible time; A more precise declination of the discipline of complaint handling, the deadline for which has been extended from forty-five to thirty days; For telephone assistance services, a dedicated option is made available to customers to submit a complaint to the first level of the IVR tree; The customer has the right to formulate the complaint through the telephone channel, registered letter with acknowledgement of receipt, and digital contact, where the operator makes this method available to the customer; The operator is obliged to communicate an identification code to the customer once the complaint has been received; For the quality indicators relating to telephone customer care services, referred to as 'average operator response time' and 'rate of calls to operator served within 20 seconds', the following obligations to achieve and meet minimum standards are established average operator response time: not exceeding 150 seconds; rate of calls to the operator served within 20 seconds: not less than 40%.

407. The Authority reserves the right to carry out periodic surveys on users' satisfaction with the various assistance services provided by operators, for the performance of which it may avail itself of the cooperation of representative consumer associations.

The new provisions will be implemented within 12 months from the publication of the measure.

§5. Dispute Resolution Ex DSA

408. The Communications Regulator, in its Council meeting of 24 July 2024, approved the Procedural Regulations for the certification of out-of-court dispute resolution bodies between providers of online platforms and recipients of services (Resolution No. 282/24/CONS) and for the issuance of the qualification of reliable reporter (Resolution No. 283/24/CONS), implementing Articles 21 and 22 of Regulation (EU) 2022/2065 (Digital Services Act or DSA).

409. The Regulations, which came into force on 15 September 2024, constitute the first measures implemented by AGCOM, in the exercise of its functions as Digital Services Coordinator for Italy, to ensure the effective and coordinated application of the DSA.

410. The Regulation for the certification of the bodies in charge of resolving disputes relating to the moderation of content between online platform providers and service recipients (Resolution No. 282/24/CONS) was adopted at the end of the public consultation, in which 11 subjects took part, including mediation bodies, trade and consumer associations and online platforms.[115]

411. As of 15 September, bodies established in Italy that carry out non-judicial dispute resolution (ADR) activities will be able to apply to the Authority for the certification necessary to be able to manage disputes relating to decisions taken by platforms with respect to the publication of 'illegal content', insofar as it is contrary to European or national legislation, or more generally with respect to the management of service recipients' accounts. For the purposes of certification, the bodies will have to prove that they meet the requirements set out in Article 21 of the DSA, including those of independence, including financial independence, from online platform providers and recipients of the service provided by online platform providers, including the persons or entities that have submitted reports, and the effectiveness of the procedures. The list of certified bodies will be published on the Authority's website.

It will thus be possible, both for those who report the publication of inappropriate content or content that violates consumer rights and for those who suffer restrictions on the use of their account on an online platform (including social networks), to access forms of alternative justice that are quick and inexpensive, although the decisions taken by the bodies will not be binding on the parties.

---

115. *See* M. Maggiore (eds.), 'Il commercio elettronico: Digital Markets act, Digital Services act e altre dimensioni giuridiche' (Giappichelli, Torino, 2024).

412. To facilitate the submission of applications for certification, the Authority has prepared a form, available on its institutional website, with a list of the necessary documentation. Furthermore, in order to ensure the uniform application of the provisions of Article 21 of the DSA, AGCOM may promote round tables with the parties concerned and, if necessary, the adoption of guidelines and codes of conduct.

413. The second Regulation (Resolution No. 283/24/CONS), relating to the procedures for issuing the qualification of reliable reporter, was adopted following a national public consultation in which 19 stakeholders from the electronic, audiovisual and Made in Italy industry, as well as service providers of online platforms and representatives of the professions and associations, took part.

414. The Regulation defines the operational procedures for granting the qualification of trustworthy reporter to any entity established in Italy that demonstrates that it meets the requirements – set out in Article 22 of the DSA – of capacity and competence, independence from online platforms and quality in its reporting activity. Interested entities will have to submit a specific request and indicate the area of competence in which they intend to exercise the activity. The qualification will last for three years and is renewable upon submission of a special application before expiry.

§6. Gambling Advertising Ban

415. The Authority for Guarantees in Communications, in the Council meeting of 24 July 2024, adopted two sanctions against subjects owning YouTube channels, which were disseminating videos promoting games and bets with cash winnings, in violation of the prohibition sanctioned by Article 9 of Decree-Law No. 96 of 12 July 2018, converted by Law No. 96 of 9 August 2018 (the so-called Dignity Decree).

416. With Resolutions No. 284/24/CONS and No. 286/24/CONS, the Authority imposed administrative fines on the companies 'PANPEG SRLS' and 'G.S.R. DI RICCI ANDREA & C. S.N.C.', amounting, respectively, to EUR 60 thousand and EUR 75 thousand, ordering, moreover, not to upload on the video sharing platform new contents identical or equivalent to those already identified (notice & stay down order) and to remove the contents that are in breach of the prohibition that may still be available (notice & take down order).

417. The proceedings were initiated as a result of numerous reports received between 2022 and 2023, in which alleged violations of the ban on the advertising of gambling with cash winnings by content creators through the dissemination of videos promoting games and betting on various video-sharing platforms, such as 'TikTok', 'YouTube', 'Instagram', 'Facebook', 'X' and 'Twitch' were alleged.

418. On the basis of the information provided by the platforms themselves, the Broadcasting and Publishing Group of the Guardia di Finanza's Special Goods and

Services Unit acquired all the elements that allowed the commencement of proceedings against the perpetrators of the offences in accordance with the provisions of Article 9, paragraph 2, of the 'dignity decree'.

419. The sanctioning proceedings initiated against the platforms have already been concluded with the adoption of the final measures (Decisions No. 316/23/CONS, 317/23/CONS, 318/23/CONS, 331/23/CONS, 50/24/CONS and 65/24/CONS).

§7. The Sanremo Festival Issue

420. The Authority's Commission for Services and Products has approved a fine of EUR 206,580.00, equal to twenty times the minimum fine, to RAI for violation of the provisions on the correct reporting of advertising messages during the '74th edition of the Sanremo Italian Song Festival'.

421. The infringement ascertained concerned the hidden advertising of a well-known shoe brand during the performance of John Travolta together with Amadeus, the presenter of the Festival. The Authority considered the episode to be extremely serious, as the exposure of the product took place during RAI's main television programme in terms of audience and during the performance of a guest of international renown, with considerable detrimental effects on viewers.

In determining the sanction, the Authority took into account the repetition of the conduct by RAI, which had already been sanctioned for episodes of surreptitious advertising during the past edition of the Sanremo Festival.

§8. Digital Citizenship and Digital Patent

422. With Resolution No. 177/24/CONS, published on 5 June, the Communications Guarantee Authority approved a guideline on digital citizenship training courses for the Regional Communications Committees (Co.re.com.).

423. For some years now, in fact, AGCOM has delegated to Co.re.com. the functions of protecting and guaranteeing users, with particular reference to minors, through decentralized media education initiatives on the national territory to be carried out in the context of the media and digital literacy activities promoted by the Authority, also in connection with other national institutions, as established in the last Framework Agreement concerning the exercise of the functions delegated to the Co.re.com., as per Resolution No. 427/22/CONS of 14 December 2022. Already after the signature of this Agreement, the Authority had adopted, by Resolution No. 182/23/CONS of 13 July 2023, guidelines for the exercise of the delegated function in the field of media education, indicating criteria and suggesting methods for the implementation of the initiatives falling within this scope.

424. With the Guideline Act that has just been adopted, the Authority has continued on its path of accompanying and guiding Co.re.com., outlining, starting with the existing initiatives on the so-called *Digital Patent*, an organic and homogeneous framework for the design and enhancement of digital and media literacy courses in first- and second-grade secondary school institutions, which promote the responsible and aware use of traditional and online media.

425. According to this Guideline Act, the training courses in question must have a minimum duration of ten hours and a maximum duration of twenty hours and must be available in hybrid mode, both in the classroom and remotely. These courses will also have to deal with some compulsory topics such as the protection of web reputation, the functioning mechanisms of algorithmic platforms, disinformation and hate speech, useful to develop students' critical sense, in line with the most recent definition of media literacy contained in the European Media Freedom Act.

426. The final objective of the Authority's work is to ensure that the digital citizenship training courses, implemented by Co.re.com. in accordance with the indications contained in the Guideline Act, can integrate, for the adhering schools, the annual timetable of civic education that all schools are required to provide pursuant to Law No. 92 of 20 August 2019, on the 'Introduction of the school teaching of civic education', for the part specifically dedicated to digital civic education.

Chapter 6. Regulation of Broadcasting Activities

§1. Broadcasting Activities in Italy

427. In Italy, the legal framework governing broadcasting activities and audiovisual services is rooted in a combination of national and European Union (EU) regulations, reflecting the country's commitment to maintaining a diverse and pluralistic media landscape while adhering to EU standards.

The Italian broadcasting sector is primarily regulated by the 'Consolidated Law on Audiovisual Media Services' ('Testo Unico dei Servizi di Media Audiovisivi'), which was implemented by Legislative Decree No. 177 of 2005 and has since been amended several times to align with EU directives, most notably the Audiovisual Media Services Directive (AVMSD).[116]

428. The framework establishes rules for public and private broadcasters, emphasizing the need for diversity in ownership to prevent media concentration and ensure pluralism. The public broadcaster, RAI (Radiotelevisione Italiana), operates under a specific service contract with the State, which outlines its obligations to provide diverse and high-quality content, including news, cultural programming, and entertainment. RAI is funded through a combination of a license fee, paid by households, and advertising revenue, although it is subject to strict rules to ensure its impartiality and independence.

429. Private broadcasters, both national and local, are regulated by the Communications Regulatory Authority (AGCOM), which oversees compliance with licensing requirements, content standards, and competition laws.

AGCOM plays a crucial role in ensuring that broadcasters respect rules regarding advertising, protection of minors, and the right to accurate and impartial information. The authority also monitors the compliance of on-demand services with content regulation, particularly in areas such as hate speech, consumer protection, and the protection of minors.[117]

430. In addition to national laws, Italy's broadcasting sector is influenced by EU legislation, particularly concerning cross-border broadcasting and the promotion of European works. Italian law mandates that a significant portion of broadcast time

116. *See* G.B. Ramello, F. Silva, A. Nicita (eds), 'La nuova televisione: Economia, mercato, regole' (Il Mulino, Bologna, 2009); F. Bassan, E. Tosi (ed.), 'Diritto degli audiovisivi: commento a nuovo Testo Unico dei servizi di media audiovisivi e radiofonici come modificato dal D. lgs. 15 marzo 2010, n. 44' (Giuffrè, Milano, 2012).

117. *See* S. Lavagnini, 'The Italian implementation of Article 17 of Directive 2019/790: complaints, appeals and the new powers of AGCOM', in 'Journal of intellectual property law & practice', Vol. 17 (5), 2022, pp. 443-449; S. Parisi, 'Right words, right actions? Il regolamento AGCOM contro l'hate speech nei mass media e la libertà di espressione', in 'Quaderni costituzionali', 2019, pp. 687-690; A. Preto, B. Carotti, 'Review of Independent Authorities: the Agcom Case', in 'Rivista trimestrale di diritto pubblico', fasc. 1, 2016, pp. 123-154; R. Mosca, '14 years of AGCOM, what has changed in the Italian TLC since 1998, in L'industria: rivista di economia e politica industriale', Vol. 33 (3), 2012, pp. 429-460.

be dedicated to European productions, with additional quotas for independent producers and Italian-language content to support the domestic creative industry.

431. Overall, the legal framework in Italy aims to balance the public interest in a free and pluralistic media environment with the need to regulate the market effectively, ensuring that broadcasting services contribute to the cultural and democratic life of the country.

§2. The Consolidated Law on Audiovisual Media Services in Brief

432. The Consolidated Law on Audiovisual Media Services in Italy serves as the primary legal framework governing the broadcasting and audiovisual media sector. This law, which has undergone several amendments, particularly to align with European Union directives, sets out comprehensive regulations aimed at ensuring the orderly functioning of the audiovisual market, promoting cultural diversity, and protecting public interests.

433. The law applies to all audiovisual media services, including traditional television broadcasting, on-demand services, and other media services delivered through electronic communication networks. It defines key terms such as 'audiovisual media service', 'broadcaster', and 'editorial responsibility', which are critical for determining the scope of its application.

434. Broadcasters and audiovisual service providers are required to obtain licenses or authorizations to operate.

The law outlines the conditions under which these licenses are granted, including compliance with technical standards, ownership transparency, and financial requirements.

This is designed to ensure that operators are capable of maintaining service quality and complying with regulatory obligations.

435. One of the central aims of the law is to promote pluralism in the media. It includes provisions to prevent the concentration of media ownership and to ensure a diverse range of viewpoints are represented. Additionally, there are content quotas requiring a certain percentage of programming to be of European origin and to promote independent productions, which helps to support the European and Italian creative industries.

436. The law enshrines the role of RAI, the national public service broadcaster, outlining its duties to provide a wide range of content that serves the public interest. RAI is required to produce and broadcast programs that cater to various audiences, including news, educational, and cultural programming, while also being subject to rules ensuring its editorial independence and impartiality.

437. There are detailed rules governing advertising and sponsorship to protect consumers and maintain a fair broadcasting environment. These include limits on the amount of advertising per hour, restrictions on certain types of advertising (e.g., targeting children or promoting harmful substances), and rules on product placement to ensure transparency.

438. The law includes strong provisions aimed at protecting minors from potentially harmful content. This includes restrictions on broadcasting certain types of content during times when children are likely to be watching, as well as the requirement for broadcasters to use content classification systems and parental control mechanisms.

439. The law guarantees individuals the right to reply to broadcasts that may affect their reputation or dignity. Broadcasters are required to provide a prompt and appropriate platform for responses, ensuring that the public receives a balanced and fair view of issues.

440. The Communications Regulatory Authority (AGCOM) is the primary body responsible for overseeing compliance with the law. AGCOM has the power to impose sanctions, including fines, suspension of licenses, or revocation of authorizations, for breaches of the law. The authority also monitors the implementation of European directives and regulations in the Italian context.

441. To foster cultural diversity, the law mandates that a significant portion of the broadcasting schedule be dedicated to European works. This includes specific quotas for programs produced by independent producers and content originally created in the Italian language.

442. The law reflects Italy's commitment to the digital transition, encouraging the development and adoption of digital broadcasting technologies. It also emphasizes the principle of technological neutrality, meaning that regulations should apply equally to similar services regardless of the technology used to deliver them.

443. In conclusion, the Consolidated Law on Audiovisual Media Services in Italy aims to create a balanced regulatory environment that supports a diverse, competitive, and culturally rich audiovisual sector while safeguarding public interests, particularly in terms of protecting minors, ensuring pluralism, and promoting European content.

§3. The 2024 Reform of the Consolidated Law on Audiovisual Media Services

444. The long-awaited Decree containing reform provisions (corrective and supplementary) to the Testo Unico dei Servizi di Media Audiovisivi ('TUSMA') was published in the Official Gazette and entered into force on 2 May 2024.

It is Legislative Decree No. 50 of 25 March 2024 ('Corrective Decree'), adopted in order to dictate supplementary and corrective provisions to Legislative Decree No. 208 of 8 November 2021, which had reformed the entire TUSMA.

445. The stated objective is to refine the regulatory framework and to give greater clarity and homogeneity to the content of the text of the new TUSMA, in continuity with the objective of ensuring the proper functioning of the single European market for audiovisual media services, in implementation of Directive (EU) 2018/1808, reordering such provisions.

446. The applicative scope of certain provisions of principle has been extended to all media service providers, both audiovisual and radio, as well as certain provisions to combat the dissemination of illegal content and to protect users, initially dictated only for video broadcasting platforms, have also been extended to audio-only content-sharing platforms.

447. At the heart of the reform, however, is the simplification of the system of programming and investment quotas for European works and original Italian works, a much-discussed subject that has caused considerable concern in the world of independent production.

448. The Corrective Decree has in fact reduced the quota for investment in European works by on-demand service providers from 20% to 16% and removed the possibility of introducing further sub-quotas for programming and investment compared to those already provided for by TUSMA or of increasing the minimum percentage. Producers' requests to maintain the existing mandatory investment quotas (reduced from 3.5% to 3% of turnover) and to introduce sub-quotas for animation were not accepted. On the other hand, the programming quota of recent works (i.e., produced in the last five years) of original Italian expression was raised from 50% to 70%.

449. Another important innovation is the establishment, in place of the Committee for the application of the Code of self-regulation on media and minors, of the Inter-Institutional Advisory Committee with promotion and research tasks on media and digital literacy issues, as well as with a consultative function (expressing its own opinion) in relation to the adoption of self-regulation and co-regulation codes for the protection of minors, whose operating rules are referred to a subsequent ministerial decree.

§4. The 2016 Reform on the Regulation of Cinema and Audiovisuals

450. Published in the Official Gazette General Series No. 277 of 26 November 2016, Law No. 220 of 14 November 2016 on the regulation of cinema and audiovisuals, with the aim of relaunching and developing a strategic sector from a cultural and social, but also economic, point of view.[118]

118. *See* L. Casini, "Il nastro dei sogni'? Il diritto (pubblico) del cinema e dell'audiovisivo', in 'Aedon', fasc. 3, 2017.

451. The objectives of public intervention, set out in Article 3, include, among others, the guarantee of the pluralism of film and audiovisual supply, the consolidation of the national film industry, the promotion of international co-productions and of the circulation and distribution, in Italy and abroad, of film and audiovisual production, the preservation and restoration of the national film and audiovisual heritage, the care of professional training, the support of image education in schools, and the enhancement of the role of cinemas and film festivals.

452. The Fondo per lo sviluppo degli investimenti nel cinema e l'audiovisivo (Fund for the development of investments in the cinema and audiovisual sector) is set up in the Mibact estimates, as of 2017, to be fed, when fully operational, by the tax revenues from the sector's activities. The funding cannot be less than EUR 400 million per year.

453. A system of automatic contributions for works of Italian nationality is introduced – from the Fund to be set up –, modifying the current procedure that provides for the allocation of funding after verification by the Commission for Cinematography (as per Article 8 of Legislative Decree 28/2004).

454. Selective contributions are introduced – again from the Fund - intended, in particular, for first and second works, works by young authors, works of particular artistic quality, newly established companies and micro-enterprises.

455. Special sections of the same Fund are envisaged to finance, respectively, the Extraordinary Plan for the strengthening of the cinema circuit and the Extraordinary Plan for the digitization of the cinematographic and audiovisual heritage.

456. Measures are introduced to strengthen the discipline of the tax credit for the film and audiovisual sector.

457. The establishment of a special section in the Guarantee Fund for small and medium-sized enterprises is envisaged to guarantee financing operations to companies for the production of audiovisual and cinematographic products.

458. In place of the Cinema Section of the Council for the Performing Arts, the Higher Council for Cinema and Audiovisual Media is established.

459. The Government is delegated to revise the current provisions on the protection of minors in the film sector – in particular, by replacing the so-called preventive censorship with a system of empowerment of operators in the sector in the classification of products – the promotion of European works by audiovisual media service providers – in particular, by introducing more transparent and effective procedures – labour relations in the sector.

460. As a result of the changes introduced, Legislative Decree 28/2004, among others, will be repealed as of 1 January 2017.

461. Law No. 220/2016 – labelled 'discipline of cinema and audiovisuals' – brings with it the feasibility of a competitive film and audiovisual market, through the precise and systematic provision of contributions and tax incentives and through a series of special rules for the works that will benefit from the various government incentives.

462. One of the main objectives of the new law is to create a 'sustainable' cinema, where sustainability is guaranteed by public and private interventions that find their source in the film industry itself, made possible thanks to the construction of an autonomous and self-sufficient system.

463. The central point of the law is thus the design of a new financing system that finds its source in the target sector itself. The disbursement of contributions, in fact, is guaranteed by the very operation of the system. External interventions constitute a collateral aspect that can support the film business.

464. The State censorship introduced in Italy with the law of 21 April 1962 is abolished. It will no longer be the ministerial commissions that will assess films. In this respect, a mechanism is planned that makes film producers and distributors responsible, who will be responsible for rating films according to their own moral criteria. It will then be up to the state to carry out an ex-post control if abuse occurs.

Chapter 7. Regulation of Online Interactive Services: Electronic Commerce, Online Platforms, B2B Platforms

§1. The Legal Framework of E-Commerce in Italy

465. In Italy, electronic commerce (e-commerce) is primarily regulated by a combination of national laws and European Union directives, which aim to create a secure and transparent environment for online transactions while protecting consumers' rights.

The main legal framework is the Legislative Decree No. 70 of 2003, which implements the EU E-Commerce Directive (2000/31/EC). This decree, along with other relevant national laws and EU regulations, outlines the responsibilities of e-commerce businesses and sets out the rights and protections for consumers. Below are the main regulations and issues related to e-commerce in Italy.[119]

466. E-commerce in Italy enjoys the same legal recognition as traditional commerce. The law ensures that electronic contracts are valid and enforceable, provided that the parties have given their consent through digital means. E-commerce businesses must ensure that the terms of sale are clear, easily accessible, and presented in a way that consumers can understand.

467. E-commerce operators are required to provide clear and detailed information about their business and the products or services they offer. This includes: The identity and address of the business. Contact details, including email and telephone numbers. VAT number or business registration number. Terms and conditions of sale, including payment methods, delivery options, and refund policies. Details about the right of withdrawal (where applicable).

This transparency is intended to build trust with consumers and ensure they have all the necessary information before making a purchase.

468. Italian e-commerce regulations place a strong emphasis on protecting consumers. Key consumer protection rules include:

Right of Withdrawal: Consumers have the right to withdraw from an online purchase within 14 days of receiving the goods, without providing a reason. This cooling-off period allows consumers to reconsider their purchase decision. The seller is obliged to refund the full purchase price, including any standard delivery charges.

Product Conformity and Warranties: E-commerce businesses must ensure that products conform to the description provided and are free from defects. Consumers have the right to a minimum two-year warranty for faulty products, during which the seller must repair, replace, or refund the item.

---

119. *See* A. Sirotti Gaudenzi, 'Il commercio elettronico nella società dell'informazione: aggiornato all'attuazione delle direttive sul copyright nell'information society (D. lgs. 69/2003) e sul commercio elettronico (D. lgs. n. 70/2003)' (Sistemi Editoriali, Napoli, 2003).

Unfair Commercial Practices: The law prohibits misleading advertising, aggressive sales tactics, and any other unfair practices that could deceive or coerce consumers into making purchases.

469. Italian law provides consumers with clear rights regarding jurisdiction and dispute resolution. In cross-border e-commerce transactions within the EU, consumers are generally entitled to bring legal action in their home country. Additionally, Italy supports alternative dispute resolution (ADR) mechanisms and online dispute resolution (ODR) platforms, which offer consumers a simple and cost-effective way to resolve disputes without going to court.

470. E-commerce businesses operating in Italy must comply with the country's tax regulations, including the collection and payment of Value Added Tax (VAT). Since the introduction of the EU VAT E-Commerce Package in 2021, rules regarding VAT on cross-border sales have been streamlined, requiring e-commerce businesses to collect VAT at the rate applicable in the consumer's country of residence. Businesses must also register for VAT in Italy if their sales exceed certain thresholds.

471. E-commerce websites must be accessible to all users, including those with disabilities. Italian law requires that websites adhere to accessibility standards, ensuring that everyone can navigate and use online services without discrimination.

§2. The Norms

472. In Italy, implementing Directive 2000/31, Legislative Decree No. 70/2003 was issued to promote the free circulation of information society services, including e-commerce.

The Italian Decree substantially takes up the content of the Directive and contains rules to guarantee the contracting party so that he can base his contractual decisions on conscious choices in a climate of trust towards the sales organization.

473. For what are the most important contractual aspects, we would like to point out Articles 12 and 13 of Legislative Decree No. 70/2003, which regulate, respectively, the information directed to the conclusion of the contract and the placing of the order.

474. The provider of information society services or the person providing a service must, without delay and by electronic means, acknowledge receipt of the recipient's order containing a summary of the general and particular conditions applicable to the contract as well as a set of information relating to the good or service, price, means of payment, withdrawal, delivery costs and applicable taxes.

475. E-commerce can be of two types: indirect e-commerce (if the transaction with the customer takes place online but the tangible good is delivered to him or her in the traditional way e.g., by a carrier) or direct e-commerce (if, on the other hand, the intangible goods do not have to be physically delivered and the user obtains the goods telematically e.g., via download. The entire transaction is completed online).

476. Distinctions were then introduced regarding the parties to the relationship: Business-to-business e-commerce (B2B): the parties are companies or professionals, e.g., business-to-supplier relationships. Business-to-consumer (B2C) e-commerce: between businesses and consumers. Consumers enjoy the advantage of being able to purchase products and services, from anywhere and without time limits, from companies located all over the world. The market is increasingly characterized by borderlessness, internationalization and so-called technological liquidity. Consumer-to-consumer (C2C) e-commerce: between consumers. Examples of an environment in which users interact are online auctions. Public Administration-to-citizen e-commerce: between public administration and citizens, e.g., there is the possibility of making payments to the PA electronically.

477. E-commerce finds its discipline in the telematic contract that is concluded at a distance through two channels that travel over the Internet: e-mail or the World Wide Web. To telematic contracts, doctrine and jurisprudence apply the discipline of contracts in general contained in the Civil Code, which, in Articles 1321-1469 deals with rules applicable to any agreement.

478. In addition to the discipline of contracts in general, the specific Italian legislation on electronic commerce, enacted by Legislative Decree No. 70/2003, applies to professional operators and consumers. If there is a consumer, the rules designed to protect him also apply. E-commerce involves legal issues concerning the formation and finalization of contracts concluded at a distance between parties not physically present in the same place at the same time.

479. Regarding the manner of conclusion of contracts consisting of the exchange of proposal and acceptance in the telematic world, according to Article 1326 of the Italian Civil Code, 'the contract is concluded at the time when the party making the proposal has knowledge of the other party's acceptance' and if the offeror requires a specific form for acceptance, the acceptance has no effect if it is given in a different form.

Knowledge of acceptance' is to be understood as cognizability, i.e., proposal, acceptance and revocation are deemed to be known at the time they reach the addressee's address.

The question of the imputability of contractual declarations, where not resolved by the use of electronic signatures, is based on the principle of reliance that characterizes all telematic contracts. The seller cannot verify who the individual buyer is, whether he is a minor and thus lacks the legal capacity to conclude contracts.[120]

120. *See* A. Fraternale, 'I contratti a distanza' (Giuffrè, Milano, 2002); F. Bravo, 'I contratti a distanza nel codice del consumo e nella direttiva 2011/83/UE: verso un codice europeo del consumo' (Giuffrè, Milano, 2013); M. P. Pignalosa, 'Contratti a distanza e recesso del consumatore' (Giuffrè, Milano, 2016).

480. The completion of the online contract may take place through the scheme of the public offer (Article 1336 of the Italian Civil Code) or through the invitation to offer (*invitatio ad offerendum*).

The difference between the two figures lies in the fact that the offer to the public is directed to an indefinite number of persons and contains a proposal with all the essential elements of the contract to be concluded, whereas the invitation to offer does not contain all the essential elements of the contract to be concluded.

481. Moreover, in the case of an offer to the public, the contract is concluded with the mere acceptance of the offer by the user, whereas in the case of an invitation to offer, the contract is not instantly concluded but there will be several exchanges of communication between the parties.

In the case of an offer to the public, the most common way of concluding a telematic contract is through the selection of the 'virtual negotiation button', which replaces the classic way of concluding a contract in the analogue world.

This is the so-called point and click or 'tap-touch', i.e., express acceptance of the agreement as a whole through the selection of the button, through the click of the mouse on the button to which legal effects follow. The negotiation key may constitute a form of weak electronic signature.

482. In other words, within an e-commerce site, the user chooses the goods or services he is interested in by placing them in a virtual shopping cart and, in order to place the order and manifest his willingness to purchase, the user must select an icon, a button or a similar function that must legibly display the words 'order with obligation to pay' or similar words. It is precisely this selection of the button that configures the 'point and click' mechanism.

483. What has raised more debate and perplexity, however, is the requirement of specific written approval pursuant to Article 1341, paragraph 2, of the Italian Civil Code for vexatious clauses unilaterally prepared by the provider of digital services.

The clauses are vexatious when they determine an imbalance of rights and obligations for one party in favour of the counterparty that prepared them.[121]

To protect the weaker party, Article 1341 of the Italian Civil Code requires that vexatious clauses be 'specifically approved in writing' or in writing and with specific approval. The question arises as to which modalities are appropriate in the online contract to integrate the requirements of Article 1341(2) of the Italian Civil Code.

484. The requirement of specific approval in writing for unfair terms is fulfilled by the simple electronic signature which, in the conclusion of online contracts by

121. G. Pedrazzi, 'Le clausole vessatorie nei contratti telematici con i consumatori', in E. Tosi (ed.), 'La tutela dei consumatori in Internet e nel commercio elettronico' (Giuffrè, Milano, 2012); G. Finocchiaro, 'Il perfezionamento del contratto on line: opportunità e criticità', in 'Diritto comunitario e degli scambi internazionali', fasc. 1, 2018, pp. 187-202.

telematic means, corresponds to authentication by means of username and password so that the user can register on the site and then receive a confirmation e-mail.

In addition, there is the need for an explicit manifestation of willingness to accept the clauses and, to this end, the user must fill in a second form specific to the clauses, in addition to the one containing the general conditions, and press the virtual negotiation button for acceptance, thereby generating the computer document containing the approval of the clauses. Jurisprudence regarding the vexatiousness of clauses in telematic contracts is not unequivocal. It is therefore necessary to adopt a cautious approach and provide for a way of signing vexatious clauses such as a double signature or a prior registration on the site, followed by a signature.

485. For doctrine and jurisprudence, the place of conclusion of the contract is where the offeror has knowledge of the acceptance. Two theories have been put forward in this respect, according to which the place is either the place where the server of the offeror receiving the acceptance is located or the place of the offeror's seat or domicile.

486. In favour of the consumer, there is a specific protection dictated by the Consumer Code and applicable exclusively when the parties to the contract about to be entered into are a consumer and a professional.

The consumer, that is to say, any natural person acting for purposes which are outside his or her trade, business, craft or profession, if he or she is negotiating a distance contract, and precisely before he or she becomes bound by it, is entitled to receive a set of information in a clear and comprehensible manner.

487. The professional seller, in fulfilling his obligations to provide information, after identifying himself by specifying his identity and contact details, must provide all the information concerning the main characteristics of the goods and services that are the subject of the contract, their costs and payment terms, the presence of product guarantees as well as the legal guarantee of conformity, the applicable law and the competent court.

488. The conditions of sale prepared by the trader must be knowable and, to this end, must be published on the site and must be expressed in clear language.

The consumer must also be informed of the content of the right of withdrawal to which he/she is entitled under Article 52 of the Consumer Code. Specifically, he/she is entitled to be informed about the conditions, terms and procedures for exercising this right as well as to receive the standard withdrawal form.

489. Except in cases where the right of withdrawal is excluded or where withdrawal is not provided for due to the particular characteristics of the product purchased or the manner in which it is made, the consumer has a period of fourteen days to withdraw from the contract without having to provide any reasons or costs.

Within the fourteen-day period, the consumer must communicate his/her will to the professional – merchant – either by filling in the form provided or by sending an explicit declaration of his intention to withdraw.

490. This period is calculated from the conclusion of the contract if it is a service or from the physical possession of the goods if it is a sale.

As far as the consequences are concerned, withdrawal terminates the parties' obligations to perform the distance contract and gives rise to specific obligations on each party: an obligation to return the goods arises on the part of the consumer (in the case of the sale of goods) and an obligation to reimburse the consumer arises on the part of the professional in favour of the consumer.

491. The consumer shall return the goods within fourteen days from the date on which he/she communicated his/her decision to exercise the right of withdrawal to the trader. The trader may withhold the refund until the material acquisition of the returned goods in order to verify its proper use and the presence of any manipulation of the good that would lead to a decrease in its value.

492. Crucial importance is given to after-sales relations because it is precisely at this stage that the consumer will express his/her level of satisfaction should he/she need assistance after the purchase. It is strategic for the professional to focus on a business that takes care of after-sales relations so as to nurture positive judgments on the service offered.

§3. The Main Case Law ('Jurisprudence')

493. According to Court of Milan, commercial court (i.e., specialized section), 20/03/2024, the provision of false reviews of goods purchased through an e-commerce platform to be published on that platform must be prevented as a matter of urgency.

Given that the offer and supply, by the owner of an internet website, of false reviews relating to goods or services purchased through an electronic commerce platform, to be published on that platform, constitutes unfair competition to the detriment of the operator of that platform and that the continuation of such unlawful conduct may contribute to causing damage that is difficult to repair in terms of the credibility of the platform itself, the performance of such activities through said website and/or any other means currently available or which will be available in the future should be prohibited with immediate effect, at the same time ordering the respondent to delete all the pages relating to said service in connection with said platform from any website he owns or controls.

494. According to Court of Civitavecchia, section I, 24/02/2023, No. 197, the contractual clause derogating jurisdiction is null and void if not negotiated between the parties.

A jurisdiction clause included in a contract between a consumer and a professional and not individually negotiated, whereby the parties have attributed exclusive jurisdiction to the court in whose jurisdiction the professional's registered office is located, is to be considered unfair, within the meaning of Article 3(1) of EC Directive No. 93/13, if, contrary to the principle of the protection of consumers, it is not subject to the exclusive jurisdiction of the court in whose jurisdiction the professional's registered office is located. 93/13 if, contrary to the requirement of good faith, it results in a significant imbalance between the parties' rights and obligations under the contract (in the present case, on the basis of the above principle, the court declared the exclusive jurisdiction clause invalid by reason of the very manner in which the contract was concluded – i.e., the so-called point and click – which showed the total absence of individual negotiation).

495. According to Corte di Cassazione, Civil section I, 09/04/2021, No. 9413, on the subject of signing computerized documents, the electronic signature (or light digital signature), understood as the set of data in electronic form, attached or connected by logical association to other electronic data, used as a method of computer authentication, is distinguished from the advanced or heavy digital signature i.e., the electronic signature obtained by means of an IT procedure that guarantees the unambiguous connection to the signatory and his unambiguous identification, in that it is created by means over which the signatory can retain exclusive control, without prejudice to the former's suitability to satisfy the legal requirement of the written form 'ad substantiam' pursuant to Article 10 of Presidential Decree No. 445 of 2000, as amended by Article 6 of Legislative Decree No. 10 of 2002, except in the cases referred to in Article 1350 of the Italian Civil Code where the written form is provided for under penalty of nullity.

In the case in point, the Corte di Cassazione upheld the decision of the Court of Appeal to consider as sufficient, for the purposes of the contractual integration enabling the negotiation of covered warrants, the mere electronic signature affixed by the saver by means of the 'point and click' in his reserved area.

For the purposes of compliance with the written form required for the integration of a contract of financial intermediation aimed at authorizing the negotiation of covered warrants, the electronic signature affixed by the investor by means of the point and click present in his reserved area is sufficient.

496. According to Justice of the Peace of Trapani, 14/10/2019, even in the case of online bookings, the clause concerning the payment of the cancellation penalty must be specifically approved. The clauses imposing the payment of a penalty in the event of cancellation, i.e., indicating the acceptance of the hotel offer as 'non-refundable' are, to all intents and purposes, vexatious clauses, effective only if signed by the customer; with the consequence that, when booking online, the possible ticking of the box in the general terms and conditions of the contract does not replace the clause relating to the payment of the penalty has no legal effect unless specifically approved.

497. According to Court of Catanzaro, section I, 30/04/2012, in telematic contracts, the acceptance of a negotiation proposal by means of the 'virtual button' or 'point and click' technique is sufficient to manifest consent and deem the contract to be perfected, inasmuch as it is a free-form negotiation bond. In the case of a contract by adhesion, outlined in uniform general terms and conditions prepared by only one of the parties, and accepted by means of a telematic system, the requirement under Article 1341 paragraph 1 of the Italian Civil Code of knowledge of the contractual proposal contained in the general terms and conditions degrades to mere knowability, which may also be satisfied by recalling the relevant clauses by means of a hyperlink.

General terms and conditions contained in telematic contracts are also cognizable if they are referred to by links, provided they are intelligible, clear and not formulated in a generic manner.

Chapter 8. Regulation of Cryptography and Dual-Use Goods

§1. Introduction (and the Italian Legal Framework)

498. The subject of encryption and data encryption, which started out as a particularly *technical topic* that was not easy to understand for the ordinary user, has in recent years also become of central importance for the jurist.

On the one hand, data encryption is seen as an indispensable cybersecurity and data protection tool. It has therefore attracted the attention of the data protection Authority, which has identified it as a minimum requirement to ensure effective cybersecurity.

On the other hand, cryptography is a technology that has entered both the system of critical infrastructures, especially that of payments and finance (use of cryptography in banking and the transfer of funds), the cloud (and data storage) and, again, the public sector (linked, for instance, to systems such as certified e-mail).

The topic is also interesting from a criminal and investigative point of view (the use of cryptography as a tool for *anti-forensics*, i.e., to cover up certain illegal activities), as a means of protecting passwords and credentials, and as an invention that may be subject to restrictions in its production or export because it is liable to criminal use.[122]

499. This has meant that a heterogeneous but interesting legal framework has had to be drawn up over the decades, which we will analyse in the following pages.

It should be made clear from the beginning that there are *no specific regulations* on cryptography in Italy, but the subject is dealt with in many sector-specific regulations.

There are, on the one hand, sectors that have a special discipline, whereby the use of cryptography is left to each administration without imposing standards and good practices that would instead be necessary for a harmonized use of technologies.

On the other hand, the subject of cryptography involves defence and national security, armaments and trade in 'dual-use goods'.

§2. Cryptography in Risk Management and Data Protection

500. In Italy, cryptography has long since entered the regulatory framework thanks to *data protection* regulations, in which cryptography is often mentioned as an appropriate tool to mitigate risk.

---

122. *See* G. Ziccardi, 'Crittografia e Diritto' (Giappichelli, Torino, 2003). *See, also*, C. Giustozzi, A. Monti, E. Zimuel, 'Segreti, spie, codici cifrati' (Apogeo, Milano, 1999). For dual-use goods, *see* https://www.esteri.it/it/diplomazia-economica-e-politica-commerciale/uama/.

We refer, in particular, to the discipline of Article 32 of the GDPR[123] and, before that, to the text of Annex B of Legislative Decree 196 of 2003,[124] the 'Privacy Code' (now partly repealed).

In this case, we are in the presence of a 'simple' technical-organizational measure that is appropriate from a regulatory point of view and explicitly provided for by law.

The European legislator, and the Italian legislator before it, have provided that the data controller and data processor must implement appropriate technical and organizational measures to ensure a level of security appropriate to the risk. Measures that include, among others, the pseudonymization and, precisely, the encryption of personal data.

The EU Regulation, therefore, does not regulate encryption as such, but indicates it as a suitable measure for protecting data both in a 'static' environment – such as cloud storage – and in a 'dynamic' environment – when an encrypted attachment is sent by email, via the cloud, and is thus not readable by unauthorized third parties.

501. In December 2003, the Italian Data Protection Authority, together with the national cybersecurity agency, published a *document* addressing the use of encryption in password management.

Nowadays, the Authors of the document write that access to most computer systems and services involves one- or multi-factor computer authentication procedures that often include the use of a password. Password management is a fundamental aspect of IT security and personal data protection. Therefore, the operators of systems and services must provide for effective technical and organizational measures for the archiving, storage and use of passwords.[125]

502. Archives in which passwords are stored increasingly fall into the hands of external parties as a result of cyber-attacks and are then published online or used to conduct other attacks.

For these reasons, the use of *robust cryptographic password hashing functions* is highly recommended. The document aims to provide guidance and recommendations on the functions that are currently considered to be the most secure.

The document is structured as follows: Chapter 2 introduces the concept of password hashing, focusing on the properties that the functions must fulfil and the possible attacks that password stores may be subject to. In Chapter 3 the most common algorithms used for password hashing are presented in detail. Finally, Chapter 4 provides information on which algorithms are recommended and their respective parameters.[126]

---

123. *See* the full official text at https://eur-lex.europa.eu/eli/reg/2016/679/oj.
124. *See* the full official text, in Italian, at https://www.normattiva.it/uri-res/N2Ls?urn:nir:stato:decreto.legislativo:2003-06-30;196!vig.
125. *See* https://www.garanteprivacy.it/web/guest/home/docweb/-/docweb-display/docweb/9962384.
126. *See* https://www.garanteprivacy.it/web/guest/home/docweb/-/docweb-display/docweb/9962384.

§3. Cryptography in the Italian Digital Public Administration Code ('Codice dell'Amministrazione Digitale')

503. In Italy, a specific reference to cryptography is also found in the *Digital Administration Code*, i.e., in that discipline that provides for the digitization of the Italian public sector and the regulation of every legal aspect of it.[127]

All provisions on the subject of digital signatures and electronic seals, or of certified electronic mail and document storage, have as their basis systems that crucially presuppose the availability of public-key and symmetric-key cryptographic technologies in several steps of their current implementations.

Cryptography is then, indispensable for the digital or electronic signature of a computer document, being the technical tool on which digital signature certificates are based for the unobjectionability of the computer document under the GDPR and eIDAS.[128]

§4. Cryptography in Electronic Commerce and Secure Communications

504. The same technology is used and underpins *electronic commerce* and all network interactions based on secure web protocols such as TLS and SSL, which are now used unknowingly when connecting, for example, to a bank account via home banking.

505. In August 2023, the Italian Data Protection Authority, deciding about whistleblowing, fixed specific guarantees for the employees who contact the Anti-Corruption Authority.

In addition to the possibility of reporting with specific guarantees of confidentiality a possible wrongdoing in one's administration or company ('whistleblowing'), there is now the possibility of sending a report directly to the Anti-Corruption Authority.

This is one of the innovations introduced by the recent reform of the whistleblowing discipline, referred to in the Anac Guidelines on the submission and management of so-called external whistleblowing reports, on which the DPA expressed a favourable opinion.

The text incorporates the indications provided by the Authority in the course of interlocutions with Anac to ensure respect for the protection of the data of the persons involved in the entire process of managing the report, with particular regard to the confidentiality of the identity of the reporter and the content of the report itself, including through the use of encryption.[129]

---

127. *See* the full official text, in Italian, at https://www.normattiva.it/uri-res/N2Ls?urn:nir:stato:decreto.legislativo:2005-03-07;82!vig=.
128. *See* the official text at https://eur-lex.europa.eu/eli/reg/2014/910/oj.
129. *See* https://www.garanteprivacy.it/web/guest/home/docweb/-/docweb-display/docweb/9918905.

506. In October 2022, the Italian DPA stated that to avert the risk of identity theft and ensure adequate protection of personal data, users' interaction with a website for the purpose of transmitting personal data must be protected with cryptographic protocols (such as 'https').

The DPA sanctioned a water service provider for 15,000 euro, for failing to adequately protect the data of customers registered on the reserved area of its website. Following a complaint, the Authority ascertained that access to the Company's website dedicated to 'online services' was via the 'http' network protocol, which was not encrypted and not secure.

The personal data of customers passing through this channel ranged from authentication credentials (username and password) to personal details, including names, surnames, tax codes/VAT numbers, e-mail addresses, telephone numbers and billing data.

The solution adopted by the company violated important principles enshrined in the Regulation, such as that of the 'integrity and confidentiality' of the data processed, according to which the data controller must implement technical and organizational measures to ensure a level of security appropriate to the risk, such as the encryption of personal data, and that of 'data protection by design', according to which it is necessary to implement, from the outset, technical and organizational measures appropriate to protect personal data and subsequently carry out periodic reviews of the security measures adopted.

§5. Cryptography and Its Relationship to International Standards and Certifications

507. Cryptography is, also in Italy, a requirement for certain international standards. Data encryption is a prerequisite for some international certification standards (document management system, information security ISO 27001, or in cloud services ISO 27017 and ISO 27018 guidelines).

For companies that want to voluntarily adhere to these certifications, data encryption is a necessary requirement in both the static and dynamic phases.[130]

§6. The Project of a National Centre for Cryptography

508. In Italy, in 2023, the government began to consider the possibility of setting up a *National Centre for Cryptography*, accepting an order of the day presented to the Chamber of Deputies.

The Centre will have to devise cryptographic algorithms and protocols, adopt a rigorous scientific methodology and issue comprehensive technical documentation. It will also have to study and assess the technologies operating in the cryptographic sector in view of their possible use, also at the request of public administrations and subject to a special agreement. It will also establish collaborative relations with the

130. *See* C. Gallotti, 'Sicurezza delle informazioni' (StreetLib, Lecce, 2022).

academic, research and industrial spheres and with similar foreign organizations, useful for the performance of its institutional tasks.

509. The National Cryptographic Centre is provided for in the *National Plan for Cyber Protection and Cybersecurity* adopted by the President of the Council of Ministers in 2017.

It is referred to in the legislation that established the National Cybersecurity Agency, whose functions include taking suitable initiatives to enhance cryptography as a cybersecurity tool, even if this leaves some modern applications of cryptography uncovered, such as the economic-financial sphere.[131]

510. Moreover, the *National Cybersecurity Strategy* 2022-2026 provides for the promotion of the use of cryptography as a cybersecurity tool, and the measures of the Implementation Plan for the aforementioned strategy specify the 'unclassified' sphere as an application area.[132]

This therefore does not include the differently and rigidly regulated 'classified' area in which cryptography has historically operated. The Centre, if requested, could also provide input in this context.

§7. The Regulation of Armaments and Dual-Use Goods

511. Dual-use goods are products, consisting of both tangible and intangible goods, such as software, designs and technologies, which, although created and sold for civil use, could also have a military use. Such products differ from weaponry in that they are not specially designed for military use.[133]

Since transactions involving dual-use items are subject to a control regime, international shippers and couriers require that the shipment of such items be accompanied by a 'dual-use declaration' by the exporter, to be placed on the invoice or on letterhead. This is a declaration in which the exporter assumes responsibility for operating in compliance with national and international dual-use regulations.[134]

512. Regulation (EU) 428/2009[135] on the establishment of a Community regime for the control of *dual-use items* was introduced with the aim of ensuring compliance with the international commitments and responsibilities of the Member States and the Union regarding non-proliferation, peace, security and stability, and respect for human rights and international humanitarian law.

Operations involving dual-use items are therefore subject to a control regime.

---

131. *See* https://www.agid.gov.it/sites/agid/files/2024-05/piano-nazionale-cyber_0.pdf.
132. *See* https://www.acn.gov.it/portale/en/strategia-nazionale-di-cybersicurezza#:~:text=National%20Cybersecurity%20Strategy%202022%20%2D%202026&text=The%20National%20Cybersecurity%20Strategy%20was,achieve%2082%20measures%20by%202026.
133. *See* D. Baliani, 'Il regime comunitario dei controlli sulle esportazioni di beni a doppio uso', in 'Il Diritto dell'Unione Euroeepa', fasc. 2, 2002, p. 265.
134. *See* F. Gaspari, 'Recenti sviluppi in materia di regolazione multilivello del commercio di armi: problemi e prospettive', in 'Rivista Italiana di Diritto Pubblico Comunitario', fasc. 2, 2015, p. 423.
135. *See* https://eur-lex.europa.eu/legal-content/EN/TXT/?uri=celex%3A32009R0428.

513. In 2021, the EU updated its legislation on controls applicable to dual-use items and technologies in light of technological, economic and political changes.

The new Regulation (EU) 2021/821[136] strengthens controls on a wider range of emerging dual-use technologies, in particular cyber surveillance items, which may be misused in connection with human rights violations.

514. By introducing *due diligence obligations* for manufacturers, the new rules also give companies an important role in countering the risks posed by dual-use items to international security.

515. The transactions subject to the control regime of the Dual-Use Regulation are different. *Export*: including the transmission of software or technology, whether oral or by electronic means. *Brokering services*: i.e., all transactions for the purchase, sale or supply of dual-use items from a third country to any other third country. *Technical assistance*: i.e., any technical support, including training and consultancy services. *Transit*: shall mean the carriage of non-Union dual-use items entering and passing through the customs territory of the Union with a destination outside the customs territory of the Union.

516. Classified dual-use items are listed in Annex I of Regulation (EU) 2021/821 and are divided into ten categories: (i) Nuclear Materials, (ii) Facilities and Equipment, (iii) Special Materials and Related Equipment, (iv) Materials Processing and Treatment, (v) Electronic Materials, (vi) Computers, Telecommunications and 'Information Security', (vii) Sensors and Lasers, (viii) Avionics and Navigation Materials, (ix) Naval Materials, and (x) Aerospace and Propulsion Materials.

517. The European Commission periodically updates the list of dual-use items. The updated version of the Regulation and thus of the list of classified items is available on the EU website.

518. To understand whether a transaction is subject to the dual-use control regime, the following actions must be carried out: Classification of the items, to check whether the item is on the list of dual-use classified items; Checks on destinations subject to embargoes or trade sanctions; Verification of parties involved and declared end uses; Verification of risk of diversion of destination; All-inclusive' controls on non-listed dual-use items.

519. A preliminary verification, in Italy, to ascertain the nature of the product can be made through the Customs and Monopolies Agency's information system (AIDA – Automazione Integrata Dogane Accise), using the product's customs code.

The TARIC (Integrated Community Tariff), in fact, is an information tool regarding the provisions, obligations and taxation to which the goods are subject.

Once the customs code of the product to be classified has been searched on the portal, it is necessary to check whether the item 'Export Authorization (Dual Use)' appears. In that case, the item is not necessarily dual-use.

---

136. *See* https://eur-lex.europa.eu/eli/reg/2021/821/oj.

In the note on the possible restriction, the corresponding dual-use code is specified. Having noted this, it is necessary to check what the dual-use regulation provides for that specific code: if the characteristics of the item correspond to those provided for, then the item falls under the dual-use control regime.

520. If the analysis of the transaction shows that it is subject to the dual-use control regime, then the export authorization must be requested from the competent authority, the UAMA (Armament Material Authorization Unit).

The best way to achieve compliance is to adopt an *Internal Compliance Programme* (ICP), which is a set of policies and procedures adopted by exporters to facilitate compliance with the provisions and objectives of the Regulation and the terms and conditions of export authorizations.

521. The sanctions regime in Italy is defined by Article 18 of Legislative Decree No. 221/2017. Anyone who carries out transactions without the relevant authorization, or in deviation from the obligations prescribed therein, shall be punished with imprisonment of up to six years or a fine of up to EUR 250,000, as well as with the confiscation of the goods used to commit the offence.

An exporter or intermediary who fails to notify the competent authority of changes in relevant information and data, or who fails to comply with the prescribed record-keeping obligations, shall also be liable to an administrative penalty of up to EUR 90,000.

522. The control of the export and import of armament materials is regulated by Law No. 185 of 9 July 1990 'New regulations on the control of the export, import and transit of armament materials'.

The legislation was amended by Legislative Decree No. 105 of 22 June 2012 to allow the transposition of 'Directive 2009/43/EC of the European Parliament and of the Council of 6 May 2009 simplifying terms and conditions of transfers of defence-related products within the Community'. Law No. 185/90 et seq. was then supplemented by the implementing regulation – Ministerial Decree No. 19 of 7 January 2013.

In 2012, the aforementioned National Authority – UAMA (Unit for the Authorization of Armament Materials) was established, called upon to ensure the application of Italian regulations, supplemented by European and international ones.

523. The operations covered by the Law must comply with Italy's foreign and defence policy. They are therefore authorized within the framework of the directives of the Government and Parliament.

As a result of the attribution to the Ministry of Foreign Affairs and International Cooperation of the competences in the field of international trade and the internationalization of the country system, the National Authority – UAMA performs the functions of Competent Authority responsible for the application of the provisions we have seen above.

524. The National Authority – UAMA issues authorizations for the export, transfer, brokering, technical assistance and transit of dual-use goods; it issues authorizations for trade in goods subject to the anti-torture regulation; it issues authorizations, for direct and indirect trade, in goods listed under Union restrictive measures.

The Director of the National Authority – UAMA chairs the Inter-Ministerial Advisory Committee called to express mandatory, but non-binding opinions on export transactions. In addition to MAECI and the Customs and Monopolies Agency, the following Ministries are represented on this Committee: the Interior, Defence, Economy and Finance, Economic Development, Cultural Heritage and Activities, and Health. The Head of the Dual-Use Materials Division acts as secretary.

§8. Cryptography in Law No. 90 of 28 June 2024

525. Law No. 90 of 28 June 2024, concerning provisions on the strengthening of national cybersecurity and computer crime, included some new, interesting rules about cryptography.

526. Article 9 is about strengthening data security measures through encryption.

1. The structures referred to in Article 8 of this Law as well as those performing similar functions for the entities referred to in Article 1, paragraph 2-*bis*, of Decree-Law No. 105 of 21 September 2019, converted, with amendments, by Law No. 133 of 18 November 2019, and Legislative Decree No. 65, verify that the computer and electronic communication programmes and applications in use, which use cryptographic solutions, comply with the guidelines on cryptography as well as those on the storage of passwords adopted by the National Cybersecurity Agency and the Guarantor for the Protection of Personal Data and do not involve known vulnerabilities that would make encrypted data available and intelligible to third parties.

527. Article 10 is about functions of the National Cybersecurity Agency in the area of cryptography.

1. In Article 7, paragraph 1 of Decree-Law No. 82 of 14 June 2021, converted, with amendments, by Law No. 109 of 4 August 2021, letter m-*bis*) is replaced by the following:

> (m-bis) shall provide, also through a special section within the strategy referred to in paragraph b), for the development and dissemination of standards, guidelines and recommendations in order to strengthen the cybersecurity of information systems, for the evaluation of the security of cryptographic systems as well as for the organisation and management of dissemination activities aimed at promoting the use of cryptography, including for the benefit of blockchain technology, as a cybersecurity tool. The Agency, also with a view to strengthening Italy's industrial and technological autonomy, also promotes collaboration with university and research centres for the enhancement of the development of new proprietary algorithms, research and the achievement of

new national cryptographic capabilities, as well as international collaboration with foreign bodies performing similar functions. To this end, a National Cryptography Centre is established within the Agency, within the framework of the human, instrumental and financial resources available under current legislation and without new or increased burdens on public finance, the operation of which is regulated by a provision of the Director General of the Agency. The National Cryptography Centre performs the functions of national competence centre for all aspects of cryptography in the unclassified sphere, without prejudice to the competences of the Central Office for Secrecy, referred to in Article 9 of Law no. 124 of 3 August 2007, with reference to the information and activities provided for by the regulation adopted pursuant to Article 4, paragraph 3, letter l) of the aforementioned Law no. 124 of 2007, as well as the competences of the bodies referred to in Articles 4, 6 and 7 of the same Law.

Part II. Online Public Services

Chapter 1. e-Government Legal Framework

§1. The 'Ten Pillars' of the Italian Legal Framework on e-Government

528. The Italian legal framework for e-Government is designed to promote the digitalization of Public Administration, improve the efficiency and transparency of public services, and enhance the relationship between the government and citizens using digital technologies.

It is possible to identify *ten pillars* as key elements, and regulations, that form the backbone of Italy's e-Government legal framework:

1. *The Digital Administration Code* (CAD, 'Codice dell'Amministrazione Digitale'). The primary legal instrument regulating e-Government in Italy is the CAD, established by Legislative Decree No. 82/2005.[137] The CAD sets the legal principles and rules for the digitalization of Public Administration and the provision of online services to citizens and businesses.
   The CAD covers a wide range of areas, including electronic documents, digital signatures, electronic identity, digital payments, and the interoperability of IT systems across different Public Administrations.
   The CAD has been *amended* multiple times to keep pace with technological advancements and EU directives, notably through Legislative Decree No. 235/2010, Legislative Decree No. 179/2016, and subsequent updates.
2. *Electronic Identity* (SPID, 'Sistema Pubblico di Identità Digitale'. Introduced by the CAD, SPID is the Italian system for *digital identity*, which allows citizens and businesses to access online services provided by Public Administrations and private entities with a single set of credentials. SPID is a key component of Italy's e-government strategy, ensuring secure and easy access to digital services.
3. *National Plan for Digital Growth* ('Piano Triennale per l'Informatica nella Pubblica Amministrazione'). The *National Plan for Digital Growth*, periodically updated, is a strategic document outlining the actions and investments required to advance the digital transformation of the public sector. The plan is coordinated by the *Agency for Digital Italy* ('Agenzia per l'Italia Digitale,

137. *See* on the Italian *Official Journal* at https://www.gazzettaufficiale.it/dettaglio/codici/amministrazioneDigitale/1_0_1.

AgID'), which is responsible for guiding the digital transformation of Public Administration and ensuring the implementation of the CAD.

4. *Electronic invoicing, digital payments and mandatory e-invoicing.* As part of its digitalization efforts, Italy has made electronic invoicing *mandatory* for B2B and B2G transactions. This requirement was introduced in 2014 for Public Administrations and extended to private sector transactions in 2019. *PagoPA* is the national platform for electronic payments to Public Administrations, enabling citizens and businesses to make payments digitally in a secure and transparent manner.
5. *Interoperability and open data.* The CAD mandates interoperability among IT systems used by different Public Administrations to ensure seamless communication and data exchange. The legal framework also encourages the release of public sector data in open formats, promoting transparency and enabling the development of innovative services by third parties.
6. *Data protection, privacy, and compliance with GDPR.* Italy's e-Government framework is aligned with the European Union's *General Data Protection Regulation* (GDPR), ensuring that digital public services respect privacy and data protection principles. Legislative Decree No. 196/2003, also known as the 'Personal Data Code', alongside the GDPR, provides additional national regulations on data protection.
7. *Electronic voting and participation* (with experiments and pilot projects). While electronic voting has not been fully implemented nationwide, Italy has conducted pilot projects and is exploring the legal and technical frameworks necessary to enable secure and reliable electronic voting. The legal framework also supports the development of *digital platforms* that facilitate citizen participation in decision-making processes, such as through online consultations and petitions.
8. *Digital public services.* Italy has developed its online presence to provide citizens with centralized access to various public services. The CAD requires Public Administrations to define and publish a *Service Charter*, outlining the services offered, quality standards, and methods of access, including digital options.
9. *Cybersecurity and national cybersecurity framework.* Italy's approach to e-government includes a focus on cybersecurity, with frameworks and regulations designed to protect the digital infrastructure of Public Administrations from cyber threats. Established in 2021, the *National Cybersecurity Agency* (ACN) coordinates Italy's cybersecurity policies, including those related to Public Administration and critical infrastructure.
10. *EU alignment and compliance with EU directives.* Italy's e-government legal framework is closely aligned with EU directives on digital services, electronic identification, and cybersecurity, ensuring that its practices are consistent with broader European standards. This framework reflects Italy's commitment to fostering a modern, digital Public Administration that is accessible, efficient, and secure, with ongoing efforts to update and refine these regulations as technology evolves.

§2. The Core of the Italian Legal Framework: The Digital Administration Code (CAD)

529. As illustrated above, over a period of about twenty years, since its enactment in 2005, the *Digital Administration Code* (CAD)[138] has seen several amendments and additions aimed both at transposing regulatory developments at the EU level and at adapting to developments in ICT technologies and tools.[139]

530. Through the CAD, the legislator has set the following objectives:

i. define a regulatory framework suitable for enabling and supporting the implementation actions, at a national level, of the *European Digital Agenda* in order to provide citizens, businesses and administrations with tools and services suitable for making digital citizenship rights effective;
ii. promote the adoption by Public Administrations, both central and local, of information and communication technologies for the provision of services, in administrative procedures and in document production, management and storage processes;
iii. regulate the evidentiary effectiveness of IT documents, and guarantee citizens and businesses the right to interact with Public Administrations by means of online services, in a simple, accessible and effective manner, also using technological tools such as *digital identity* and *digital domicile*;
iv. allow citizens and businesses to effectively participate in administrative proceedings by electronic means;
v. promote the integration and interoperability between public services provided by the various public administrations to create a network of data, information and services with the aim of streamlining procedures and reducing the complexity, redundancy and inefficiency of administrative action.

531. On a first reading, the CAD may appear as a collection of provisions that are sometimes organized in a non-homogeneous and harmonious manner. However, it serves as a sort of digital 'constitution', mandating digital innovation within the PA, including the digitization of administrative procedures, services, data and documents.

§3. The Main Principles of the CAD

532. Articles 2 and 3 establish:

i. the PA's duty to ensure access, transmission, preservation, and usability of information in digital mode for its users;

---

138. *See* at https://www.normattiva.it/uri-res/N2Ls?urn:nir:stato:decreto.legislativo:2005-03-07;82.
139. *See* F. Minazzi, 'Il codice dell'amministrazione digitale riformato', Giuffrè, Milano, 2017; G. Vitrani, R. Arcella, 'Il codice dell'amministrazione digitale', Giuffrè, Milano, 2024; F. Trojani, 'Il nuovo codice dell'amministrazione digitale', Maggioli Editore, Rimini, 2016.

ii. the right of citizens and businesses to relate with Public Administrations through the use of information technologies in order to be able to access and participate in administrative procedures, use public data, and exchange information and documents.

The PA must organize itself and act using information and communication technologies in the most appropriate manner and in the most suitable way to satisfy users' interests.

533. With regard to digital identity and the digital domicile of citizens and businesses, the Code states that:

i. all citizens and businesses have the right to be assigned a digital identity through which they can access and use the services provided online by Public Administrations;
ii. all those registered in the *National Register of Resident Population* (ANPR) have the right to be identified by Public Administrations through a digital identity, as well as to send communications and documents to Public Administrations and to receive them from them through a digital domicile;
iii. Public Administrations, professionals required to be registered in registers and lists, and persons required to be registered in the business register are obliged to have a digital domicile.

534. The index of the digital domiciles of professionals required to be registered in registers and lists and persons required to be registered in the business register is INI-PEC, managed by the MISE.

Digital domiciles for communications and the exchange of information and documents with Public Administrations and public service providers are registered in a special public list called the *Index of Digital Domiciles of the Public Administration and Public Service Providers* or IPA. The creation and management of these are entrusted to AgID.

The digital domiciles of natural persons, professionals and other private law entities not required to be registered in the index referred to in Article 6-*bis* are registered in a special index, the INAD, also created and managed by AgID.

535. In short, citizens and businesses can access the services of Public Administrations and participate in administrative procedures by authenticating themselves on the relevant portals with their SPID digital identity or *Electronic Identity Card* (CIE).

Communication between citizens and businesses on the one hand and Public Administrations on the other can take place in fully digital mode through the PEC, which fully replaces paper communications.

536. In addition, administrations are obliged to accept electronic payments through the technological platform for interconnection and interoperability between Public Administrations and authorized service providers referred to in Article 5(2) ('pagoPA').

§4. Digitalization and Computer Literacy

537. The CAD recognizes in the *computer literacy of citizens* as an *enabling element* for a pervasive diffusion of digital culture and for fostering a greater use of computer services by citizens, and therefore provides that administrations promote initiatives and implement concrete actions aimed at fostering the development of skills in this area, at all levels and in particular in relation to minors and categories at risk of exclusion.

538. To guarantee citizens and businesses the right to use technology, Article 12, paragraph 1 of the Code states that administrations shall use ICT technologies and tools to achieve the objectives of efficiency, effectiveness, cost-effectiveness, impartiality, transparency, simplification and participation of citizens and businesses in administrative procedures.

539. Digitalization is therefore a tool available to the PA to achieve the following capabilities:

i. to use resources in a sustainable and timely manner;
ii. to produce results that meet the expectations and needs of users, both internal and external;
iii. to endure by maximizing the efficiency of the resources used while respecting the conditions of economic equilibrium;
iv. to act in the absence of discrimination and favouritism;
v. to allow real knowledge of administrative activity;
vi. to foster the active participation of citizens and businesses;
vii. to simplify administrative action.

§5. Simplification, Performance and Management

540. With particular regard to the aspect of simplification, in Article 15, paragraph 2 the legislator draws attention to a key aspect of the digital transformation process: even before digitalizing, administrations must rationalize and streamline administrative procedures, management activities, documents, forms, etc.

In fact, a preparatory activity for the transition to digital is necessarily the *simplification* of administrative activities, which is essential to eliminate redundant and irrelevant steps and data, which weigh down processes and the document system, lengthen the time of proceedings, and at the same time increase the costs and inefficiency of administrative action.

541. In paragraphs 1-*bis* and 1-*ter* of Article 12, the legislator then emphasizes the fundamental role of management and recalls the Legislative Decree No. 150 of 2009[140] as a tool for implementing, through the *Performance Plan*, the provisions of the CAD.

---

140. *See* at https://www.normattiva.it/uri-res/N2Ls?urn:nir:stato:decreto.legislativo:2009-10-27;150!vig=.

In relation to the functions of implementing and monitoring the digitization process at the level of each administration, Article 17 of the CAD identifies the role of the *Digital Transition Manager* (RTD).

In particular, to ensure the implementation of the strategic lines for the reorganization and digitalization of the services of Public Administrations, Public Administrations must entrust a specific office with the transition to the digital mode of operation and the consequent reorganization processes aimed at achieving a digital and open administration.

542. This office is assigned specific tasks such as:

i. the strategic coordination of the development of the administration's information, telecommunication and telephony systems;
ii. the direction and coordination of the development of the services, both internal and external, provided by the systems;
iii. the direction, planning, coordination and monitoring of IT security with regard to data, systems and infrastructures;
iv. the periodic analysis of the consistency between the organization of the administration and the use of information and communication technologies;
v. the planning and coordination of initiatives relevant to the more effective delivery of networked services to citizens and businesses;
vi. the dissemination within the administration of the knowledge of the concepts inherent to the digital transition.

543. Article 17 also defines the office of the *Digital Ombudsman*, established at AgID.

This office is headed by a person who must necessarily have the requisites of third-party status, autonomy, impartiality, and competence.

Anyone may submit reports to the *Digital Ombudsman*, through a specific area on AgID's institutional website, concerning alleged violations of the Code and any other rules on the digitization and innovation of public administration by persons to whom the CAD applies.

Upon receiving the report, the ombudsman, if he considers it well-founded, invites the responsible party to rectify the violation promptly or in any case within thirty days. The ombudsman's decisions are published in a designated area of the institutional website.

§6. The Digitalization of the Documental System

544. The Code extensively regulates aspects relating to the digitalization of the *document system* as a fundamental step for the modernization of Public Administrations.

In fact, the document system represents the information assets of an administration and the founding element of its administrative procedures.

It is made up of data, information – i.e., related and structured data – and documents formed by citizens and businesses, by the administration itself and by other administrations in response to requests, applications, communications, etc.

545. In Article 1 of the Code, we find, among others, definitions of data, information, documents, both analogue and computerized, and copies thereof.

In Article 2(1), the Code stipulates that all Public Administrations, both local and central, must ensure the processing and management of information – and therefore of the data comprising it and the computerized administrative documents containing it – in digital mode.

546. Furthermore, the CAD recognizes full autonomy of the digital document system as a system of primary and original information.

This important principle unties the value of the digital document from the existence of the related written document, putting the two types of document on an equal footing.

Therefore, the digital document does not require any additional documents to guarantee its originality and inherently possesses full evidentiary and administrative effectiveness.

547. With the aim of facilitating and streamlining document management, reducing the burdens associated with the transition from paper to digital documents, paragraph 3 of Article 23-*ter* establishes that the preservation of documents originally produced on analogue support, for which a digital copy has been made – a copy made guaranteeing conformity with the original by means of a digital signature or other qualified electronic signature affixed by a delegated official and in compliance with the technical rules dictated by AgID (Article 71) – is satisfied on the digital copy and there is no obligation to preserve the relative paper document.

§7. THE CONCEPT OF 'DIGITAL SIGNATURE'

548. The digital signature, or equivalently the qualified electronic signature (FEQ), is the result of a computer procedure, called *validation*, that guarantees the authenticity, integrity and non-repudiation of computer documents.

It guarantees full legal validity and is equivalent to a handwritten signature.

The digital signature is based on a certificate and a pair of keys, private and public (asymmetric encryption): the private key is used by the subscriber to encrypt the document to be signed and the public key by the recipient to decrypt the message received.

549. The signing process technically takes place according to the following steps:

i. a digital fingerprint of the document is generated using a *hash function* (algorithm). This generated string is unique and non-invertible;

ii. encryption with a private key is applied to this fingerprint. This ensures that the digital signature is linked to both the subscribing party (via the private key) and the signed document (via the fingerprint);
iii. the subscriber's signature is affixed, e.g., in a predefined position within the document.

550. The following are sent to the recipient of the document:

i. the document signed using the procedure described above;
ii. the certificate (issued by the certification body to the subscriber) which guarantees ownership of the public key to decrypt the digital signature.

In the verification phase, the recipient decrypts the digital signature string and compares it with the one generated by the hash function on the document. If the two fingerprints match, the recipient is sure of both the integrity and authenticity of the received document. Digital signature certificates are issued by Certification Authorities (CA) authorized through AgID's public list.

551. In addition to the provisions of Article 23-*ter*, Article 40(1) establishes a general principle requiring that administrations produce the *originals* of their documents, including those relating to registers, lists and public records, in digital form from the outset and in accordance with the provisions of the CAD and the guidelines referred to in Article 71.

§8. Digital Copies, Management, Storage and Transmission of Documents

552. Again in relation to the digitalization of the document system, the Code regulates the conditions for the validity and evidentiary effectiveness of digital documents and their copies.

In particular, Article 20, paragraph 1-*bis* of the CAD provides that the requirements for a written form and evidentiary effectiveness of a digital document are satisfied if the document is signed with a digital signature, or with other qualified or advanced electronic signature. Alternatively, it can also be satisfied if the document is formed through an IT process that guarantees traceability to the author and ensures the security, integrity and immutability of the document, in compliance with the requirements established by AgID pursuant to Article 71.

553. The following Articles 22, 23 and 23-*bis* regulate the evidentiary effectiveness in the three possible cases of copies:

i. image copy of an analogue original document on IT support: the copy has the same evidentiary effectiveness as the original from which it is extracted if its conformity is certified by a notary public or other public official authorized to do so, always in line with the requirements established by AgID pursuant to Article 71 of the Code;

ii. analogue copy of an IT document: the copy is certified by a notary public or other public official authorized to do so, always in line with the requirements established by AgID pursuant to Article 71 of the Code;
iii. analogue copy of an IT document: the copy is certified by a notary public or other public official authorized to do so, always in line with the requirements established by AgID pursuant to Article 71 of the Code. 23, paragraph 1). The evidentiary effectiveness of the copy is guaranteed if its compliance with the original is certified by an authorized public official;
iv. computer duplicate of a computer document: in this case, the evidentiary effectiveness is guaranteed if the copy is produced in line with the requirements established by AgID pursuant to Article 71 of the Code.

554. In Chapters III and IV the Code deals with aspects relating to the management, storage and transmission of documents.

In particular, Article 40-*bis* provides that all communications exchanged by the digital domiciles of administrations and citizens are subject to *registration* by the computerized protocol system, which constitutes the incoming and outgoing 'gateway' for documents and information.

The protocol records a series of document information to guarantee its legal value.

The rules on protocol were laid down by Presidential Decree No. 445 of 2000,[141] which, in Article 53, also regulates the specifications of the protocol system, including those relating to the registration phase.

555. Article 41 of the CAD deals with the computer file, the function of which is to collect the acts, documents and data of the administrative procedure, regardless of who formed them.

It is also established that the computer file must be able to be consulted and fed by all the Public Administrations involved in the procedure. In particular, in paragraph 2-*ter* of the same article, the Code indicates which information must be contained in the computer file.

556. The subsequent Article 42 lays down a general criterion in relation to the dematerialization of the documents of Public Administrations, stating that they must assess in terms of cost-benefit ratio the recovery in computerized form of paper documents and deeds for which preservation is envisaged, thus replacing paper preservation with digital preservation, always in accordance with the guidelines of Article 71.

Furthermore, the preservation and exhibition obligations are fulfilled for all legal purposes by means of computerized documents if conformity to the original is guaranteed over time and procedures are used that comply with the guidelines of Article 71.

557. In Article 44, the Code establishes the necessary characteristics for the preservation of computerized documents, stipulating in paragraph 1-*ter* that in all

141. *See* https://www.normattiva.it/uri-res/N2Ls?urn:nir:presidente.repubblica:decreto:2000-12-28;445.

cases in which the law prescribes preservation obligations, also for private parties, the computerized document preservation system shall ensure, for what is preserved in it, characteristics of authenticity, integrity, reliability, readability, retrievability, according to the methods indicated in the Guidelines.

558. As regards the transfer of computerized documents, the Code provides that they must be transferred electronically by ascertaining the source of origin of the document (Article 45) and, in particular, for the transmission of documents between Public Administrations, it is provided that it may take place by electronic mail or application cooperation and that, for the purposes of verifying the source, communications are valid if they are signed with a digital signature or other qualified electronic signature or if they have a protocol signature or if it is in any case possible to ascertain their source (Article 47).

§9. Institutional Databases and Websites

559. In Chapter V, sections I and II, the legislator defines the requirements that government data must meet and identifies *several databases* of national interest.

The first data requirement is *availability*. Precisely to ensure data availability, administrations must define business continuity and disaster recovery plans and adopt, in general, all the necessary technical solutions of the Guidelines in relation to the security of systems and infrastructures in order to guarantee the aspects of data protection, availability, accessibility, integrity and confidentiality.

560. In Article 53, the CAD stipulates that Public Administrations must create institutional websites that are accessible and usable and that guarantee the right of access to information and interaction between them and citizens.

It provides that these sites contain the data relating to publicity and transparency obligations as well as the forms necessary for interaction between citizens and administrations.

561. As regards the databases of national interest set out in the Code, we mention in particular: in Article 57-*bis*, the index of Public Administration addresses (IPA) containing the *Certified Electronic Mail* addresses to be used for communications and for exchanging information and sending documents between Public Administrations, public service providers and private individuals; in Article 59, the *National Directory of Spatial Data*; in Article 62, the *National Register of Resident Population* (ANPR); in Article 62-*bis*, the national bank of public contracts (BDNCP), set up to foster the reduction of administrative burdens and to prevent corruption in public spending; in Article 62-*ter*, the National Register of Patients (ANA), established with the aim of strengthening interventions in the area of monitoring expenditure in the health sector; in Article 62-*quater*, the national registry of education (ANIST) and, in Article 62-*quinquies*, the national registry of higher education (ANIS); in Article 60, the criminal record and the business register.

562. Article 63 establishes that Public Administrations must identify the modalities for the provision of online services on the basis of assessment criteria of effectiveness, cost-effectiveness and usefulness and in compliance with the principles of equality and non-discrimination, bearing in mind, however, aspects such as the size of users, the frequency of use and the possible destination of use by categories in disadvantaged situations, and designing them to better meet the needs of users and facilitate the fulfilment of obligations for citizens and businesses.

As regards access to these online services, Article 64 provides that the CIE, the *National Services Card* (CNS) and identification through SPID may be used.

563. Moreover, in Article 65, the Code regulates the conditions of validity for submitting applications and declarations electronically to Public Administrations and public service providers.

In particular, validity is ensured: under the conditions set out in Article 20, i.e., in one of the forms in which the validity and evidentiary effectiveness of computer documents is ensured; i.e., if the declarant is identified by means of a CIE, CNS or SPID; i.e., if the applications and declarations are signed and submitted together with a copy of an identity document or if they are transmitted by the declarant through his digital domicile.

564. Article 64-*bis* also regulates the App IO, which is defined as the single telematic access point to the services of the administrations from smartphones, and requires them to launch the relevant digital transformation projects aimed at making services available through this platform.

§10. Software

565. Public Administrations must acquire computer programmes or parts of them in compliance with the principles of cost-effectiveness and efficiency, protection of investments, reuse and technological neutrality by carrying out a comparative technical-economic assessment of the following options available on the market:

1. software developed on behalf of the Public Administration;
2. reuse of software or parts of it developed on behalf of the Public Administration;
3. free or open source software;
4. software usable in cloud computing mode;
5. proprietary software through the use of licences;
6. software combining the previous solutions.

566. With regard to reuse and open standards, Article 69 of the CAD states that Public Administrations that own IT solutions and programs realized according to the specific indications of the public purchaser, are obliged to make the relevant source code, complete with documentation and released in the public domain under an open licence, available and free of charge for use by other Public Administrations or legal entities that wish to adapt them to their own needs, except for justified reasons of public order and security, national defence and electoral consultations.

567. *Developers Italia*, the community dedicated to the development of free software in support of Italian public digital services, is set in this context.

This project arose from the collaboration of AgID and the *Department for Digital Transformation* (DTD) with the aim of facilitating *reuse processes* by the PA. It provides a catalogue of software that administrations can reuse and adapt to their specific needs.

§11. Technical Rules for the Digital Transition and Connectivity

568. Article 71 provides that AgID is to adopt *Guidelines* containing the technical and policy rules for the implementation of the Code.

569. Articles 73 to 87 then regulate the *Public Connectivity System* (SPC), which represents the set of technological infrastructures, governed by the technical rules referred to in Article 71 and aimed at the development, sharing, integration and dissemination of the Public Administration's information assets and data, necessary to ensure the interoperability of the PA's IT systems.

The SPC is structured to facilitate and make possible the exchange of IT documents and data between administrations through a network and application cooperation in compliance with technical and security rules to streamline the entire administrative process by removing redundancies and reducing administrative inefficiencies.

The interoperability of the SPC system allows administrations to interact with each other, enabling the exchange and reuse of information even in the presence of non-homogeneous systems.

570. The requirements of digital transition imply the need for *managers* of Public Administrations, both central and local, to possess skills and tools for evaluating and governing ICT interventions and projects for e-Government.

At the same time, the absence or laxity of in-house skills in the PA and the fact that these are not always up to date generates the need to resort to suppliers and consultants of technologies and services external to the administrations, among other things in situations of cost and time constraints.

Under these conditions, the evaluation process of innovation initiatives and related ICT projects – an aspect also highlighted in Article 15 paragraph 2-*bis* of the CAD – and the governance of project risks represent a fundamental aspect not only *ex ante* but also *in itinere* and *ex post*.

This assessment process can be effectively carried out by adopting best practices, methods and techniques, also supported by the use of tracking and management tools (both design and economic).

§12. Conclusions: The Importance of the CAD

571. At its core, the CAD emphasizes the principles of accessibility, efficiency, and transparency in Public Administration. It mandates the digitalization of administrative processes, aiming to ensure that all interactions with public entities can be conducted online, reducing bureaucratic burdens and making government services more user-friendly. This digital transformation is not just about the adoption of new tools but about fundamentally *rethinking* how public services are delivered.

572. The Code introduces the concept of the 'digital citizen', ensuring that all citizens have the right to access digital services and participate in digital governance. To support this, it outlines requirements for *digital identities*, which allow secure and authenticated access to government services online. Additionally, the CAD promotes *interoperability* among public administrations, ensuring that different systems can communicate and share information efficiently, which is crucial for providing seamless services across various sectors.

573. The code also advocates for the use of *open data*, encouraging Public Administrations to make non-sensitive data freely available to the public. This is seen as a way to foster transparency, stimulate innovation, and support economic growth by allowing businesses and individuals to develop new services and products based on public data.

574. Another significant aspect of the CAD is its push for *digital literacy* and the inclusion of all citizens in the digital transformation. It recognizes that access to technology alone is not sufficient; people must also have the skills to use digital tools effectively. To this end, the code supports initiatives aimed at improving digital literacy across all segments of the population.

575. In conclusion, the Italian Code of Digital Administration is a *pivotal* piece of legislation that guides the country's efforts to modernize its Public Administration through digital means. It seeks to create a more accessible, transparent, and efficient government that can better serve its citizens in the digital age.

Chapter 2. Legal Framework for eHealth

§1. Introduction

576. The *Strategy for Digital Growth* and the *Three-Year Plan for Information Technology in Public Administration* have defined, in the last ten years, the intervention actions dedicated to the *digital health ecosystem* and the main solutions aimed at improving health services, limiting waste and inefficiencies, improving the cost-quality ratio of health services, and reducing differences between territories.

577. Within the Three-Year Plan, for the Health Ecosystem, three projects were highlighted as examples:

i. *Electronic Health File* ('Fascicolo Sanitario Elettronico', FSE), as an example of enabling infrastructure.
ii. *Single Booking Centre* (CUP), as an example of simplifying interaction between the Public Administration and the citizen.
iii. *Telemedicine*, as an example of the relationship with the territory.

578. *Electronic Health Record* is the tool through which citizens can trace, consult and share their health history.

The standard establishes that the infrastructure manages the set of data and digital documents of a health and social-health nature generated by present and past clinical events concerning the patient. The reference site is www.fascicolosanitario.gov.it

579. *Single Booking Centre* (CUP) is the centralized computerized system for the unified booking of services, to facilitate the accessibility of care and the reduction of waiting times.

580. *Telemedicine* is the project to offer services that improve the accessibility of care, diagnostic services and remote medical advice, as well as the constant monitoring of vital parameters.

581. The *Health Insurance Card* (TS) enables access to healthcare services provided by the NHS throughout the national territory and is a health insurance card for the purposes of recognizing healthcare in EU countries, as well as acting as a tax code.

582. *Digital recipes* constitute a process towards the complete dematerialization of pharmaceutical and specialist paper prescriptions, replacing them with the equivalent digital documents, throughout the national territory.

583. The *dematerialization* of medical reports and medical records is a process that aims to create a flow of digital documents with full legal value that will lead to the replacement of all paper equivalents, in order to improve services to citizens.

In this context, the 'Guidelines for the Dematerialisation of Informed Consent in Diagnostic Imaging' have been drawn up in collaboration with the *Italian Society of Medical and Interventional Radiology* (SIRM).

Actors involved are the Ministry of Health, Ministry of Economy and Finance, Data Protection Authority, and Treating Facilities (public or private).[142]

§2. The Single Reservation Centre

584. One of the areas of digital health that can contribute to facilitating access to care in rapid time is the presence of advanced systems for the unified booking of services, through *Single Reservation Centres* (CUP), which enables citizens to book health services through various digital communication channels (Internet portal, mobile applications, e-mail and/or totems located in municipalities or supermarkets, as well as at pharmacies) which, through integrated management of booking agendas, favours the accessibility of care and the reduction of waiting times.

585. By *Single Booking Centre*, we mean the centralized computerized booking system for healthcare services, responsible for:

i. efficiently managing the entire supply (NHS, contracted regime, intramoenia freelance work);
ii. structuring the activities of the supplying units in an organized manner with regard to the supply of services;
iii. interfacing the various procedures for managing supply, access and related information;
iv. supporting supply planning methods and communication to citizens aimed at reducing waiting times.

The System, made up as a whole of several procedures, must make it possible to optimize the offer to the citizen and to standardize the analyses to reshape it, comparing estimates of need and offer, and what has been booked and supplied.

§3. The Italian National Guidelines

586. With a view to defining a reference model at a national level, through which to allow a complete and fully integrated vision of the health services supply network, the Ministry of Health, in collaboration with the Regions, has prepared the *National Guidelines*.

The purpose of the Guidelines is to harmonize the CUP systems, by defining minimum and uniform characteristics for these systems at a national level, in order to make it possible to make 'extended and cross-booking' of services at various types of facilities (public and private accredited facilities), for the various supply

142. *See* https://www.agid.gov.it/it/piattaforme/sanita-digitale.

regimes (SSN services, *intramoenia* freelance work and extended *intramoenia*), and for the various access modes (ordinary hospitalization, day hospital, outpatient specialist care, etc.).

587. The Guidelines provide an examination of the possible access channels through which citizens can make use of booking services, including the manned counter, the telephone, access via the Internet, territorial pharmacies, etc.

It is envisaged that the CUP systems should centrally manage all the Agendas of public and private accredited facilities both for institutional activity and for activity provided on a freelance basis.

Moreover, the CUP systems must provide functions capable of intercepting any simultaneous bookings for the same service by the same user.

Moreover, the Plan provides for the development of online CUP systems that allow real-time consultation of waiting times for examinations or examinations in institutional and freelance activities, according to actual availability, and promotes access to bookings also through community pharmacies.

§4. The Introduction of the Electronic Health Record

588. The Electronic Health Record (Fascicolo Sanitario Elettronico, FSE), also known as EHR, is a set of health and social-health data and digital documents generated by clinical events, concerning the patient, referring to services provided by the *National Health Service* (Servizio Sanitario Nazionale – SSN) and, as of 19 May 2020, also by private health facilities.

The ESF is established under Article 12 of Decree-Law No. 179 of 18 October 2012.

The ESF is a key element within the set of initiatives that are part of digital health and represents an important tool for improving the quality of care that healthcare facilities, at all levels, offer the patient.

The ESF is made available by the Regions and Autonomous Provinces, in compliance with the regulations in force on the protection of personal data, for the purposes of prevention, diagnosis, treatment and rehabilitation; study and scientific research in the medical, biomedical and epidemiological fields; healthcare planning, verification of the quality of care and evaluation of healthcare.

589. At present the Electronic Health Record collects and makes available to patients and, with their consent, to the healthcare personnel, the patient's identification and administrative data, information from the general practitioner chosen by the patient, specialist and pharmaceutical prescriptions, laboratory reports, the summary health profile drawn up and updated by the general practitioner or paediatrician of free choice summarizing the patient's clinical history and his known current situation.

Moreover, the patient has a notebook in which he/she can enter, at his/her own discretion and autonomously, the personal data and documents that he/she deems of interest to the health professionals who should take care of him/her.

Soon, it will also be possible to enter hospital discharge letters, emergency room reports, radiology reports, exemption documents, outpatient specialist reports, pathology reports, dematerialized prescriptions, pharmaceutical and specialist dispensing, notebooks, pharmaceutical dossiers, and vaccinations.

On the website www.fascicolosanitario.gov.it is published the progress of the implementation of the ESF in the regions and autonomous provinces and its dissemination throughout the country.

590. The information contained in the Electronic Health Record is governed by the Decree of the President of the Council of Ministers 29 September 2015, No. 178, Regulation on the electronic health record, and is distinguished between:

i. minimum core, and
ii. supplementary data and documents.

591. The so-called Minimum Core is the same for all ESFs established by regions and autonomous provinces.

It consists of the data and documents identification and administrative data of the assisted person reports; emergency room reports; discharge letters; summary health profile; pharmaceutical dossier; consent or refusal to organ and tissue donation.

592. Supplementary data and documents, the supply of which depends on the health policy choices of the regions/autonomous provinces and the level of maturity of the digitization process, such as prescriptions (specialist, pharmaceutical, etc.); bookings (specialist, hospitalization, etc.); medical records; health budgets; home care: card, programme and clinical-assistance folder; diagnostic-therapeutic plans; residential and semi-residential care: multidimensional assessment form; drug supply; vaccinations; specialist assistance services; emergency services (118 and first aid); in-patient hospital care services; medical certificates; the patient's personal notebook; reports on services provided by the continuity of care service; self-certifications; participation in clinical trials; exemptions; prosthetic assistance services; data supporting telemonitoring activities; data supporting the integrated management of diagnostic-therapeutic pathways; other documents relevant to the patient's care pathways.

593. In order to speed up the activation and use of the ESF by all assisted persons, Article 11 of Decree-Law No. 34 of 19 May 2020 provided that, as of the date of publication of the decree, the activation and feeding of the ESF would take place automatically (elimination of the 'feeding consent').

594. The Circular of the Ministry of Health and the Ministry of Economy and Finance of 17 February 2021 provides precise indications for feeding the ESF of all assisted persons as of 1 March 2021, also attaching a model of information for a uniform application of this novelty throughout the country.

This allows each assisted person to have their health records at their disposal in an immediate and organized manner, without them being available to others unless they explicitly consent to consultation.

595. An assisted person's ESF is thus automatically fed with the data and documents relating to healthcare events received after 19 May 2020, both within and outside the National Health Service and the regional social and health services.

Health documents relating to services that a patient can access anonymously do not feed into the ESF.

596. Concerning health data and documents prior to 19 May 2020, data and documents relating only to services received within the National Health Service and regional health and social services, prior to that date, feed into the ESF only if the patient has not expressed a contrary will.

597. In fact, on 5 October 2020, following this regulatory change, the Italian Data Protection Authority issued a specific opinion on the feeding of the ESF with data prior to 19 May 2020, stating that, in order to guarantee the rights of the data subjects an adequate *information campaign* should be carried out at national and regional levels aimed at making data subjects aware of the characteristics of the processing carried out through the ESF, with particular reference to the new features introduced by the rule, the interested party is guaranteed to be able to exercise the right to object to the feeding of the ESF with health data generated by clinical events prior to 19 May 2020, within a pre-established deadline, not less than thirty days.

598. Individuals and health professionals who take care of a patient – both within and outside the NHS and regional health and social services – can only access the data and documents contained in the ESF if the patient has given their consent beforehand. This consent may be expressed online, by accessing the personal ESF, or according to the methods made available by each region or autonomous province.

For minors, consent to consultation is expressed by the person exercising parental responsibility or by the legal representative, after identifying the latter.

For disqualified or incapacitated persons, consent shall be given by the representative appointed by the judge.

599. Failure to consent to consultation of the FSE does not entail any consequences in the provision of healthcare services, but it does not ordinarily allow healthcare professionals treating a patient to consult his or her FSE and thus acquire information useful for safer and more appropriate care. In the absence of consent, only the patient can view the documents contained in his or her FSE.

An assisted person's ESF data is automatically deleted thirty years after the date of death of the assisted person.

600. The assisted person has the right not to make visible on the ESF data relating to a service he or she has received (the so-called right to obfuscation).

The 'higher protection' data (data and documents governed by the regulations for the protection of HIV-positive persons, women undergoing voluntary termination of pregnancy, victims of sexual violence or paedophilia, persons who use drugs, psychotropic substances and alcohol, as well as data and documents relating to the services offered by family counselling centres) are automatically uploaded in blacked-out form to the patient's ESF.

601. The National Infrastructure for the Interoperability of the ESF (INI) has been set up to allow the healthcare personnel or the assisted person to consult the ESF documents relating to clinical events which took place in regions or autonomous provinces other than the assisted person's residence.

This infrastructure, designed by the Agenzia per l'Italia Digitale (AgID) and implemented at the Ministry of Economy and Finance, also enables the transfer of ESFs to different regions or autonomous provinces in the event of a change of residence of the assisted person.

The progress of ESF implementation in the regions and autonomous provinces and its dissemination throughout the country is published at www.fascicolosanitario.gov.it.

602. The European initiative 'MyHealth@EU' is developing tools to enable European citizens to use healthcare in the country they are travelling to in the same way as in their country of residence.

To this end, Italy is setting up the ESF data interchange node with the other countries participating in the initiative (National Contact Point for eHealth – NCPeH, within the eHealth Digital Service Infrastructure – eHDSI). At the time of start-up, it is envisaged that only e-prescription and summary health profile information will be exchanged with the consent of the patient.

603. 'The Electronic Health Record 2.0 represents a significant step forward in the digitalization of health data, one of the most important objectives of the PNRR, and towards a new vision of healthcare in which technological innovation contributes to strengthening territorial care and overcoming inequalities' stated Minister Orazio Schillaci regarding the favourable opinion given on 2 August 2023 at the State-Regions Conference on the decree that makes the new Electronic Health Record operational.

604. The decree identifies the contents of the ESF, the limits of the responsibilities and tasks of the parties involved in its implementation, the guarantees and security measures to be adopted in the processing of personal data in respect of the rights of the assisted person, and the modalities and diversified levels of access, and consists of three technical annexes.

605. In particular, the ESF will contain the citizen's identification and administrative data, emergency room reports and minutes, discharge letters, the summary health profile (i.e., the computerized socio-health document drawn up and updated by the general practitioner or free-choice paediatrician that summarizes the patient's clinical history and his or her known current situation), specialist and pharmaceutical prescriptions, and other documents such as, among others, medical records, vaccinations, and implant card data.

606. The new FSE responds to the needs of citizens who will be able to consult clinical data, access telemedicine, emergency and drug delivery services, and book health services.

Citizens will have the right to access the 'Personal Notebook', a reserved section of the FSE where they will be able to enter, modify and delete data and personal documents relating to their care pathways.

607. It will enable general practitioners, paediatricians and specialists to consult and analyse the clinical data of their patients in support of diagnosis and treatment activities, for the preventive assessment of prescriptive appropriateness and the monitoring of the patient's adherence to treatment, for primary and secondary prevention and the booking of services for their patients.

It will also be a useful tool for the activities of pharmacists, including the dispensing of drugs and verification of therapy dispensed, recording and reporting allergies and adverse drug reactions; of nurses and other health professionals for searching and consulting the clinical data of the patients whose care they follow of the Regional Health Directorates, within the framework of prevention and health planning activities; of research bodies to support research activities in the medical and biomedical field.

608. The supply of the ESF will be ensured by the Local Health Authorities, the public and accredited health facilities of the National Health Service and the Regional Health and Social Services, and the Territorial Services for the Health Care of Aircraft Personnel (SASN), as well as by the authorized health facilities and health professionals, including those affiliated with the National Health Service, when they operate autonomously.

The interoperability of the ESF, in the event that the patient has to go to healthcare facilities in Regions other than the region of care, is guaranteed by the National Infrastructure for Interoperability between ESFs (INI).

609. The Decree of the Minister of Health of 7 September 2023, published in the G.U. Serie Generale of 24 October 2023, identifies the contents of the Electronic Health Record (Fascicolo sanitario elettronico – FSE) 2.0.

The Decree also defines the limits of the responsibilities and tasks of the subjects that contribute to its implementation, the guarantees and security measures to be adopted in the processing of personal data in respect of the rights of the assisted person, the modalities and diversified levels of access to the ESF.

610. The Decree is issued in implementation of the provisions set forth in paragraph 7 of Article 12 of Decree-Law No. 179 of 18 October 2012, converted, with amendments, by Law No. 221 of 17 December 2012, and subsequent amendments.

611. The ESF 2.0 will contain the following data and documents, also referring to services provided outside the National Health Service: identification and administrative data of the patient (exemptions for income and pathology, contacts, proxies), reports, emergency room reports, discharge letters, summary health profile, specialist and pharmaceutical prescriptions, medical records, dispensing of medicines charged to the SSN and not charged to the SSN, vaccinations, provision of specialist assistance services, patient's personal notebook, implant card data, invitation letter for screening.

612. The following shall contribute to the correct feeding and updating of the ESF with the data and documents referring to the assisted person: the local health authorities, the public health facilities of the NHS and of the regional socio-health services and the SASN, through the different organizational articulations, the healthcare facilities accredited with the SSN and the regional social-health services, the authorized healthcare facilities, the health professions, including those affiliated with the NHS when they operate independently.

613. The Fascicolo is a tool available to the patient, who can access it for consultation by the subjects of the National Health Service and of the regional socio-health services and by the practitioners of the health professions who take care of him/her, also outside the NHS.

The data and documents in the ESF are always consultable not only by the patient but also by the subjects who produced them.

§5. Telemedicine

614. The use of telemedicine, through the remote care and monitoring of patients, offers the appropriate healthcare response to the needs of a population that is ageing rapidly and with an increase in chronic diseases.

Telemedicine is an indispensable element of the restructuring and rationalization of the healthcare system, through the use of advanced technologies and new organizational models of home care.

615. The term telemedicine refers to all healthcare services in which, thanks to the use of innovative technologies, the health professional and the patient are not in the same place.

Telemedicine makes it possible to assist and make check-ups on patients, remotely check patients' vital parameters, bring health professionals together for consultations on particular clinical cases, and send and receive documents, diagnoses and reports.

616. Telemedicine is especially indispensable for categories of people who require continuous care, as they suffer from chronic diseases, for example. These patients may need constant monitoring of certain vital parameters to reduce the risk of complications.

In this case, a better service can be provided to the patient, through a more rapid availability of information on the state of his or her health, making it possible to increase the quality and timeliness of decisions by healthcare professionals, particularly useful in emergency-urgency conditions. In this sense, technology and telecommunications play a fundamental role as they help improve the efficiency and safety of care, as well as the confidentiality and protection of patients' personal data.

617. Telemedicine, which is one of the main areas of application of e-health, offers potential of great relevance especially for increasing equity in access to social and health services in remote territories, thanks to decentralization and flexibility in the services provided, which are made possible by innovative forms of home care redistribute human and technological resources between different centres, making it possible to cover the need for professional skills that are often lacking and ensure continuity of care in the area offer, thanks to the availability of teleconsultation services, support for mobile emergency services or for remote areas, through the reorganization of health services, possibly by using remote clinical resources, even deployed directly on board ambulances.

618. Within Mission 6 Health, envisaged in the *National Recovery and Resilience Plan* (PNRR), telemedicine takes on a primary role through specific areas of intervention. In the PNRR, as part of the reform of territorial care, the person in his or her own community is placed at the centre through the investment of the home as the first place of care and telemedicine and the strengthening of health care in all its forms. In this reorganization, digital solutions can play a fundamental role in reducing waiting times for visits, improving accessibility to health services, and generally increasing the efficiency of the health system.

619. The minimum telemedicine services envisaged in the NRP, in order to ensure their uniform implementation throughout the country, are: Telehealth, Teleconsultation and medical teleconsultation, Telecare, and Telemonitoring. These services are defined in the National indications for the provision of telemedicine services (State-Regions Agreement of 17 December 2020).

620. For a systematic use of telemedicine within the National Health Service and to implement the European Communication, a Technical Table on Telemedicine was established at the Consiglio Superiore di Sanità, which drew up the National Guidelines, in order to: identify the priority areas of application of telemedicine; analyse models, processes and methods for integrating telemedicine services in clinical practice; define common taxonomies and classifications; define aspects concerning legal and regulatory profiles and the economic sustainability of telemedicine services and services.

The first National Guidelines on Telemedicine were approved by the General Assembly of the Consiglio Superiore di Sanità on 10 July 2012.

621. On 20 February 2014, in order to ensure 'a coordinated, harmonious and coherent development of telemedicine within the National Health Service' the Agreement was signed between the Government, the Regions and the Autonomous Provinces of Trento and Bolzano on the document entitled 'Telemedicine – National Guidelines (Repertory of Acts No. 16/CSR of 20/02/2014)'.

The Agreement represents a particularly significant result in view of the need to rethink the organizational and structural model of the National Health Service in Italy, with respect to which the territorial distribution of Telemedicine services can be an important enabling factor.

§6. The Dematerialization of Prescriptions

622. The electronic prescription, regulated by the Interministerial Decree of 2 November 2011, is now a widely used tool for citizens to access pharmaceutical and outpatient services of the National Health Service.

Among other things, the electronic prescription has made it possible to ensure the circularity of pharmaceutical prescriptions under the conventional system throughout the country: a citizen can go to a pharmacy in another region and still be entitled to the dispensing of medicines.

The digitization of the services provided by the National Health Service also makes it possible to activate control tools, both in terms of pre-dispensing checks and reporting by the dispensers themselves.

623. The doctor registers the citizen's and prescription data on the Health Card System. To the citizen, he issues: the electronic prescription number (NRE); and the paper reminder of the prescription.

The paper reminder is issued to guarantee the provision of the service even in the event of computer system unavailability. However, with the Interministerial Decree of 25 March 2020, which extended the electronic alternative to the paper reminder beyond the emergency phase, a path was set in motion to make the prescription completely digital.

The spread of dematerialized prescriptions has reached a very high level of coverage for pharmaceuticals. The level of coverage for outpatient prescriptions is lower.

624. The COVID-19 emergency has given further impetus to the dematerialization of prescriptions, in order to ensure the availability of medicines to the most fragile individuals and, in general, to reduce the influx of patients into doctors' offices (Order of the Head of Civil Protection of 19 March 2020).

The Interministerial Decree of 25 March 2020 provided for the extension of the dematerialized prescription to medicines with an AIFA therapeutic plan and to medicines distributed on behalf of the National Health Service.

The enhancement of the dematerialization process then continued with the decree of 30 December 2020 of the Ministry of Economy and Finance, in agreement with the Ministry of Health, which extended the dematerialization of medical prescriptions to the prescription of medicines not paid for by the National Health Service and provided for ways of issuing the electronic prescription reminder through additional channels, both when fully operational and during the emergency phase from COVID-19.

625. As clarified by the Note of 14 May 2020, medicinal products based on narcotic and psychotropic substances included in sections B, C, D, and E of the Table of Medicinal Products and medicinal products with strong analgesic activity, as provided for in Annex III-*bis*, for the treatment of patients with severe pain, marked in section A of the Table of Medicinal Products with (**), can also be prescribed with a dematerialized prescription (*see also* Note of 28 July 2020).

626. Prescriptions for medicines included in section A of the Table of Medicinal Products, with indications other than pain therapy, remain excluded from dematerialization.

In addition, a working group at the Ministry of Health is working on the dematerialization of vouchers for the dispensing of gluten-free products for coeliac disease sufferers, vouchers that will be spendable anywhere in Italy, even outside their region of residence.

Another sector recently affected by the dematerialization of paper prescriptions is veterinary medicine. In this case, it does not fall within the scope of initiatives created to control expenditure on the National Health Service as those that have addressed the sector dedicated to citizens, but within an area that exclusively concerns the protection of public health.

627. The decree of 30 December 2020 of the Ministry of Economy and Finance, in agreement with the Ministry of Health, continues the strengthening of the process of dematerialization of drug prescriptions already started during the COVID-19 emergency.

The COVID-19 emergency gave particular impetus to the dematerialization of prescriptions. In order to ensure the availability of drugs to the most fragile individuals and, in general, to reduce the influx of patients into doctor's offices, more measures were implemented to dematerialize prescriptions and paper reminders.

628. The Order of the Head of Civil Protection of 19 March 2020 introduced alternative methods to the paper memo to limit access to the offices of NHS doctors.

The Interministerial Decree of 25 March 2020 provided for the extension of the dematerialized prescription to medicines with an AIFA therapeutic plan, to medicines distributed on behalf of the National Health Service, and extended the alternative electronic modalities to the paper memo beyond the emergency phase.

The decree of 30 December extends the dematerialization of prescriptions to prescriptions for medicines not paid for by the National Health Service and provides for ways of issuing electronic prescriptions and paper reminders through additional channels, both when fully operational and during the emergency phase from COVID-19.

629. As part of the Tessera Sanitaria system, the dematerialization of prescriptions for drugs not paid for by the National Health Service, the so-called white prescription, became operational on 31 January 2022, based on the provisions of

Article 2 of the Decree of the Ministry of Economy and Finance in agreement with the Ministry of Health of 30 December 2020, approved by the Garante per la protezione dei dati personali.

Moreover, with the signing of the joint Circular of the Ministry of Economy and Finance and the Ministry of Health on 3 March 2022, the application indications for operators are provided.

Chapter 3. Online Voting

§1. A Brief Introduction

630. The subject of online voting has been discussed, in Italy, at least since the 1990s. When the discussion began in 1992 about the digitalization of public administration and its activities, thanks to the then Minister Franco Bassanini, this issue was immediately recognized as being of great importance.

At the same time, however, the security problems associated with such a critical technology were immediately highlighted.

This is the reason why, to date, the path to full implementation has not yet been completed, although in the last ten years, partly because of the pandemic, there have been some very interesting experiments that seem to have identified the most correct regulatory path.[143]

On the one hand, therefore, there is still no complete legal framework with specific regulations. On the other hand, however, the world of politics is devoting a great deal of attention to trying to set up a useful and operational legal framework for the near future, incorporating the issue of implementing online voting into the broader one of digitizing all public sector processes.[144]

631. Even in Italy, doctrine and politics clearly distinguish between the concept of 'E-voting', i.e., a process in which the vote is cast through voting machines that are physically placed at the polling station, and 'I-Voting', or true online electronic voting, which consists of the expression of the vote through devices connected to the Internet (e.g., smartphones, tablets and computers).[145]

The three objectives underlying the Italian legislative reform in the coming years are, in particular,

i. the simplification of voting processes;
ii. the reduction of the costs of elections, and
iii. the ability to involve voters as much as possible, at a time when absenteeism, especially during political elections, is very high.

632. In Italy, the use of online voting outside actual elections is, for the time being, confined to universities, associations and companies, and is used for certified

---

143. *See* a simulation project at https://dait.interno.gov.it/elezioni/notizie/e-vote-simulazione-del-voto-elettronico and L. Zorloni, 'Come funziona la prima simulazione di voto elettronico in Italia', at https://www.wired.it/article/voto-elettronico-simulazione-ministero-interno-13-14-dicembre/. *See also* R. Scarfato, 'Voto digitale: una soluzione contro l'astensionismo?' at https://www.agendadigitale.eu/cultura-digitale/voto-digitale-una-soluzione-contro-lastensionismo/.

144. *See* G. Rigobello, 'Questioni digitali e analogiche: la 'digital democracy' nuovamente alla prova della Corte Suprema del Kenya', in 'Diritto dell'Informazione e dell'Informatica' (Il), fasc.2, 1 Apr. 2023, pag. 363. *See, also*, M. Cian, 'L'intervento e il voto elettronici nelle assemblee di s.p.a.', in Riv. soc., fasc.6, 2011, pag. 1065. L. Trucco, 'Il voto elettronico nella prospettiva italiana e comparata', in Dir. informatica, fasc.1, 2011, pag. 47. *See* P. Costanzo, 'Quale partecipazione politica attraverso le nuove tecnologie comunicative in Italia', in Dir. informatica, fasc. 1, 2011, pag. 19.

145. *See* G. Gometz, 'Democrazia elettronica. Teoria e tecniche', Edizioni ETS, 2017.

internal polls, for amendments to statutes and regulations and for elections to administrative bodies, and in some pre-electoral or internal political processes that will be analysed below.

§2. Online Voting in Universities Governance

633. The sector where, in Italy, the online voting system is proving itself is the academic one: dozens of universities in Italy use electronic voting platforms made available since 1999 by Cineca, a large inter-university consortium that provides telematic assistance to the main Italian universities.

'Eligo', in particular, is one of the online voting platforms used by most universities. These are used in all voting processes involving students, faculty and staff and in internal procedures.[146]

The convenience, in concrete terms, consists of an increased time window for voting, the fact that it is not necessary to travel from home, that the counting of votes is immediate, and that there is no need to set up ad hoc facilities. The system is used from student voting to the election of the Rector.

§3. The Market of Online Voting in Italy

634. The e-voting market is growing steadily in Italy, with an estimated value of EUR 285 million in Europe by 2027 and, in Italy, rising from 20.52 million in 2017 to 33.23 million in 2027. Italy's average growth rate is 4.9%, in line with the European (5.5%) and US (5.4%) averages.

One of the market leaders in Italy is the company producing the aforementioned 'Eligo' software and service, which was founded in 2005. It is a cloud and web-based platform that in recent years has been used for 45,000 online votes in Italy, on behalf of 3,500 public and private entities, involving 18 million voters, or an average of over 7 elections per day.

635. The sectors that use e-voting in Italy, and are therefore interested in the development of this market, are very varied, ranging from the public to the private sector. These are associations that have to carry out voting, deliberative and elective assemblies required by their own regulations and statutes.

Then there are small and medium-sized enterprises and large companies that use this instrument for elections of trade union representatives, votes for elections of boards of directors of supplementary funds and funds for internal company employees and consultations.

On the public administration side, at the same time, the platform cooperates with municipalities for votes related to participatory budgets or neighbourhood councils and is also active in the area of cooperation. There is, then, a very great democratic

146. *See* https://www.eligo.social.

potential that is emerging in this world, for example, the whole world of associations and the third sector: consider that there are more than 109,000 associations in Italy that could take advantage of this system.

§4. Cybersecurity Issues

636. The security and confidentiality of the data entered and processed by the system must be adapted to the highest standards. One of the main reasons for mistrust and fear regarding the large-scale use of such systems is precisely the aspect of possible attacks.

First of all, the support of end-to-end encryption is seen as central: the information that passes through users' browsers must be compulsorily encrypted with asymmetric encryption, which does not allow the voting preferences expressed to be intercepted and deciphered.

637. The secret vote should, then, be created directly on the client, i.e., on the mobile phone, the tablet, in practice the instrument with which one votes that is owned or used by the voter.

This will result in there being no link between the vote and the voter in the databases. The system storing all voting and polling data would then have to apply an additional layer of encryption. Only the voter, the user, then has access to the data, which remains inaccessible even to the owners of the technology itself.

638. The fear that e-voting may expose people to identity theft or tampering with election results can also be mitigated by certification processes such as, for example, ISO 27001 certification.

This is a quality certification related to information security that not only concerns the platform itself but the entire environment around it. Fundamental, for example, is the aspect that the data cannot even be accessed by the operator, who thus cannot even change a vote or intervene in the process (except to block it in the event of an attack).

§5. Online Voting and Digital Skills: The CEI Case

639. A barrier to the use of e-voting, according to some, might be the difficulty of this system for the elderly, who might have difficulties, especially given the worrying digital literacy figures in Europe, or for anyone without basic technological skills.

640. The aforementioned Eligo software, in Italy, was used for the election of the trio from which the new president of the Italian Bishops' Conference (CEI) was then appointed. Voting was done in presence, with an average age of voters over 75. All the bishops with voting rights, around 300 people, took part. It is a complex voting mechanism, the one envisaged by this type of election, but the two scheduled votes were conducted with great agility: the first vote took 8 minutes and the second 3 minutes. Thus, it seems that the myth of age preventing access to this instrument can be dispelled.

§6. The Italian Legal Framework

641. The implementation in Italy of a legal framework on online voting must, of course, respect the indications of the European Union, albeit with the possibility of specific local adaptations.

With the Communication '2030 Digital Compass: the European way for the Digital Decade' of 9 March 2021, the European Commission presented the guidelines and ground rules for the digital transformation of Europe by 2030, which have also been transposed by the Italian legislator.

In fact, one of the EU's objectives is to ensure that by 2030 democratic life and online public services are fully accessible to all, including people with disabilities, also through e-voting, which would encourage greater citizen participation in democratic life.

642. The experimentation of e-voting was provided for in Italy by the 2020 Budget Law (Article 1, paragraphs 627-628, L. 160/2019), which established the 'Fund for e-voting' with an initial allocation of EUR 1 million. The Fund is aimed at the experimental introduction of digital voting in European and general elections and for referendums. The experimentation refers to voting by Italians abroad and voters temporarily away from their municipality of residence for work, study or medical treatment.

This provision was amended by Decree Law 77/2021 (Article 38-*bis*, paragraph 10), which extended the experimentation to regional and local elections as well. The experimentation was then postponed to subsequent years with a concomitant increase in the funds for electronic voting.

643. The experimentation is limited to models that guarantee the concrete exercise of the right to vote by two specific categories of voters: (i) Italians abroad; and (ii) voters who, for reasons of work, study or medical treatment, are in a municipality of a Region other than that of the municipality on whose electoral roll they are registered.

§7. Online Voting Specific Government Guidelines

644. The implementation modalities of the use of the Fund, and of the related experimentation, were delegated to a decree of the Minister of the Interior, adopted in agreement with the Minister of Technological Innovation and Digitalisation with the Ministerial Decree of 9 July 2021, which approved the guidelines for the experimentation of digital ways of expressing votes.

On 21 October 2021, a new ministerial decree supplementing the previous one was issued in order to dictate the modalities for applying the experimentation to regional and local elections.

645. The delay in the full implementation in Italy is motivated by the fact that a series of extremely delicate and complex technical aspects, peculiar to the electoral process, need to be analysed in detail.

These aspects reflect on the respect of the constitutional principles of secrecy and of the personality of the vote, on the need to ensure the correct counting of votes for the purposes of the official proclamation of the elected, on the possible litigation and on the related need to extract all the data that led to the formation of the official results.

§8. A Case History in Lombardy

646. An interesting experiment, at the local level, of electronic voting, in a Region of fundamental importance for the economic life of the country, was recorded on the occasion of the regional referendum on the so-called differentiated regionalism, held in Lombardy on 22 October 2017.

The novelty of the referendum consisted of voting on electronic media called 'voting machines' and the subsequent ballot, also in digital mode. Voting, in this case, did not take place remotely, but in the presence, of special polling stations.

§9. Preparatory Process for Elections

647. In the Italian legal system, legislative initiatives for the computerization of some phases of the 'preparatory' electoral process have been envisaged in recent years.

The electoral reform law (L. 165/2017), in particular, has delegated (Article 3, paragraph 7) to a ministerial decree, to be adopted within six months of the date of entry into force of the law, the definition, on an experimental basis, of the collection in digital mode of the subscriptions necessary for the presentation of lists of candidates, including through the use of digital signatures and qualified electronic signatures. The decree has not yet been adopted.

A series of measures aimed at digitization in the electoral preparation process was then introduced by Decree-Law 77/2021 (Governance of the PNRR and simplifications), providing, in particular, the following very interesting aspects.

648. The filing of the countersign by political parties intending to submit lists of candidates for the elections may take place in digital form.

The deed of designation of list representatives may also be submitted by certified email; moreover, the deadline for submitting the aforementioned deed of designation, either in person or by PEC, is brought forward to the Thursday before the vote (instead of the Friday before the vote, as provided for under current legislation).

Authentications of the deeds of designation of list representatives are not necessary when the deeds of designation are signed digitally or with another type of qualified electronic signature by the persons authorized by the same delegates with a digitally signed deed, provided that such documents are transmitted by certified electronic mail.

649. The certificate of registration on the electoral roll, required for the signature in support of lists of candidates for political, European and local elections, as well as for proposals for referendums and for popular legislative initiatives, may be requested in digital format by certified electronic mail.

The legal representatives of the political parties and movements and of the lists competing in local elections in municipalities with at least 15,000 inhabitants may also request by certified email the criminal record certificates issued by the criminal records offices for their candidates, in order for the parties to comply with the obligation to publish the curriculum vitae and the criminal record certificate of the candidates on their website.

650. Provision is made for the timely publication on the Order's institutional website of the names of the lawyers on the register who have notified the order to which they belong of their willingness to carry out the authentication of electoral subscriptions.

The experimentation with electronic voting for out-of-office voters provided for by the 2020 Budget Law for general and European elections and referendums is also extended to regional and local elections.

§10. The Use of Online Voting in Referendums

651. The Budget Law 2021 introduced the possibility of digitally collecting the signatures required for submitting popular referendum requests. To this end, a special fund was established in the estimates of the Ministry of the Economy and Finance, to be transferred to the Prime Minister's Office, for the creation of a digital platform dedicated to the collection of signatures, with an allocation of EUR 100,000 per year starting from 2021.

Subsequently, Decree-Law No. 77/2021 (Article 38-*quater*), containing provisions on the governance of the PNRR and simplification, introduced a series of measures aimed at the digitalization of the preparatory electoral process, including some that modify the discipline of the platform for the digital collection of signatures for referendums.

652. First, the scope of the digital collection of signatures is extended to include those required for submitting citizens' initiative bills to Parliament. Furthermore, as far as referendums are concerned, it is specified that the digital collection of signatures covers the referendums referred to in Articles 75 (abrogative) and 138 (constitutional amendment) of the Constitution.

653. The collection takes place not only in paper format but also by means of SPID, electronic identity card or national services card. According to the procedure, the platform for the collection of digital signatures is required to be made available to the signatory, depending on the purpose of the signature collection, and the specific indications prescribed, respectively, by Articles 4 (constitutional referendum), 27 (abrogative referendum) and 49 (popular initiative bill) of Law 352 of 25 May 1970.

654. The platform also acquires the name, surname, place and date of birth of the subscriber and the municipality on whose electoral roll he/she is registered or, for Italian citizens residing abroad, their registration on the electoral roll of the single registry of Italian citizens residing abroad.

§11. The First Application in Italy

655. The transitional rules in force in Italy were first implemented for three abrogative referendums for which signatures were collected in 2021 and then deposited at the Central Referendum Office. These are referendums on the cultivation, production and illicit trafficking of drugs, murder of a consenting person, and hunting.

656. For the collection of signatures, the promoters of the referendums used a platform operated by a company under private law. The platform also allows the signing of citizens' initiative bills. In all three cases, digital signatures were also deposited along with paper signatures.

657. As for the signatures in digital format, the initiators deposited an external hard disk containing the computer duplicate of the signatures collected electronically and the certificates of registration on the electoral roll attached to the certified e-mail messages received from the municipal administrations.

§12. The Preparation of the 2024 Referendum

658. For the first time in Italy, the 2024 referendum can only be signed online, via SPID. To sign the 14 questions, in fact, it is sufficient to access the specific digital platform of the promoting committee with your SPID.

659. To sign, one has to pay EUR 1.65, regardless of the number of questions one signs. This is a small contribution that the organizing committee asks subscribers to make, in exchange for the convenience of being able to sign with a few simple clicks, whenever and wherever they want, without having to physically move in search of the traditional stall in the square.

660. The EUR 1.65 fee charged for signing online referendums with SPID serves to cover the costs of the technical management of the entire referendum process. These costs are represented, in particular, by the authentication to affix the qualified electronic signature and the affixing of the time stamps necessary for the legal validity of the signature.

661. The need to cover these costs stems from the fact that, to date, Italy still lacks a public technological platform that can be used for the digital collection of signatures. A state online platform was envisaged by the Budget Law 2021 but has not yet been implemented. Therefore, in order to provide Italian citizens with the possibility of signing the new referendums online, the promoting committee had to turn to a private operator accredited with AgID, which provided a private platform.

662. To subscribe to the referendums digitally, one must first register with the platform. To register, one must enter one's e-mail address, indicate which is one's municipality of residence (or, if one is resident abroad, which was one's last municipality of residence in Italy), and read and accept the site's privacy policy. After clicking on 'Send', the platform sends to the email that the user has indicated a link that allows the user to subscribe to the referendum questions. Clicking on the link takes you to a page on the platform where you have to tick a box declaring that you have a personal and active SPID account. Continuing on, one arrives at the point where one is asked to pay the contribution of EUR 1.65, after which one arrives at the section of the platform where one can find all the proposed questions and can finally choose which questions to subscribe to.

663. Do not confuse the collection of signatures with the actual vote. SPID can only be used to sign the questions and reach the quorum of 500,000 signatures, but not for online voting, which is not yet allowed in Italy. Voting on individual referendums, planned for 2024, will still take place in the classic in-person mode and will still involve going to the ballot box to mark your preference on the ballot paper.

§13. Online Voting and Data Protection Authority

664. On 18 February 2022, the Minister for Technological Innovation and Digital Transition at the Presidency of the Council of Ministers forwarded to the Garante per la protezione dei dati personali, for the purpose of acquiring the required opinion, the draft decree of the President of the Council of Ministers regulating the platform for the collection of voters' signatures required for referendums and for popular initiative bills.

The Garante issued its opinion noting that the scheme submitted to the Authority lacks adequate safeguards for the full respect of citizens' fundamental rights and freedoms. Therefore, the Garante did not issue a favourable opinion and indicated a number of conditions to be complied with in order to prevent non-compliant data processing.

665. Both the Garante and the Ministry of Justice made a number of more general considerations regarding the need for greater regulatory coordination between the regulation of signature collection by means of the so-called referendum platform and the entire analogical process regulated by the law of 25 May 1970 on planned referendums and legislative initiative.

666. In any case, the minister pointed out that the legislation only guarantees the digitalization of signature collection, which is the initial segment of the initiative promotion process but does not allow for complete digitalization, extended, for example, to the authentication of signatures or the collection of electoral certificates, which are still regulated analogically. These considerations are beyond our own technical scope and that of the decree currently being drafted and are left to the prerogatives of the legislator. Thus, it is only one part of the process, not the whole.

§14. Online Voting for Italians Abroad

667. Electronic voting was tested in the 3 December 2021 election of the Committees of Italians Abroad. Decree-Law No. 67 of 30 May 2012, converted, with amendments, by Law No. 118 of 23 July 2012, postponed the elections that should have taken place in 2012, with a view to reorganizing the sector's regulations (Law No. 286 of 23 October 2003). In addition, it introduced the mode of computer voting for this type of election, postponing – for the implementation of the provision – to a subsequent regulation that, on the one hand, regulates the modalities for carrying out the voting operations in special polling stations, albeit with computerized modalities, and, on the other, regulates the hypothesis of carrying out these operations, where technically feasible, remotely, through the use of personal computers and the Internet network.

668. The 2021 Budget Law (L. 178/2020, Article 1, paragraph 648) authorized the expenditure of EUR 9 million for the year 2021 for the holding of votes for the renewal of the Committees of Italians Abroad and of the General Council of Italians Abroad, as well as for the experimental introduction of digital methods of expressing the vote for the holding of the same votes.

669. On 3 December, all voters who requested to be registered in the list of voters for the 'Comites' elections through the 'Fast it' portal were able to cast their vote for the 2021 Comites elections also in digital mode. Until 3 December, they were able to connect to the 'IOvoto' Portal to vote with their level II SPID. Voters also voted in paper mode, as only that vote counts for counting purposes. Electronic voting did not replace traditional postal voting.

§15. Online Voting and Political Parties: Movimento 5 Stelle and Partito Democratico

670. At present, within the Italian political parties, few have had the courage to experiment with online voting. The 5 Star Movement is in fact the first to have introduced the issue of e-voting and digital democracy, through the Rousseau platform. While Rousseau had the merit of bringing the issue of online voting to the attention of the public debate, it also highlighted the security and privacy problems associated with it.[147]

671. In 2019, the Data Protection Authority snapped up the Rousseau Association because it did not protect the anonymity of users or shield them from possible manipulation of their preferences. In the face of the problems that emerged with Rousseau, the 5 Star Movement opted for the Skyvote Cloud platform for the latest votes, developed and managed by the Italian company Multicast, which was identified after careful market research as the most suitable for guaranteeing anonymous, unambiguous and privacy-secure voting operations.

672. The Democratic Party, for its part, announced the modalities for electronic voting in the 26 February 2023 primaries. A compromise position was reached on the issue of e-voting in the primaries, which allowed access to this tool only for certain categories of people who otherwise would not have been able to travel to party headquarters to cast their vote: these are residents abroad, students away from home, the elderly, the disabled and people living in areas that are too inaccessible.

673. For remote voting operations, the resolution of the National Congressional Commission No. 19 of 3 February 2023 merely stipulated that SPID was compulsory without specifying anything about the platform chosen.

674. A separate document, entitled 'Vademecum for pre-registration and online voting in the primaries of 26 February 2023 for the election of the secretary and the national assembly', presents the chosen platform for voting operations, providing members with instructions on how to access it.

675. Point 4 of the vademecum presents it as 'a digital tool created by the Partito Democratico Nazionale to carry out two-way communication campaigns' capable of managing e-voting sessions in full compliance with European recommendations and personal data protection legislation, according to transparent criteria based on the reliability, security and secrecy of the vote.

676. The 'Participate Platform', according to the vademecum, was built on an infrastructure managed by a hypervisor distributed on a high availability cluster of servers and uses the latest technological solutions to guarantee speed, reliability,

---

147. *See* F. Orazi and M. Socci, 'Il grillismo. Tra democrazia elettronica e movimento personale', Carocci, Roma, 2014; *see, also*, D. Pitteri, 'Democrazia elettronica', Laterza, Bari-Roma, 2007, and G. Fioriglio, 'Democrazia elettronica. Presupposti e strumenti', CEDAM, Padova, 2017.

security and redundancy. The hardware is hosted within the data centre of Unidata S.p.a., a company with ISO 9001:2015 and ISO 27001:2017 certifications. The data centre, located in Italy, adopts the Tier 4 standard and is equipped with a redundant conditioning system according to the N+1 principle.

677. In particular, the platform guarantees compliance with the principles set out in Article 48 of the Constitution (the vote must be personal, free and secret), the impossibility, at any level of computer skills and operations, of making the vote cast by the individual voter knowable, and that the vote, once cast and confirmed, is not repeatable, modifiable or revocable.

Chapter 4. Other e-Government Services

§1. Electronic Invoice

678. Electronic invoicing is a digital method of exchanging business documents such as invoices and purchase orders between buyers and suppliers. It enables the transmission of electronic data between businesses, eliminating the need for manual processing, reducing the costs associated with producing and distributing paper invoices, and providing error-free transactions.[148]

Electronic invoicing eliminates the hassle associated with traditional paper invoices and improves the accuracy and timeliness of payments.

This results in improved cash flow and reduced administrative burdens for both parties involved in the transaction.

In addition, e-invoicing offers greater visibility into financial processes, providing real-time monitoring information that helps organizations better understand spending patterns and improve internal controls.

679. As of 1 January 2019, electronic invoicing is mandatory in Italy for both B2B and B2C transactions. The obligation was introduced by the 2018 Budget Law[149] and applies to all invoices issued as a result of supplies of goods and services made between persons resident or established in Italy.

680. To ensure compliance with this obligation, businesses must adopt an electronic invoicing system capable of generating, sending, receiving and storing electronic documents in line with Italian regulations.

Electronic invoices must include certain data such as tax code/VAT number, name and address (or other identifier) of the supplier, date of issue/payment, etc.

The Italian government also requires all companies to have a *Digital Invoice Register* (DRF), which serves as an electronic archive for all electronic invoices sent and received by companies. This digital registry aims to simplify the entire electronic invoicing process, allowing companies to quickly access information on their financial transactions at any time.

681. However, companies should be aware that there are certain deadlines that must be met to avoid penalties. For example, the first moratorium by flat-rate taxpayers for July transactions expired on 31 August 2022; subsequent late filers will trigger the first penalties as of 1 October 2022. It is therefore important that companies issue electronic invoices within 12 days of receiving payment, otherwise, they risk administrative penalties ranging from 5% to 10% of the amount of undocumented or unpaid invoices.

148. *See* V. E. Vertua, 'La fatturazione elettronica' (Giuffrè, Milano, 2019). *See, also*, N. Santangelo, 'Guida alla fatturazione elettronica tra privati' (Maggioli Editore, Rimini, 2019). *See* M. Zavani, P. Di Toma, 'L'innovazione nei processi amministrativi delle PMI. Opportunità e vincoli della fatturazione elettronica' (Franco Angeli, Milano, 2013).

149. *See* https://www.gazzettaufficiale.it/eli/id/2017/12/29/17G00222/sg.

682. An e-invoice differs from a paper invoice in general only in two respects: (i) it must necessarily be drafted using a PC, tablet or smartphone, and (ii) it must be transmitted electronically to the customer via the so-called *Sistema di Interscambio* (SdI).

The SdI is a kind of 'postman' that performs the following tasks: it checks whether the invoice contains at least the data required for tax purposes (Article 21 or 21-*bis* of Presidential Decree No. 633 of 26 October 1972[150]) as well as the telematic address (so-called addressee code or PEC address) to which the customer wishes the invoice to be delivered; checks that the supplier's VAT number (the so-called transferor/provider') and the customer's VAT number or tax code (the so-called transferee/purchaser) exist.

683. In the event of a positive outcome of the above checks, the Interchange System securely delivers the invoice to the addressee by notifying, by means of a 'delivery receipt', the person who transmitted the invoice of the date and time of delivery of the document.

Ultimately, therefore, the mandatory data to be reported on the electronic invoice are the same as on paper invoices in addition to the telematic address where the customer wants the invoice delivered.

684. The rules allowing the so-called deferred (electronic) invoice to be prepared by the 15th day of the month following the month in which the transaction is carried out, in compliance with the provisions of Article 21(4)(a) of Presidential Decree No. 633/72, remain valid.

From an operational point of view, this provision may allow the user more time to prepare and transmit to the SdI the electronic invoice, without prejudice to the obligation to issue to the customer – at the time of the transaction – a transport document or other equivalent document also on paper.

685. Electronic invoices must always be sent to your customers via the SdI (Sistema di Interscambio). Otherwise, they are deemed not to have been issued. When filling in the customer data, the e-invoice must include the e-invoice address communicated by the customer (which can be a 7-digit alphanumeric 'recipient code' or a PEC address) – otherwise the e-invoice will not reach the recipient.

686. There are several ways to transmit the XML file of the e-invoice to the SdI: you can use an online service available on the 'Fatture e Corrispettivi' portal, you can use the web procedure or the Invoice App made available free of charge by the Revenue Agency, or you can use a PEC (Certified Electronic Mail) by sending the invoice file as an attachment to the PEC message to the address 'sdi01@pec.fatturapa.it'.

687. As already said, an electronic invoice is an electronic document issued and transmitted via telematic systems in a manner that guarantees the integrity of content, authenticity of origin and legibility and for which there is acceptance by the recipient.

---

150. *See* https://www.normattiva.it/uri-res/N2Ls?urn:nir:presidente.repubblica:decreto:1972;633.

But what is meant by integrity of content, authenticity of origin and legibility? Authenticity of origin means that the identity of the supplier, provider of goods or services or the issuer of the invoice must be certain. Integrity of content: means that the content of the invoice and, in particular, the mandatory data (e.g., taxable amount and VAT) cannot be altered. Legibility means that the invoice must be rendered human-readable in accordance with the Explanatory Notes to Directive 2010/45/EU.

688. In Italy, as of 1 January 2019, an electronic invoice issued: (i) between VAT taxable persons resident or established in Italy (B2B transactions) to be sent through the Interchange System (so-called SDI) managed by the Revenue Agency; (ii) to final consumers (B2C transactions), the invoice will be made available to consumers by the telematic services of the Revenue Agency and an electronic or analogue copy will be made directly available by suppliers. Consumers may opt out of receiving either an electronic or analogue copy of the invoice.

689. As of 1 July 2019, the electronic invoice can be issued (and transmitted to the SDI) within 12 days (deadline amended by Law No. 58/2019 – previously the deadline was 10 days) after the transaction has taken place (Article 6 Presidential Decree No. 633/1972) (Article 11 DL 34/2019, converted into Law 58/2019 – Growth Decree 2019).

As of 1 July 2022, smaller taxpayers (flat-rate and minimum taxpayers) who exceeded the threshold of EUR 25,000 in revenue/compensation during the previous tax year are also required to submit an electronic invoice.

690. Concerning penalty profiles, in the event of an invoice being issued, between persons resident or established in the territory of the State for whom the obligation to issue an electronic invoice returns (according to the deadlines identified above), in a manner other than electronically, the invoice is deemed not to have been issued and a penalty of between 90% and 180% of the tax relating to the taxable amount that has not been correctly documented applies.

691. To understand how electronic invoicing works, it is necessary to understand the tasks assigned by the *Revenue Agency* to the SdI, the Interchange System that manages the entire flow of digital accounting documents. The SdI, in fact, verifies the presence and correctness of all mandatory data for tax purposes and the recipient code, the PEC address to which the document will be delivered.

692. From a technical point of view, the process on which the operation of electronic invoicing is based involves the digital creation of a document in XML format, containing a series of parameters and mandatory information indicated by the Revenue Agency, which must be digitally signed and transmitted to the other party through the *Interchange System* (Sdl).

Documents issued in a different manner will be considered as not issued and will incur the penalties provided for in Article 6 of Legislative Decree 471/1997.

Part III. Online Transactions

Chapter 1. Electronic Contracting (Including Smart Contracts and Blockchain)

693. Smart contracts are computer programmes that execute automatically when predetermined conditions occur.

The inclusion of such programmes in an unalterable and immutable (tendentially) distributed ledger such as a blockchain makes it possible to guarantee the automatic and irreversible execution of contractual clauses transposed into computer language.[151]

694. The Italian legal system offers a definition in Article 8b co. 2 of Decree-Law No. 135/2018: 'A "smart contract" is defined as a computer program that operates on distributed ledger-based technologies and whose execution automatically binds two or more parties on the basis of effects predefined by them.'

To supplement the definition, where the legislator mentions 'distributed ledger technologies' (DLT), which in turn are defined, albeit too rigidly, in paragraph 1 of the aforementioned decree, blockchain technology is essential to be understood.

695. Moreover, the definition of a smart legal contract would be more correct to connote the legal aspect to which the computer code would represent a mere transposition.

The statement presupposes knowledge of the functioning underlying blockchain, the if-then computer concept and the regulation of legal relations according to contractual schemes.

696. Since the operation of this instrument takes place on a computerized level, parties wishing to regulate their interests through a smart contract will have to equip themselves with accounts suitable for exchanging tokens on the blockchain. Second, the asset or right that is the subject of the transaction will have to be digitally represented through a token.

697. Having set up the IT tools to identify the subjects and objects of the contract, the parties identify the interest to be settled through a traditional agreement

151. *See* R. Battaglini, M.T. Giordano (eds), 'Blockchain e smart contract: funzionamento, profili giuridici e internazionali, applicazioni pratiche' (Giuffrè, Milano, 2019).

with clauses. Subsequently, this agreement is translated into a computer program with clauses that are self-executing as a consequence of the occurrence of predetermined circumstances. Finally, this programme is inserted into a blockchain so as to make it virtually unchangeable.

698. The above definitional attempts place the emphasis on automatic execution, leaving out the moment of the formation and conclusion of the contract, which will be regulated by traditional institutions.

It follows that the elements provided for by the Italian Civil Code (Article 1325 of the Italian Civil Code) for the validity of the contract can also be found in the formation of a smart contract.

699. The element that gives rise to most thought is the moment of agreement between the parties. A smart contract formed as a result of a negotiation between the parties and a subsequent agreement would only be representative of the manner of execution of the contract, otherwise replicating the traditional consensualist principle in the formation of the contract itself.

700. Law converting the Simplifications Decree Law, 11/02/2019, No. 12, Official Gazette 12/02/2019, Article 8-*ter*: Article 8-*ter* (Technologies based on distributed ledgers and smart contracts). – (1) 'Distributed ledger-based technologies' shall be defined as computer technologies and protocols that use a shared, distributed, replicable, simultaneously accessible, architecturally decentralized ledger on a cryptographic basis, such as to enable the recording, validation, updating and storage of both unencrypted and further cryptographically protected data verifiable by each participant, not alterable and not modifiable.

701. A 'smart contract' is defined as a computer program that operates on distributed ledger technologies and whose execution automatically binds two or more parties on the basis of effects predefined by them. Smart contracts meet the requirement of being in writing upon computer identification of the parties concerned, through a process having the requirements established by the Agency for Digital Italy with guidelines to be adopted within ninety days from the date of entry into force of the law converting this decree.

702. The storage of an electronic document through the use of technologies based on distributed registers shall produce the legal effects of electronic time stamping referred to in Article 41 of Regulation (EU) No. 910/2014 of the European Parliament and of the Council of 23 July 2014.

703. Within ninety days from the date of entry into force of the law converting this decree, 'the Digital Italy Agency shall identify the technical standards that technologies based on distributed registers must possess in order to produce the effects referred to in paragraph 3.'

704. Article 8b, 1st paragraph, Law No. 12/2019:

> Distributed ledger-based technologies are defined as those information technologies and protocols that use a shared, distributed, replicable, simultaneously accessible, architecturally decentralised ledger on a cryptographic basis, such as to enable the recording, validation, updating and storage of both unencrypted and further cryptographically protected data verifiable by each participant, not alterable and not modifiable.

705. This first paragraph, on the one hand, highlights the legislator's desire to create a regulatory basis that allows companies to invest and experiment with the possible uses of technology, on the other hand, it leaves a significant margin of uncertainty as to which networks may fall within the definition, as it does not specify whether they should be public, private, permissionless, permissioned, or which consent algorithm should be used (PoW, PoS, other).

706. Article 8b, 2nd paragraph, Law No. 12/2019:

> A 'smart contract' is defined as a computer programme that operates on distributed ledger-based technologies and whose execution automatically binds two or more parties on the basis of effects predefined by them.
>
> Smart contracts meet the requirement of written form after computer identification of the parties involved, through a process having the requirements set by the Agency for Digital Italy with guidelines to be adopted within ninety days from the date of entry into force of the law converting this decree.

707. Article 8b, paragraphs 3 and 4, Law No. 12/2019:

> 'The storage of an electronic document through the use of distributed ledger-based technologies shall produce the legal effects of electronic time stamping referred to in Article 41 of Regulation (EU) No. 910/2014 of the European Parliament and of the Council of 23 July 2014.'
>
> 'Within ninety days of the date of entry into force of the law converting this decree, the Digital Italy Agency shall identify the technical standards that technologies based on distributed registers must possess in order to produce the effects referred to in paragraph 3.'

708. The two paragraphs do not present any particular problems of interpretation. DLT technologies can be used for 'electronic time validation', i.e., the so-called notarization of documents.

709. We have seen how the Italian legislation does not provide a detailed discipline but lays the groundwork for experimentation to begin, bringing to light the critical issues that the law will have to deal with.

Chapter 2. Electronic Signatures

§1. Introduction

710. In Italy, electronic signatures are regulated primarily by Regulation (EU) No. 910/2014, commonly known as the eIDAS Regulation, and by Legislative Decree No. 82/2005 (the 'Digital Administration Code' or CAD).

711. eIDAS Regulation (EU) No. 910/2014 provides the legal framework for electronic signatures across the European Union, including Italy.

Types of Electronic Signatures: Simple Electronic Signature (SES): This includes scanned signatures or email signatures. It is the most basic form and may be sufficient for some transactions but offers the least security and verification. Advanced Electronic Signature (AES): This type must be uniquely linked to the signatory, capable of identifying the signatory, and linked to the data being signed. AES provides more robust security than SES and is used for more sensitive transactions. Qualified Electronic Signature (QES): This is the most secure form of electronic signature, requiring a qualified digital certificate and a secure signature creation device. QES has the same legal effect as a handwritten signature.

712. Legislative Decree No. 82/2005 (Digital Administration Code): This decree implements the eIDAS Regulation in Italy and establishes how electronic signatures are used in Italian law. The decree recognizes the validity of electronic signatures as long as they meet the requirements set forth by eIDAS. This means that AES and QES have legal equivalence to traditional handwritten signatures, depending on the level of assurance provided. The decree supports the use of PKI for the creation and verification of qualified electronic signatures.[152]

713. For QES, the use of qualified digital certificates is mandated. These certificates are issued by Qualified Trust Service Providers (QTSPs) and must be stored in a secure signature creation device, such as a smart card or USB token. The process involves generating a digital signature using the private key associated with the qualified certificate. This signature is then validated using the corresponding public key.

714. Verification involves checking that the digital signature corresponds to the signatory's public key and that the document has not been altered since the signature was applied. Blockchain technology can also be used to further enhance the integrity and traceability of electronic signatures.

715. Italian law adheres to international standards for electronic signatures, including those specified by the eIDAS Regulation. This ensures interoperability and reliability across different systems and jurisdictions.

---

152. *See* E. Carloni (ed.), 'Codice dell'amministrazione digitale: commento a D.lgs. 7 marzo 2005 n. 82' (Maggioni, Santarcangelo di Romagna, 2005); R. Arcella, G. Vitrani, 'Il codice dell'amministrazione digitale: disciplina e applicazioni' (Giuffrè, Milano, 2024).

§2. The Italian Law in Details

716. In Italy, the Digital Administration Code (CAD) identifies four types of electronic signatures, each with specific characteristics and values.

717. Electronic signature (simple): Lacking the guarantees of paternity and integrity of the document, it represents the weakest form of signature in the IT field. It takes on the value of a mere signature instrument. This includes, for example, logging in using a username and password. The low legal value clearly emerges in the event that we wish to identify with absolute certainty the person who has logged in with certain credentials.

718. Advanced electronic signature: As the name suggests, this type of signature provides a higher degree of protection and security than the simple electronic signature. It presupposes the prior identification of the signatory by means of an acknowledgement that can take place de visu or remotely by means of audio and/or video recording tools made in compliance with the regulations in force. The most widespread type of advanced electronic signature is the graphometric signature using a tablet. From a legal point of view, it has the same probative value as a private contract for which the presumption of traceability of the signature to the holder applies. In court, it is then up to the other party to prove the invalidity of the deed.

The CAD limits the application of the advanced electronic signature to documents within an administrative procedure.

719. Qualified electronic signature: this is one of the most advanced forms of electronic signature and is characterized by two elements: (i) a secure physical device for creating the signature, (ii) a certification attesting to the identity of the signatory and the originality and integrity of the signed documents. Compared to the previous ones, this signature is based on a signature certificate issued by an authority guaranteeing the authenticity of the signatory and the absence of changes to the document after the signature.

720. Digital signature: This is by far the most advanced form of electronic signature. It makes use of a digital signature kit consisting of: (*i*) a physical device (except for remote signature), (*ii*) a subscription certificate with a validity of 3 years issued by a certifying body that identifies and certifies with certainty the identity of the holder of the signature, (*iii*) a PIN known only to the signatory. With the PIN, a further step is added to strengthen the entire signing process, a step that can only and exclusively be performed by the holder. As mentioned above, the legal value of the digital signature is maximized; this results in a reversal of the burden of proof, in other words, in the event of a court case, it will be up to the signatory to prove or deny the validity of the signature.

721. Both electronic and digital signatures are governed by the Digital Administration Code, Legislative Decree No. 82 of 7 March 2005, as amended and supplemented, as well as by the eIDAS Regulation, Reg. EU No. 910/2014, i.e., the

European Regulation governing electronic identification and trust services for electronic transactions in the European market, replacing the previous Directive 1999/93/EC. Unlike in the previous regulation, in the current one, electronic signatures – as well as time stamps – outside national borders and throughout the EU assume the same legal status.[153]

722. The eIDAS Regulation sets out certain security and transparency requirements and minimum obligations for all trust service providers wishing to be accredited in the European area. The same eIDAS Regulation also defined the types of signatures envisaged and usable within the EU, namely: simple electronic signature, advanced signature and qualified signature. Among these, we can include the digital signature, a particular type of advanced electronic signature provided for by the CAD but not expressly taken up by the eIDAS Regulation.

723. An electronic signature is defined by the eIDAS Regulation as 'a set of data in electronic form, attached to or logically associated with other electronic data, used as a method of computer identification'. The digital signature, on the other hand, is only envisaged by the Italian state; it is defined by the digital administration code as 'a particular type of Advanced Electronic Signature based on a qualified certificate and on a system of cryptographic keys, one public and one private, correlated with each other, which allows the owner by means of the private key and the addressee by means of the public key, respectively, to make manifest and to verify the provenance and integrity of an IT document or a set of IT documents'. Thanks to these regulations, a digital document satisfies the requirement of written form and has the effectiveness provided for in Article 2702 of the Italian Civil Code when a digital signature or other type of qualified or advanced electronic signature has been inserted. In fact, Article 2702 of the Italian Civil Code provides as follows: 'a private contract is full proof, up to a claim of forgery, of the origin of the declarations made by the person who signed it, if the person against whom the contract is produced recognises the signature, or if it is legally considered as recognised'.

724. In all other cases, the suitability of the computer document and its probative value are freely assessable in court, in relation to the characteristics of security, integrity and immodifiability. A document signed with an advanced, qualified and digital electronic signature therefore has full legal effect in our legal system, provided that it is not modified after the signature has been affixed. In order to acquire qualified and digital electronic signatures, however, it is necessary to refer to a qualified trust service provider, authorized by the Agenzia per l'Italia Digitale (AgID), which guarantees the identity of the persons using the digital signature and the appropriateness of the technologies used.

725. The simple electronic signature does not require any special requirements for its constitution, its evidentiary value is freely assessable in court, taking into

153. *See* M. Vincenti, M. Sala, 'Manuale di diritto di internet' (La Tribuna, Piacenza, 2003).

account the objective characteristics of quality, security, integrity and immodifiability pursuant to Article 21 CAD. The eIDAS Regulation leaves the determination of its legal effects to the national law of the individual countries.

726. The advanced electronic signature is suitable for guaranteeing the identity of the author and the integrity and unchangeability of the document to which it is affixed. To guarantee the certified identity of the holder, it is necessary to use a recognition process that can be implemented by the service provider or by a QTSP (Qualified Trust Service Provider). The advanced electronic signature has the evidentiary effect of a handwritten signature.

727. The qualified electronic signature requires the use of a technology identified and required by the legislator and must be affixed after the issuance of a 'qualified certificate', i.e., a document issued by a Qualified Trust Service Provider, which certifies the identity of the person affixing it and must be generated by means of a secure device. As with the advanced electronic signature, a procedure is required to guarantee a unique connection to the signatory. In addition, this type of signature must technologically comply with the standard protocols defined by ETSI (European Telecommunications Standards Institute) and must be created by suitable means over which the signatory can retain exclusive control, and it must be linked to the data to which it refers in such a way that it is possible to detect that they have subsequently been changed. As with the advanced electronic signature, documents signed with a qualified electronic signature have evidentiary effect, but in this case, the burden of proof is reversed, i.e., it is the person who claims that the signature is invalid who has to prove it.

728. The digital signature is a special type of qualified electronic signature based on a system of asymmetrical key pairs, one public and one private, that allows the holder by means of the private key and the recipient by means of the public key, respectively, to verify the provenance and integrity of an IT document or set of IT documents. The digital signature must refer uniquely to a single subject and to the document or set of documents to which it is affixed or associated. Exactly as for the qualified electronic signature, in the event of disallowance of a document to which a digital signature has been affixed, the burden of proof is reversed.

729. The data published by AgID on its website[154] continues to show a large spread for the various components involved in the system, in particular: The number of remote digital signatures in the first half of 2023 reached a remarkable figure of approximately 3.361 billion. In the same period, the number of active digital signature devices (with the associated qualified certificates) exceeded almost 34.5 million. The number of time stamps also reached over 2 billion. 70% of users are freelancers, 20% private citizens and 10% companies. The service is mainly used

---

154. *See* https://www.agid.gov.it/it/notizie/online-i-dati-sulla-diffusione-dei-servizi-fiduciari-qualificati-nel-2deg-semestre-2023.

for communications with the PA (28%), for signing contracts (24%), for projects and building practices (21%), for business management procedures (19%), and to manage electronic invoices (10%).

§3. Some Interesting Case Law

730. According to Court of Cassation, Criminal section VI, 3 July 2023, decision No. 34099, appeal without the digital signature of the defendant is inadmissible even if the lawyer verifies the integrity of the signature using software recognized by AgID.

The notice of appeal transmitted electronically without the digital signature of the defendant is inadmissible, as neither the validity of the signature of the lawyer on the brief nor the fact that the lawyer subsequently used an application approved and recognized by the Agenzia per l'Italia Digitale (AgID) to verify the validity and integrity of the signature are relevant, as this is a verification carried out 'in-house' on the basis of documents not necessarily corresponding to those transmitted and received by the court registry, and as such not sufficient to refute the latter's certification. (In this case, the Court of Cassation declared the order of the court of merit immune from criticism when, having noted the certificate of the clerk's office that had found the absence of a digital signature in the appeal, it had complied with the legal provision governing the current system of digital appeals, declaring the appeal inadmissible and ordering the execution of the contested measure pursuant to Article 24, paragraph 6-*septies*, Decree No. 137/2020, converted, with amendments, into law No. 176/2020, highlighting, among other things, the inapplicability to the case under examination of the general principle of *favor impugnationis*, which certainly cannot prevail over the peremptory provisions that censure with inadmissibility the non-compliance with the discipline on the formal requirements placed to protect the certainty of the origin of the deed from its author).

Chapter 3. Trust Services

§1. Digital Trust Services Regulation in Italy

731. There is no specific legislation in Italy that regulates in a homogeneous and orderly manner qualified, accredited and trusted digital services for citizens. It is therefore necessary to identify, in the individual disciplines, detailed regulatory regulations. To date, the areas that have been regulated the most are those of electronic signatures, certified e-mail, digital storage of documents and the single digital identity of every citizen (SPID).

732. AgID, the Digital Italy Agency, also has the task of supervising the development of these services in Italy. To this end, it has set up a monitoring system of qualified or accredited digital services, with a platform dedicated to those services that enable secure transactions between public administrations, businesses and citizens ('digital trust services'). These are, for example, digital signature services, digital identity (SPID),[155] in addition, certified electronic mail and document storage in accordance with the law. These are all services provided by entities registered in public trusted lists, over which AgID exercises supervisory functions.

733. AgID's service is aimed at digital users (citizens, businesses, public administrations) and is designed to improve knowledge and awareness of the use of these services, in the potential they offer in mutual relations, in the limitations and precautions to be adopted to prevent unintended use. At the same time, it is aimed at insiders (the qualified or accredited service providers) to support their activities, making available, in restricted access sections, special functions for reciprocal interactions.[156]

734. This system generates interesting and very useful rights for users. Users can, for instance, send in reports on alleged management anomalies encountered in the provision of services or violations of the relevant regulations by digital service providers. In addition, the citizen can acquire information or guidance in the use of services, improve knowledge about services for a more conscious use, become aware of recurrent issues and view indicators on the performance of services.

735. Qualified trust services include a set of electronic services, normally provided against payment, that meet a set of requirements valid throughout the European Union (requirements established by the eIDAS Regulation) providing users with mutual guarantees of security and quality. Trust services are services for the creation, verification and validation of electronic signatures, electronic seals, electronic time stamps, electronic certificate delivery services; certificates related to these services, services for the creation, verification and validation of website authentication certificates, services for the preservation of signatures; electronic seals or certificates related to these services. It is possible to identify all qualified

155. *See* https://www.spid.gov.it/.
156. *See* https://www.agid.gov.it/it/agenzia.

trust service providers in each Member State and the trust services they provide by using an online application made available by the European Commission. AgID publishes the list of trust service providers established in Italy, together with information on the services they provide. AgID performs supervisory functions on these entities.

§2. SPID (Public System for Digital Identity)

736. SPID (Sistema Pubblico di Identità Digitale – Public Digital Identity System) is the solution that allows citizens to access online services of the public administration with a single digital identity (username and password) that can be used by computers, tablets and smartphones. SPID is free of charge and can be requested from one of the Identity Providers by registering on the site, entering your personal data, creating your SPID credentials and performing the recognition process. Usually, recognition takes place in person, by means of an Electronic Identity Card (CIE), National Services Card (CNS), Digital Signature or via webcam.[157]

737. The Agenzia per l'Italia Digitale monitors compliance with the rules in collaboration with the Garante per la Privacy, both with regard to the activities of identity providers and with regard to the services made available by public administrations and private individuals.

738. To request and obtain SPID credentials, the Sistema Pubblico di Identità Digitale (Public Digital Identity System), one must be of legal age. SPID is free, but Identity Providers provide different ways of registering, some for a fee. The health card or tax code are additional elements supporting the identity verification process that help to combat identity theft by verifying their authenticity on national non-public databases.

739. The Simplifications Decree (Decree-Law No. 76/2020) established that, as of 1 March 2021, all local and central administrations, public bodies and agencies should allow citizens to access their digital services subject to computer identification carried out exclusively through the Public System for Digital Identity (SPID), or through the Electronic Identity Card (CIE). In fact, Article 24 of the Decree provides for the equivalence of SPID and CIE and indicated 28 February 2021 as the date for the switch-off of the different methods of identification for access to the online services of public administrations (amendment to Article 64 of the CAD). From 1 March 2021, therefore, administrations may no longer issue or renew credentials for the identification and access of citizens to their online services other than SPID or CIE, without prejudice to the use of those already issued until their natural expiry date and, in any case, no later than 30 September 2021.

740. SPID is therefore based on a federated and collaborative model. The subjects participating in the SPID federation (Article 3, Prime Ministerial Decree of 24

157. *See* https://www.spid.gov.it/.

October 2014) are as follows: (i) digital identity managers (identity providers): legal persons accredited by AgID who, in their capacity as public service managers, after certain user identification, assign, make available and manage the attributes used by the same user for their computer identification. Citizens and businesses can freely choose their digital identity manager; (ii) qualified attribute managers: subjects accredited pursuant to Article 16 who have the power to certify the possession and validity of qualified attributes, at the request of service providers. They are therefore subjects who, according to a regulation, have the power to certify qualifications, personal statuses, and powers of natural persons (e.g., professional orders and colleges, professional associations, chambers of commerce, national councils and public administrations); (iii) service providers: these, in order to provide online services, forward requests for computerized user identification to digital identity managers and receive the outcome. Service providers adhere to SPID through a special agreement (Article 13, Prime Ministerial Decree of 24 October 2014) and may be: (a) public administrations: Access to networked services provided by public administrations that require computer identification is via SPID (Article 64, paragraph 2-*quater*, CAD); (b) private entities: it is also recognized that private entities, according to the modalities defined by the decree referred to in paragraph 2-*sexies*, have the right to use the SPID system for the management of the digital identity of their users (Article 64, paragraph 2-quinquies, CAD), (c) AgID (role defined by Article 4, Prime Ministerial Decree of 24 October 2014): takes care of the activation of the SPID, managing in particular the accreditation of identity providers and managers of qualified attributes (through special agreements); updates the SPID register (which contains the list of entities that have gone through the accreditation process to join thc SPID federation) and supervises the entities that participate in the SPID; enters into special agreements with entities that certify the validity of identity attributes and enable the verification of identity documents; users: natural or legal persons, holders of a SPID digital identity, who use the services provided on the network by a service provider, following computer identification.

§3. Electronic Signatures

741. Among the most widespread qualified trust services in Italy are qualified electronic signature (FEQ) services (aka ‘digital signatures’).

All natural persons can have a digital signature: citizens, directors and employees of companies and public administrations.

742. The digital signature is generated thanks to a pair of asymmetric digital keys uniquely assigned to a subject, called the owner: the private key is known only to the owner and is used to generate the digital signature to be affixed to the document; the key to be made public is used to verify the authenticity of the signature.

This method is known as dual-key encryption and guarantees full security as the public key cannot be used to reconstruct the private key.

743. There are two ways of using digital signatures: ‘locally’: the digital signature is generated through a device in the holder’s possession (smartcard or token);

'remotely': the digital signature is generated using authentication tools (typically user id+ password +OTP or mobile phone) on a device (HSM) held by the certifier (in European terminology, qualified trust service provider). Those wishing to acquire a digital signature device must contact qualified trust service providers for this service. The digital signature can also be obtained by using the SPID as a recognition system.[158]

§4. PEC

744. Certified Electronic Mail (CEM) is a communication system similar to standard electronic mail with the addition of certain security and transmission certification features that make messages enforceable against third parties.[159] These features have been defined in Presidential Decree No. 68 of 11 February 2005 and in related technical documents. These rules serve to guarantee the validity of the overall service and interoperability between the different certified mail operators.

745. The CAD (Legislative Decree No. 82/2005 amended and supplemented by Legislative Decree No. 235/2010), further reaffirms the legal value of Certified Electronic Mail as a telematic transmission tool. Article 16 of Legislative Decree No. 185/2008, converted into Law No. 2/2009, stipulates that new companies are required to declare their CEM address when registering with the companies register, that professionals must declare their CEM address to their respective orders within one year, that existing companies must declare their CEM address to the companies register within three years, and that all public administrations must declare their CEM address. Decree Law No. 179/2012, converted with amendments into Law 221 of 2012, completes the regulatory framework on CEM. In particular, Article 5 stipulates that new sole proprietorships that register with the business register or the register of craft businesses must communicate their CEM address at the time of registration and that active sole proprietorships are required to file their certified email address with the competent business register by 30/06/2013.

746. In addition, the public list of Certified Electronic Mail (CEM) addresses of companies and professionals called the National Index of Certified Electronic Mail Addresses (INI-PEC) is established at the Ministry for Economic Development. Access to the INI-PEC is granted to public administrations, professionals, businesses, managers or operators of public services and all citizens via a website and without the need for authentication. In accordance with the provisions of Ministerial Decree No. 44/2011, the General Register of Electronic Addresses (ReGIndE), managed by the Ministry of Justice, contains the identification data as well as the certified electronic mail (PEC) address of external qualified subjects, i.e: (a) belonging to a public body; (b) professionals registered in registers and lists established by

---

158. *See* C. Leanza, 'L'identità personale nell'era telematica: l'identità digitale', in 'Il diritto di famiglia e delle persone', fasc. 4, 2023.
159. *See* B. Brunelli, 'Le notificazioni civili nella riforma Cartabia', in 'Rivista trimestrale di diritto e procedura civile', fasc. 1, 2024.

law; (c) auxiliaries of the judge who do not belong to a professional body/order or who belong to a professional body/order that has not yet sent the register to the Ministry of Justice (this does not apply to lawyers, whose specific role as defence counsel implies that the sending of the register must always be done by the order to which they belong or by the body they are defending).

747. Particularly interesting, and useful, are the institutional P.A. boxes, provided for in the protocol legislation, and the General Index of Italian Public Administrations, a site that allows Italian P.A. to be identified using different search criteria and, for each P.A., which provides information including the institutional box (where present). The P.A. index represents the main certified mail address book on the Net.[160]

748. A transmission can only be considered certified mail if both the sender's and the addressee's boxes are certified mailboxes. If this is not the case, the system can only provide part of the certification functionalities envisaged (e.g., a delivery receipt is not provided).

749. Certified mail operators are obliged to record all transmission events for thirty months if requested by interested parties. Managers are also required to always use a time reference aligned with official institutes that guarantee exact time; for this reason, records but also other elements such as receipts, pay slips, etc. will always contain exact time.

750. Certified mail services use exclusively secure protocols (managed for some time by the most widespread mail tools), to prevent any tampering with the message by third parties. Identification may be by user and password or by digital certificates.

751. When a regular message is sent from a certified mailbox, one receives from one's own certified mail provider an acceptance receipt, signed by the manager, certifying the time of sending and the recipients (distinguishing between normal and CEM recipients); the information is available in both text and XML format.

752. The sender's certified mail operator creates a new message, known as a transport envelope, which contains the original message and the main dispatch data; the envelope is signed by the provider so that the recipient's provider can verify its integrity (i.e., that it has not been tampered with in transmission).

To guarantee the integrity of the message, sender and receiver are obliged to use the CEM box only via secure protocols.

753. A certified mail message is delivered to the recipient's box in its 'transport envelope'. As soon as delivery has taken place, the addressee's provider sends the sender a delivery receipt, an e-mail message, signed by the operator certifying: (i) delivery, (ii) the date and time of delivery, and (iii) the content delivered.

---

160. *See* https://indicepa.gov.it/ipa-portale/consultazione/pec/ricerca-pec.

754. Certified mail provides the sender with proof, signed by the provider chosen by the recipient, of all content that has been delivered (with date and time of delivery). This is one of the most significant features that distinguishes certified mail from normal means of sending official documents in paper format.

755. All companies, VAT numbers and sole proprietorships, are obliged to declare their PEC box to the Company Registry. It therefore follows that for companies, the CEM is mandatory. As of October 2021, the sanctions regime for companies and professionals that do not have a CEM with penalties of up to EUR 2,000 was triggered.

756. With Determination No. 233 of 9 August 2022, AgID adopted the 'Technical rules for certified delivery services in accordance with the eIDAS Regulation 910/2014'. These technical rules enabled the start of the migration of the PEC system to the REM (Registered Electronic Mail – a particular Certified Electronic Delivery Service – SERC) messaging system compliant with the aforementioned eIDAS Regulation. The objective is to have a Community interoperability standard, consistent with the eIDAS Regulation, that allows the exchange of messaging usable as registered mail at the Community level. The completion of the migration will be characterized by the issuance of a Prime Ministerial Decree that will sanction on the basis of national primary legislation the abrogation of Article 48 of the Digital Administration Code and thus of the CEM.

757. The PEC has the same legal value as the traditional registered letter with acknowledgement of receipt; it therefore allows the opposability to third parties of the successful delivery (the legal value is sanctioned by Presidential Decree No. 68 of 11 February 2005).

The Certified Mail was disseminated with the obligations for persons required to register in the business register (including new VAT numbers and sole proprietorships) and professionals registered in registers and lists. Registration in the commercial register could only take place by communicating the specific box. Even a taxi driver is a holder of a PEC box.

PEC is compulsory in the context of document exchanges in telematic processes. It is used in many other situations, such as registration for public competitions, requests for information from PAs within the framework of transparency rules (FOIA) and exchanges of data between the financial world and the tax authorities.

Chapter 4. Online Financial Services

§1. The Italian Law

758. The European Union has long intended to create a single market for financial services and activities in all European countries, and for this reason, the MiFID Directive came into force in Italian law on 1 November 2007.

With the aim of pursuing the same goals as the MiFID and, at the same time, further strengthening the safeguards for Investors, MiFID II will enter into force on 3 January 2018.[161]

759. Various new features have been introduced by the MiFID II Directive, also with reference to information transparency towards clients.

The regulatory intervention introduced by MiFID II entails the need for intermediaries to assess the characteristics of the client for whom the products are intended from the moment the product is designed.

Regulators (European and national) will be able to intervene before products are distributed if they are deemed unsuitable for the market in question.

760. At the European level, there will also be a restriction on the possibility of selling a financial product without it being accompanied by an adequacy assessment.

Finally, an adequate level of competence and professional experience of the staff in contact with clients will be required.

761. The objective of providing the client with more transparent cost aggregation for each instrument or service is one of the most important aspects.

The purpose of the regulatory intervention is to put the customer in a position to understand exactly the cost he is incurring even before making the investment choice, also in order to be able to identify, through comparison and for the same product, which Intermediary offers the best service.

762. Again with a view to greater transparency, MiFID II has introduced an extension of the contents of the periodic reports to be provided to clients, with particular reference to costs, charges and incentives, as well as an increase in the frequency of their transmission.

763. MiFID II has also stipulated that investment firms must explain in a clear and concise manner whether and why investment advice is independent or non-independent; in the case of investment advice on an independent basis MiFID II provides for the prohibition of receiving and retaining inducements.

---

161. *See* F. Annunziata, 'Il recepimento di MiFID II: uno sguardo di insieme tra continuità e discontinuità', in 'Rivista delle Società', fasc. 4, 2018; F. Della Negra, 'MiFID II and private law: enforcing UE conduct of business rules' (Hart, Oxford, 2019); F. Della Negra, 'I rimedi per la violazione di regole di condotta MIFID II: una riflessione di diritto UE', in 'Banca, Borsa, Titoli di Credito', fasc. 5, 2020.

764. In addition, when the same client is offered or given advice on both an independent and a non-independent basis, a clear explanation of both services must be provided so that the client can understand the differences between one service and the other.

As in the past, the client must be informed about the bank's order transmission and execution method; decide whether to accept it and, if so, state this explicitly.

The regulations also oblige intermediaries to handle orders to buy or sell financial instruments under the best possible conditions (best execution).

As in the past, the advisory service, i.e., the provision of personalized recommendations on financial transactions, is regulated and only an Intermediary expressly authorized by the Supervisory Authority, such as UniCredit, may provide investment advice.

765. The regulations also require that investment firms providing investment advice (whether on an independent or non-independent basis) also represent to the client, in view of the range of financial instruments they may recommend, the firm's relationship with the Issuers/Offerors of those instruments.

766. When providing investment services, the bank must establish appropriate organizational measures to prevent and manage conflict of interest situations. In cases where the measures taken to manage conflicts of interest are not considered sufficient to ensure, with reasonable certainty, that the risk of harm to the interests of the client is avoided, the bank, before acting on their behalf and according to the manner in which the service is provided, informs the client of the nature and sources of such conflicts of interest and the measures taken to mitigate them, so that the client can make an informed decision on the services provided.

767. The bank may pay or receive inducements from a party other than the Client only if the Client has been informed in advance and provided that such inducements enhance the quality of the service rendered to the Client.

768. As in the past, in order to protect its investors' interests, the bank must ask its investors for the information necessary to identify their characteristics, objectives and investment needs and thus be able to recommend suitable financial services and products.

769. Through an in-depth interview and the completion of two separate questionnaires (known as the Appropriateness Interview and the Adequacy Interview, jointly known as the MiFID Interview), the bank verifies with the client his knowledge and experience in investment matters, his investment objectives and his financial situation in order to accompany him in identifying an appropriate investment choice.

§2. Some Interesting Case Law

770. According to Court of Cassation Criminal section II, 26 October 2022, decision No. 44378, virtual currency must be considered an investment instrument because it is a financial product, and must therefore be regulated by the rules on financial intermediation (Articles 94 et seq. of the Consolidated Law on Finance), which guarantee the protection of the investment through a unitary discipline of special law; therefore, those who provide such services are obliged to increase their obligations to inform the consumer, in order to allow the consumer to know the contents of the economic-contractual operation and to make a well-considered negotiating choice (case in point concerning the existence of the offence of abusive exercise of financial activity under Article 166 of the Consolidated Law on Finance, which in the specific case consisted in the online funds request through collective financing declared as an investment offer, and the preventive seizure of a wallet containing 30 bitcoins considered to be the object of the crime of self-laundering under Article 648-*ter* of the Criminal Code).

771. According to Court of Cassation, Criminal section II, 7 July 2022, decision No. 27023, the hypothesis of self-money laundering exists in case of reinvestment in the purchase of bitcoins of the money coming from online scams.

The physiognomy of the bitcoin purchase system 'lends itself to facilitating unlawful conduct', given that it is able to ensure a high degree of anonymity: ok to the precautionary measure for fraud and self-laundering.[162] In confirming the precautionary measure also for the reuse of the proceeds of the offences of aggravated fraud in speculative activities such as the purchase of cryptocurrencies, the Supreme Court rejected the defence's appeal which argued that the transactions were not for speculative purposes and that the rules of the reference market do not allow the identity of the purchaser to be concealed because they are marked by maximum transparency. The Supreme Court did not share this view and, on the contrary, stated that the regulatory indication provided by the article on self-laundering (648-*ter*.1, Cp) on the activities in which the money resulting from the predicate offence may be used or transferred does not constitute a formal list, but rather identifies macro-areas, all linked by the characteristic of use for the purpose of obtaining a profit, thus polluting the economic circuit. In this perspective, a plurality of activities can be brought under the notion of 'speculative activities'. As for virtual currencies, it is pointed out that they can be used for purposes other than payment and include store-of-value products for savings and investment purposes. Contrary to what the defence had argued, which had valued blockchain and distributed ledger registrations in terms of transparency, it is instead possible to guarantee maximum 'anonymity (permissionless system), without any provision for controlling the entry of new 'nodes' and the origin of the converted money'. Finally, the high number of cryptocurrencies used in the darkweb was noted, precisely because of their opacity characteristics.

772. According to Criminal Cassation section II, 17/09/2020, No. 26807, cryptocurrencies (virtual currencies or bitcoins) are financial products where their sale is advertised as an investment proposal and, in such a case, since it is an activity

162. *See* M. Tola, 'Valute virtuali e frode alla legge', in 'Banca, Borsa, Titoli di Credito', fasc. 6, 2023.

subject to the requirements set forth in the Consolidated Law on Financial Intermediation (TUF), the omission constitutes the offence of financial abuse pursuant to Article 166(1)(c) of the TUF (Legislative Decree No. 58 of 24 February 1998).

773. According to Court ('Tribunale') of Verona, section II, 24 January 2017, No. 195, bitcoins represent a financial instrument consisting of a currency that can be minted by any user and can be exploited to carry out transactions, which are possible thanks to open source software and a peer-to-peer network.

The transaction of exchange of traditional currency against units of the virtual currency bitcoin and vice versa is carried out against payment of a sum corresponding to the margin made up of the difference between the purchase price of the currencies and the selling price charged by the operator to its customers, can be qualified on the operator's side as a professional activity of provision of services for consideration, carried out in favour of consumers.

The purchase and sale of virtual currencies (e.g., bitcoins), which can be qualified as financial instruments, is an operation that can be defined as high risk for the saver, which obliges the person who advertises the sale, on his own behalf or on behalf of third parties, to first inform the user interested in the purchase about the risks connected to the investment (so-called pre-contractual information), as well as the risks of the investment, pre-contractual information), as laid down in Articles 67 et seq. of the Consumer Code on the subject of distance marketing of financial services to consumers; in particular, the promoter of the sales transaction is required to apply the stricter provisions laid down by the sector legislation governing the offer of the service or product concerned.

Chapter 5. Law of Evidence in the Digital Environment

§1. Introduction

774. In the Italian legal system, 'digital preservation', or 'digital preservation of computer documents', means a legal/informatic process, regulated by law, which allows the creation of computer documents with full legal value. Digital preservation means, therefore, replacing paper documents (which some legal entities are required by law to preserve) with the equivalent document in digital format, which is 'locked' in form, content and time, through digital signature and time stamp.[163]

775. Substitute storage serves to equate paper documents with electronic ones and allows private companies and public administrations to eliminate, or reduce, the costs associated with printing, storage, archiving and stamp duty on stamped newspapers. The Agenzia per l'Italia Digitale (AgID) defines the operating methods for implementing the preservation activity for this service, over which it performs supervisory functions.

776. The Agenzia per l'Italia Digitale shall also define the operating procedures for carrying out the preservation activity, with the clear identification of the nature and function of the system, the organizational models, the roles and functions of the subjects involved, the description of the preservation process and the professional profiles of the managers employed in the preservation process. In particular, those providing the service are registered in the public list of accredited conservators and subject to the Agency's supervisory functions.

777. The ever-increasing volume of documentation produced, with the need to give it the correct civil and fiscal value, has led, over the years, to a progressive updating of the Italian regulatory framework on digital preservation. In fact, we are in the presence of services regulated by national law: Legislative Decree No. 82 of 7 March 2005, and subsequent amendments and additions, 'Digital Administration Code-CAD', by the Prime Ministerial Decree of 13 November 2014, containing 'Technical rules on the formation, transmission, copying, duplication, reproduction and temporal validation of computer documents', by the Prime Ministerial Decree of 3 December 2013, containing 'Technical rules on the preservation system', and by international standards.

778. Document management, for the Italian legislator, is a process that can be divided into three main phases: formation, management and preservation. Within each of these phases a series of activities are envisaged, and take place, that differ

163. *See* G. Corasaniti, 'Prove digitali e interventi giudiziari sulla rete nel percorso della giurisprudenza di legittimità', in 'Diritto dell'informazione e dell'informatica', fasc. 3, 2011; M. Daniele, 'La formazione digitale delle prove dichiarative: l'esame a distanza tra regole interne e diritto sovranazionale' (Giappichelli, Torino, 2012); S. Aterno, 'Le investigazioni informatiche e l'acquisizione della prova', in 'Giurisprudenza di merito', fasc. 4, 2013; M. Rocchi, 'Le prove digitali nel processo civile: profili giuridici e informatico-forensi' (Pacini giuridica, Pisa, 2021).

in complexity, impact, nature, purpose and/or effect, including legal, to which distinct methodological approaches and operating practices correspond.

779. The computerized document management system, the maintenance of which may also be delegated to third parties, in order for it to be efficient and secure, must necessarily be governed by specific computer procedures and tools, capable of effectively governing each and every event that involves the life of the document and carried out in accordance with the general principles applicable to the processing of personal data, also by means of an adequate risk analysis. Moreover, proper document management from the time of their creation is the best guarantee for the correct fulfilment of administrative, legal and archival obligations typical of public archives management.

780. From an archival point of view, a distinction can be made between three management phases according to the different ways in which documents are organized and used: (*i*) current archive (concerning documents necessary for current activities), (*ii*) deposit archive (concerning documents still useful for administrative or legal purposes, but no longer indispensable for current activities), and (*iii*) historical archive (concerning historical documents selected for permanent preservation).

781. At the training stage, the objectives of quality, efficiency, rationality, systematicity, accessibility and consistency with the technical rules that govern the formation of computerized documents must be pursued, taking due account of the requirements and practical needs of daily work. To this end, it is essential to use a valid and complete document management manual, document workflows and Document & Content Management systems and IT applications, for the Public Administration pursuant to Articles 68 and 69 of the CAD, based on high levels of automation and interoperability capable of operating on the web.

782. In an ever-changing context, the document management manual must be subject to continuous updating, due to the technological evolution and obsolescence of the digital objects and tools used. In the same way, the processes and activities that govern the formation phase of computerized documents must also undergo constant evaluation, monitoring, redesign and re-engineering. The adoption of the document management manual and the storage manual does not only respond to practical-operational needs but represents a precise obligation for the Public Administration followed by the further obligation of their publication on the institutional website of the entity.

783. Computerized document management continues with its transfer to a preservation system to be implemented in compliance with the provisions of the CAD and the Guidelines. Document preservation is typically carried out within a preservation system dedicated to this function. However, attention must be paid to the preservation profile from the moment the document is created, in order to guarantee its preservation within the computerized document management system and possible long-term preservation within dedicated systems.

784. In the context of document management, it may be necessary to transfer documents in a different format from the original one. This reversion may occur several times in the management of the computer document and at different times for management or preservation purposes.

785. Finally, in the digital sphere, the obligations of publication of administrative acts and measures having the effect of legal publicity or in any case deriving from transparency regulations must be fulfilled with publication on the respective institutional websites. In order for the online publication process to generate a product capable of fulfilling the aforementioned obligations, it must guarantee the conformity of what is published with the original, the authoritativeness of the issuing body and the website, the legal validity of the documents and therefore their truthfulness, effectiveness and durability over time.

§2. The Norms

786. Digital preservation of documents was introduced by Legislative Decree No. 82 of 7 March 2005, better known as the 'Digital Administration Code' (CAD). Chapter III of the CAD outlines the legal framework for the formation, management and preservation of computerized documents, laying the foundations for the dematerialization of documents in accordance with the law in public administration and beyond. The CAD also contains the definition: 'Digital Preservation means the set of processes and activities that guarantee the accessibility, usability, authenticity and retrievability of digital documents and computer files in the medium and long term, thanks to the use of practices and technologies identified by the standard'.

787. The ultimate purpose of the regulation-compliant preservation of digital documents aimed at by the Italian legislator is to make the documents themselves available even decades later, ensuring the integrity of the information contained and its form.[164]

788. The Italian legislator started with the definition of the characteristics of the digital document according to the reference standards and, in particular, Article 44 of the CAD, to precisely identify the four fundamental tasks performed by this preservation system. In particular, the system ensures (i) the certain identification of the subject producing the document, (ii) the integrity of the document, (iii) the readability and easy retrieval of the documents and identifying information, and (iv) compliance with the security measures for the data and documents stored.

789. According to Italian law, this framework covers documents of entities and companies such as the journal, inventory book, auxiliary records (assets, income

164. *See* G. Rognetta, 'L'archiviazione ottica dei documenti: profili giuridici della conservazione digitale dei documenti' (Giuffrè, Milano, 2003); F. Ruggieri, 'Novità. il protocollo 16 alla cedu in vigore dal 1° agosto 2018. la proposta per l'ordine europeo di conservazione o di produzione della prova digitale', in 'Cassazione Penale', fasc. 7, 2018.

and stock), depreciable assets register, registers useful for VAT purposes, tax returns, company books, financial statements, management reports, active and passive invoices and tax receipts, transport documents, customs records, payroll and employee register.

790. The central role in the digital preservation process is entrusted to the 'Preservation Officer'. He is entrusted with the task of affixing the digital signature and time stamp to the preserved documents, certifying that the digital preservation process has been carried out correctly. His contribution is constitutive of the Preservation system because he defines the system's characteristics and requirements.

791. Specifically, the functions of the Conservation Manager are as follows: drafting and keeping the Conservation manual, verifying the correct operation of the Conservation system and management programmes, defining security procedures, managing information on document content, identifying the Conservation Manager and any delegated powers, verifying, at regular intervals not exceeding five years, the actual usability of the preserved documents, proceeding with the direct or replacement transfer of content, ensuring the presence of a public official in cases where this is required.

792. Outsourcing of the Digital Preservation process is provided for in Article 44-*bis* of the CAD. Public or private entities that perform the activity of Digital Document Preservation on behalf of third parties must be accredited according to the modality defined by AgID in Circular No. 65 of 10 April 2014.

793. In a constantly evolving framework, the standards and technical rules that regulate the issue of digital substitution have stratified over time and to date they are: the technical rules laid down in the Decree of 3 December 2013 of the President of the Council of Ministers, the Digital Administration Code or CAD (Legislative Decree No. 82 of 7 March 2005), the preservation of cultural heritage (Legislative Decree 22 January 2004 No. 42), data protection legislation (Personal Data Protection Code – Legislative Decree No. 196 of 30 June 2003) and GDPR, the provisions on administrative documentation (Presidential Decree No. 445 of 28 December 2000), the rules on administrative procedure (Law No. 241 of 7 August 1990) and the computerized document (Civil Code Article 2215-*bis*).

794. The Agenzia per l'Italia Digitale (Digital Italy Agency) defines the operating methods for carrying out the preservation activity, i.e., nature and function of the system organizational models; roles and functions of the subjects involved; description of the preservation process; professional profiles of the managers involved in the preservation process.

795. Public administrations are required to preserve all documents formed in the course of their administrative action. Also the daily protocol register, as of 11 October 2015, according to Article 7, paragraph 5 of the Technical Rules for IT Protocol, must be sent for preservation within the next working day.

796. Determination No. 455/2021 adopted the Regulation on the Criteria for the Provision of Computerised Document Preservation Services, accompanied by Annex A, which contains the general requirements as well as the quality, security and organizational requirements necessary for the provision of the service, and Annex B, which contains the indications for the service termination plan.

797. By Resolution No. 629/2021, the amended text of the Regulation was approved with regard to the platform through which it will be possible to submit the application for qualification.

798. Administrations that entrust the computerized document preservation service to parties not registered in the 'preservation services' section of the Cloud Marketplace are obliged to transmit the relevant contracts to AgID within thirty days of signing them so that the Agency can carry out the verification activities of the general requirements as well as the quality, security and organizational requirements set out in Annex A to the Regulation.

799. The Regulation supplements what has already been defined in the Guidelines on the formation, management and preservation of computerized documents, issued in September 2020.

800. Consisting of two technical annexes, the Regulation is issued in accordance with the provisions of Article 34, paragraph 1-*bis* of Legislative Decree No. 82/2005, as supplemented and amended by the Simplification Decree (Decree-Law No. 76/2020), converted by Law No. 120/2020 and entered into force on 1 January 2022, the date from which Circular No. 65/2014 is repealed.

801. The role of preservation manager may only be held by a natural person employed by the party producing the documents to be preserved, who entrusts the preservation activities to the preservation manager. Consistent with what is indicated in relation to the subjects to which the Guidelines apply, this constraint applies to all subjects. For parties other than the Public Administration, pursuant to paragraph 4.6 Preservation Officer of the Guidelines, the role of the preservation officer may be performed by a person external to the organization, with suitable legal, IT and archival skills, provided that he/she is third party with respect to the Preservation Officer in order to guarantee the function of the Preservation Holder with respect to the preservation system.

802. Pursuant to Article 2(3) of the Digital Administration Code, it follows that the Guidelines issued apply to all entities, including private entities, unless otherwise provided, that perform preservation activities.

Chapter 6. Consumer Protection in Online Sales and Services

§1. The Protection of Online Consumers

803. In the Italian regulatory framework, 2023 was an important year for the protection of online consumers: there was, in fact, a great deal of legislative activity to supplement the rules on e-commerce, and the *Consumer Code*, with specific rules that would better protect users of online services in particular.[165]

In particular, e-commerce and marketplaces are affected by the new rules, effective as of 2 April 2023, introduced by Legislative Decree No. 26 of 7 March 2023,[166] implementing the EU *Consumer Protection Directive* 2019/2161.

804. E-commerce and online platforms must now update their general terms and conditions of sale and, in some cases, revise the commercial policies they follow, especially with regard to prices and online reviews.

Already at the end of 2021, new provisions, also of EU derivation, were added to the *Consumer Code* concerning contracts for the supply of digital content and digital services (Article 135-*octies* ff.), which affected e-commerce and are now further amended.

805. The changes to the Consumer Code for e-commerce in 2023 intended, for the first time,

i. to define digital marketplaces, so-called platforms that intermediate sales between several professionals and consumers or between consumers, and to regulate their transparency, in particular with regard to the positioning of products online;
ii. to regulate online reviews, and price and product transparency concerning both online shops and physical shops;
iii. to regulate (further) information concerning e-commerce and the right of withdrawal;
iv. to apply new rules to the provision of consumer data in exchange for a service or digital content and higher penalties with consumer's right to damages.

806. The Consumer Code defines 'online marketplace' a service using software, including websites, part of websites or an application, operated by or on behalf of the trader, which enables consumers to conclude distance contracts with other traders or consumers.

---

165. *See* C. Dalia, 'Sanzioni e rimedi individuali 'effettivi' per il consumatore in caso di pratiche commerciali scorrette: le novità introdotte dalla direttiva 2161/2019/UE', in 'Rivista di diritto industriale', fasc. 6, 2020; L. Guffanti Pesenti, 'Pratiche commerciali scorrette e rimedi nuovi. La difficile trasposizione dell'art. 3, co. 1, N. 5), dir. 2019/2161/UE', in 'Europa e diritto privato', fasc. 4, 2021; A. Purpura, 'Private enforcement delle pratiche commerciali scorrette: il nuovo comma 15-*bis* dell'art. 27 c. cons', in 'Europa e diritto privato', fasc. 4, 2023.
166. *See* the full text at https://www.normattiva.it/uri-res/N2Ls?urn:nir:stato:decreto.legislativo:2023;026.

807. Article 45(1)(q-*ter*) of the Consumer Code states information obligations of digital marketplaces. Digital marketplaces have specific and additional information obligations with respect to e-commerce, both with regard to the positioning of products and the identity and role of sellers operating on the platform.

808. The new regulation now requires that the consumer who is about to make a purchase on a marketplace receive the following information:

i. The criteria that determine the positioning (ranking) of the products listed as a result of a search carried out by a consumer and, in particular, whether such positioning is due to the payment of a sum by the seller [Article 49-*bis* letter a]. As is well known, the products at the top of the rankings and with greater visibility are those most chosen by the consumer: the Consumer Code requires that the same consumer be informed in advance of the criteria chosen by the marketplace to display the products and whether the sellers pay for the positioning. The Consumer Code wants to prevent the consumer from being *induced to buy* on the marketplace erroneously convinced that the products shown are more convenient for him on the basis of neutral criteria or the real opinions of customers.
ii. The presence of sellers who are themselves consumers is not subject to the obligations of the Consumer Code. The online platform must inform that the advertisement or the product displayed is not of a professional, but of a *private individual* and 'must inform the consumer making the purchase that the rights ... arising from European Union law on consumer protection do not apply to the contract' [Article 49-*bis* letter b-c].
iii. Search engines, in fact, are also required to disclose the criteria that affect ranking not only for the benefit of the consumer but especially for the benefit of e-commerce and marketplaces themselves, which must also understand the reasons for decisions that affect them, e.g., the change or deletion of a search engine ranking due to a third party's report.
iv. E-commerce and platforms that publish reviews must disclose whether and how they guarantee that the published reviews come from consumers who have actually purchased or used the product.

809. In this regard, the following conduct is expressly considered misleading business practices:

i. Stating reviews as verified without taking reasonable and proportionate steps to verify that the reviews come from such consumers.
ii. Publishing false reviews or posting and causing to be posted false reviews of consumers or instructing others to post or provide them.

In practice, e-commerce companies will be able to publish on their website or reviews of consumers with verified purchases on their website or to engage third-party providers to issue reviews that give guarantees of reliability. The alternative of stating that reviews are not verified is for many small e-commerce companies an unfeasible route because consumers would not be enticed to buy.

810. Among the most important new features is the regulation on *price reduction announcements* (Article 17-*bis*), announcements that, by attracting consumers' attention, influence their purchasing decisions.

The announcements, both online and in physical shops, must indicate both the reduction and the previous price, with the clarification that previous price means the lowest price applied by the trader at least thirty days before the reduction.

811. During sales, where the physical or online shop gradually increases the discount, the previous price to be indicated is always the price before the first reduction. This also applies to the identification of the normal selling price to be displayed during extraordinary sales, while sales below cost remain governed by Articles 15(5) and (7) of Legislative Decree No. 114/1998, reforming the regulations in the trade sector.

Violation of the new rules on price reduction announcements will result in fines ranging from EUR 516 to EUR 3,098.

812. For online sales and contracts negotiated away from business premises, a new provision of the Consumer Code (Article 49 letter e-*bis*) requires that the consumer be informed if the price has been personalized on the basis of an *automated decision-making process* (and if it is admissible under the GDPR). This is the case, for example, with airline tickets.

If the price is the result of online profiling, it must of course be verified that this is in line with the privacy regulation and that all disclosures are complete, and it must also be specified in the general conditions of sale of the e-commerce.

813. Especially with a view to *preventing fraud* in the agri-food sector, it is also specified that any marketing activity that promotes a good, in a Member State of the European Union, is identical to a good marketed in other member states, while this good has a significantly different composition or characteristics, is misleading unless justified by legitimate and objective factors.[167]

814. Among the novelties, the Consumer Code contains new mandatory information that e-commerce must provide, in particular:

i. The geographical address where the trader is established, his telephone number and his electronic address. Moreover, all means of communication provided by the trader must enable the consumer to contact him quickly and communicate with him effectively. Where applicable, the trader shall also provide the geographical address and the identity of the trader on whose behalf he is acting.

167. *See* R. Palma, 'Agro-ecologia e indicazioni geografiche tra magia e razionalità nel diritto dell'UE e dell'OMC: 'reinventare' le designazioni d'origine per preservare l'economia rurale, il patrimonio culturale e l'ambiente', in 'Rivista di Diritto Industriale', fasc. 6, 2017; M. Imbrenda, 'Filiera agroalimentare e pratiche commerciali sleali', in 'Europa e diritto privato', fasc. 4, 2019; G. Spoto, 'Le filiere agroalimentari e i divieti di pratiche commerciali sleali', in 'Europa e diritto privato', fasc. 1, 2022.

ii. A reminder of the existence of the legal guarantee of conformity for goods, digital content and digital services.
iii. E-commerce shops must specify in their general terms and conditions of sale that the right of withdrawal lapses if the consumer accepts the service during the withdrawal period and is thus made aware of the loss of his right.

§2. PROVISION OF DATA

815. The provisions of the Consumer Code (Articles 48-67) now also apply to any supply or undertaking to supply the consumer's personal data in exchange for digital content through a non-material medium or a digital service promised or provided by the trader to the consumer.

816. This excludes cases where the personal data provided by the consumer are processed by the trader exclusively for the purpose of supplying the digital content on a non-material medium or the digital service [...] or to enable the performance of legal obligations to which the trader is subject, and the trader does not process those data for any other purpose.

817. The definition of *digital service* has been changed by the new Article 45(1)(q-*bis*) of the Consumer Code and now includes a service enabling the consumer to create, transform, store or access data in digital form; or services enabling the sharing of data in digital format uploaded or created by the consumer or other users of that service or any other interaction with such data.

818. The maximum administrative fine for unfair commercial practices has been doubled to EUR 10 million.

For example, the operator of a platform who, without clearly indicating this to the consumer, is paid to get sellers to rank products better in the search results, in addition to having to cease the aforementioned practice, may be sanctioned by the Italian Competition Authority with a fine ranging from EUR 5,000 to EUR 10 million.

The same ceiling applies to the sanction resulting from the detection of the use of unfair terms by the Competition Authority (Article 37-*bis*, paragraph 2-*bis*). In both cases, if the infringements concern more than one Member State (as specified by Regulation (EU) 2017/2394), the sanction may be up to 4% of the trader's annual turnover achieved in Italy or in the EU States concerned.

Furthermore, for unfair commercial practices, where information on annual turnover is not available, the maximum amount is EUR 2 million.

Finally, in the case of unsafe products or products sold through unfair commercial practices that threaten, even indirectly, the safety of children and adolescents, the minimum penalty is still EUR 50,000.

819. As for civil actions, it is made explicit that injured consumers may bring an action before the ordinary courts in order to obtain proportionate and effective remedies, including compensation for the damage suffered and, where applicable, reduction of the price or termination of the contract, taking into account, where appropriate, the seriousness and nature of the unfair commercial practice, the damage suffered and other relevant circumstances, without prejudice to other available remedies.

§3. Goods with Digital Elements

820. Goods with digital elements are also covered by the legal guarantee of conformity and include goods with digital content, i.e., goods whose data are produced and supplied in digital form; and goods sold with digital services.

821. When selling goods with digital elements, the seller (whether e-commerce or physical retailer) is obliged to inform the consumer about available updates, including security updates, necessary to maintain the conformity of the goods and to provide them to the consumer.

If the supply of the digital content or service is continuous, this obligation extends for the statutory two years or, in any case, for the longest time stipulated in the contract. The law thus makes it incumbent on the seller to inform about digital updates to the goods and provide them to the consumer.

822. The seller may be held liable for the non-compliance of the product if the consumer does not receive them, or if he fails to complete the installation or updates, due to a deficiency in the installation instructions or updates provided by the manufacturer.

This may be the case, for example, with products that provide installation/update instructions only in English, which the average consumer cannot understand.

823. The seller is only exempt from liability if he proves that the product's deficiencies are due to the consumer not having been informed and having received adequate update instructions.[168]

824. The remedies available to consumers due to product non-conformity are: repair, replacement, price reduction and termination of the contract.

The consumer may refuse to make payment of the price as long as the seller has not fulfilled its warranty obligations for the product.

825. In the first instance, in the event of non-conformity, the consumer may request, at his or her choice, the repair or replacement of the goods. Repair or replacement is free of charge for the consumer, who need only make the goods available. The seller repairs or takes back the replaced non-conforming products at his own expense. Moreover, if the non-conforming product has already been installed, the seller shall uninstall and re-install the replaced or repaired product.

---

168. A. Sardini, 'La 'product liability' e il commercio elettronico', in 'Il diritto dell'informazione e dell'informatica', fasc. 1, 2021.

826. The consumer is not obliged to pay for the normal use of the goods prior to replacement. The seller or e-commerce may refuse to carry out the repair or replacement if this is impossible or the costs are disproportionate. In that case, the consumer shall be entitled to a price reduction or termination of the contract.

827. A proportional price reduction or termination of the contract may occur if: the seller does not carry out the repair or replacement, or the seller declares that it cannot carry them out because they are impossible or uneconomic; if the lack of conformity becomes apparent after repair or replacement; if the defect is so serious as to justify immediate price reduction or termination of the contract.

The consumer is not entitled to a price reduction if the lack of conformity is minor; it is for the seller to prove that the defect is minor.

The seller must reimburse the part of the price proportionate to the reduction in value suffered by the goods as a result of the lack of conformity.

828. Termination of the contract may be exercised by the consumer by means of a declaration of will to that effect addressed to the seller. Termination may concern all the contractual goods or, at the consumer's choice, only some of the goods received. In particular, the consumer may terminate the entire contract if he has no interest in keeping only the goods free from defects.

Upon termination of the contract, the goods are returned to the seller at the seller's expense and the seller or e-commerce will refund the consumer the price upon receipt of the goods or proof that the goods have been shipped.

829. The consumer may assert the statutory warranty within twenty-six months after delivery.

Defects are presumed to exist (and thus to be borne by the seller), for one year after delivery of the product, instead of six months. The consumer is no longer required to report defects within two months of discovery.

The consumer protection provisions of the Consumer Code are mandatory and prevail, rendering all contrary provisions in the general terms and conditions of sale or consumer contracts null and void.

830. The nullity may be asserted by the consumer and detected ex officio by the judge. The consumer is also entitled to compensation for damages under the Italian Civil Code. In addition, he may rely on any additional, more favourable commercial guarantees, if any, provided by the seller.

§4. Main Case Law ('Jurisprudence') of Court of Justice on the Topic

831. Court of Justice EU section V, 30/05/2024, No. 400. In a contract to be concluded online, the automatism between the placing of the order and the obligation to pay must be clear. In the case of contracts concluded at a distance through Internet sites, it is important to ensure that the consumer can determine *the moment* at which he assumes the obligation to pay the trader and to specifically draw the consumer's attention, by means of unambiguous wording, to the fact that placing an order entails an obligation to pay the trader. The order placing button or a similar function must clearly indicate that, by clicking on it, the consumer enters into an obligation to pay, and this applies even if the obligation to pay depends on the fulfilment of an additional condition.

832. ECJ section III, 05/05/2022, No. 179. A trader who sells goods made by others online must inform the consumer of the manufacturer's guarantee only if he makes it a determining factor in his offer.

A trader who sells online a good made by others must inform the consumer of the manufacturer's warranty only if he makes it a determining element of his offer. For the EU Court, it is right to protect the buyer, but an unconditional obligation to provide all warranties attached to the good, including the manufacturer's commercial warranty, is disproportionate. In order to determine whether the manufacturer's commercial guarantee is an essential condition, account must be taken of the content and general scheme of the offer in relation to the good, the importance, in terms of sales argument or advertising message, of the mention of the manufacturer's commercial guarantee, the position occupied by that mention in the offer the risk of error or confusion that such an indication might induce in the average consumer, who is reasonably well informed and reasonably observant and sensitive to the types of guarantees that he may exercise, the presence or absence in the offer of explanations relating to other guarantees attached to the goods, and any other element capable of establishing a need for consumer protection.

833. EU Court of Justice VI, 25/06/2020, No. 380. General terms and conditions of online sales or service contracts with consumers must include information about the alternative dispute resolution body. Article 6(1) of Directive 2011/83 is intended to ensure the provision to the consumer, prior to the conclusion of a contract, both information concerning the contractual terms and conditions and the consequences of that conclusion, enabling that consumer to decide whether he wishes to be bound by a contract with a trader, and of the information necessary for the proper performance of that contract and, in particular, for the exercise of his rights. In order for the consumer to be able to benefit from that information for that purpose, he must receive it in good time before the conclusion of the contract and not only at the stage of its conclusion, since the information provided prior to that conclusion is, for the consumer, of fundamental importance.

834. EU Court of Justice section I, 10/07/2019, No. 649. An e-commerce website is not obliged to make available to the consumer a telephone number, but any means of rapid and accessible contact. An e-commerce platform is not obliged to make a telephone number available to the consumer. Indeed, in order to ensure due protection, it is only necessary to ensure rapid contact and effective communication by accessible, clear and comprehensible means, the choice of technical means remaining at the discretion of the business. Thus, the Court of Justice of the European Union ruled out the obligation for professionals to activate a dedicated telephone line, shielding online sellers from overly rigid national rules that could create excessive burdens. In the case at hand, the Federal Union of German Consumer Associations argued that the company Amazon EU had failed to adequately provide telephone and fax facilities, as required by German law, in violation of the Consumer Rights Directive 2011/83. For the Luxembourg judges, however, this reading is wrong, as the unconditional obligation to provide the consumer with a telephone line or to create a new email address is a disproportionate burden.

835. Court of Justice EU section VI, 27/03/2019, No. 681. Mattress bought online: a consumer who removes the protective film is entitled to a right of withdrawal unless the seller is compensated if it reduces the value. It does not fall within the notion of 'sealed goods that are not suitable to be returned for hygienic or health protection reasons and opened after delivery' those goods such as a mattress where the protective film is removed by the consumer after delivery following an online purchase, the consumer, in these cases, may exercise the right of withdrawal guaranteed by Directive 2011/83. However, if his action causes a decrease in the value of the returned goods, he will have to compensate the seller.

Chapter 7. Liability of Online Service Providers

§1. Introduction to the Topic, and First Definitions

836. The issue of the liability of *Internet Service Providers* (ISP) and platforms is experiencing a moment of *great change* in Italy in 2024.

In fact, there is an ongoing process of updating and adapting to European Union regulations – in particular the *Digital Markets Act* and the *Digital Services Act* – which will lead, in the coming months/years, to a *new framework* that will overcome a discipline that has been in place in Italy for almost twenty-five years, i.e., since the 2000s.[169]

It was, in fact, at the end of the old millennium, with the start of e-commerce and of the first services on platforms also in Europe, that the Italian legislator began to acknowledge the indications of the European Union aimed at creating a single digital market that would allow the start-up of this new, fundamental economy also in the Old Continent.[170]

The principle underlying the reform of that time, which remains, albeit with some adaptations, also in today's framework, is that of the *general non-liability* of the provider for the content that is received and circulates on its systems, with, at the same time, a *duty to intervene* for the removal or control of the content when the entrepreneur is alerted to the presence of unlawful content.[171]

837. Briefly, the regulation of Internet service provider liability is derived, also in Italy, from European Union rules, which have been implemented, over the years, in domestic law.

This means, in concrete terms, that the Italian regulatory framework does not present any particular *original* characteristics compared to the other countries that are part of the European Union. We will, therefore, sketch a very brief outline below.

838. From a *definition* point of view, in Italy, the locution 'Internet Service Provider' refers to the organization, or infrastructure, of an *entrepreneurial nature* that

169. *See* A. Manganelli, 'Piattaforme digitali e social network, fra pluralità degli ordinamenti, pluralismo informativo e potere di mercato', in 'Giurisprudenza Costituzionale', fasc. 2, 2023, p. 883; V. Falce, 'Piattaforme ed ecosistemi digitali. Scelte pro-concorrenziali', in 'Rivista di Diritto Industriale', fasc. 4-5-6, 2022, p. 172; A. Alù, 'La responsabilità dei motori di ricerca: quale regime applicabile?', in 'Diritto di Famiglia e delle Persone' (Il), fasc. 1, 2021, p. 338; R. Panetta, 'Il ruolo dell'Internet Service Provider e i profili di responsabilità civile', in 'Responsabilità Civile e Previdenza', fasc. 3, 2019, p. 1017.

170. *See* R. Petruso, 'Responsabilità degli intermediari di Internet e nuovi obblighi di conformazione: robo-takedown, policy of termination, noice and take steps', in 'Europa e Diritto Privato', fasc. 2, 2017, p. 451.

171. *See* G. Mirabile, 'Le tendenze evolutive della giurisprudenza riguardo alla nozione di attività pericolosa', in 'Responsabilità Civile e Previdenza', fasc. 2, 2018, p. 454. *See, also*, M. De Cata, 'La responsabilità civile dell'Internet service provider'(Giuffrè, Milano, 2010); E. Apa, O. Pollicino, 'Modeling the liability of internet service providers: Google vs. Vivi down. A constitutional perspective' (EGEA, Milano, 2013); R. D'Arrigo, 'Recenti sviluppi in tema di responsabilità degli Internet Services Providers'(Giuffrè, Milano, 2012).

offers users, by means of a *supply contract*, services relating to the Internet (e.g., access to the web and e-mail, data sharing or storage, etc.).

From a regulatory point of view, Internet service providers are called 'information society service providers', and their activity is regulated in Italy by Legislative Decree No. 70/2003,[172] issued in implementation of European Directive 31/2000/EC[173] on *electronic commerce.*

839. As is well known, this regulatory framework identifies *three* different figures of ISPs, corresponding to three different types of services:

i. *mere transport* (cd. 'mere conduit'), which consists of transmitting, over a communication network, information provided by a 'recipient of the service' (the user) or in providing access to the communication network;
ii. *temporary storage* (so-called caching), which consists of the 'automatic, intermediate and temporary storage' of information provided by a user, carried out for the sole purpose of making more effective the subsequent forwarding to other recipients at their request, and
iii. *information storage* (so-called hosting); an activity consisting in the storage of information provided by a user.[174]

§2. The General Principles of Responsibility

840. The Italian Decree No. 70/2003 establishes some *general principles* of responsibility that apply to all ISPs, and some *specific rules* that vary for each of the three types of activity.[175]

A general principle is that ISPs are *not responsible* for the information processed and the operations carried out by the users who use the service unless they *intervene* in the content or performance of the operations themselves.

Furthermore, there is no *general duty of vigilance*, so the provider has no obligation to monitor the information it transmits or stores, nor to actively seek out facts or circumstances indicating the presence of illegal activities.

In view of this, the provider has *two fundamental duties* of disclosure and cooperation with the authorities:

i. when it becomes aware of alleged unlawful activities or information concerning a user, it must inform the supervisory (judicial or administrative) authorities without delay;

---

172. *See* the full official text, in Italian, at https://www.normattiva.it/uri-res/N2Ls?urn:nir:stato:decreto.legislativo:2003-04-09;70.
173. *See* the full official text at https://eur-lex.europa.eu/legal-content/IT/TXT/?uri=CELEX%3A32000L0031.
174. *See* M. Iaselli, 'Responsabilità del provider: la Cassazione detta rilevanti principi di diritto', at https://www.altalex.com/documents/news/2019/03/20/diritto-d-autore-responsabilita-dell-hosting-provider.
175. *See* R. Panetta, 'Il ruolo dell'internet service provider e i profili di responsabilità civile', in 'Responsabilità civile e previdenza', fasc. 3, 2019, p. 1017.

ii. it must provide without delay, at the request of the authorities, the information in its possession that is useful for *identifying* the user with whom it has data storage agreements, in order to identify and prevent unlawful activities.

841. The provider is liable under civil law for the *content* of the services (i.e., it is obliged to compensate for damages suffered by third parties) when requested by the supervisory authorities, it does not act promptly to prevent access to the content or does not inform the authorities having become aware of the unlawful or harmful nature of the content.

According to Article 15 of Legislative Decree No. 70/2003, the *cache provider* is exempt from liability for content posted by others when he is in no way involved in the information transmitted, does not modify it, and does not actively collaborate in the offence.

842. The liability of *hosting* is regulated by Article 16 of the Decree, which states that hosting is not liable for the information stored if it is not *actually aware* that the activity or information is unlawful, or if, as soon as it becomes aware of unlawful facts, upon notification by the competent authorities, it takes *immediate action* to remove the information or to disable access to it.

This *favourable regime* applies to so-called passive hosting, which performs a purely technical, automated service.

843. In the sphere of information society services, the liability of the hosting provider, provided for in Article 16 of Legislative Decree No. 70 of 9 April 2003, applies to a service provider who has failed to immediately remove unlawful content, as well as if it has continued to publish it, even where the following conditions are jointly met:

i. it has legal knowledge of the unlawfulness perpetrated by the recipient of the service, either because it has had knowledge of it from the holder of the right infringed or *aliunde*;
ii. the unlawfulness of another's conduct is reasonably ascertainable so that he is grossly negligent for not having ascertained it, in accordance with the degree of diligence reasonably to be expected of a professional network operator at a given time;
iii. has the possibility of taking useful action, inasmuch as he has been made sufficiently aware of the unlawful content to be removed.

§3. 'Protected Content' in the Copyright Framework

844. The *Copyright Directive* (EU) 2019/790[176] and the implementing decree in Italy of the directive (Legislative Decree No. 177/2021[177]) introduced Title

176. *See* the official text at https://eur-lex.europa.eu/eli/dir/2019/790/oj.
177. *See* the official text at https://www.normattiva.it/uri-res/N2Ls?urn:nir:stato:decreto.legislativo:2021-11-08;177.

II-*quater* to Law No. 633/1941[178] establishing specific provisions on the 'Use of protected content by providers of online content-sharing services', consisting of Articles 102-*sexies* to 102-*decies*.

845. Article 102-*sexies* defines a provider as a service provider with the following requirements:

i. the main purpose is to store and give public access to large quantities of works or other materials protected by copyright;
ii. the works or other protected materials are uploaded by users;
iii. the protected works are organized and promoted for the purpose of profiting from them either directly or indirectly.

The rule specifies that the following *cannot be considered* as providers of online sharing services:

i. providers that give access to non-profit online encyclopaedias and educational or scientific directories;
ii. open source software development and sharing platforms;
iii. providers of electronic communication services;
iv. providers of online marketplaces, business-to-business cloud service providers;
v. cloud service providers that allow users to upload content for personal use.

Sharing service providers, however, include providers of online marketplaces or cloud services that allow protected works to be shared between multiple users.

846. Article 102 clarifies, also, that providers perform an act of communication to the public when they allow access to copyrighted works or other protected material uploaded by their users.

In order to legitimately carry out this type of activity, they must obtain *authorization* from the right holders by concluding a *licence agreement.*

Authorization also covers acts performed by users of services that upload protected content onto the platform if they are not acting on a commercial basis or if their activity does not generate significant revenue.

847. Article 102-*septies* regulates the liability regime of providers and users in the event of failure to obtain authorization from right holders.

In the event of failure to obtain authorization, service providers are held liable for unauthorized acts of communication to the public.

Liability is, however, excluded when service providers *can prove* that they have made *every effort* to obtain an authorization according to high standards of professional diligence prevent works and other materials for which they have received

178. *See* the official text, in Italian, at https://www.normattiva.it/uri-res/N2Ls?urn:nir:stato:legge:1941-04-22;633.

information from right holders from not being made available, disable access to or remove the reported works or other materials from their websites and prohibit them from being uploaded in the future (action must be taken *promptly* after receipt of a substantiated report from the right holders).

848. Article 102-*octies* provides that mitigated obligations regarding the control and removal of unauthorized content apply to providers of sharing services that have been publicly available for less than three years and have an annual turnover of less than EUR 10 million.

849. Article 102-*nonies* contains the rules on *cooperation* between platforms and right holders.

This cooperation facilitates the availability of works or other materials uploaded by users (which do not infringe copyright or related rights), while also safeguarding the case where such works or other materials are subject to an exception or limitation.

In fact, users may make use of the exceptions or limitations for the cases of:

i. quotation, criticism, review;
ii. use for the purpose of caricature, parody or pastiche.

Notice of this opportunity is given by the service providers in their terms and conditions.

850. Article 102-*decies* regulates the complaint and removal procedures in the event of disputes regarding the disabling or removal of content made available by users in the presence of alleged infringements of rights.

§4. The Most Recent Case Law ('Jurisprudence') in Italy Regarding ISPs Liability

851. De-indexing: Court of Milan, section I, 31 March 2023, decision No. 1378, about procedure for applying for de-indexing. It is the *onus* of the applicant claiming his right to be forgotten to identify *precisely* the URLs in respect of which he requests de-indexing, since the Internet Service Provider is not obliged to carry out an 'active search' of the allegedly unlawful contents it indexes, as established by Article 17 of Legislative Decree No. 70 of 2003.

852. Limits to the hosting provider's liability: Court of Milan, section I, 15 February 2023, decision No. 1208. The hosting provider is not, in general, subject either to a widespread obligation to monitor the information it transmits or stores, or to a general obligation to actively seek facts or circumstances indicating the presence of unlawful activities on the platforms it manages, unless it fails to remove content it knows to be manifestly unlawful.

853. *Knowledge of falsity of contents:* Court of Cassation, Civil section I, 8 June 2022, decision No. 18430. The hosting service provider is liable for the information and for the storage of information provided by a recipient of the service, if it has been warned of the falsity or erroneous nature of the information, and has failed to de-index the URLs indicated in the request by the applicant.

854. *Precision of indication of the content to remove:* Court of Cassation, Civil section I, 13 December 2021, decision No. 39763. In the context of the assessment of the actual knowledge of the unlawful act required in order to establish the liability of the hosting provider pursuant to Article 16 of Legislative Decree No. 70/2003, it is for the court of the merits to ascertain whether the identification of videos broadcast in breach of another person's right is possible by indicating only the name or title of the broadcast from which they are taken, or whether it is indispensable to communicate the URL address of the web page where the videos are located, in the light of the state of the art at the time of the events.

In the context of information society services, the liability of the hosting provider is incurred by the service provider who does not immediately remove the unlawful content when the following conditions are jointly fulfilled:

i. the service provider is aware of the unlawful act perpetrated by the recipient of the service by reason of having been informed of it by the holder of the right affected or aliunde;
ii. the unlawfulness of the conduct of another person is reasonably ascertainable, and there is therefore gross negligence for not having detected it in a positive manner in accordance with the diligence that can reasonably be expected of a professional network operator at a given moment in time; and
iii. the service provider has the possibility of taking useful action since it was made sufficiently aware of the unlawful content to be removed.

The active hosting provider is the provider of the services of the information society who performs an activity that goes beyond a merely technical, automatic and passive service, and instead engages in active conduct by participating in the commission of the unlawful act of others so that he is exempt from the exemption regime provided for in Article 16 of Legislative Decree No. 70/2003.

855. *Right to be forgotten:* Court of Cassation, Civil section I, 21 July 2021, decision No. 20861. On the subject of the right to be forgotten, the judicial application for the de-indexing of certain web pages must contain the precise identification of the search results to be removed, both for procedural reasons, since the document instituting the proceedings requires, on pain of nullity, the indication of the mediated '*petitum*', and for substantive reasons, since the obligation for the 'provider' to intervene presupposes the latter's knowledge of the existence of content liable to be removed.

Moreover, it is the identification of said results that enables the judge to carry out, in the individual case, the fundamental balancing act between the right to protection of personal data and the public interest in information, on the basis of factual elements acquired at the trial and submitted to the contradictory nature of the parties.

856. Delay in removing illegal content: Court of Rome, Section Specialized in Enterprise, 22 January 2021. A neutrality of the provider that is in fact a lack of control over its own digital platform constitutes in itself a form of liability for omission, for having allowed the infringement of third party rights.

In the case in point, the provider had not acted promptly to remove the contested content, taking an average of *forty days* to do so, and had not acted to identify, even autonomously and in advance, the programs illegally spread on the platform even though they had already been reported.

It is up to the provider to prove that it meets the requirements to enjoy the exemption from liability provided for by Article 16 of Legislative Decree No. 70/2003, namely that it has a business structure and an organization of employees and of the management of the platform compatible with its alleged role of passive provider.

In order to consider that the provider is aware of the unlawful use of the platform carried out by the users through the dissemination of content in violation of the copyrights of others, it is necessary and sufficient that the organization of the site, or rather its search channels, is configured in such a way as to allow and facilitate the selection and grouping of the unlawfully stored content so as to favour its retrieval by the users.

857. Exemption of liability for the hosting provider: Court of Rome, 21 September 2020, Decision No. 17278. The hosting provider's exemption from liability, as enshrined in Article 16 of Legislative Decree No. 70 of 9 April 2003, is waived if the service provider is actually aware of the unlawfulness of the information stored, if it appears to be 'manifestly' unlawful, or when, having become aware of a fact that makes the content unlawful, it does not immediately take action to remove it or disable access to it.

In any case, in the presence of online content potentially damaging to the dignity of others, the judge is required to assess their objectivity and continence in relation to the topic of discussion, ordering the provider to remove the defamatory and untruthful information.

858. Difference between active and passive hosting providers and different liability profiles: Court of Rome, section XVII, 2 October 2019, decision No. 18727. The distinction between active and passive providers is relevant for the purposes of ascertaining the liability of the service provider: where the activity carried out is that of an active hosting provider, the specific rules on the exclusion of liability, provided, on the other hand, only for the operator carrying out passive hosting activities, are not applicable; in any event, the exemption from liability is also applicable to the latter where it:

i. is not actually aware of the fact that the activity or information disseminated is unlawful and, as regards actions for damages, is not aware of facts or circumstances that make manifest the unlawfulness of the activity or information;
ii. as soon as it becomes aware of such facts, upon notification by the competent authorities, acts immediately to remove the information or to disable access thereto.

859. *Definition of 'active' provider:* Court of Rome, Section Specialized in Enterprise, 12 July 2019, decision No. 14760. The failure to adopt simple and easily enforceable preventive control measures for the protection of the copyright of others, in addition to entailing a breach of the general principle of good faith, contributes to the classification of the ISP as an 'active' hosting provider. A hosting provider is considered an 'active' hosting provider when it carries out an interference with the stored data which may consist in activities of filtering, selection, indexing, organization, cataloguing, aggregation, evaluation, use, modification, extraction or promotion of the content, carried out by means of an entrepreneurial management of the service, as well as the adoption of a technique of behavioural evaluation of users in order to increase their loyalty.

In the present case, the hosting provider had an 'editorial team' to manage content; it carried out user profiling activities in order to submit to them content similar to that already viewed; it had set up cookies in order to associate content with each other; it directly suggested content, so-called staff picks, to users in order to increase their loyalty.

The regime of exemption from liability under Article 16 of Legislative Decree No. 70/2003 is reserved only for so-called passive hosting providers, i.e., ISPs that merely operate the permanent storage of data in a technical, automatic and passive manner, without knowledge and control of the stored data, and does not apply instead to so-called active hosting providers, i.e., ISPs that actively operate by exploiting, manipulating, processing, classifying and profiling data, in a non-automated manner.

Article 16 of Legislative Decree No. 70/2003, which provides for an exemption of the hosting provider's liability with respect to the information stored, derogates from a general principle of law.

Therefore, this rule must be interpreted *restrictively* (with the prohibition of analogical or extensive application) and the party that intends to make use of it must allege and prove its nature as a hosting provider (so-called passive).

A hosting provider may perform both active and passive functions, even simultaneously. The *verification* of the active or passive nature of the hosting provider therefore does not concern the legal entity as such, but the specific activity brought to the attention of the judge, who must ascertain in concrete terms the behaviour of the provider in relation to the data at issue.

860. *Civil liability:* Court of Milan, section XIV, 10 June 2019. Injunction orders taxable against intermediary providers of network access services by the judicial authority may not be postponed by the 'provider' of such services for any reason whatsoever, not even related to possible organizational difficulties, since no discretion as to the time in which to execute the order is left to the 'provider'.

Only a possible impossibility for reasons not attributable to the 'provider' could exempt the latter from the consequent liability for the non-execution or delayed execution of the judicial authority's order.

861. Copyright infringement: Court of Milan, Section Specialized in Enterprise, 22 May 2019. The intervention of the Internet Service Provider, when faced with a precautionary measure for copyright infringement, must be *rapid* in order not to nullify its effect.

In the case of infringements of copyright or related rights carried out through the Internet, where a precautionary measure requires an ISP to 'immediately take the most appropriate technical measures' to implement an injunction, the technical time required for this must be limited and must be assessed according to criteria of reasonableness taking into account both the need not to nullify the effectiveness and effectiveness of the measures adopted and the responsibility of service providers, including mere conduit providers, to take appropriate organizational measures to implement promptly any orders issued as a matter of urgency by the judicial authority.

862. Caching liability: Court of Cassation, Civil section I, 19 March 2019, decision No. 7709. In the field of information society services, liability for the removal of content in the context of so-called caching, an activity consisting in the transmission over a communication network of information provided by a recipient of the service, governed by Article 15 of Legislative Decree No. 70 of 2003, exists for the service provider who has not immediately removed the unlawful content, when the administrative or jurisdictional authority has ordered him to do so; otherwise, the service provider who provides a mere neutral 'caching' activity, the law does not require him to spontaneously remove certain contents only because he has been made aware of their unlawful nature by means of an extra-judicial warning or the submission of a judicial request.

863. Wikimedia: Court of Appeal Rome, section I, 19 February 2018, decision No. 1065. Wikimedia is a *mere hosting provider*, i.e., a provider of an information society service consisting in the 'storage of information provided by a recipient of the service', and this on the basis of the definition provided by the special rules dictated for ISPs by Directive 31/2000/CE and by the national legislation transposing it (Legislative Decree No. 70/2003), and thus by a legislative compendium that is not directly applicable in this case but contains the necessary legal guidelines of reference for the framing of the case.

In its capacity as hosting provider, Wikimedia is under no obligation to carry out a prior check on the quality of the content, when the person concerned does not activate the procedure envisaged by Wikimedia for the modification and deletion of the encyclopaedia entries in accordance with the site's rules, and the unlawfulness of the content does not appear *aliunde*, and in particular not even the existence of previous measures by the competent authority.

The liability of the Internet Service Provider must be held to exist for the information hosted (durable storage) only when the provider has actually become aware of the fact that the information is unlawful and has not acted to prevent the further dissemination thereof, and this in the absence of a general obligation to actively seek facts or circumstances indicating the presence of unlawful activities, nor can any position of guarantee be held to exist, in the absence of rules establishing the objective liability and position of the provider or the existence on his part of an obligation to monitor.

In the present case, therefore, I.S.P. had no prior obligation to carry out a check on the quality of the contents of the biography, since the person concerned had not activated the procedure for the amendment and deletion of the entries in accordance with the rules of the site and the alleged unlawfulness of the contents did not result aliunde, in particular not resulting from measures taken by the competent authority.

864. Audiovisual contents and liability: Court of Appeal Rome, Section Specialized in Enterprise, 29 April 2017, decision No. 2833. On the subject of copyright infringement through the uploading onto a digital platform of content covered by copyright, the exemption from liability provided for the provider under Article 14 of Directive 2000/31/EU and Article 16 of Legislative Decree No. 70/2003 operates only if the so-called hosting service is of a merely technical, automatic and passive nature, i.e., when it has carried out a neutral activity with respect to the unlawful content uploaded onto its digital platform.

This exemption, however, cannot be applied when the copyright owner has notified the provider of the unlawful activity consisting in the unlawful distribution and use of audio and video programmes by means of a digital platform.

Therefore, there is the liability of the so-called active provider (content-provider), when the activity, far from being limited to a neutral service of hosting provider, takes the form of an *audiovisual entertainment service*, in competition with the entrepreneurial activity of the owner of the copyright on the content disseminated, by means of the sorting and dissemination, for economic purposes, of that content.

When the hosting provider carries out activities for the management of the content uploaded by users, its role cannot be considered passive, with the consequent inapplicability of the regime of exemption from liability under Article 16 of Legislative Decree No. 70/2003.

In the present case, the provider had implemented an operating system for the creation and distribution of digital entertainment content that was *linked* to the selection of video content entered by users and also proceeded to the selection of that content for the purposes of advertising exploitation on the basis of the minor or major displays.

In any case, this exemption from liability does not apply when the injured party, the owner of the copyright, has reported the offence to the provider, and the latter has remained inactive.

Since the activity of the provider concerns, among others, that of sorting the audio video contents to be linked to advertising on the basis of the data of greater or lesser viewing, the direct interest of said provider in the nature and type of contents existing in its own digital platform for the aforesaid direct purpose is evident precisely for evident reasons of economic advantage, i.e., an activity certainly not ascribable to the mere function of technical and neutral support of the provider for the diffusion of the aforesaid contents.

It therefore appears evident that in this case the factual condition from which the legislation in question and the same elaboration made by the European and national jurisprudence gives rise to the liability of the provider without any limitation in the event of unlawful acts and infringement of the rights of third parties, being recognizable an activity voluntarily aimed at concurring or cooperating with the third party in the unlawful act, is exactly present.

865. YouTube contents: Court of Turin, section I, 7 April 2017, decision No. 1928. Although there is no obligation for the YouTube platform to carry out a prior assessment of the actual ownership of copyright owned by the individuals uploading the videos, it is nevertheless legally obliged to *prevent* new uploads of videos already reported as copyright infringement, and this on the basis of the clear regulatory provision of Article 16 Legislative Decree No. 70/2003, which states that the provider is not responsible for the information stored at the request of a recipient of the service, but only on condition that it does not actually know that the activity or information is unlawful.

Once aware of the unlawfulness, the operator of the video-sharing platform is indeed obliged to take action and cooperate with the holder of the infringed copyright in order to effectively stop the infringement reported to it and prevent its perpetuation.

A special-preventive filtering obligation exists when the provider – without suffering a disproportionate sacrifice – using minimum technical functionalities is able to prevent new uploads of videos that have already been reported and removed following a court order.

The legislation currently in force excludes that there is a general obligation of supervision of Internet service providers, and therefore also of the provider of the video-sharing service, on the actual ownership of copyrights by the persons who upload a video on the storage space made available to them (by YouTube); the provider is, instead, liable for infringement of intellectual property rights if, duly informed, it has not removed the files reported by the legitimate owner of the copyright infringed or when it does not fulfil a specific obligation of supervision a posteriori, arising as a result of a report or warning.

866. Defamation contents: Court of Cassation, Criminal section V, 14 July 2016, decision No. 54946. The legal representative of a company operating a website hosting messages published directly by users contributes to the *offence of defamation* if, although aware of the unlawfulness of the publication of others, he has kept it visible on the website, thus allowing it to exercise its defamatory effect.

867. Editing of material published online (minimal contribution): Court of Rome, section. IX, 27 April 2016, decision No. 8437. On the subject of provider liability, even a minimal contribution to the editing of material published on the net (in this case, the selection, organization and aggregation of videos by an editorial team of a well-known American portal), damaging protected interests, represents an activity that does not fall within the figure of hosting provider outlined in Article 16 of Legislative Decree No. 70/2003, with the ensuing liability to be defined under the common rules.

Part IV. Intellectual Rights ('Digital Rights')

Chapter 1. Patent Law

868. In Italy, in keeping with the main countries adhering to the European Patent Convention, computer programs 'as such' are excluded from patent protection. However, software can be patented if presented as a 'method', or as a 'technical means implementing a method'.

869. This is referred to as 'computer implemented inventions' and not as software patents.

It is essential that there is a technical effect resulting from the execution of the computer program that goes beyond the normal interaction between program and computer.

The further technical effect of the software action may be found either outside the PC (e.g., in process/equipment control systems) or within the PC itself (for example, in the management of data in the computer's memory or in the management of hardware resources).

Thus, software that processes technical data (and not abstract numerical entities), such as image processing, data compression, noise suppression, and encoding/decoding, is patentable.

870. In addition, computer programs are protected by copyright, in whatever form they are expressed, as long as they are original, i.e., the result of the author's intellectual creation.

The protection relates to the program expressed in its source code, to its output (sounds, words or images: e.g., in video games) as well as to the user interfaces (set of graphic images, messages and sounds that guide the user to the computer's commands). The author shall have the exclusive right to reproduce, translate, adapt, transform, modify and distribute the program itself.[179]

871. A software patent refers, according to the definition adopted by the European Union, to a patent applied to an 'invention realized by means of a computer'.

Italy is a party to the European Patent Convention (EPC) and the Industrial Property Code and its interpretation are substantially harmonized with the EPC and the Guidelines of the European Patent Office.

179. *See* https://uibm.mise.gov.it/index.php/it/brevetti/brevetto-per-invenzione-industriale/brevetti-e-software.

In accordance with Article 52 of the EPC, Article 45 of the *Industrial Property Code* states that computer programs, considered as such, are not considered inventions.

Following the TRIPS Agreement, which does not exclude the patentability of software, and recent international developments (mainly in the United States and Japan), which allow the patentability of software, a new interpretation of Article 52 of the EPC is currently emerging which results in a narrowing of the patent prohibition and in considering patentable those software inventions that have a technical nature, i.e., software inventions that are technical solutions to technical problems.

872. Therefore, if a software invention represents a technical contribution to the state of the art, that software invention is patentable at the European Patent Office and also in Italy.

This is the case, for example, with inventive software that implements a process for operating a computer by optimizing its resource management or that controls a production process or implements an automation process or implements a method for processing data representing physical entities.

A Patent protects the algorithms and/or logic underlying the software, regardless of its specific implementation.

873. The European Patent Office (EPO) has granted many patents on inventions based at least partly on software since the European Patent Convention has been in force since the 1970s.

Article 52 of the convention, as mentioned, explicitly excludes computer programs from patentability (paragraph 2), understood as computer programs as such (paragraph 3).

The interpretation given to the Article is that a new technical solution which solves a technical problem in an inventive (i.e., non-obvious) manner may be patentable.

In the case of inventions implemented using a computer, expressed in terms of steps, there must necessarily be an Additional Technical Effect beyond the normal interaction of the software with hardware elements and devices in order to fulfil the patentability requirements.

In the absence of a Technical Problem, it is often possible to distinguish 'software' that is an end in itself (i.e., a program for a computer as such) from a program that is able to achieve a Technical Solution capable of solving a Technical Problem in a new and inventive manner with respect to the State of the Art.

The State of the Art is all that is known and accessible to the public by any disclosure, written or oral, up to the day before the filing date of a patent application.

For example, a program that processes images is not patentable. On the other hand, a new algorithm that allows images from a telescope to be processed in a new and inventive way, enabling the resolution and quality of the telescope's images to be increased, is patentable. A computer-based invention that only solves a business problem and not a technical problem is not considered patentable. However, the fact that an invention is useful in the commercial sector does not automatically mean that it is not patentable.

874. Drafting a patent application, especially in this area, and following it through to the granting stage is a complex task. Filing a patent application and following it through to grant means: conducting a search of the existing state of the art to identify pre-existing documents or inventions that may make the invention unpatentable; drafting the claims as well as the complete description of the invention according to technical and legal terminology; liaise with the relevant national or regional patent office, especially during the substantive examination of the patent application; make any changes requested by the patent office to the application. All these aspects require an in-depth knowledge of patent law and the work of patent offices.

Therefore, although technical or legal assistance is generally not mandatory, it is in fact strongly recommended. It is therefore advisable to appoint an industrial property attorney who has both adequate legal expertise and experience and technical knowledge of the invention.[180]

875. Patenting an app or software is possible if the app or software contains one or more innovative algorithms that make a technical contribution to the state of the art.

Patentable software is, for example, those relating to data compression, video acceleration, or calculation of operating parameters.

To apply for a software or app patent, it is not necessary to provide lines of code, but it is necessary to describe the innovative algorithms and their interaction with the software in detail, in particular by means of a document containing, for example, metalanguages, flow diagrams, block diagrams of the hardware and software systems used.

In any case, software and apps must also meet the patentability requirements for traditional inventions, in particular novelty and inventive step.

876. Icons, fonts and graphic symbols can also be protected by design registration as long as they meet the normal registration requirements.

Software and apps also enjoy (significantly more limited) copyright protection and can be filed with a special register.

877. The owner of patent rights for software or apps or copyright on the software or app is entitled to customs protection, i.e., to request customs detention of counterfeit goods.[181]

---

180. *See* https://lu.camcom.it/quesiti/1/4985.

181. https://www.sib.it/brevetti/approfondimenti-invenzioni/brevetto/brevetto-per-software/.

Chapter 2. Trademarks

878. A trademark is a 'sign' used to identify a company's products/services and distinguish them from those of its competitors.

All signs, in particular words, including names of persons, or designs, letters, numerals, colours, the shape of the product or its packaging, or sounds, may constitute trademarks, provided that such signs are suitable for distinguishing the goods or services of one undertaking from those of other undertakings; and that they are represented in the register in such a clear manner as to clearly and precisely determine the subject matter of the protection conferred on the proprietor.

879. The Code indicates that the trademark must: Have distinctiveness: it cannot be limited to words that only convey the type of activity carried out or product (Article 13 IPC). Be lawful: it cannot be contrary to public order and must not violate the provisions of the law (Article 14 IPC) – for example, it is not possible to register a trademark that incites violence.

880. Depending on its elements, the trademark can be distinguished into: a wordmark, which consists only of words, figurative trademark, which consists of a figure or a reproduction of real or imaginary objects. A mixed mark (consisting of words and figurative elements) is also considered figurative for filing purposes, shape or three-dimensional mark, which consists of a three-dimensional shape and may include containers, packaging, the goods themselves or their appearance, sound mark which consists exclusively of a sound or a combination of sounds, movement mark which is characterized by a change in position of the elements of the mark, multimedia mark consisting of the combination of image and sound, mark with repeated patterns,

position mark, holographic mark, consisting of elements with holographic features.

Sound, movement, multimedia and holographic marks have recently been introduced in the national discipline.

881. The protection of the trademark is limited to the goods or services to which it is related that are indicated in the Nice Classification.

Protection is limited to the classes applied for and it is not possible to extend protection after the application is filed.

It is possible to apply for trademark registration in more than one class. Costs vary depending on the number of classes indicated.

882. The filing of an Italian trademark application is valid only on the territory of Italy.

It is possible to apply for protection valid throughout the European Union by filing an EU trademark application (MUE), directly with the EU office EUIPO.[182]

182. *See* https://www.euipo.europa.eu/.

883. The trademark is valid for ten years from the filing of the application and can be renewed indefinitely every ten years.

884. All signs may be registered as trademarks: words (including names of persons), designs, letters, figures, sounds, shape of the product or its packaging, colour combinations or shades provided that they are (a) capable of distinguishing the goods or services of one undertaking from those of other undertakings; and (b) capable of being represented in the register in such a way as to enable the competent authorities and the public to determine with clarity and precision the subject of the protection conferred on the proprietor.' (Article 7 IPC).

885. What cannot be registered? Portraits of persons, names and well-known signs if consent is not given, Coats of arms, flags and other symbols of public interest, Marks containing words, figures or signs with political signification or high symbolic value, or containing heraldic elements; Coats of arms of political parties; Signs contrary to law, public order or morality (under the Criminal Code and criminal laws); Geographical indications (Article 29-30 IPC); Reproductions of works of art or cultural assets. For shape marks, further limitation applies: they cannot be pretected in cases where the shape imposed by the very nature of the product or the shape of the product necessary to obtain a technical result or the shape that gives substantial value to the product (Article 9 IPC).

886. Who can own a trademark? Anyone: natural person, legal person, associations, entities, etc. More than one person can be the owner of a trademark.

The owner can also be a foreigner, as long as they are domiciled in one of the EU countries.

Also, minors can file a trademark application.

887. The trademark is not the only distinctive sign.

There are others such as the trade name, company name or business name, sign and domain name, each of which is related to an undertaking that produces goods or provides services. Although they fulfil different functions from the trademark, they may equally lead to the lack of novelty of a trademark (and, therefore, its non-registrability).

888. The company – The company is the name under which the individual entrepreneur carries on business. The firm (like the company name or business name) identifies the entity that produces goods or performs services; the trademark, on the other hand, identifies the goods produced or services offered.

The company name or business name – all companies (partnerships or corporations) must have a name. In the case of partnerships – i.e., simple partnerships, general partnerships and limited partnerships – this is called the company name, whereas in the case of corporations – i.e., joint stock companies, limited partnerships and limited liability companies – it is called the company name.

The sign traditionally serves to identify and distinguish the premises where the activity is exercised (i.e., the shop, workshop, warehouse, etc.).

The domain name – The domain name is the distinctive sign that distinguishes an Internet site (e.g., 'uibm.gov.it'). The rule is that you cannot register a sign known as a domain name as a trademark unless you are the owner of the domain itself, nor can you register someone else's trademark as a domain name.

889. A 'de facto trademark' is a trademark that has not been registered, but has been used for some time for the marketing of services or products and has gained visibility and distinctiveness with respect to the target clientele and the reference territory. Pursuant to Article 2571 of the Civil Code, a person who has made use of an unregistered trademark has the right to continue using it, notwithstanding the registration obtained by others, to the extent that he has previously made use of it.

The protection of the right to the de facto trademark is based on the use and renown achieved, mere use is not enough: the person who claims ownership of the unregistered trademark must first prove both the pre-use and the renown achieved.

The de facto trademark enjoys less protection than the registered one because it is limited to the area within which the pre-use took place.

890. To find out if a trademark is new, you need to search the databases of the offices that register trademarks.

A trademark is protected in Italy if it is registered as an Italian national trademark, as an EU trademark (MUE) or as a designation of an International Registration extended to Italy or the EU. It is therefore necessary to carry out specific searches on UIBM's National Filing Database and in the EU and WIPO databases.

891. Is it possible to check trademarks filed in Italy in the EUIPO database for European Deposits and in the WIPO database for International registration to know if the validity of a trademark has been extended in Italy?

The Italian Patent and Trademark Office does not conduct prior art searches when examining an application for registration of a trademark.

892. Exclusive rights are conferred upon registration.

The effects of the first registration start from the filing date of the application (the filing date is the date of payment of the application fees).

In case of renewal, the renewal effects run from the expiration date of the previous registration.

To keep the trademark alive after ten years is possible to apply for renewal of the trademark. You can apply twelve months earlier; you can renew with a delay of up to six months by paying late fees. Beyond this date, the trademark is not renewable and a new first filing trademark application must be filed.

The trademark must be identical to the trademark being renewed. Changes cannot be made: you cannot change the graphics and you cannot increase the classes but you can limit them.

The renewal application is subject to a formal examination to ensure that no changes have been made; the trademark renewal examination process does not include an opposition procedure.

If, at the time of renewal of a trademark, circumstances have changed with respect to those of the first filing (e.g., the proprietors have changed, or the elective domicile has changed), updated data must be recorded.

893. If you need to extend protection after filing to other classes or to other goods or services, you have to file a new trademark application for the new classes, totally independent from the one you have already filed.

894. An application is filed with a EUR 16 revenue stamp together with the form.

The application can be filed at the CCIAA of filing through the telematic service (it is necessary to be registered with a digital signature); in this case, the stamp duty is EUR 15.

895. To surrender the ownership of the trademark an application must be submitted on a EUR 16 revenue stamp together with the original (or certified copy) of the renouncement document already filed with the Revenue Agency (since you are renouncing an acquired right, it is necessary to carry out the procedure at the Revenue Agency according to the procedures and forms indicated by the Revenue Agency) and the form.

The application may be filed at the CCIAA of filing via the telematic service (it is necessary to be registered with a digital signature); in this case, the stamp duty is EUR 15; (c) filed at the Public Hall, via San Basilio 14 – Rome (d) sent by registered mail with return receipt to UIBM, Div. XI- Transcrizioni Via Molise 19 – 0187 Roma.

896. According to Court of Rome Sez. spec. Enterprise, 20/07/2022, an injunction should be ordered against the company marketing NFT with a photo of a former football player reproducing the club's uniform and trademark without a licence from the company.

An injunction must be ordered against the company which markets, produces and offers for sale NFT (Non-Fungible Tokens) bearing the photograph of a well-known former football player, also reproducing the Juventus Club uniform and trademark, in the absence of a licence from the company; consequently, the withdrawal from the market and removal from each website and/or from each page of the website on which such products are offered for sale and/or advertised, the NFT and the digital content associated with them must be ordered.

The fact that a player has actually played in a team and that he has been granted permission for the use of his image through the creation of Cards reproducing the player with the various shirts of the teams in which he played does not exclude the need to request permission to use the registered trademarks relating to the teams whose shirts and names are reproduced, since these are goods intended for commercial sale, in relation to which also the reputation of the different teams in which the player has played contribute to giving value to the digital image to be purchased (in the present case, the Court issued an order prohibiting the marketing of Non-Fungible Tokens – NFT associated with digital cards bearing the photograph of a player wearing a Juventus jersey).

897. According to Court of Rome, 19 July 2022, the creation and marketing of non-fungible tokens (in this case digital cards) incorporating another person's registered trademark constitutes an infringement and is also an act of unfair competition, owing to the likelihood of confusion caused by the identity of the signs used, which is liable to mislead the public as to the existence of a particular commercial link between the creator of the digital product and the proprietor of the registered distinctive sign.

898. The Courts already offer some examples of protection granted to well-known brands that complained of an infringement of their patent rights in the metaverse.

An Italian case involved Juventus Football Club Spa, which accused a party operating in the metaverse of counterfeiting the word marks Juve and Juventus and the figurative mark consisting of the black and white striped shirt with two stars on the chest and of unfair competition consisting of the unauthorized use of the marks through the online marketing of digital playing cards reproducing the aforementioned distinctive signs.

The Court of Rome, by order dated 20 July 2022, found that there was a substantial likelihood of confusion, i.e., that the relevant public would believe that the disputed products originated from Juventus itself or from a related party; it also found that the registered trademarks also related to downloadable electronic publications and that the company Juventus had proved that it was also active in the crypto game or blockchain game sector, for which the Court also found unfair competition.

899. The Court of Rome therefore ordered an injunction against the further production, marketing, promotion or sale of NFT and related digital content, and also ordered the withdrawal from the market and from any website.

900. A case known worldwide concerned the famous Birkin bags by Hermès: a well-known designer had in fact created a collection of NFTs inspired by the iconic bag and then sold them on marketplaces dedicated to crypto art.

Hermès has for years registered both the word mark Birkin and the figurative mark depicting the image of the bag in the United States, but has never registered the mark in the class of digital goods; Hermès has therefore turned to the US courts requesting a declaration of infringement and unauthorized use of the mark in this case as well.

The U.S. District Court for the Southern District of New York on 14 February held that a collection of NFT whose value essentially lies in the luxury product value of the Birkin trademark could indeed mislead consumers.

Trademark registration for digital goods

901. More and more brands, in order to protect themselves against the possible counterfeiting of their registered trademarks for physical goods, are also requesting the registration of corresponding trademarks for digital goods.

902. As of 1 January 2023, the 12th edition of the Nice Classification is in force, which introduced the term 'download digital files authenticated by non-fungible tokens' in class 9.

However, NFTs are distinct goods from authenticated digital goods, which is why EUIPO in its 'Guidelines concerning examination before the European Union Intellectual Property Office of European Union trademarks and registered Community designs' stated that the term 'virtual goods' per se lacks clarity and therefore the content of the virtual goods (e.g., virtual footwear) must be specified, regardless of whether they are considered in Class 9 as goods or in relation to retail services in Class 35.

The term 'non-fungible tokens' as such is ineffective for classification purposes without further specification as to the object to which the NFTs refer, again the type of goods to which they refer must therefore be indicated.

Trademark registration for digital goods is important because it has the dual purpose of paving the way for and protecting brands in the virtual world and contestably protecting corresponding brands in the real world, highlighting risks of confusion, parasitic entanglement and loss of value of one's own brand.[183]

903. The year 2023 will undoubtedly be the year that will be characterized for trademark protection in the metaverse. By now, in fact, the importance of protecting one's brand in the digital world is a necessity and no longer a mere opportunity that one may or may not choose to take.

904. Highlighting the importance of such protection are the increasing number of cases of decisions and judgments pending in various jurisdictions concerning the infringement (or alleged infringement) of trademarks in the digital environment by third parties. This is the case, for example, of the alleged trademark infringement of the Hermés Birkin handbag decided by a US court or the now well-known judgment of the Court of Rome of 20.07.2022 that condemned a company that had used the famous 'Juventus' trademarks on the T-shirts worn by the footballer Bobo Vieri depicted on digital content in NFT format (so-called CARDS), which can be purchased on various online platforms. In the latter case, in fact, although the defendant company had obtained the authorization of the well-known footballer to use his image and name for the creation of CARDS depicting the footballer himself wearing the shirts of the various teams in which he has played over the years, this did not exclude the 'need to request [also] authorization to use the registered trademarks relating to the teams whose shirts and names are reproduced, insofar as these are goods intended for commercial sale, in relation to which the reputation of the various teams in which the player has played also contributes to giving value to the digital image to be purchased', an authorization which, clearly, had not been requested from Juventus Football Club S. p.A.

905. Therefore, the judge in Rome held (correctly) that such use constituted infringement of the 'Juventus' trademarks, essentially for two reasons: (i) because

183. *See* https://www.studiolegalestefanelli.it/it/approfondimenti/tutelare-il-marchio-nel-mondo-virtuale/.

such trademarks are certainly protected also for digital products since they are well-known trademarks, enjoying ultra-merchandise protection (i.e., also for products/ services other than those for which they have been registered); and, in any case, (ii) because the 'Juventus' trademarks were also registered in class 9, designating – albeit generically – 'downloadable electronic publications'.

906. Thus, as emerges in the case decided by the Court of Rome, the reputation of the mark – and the consequent possibility of ultra-merchandise protection – undoubtedly constituted an element of particular importance (and in some cases even decisive) to be able to enjoy the protection of the mark also in the digital environment. Due, in fact, to doubts about the correct classification of NFTs and, above all, to the absence of an express indication of the same within the Nice Classification of Goods, the only way to 'defend' a trademark in the digital world was to demonstrate its notoriety (and consequent ultra-commercial protection), thus excluding the protection of all other trademarks that are not well-known.

907. This was true until 31.12.2022. This protection gap was filled by the European Intellectual Property Office (EUIPO), which confirmed that as of 1 January 2023, the product headings 'downloadable digital files authenticated by non-fungible tokens [NFTs]' and 'downloadable e-wallets' have been added to Class 9 of the Nice Classification. In this regard, the EUIPO also made it clear that the term 'virtual products' used to date by some to try to ensure their brand some protection in the digital world was not sufficiently clear and precise.

908. As of today, it is therefore possible (and, indeed, undoubtedly advisable) to register one's trademark for NFTs in class 9 by expressly designating 'downloadable digital files authenticated by non-fungible tokens [NFTs]' and/or 'downloadable e-wallets', in order to protect it also for this kind of goods. This is particularly important, as we have seen, for all those trademarks that, although they have distinctive capacity, are not well-known and therefore do not enjoy ultra-commercial protection. Concretely, it will be necessary to file a new trademark application for those specific products, since it is not possible to extend the scope of an already registered trademark.

909. Beyond trademark registration in Class 9 for NFT, the year 2023 will certainly see an increasing focus on trademark exploitation contracts in the virtual world. The importance and care with which these aspects will have to be regulated contractually emerges clearly once again from the aforementioned decision of the Court of Rome, which most likely resulted from an 'oversight' in the drafting of a licence agreement. In fact, in this type of contract, it is always necessary to provide for the granting of all necessary authorizations for the use of trademarks/images/ names of others, in addition to assessing the possibility/opportunity of including an indemnity in the event of disputes by third parties (where applicable).

910. Ultimately, therefore, one of the good intentions for 2023 that has just begun is to evaluate, together with one's trusted lawyers, experts in the field of industrial and intellectual property, the possibility and/or opportunity to extend the protection of one's trademark in the metaverse, as well as to be assisted in the revision/redaction of contracts that imply the exploitation of one's trademarks in the digital world, in order to be able to take advantage of all the new challenges and opportunities that this 'new world' offers and will continue to offer, without running into unpleasant inconveniences.[184]

184. *See* https://it.andersen.com/proteggere-i-marchi-nel-metaverso/.

Chapter 3. Design Protection

911. Designs are governed by Articles 31 to 44 of the IPC.

A design means the appearance of the whole or a part of the product as it results, in particular, from the features of the lines, contours, colours, shape, surface texture and/or materials of the product itself and/or its ornamentation, provided they are new and have individual character.

The protection concerns the outward appearance as a whole and not inscriptions. If there are writings, they are not protected. Product means any industrial or handicraft object, including, *inter alia*, components that must be assembled to form a complex product, packaging, presentations, graphic symbols and typographic characters, excluding computer programs. A complex product is defined as a product consisting of several components that can be replaced, allowing for disassembly and reassembly of the product.

912. The design protection period lasts 5 years from the date the application is filed and can be renewed, by paying the renewal fee, for 4/5 year periods, up to a maximum total of 25 years.

Protection is only valid in the country where the application is made. In addition to applying for registration in Italy, it is possible to apply for registration with validity throughout the EU by applying to the EUIPO, or to apply for registration in many foreign countries directly by applying to the WIPO.

The application, with attached documentation, is made available to the public immediately, unless the applicant has excluded its accessibility for a period not exceeding 30 months from the filing date or the date of priority (inaccessibility).

The application may be filed for a single design or for several designs (MULTIPLE), provided they belong to the same 'class' of the Locarno Classification (e.g., collections).[185]

913. Design protection rules in the European Union will soon undergo changes to update the system to new technologies, make design protection more attractive to small businesses, and limit design protection for spare parts of complex products.

New European rules finally approved by the European Parliament in March 2024 will amend the EU's current legislation on design protection, namely Regulation No. 6/2002 on Community Designs and Directive No. 98/71 on the legal protection of designs.

914. The amendments essentially aim to update the system to new technologies such as 3D printing and artificial intelligence, to make design protection more attractive to small businesses and to align EU design law with trademark law.

The changes will enter into force gradually over a period from the beginning of 2025 to the end of 2027.

185. *See* https://uibm.mise.gov.it/index.php/it/disegni-e-modelli.

915. We summarize here the main changes of interest to users of the EU design protection system.

916. Protection extended to digital and 3D printed designs: The amended definitions of 'design' and 'product' have been extended to cover digital and 3D printed designs; the changes introduced make it clear that protection is no longer limited to physical objects and can also cover digital designs and dynamic elements – such as movement, transitions or any kind of animation – that determine the appearance of the product or a part of it: think of virtual objects, parts of video games, light shows, dynamic billboards.

The rules on representation of designs in applications will also have to be amended accordingly, allowing video files to be attached and raising the ceiling on the number of views to be included in the application.

917. Updated infringement acts: Under the new rules, creating, downloading, distributing or sharing multimedia content or software that includes copies of a protected design may constitute design infringement. The aim is for the rules on the enforcement of design rights to apply to 3D printing of protected objects.

918. Parts: Component designs of complex products will not be protectable with an EU registration if their sole purpose is to restore the original appearance of the product. A harmonized transitional period of protection (eight years) will be introduced for designs already granted.

919. Fees: Filing fees for an EU design will remain low and renewal fees will be adjusted to be more attractive to small businesses and individuals: the renewal fee for the first five years will be EUR 150 and will gradually increase with each subsequent renewal up to EUR 700.

The abolition of the class unity requirement – which means that several designs from different Locarno classes can be included in a single application – will simplify the procedure and maximise savings in the case of multiple applications. On the other hand, however, a cap will be introduced on the number of designs that can be included in a single application.

920. Name and symbol: The Community Design will be renamed the European Union Design (to correspond to the European Union Trade Mark), and the symbol to represent it will be a circled D, similar to the ® of the registered trademark and the © of the copyright.[186]

---

186. *See* https://www.sib.it/flash-news/nuove-regole-sulla-tutela-del-design-nellunione-europea-cosa-cambia/.

Chapter 4. Copyright Protection in the Digital Context

§1. Normative Sources

921. In Italy copyright is mainly regulated by Law No. 633/1941 (Italian copyright Law), which has been amended several times to comply with the ratified International Treaties and with European Law.

In particular, Law No. 923/1956 ratified the Universal Copyright Convention; Law No. 866/1973 implemented the Convention of Rome for the protection of interpreters and performer artists, producers of phonograms and radio-diffusion organizations (subsequently revised by the Beijing Treaty on Audio-visual Performances – entered into force on 28 April 2020 – extending digital protection to the work of actors, singers, musicians and dancers in audiovisual performances; Law No. 399/1978 ratified the Berne Convention for the Protection of Literary and Artistic Works; Law No. 747/1994 ratified the TRIPS Agreement, part of the Uruguay Round multilateral commercial negotiations; Law No. 37/2019 implemented Directive No. 2017/1564 ratifying the Marrakesh Treaty to facilitate access to published works for blind, visually impaired, or otherwise print disabled (specifically, paragraphs from 2-*bis* to 2-*terdecies* were added in Article 71-*bis* of Law No. 633/1941).

922. Following the WCT (WIPO Copyright Treaty) and the WPPT (WIPO Performances and Phonograms Treaty), the European Union enacted Directive No. 2001/29/EC on the harmonization of certain aspects of copyright and related rights in the information society. In Italy, such Directive was implemented by Legislative Decree No. 68/2003, which – by amending section 13 of the Italian copyright Law – included temporary reproduction of works subject to copyright to the definition of the exclusive right of reproduction.

923. Directive No. 91/250/EEC on the legal protection of computer programs and Directive No. 96/9/EC on the legal protection of databases were adopted by Legislative Decrees No. 518/1992 and No. 169/1999, granting the use of technological protection measures (TPM) on copyrighted works.

924. Specific provisions on rental and lending rights, as well as certain rights related to copyright in the field of intellectual property, were introduced in the Italian copyright Law through the implementation of Directive No. 92/100/EEC by Legislative Decree No. 685/94. Directive No. 93/98/EEC harmonizing the term of protection of copyright (and certain related rights) was implemented by Legislative Decree No. 154/97.

925. Law No. 140/2006 incorporated Directive No. 2004/48/EC, establishing new rules for the enforcement of intellectual property rights (as such, integrated in the intellectual property Code disciplined by Legislative Decree No. 30/2005). In such perspective, said Law has introduced a new set of measures, procedures, and remedies in favour of the copyright holder.

Through Law No. 2/2008, part 1-*bis* was added to section 70 of the Italian copyright Law, granting the possibility to freely publish low resolution or degraded quality contents (images or music) for educational or scientific non-profit use only.

Directive No. 28/2012 on certain permitted uses of orphan works was implemented by Legislative Decree No. 163/14, which introduced sections to 69-*bis* to 69-*septies* to the Italian copyright Law.

926. Legislative Decree No. 168/2013 has fixed the competence and venue of judicial actions concerning IP rights and copyright – including economic rights and rights on software and database – before specialized business sections of Court.

The so-called Barnier Directive (Directive No. 2014/26/EU), transposed in the Italian framework by Legislative Decree No. 35/2017, implemented significant changes for the collective management of copyright, providing for new rules in terms of reductions and exemptions from the relating payment. Although section 4.2 of Legislative Decree No. 35/2017 specifically established the right for copyright-owners to entrust independent entities with the power of managing their rights, the market was liberalized only partially.[187]

927. Legislative Decree No. 73/2021, then converted into Law No. 106/2021, provided for the amendment of section 71-*octies* of the Italian copyright Law and established differentiated criteria for audio and video private reproduction.

Directive (EU) No. 790/2019 on Copyright and related rights in the Digital Single Market (and amending Directives 96/9/EC and 2001/29/EC) was incorporated by Legislative Decree No. 177/2021, which introduced relevant novelties to the Italian copyright Law, especially concerning copyrights of online works (*see* paragraph 4.7 below).

928. Recently, Law No. 93/2023 introduced specific provisions against cinematographic, audiovisual, and editorial piracy in the copyright Law.

In a broader view, the Italian copyright regulation cannot be analysed and interpreted without taking also into consideration Legislative Decree No. 70/2003 (implementing Directive No. 2000/31/EC on E-commerce), Regulation (EU) Bo.

---

187. After the entry in force of the Legislative Decree No. 35/2017, an important and very debated case held in Italy among SIAE, the Italian Society of Authors and Publishers, a public company established for the collective management of authors' rights, SOUNDREEF EST, an English independent management entity, and LEA, a no profit entity strictly linked to this latter. SOUNDREEF EST filed before the AGCM, Italian Competition Authority, a request for ascertaining whether SIAE was in abuse of dominant position as intermediary entity or not. The AGCM uphold the request of SOUNDREEF, but SIAE filed an appeal before the Administrative Court. On its turn SOUNDREEF brought an action before the Court of Rome against SIAE for alleged unfair competition but the Court suspended the judgment and submitted the question to the Court of Justice for the correct interpretation of Directive No. 2014/26/EU about the collective management entities (to be intended as collective management entity or as independent collective entity, even established in other member States). On 2019 SIAE, SOUNDREEF LTD and LEA announced that they have reached an agreement aimed at settling all existing disputes between them and preventing further disputes. *See* G. Remotti, Il nuovo mercato della gestione collettiva dei diritti d'autore tra resistenze monopolistiche (illecite) e funzioni di interesse economico generale (lecite)', in 'AIDA', 2020,.

2022/2065 (so-called Digital Services Act, *see* paragraph 4.8 below), Regulation (EU) Bo. 679/2016 (GDPR) and Law Bo. 196/2003 (Italian privacy Law).

§2. Protected Works

929. Under section 1 of the Italian copyright Law, all intellectual works having creative nature and pertaining to literature, music, figurative arts, architecture, theatre, and cinematography, whatever their form of expression, shall be protected.

Computer programs shall equally be protected as literary works according to the Berne Convention for the protection of literary and artistic works (ratified and enforced by Law Bo. 399/1978). The law includes in the definition of computer programs all preparatory materials for the development of the final products. For what specifically regards databases, the relating copyright protection shall not extend to their contents and shall be without prejudice to any subsiding right.

930. Pursuant to section 2 of the Italian copyright Law, the following works are protected: (i) literary, dramatic, scientific, educational, and religious works, whether in written or oral form; (ii) musical works and compositions, with or without words, dramatic-musical works and musical variations constituting original works; (iii) choreographic and pantomimic works, whether fixed in writing or otherwise; (iv) works of sculpture, painting, drawing, engraving and similar figurative arts, including scenography; (v) designs and works of architecture; (vi) works of cinematographic art, whether in silent or sound form; (vii) photographic works and those expressed by processes similar to photography; (viii) computer programs, whatever may be the form of expression, on the condition that they result from the author's intellectual creation[188] and including all preparatory materials for the development of the final products; (ix) databases, meant as collections of works, data or other independent materials systematically or methodically arranged, that can be individually accessed by electronic or other means; and (x) works of industrial designs that exhibit creative character and artistic value.

931. With reference to software, case law has clarified that the Italian copyright Law does not protect neither its purpose and the mathematical algorithms implementing the functions to be performed by the program, nor the so-called flow chart describing how different parts interact with each other.[189] It does indeed safeguard both the source code (i.e., the set of steps and commands expressed by the author and comprehensible to humans) and the object code (i.e., the translation of the source code into machine language).

188. According to undisputed case law (Court of Cassation No. 581/2007), the elements of creativity and originality required to grant legal protection to software '*subsists even when the work is composed of simple ideas and notions included in the intellectual property of persons having experience in the subject-matter of the work itself, provided that they are formulated and organised in a personal and autonomous manner with respect to the previous ones*'; in the same direction, *see also* Court of Torino, ruling on the case No. 33273/2016 published on 16 Oct. 2020 in DARTS IP.

189. In this sense, *see* Court of Naples No. 20635/2018, in DARTS IP.

932. In order to be protected under the Italian copyright Law, works should be creative and new;[190] they do not need to be legal nor valuable. In particular, works:

- shall have creative character, to be intended as the form of expression of the idea, or the specific expression made by its author, implying that the same idea may be the base of different works;[191] and
- shall be new and original. Even if the creative act is minimal, it shall however be susceptible of manifestation in the external world; the elements of novelty and originality shall emerge from the personal contribution of the author and differentiate the works form the pre-existing.[192]

933. According to section 3 of the Italian copyright Law, collective works, consisting of the assembly of works or parts of works, that have the character of autonomous creation as a result of selection and coordination for a specific literary, scientific, educational, religious, political, or artistic purpose, such as encyclopedias, dictionaries, anthologies, magazines, and newspapers, are protected as original works, without prejudice to the copyright of the works, or parts thereof, of which they are composed. Without prejudice to the rights belonging to the original works, all creative elaborations (such as the translation into another language, the transformation into any other literary or artistic form, modifications or additions constituting a substantial recasting of the original work, including adaptations, reductions, abridgements, and variations which do not constitute an original work) are also subject to protection.[193]

---

190. *See* Court of Cassation No. 10300/2020 stating that '*Copyright protection postulates the requirement of originality and creativity, consisting not in the idea underlying its creation, but in the form of its expression, that is, by its subjectivity, presupposing that the work reflects the personality of its author, manifesting his free and creative choices*' (in the same sense, *see also* Court of Cassation No. 13524/2014, in DARTS IP).
191. *See* Court of Cassation No. 25173/2011, in DARTS IP, establishing that '*the legal concept of creativity, to which section 1 of Law No. 633 of 1941 refers, does not coincide with the concept of creation, originality, and absolute novelty, referring, on the contrary, to the personal and individual expression of an objectivity belonging to the categories listed, by way of example, in section 1 of Law No. 633 of 1941. [...] An original work receives protection on the condition that it contains a creative act, albeit minimal, capable of manifestation in the external world, with the result that creativity cannot be excluded merely because the work consists of simple ideas and notions, included in the intellectual heritage of persons with experience in the field; intellectual property of persons having experience in the subject-matter; moreover, creativity does not consist of the idea in itself, but in the form of its expression, that is to say, in its subjectivity, so that the same idea may be the basis of several works that are or may be different because of the subjective creativity that each of the authors expends and that, as such, is relevant for the purposes of protection*'.
192. *See* Court of Milan No. 4863/2017, in DARTS IP.
193. *See* Court of Cassation No. 20925/2005, in DARTS IP, stating that '*a creative elaboration is characterised by an elaboration of the original work with recognisable creative contribution, and the consistency of that contribution must be appreciated in the light of the importance that the creative act receives protection even if it is minimal, provided that it is susceptible of manifestation in the external world, with the consequence that creativity cannot be excluded merely because the work consists of simple ideas and notions, included in the intellectual heritage of persons having experience in the subject matter*'.

§3. SUBJECTS

934. Under section 6 of the Italian copyright Law, copyright protects the creation of a work resulting from an intellectual effort and its author shall be considered the one who has created the work.[194]

For collective works, the person who organizes and directs its creation shall be deemed to be the author. For databases, the author is whoever makes relevant investments in terms of time, labour, or financial resources to allow its verification or presentation.[195]

Within the limits of its contribution, the person who has elaborated a work shall be deemed to be the author of such elaboration, being understood that the rights of economic use and moral rights on the creative work do belong (at least originally) to the person who realized it. The exploitation of copyrights on derivative works is subject to the consent of the original author.

935. In compliance with section 8 of the Italian copyright Law, the author of a work – unless proven otherwise – is the one indicated as such in the customary forms of use, or announced as such in the recitation, performance, representation, or broadcasting of the work. This general rule is intended to facilitate, at a procedural level, the position of the person who claims to be the author and has the burden of proving his active legitimacy. Pseudonyms, stage names, initials, or conventional signs that are widely known as equivalent to the real name are valid as real names. Anyone who has represented, performed, or otherwise published an anonymous or pseudonymous work is allowed to exercise the rights of the author, until the true author is revealed.

936. If a work has been created with the indistinguishable and inseparable contribution of multiple individuals, the copyright is jointly owned by all co-authors. Undivided parts are presumed to be of equal value unless there is written proof of a different agreement. In this case, the provisions governing joint ownership apply. However, the defence of moral rights can always be individually exercised by each co-author, and the work cannot be published – if unpublished – nor can it be modified or used in a manner different from the initial publication without the agreement of all co-authors. Nevertheless, in case of unjustified refusal by one or more co-authors, the publication, modification, or new use of the work can be authorized by the judicial authority, under the conditions and terms it may rule.

937. Differently from the patents' regulation, the copyright Law does not determine specific rules on the ownership and exploitation of a work created by the employee or the co-worker in the fulfilment of an employment relationship. Therefore, for these rights to be exercised by employers, they shall be transferred from the employee or the co-worker by specific deed. Only in particular cases, the Law

194. According to case law, the individual who claims or acts for copyright infringement has the burden of proof of its active legitimacy (*see* Court of Cassation No. 5388/1998 and Court of Cassation No. 5359/2010, in DARTS IP).

195. *See* Court of Rome No. 152/2022, in DARTS IP.

provides for explicit rules. Under sections 12-*bis*[196] and 12-*ter*[197] of the copyright Law, unless otherwise agreed, the employer holds the exclusive right to the economic use of the computer program or the database or the industrial design created by employees in the performance of their duties or based on instructions provided by the employer.

§4. The Right of Economic Use

938. Pursuant to section 12 of the Italian copyright Law, the author has the exclusive right to publish the work and economically use it in every form and manner, whether original or derivative, within the limits fixed by the Law, and particularly through the exercise of the exclusive rights listed under sections from 13 to 18-*bis*. The first publication is considered the first exercise of the right of economic use. Specific provisions are set forth in relation to computer programs (section 64-*bis*) and database (section 64-*quinquies*).

939. The Law makes a list of the exclusive rights relating to the economic use of a work. Such list is non-exhaustive, and the exercise of each right is independent from those of the others. Such exclusive rights are the following:

- to reproduce the work (that is the multiplication of copies by any means, such as hand copying, printing, lithography, engraving, photography, phonography, cinematography and any other process of reproduction);
- to transcribe the work (transforming an oral work into a written work, or into a work reproduced by one of the methods indicated by the Law);
- to perform the work, play it or act it in a musical, dramatic, cinematographic, public performance, either free of charge or upon the payment of a fee;[198]
- to communicate the work to the public by any means of diffusion, such as telegraphy, telephony, radio or television broadcasting and other analogous means;[199]

196. *See* Court of Rome No. 42661/2009, in DARTS IP.
197. *See* Court of Milan No. 3115/2017, in DARTS IP.
198. The performance or recitation of a work within the family circle, or within a college, school or institute of retreat or treatment, shall not be considered as a public performance or recitation. Acting in public museums, archives and libraries for the exclusive purpose of cultural promotion and enhancement of the works, as specifically agreed on the basis of memoranda of understanding between the SIAE and the Ministry of Cultural Heritage and Activities and Tourism, shall not be considered to be public.
199. In accordance with the settled case law of the Court concerning Art. 3(1) of Directive 2001/29, the concept of 'communication to the public' includes two cumulative criteria, namely an act of communication of a work and the communication of that work to a public (judgments of 31 May 2016, Reha Training, C-117/15, EU:C:2016:379, para. 37, and of 19 Dec. 2019, Nederlands Uitgeversverbond and Groep Algemene Uitgevers, C-263/18, EU:C:2019:1111, para. 61 and the case law cited). Any act by which a user gives access to protected works, with full knowledge of the consequences of that action, is liable to constitute an act of communication for the purposes of Art. 3(1) of Directive 2001/29 (judgment of 14 Jun. 2017, Stichting Brein, C-610/15, EU:C:2017:456, para. 26).

– to distribute the original work (or its copies), commercialize it, circulate it, or otherwise make it available to the public, whatever the means and for whatever purpose. It includes the exclusive right to introduce reproductions made in non-EU countries into the territory of the European Union, for the purpose of distribution;
– to translate the work in other languages or dialects;
– to modify, elaborate or transform the work (authors own the exclusive right to publish their work in a collection and to introduce in it any modification);
– to lease the use of originals, copies, or media of works protected by copyright, for a limited period and for the purpose of direct or indirect economic or commercial benefit, and to lend the use of originals, copies, or media of works protected by copyright, to institutions open to the public, for a limited period, for purposes other than those mentioned for the lease. Authors, even in the case of transferring the leasing right to a producer of phonograms, cinematographic, audiovisual works, or sequences of moving images, retain the right to receive fair remuneration for the lease subsequently concluded with third parties. Any contrary agreement is void.

§5. Duration of the Right of Economic Use

940. Under section 25 of the Italian copyright Law, the right of economic use endures throughout the lifetime of the author and until the end of the seventieth calendar year after their death.

941. For works created with the indistinguishable and inseparable contribution of multiple individuals, and for dramatic-musical, choreographic works and pantomimes, the duration of the right of economic use is determined by the life of the co-author who survives the longest. For collective works, the duration for each contributor is determined by their individual life. The duration of a work as a whole shall be considered as seventy years from the first publication, whatever the form of publication, except for magazines, newspapers, and other periodical works to which section 30 of the Italian copyright Law applies.[200] For anonymous or pseudonymous works (except when pseudonymous are widely known as equivalent to the real name), the duration of the right of economic use is seventy years form the first publication, whatever the form of publication.

942. To acquire the benefit of normal duration of the right of economic use, the revelation of identity must be made by means of declaration to the Office of literary, scientific, and artistic property at the chairman office of the council of Ministers. Under section 28 of the Italian copyright Law, the revelation of identity is

200. Under s. 30 of the Italian copyright Law, when the parts or volumes of the same work are published separately, at different times, the duration of the right of economic use, if specified in years, starts for each part or volume from the year of publication. Fractions of a year benefit the author. If it is a periodic collective work, such as a magazine or newspaper, the duration of the right is calculated from the end of each year from the publication of individual issues or numbers.

effective before third parties having acquired rights to the work as anonymous or pseudonymous from the date of its deposit.

943. The duration for works belonging to the State, the Provinces, the Communes, the Academies, or public cultural organizations, as well as non-profit private entities, is twenty years from the first publication, whatever the form of publication.

Under section 31 of the Italian copyright Law, for works published for the first time after the death of the author, the duration of the economic use is seventy years from the death of the author.

§6. Moral Rights of the Author

944. Moral rights last for the author's entire life and are not transferrable due to their strictly personal nature. According to a widespread position,[201] moral rights should be considered inalienable,[202] imprescriptible and untransmissible *mortis causa.*

945. A relevant distinction exists between moral rights and exclusive rights of economic use. Whereas the first concerns the author' right to be recognized as such, preventing others from unduly attributing such authorship, the latter allow the author to economically use and exploit the work.[203] According to case law, '*the moral right consists of the right to be recognised as the author of a work. This right includes the right to claim authorship of the work. Claiming authorship of the work means preventing others from qualifying and passing themselves off as the author by substituting their name for that of the real author, as well as preventing a co-author of the work from presenting himself as the sole author of the work or otherwise failing to properly indicate the share due to the contributor*'.[204]

946. Regardless of the exclusive rights of economic use of the work, and even after the transfer of these rights, the author retains the right to claim authorship of the work and to oppose to any distortion, mutilation, or other modification or act to the detriment of the work that could prejudice their honor or reputation. The purpose thereof is to avoid not only the acts that may materially affect the work and modify it, but also to prevent those that may alter the way it is presented to the public from how it was intended by the author.[205] However, in architectural works,

201. *See* under s. 20, L. C. Ubertazzi, 'Commentario breve alle leggi su proprietà intellettuale e concorrenza' (Cedam, Padova, 2019).
202. *See* Court of Cassation No. 15104/2015, stating that '*section 21 of the law n. 633/1941 sets forth the prohibition on the alienation of the moral right revealing how the guarantee of the authorship of the work and its integrity not only protects the author himself, but also has a public purpose*'.
203. *See* Court of Rome No. 10264/2021, in DARTS IP.
204. *See* Court of Rome No. 2350/2022, in DARTS IP.
205. For instance, the following have been considered violations of the moral right of the author, with respect to the integrity of the work: distribution of live-recorded music with serious defects and imperfections, combination of literary or musical works with advertising campaigns, deterioration

authors cannot object to modifications deemed necessary during construction. Similarly, they cannot object to other modifications necessary for the completion of the work.[206]

947. Authors of anonymous or pseudonymous works maintain the right to reveal themselves at any time and to have their status recognized in court. On the matter, case law has clarified that the original declaration by which the author of musical lyrics asked not to be named as such, is always and at any time withdrawable.[207]

Under section 22 of the Italian copyright Law, those rights are inalienable. However, authors who have known and accepted the modifications to their work are no longer entitled to take action to prevent its execution or to request its suppression.

948. After the death of the author, rights may be asserted, without limitation of time, by the spouse and children and, in their absence, by the parents and other direct ascendants and direct descendants. In the absence of ascendants and descendants, by siblings and their descendants. Under section 24 of the Italian copyright Law, the right to publish unpublished works belongs to the heirs of the authors or the legatees of the works, unless the author has expressly prohibited publication or has entrusted others to do so. If the author has set a deadline for publication, unpublished works cannot be published before its expiration. When heirs are multiple and there is a disagreement among them, the judicial authority decides.

949. Heirs have the right to oppose to any modification to the work that may be detrimental to the author's honour and reputation, on the condition that such prejudice shall be objective – meaning beyond the subjective sensitivity of the author or of those entitled to moral protection – and strictly related to the work[208] – and not merely to the context in which the work is presented.

950. Whether or not moral rights can belong to legal entities is still debated, especially for creations made by artificial intelligence. In the current legal framework, copyrights are recognized to the natural individuals who created the work.

According to Court of Milan 'the moral right – which includes the right to mention the author's name – constitutes a strictly personal subjective position. […] The moral right cannot be attributed to persons other than natural persons, since it is a sphere relating to the protection of the creator's personality that is closely connected to the material creative process preparatory for the creation of the work. The

---

of a painting due to the passage of time together with other negative factors attributable to the owner, failure to include subtitles in specific parts of a movie (essential to understand the plot), production of a screenplay/film that deviates significantly from the inspirational subject, as in L. C, Ubertazzi, cited above, under s. 21.

206. The provision seems to refer only to architectural works and its application should be restrictive. However, some believe it could be applicable to design creations and software. Required changes are considered not only those for technical, urban planning, legal and environmental reasons, but also for economic reasons. In this sense, *see* Court of Venice, decision 9 Apr. 2020, p. 179, in 'AIDA' 2020, and relevant comments.

207. *See* Court of Cassation No. 29176/2017, in DARTS IP.

208. *See* Court of Milan No. 9232/2016, in *Giurisprudenza delle Imprese*.

necessary creative capacity is indeed a quality that can be attributed only to natural persons (and in fact, the moral right, from a genetic point of view, arises at the time of the creation of the work and, from a functional point of view, refers to the link of intellectual authorship to which the various moments of the right are related). EU Copyright rules – in typifying the content of intellectual property rights – are expressly assigned *ab origine* to the intellectual creator'.[209]

§7. Directive (EU) No. 790/2021

951. Directive (EU) No. 790/2021, enforced in Italy by Legislative Decree No. 177/2021, has introduced relevant novelties to the Italian copyright Law, especially concerning copyrights of online works. Resolution 95/24/CONS, regulating issues related to copyright, licences for the use of audiovisual works on video on demand services, and dispute resolution. This new Regulation expands the Authority's powers to include contractual supervision and sanctions for non-compliance.[210] In particular, the following relevant provisions were added to the Italian copyright Law:

- section 32-*quarter*, according to which, at the expiration of the protected period of a work of visual arts, all materials resulting from the reproduction of said work is not subject to copyright or related rights, unless it constitutes an original work, introducing the right to disseminate, share (including online) and reuse (also for commercial purpose) non-original copies of works that have become of public domain;
- section 43-*bis*, establishing that journalistic publishers shall be granted, by information services providers, with the exclusive rights of reproduction and communication (pursuant to section 13 and 16 of the Italian copyright Law) for online use of their publications. For such use, information services providers shall recognize authors fair compensation, the determination of which also depends on the number of online visits of the work. The determination of fair remuneration for the online use of journalistic publications, pursuant to Article 43-*bis* of the Copyright Act, has been established by Regulation No. 3/23 of AGCOM;
- section 70-*bis*, determining that summarizing, quoting, reproducing, translating, and adapting excerpts or parts of works and other materials, and their communication to the public through digital means, are free only for educational purposes, within the limits justified by the non-profit goal. Said acts shall be done under the responsibility of an educational institution, either within its premises or in another location or in a safe electronic environment, accessible only to the teaching staff and the enrolled students of the course of study where the works or other materials are used;

---

209. *See* Court of Milan, No. 7333/2018, in *Giurisprudenza delle Imprese*.
210. *See* S. Lavagni, 'Regolamento Agcom sul diritto d'autore: novità e problemi', 2024, at https://www.agendadigitale.eu/mercati-digitali/nuovo-regolamento-agcom-sul-diritto-dautore-novita-e-problemi/.

- section 70-*ter*, according to which reproductions carried out by research institutions and institutions for the protection of cultural heritage are allowed for scientific research purposes, for the extraction of text and data (i.e., any automated technique aimed at analysing large quantities of text, sounds, images, data, or metadata in digital format with the purpose of generating information, including patterns, trends, and correlations) from works or other materials available in networks or databases to which they have legal access. The communication to the public of the results of such research, expressed through new original works, is permitted.

952. The Directive has introduced a specific set of provisions regarding the use of protected contents by providers of online content-sharing services, defined as information services providers that meet, cumulatively, the following requirements:

a. have as their main purpose, or among its main purposes, to store and give access to the public to large quantities of copyrighted works or other protected materials;
b. the copyrighted works or other protected materials shall be directly uploaded by its users;
c. the copyrighted works or other protected materials shall be organized and promoted for the purpose of directly or indirectly profiting from them.

953. Under section 102-*sexies* of the Italian copyright Law, providers of online content-sharing services do not include those that provide access to online encyclopedias without a profit purpose, non-profit educational or scientific inventories, as well as open-source software development and sharing platforms, electronic communication service providers, online marketplaces, business-to-business cloud service providers, and personal cloud service providers that allow users to upload content for personal use, unless the online marketplace or cloud service allows the sharing of copyrighted works among multiple users. When providing public access to copyrighted works or other protected materials uploaded by their users, providers of online content-sharing services perform an act of communication to the public or an act of making available to the public, for which an authorization from the right holders is needed. Such authorization shall be obtained also through the conclusion of a licensing agreement and includes all acts performed by users who upload copyrighted works to the service provider's platform, when not acting for commercial purposes or their activity does not generate significant revenues.

954. In absence of said authorization, providers of online content-sharing services shall be held liable for unauthorized communication to the public and for making protected works available, unless they demonstrate that they have, cumulatively satisfied the following conditions:

a. made the best efforts to obtain the authorization, according to high standards of professional diligence;

b. exercised, according to high standards of professional diligence, the best efforts to ensure that specific works and other materials for which they have received relevant information from rights holders are not made available;
c. promptly disabled access or removed from their websites the works or other materials referred to in sufficiently motivated notice received from rights holders and, according to high standards of professional diligence, made the best efforts to prevent their future uploading.

955. Under section 102-*septies*, point 2 of the Italian copyright Law, to determine, according to the principle of proportionality, whether the provider of online content-sharing services is exempt from liability, the type, audience, and size of the service, as well as the type of works or other materials uploaded by users of the service, are considered on a case-by-case basis. The availability of appropriate and effective tools and their cost is also considered. In any case, providers that engage in, or facilitate in any way, copyright piracy is not exempt from liability.

956. Under section 102-*decies*, providers shall make fast and effective complaint mechanisms available to users. Rights holders can request providers to disable access to specific works or to remove them, upon motivated notice. Providers promptly notify users of the disabled or removed content and, pending the decision on the complaint, disputed content remains disabled. Decisions on such requests are subject to human review and can be contested by filing an appeal before the Communications Authority.[211]

§8. Digital Services Act

957. One of the main goals of the Digital Services Act (DSA),[212] is to limit the proliferation of online illegal content, on the assumption that what is illegal offline should also be considered illegal online. Activities such as the use, reproduction, or dissemination – even online – of copyrighted works (or parts thereof), without the prior authorization of rights holders, shall be considered in violation of the law. For this reason, service providers that allow users to share such content online are subject to a specific liability regime, harmonized at the European level.

958. Under section 2.4 of the DSA, the DSA is without prejudice to the rules laid down by other Union legal acts regulating other aspects of the provision of intermediary services in the internal market, including Union law on copyright and related rights. Therefore it shall be considered complementary to existing specific

211. *See* https://www.agcom.it/sites/default/files/media/allegato/2024/Linee%20Guida.pdf about the guidelines concerning complaint procedures set up by providers of online content-sharing services and regulation concerning the resolution of disputes between content-sharing service providers of online content-sharing services and users, implementing Art. 102-*decies* of law No. 633 of 22 April 1941. https://www.agcom.it/sites/default/files/migration/delibera/Delibera%20115-23-CONS.pdf.
212. Regulation (EU) No. 2022/2065.

sector legislation, such as Directive (EU) No. 790/2021, which shall continue to apply as a *lex specialis* regulating certain aspects of information services providers (*see* section 4.7 above).

959. In other terms, even if the DSA does not directly regulate copyright and related rights, it does complete the general framework implemented by Directive (EU) No. 790/2021.

In particular, the DSA provides for a definition of the 'sufficiently motivated notice', required for the request by right holders to disable access to specific works or to remove them. Under section 16 of the DSA, providers of hosting services shall put mechanisms in place to allow any individual or entity to notify them of the presence on their service of specific items of information that the individual or entity considers to be illegal content. Those mechanisms shall be easy to access and user-friendly, shall allow for the submission of notices exclusively by electronic means and facilitate the submission of sufficiently accurate and adequately substantiated notices. To that end, providers of hosting services shall take the necessary measures to enable and to facilitate the submission of notices containing all the following elements:

a. a sufficiently substantiated explanation of the reasons why individuals or entities allege the information in question to be illegal content;
b. a clear indication of the exact electronic location of that information, such as the exact URL or URLs, and, where necessary, additional information enabling the identification of the illegal content adapted to the type of content and to the specific type of hosting service;
c. the name and email address of the individual or entity submitting the notice (except in the case of information considered to involve one of the offences referred to in sections from 3 to 7 of Directive 2011/93/EU);
d. a statement confirming the *bona fide* belief of the individual or entity submitting the notice that the information and allegations contained therein are accurate and complete.

960. Where the notice contains the electronic contact information of the individual or entity that submitted it, the provider of hosting services shall, without undue delay, send back a confirmation of receipt of the notice. The provider shall also, without undue delay, notify that individual or entity of its decision in respect of the information to which the notice relates, providing information on the possibilities for redress in respect of that decision. Providers of hosting services shall process any notices that they receive and take their decisions in respect of the information to which the notices relate, in a timely, diligent, non-arbitrary and objective manner. Where they use automated means for that processing or decision-making, they shall include information on such use in the notification of the decision to which the notice relates.

§9. LEGAL PROTECTION AND SANCTIONS

961. Law No. 140/2006 has introduced in the Italian copyright Law a new set of measures, procedures, and remedies for copyright holders.[213]

Anyone who has a legitimate fear of infringement of an economic use right vested in them under the copyright Law or intends to prevent the continuation or repetition of an already occurred infringement, both by the perpetrator of the violation and an intermediary whose services are used for such violation, can take legal action to have their right recognized and the continuation of the infringement prohibited.[214] When issuing an injunction, the judge may set a sum due for each subsequently ascertained violation or non-compliance or for any delay in the execution of the measure.

Procedurally, for the protection of the rights of economic use and neighbouring rights, as well as for the ascertainment of damages and relative proofs on its quantification, provisional and ordinary protection is provided. Legal standing is held by the author, by the holder of the economic use rights, by those in legal possession of said rights and by those who may act on behalf of rights holders.

962. Regarding provisional measures, owners of the right may act to obtain (i) under section 161 of the copyright Law, the description and ascertainment, and the expert's report (with investigative character), (ii) under section 162-*ter*, the seizure (with sanctioning and injunction character, and (iii) under section 163, the injunction. As requirements for the issue of provisional measures, there are the appearance of the right based on which the party is proceeding and the danger in delay (prejudice resulting from the continuation of the illegal activity). Description and seizure are carried out by a judicial officer with the assistance of one (or more) experts, with the use of technical means of investigation, photography or otherwise. Seizure may not be affected in the case of works resulting from the collaboration of two or more persons, except in case of special severity or when the infringement is imputable to all the co-authors. The Judge may, in severe cases, order the seizure of profits due to the author of the disputed work or product. These provisions shall also apply to any person circulating, in whatever manner, or detaining, for commercial purposes, unauthorized copies of computer programs and any device intended exclusively for allowing or facilitating the unauthorized removal or the operational disconnection of protection devices for computer programs.

963. Apart from an injunction, which is a measure with anticipatory content, proceedings on the merits shall be instituted, under penalty of forfeiture of the obtained measures, within the time limit set by the judge who issued the injunction or within twenty working days or thirty-one calendar days (whichever is longer),

---

213. With reference to provisional measures, the new wording of s. 161 not only includes providers among possible recipients of description and seizure measures, but also provides that those measures may relate to evidence of infringement. In essence, more attention is given to the protection of economic interests than to moral rights.

214. Settled doctrine and case law consider ss 156 et seq. of the copyright Law regarding the judicial protection as applicable also in case of infringement of neighbouring right, in this sense *see* Court of Venice No. 6586/202, in DARTS IP.

starting from the pronouncement of the measure or its communication. The injunction, which is intended to prevent the infringement or to prevent its repetition, may be accompanied by monetary penalties for each infringement, non-compliance, or delay in the execution of the injunction. The rules of the Code of Civil Procedure may apply, unless otherwise provided for in the copyright Law.

964. As to the merits, section 156 provides for an action to ascertain one's right (copyright or related) and the related infringement with a final injunction against the infringer or intermediary, including the fixing of penalties for non-compliance. From an evidentiary point of view, the plaintiff must prove the asserted facts.

Under section 158 of the copyright Law, anyone who is harmed in the exercise of an economic use right vested in them can take legal action to obtain, in addition to compensation for damages, the removal or destruction, at the expense of the violator, of the actual condition resulting in the violation. The compensation owed to the injured party is determined pursuant to sections 1223, 1226, and 1227 of the Civil Code. The loss of profit is assessed by the judge in accordance with section 2056, second paragraph of the Civil Code, considering the profits made in violation of the right. The judge may also assess damages in a lump sum based on at least the amount of the rights that should have been recognized if the violator had requested permission from the right holder for the use of the right. Non-pecuniary damages are also due under section 2059 of the Civil Code, but the relevant burden of the proof must be satisfied.[215]

965. According to case law: (1) 'the criterion of retroversion of profits in copyright matters, even if more favourable to the injured party, nevertheless remains anchored to the rule of the necessary causal derivation under section 1223 of the Civil Code from the wrongful act: therefore, the sum, as ascertained as revenue for the exploitation of the work carried out by the responsible person, must be adjusted, on the one hand, by the costs incurred by him, and, on the other hand, by the autonomous contribution to the success of the work (...), favoured by the notoriety of the performer and by his concrete executive and evocative abilities, such as to arouse the interest of the public'; (2) 'Among the 'moderating factors' of the reimbursable profits, in accordance with the criterion of the retroversion of profits, under section 158, costs incurred by the author of the plagiarism (who has the burden of providing concrete elements of calculation, such as balance sheets, accounting records, contracts, etc. must be considered, while the Judge may order an Expert to give an

215. The allegation of this damage must necessarily be claimed and proven specifically: *see* Court of Torino decision No. 5252/2020 published on 14 May 2021, 'Regards the proof of such damage, the College points out that it must always be provided by the injured party as damage-consequence and not as damage-event: in fact, according to settled case law, "damage to reputation and image, according to the settled case law of this Court, is a consequential damage that requires, therefore, specific proof by the party seeking compensation" (Court of Cassation No. 20558/2014); Court of Milan, decision No. 3681/2022 published on 29 April 2022 "It is therefore common ground that non-pecuniary damage is recoverable in the case of injury to the right to the image. It should also be pointed out that the compensability of such damage does not exempt the plaintiff from burden of allegation"'; Court of Rome decision No. 19321/2021 published on 12 Dec. 2021, all in DARTS IP.

account of the average incidence of the costs on the revenues in the specific market sector, and in any event, to draw arguments of proof pursuant to section 116.2 of the Procedural Code, the autonomous contribution to the success of the work by the author or authors of the offence, to be ascertained by the judge, also in a presumptive manner, on the basis of the most objective indicators, such as the sales achieved by the responsible party, also for other works, within a significant and sufficiently extended period of time, and this in comparison with that of the author of the plagiarised work'.[216] Currently the Italian legal system does not expressly provide for punitive damages.[217]

966. In addition to damages, anyone injured by the exercise of a right of economic use belonging to them may institute legal proceedings for the removal or destruction of the material constituting the infringement. The removal or destruction may be affected only as regards to specimens or copies illegally reproduced or disseminated and contrivances employed for reproduction or dissemination which, by their nature, are not capable of use for reproduction or dissemination. If a part of the specimen copies or contrivance is capable of use for reproduction or dissemination the interested party may, at their expense, request the separation, in their interest, of such part. If the specimen, copy or contrivance of which the removal or destruction is requested has special artistic or scientific value, the judge may order, ex officio, its deposit in a public museum. The injured party may, at any time, ask that the specimens, copies, and contrivances liable to destruction to be delivered to them and their appraised value applied to reparation. The provisions for destruction and delivery shall not apply to infringing specimens or copies acquired in good faith for personal use. Removal or destruction shall not be demanded in the last year of the term for which the right endures.

967. The Law sets forth a prohibition of representation or performance: in particular, any person who is entitled to exercise the rights of public performance of a

---

216. *See* Court of Cassation, s. I, 29 Jul. 2021 No. 21833. As far as the loss of profits, Court of Cassation, by decision of 26 Jan. 2018, No. 2039 held that 'In the award of damages suffered by the owner of the right of economic use of a work, the judge has the power-duty to commensurate it, in the appreciation of the concrete circumstances, with the benefit derived from the prohibited activity, which rises to the useful criterion of loss of profit, when it is related to the profit of the damaging party, having exploited in its own favour opportunities for profit pertaining to the injured party and by decision of 29 May 2015, No. 11225 that 'On the subject of quantifying the damage suffered by the owner of the right to the economic use of a song whose plagiarism has been ascertained, the judge has the duty to commensurate it, by assessing the circumstances of the concrete case, with the benefit derived from the prohibited activity, which becomes a useful reference criterion for loss of profit, especially when it is related to the profit of the damaged party, in the sense that the latter has exploited in its own favour opportunities for profit pertaining to the damaged party, taking them away from the latter'.

217. A recent decision of Court of Cassation has been construed as a possible recognition by the Italian legal system also to punitive damages. In particular, the order of the Supreme Court of Cassation, after examining a broad analysis of the various compensation criteria provided for in Art. 125 of the Code of Industrial Property Rights, highlights its function, which is also punitive, and proposes interesting clarifications concerning the burden of proof, *see* Court of Cassation, s. I, 2 marzo 2021, No. 5666, G. Morretta e L. Brandoli 'Condotta contraffattiva: porta aperta ai danni punitivi', in 'Il Diritto industriale', fasc. 4, 2021.

work suitable for such performance, including a cinematographic work or a work of musical composition may request the Prefect of the province to prohibit any performance for which written proof of their consent is not shown.[218] The Prefect shall, upon request and based on any documents submitted, authorize or forbid the performance, subject to the right of the interested party to turn to the judicial authority for final decision.

968. If legal action is taken by one of the official legal entities referred to in sections 180 to 184, the following rules shall be observed: (1) officers may, without special authorization and upon proof of their status as such, institute actions in the interests of the rights' owner; (2) such legal entities shall be relieved of the obligation of granting security for carrying out acts in respect of which security is prescribed or authorized; (3) such legal entities may access to the procedure for securing an injunction (under the conditions set forth in sections 3 and 12 of the Royal Decree of 7 August 1936 No. 1531).

969. Authors of a work granted with the right of economic use may, after the assignment of such right, intervene at any time to protect their interests, in proceedings instituted by the assignee.

The judge may, at the instance of the interested party or ex officio, and at the expense of the unsuccessful party, order the operative portion of the judgment to be published, more than once, if necessary, in one or more newspapers. The rights of economic use may also be judicially enforced by any person legitimately entitled to such rights.

970. All mentioned rules shall be applicable in proceedings concerning the exercise of moral rights, safe the application of the following provisions:

- actions in defence of the rights bearing upon the authorship of the work shall give rise to sanctions of removal and destruction only when the injury cannot be remedied by means of addition or suppression of indications on the work which refer to its authorship or by other means of publicity;
- actions in defence of the rights bearing upon the integrity of the work shall give rise to removal or destruction of the deformed, mutilated or otherwise modified copy of the work only when it is not possible to re-establish said copy in its original form at the expense of the party interested in avoiding removal or destruction.

971. Under sections from 171 to 174-*quinqueis*, the Italian copyright Law also provides for *criminal sanctions* in relation to certain conducts in breach of copyright. In particular, the reproduction and dissemination of a protected work, the

218. SIAE, in exercising the protection of representation and performance rights for most works in the interest of owners, submits the request to the Prefect. This is an administrative measure that concerns only one representation or performance so that others are prohibited. The request must be submitted in writing at least eight hours before the announced start time of the performance, *see* under Art. 157 in L. C.Ubertazzi above.

unauthorized duplication, duplication and sale of protected works, the rental (including a sale with a ransom or under resolutive condition) or unauthorized use of originals, copies, or media, are subject to criminal punishment.[219]

The judicial authority may order the destruction of seized works when it results – by its nature or entity – difficult to keep. The confiscation of the means and materials used for (or intended to) committing offences is permitted.

§10. Public Entities for the Protection of Copyrights

972. The right to act as an intermediary in any way, whether by direct or indirect intervention, mediation, agency, or representation, or by assignment of the exercise of the rights of performance, recitation, broadcasting, and mechanical and cinematographic reproduction of protected works shall be reserved exclusively[220] to S.I.A.E. (Società Italiana degli autori ed editori).

973. Its activities shall be exercised to: (1) grant licences and authorizations for the economic use of protected works, in the account and interest of the entitled persons; (2) collect the profits arising from said licences and authorizations;[221] (3) distribute said profits among the persons entitled thereto. SIAE shall carry on its activities, in accordance with the provisions established by regulations of foreign countries in which it possesses organized representation. Said exclusivity of powers shall not prejudice the right of authors or their successors to exercise directly the rights recognized in their favour by the copyright Law. In the distribution of the profits mentioned under (4), a portion shall be reserved to the author.

974. If the rights of economic use of the work give rise to the collection of funds abroad on behalf of Italian citizens domiciled or resident within Italy, and the owners of these rights do not – for any reason – effect the collection of such funds, then,

219. Criminal proceedings may not be commenced or continued against a person who has already been administratively sanctioned for the same copyright infringement. In particular, by a very recent decision No. 149/2022 of 16 Jun. 2022, the Constitutional Court declared the constitutional illegitimacy of s. 649 of the Code of Criminal Procedure, in the part in which it does not provide that the judge pronounces a judgment of acquittal or not to proceed against a defendant for one of the offences provided for by sec. 171-*ter* of copyright Law which, in relation to the same act, has already been the subject of proceedings, finally concluded, for the administrative offence referred to in s. 174-*bis* of the same law.

220. The activity of copyright intermediation may also be exercised by collective management organizations, but – after the introduction of the so-called Barnier Directive – the liberalization of the market happened only partially.

221. On 21 Mar. 2024 in Case C-10/22 the Court of Justice ruled that Art. 56 TFEU, read in conjunction with Directive 2014/26/EU of the European Parliament and of the Council of 26 Feb. 2014 on collective management of copyright and related rights and multi-territorial licensing of rights in musical works for online use in the internal market, must be interpreted as precluding legislation of a Member State which generally and absolutely excludes the possibility of independent management entities established in another Member State providing their copyright management services in that first Member State.

Therefore on the basis of such decision Art. 180 of the Italian Copyright Law is contrary to the freedom to provide services under Art. 56 TFEU.

after the lapse of one year from the date when liability for payment arose, S.I.A.E. shall be empowered to exercise the rights in the account and interest of the authors or their successors in title.

975. The funds collected by S.I.A.E., shall (after deduction of expenses) be held at the disposal of claimants for a period of three years. If this period elapses without such funds being claimed, they shall be paid to the National Federation of professional artists (Confederazione Nazionale professionisti ed artisti) to assist categories of authors, writers, and musicians.

976. In addition, S.I.A.E. may, pursuant to its statutes, exercise other activities connected with the protection of intellectual works. It may undertake, for the account of the State or of public or private institutions, the services of ascertaining and collecting taxes, contributions, and fees.

S.I.A.E., to prevent and ascertain infringements to the copyright Law, is entrusted with supervising: (a) the reproduction and duplication, by any means, on audiovisual and phonographic support, and any other support, as well as with supervising premises where the use in public by air or by cable takes place, and the broadcasting activity made by any means; (b) the public show in cinemas of copyrighted works and recordings or those protected by neighbouring rights; (c) the distribution, sale, rental, broadcasting and utilization in any form of the supports under point (a); (d) public or private reproduction centres, which use in their own premises or make available to third parties, even for free, photocopiers, xerox copiers or analogous reproduction system; (d-*bis*) the manufacturing, import and distribution of devices and media under section 71-septies. Within the tasks it is entrusted with by Law, S.I.A.E. shall coordinate its activity with the Authority for telecommunications.

§11. Field of Application

977. The Italian copyright Law applies to all works by Italian authors, wherever first published, (except for provisions as of section 189). It equally applies to works by foreign authors domiciled in Italy for works which have been first published in Italy.

The Law may likewise be applied to the works of foreign authors, when the following conditions are fulfilled:

- international conventions for the protection of copyrighted works shall govern the field of application of the Italian copyright Law to works of foreign authors;
- if the conventions contain general stipulation of reciprocity or equality of treatment, such stipulation shall be interpreted according to the rules of actual equivalence of the two protections;
- in absence of international agreements, works of foreign authors which do not comply with the conditions specified in the second paragraph of section 185 shall, within the limits of actual equivalence, enjoy the protection granted by the copyright Law, provided that the State of which they are citizens grants the works of Italian authors effectively equivalent protection;

– if foreigners are stateless or if their nationality is uncertain, the rule of the preceding paragraph shall operate with reference to the State in which the work is first published.

978. Actual equivalence shall be certified and regulated by Presidential Decree. The duration of protection of a foreign work shall in no case exceed that one granted to the work in the State of which the foreign author is citizen. If the law of said State includes a period of compulsory licensing during the term of protection, the foreign work shall be submitted to an equivalent rule in Italy. If the law of said State subjects protection to the fulfilment of formalities, declarations of reservation, or the deposit of copies of the work, or any other formality, the foreign work shall, in Italy, be subject to equivalent formalities, as determined by Presidential Decree.

979. The provisions of section 185 shall apply to cinematographic works, phonograph records or contrivances, to the rights of performing actors or artists, to photographs and engineering works, if such works or products are created in Italy or may be considered national works according to the copyright Law or any other special law.

§12. The Right of Economic Use for Certain Categories of Works

980. Musical drama, musical compositions with words, film and pantomime works.

In the absence of a special agreement between collaborators in respect of operas, operettas, monologues, musical compositions with words and dance and ballet music, the following provisions shall apply. The author of the musical part shall be entitled to exercise the rights of economic use; however, the rights flowing from the common ownership of the parties are not affected. The profits derived from economic use shall be shared in proportion to the values of the respective literary and musical contributions. For operas, the value of the musical part shall be regarded as being three-quarters of the total value of the work. In operettas, in monologues, in musical compositions with words, and in dance and ballet music, the value of two contributions shall be considered equal.

981. Subject to the provisions of the following points, each collaborator shall be entitled to use their own work separately and independently.

The author of the literary part may dispose thereof for the purpose of its union with some other musical work, only in the following cases: (i) if, after the final text of the manuscript of the literary contribution has been sent to the composer, they do not set it to music within five years in the case of a libretto for an opera or operetta, or within one year in the case of any other literary work to be set to music; (ii) if, after having been set to music and considered by the parties as being ready for performance, the work is not performed within the period specified in the preceding subsection, except as longer periods may be granted for performance in accordance with sections 139 and 141; (iii) if, after a first performance, the work ceases to be performed for a period of ten years in the case of an opera, an oratorio, a symphonic poem or an operetta, or for a period of two years in the case of any other composition.

The *composer*, in the cases specified in points (ii) and (iii), may make use of the music in other ways.

In the case as of point (i), the author of the literary part shall reacquire the right of unrestricted disposal thereof, without prejudice to any ultimate action for damages that they may take against the composer. In the cases as of points (ii) and (iii), and without prejudice to any action for damages referred to in the preceding paragraph, the community rights as such shall be maintained in respect of the work which has already been set to music, but the work itself may not be performed without the consent of both collaborators.

With reference to *choreographic works or pantomimes*, or *other works consisting of music with words, dancing or mimicry, such as musical reviews and similar works*, in which the musical part does not constitute the principal function or value, the right of economic use shall, in the absence of different agreement, belong to the author of the choreographic or pantomimic part (in case of musical revues to the author of the literary part).

982. For collective works, the right of economic use shall, in the absence of different agreement, belong to the *publisher of the work*,[222] without prejudice to any right deriving from the application of section 7 (according to which the author of the collective work is the person who organizes and directs the creation of the work).

983. The right to use their own contributions separately shall be reserved to the individual collaborators in collective works,[223] provided they observe any subsisting agreements, or, in the absence of agreements, the rules set out below.

---

222. *See* Court of Cassation, ruling on case No. 20410/2006, held that 'On the subject of copyright, pursuant to Articles 7 and 38 of Law No. 633/1941 , for collective works - which include magazines and newspapers - while the moral right belongs to the person who directs and organises the overall work, the right of economic use belongs, unless otherwise agreed, to the publisher, who assuming the risk of publication, is entitled to the receipt of the relevant economic result. This right extends to the whole work, including - for the purposes of protecting the exclusivity of exploitation - each of its parts.' In the same sense, Court of Cassation, ruling on the case 10612/1999, held that 'Pursuant to Articles 38, 7, and 42 respectively of Law No. 633 of 22 April 1941, for collective works, to which magazines and newspapers belong, the moral right of authorship belongs to the editor, creator of the overall work; the right of economic use to the publisher and the right to use his contribution in other magazines or newspapers to the contributor. These rules, however, shall apply in the absence of a different agreement between the parties', in DARTS IP.
223. In a recent decision of the TAR (Tribunale Amministrativo Regionale) of Lazio, ruling on case No. 3437/2020 published on 3 Mar. 2021, it has been stated that 'According to Art. 3 of the Copyright Law, the author's right to the individual newspaper article is flanked by the author's right to the newspaper as a collective work, which is intended to protect the activity of choosing and coordinating the individual contributions. Article 38 of the Copyright Law assigns the patrimonial rights on the collective work newspaper not so much to the editor, who directs the creation of the work, carrying out the choice and coordination of the individual contributions and who, under Art. 7 of the Copyright Law is the holder of the moral rights, but to the publisher, thereby rewarding the contribution of organisation and the employment of means and capital', in DARTS IP.

If, without prior agreement, an article is sent to a magazine or newspaper by a person outside the editorial staff, for the purpose of reproduction, the author shall reacquire the right to dispose of it unrestrictedly if he does not receive notice of acceptance within one month from notification of such acceptance.

In the absence of agreement to the contrary, the collaborator, in a collective work other than a magazine or newspaper, shall be entitled to have their name appear in a customary manner in the reproduction of his work.

984. The *director of a newspaper* shall, in the absence of agreement to the contrary, be entitled to introduce into an article submitted for reproduction such modifications of form as are required by the nature and objects of the newspaper.

985. Authors of an article or other work reproduced in a collective work shall be entitled to reproduce it in a separate form, or to include it in a volume, provided they indicate the collective work from which it has been taken and the date of publication. In the case of articles appearing in magazines or newspapers, the author shall, in the absence of agreement to the contrary, also have the right to reproduce them in other magazines or newspapers. The author of the subject, the author of the scenario, the composer of the music and the artistic director shall be considered co-authors of a cinematographic work.

986. As seen in section 4.7 above, following the implementation of Directive (EU) 2019/790, section 43-*bis* was introduced, regulating the new right granted to publishers of journalistic publications.[224] The provision regulates analytically the relationship between the author and the platform, whereby in the event of failure to agree on the amount of remuneration, the parties may refer the matter to the Guarantee Authority Communications Authority (AGCOM); in case of non-compliance with the Authority's decision, they can turn to the section of the ordinary Court specialized in Business Sections. Providers, including media monitoring and review companies press, are obliged to make any appropriate data to determine the measure of fair compensation available. The fulfilment of this obligation is monitored by AGCOM, which – in the event of failure to communicate – applies administrative pecuniary sanctions, up to 1% of the turnover achieved in the last financial year closed prior to the notification of the contestation.

224. A publication of a journalistic character means a set composed principally of literary works of a journalistic character, which may include other works and protected subject matter, such as photographs or videograms, and constitutes a single item within a periodical or regularly updated publication bearing a single title, such as a newspaper or magazine of general or specific interest, with the function of informing the public about news, or other subjects, published in any medium under the initiative, editorial responsibility and control of a publisher or news agency. For the purposes of this Article, periodical publications for scientific or academic purposes are not considered to be journalistic publications. The rights of reproduction and communication shall not be granted in the case of private or non-commercial use of journalistic publications by individual users, nor in the case of hyperlinks or use of single words or very short extracts from journalistic publications. A very short extract from a journalistic publication is any portion of such publication that does not dispense with the need to consult the journalistic article in its entirety.

In particular, (*1*) Publishers of journalistic publications, whether single or associated or consortia, are recognized for the online use of their journalistic publications by information society service providers referred to in Article 1(1)(b), of Legislative Decree No 223 of 15 December 2017, including media monitoring companies and press reviews, the exclusive reproduction and communication rights referred to in Articles 13 and 16. (*2*). A journalistic publication means a set composed primarily of literary works of a journalistic character, which may include other works and protected materials, such as photographs or video grams, and constitutes a single element within a periodical or regularly updated publication bearing a single title, such as a newspaper or magazine of general or specific interest, with the function of informing the public about news, or other subjects, published in any medium under the initiative, editorial responsibility and control of a publisher or news agency. For the purposes of this Article, publications periodicals for scientific or academic purposes are not considered to be journalistic publications. (*3*). Publishers of journalistic publications are defined as persons who, either as single, associated or consortium form, in the exercise of an economic activity, publish the publications referred to in paragraph 2, even if they are established in another Member State. (*4*). The rights recognized by the copyright Law in favour of authors and other right holders concerning works or other materials included in a journalistic publication, including the right to exploit them also in forms other than journalistic publication shall in any case be ineffective. (*5*). Where works or other protected materials are included in a journalistic publication based on a non-exclusive licence, the rights referred to in paragraph 1 may not be invoked to prevent use by other authorized users or to prevent the use of works or other materials whose protection has expired. (*6*) The rights referred to in paragraph 1 shall not be granted in case of private or non-commercial use of journalistic publications by individual users, nor in the case of hyperlinks or the use of single words or very short extracts from journalistic publications. (*7*) A very short extract of a journalistic publication means any portion of such publication that does not dispense with the need to consult the journalistic article in its entirety. *(8)* For the online use of journalistic publications, the providers of information society services shall pay the persons referred to in paragraph 1 fair compensation. (9) The negotiation, for the conclusion of the contract for the use of the rights referred to in paragraph 1, between information society service providers, including media monitoring and press review companies, and the publishers referred to in paragraph 3, shall also be conducted considering the criteria defined by the regulation referred to in paragraph 8. During the negotiation, information society service providers shall not limit the visibility of publishers' content in search results. The unjustified restriction of such content during negotiations may be assessed for the purpose of verifying compliance with the obligation of good faith pursuant to section 1337 of the Civil Code. (10) Without prejudice to the right to refer the matter to the ordinary judicial authorities, if no agreement on the amount of compensation is reached within thirty days from the request to start negotiations by one of the parties concerned, either party may solicitate the AGCOM to determine fair compensation. Within sixty days from the request of the interested party, even when a party, though duly summoned, has not presented itself, the Authority shall indicate, on the basis of the criteria established by the regulation referred to in paragraph 8, which one between the economic formulated proposals complies with the aforementioned criteria or, if it does not consider any of the proposals to be compliant, it shall indicate ex officio the amount of fair compensation. (11) When, following the determination of fair compensation by AGCOM, the parties fail to conclude the contract, either party may refer the matter to the section of the ordinary courts specialized in enterprise matters, competent pursuant to section 3(1)(b) of Legislative Decree No. 168 of 27 June 2003, also with a view to bringing the action referred to in section 9 of Law No. 192 of 18 June 1998. (*12*) Providers of information society services, including media monitoring and press review companies, shall be obliged to make available, at the request of the interested party, including through the collective management bodies or independent management entities referred to in Legislative Decree No. 35 of 15 March 2017, where mandated, or AGCOM, the necessary data to determine the measure of fair compensation. The fulfilment of the obligation referred to in the first sentence shall not exempt the publishers referred to in paragraph 3 from respecting the confidentiality of the commercial, industrial, and financial information of which they have become aware. Compliance with the obligation to provide information by service providers shall be monitored by AGCOM. In the event of failure to communicate such data within thirty days from the request pursuant to the first sentence, the Authority shall impose an administrative pecuniary sanction on the defaulting party, up to 1% of the turnover achieved in the last financial year closed prior to notification of the dispute. For the administrative sanctions referred to in the fourth sentence, the benefit of reduced payment provided for by section 16 of Law No. 689 of 24 November 1981 is excluded. (*13*) Publishers referred to in paragraph 3, whether individually or in association or consortium, shall pay the authors of journalistic articles a share, between 2% and 5%, of fair compensation referred to in paragraph 8, to be determined, for self-employed workers, on a conventional basis. For employed workers this share may be determined by collective agreement. (*14*) The rights referred to in this section shall expire two years after the publication of the work of journalistic nature. This period shall be calculated from 1 January of the year following the date of publication of the work. (*15*) The provisions of this section shall not apply to journalism publications published for the first time before 6 June 2019. (*16*) The provisions relating to the exceptions and limitations are provided for in Chapter V of Title I, the technological protection measures are provided for in Title II-*ter*, the defences and judicial sanctions are provided for in Chapter III of Title III, as well as in section 2 of Law No. 167/2017.

§13. Cinematographic Work

987. The rights of economic use of *cinematographic works* shall belong to the person who has organized the relating production. The evolution of the means of production and dissemination of intellectual works has led to the emergence of new audiovisual cultural products, and the interpretation of the notion of cinematographic work must be carried out in an evolutionary and extensive way. Therefore, protection shall be granted to creative works, e.g., documentaries, works of fiction, reality shows, the television format, audiovisual advertising clips, music videos.[225]

988. The rights of economic use belonging to *producers*,[226] namely the person who is indicated in the cinematographic film, shall have as its object the cinematographic exploitation of the produced work. In absence of agreement to the contrary, the producer shall not make or show elaborations, transformations, or translations of the produced work without the consent of the authors indicated in section 44.

Authors of music, of musical compositions and of the words which accompany music shall be entitled to collect directly from the persons publicly showing the work a separate payment in respect of such showing.

Authors of the subject, of the scenario and artistic directors, in cases where they are not remunerated upon the basis of a percentage of the receipts derived from public showing, shall, in absence of an agreement to the contrary, be entitled to receive an additional payment when the receipts have attained a level to be fixed by contract with the producer. The form and amount of such payment shall be fixed by agreement between the categories of persons interested.

In compliance with Legislative Decree No. 177/2021, fair remuneration shall be proportionated: the modalities for determining remuneration in absence of an agreement between the parties have been amended and updated, referring their definition to AGCOM instead of the arbitration board provided for in section 4 of Legislative Decree No. 440/ 1945, the mechanism of which was scarcely used. These changes are also consistent with the new powers attributed to AGCOM and with the aims of the directive aimed at a more effective protection of copyright and related rights.

Producers shall have the right to make modifications in cinematographic works when necessary for their cinematographic adaption. Authors of a cinematographic work shall be entitled to have their names, together with an indication of their professional functions and their contributions, mentioned in the act of showing the final work.

Authors of literary or musical parts of a cinematographic work may reproduce them or utilize them separately in any manner, provided no damage is thereby occasioned to the rights of use, the exercise of which belongs to the producer. If the producer fails to complete the cinematographic work within a period of three years[227] from the delivery of the literary or musical parts or does not show the completed

225. L. C. Ubertazzi, under ss 44-50, as cited above.

226. *See* Court of Naples on case No. 12144/2016 by decision No. 4476/2020 published on 27 Jun. 2020 'Art. 45 provides that The exercise of the rights of economic exploitation of the cinematographic work belongs to those who have organised the production itself, within the limits indicated in the following articles. The regulatory provision is clear in attributing to the producer (i.e., the person who is not only responsible for the technical and financial organisation necessary for the creation of the cinematographic work but secures by contract all the contributions, also creative ones, necessary for the realisation of the same) the exercise and therefore the ownership of the patrimonial rights of the film, as also confirmed by relevant case law' (*see* Court of Rome of 30.05.1984; Court of Rome of 01.09.1980 and Court of Milan of 31.05.2010), in DARTS IP.

227. L. C. Ubertazzi, under art 50, 'The three-year time limit is the result of balancing the interests at stake, considering the technical lead time and the possible immediate usability of the literary parts of the work. It is provided for the protection of authors as weaker contracting parties, so it cannot be waived by prior agreement between the parties', *see* as cited above.

work within three years from its completion, the authors of said parts shall be entitled to dispose unrestrictedly of the work.

Broadcasting. In view of the nature and purposes of broadcasting, as a service reserved for the state, which exercises it directly or through concessions, the exclusive right of broadcasting, directly or by any intermediary means, is regulated by the following special rules.

The entity operating the broadcasting service has the authority to broadcast intellectual works from theatres, concert halls, and any other public place, under the conditions and within the limits specified in this article and the following ones. Owners, impresarios, and all those involved in the performance are required to allow the installation and technical tests necessary to prepare the broadcast. The consent of the author is necessary to broadcast new works and the first seasonal performances of non-new works. A theatrical work publicly performed in three different theatres or other public places is not considered new.

During performance or concert seasons lasting no less than two months, the right of the entity mentioned in the previous article can be exercised for performances once a week and for concerts every five or fractions of five concerts. The duration of the theatre or concert season is understood to be that resulting from posters or programs published before the start of the season.

The verification of compliance with good technical standards for broadcasts is the exclusive responsibility of state bodies responsible for monitoring broadcasts, with the powers established by section 2, paragraph of Law No. 1352/1928, and section 2 of Royal Decree-Law February 3, 1936-XIV, No. 654, converted into Law No. 1552/1936. The name of the author and the title of the work must be broadcast simultaneously with the work.

Without prejudice to the rights of the author on the broadcast of their work, the entity operating the service is authorized to record on a disc or on another medium the same work for deferred broadcasting due to schedule or technical needs, provided that the recording is, after use, destroyed or rendered unusable. The preservation in official archives of recordings referred to in paragraph 1 that have an exceptional documentary character is allowed, with no possibility of further use for economic or commercial purposes, except for the latter, with the authorization of the author of the work and the holders of related rights.

The author of the broadcasted work, as provided in the preceding articles, has the right to obtain from the entity operating the broadcasting service the payment of compensation, to be settled, in case of disagreement between the parties, by the judicial authority. The claim cannot be brought before the judicial authority before attempting conciliation in the ways and forms that will be established in the regulations.

Compensation is calculated based on the number of broadcasts.

For the public performance of radio broadcasted works through sound radio receiving devices equipped with a loudspeaker in public establishments, the author is entitled to fair compensation. This compensation is periodically determined through agreement between SIAE and the representation of the relevant trade union.

The broadcasting of intellectual works from the premises of the entity providing the broadcasting service is subject to the author's consent in accordance with the provisions contained in the third chapter of this title; the provisions of the preceding articles do not apply to it, except for those of section 55.

§14. Special Provisions on Computer Programs

989. The exclusive rights granted by this law on computer programs include the right to perform or authorize (a) the reproduction, permanent or temporary, total, or partial, of the computer program by any means or in any form. To the extent that operations such as loading, displaying, executing, transmitting, or storing the computer program require reproduction, such operations are also subject to the authorization of the rights holder; (b) translation, adaptation, transformation, and any other modification of the computer program, as well as the reproduction of the resulting work, without prejudice to the rights of those modifying the program; (c) any form of distribution to the public, including rental, of the original computer program or copies thereof. The first sale of a copy of the program in the European Economic Community by the rights holder, or with their consent, exhausts the distribution right of that copy within the Community, except for the right to control further rental of the program or a copy thereof.

Unless otherwise agreed, the activities specified in section 64-*bis*, letters a) and b), are not subject to the authorization of the rights holder when these activities are necessary for the use of the computer program in accordance with its intended purpose by the rightful acquirer, including error correction. It is not prohibited by contract for those with the right to use a copy of the computer program to make a backup copy of the program if such a copy is necessary for use. The person with the right to use a copy of the computer program may, without the authorization of the rights holder, observe, study, or test the program's operation to determine the ideas and principles on which each element of the program is based, provided that these actions are performed during loading, displaying, executing, transmitting, or storing the program that the person has the right to perform. Contractual clauses agreed in violation of this paragraph and paragraph 2 are void.

Authorization from the rights holder is not required if the reproduction of the computer program's code and the translation of its form, as referred to in section 64-*bis*, letters a) and b), carried out to modify the code's form, are essential to obtain the information necessary for achieving interoperability with other independently created computer programs, provided the following conditions are met: (a) the aforementioned activities are carried out by the licensee or others who have the right to use a copy of the program or, on their behalf, by someone authorized for this purpose; (b) the information necessary for achieving interoperability is not readily and quickly accessible to the parties indicated in letter a); (c) the aforementioned activities are limited to the parts of the original program necessary to achieve interoperability.

The provisions of paragraph 1 do not allow the information obtained under their application to: (a) be used for purposes other than achieving the interoperability of the independently created program; (b) be communicated to third parties, except to enable the interoperability of the independently created program; (c) be used for the development, production, or marketing of a computer program substantially similar in its expressive form, or for any other activity that violates copyright. Contractual clauses agreed in violation of such rules are null and void.

990. The duplication of software is permitted only when necessary to achieve interoperability with other programmes of independently created software. As clarified by the Court of Milan, 'what matters, to make the analysis activity, performed by a person who is not the author, lawful, is the purpose of the activity, which must be the typical destination of the work, the object of protection, (…). The activity of analysis is also permitted, (.), when it is indispensable to obtain the information necessary to achieve interoperability with other programmes. It should be noted, however, that even in this hypothesis, the lawfulness of the analysis is subject to compliance with certain conditions and, specifically, the non-use of the information for 'purposes other than the achievement the interoperability of the independently created programme' and the non-use of the information for exploitation 'for the development, production or marketing of a programme substantially similar in its expressive form' (section 64c), in other words, for commercial purposes; a provision that too, as expressly provided, cannot be derogated from by contractual clauses, under penalty of nullity. In conclusion, analysis operations, aimed at understanding the functioning mechanisms of the programmes, are permitted to the extent that they are aimed at the use and typical destination of the programmes, while they are never permitted for commercial purposes'.[228]

§15. Free Use

991. Case law indicates that 'free uses are exceptional cases, subject to restrictive interpretation and their scope of application is limited to the strict cases expressly determined'.[229]

The provisions of sections 65 and seq. of the copyright Law, identify a regulatory area within which, for purposes of collective interest – such as teaching, research, information, and criticism –, the author's exclusive right is 'weakened' and third parties are allowed, within specific limits, to freely use the work. This is the result of balancing the need to protect the author and that of disseminating knowledge, encourage the free exchange of ideas and, ultimately, produce culture.[230]

992. The rules on exceptions and limitations do not affect the authors' moral rights.

Free uses are mainly referred to the following cases: articles of economic, political or religious interest, published in magazines or newspapers, discourses upon matters of political or administrative interest delivered in public assemblies or in any other public manner, works or portions of works that may be reproduced for use in judicial or administrative proceedings, reproduction of single works or portions of works for the personal use of readers, photo-copying of works existing in

---

228. *See* Court of Milan No. 68360/2013, BUSINESS COMPETENCE vs FACEBOOK, in DARTS IP.
229. *See* Court of Rome, decision of 22/4/2008, in DARTS IP.
230. *See* Court of Milan No. 32236/2014, published on 8 Feb. 2017, in DARTS IP.

libraries, when made for personal use or the services of the library. These free utilizations and the relevant characteristic thereof are set forth in section from 65 to 71-*decies* of the copyright Law.

993. As far as free uses are concerned, Directive (EU) No. 790/2021, enforced in Italy by Legislative Decree No. 177/2021, has introduced section 70-*bis* to the copyright Law.

Chapter 5. Legal Protection of Software

§1. The Legislative Framework

994. The legal protection of software in Italy is primarily governed by intellectual property laws, particularly focusing on copyright protection. The Italian legal framework for software protection is influenced by European Union directives and international treaties, which Italy has incorporated into its national legislation. Below is an overview of the fundamental principles and key aspects of how software is protected under Italian law:

995. Legal Basis
Software is protected as a literary work under the Italian Copyright Law (Legge sul Diritto d'Autore), which implements the European Directive 2009/24/EC on the legal protection of computer programs. This directive harmonizes the protection of software across EU member states, including Italy.[231]

996. Scope of Protection
Source Code and Object Code: Both the source code (the human-readable form of the program) and the object code (the machine-readable form) are protected by copyright. This protection covers the expression of the software, not the underlying ideas, algorithms, or principles that the software implements.
User Interfaces: Certain elements of the user interface may be protected if they meet the criteria of originality, although the extent of this protection can be more limited compared to the code itself.
Documentation and Manuals: Documentation that accompanies software, including user manuals and technical instructions, are also protected under copyright as part of the software package.

997. Originality Requirement
For software to be protected, it must be original, meaning it is the author's own intellectual creation. This requirement is consistent with broader EU copyright principles.
Rights Conferred: The copyright holder of software enjoys several exclusive rights, including:
Reproduction Right: The right to make copies of the software, including copying it onto a computer or other device.
Modification Right: The right to modify the software, including creating derivative works or adaptations.
Distribution Right: The right to distribute copies of the software, whether by sale, lease, or other means.
Right of Communication to the Public: The right to make the software available to the public, including through online distribution.

231. *See* G. Ghidini, E. Arezzo, 'Il software fra brevetto e diritto d'autore. primi appunti sulla proposta di direttiva comunitaria sulle «invenzioni attuate per mezzo di elaboratori elettronici»', in 'Rivista di diritto industriale', fasc. 1, 2005, p. 46.

998. Duration of Protection

Term of Protection: The copyright protection for software in Italy lasts for the lifetime of the author plus 70 years. If the software is created by an entity (such as a company), the protection lasts for 70 years from the date of first publication or creation, depending on the circumstances.

999. Moral Rights

Moral Rights of the Author: In Italy, authors have moral rights over their works, including software. These rights are inalienable and include:

Right of Attribution: The author has the right to be recognized as the creator of the software.

Right of Integrity: The author can prevent any distortion, mutilation, or other modifications of the software that would harm their reputation.

1000. Licensing and Transfer of Rights

Licensing: The rights holder can grant licenses to third parties to use, reproduce, or modify the software. These licenses can be exclusive or non-exclusive and are often governed by detailed contractual agreements.

Transfer of Rights: Copyright in software can be transferred or assigned, typically through a contractual agreement. This allows the original author or rights holder to sell their rights to another party.

1001. Protection Against Infringement

Infringement Actions: The copyright holder can take legal action against anyone who infringes on their rights. This includes unauthorized copying, distribution, or modification of the software. Italian courts can grant injunctions, order the seizure of infringing copies, and award damages to the rights holder.

Criminal Sanctions: In addition to civil remedies, Italian law also provides for criminal sanctions in cases of wilful infringement, particularly in cases involving commercial piracy or large-scale unauthorized distribution of software.

1002. Exceptions and Limitations

Backup Copies: Users who legally own a copy of the software are allowed to make backup copies for personal use.

Decompilation: Under certain conditions, the decompilation (reverse engineering) of software is allowed, particularly for achieving interoperability with other software, provided that such actions are not used to create a competing product.

Fair Use: Certain uses of software may fall under exceptions similar to 'fair use,' such as using software for teaching or research, provided it does not conflict with the normal exploitation of the software or unreasonably prejudice the legitimate interests of the rights holder.

1003. Patent Protection for Software-Related Inventions

Software Patents: While software as such is generally not patentable in Italy, inventions that involve software can be patented if they provide a technical solution to a technical problem. This means that if software controls a technical process or is integral to the functioning of a machine, it may be eligible for patent protection under the Italian Industrial Property Code.

1004. International Considerations

WIPO Treaties: Italy is a signatory to several international treaties administered by the World Intellectual Property Organization (WIPO), such as the Berne Convention and the WIPO Copyright Treaty, which provide international protection for software.

EU Harmonization: As part of the European Union, Italy adheres to EU directives and regulations that harmonize software protection across member states, ensuring consistency and mutual recognition of rights within the EU.

§2. Practical Issues

1005. Protecting the value of software: Software can be protected

- by copyright when it meets the requirements of creativity and originality;
- by patent when it contains one or more technically innovative algorithms.

It is also possible to register software with the Special Public Register held by S.I.A.E. This section of the site contains an information sheet on software copyright protection.

1006. Which software is protected by copyright? If it meets the legal requirements, software is protected by copyright without any special formalities. In order to prove creation, the software can be registered with the Special Public Register for Computer Programs or filed as an unpublished work if the software itself has not yet been published or used. It is also possible to patent software, but only in cases where it contains one or more technically innovative algorithms.

1007. Territory: Copyright protection for software extends to the entire territory of Italy, the State of San Marino and the Vatican City (a total of 324,000 sq. km, about 60 million inhabitants).

1008. Creativity and Originality: All software that meets the requirements of creativity and a minimum of originality with respect to pre-existing works, including elaborations and variations of previous software, may be registered.

1009. Registration of Software: The registration of software in the Special Public Register held at the OLAF Section of the SIAE (Italian Society of Authors and Publishers), must be carried out directly by the authors or their assignees, or, on their behalf, by their authorized representatives, by submitting a special form and the software to be registered.

1010. Effects of Registration: The effects of registration are to constitute a means of proof of the date of creation of the software and the data contained in the application submitted: authorship, title, date of publication.

1011. Exclusive rights to the software: Exclusive rights to the software include the right to economically exploit the software as well as the right to make or authorize reproduction, translation, adaptation, transformation, modification and distribution in any form of the software.

1012. Ownership: Ownership of the registration and hence of the software shall belong to the author or his Italian or foreign successor in title.

1013. Transfer: The rights to the software and the registration in the Special Public Register are freely transferable to third parties. The assignment shall be transcribed in the Special Public Register.

1014. Infringements and offences: Infringements and offences concerning software copyrights can be prosecuted and sanctioned both civilly (Articles 156–170 Copyright Law) and criminally (Article 171-*bis* and, residually, Article 171 Copyright Law). Legislative Decree No. 658/94 also provides for an administrative sanction (Article 171-*quater* of the Copyright Law) in the case of abusive rental of media reproducing software, even if lawfully produced.

1015. Customs Protection: Copyright in software entitles the holder to customs protection, i.e., to have counterfeit goods stopped at customs.

1016. Applicable laws: EEC Directive No. 91/250 of 14 May 1991, Legislative Decree No. 518 of 29 December 1992. Prime Ministerial Decree No. 244 of 3 January 1994.

§3. Main Case Law

1017. According to Court of Cassation, Criminal section V, 20/10/2023, No. 3211, the offence of revealing scientific or trade secrets can be committed if a secret of part of the production process is unduly disclosed.

The offence of disclosing scientific or commercial secrets can be committed whenever a secret concerning even a single part of the production process (in this case, by means of the technique of 'reverse engineering') is unlawfully disclosed, since it is not necessary for the disclosure to relate to all the components of the product.

1018. According to Court Bologna, Specialized Section in Enterprise, 03/11/2022, No. 2713, the protection of copyright concerning computer programs ('software'), like that concerning any other work, presupposes the requirement of originality, and it is therefore necessary to establish whether or not the program is the result of an original creative elaboration with respect to previous works, it being understood that creativity and originality also exist when the work is composed of simple ideas and notions, included in the intellectual patrimony of persons having experience in the subject matter of the work itself, provided that they are formulated and organized in a personal and autonomous manner with respect to previous works.

1019. According to Court Bologna, Specialized Section in Enterprise, 04/11/2021, No. 2581, the insertion of access codes in software constitutes a technological protection measure.

Activation codes for access to a computer program qualify as technological protection measures under Article 102-*quater* of the Copyright Law.

1020. According to Court of Turin, Specialized Section in Enterprise, 16/11/2020, No. 3959, a very similar user interface between two pieces of software may constitute evidence of copying.

Graphical similarities between the user interfaces of two pieces of software may constitute evidence of the derivation of one from the other.

The presence in the source codes of two pieces of software of the same typing errors constitutes the indelible chromosomal trace of their parent/child relationship, even when the software has been processed over time and can no longer be easily compared.

1021. According to Tribunale Firenze, Specialized Section in Enterprise, 23/05/2019, No. 1598, the owner of a software copyright has the right to oppose the execution of the program remotely.

In the case of software that can be accessed remotely, the right of the author of the program or his assignees to control its rental pursuant to Article 64-*bis*, 1(c) Copyright law includes the right to oppose the execution of the program by opening a remote connection to the server on which it is installed.

1022. According to Court of Cassation, Criminal section III, 27/04/2017, No. 38204, on the subject of copyright, consoles enjoy the same broad protection as video games.

Video games are not mere computer programs and cannot be brought under the concept of computer program. In fact, they are moving images, i.e., complex multimedia works that enjoy broad copyright protection. This also applies to consoles. The Court of Cassation takes stock of the legal protection of videogames by rejecting the request for referral to the United Sections to update the 'digital question', on the basis of a complained of potential conflict between judges of merit and Community jurisprudence. According to the Court, called to rule on a case of tampering with the Mtp (technological protection measures) of consoles, it is not necessary that the tampering occurs directly and exclusively on the videogame product (software), because if the console (hardware component) is necessary to 'run' the original software program, its role is that of a 'key' device placed to directly protect the copyright covered by the incriminating norm.

1023. According to Court Milan, Specialized Section in Enterprise, 06/11/2015, technological measures for the protection of copyright on a video game do not necessarily have to be incorporated on the work itself, but may instead be affixed to the physical supports of the video games or the consoles, operating in a relationship of interaction.

A video game has the quality of a complex and multimedia work; the protection of intellectual property applies to it, and in particular that of Article 171-*ter* lett. f/*bis*), in relation to Article 102-*quater* of the copyright law.

1024. According to Court of Appeal Venice, 09/07/2014, copyright protection concerning computer programs (the so-called software, which represents the creative substance of computer programs), like that concerning any other work, postulates the requirement of originality. Therefore, it is necessary to establish whether the work (i.e., the program) is or is not the result of an original creative elaboration with respect to previous works, but with an important clarification that creativity and originality subsist even when the work is composed of simple ideas and notions, included in the intellectual heritage of persons having experience in the subject matter of the work itself, provided that they are formulated and organized in a personal and autonomous manner with respect to previous works.

1025. According to Court of Cassation, Civil section I, 13/06/2014, No. 13524, the protection of copyright in respect of computer programs ('software', which is the creative substance of computer programs), like that in respect of any other work, presupposes the requirement of originality, and it is therefore necessary to establish whether or not the program is the result of an original creative process compared with previous works, it being understood that creativity and originality also exist when the work is composed of simple ideas and notions included in the intellectual wealth of persons having experience in the field of the work itself, provided that they are formulated and organized in a personal and autonomous manner with respect to previous works. The consistency in concrete terms of such autonomous contribution is the subject of an assessment destined to be resolved in a judgment of fact, as such reviewable in a court of law only for any flaws in the reasoning. (In the case in point, the Supreme Court upheld the judgment on the merits which found that the 'Giava' programme, designed for travel agencies and consisting of an accounting section and a section for ticket sales, was worthy of protection, evaluating it as original both from the point of view of its functionality and from the structural and algorithmic point of view of the 'software').

1026. According to Court of Catania, 12/07/2012, an unlawful servile imitation of the software relating to an electronic game exists when the two games have an almost identical name ('Fowl Play Summer 4' and '4 Fowl Play'), except for the addition of the word 'summer' which evokes, however, a mere summer edition of the same game; the screens of the game are substantially identical in terms of their basic graphic characters; the rules, scores, bonuses and instructions of the game are absolutely identical.

1027. According to Court of Florence, Section of Industrial and Intellectual Property, 17/06/2006, Articles 1 and 2 of Law No. 633/1941 extend the protection of intellectual works to computer programs. Pursuant to Article 12 of the same law, the owners of the rights have the exclusive right to use the programs they have created, and pursuant to Article 64-*bis* the exclusive right to proceed with the reproduction, permanent or temporary, total or partial, of the computer program by any means and in any form.

Pursuant to Article 156 Law No. 633/1941, anyone who has reason to fear the infringement of a right of economic use to which he is entitled or who intends to prevent the continuation or repetition of an infringement that has already occurred may take legal action to have his right ascertained and the infringement stopped.

The last paragraph of Article 161 Law No. 633 provides that the provisions of the regulations (which allow the Judicial Authority to order the description, ascertainment, appraisal or seizure of what is considered an infringement of the right of use) are also applicable to anyone who puts into circulation in any way or possesses for commercial purposes unauthorized copies of programs and any means aimed at allowing or facilitating the arbitrary removal or functional circumvention of the devices applied to protect a computer program.

The circumstance that the user company had a need to manage and update payment and accounting procedures and programmes cannot constitute a presumption of undue use of a programme.

In order to realize the probative effects referred to in Article 2727 of the Italian Civil Code, it is necessary that the unknown fact is a reasonably possible consequence according to a canon of probability of the fact ascertained, with reference to a connection of possible and likely events, according to a criterion of normality and according to the rules of experience taken by the Judge and according to the *id quod plerumque accidit*. There is no such link between, on the one hand, the need to update the accounts, to manage payments and to maintain administration and, on the other, the use of the 'Office' package programmes, events which are entirely unconnected and influenced by a multiplicity of facts which escape a causal relationship. The granting of the precautionary measure *inaudita altera parte* is justified where the information of the counterparty about the need to issue the measure, concerning objects that are easy to conceal, may determine the risk of the measure being unsuccessful or of the counterparty being deprived of the effects thereof.

1028. According to Court of Bologna, section of Industrial and Intellectual Property, 17/05/2006, the originality of a computer program is detectable only when its form of expression (programming language, user interface, processors) is the result of a creative effort, and not merely repetitive, of the author's ingenuity, even if the content of the program (represented by the algorithms) is identical to other previous ones. Therefore, the albeit modest level of this defining requirement cannot, in any event, disregard an activity with a certain degree of expressive complexity, which – at the very least – necessitates the underlying choice between different computer options, in addition to implying the adoption of the relevant formal representation by the author of the software.

Obviously, the minimum degree of originality considered appropriate for the purposes of the protection ensured by the L.d.A. – also on the basis of the prevailing interpretation of the relevant Article 2(8) – reverberates in specular terms on the limits of the exclusive right, in the sense that an equally low level of creativity in the subsequent one is then sufficient to exclude the infringement of the relevant programme.

Computer programs, in whatever form they are expressed, fall squarely under the protection of copyright law provided they are original, i.e., the result of the author's intellectual creation. Therefore, the originality of the software is recognizable only when its form of expression – in the form of programming language, user interface, processors – is the result of a creative effort and not merely repetitive of the author's ingenuity, even though the content of the program may be identical to others before it and therefore identical to others in its functionality. In such a context, the originality required for the purposes of the application of the legal protection cannot, however, disregard an activity with a certain degree of expressive complexity, which makes it at least necessary to choose between different computer options, it being at the same time necessary for the author of the software to give adequate formal representation to his work.

A computer program or software, which may be defined as the expression of an organized and structured set of instructions (or symbols) contained in any form or medium, capable directly or indirectly of causing a particular function, task or result to be performed or obtained by means of an electronic information processing system, is currently protected by Articles 1(2) and 2(8) of the Copyright Act.

It follows unquestionably from the regulatory definition that, with regard to software, neither its purpose, understood as the end it proposes (as a whole and in its modules), nor the mathematical algorithms that implement the functions that the program must perform, nor the flowchart, which describes at a detailed level the manner in which the various parts interact, are protected; On the other hand, both the source code, i.e., the set of steps and commands prepared by the author in an express form consisting of a language comprehensible to man, and the c. so-called object code, that is to say, the translation of the source code into machine language (which, although not being an expression comprehensible to man, falls under the protection of Article 2(8) by virtue of the textual reference 'in any form expressed').

1029. According to Court of Bolzano, 20/12/2005, computer products for consoles, that is to say, video games, are to be regarded for all intents and purposes as software. It follows that in the present case, Article 171-*bis* of Law No. 633 of 1941 must be applied (on the basis of which the criminal sanction would be applicable only and exclusively if a modchip were to be considered a means intended solely to allow or facilitate the arbitrary removal or functional circumvention of devices applied to protect a computer program) and not Article 171-*ter*, the latter being applied exclusively to phonograms and videograms. More specifically, the Community legislation set forth in Directive No. 29/2001/Ce is expressly applicable only to matters concerning phonograms and videograms. Consequently, since computer products for 'consoles' (in the case 'de quo' video games) are legally to be considered software, such discipline cannot be applied in the present case.

1030. According to Court Milan, 13/03/1987, software is the result of an intellectual activity falling within the scope of protection of copyright law and Articles

2575 et seq. of the Italian Civil Code. A derivative work is illegitimate where it repeats, albeit modifying it, the core and the original aspects of the 'derivative' programme; where the derivation is resolved in the repetition and reworking of the obligatory, non-new aspects of the programme, it does not appear well founded to invoke the protection under Article 18 of the copyright law, otherwise protection would be given to what 'ab origine' is not susceptible of being qualified as an intellectual work. Contractual ties between software companies can take on a broader applicative effectiveness that is free from the copyright regime.

Chapter 6. Protection of Databases

§1. Main Issues

1031. The legal protection of databases in Italy is governed by a combination of national laws, European Union directives, and international treaties.

The protection covers both the structure of the database and the contents under certain conditions.[232]

The key legal instruments include the Italian Copyright Law (Legge sul Diritto d'Autore) and the Database Directive 96/9/EC implemented into Italian law.

1032. In Italy, databases can be protected under two main legal frameworks: Copyright Protection: This applies to the original structure or arrangement of the database if it constitutes the author's own intellectual creation.

Sui Generis Database Right: This provides protection for the substantial investment made in obtaining, verifying, or presenting the contents of the database, even if the database itself is not eligible for copyright protection.

1033. A database is eligible for copyright protection if it is original, meaning the selection or arrangement of the content reflects the author's own intellectual creation. The content of the database itself does not need to be original—only the structure or arrangement must be.

1034. The copyright holder has exclusive rights to reproduce, distribute, and make available to the public the structure of the database. This includes the right to authorize or prohibit any adaptation, translation, or alteration of the database.

1035. The copyright protection for a database lasts for 70 years after the death of the author. If the author is a legal entity (such as a company), the protection lasts for 70 years from the date of creation or publication.

1036. The *sui generis* right protects databases that result from a substantial investment in the obtaining, verification, or presentation of their contents. This protection applies even if the database does not qualify for copyright protection due to a lack of originality.

1037. The *sui generis* right grants the database maker exclusive rights to prevent the extraction and/or reutilization of the whole or a substantial part of the contents of

232. *See* V. Falce, 'La disciplina comunitaria sulle banche dati. Un bilancio a dieci anni dall'adozione', in 'Rivista di diritto industriale', fasc. 6, 2006, p. 227; V. Falce, 'L''insostenibile leggerezza' delle regole sulle banche dati nell'unione dell'innovazione', in 'Rivista di diritto industriale', fasc. 4, 2018, p. 337; C. Sganga, 'Ventisei anni di Direttiva Database alla prova della nuova Strategia Europea per i Dati: evoluzioni giurisprudenziali e percorsi di riforma', in 'Diritto dell'informazione e dell'informatica', fasc. 3, 2022, p. 651.

the database. 'Extraction' refers to the permanent or temporary transfer of content to another medium, while 'reutilization' involves making the content available to the public.

1038. The *sui generis* right lasts for 15 years from the date of completion of the database. If the database is made publicly available during this period, the 15-year term begins from the date of first public availability. If substantial changes are made to the database, resulting in significant investment, a new 15-year term can begin, effectively renewing the protection.

1039. Italian law allows for certain exceptions to database protection, similar to fair use in copyright law. For example, extraction for private study or research, as long as it does not conflict with the normal exploitation of the database and does not unreasonably prejudice the legitimate interests of the right holder.

1040. In some cases, databases of significant public interest, such as those related to national security or public health, may be subject to mandatory licensing, where the government allows third parties to access the database under specified conditions.

1041. Database rights holders can enforce their rights through civil litigation in Italian courts. Remedies may include injunctions to prevent further infringement, damages for losses incurred, and orders for the seizure of infringing copies.

1042. In cases of deliberate infringement, particularly when it involves commercial exploitation, criminal sanctions may apply. This can include fines and, in some cases, imprisonment.

1043. Database rights holders can also request that customs authorities detain goods suspected of infringing database rights at the border, preventing their importation into Italy.

1044. One of the main legal challenges is determining what constitutes a 'substantial part' of a database, as this can vary depending on the content and context of use. Italian courts have developed case law to interpret these concepts, often in alignment with EU jurisprudence.

1045. The rise of big data and AI-driven databases raises questions about the applicability of traditional database protection frameworks. As databases become more dynamic and integrated with other technologies, Italian law will need to adapt to address these new challenges.[233]

---

233. *See* M. W. Monterossi, 'Estrazione e (ri)utilizzo di informazioni digitali all'interno della rete internet. il fenomeno del c.d. web scraping?', in 'Diritto dell'informazione dell'informatica', fasc. 2, 2020, p. 327.

1046. Given that databases are often used and accessed internationally, enforcing Italian database rights in other jurisdictions can be complex. This often requires cooperation with international bodies and alignment with EU regulations.

1047. Italy's database protection regime is aligned with the broader European Union framework, ensuring consistency across member states. The Database Directive 96/9/EC is crucial in harmonizing the protection standards, and Italy's participation in international treaties like the Berne Convention and TRIPS (Trade-Related Aspects of Intellectual Property Rights) ensures that Italian database rights are recognized internationally.

§2. Jurisprudence

1048. According to Court of Appeal Milan, 16/04/2018, an app that organizes information already existing in the database of a social network must be qualified as a database and not as software.

A software application that reinterprets already existing information and organizes that information in an original way must be qualified as a creative database.

An 'application' which reinterprets already existing information by cross-referencing the data present in the database of users of a social network with the geolocation function, which makes it possible to identify the geographical position of the person using the application, and organises that information in an original way must be classified as a database protected under Directive No. 9/1996 and not as a computer program.

The activity of testing a social network application carried out by the operator of the platform in breach of Article 64-*ter* of the Copyright Law relating to the analysis of a copy of a computer program and the consequent launch of an application identical to the first in its functions and purposes, infringes the copyright on the database recognized to the developer of the original application, producing to the latter's detriment a parasitic anti-competitive effect.

1049. According to Court of Cassation, Civil section I, 30/05/2017, No. 13543, if significant modifications are made to the content of a database, a new 15-year term of protection begins to run.

According to Article 102-*bis* Copyright Law, 'if significant new investments are made to the contents of the database [...] an autonomous term of protection begins': which is also 15 years, and concerns the term of protection of the entire database as modified by the new investments, and not only its modifications.

1050. According to Court of Appeal Rome, Specialized Section in Enterprise, 16 February 2021, No. 1199, databases are intellectual works, as intangible goods. As such, they must be protected in accordance with the provisions of Legislative Decree No. 169 of 6 May 1999; this protection is divided into two distinct profiles: that in favour of the author of the new creation (in the form of exclusive copyright) and that in favour of the so-called creator of the database, which takes the form of a special protection that presupposes proof by the applicant of the substantial investments made for the creation of the database.

1051. According to Court of Rome, section XVII, 27 January 2020, No. 11047, company databases containing policyholders' data are protected by secrecy.

Company databases containing policyholders' data are protected by secrecy pursuant to Articles 98 and 99 of the IPC. The undue retention by the former agent of the availability of these data and databases is in breach of basic rules of the agency contract and of industry regulations, as well as in violation of the normal rules of fairness and good faith.

1052. According to Court of Rome, Specialized Section in Enterprise, 17 January 2020, No. 1139, in order to prove the violation of a protected database, the time, place, extraction and re-use of data must be specified and proven.

For the purposes of the protection of the database pursuant to Article 102-*bis* of the Copyright Law, it is necessary to specify and prove the conduct allegedly carried out in breach thereof by means of the extraction and re-utilization of the data contained therein, as well as the data themselves and the modalities of time and place through which such breach allegedly occurred.

1053. According to Civil Cassation, Criminal section III, 29 May 2018, No. 6734, the maker of a database enjoys protection independent of that relating to the creative character of the work.

Pursuant to Article 102-*bis* of Italian Law No. 633 of 22 April 1941, introduced by Legislative Decree No. 169 of 6 May 1999, the database maker enjoys protection independent of the creative character of the work. The maker of a database – i.e., the person who makes a significant investment, from a qualitative or quantitative point of view, in its creation, verification or presentation – enjoys a protection independent of that relating to the creative or original character of the work, which consists in the right to prohibit the operations of extraction or re-use of the whole or of a substantial part thereof, with the consequent exclusion of the possibility of recourse by the same to the protection typical of copyright, both civil, as regards the moral right and the right of economic use, and criminal, with reference to the criminal offences provided for in Articles. 171 et seq. law No. 633 of 1941.

The legal protection granted to databases on the basis of copyright can only be applied if the choice or arrangement of the content constitutes an intellectual creation of its author. That being said, it must be ruled out that such characteristics correspond to the data published on the websites of the entities managing the advertising provided for in respect of judicial sales, expressly authorized by the Ministry itself in accordance with the directives set out in Ministerial Decree 31.10.2006 and contained in a specific list. The regulatory provisions provide that all notices of sale relating to ongoing proceedings must be uploaded on the portal, at the request of the persons who have been appointed in the proceedings. It is clear from such a system that the website is merely an entity managing the publicity of judicial sales, which in that capacity collects and publishes, without any margin of autonomy, let alone processing, the data transmitted to it from the Ministry's portal, intended to remain there for a limited time. It is therefore neither a question of a selective database, the contents of which are chosen in an original manner by the author, nor of a database in which, although the selection is not creative, the arrangement of the materials in the database is nevertheless original.

1054. According to Court of Appeal Milan, 16/04/2018, an app that organizes information already existing in the database of a social network must be qualified as a database and not as software.

A software application that reinterprets already existing information and organises that information in an original way must be qualified as a creative database.

An 'app' which reinterprets already existing information by cross-referencing data present in the database of users of a social network with the geolocation function, which makes it possible to identify the geographical position of the person using the app, and organises that information in an original way must be classified as a database protected under Directive No. 9/1996 and not as a computer program.

Chapter 7. Chips Protection

§1. Chips Protection

1055. A semiconductor product is a finished or intermediate product consisting of an assembly of materials comprising a layer of semiconductor material containing one or more composite layers of conducting, insulating or semiconducting material arranged in a predetermined three-dimensional pattern intended to perform, exclusively or in conjunction with other functions, an electronic function.

The topography of a semiconductor product is a series of related patterns, however fixed or encoded, representing the three-dimensional pattern of the layers of which a semiconductor product is composed and in which series each image reproduces in whole or in part a surface of the semiconductor product at any stage of its manufacture.

1056. From a global perspective, the weight of the Italian semiconductor industry is marginal: the value of production of semiconductors alone is around 3÷4 billion dollars against a world market that will reach 533 billion dollars in 2023, according to Gartner; overall, the turnover of our sector, considering manufacturers of equipment, substrates, materials and research is around 6÷8 billion dollars, relegating Italy to fifth/sixth place in Europe, while Italian manufacturing as a whole ranks second in Europe after Germany.[234]

1057. Pursuant to Article 88 of the Italian Code of Intellectual Property, the requirements for obtaining an exclusive right to a semiconductor product are: (*i*) be the result of the creative intellectual effort of their author that are not common or familiar within the semiconductor product industry; (*ii*) possibly be a combination of common or familiar elements, provided that taken together they are not common or familiar within the semiconductor industry; (*iii*) the exclusive rights arise on the first, in order of time, of the following dates: the date of the first commercial exploitation of the topography in any part of the world; the date on which the application for registration is filed in due form.

1058. The rights shall expire 10 years after the earlier of the following dates in order of time: the end of the calendar year in which the topography was first commercially exploited in any part of the world; the end of the calendar year in which the application for registration was filed in due form.

1059. Pursuant to Article 198 of Legislative Decree No. 30/2005, applications for protection relating to a semiconductor product are subject – like patent applications – to prior examination by the Ministry of Defence, which may request deferment of the grant or the granting of the title in secret form.

234. *See* https://www.elettronicaemercati.it/litalia-dei-chip-una-panoramica-dellindustria-italiana-dei-semiconduttori/.

Subject to these exceptions, the deadline for registering applications that have as their subject matter the topography of a semiconductor product is 90 days from filing (Prime Ministerial Decree No. 272/2010).

Any other information is in section VI of Legislative Decree No. 30 of 10 February 2005.[235]

§2. Chips General Regulation

1060. The first semiconductor protection legislation was introduced in the US in the second half of the 1980s with the enactment of the Semiconductor Chip Protection Act or SCPA in 1984.

Subsequently, there was the diplomatic conference in WIPO that led to the Washington Treaty on Intellectual Property in Integrated Circuits on 26 May 2019. This treaty was signed by very few states, of which Italy was not one.

In Japan, too, legislation came into force that followed the SCPA in 1985.

Within the EU, the protection of semi-conductors was granted through EEC Directive 87/57/EEC of 16 December 1986.

In compliance with this directive, at national level, a special regulation was issued by Law No. 70 of 21 February 1989, which was then amended in 1996 to transpose the changes to adapt to TRIPs, and finally merged into the Property at Articles 87-97. The latter give special protection to semiconductor topographies.

The ad hoc protection was in fact necessary because the other traditional forms of intellectual and industrial property protection were difficult to apply.

1061. The so-called Chips Act is the proposal for a European regulation to prevent and remedy semiconductor shortages, which was approved on 8 February 2022 by the European Commission, and for which an agreement was finally reached on 18 April 2023, leading to the formal adoption of the Chips Act in the coming months.

The Chips Act provides for the allocation of EUR 43 billion for the creation of a European chip design and manufacturing supply chain: the main goal is to double the production of semiconductors in Europe by 2030.

1062. The legal protection of microchips (semiconductor integrated circuits) in Italy is so governed by a combination of national laws, European Union directives, and International treaties.

These legal frameworks cover various aspects of intellectual property rights, including patents, designs, and the protection of semiconductor topographies (the layout-designs of integrated circuits).

1063. In Italy, microchips can be protected under *patent law* if they meet the requirements for patentability, such as novelty, inventive step, and industrial applicability.

---

235. *See* https://uibm.mise.gov.it/index.php/it/brevetti/topografie-di-prodotti-a-semiconduttori.

The Italian Industrial Property Code ('Codice della Proprietà Industriale', CPI) governs the granting of patents. Patents can cover various aspects of microchips, including their manufacturing process, specific functionalities, and technical innovations.

1064. Patent protection grants the patent holder exclusive rights to prevent others from making, using, or selling the patented microchip in Italy for a period of 20 years from the filing date.

1065. Specific legal protection for the topographies (layout-designs) of semiconductor products is provided under the European Union Directive 87/54/EEC, which has been implemented into Italian law through Legislative Decree No. 70/1989.

This law grants exclusive rights to creators of semiconductor topographies, allowing them to authorize or prohibit the reproduction and commercial exploitation of their designs.

The protection is granted for a period of 10 years, starting from the first commercial exploitation or the date of registration, whichever occurs earlier.

1066. Microchips, particularly their external designs or any unique visual features, can also be protected under *design rights* as provided by the CPI and related EU regulations. However, these rights are more commonly applied to the aesthetic aspects of products rather than the functional elements of microchips.

1067. Italian law, in line with the EU Trade Secrets Directive (2016/943), protects confidential business information and trade secrets.

If a company maintains the confidentiality of certain technical information related to microchips, it can seek legal protection against unauthorized disclosure or use by third parties.

Trade secret protection is indefinite, lasting as long as the information remains confidential and holds economic value.

1068. Rights holders can initiate civil litigation in Italian courts to enforce their intellectual property rights, including seeking injunctions, damages, and the seizure of infringing goods.

The Specialized IP Courts in Italy handle disputes related to patents, designs, and semiconductor topographies, offering expertise in these complex technical matters.

1069. In cases of willful infringement, particularly where counterfeiting or piracy is involved, *criminal sanctions* can also be pursued under Italian law. This includes fines and imprisonment for the offenders.

1070. Italy, as part of the EU, also allows for customs enforcement of intellectual property rights. Rights holders can request customs authorities to detain suspected infringing goods, including counterfeit microchips, at the border.

1071. Patent disputes involving microchips can be highly complex, often involving questions of technical expertise, patent validity, and infringement. Italian courts rely on expert opinions to resolve these issues.

The importation of microchips from markets outside the EU can raise issues of patent exhaustion and the legality of parallel imports, which are subject to specific rules under Italian and EU law.

Given the global nature of the semiconductor industry, enforcement of rights often involves cross-border considerations, requiring coordination with international legal frameworks and cooperation with authorities in other jurisdictions.

§3. Chips and Patent Law in Italy

1072. As seen before, microchips, like other technological inventions, can be protected under patent law in Italy if they meet certain criteria established by the Italian Industrial Property Code ('Codice della Proprietà Industriale', CPI).

1073. These criteria include: (i*) novelty* (the microchip must be new, meaning it has not been publicly disclosed anywhere in the world before the date of the patent application. Any prior public disclosure, use, or publication of the invention can invalidate the novelty requirement); *(ii) inventive step* (the microchip must involve an inventive step, meaning it is not obvious to a person skilled in the relevant technical field. The inventive step requirement ensures that the patent is only granted for genuine technological advances, not for trivial modifications of existing technology); *(iii)* industrial applicability (the microchip must be capable of being made or used in some kind of industry, which is a broad category including any useful and practical application. This requirement is easily met by microchips since they are designed for use in electronic devices and systems).

1074. In Italy, patents can be granted for various aspects of microchips, including but not limited to: *Manufacturing Processes* (patents can cover specific methods of manufacturing microchips, including innovations in semiconductor fabrication techniques, materials used in chip production, and processes that improve efficiency, cost-effectiveness, or performance); *technical innovations* (patents can also protect the technical innovations embodied in the microchip itself, such as novel circuit designs, architecture, or methods of data processing. For example, a new design that improves processing speed, reduces power consumption, or enhances security could be patentable); *functionalities* (specific functionalities provided by the microchip, such as unique ways of handling data, processing signals, or interfacing with other hardware, can also be the subject of patent protection).

1075. Once a patent is granted for a microchip in Italy, the patent holder obtains exclusive rights to the invention. These rights allow the patent holder to control how the microchip is used commercially. Specifically, the patent holder can: *(i)* prevent others from making (the patent holder can stop other companies or individuals from manufacturing the patented microchip without permission. This includes any reproduction of the patented design, process, or technology); *(ii)* prevent others from using (the patent holder can prevent the use of the patented microchip in products or processes, ensuring that only authorized parties can use the patented technology); *(iii)* prevent others from selling (the patent holder has the exclusive right to commercialize the microchip. This means that others cannot sell, offer for sale, or distribute the patented microchip without the patent holder's consent).

These exclusive rights are enforceable in Court, allowing the patent holder to seek remedies such as injunctions to stop infringing activities and damages to compensate for unauthorized use of the patented technology.

1076. The patent protection for microchips in Italy lasts for 20 years from the date of filing the patent application. This period is generally not extendable, although there are some exceptions in specific fields like pharmaceuticals and plant protection products.

To keep the patent in force for the full 20 years, the patent holder must pay annual maintenance fees to the *Italian Patent and Trademark Office* ('Ufficio Italiano Brevetti e Marchi', UIBM). Failure to pay these fees can result in the patent lapsing before the full term is reached.

1077. If a patent holder believes that their patent is being infringed, they have several legal options: *(i) civil litigation* (the patent holder can file a lawsuit in one of Italy's specialized intellectual property courts. The courts can grant remedies such as injunctions to prevent further infringement, orders for the seizure of infringing products, and monetary damages); *(ii) customs actions* (patent holders can also request Italian customs authorities to detain goods suspected of infringing patents as they enter the country); *(iii)* criminal sanctions (in cases of willful infringement, particularly involving counterfeit goods, the patent holder can also pursue criminal action, which may result in fines or imprisonment for the infringers).

1078. Concerning competence for chips, according to Court of Appeal Brescia, Specialized Section in Enterprise, 19 February 2021, decision No. 183, before the 2005 reform, disputes concerning *know-how* did not fall within the original competence of the specialized sections. According to the judges, it was only with Legislative Decree No. 30 of 2005, the so-called Industrial Property Code, that the list of matters attributed to the competence of the specialized sections by Article 3 of Legislative Decree No. 168/2003 was *extended* and (in addition to geographical indications, appellations of origin, topographies of semiconductor products and other distinctive signs other than trademarks) also reserved business information, constituting a company's know-how.

It follows that prior to the entry into force of the aforesaid Industrial Property Code, the case of unfair competition concerning know-how could not be said to interfere, even indirectly, with an industrial property right, precisely because know-how did not fall within intellectual property rights, with the result that cases concerning the protection of confidential information did not fall within the jurisdiction of the specialized intellectual property sections introduced by legislative decree No. 168 of 2003.

Chapter 8. Protection of Internet Domain Names

§1. The Italian Legal Framework

1079. In Italy, registered domain names are subject: *(i)* to the discipline on the right to the name, as protected by Articles 6, 7, 8 and 9 of the Italian Civil Code, where Article 9 refers to the pseudonym when it has acquired the importance of the name; *(ii)* to the discipline of trademarks and distinctive signs (provided for in Articles 2569 et seq. of the Italian Civil Code and Legislative Decree No. 30/2005 – Industrial Property Code); *(iii)* to the code discipline on unfair competition (Articles 2598–2601 of the Italian Civil Code); *(iv)* to the regulations on trademarks provided for by the European Union (First Directive 89/104/EEC, replaced by Directive 2008/95/EC of the Parliament and of the Council; Regulation No. 2868/1995 of the Commission, laying down implementing rules of Council Regulation No. 40/1994 on the Community trademark, codified in Council Regulation No. 207/2009 on the Community trademark).

1080. As regards personal names, the Italian Civil Code (Article 7) establishes that a person who contests the appropriation or undue use of his own name by a third party may request the cessation of the damaging fact (an action of claim, to protect the person's right to use his own name against the act of the third party that prevents its use, and an action of usurpation, which requires even only potential damage), in addition to compensation for pecuniary and moral damages, if proven.

1081. When the domain name constitutes a distinctive sign for commercial use, connected to business activity, realized through the corresponding website (or company domain name), the domain name assumes its own distinctive and advertising value of the company operating in the market and must possess the requirements of *distinctive capacity* (suitable for distinguishing a product or service from that of others), *novelty* (suitable for not being confusable with earlier distinctive signs of others (trademarks, domain names, trade names), *lawfulness* (not contrary to law, public order and morality and suitable for not misleading consumers as to the origin, characteristics and qualities of the relevant products or services).

1082. The Italian legislator (Legislative Decree No. 30/2005) has equated the domain name with the other distinctive signs of the entrepreneur (company, sign, trademark), establishing in Article 22 (Uniformity of distinctive signs) the prohibition of using in economic activity distinctive signs equal or similar to other marks (registered for products or services, even if not similar, or that enjoy a reputation in the State), which may determine for the public a 'risk of confusion or association between two signs', with a consequent undue economic advantage for the person using them.

Therefore, domain names are given the same protection as distinctive signs: precautionary protection, Article 133, and ordinary protection, action of claim, Article 118.

1083. In particular, Article 133 provides for the possibility for the judicial authority to order, as a precautionary measure, not only the injunction for the use of the illegally registered domain name, but also its provisional transfer to the opposing party.

1084. Thus, the owner of a registered trademark has the right to use it exclusively, and thus also to register it as a domain name.

If others use the trademark by registering it as a domain name, the proprietor may take legal action also by emergency procedure (*ex* Article 700 c.p.c.) to inhibit its use.

1085. Competent to decide are the Specialized Sections for Companies, set up at all the courts and at the courts of appeal of Bari, Bologna, Catania, Florence, Genoa, Milan, Naples, Palermo, Rome, Turin, Trieste and Venice, provided for by legislative decree No. 168 of 27 June 2003.

1086. With regard to acts of unfair competition, the code (Article 2598 No. 1, Italian Civil Code) establishes that acts of unfair competition are committed by anyone who uses names or distinctive signs capable of producing confusion with the names or distinctive signs legitimately used by others, or slavishly imitates the products of a competitor, or commits by any other means acts capable of creating confusion with the products and activity of a competitor.

1087. These are generic offences that will have to be identified by the judge on a case-by-case basis. Considering that there are often acts of unfair competition that also constitute counterfeiting of the trademark, the relevant actions for protection can be asserted jointly in court.

1088. Indeed, counterfeiting and unfair competition, although having distinct purposes and marked by a different nature (respectively 'real' and 'personal'), may have an important element in common, i.e., the undue appropriation of the distinctive sign, which generates confusion and damage.

1089. Thus, in order to protect oneself against acts of unfair competition relating to domain names, such as 'domain grabbing', it is sufficient that the act be harmful, i.e., the registration by the respondent of the offending domain. The existence of concrete damage is necessary only for the purposes of its compensation.

1090. Moreover, it should be noted that the legislation on unfair competition is also closely linked to the prohibition of 'unfair commercial practices' for the protection of consumers in their relations with professionals (*see* Articles 18 et seq. of the Consumer Code, Legislative Decree No. 206/2005), in respect of which the sanctioning intervention of the Antitrust Authority is provided for. While in favour of the consumer, the civil judge may provide the compensatory remedy and/or the annulment of the contract due to a defect of will.

1091. As an alternative to judicial proceedings, the *Italian Registration Authority* has provided for a 'reassignment procedure' and an 'irritual arbitration' ('Regulation for the resolution of disputes in the ccTLD 'it' of 30 March 2006').

1092. The reassignment procedure is conducted by 'experts' who verify, in an adversarial process between the parties, whether or not the declaration not to infringe the rights of others, made by the person who originally registered the domain name, is truthful.

If at the outcome of the procedure it appears that: *(i)* the registered domain name is identical or similar to another name or distinctive sign or mark on which the complainant boasts rights and such as to mislead the public; *(ii)* the assignee has no rights or legitimate interests in the domain; *(iii)* bad faith exists, the domain name is considered to be registered abusively and is reassigned to the complainant.

1093. According to Court of Rome, Specialized Section in Enterprise, 3 February 2021, No. 1937, registration as a domain of a name in common use is lawful if it is not intended to create confusion or take advantage of another person's trademark.

Registration of a domain name coinciding with a common word or expression may be lawful, but on condition that the domain name is used in a manner that is genuine and consistent with its meaning, and not for the purpose of profiting from another person's trademark rights or causing confusion among Internet users. In making this assessment, the reputation and status of the earlier mark, the circumstances of the case and the overall conduct of the registrant must be taken into account.

The registration of a website 'domain name' reproducing or containing someone else's trademark constitutes an infringement of the trademark since it allows the activity to be *linked* to that of the proprietor of the trademark, taking advantage of the reputation of the sign and thus taking unfair advantage of it, so that only the proprietor of a registered trademark could legitimately use it on his own website or as a domain name.

The action brought pursuant to Article 3.1 of the 'Regulations for the resolution of disputes in the country code Top Level Domain.it' for reassignment and the relative outcome do not preclude recourse to the judicial authorities, given that, pursuant to Article 3.2, paragraph 3, of the above-mentioned reg., the procedure for reassignment of a domain name subject to opposition is not judicial in nature, and as such does not preclude the parties from resorting, even subsequently, to the courts or arbitration.

1094. Court of Cassation, Civil section I, on 21 February 2020, decision No. 4721, stated that the Intellectual Property Code applies to Internet domain names, even if they are atypical distinctive signs. According to the Court, the Intellectual Property Code must also be applied to (Internet) domain names, even though they are atypical distinctive signs, since they are tools through which to access, in the context of the Internet, a vast commercial market of global dimensions that enable the owner of the website and the products and services offered to the public to be identified.

The registration of a domain name that reproduces or contains someone else's trademark constitutes trademark infringement, since it allows the registrant's activity to be linked to that of the trademark owner, exploiting the sign's notoriety and thus taking unfair advantage of it.

1095. Also according to Court of Cassation, Civil section I, on 18 August 2017, decision No. 20189, the domain name is *assimilable* to a *distinctive sign.*

Articles 13 and 17 of the Trademarks Law (and the corresponding provisions of the Industrial Property Code) recognize the principle of the unitary nature of distinctive signs, whereby the infringement of one of them (trademark, company or sign) is realized even if it is carried out through the counterfeiting or abusive use of a different distinctive sign.

Therefore, even before the enactment of the IPC, the domain name, as an atypical distinctive sign, enjoyed the same treatment as other distinctive signs other than the registered trademark.

In the period before the entry into force of the IPC, the law on trademarks applied to the domain names of Internet sites even if they were atypical distinctive signs, since such names allow access, in the context of the Internet, to a vast commercial market of global dimensions and make it possible to identify the owner of the website and the products and services offered to the public. In fact, such names have a true and proper distinctive capacity, since, according to the current conception of the nature and function of trademarks, they do not merely indicate the origin of the product or service, but perform an advertising and suggestive function, the purpose of which is to attract the consumer, inducing him to purchase.

The use, as an Internet domain name, of a name corresponding to an earlier registered trademark of another person that is not well-known is *unlawful* and the trademark proprietor may apply to have that use stopped and the domain name reassigned, provided that the two signs refer to goods or services that can be confused, since they are similar.

1096. According to Court of Milan, 11 January 2016, Article 133 of the IPC, as a special rule dictated for domain names, cannot be applied extensively to trademarks.

1097. According to Court of Rome, on 15 June 2012, in the case of domain names coinciding with reputed trademarks, the effect of coupling is represented by the greater frequentation of the site compared to the case where the domain name was different and occurs before – and therefore without the fact that – the consumer can become aware of the fact that the site in question has no connection with the trademark it includes.

The presence of an inactive domain name of a site coinciding with a trademark of renown is such as to cause the proprietor of that trademark unfair prejudice, since it indicates a lack of commercial vitality which is inconsistent with that of the proprietor of the trademark of renown.

Part V. Cybersecurity Law

Chapter 1. Institutional Framework

§1. The National Cybersecurity Agency

1098. Italy has been slow to develop a *clear structure* dedicated to cybersecurity at the national level, due to both a lack of attention to the issue by the political class and the low level of information in the Country on the subject.[236]

In the last four years, however, there has been a noticeable acceleration that has led to the *National Cybersecurity Agency* (ACN) being identified as the main government-issued agency around which most of the activities, including regulatory ones, on the topic revolve.[237]

1099. The ACN is today the national cybersecurity *authority* for the protection of national interests in the field of cybersecurity.

The Agency is responsible for safeguarding security and resilience in cyberspace, for preventing and mitigating as many cyberattacks as possible, and for promoting the achievement of technological autonomy.

Among the Agency's main tasks is the implementation of the *National Cybersecurity Strategy*, adopted by the President of the Council of Ministers, which contains the goals to be pursued by 2026.[238]

1100. The Agency was established by Decree-Law No. 82 of 14 June 2021,[239] which redefined the national cybersecurity architecture, aiming to rationalize and simplify the system, enhancing the aspects of cybersecurity and resilience.

The organization of ACN is regulated by President of the Council of Ministers' Decree No. 223 of 9 December 2021.[240]

236. *See* T. F. Giupponi, 'Il governo nazionale della cybersicurezza', in 'Quaderni costituzionali', fasc. 2, 2024, p. 277.
237. *See* https://www.acn.gov.it/portale/en/home.
238. *See* https://www.acn.gov.it/portale/en/2023-year-in-review.
239. *See* https://www.normattiva.it/uri-res/N2Ls?urn:nir:stato:decreto.legge:2021-06-14;82.
240. *See* https://www.normattiva.it/uri-res/N2Ls?urn:nir:presidente.consiglio:decreto:2021;223.

§2. The National Cybersecurity Strategy 2022–2026

1101. The National Cybersecurity Strategy aims at planning, coordinating and implementing security measures to make the Country safer and more resilient.

The strategy seeks to achieve *82 measures* by 2026. A path of innovation is defined by the National Cybersecurity Agency which is also responsible for checking that the objectives are achieved in due time.[241]

1102. The *Italian Cloud Strategy*, on its side, contains the guidelines for the migration to the qualified cloud of the Public Administration.

It was published in September 2021 and implemented by the Department for Digital Transformation of the Presidency of the Council of Ministers and the National Cybersecurity Agency.

1103. The strategy responds to three main challenges:

i. ensuring the Country's technological autonomy,
ii. guaranteeing control over data, and
iii. increasing the resilience of digital services.

Consistent with the objectives of the *National Recovery and Resilience* Plan, the document outlines a defined path to accompany approximately 75% of Italian Public Administrations in migrating their data and IT applications to a qualified cloud environment.

Through the *cloud-first approach*, the aim is to guide and foster the secure, controlled and complete adoption of cloud technologies by the public sector, in line with privacy protection principles and the recommendations of European and national institutions. In this way, digital infrastructures will be more reliable and secure and the Public Administration will be able to respond in an organized manner to cyberattacks, guaranteeing continuity and quality in the use of data and services.

§3. The Prevention and Management of Cyber Events

1104. During 2023, in a context characterized by a considerable overall increase of cyber threats, the ACN renewed and strengthened its commitment to provide early warning, alerts, dissemination of information on cyber risks as well as assistance to victims, enhancing national cybersecurity and resilience in cyberspace.

Through its technical-operational structure, CSIRT Italia,[242] the Agency has constantly monitored the evolution of the threat landscape, which appeared increasingly characterized by *ransomware* and *distributed denial of service* (DDoS) events

---

241. *See* https://www.acn.gov.it/portale/strategia-nazionale-di-cybersicurezza.
242. *See* https://www.csirt.gov.it.

– but also malware distribution via e-mail and phishing – and addressed to government and public bodies as well as to private entities in many different sectors (e.g., telecommunications, transportation, and financial services).

1105. In 2023, CSIRT Italia handled 1,411 cyber events, for an average of approximately 117 per month, with a peak of 169 in October. Of these, 303 were classified as incidents, for an average of 25 per month. Both figures registered significant increases compared to 2022, when cyber events amounted to 1,094 (+29% in 2023) and cyber incidents to 126 (+140,5%).

Cyber events handled by the Agency span many different types, among them DDoS, malware distributed via email, phishing, ransomware, and brand abuse were the most detected. It should be noted that each of these events may have been associated with one or more categories: for example, a phishing event is often also aimed at spreading malware, which can in turn be a ransomware.

1106. Regarding the sectors and industries of the targeted entities, telecommunications and the public sector prevail, both at the local and central level, followed by transportation and financial services.

Two of the most insidious cyber threats detected by CSIRT Italia are DDoS and ransomware attacks, both of which mostly targeted the private sector (respectively 65% and 84%).

1107. In particular, DDoS events have shown a worrying trend in 2023, as they grew by 625% compared to the previous year. Such events are strongly associated with cyber activism (so-called *hacktivism*), often related to the ongoing conflicts in Eastern Europe and in the Middle East.

Ransomware events also showed a notable increase (+27% compared to 2022), but it should be noted that the actual figure could well exceed the 165 events registered by CSIRT Italia, as firms are often *reluctant* to make such attacks *public* for reputational reasons. Ransomware attacks have for the most part been attributed to a limited number of threat actors, generally in line with those detected in 2022.

1108. In 2023, ACN personnel provided support to the targets of cyber incidents intervening, remotely or on site, 44 times.

Moreover, the Agency detected hostile activities carried out by the so-called Advanced Persistent Threats (APTs). The analysis of such attacks allowed the identification of connections to activities that have been publicly attributed to known groups, namely APT28, APT29, APT33, Storm-0558, and Lazarus.

1109. In this context, the periodic meetings of the *National CyberSecurity Cell* ('Nucleo per la cybersicurezza', NCS) have allowed the Agency to ensure regular information sharing on the state of the cyber threat landscape, as well as inter-institutional coordination at the technical-operational level among the various administrations involved.

1110. The *National CyberSecurity Cell*, established within the ACN, acts in support of the President of the Council of Ministers for the prevention of and preparedness for possible cyber crisis situations and for the activation of warning procedures.

The NCS is chaired by the ACN's Director General and is composed of the President of the Council of Minister's Military Adviser, representatives from the three intelligence agencies (the Department of Security Intelligence, the External Intelligence and Security Agency, and the Internal Intelligence and Security Agency), and of representatives from each of the Ministries represented in the Inter-Ministerial Committee for Cybersecurity ('Comitato interministeriale per la cybersicurezza', CIC) as well as from the Department of Civil Protection of the Presidency of the Council of Ministers. In case classified information be discussed, the NCS also includes a representative from the Central Office for Secrecy of the Department of Security Intelligence.

1111. The NCS's technical-operational evaluation of the cyber threat can lead to the convening of the CIC – whose functions include consultation, proposal, and oversight over cybersecurity policies – for a political-strategic analysis of the state of cybersecurity.

The CIC is chaired by the President of the Council of Ministers and composed of the Ministers of Foreign Affairs and International Cooperation, Interior, Justice, Defence, Economy and Finance, Enterprises and Made in Italy, Environment and Energy Security, University and Research, and Infrastructures and Transport. The Director General of ACN is the CIC's Secretary. The Committee has been solicited particularly due to the geopolitical tensions stemming from the conflicts in the Middle East and Eastern Europe. As a result of the topics under examination, in 2023 the composition of CIC has been on some occasions extended to other members of the Council of Ministers as well as to other interested public authorities.

The ACN also contributed to the consolidation of the European mechanisms for the prevention and preparation of cyber crises, by participating in the newly established *Cyber Crisis Liaison Organisation Network* (CyCLONe).[243]

1112. CyCLONe was created in 2020 and formally established by the NIS 2 Directive, which entered into force on 16 January 2023. CyCLONe is the network of Member States' national authorities in charge of cyber crisis management, aiming to allow them to collaborate and develop timely information sharing and situational awareness. It is chaired by a representative of the Member State holding the rotating Presidency of the EU Council while ENISA acts as the Network's Secretariat. The Commission participates as an observer to CyCLONe activities, while it is a regular member in case of large-scale cybersecurity incidents that have or are likely to have a significant impact on services and activities falling within the scope of the NIS 2 Directive.

1113. A further tool to become better prepared to manage cyber crises is represented by *cyber exercises* (or exercises with a cyber dimension) developed to test

243. *See* at https://www.enisa.europa.eu/topics/incident-response/cyclone.

critical IT security infrastructure and the ability to coordinate responses with different administrations and/or across borders. Such exercises have been conducted in the framework of NATO (Crisis Management Exercise and Short Notice Exercise) and of the European Union (BlueOLEx and European Election Cyber Exercise 2023) as well as at the national level (to strengthen the capacity of the administrations represented in the NCSC and of the subjects included in the National Security Perimeter for Cyber, and to test the preparedness of CSIRT Italia). The Agency has also been working on the preparation for Cyber Europe 2024, the main EU exercise organized by ENISA every two years.

§4. Resilience of Digital Infrastructures and Technological Security

1114. Strengthening national cyber resilience is among the primary objectives of the Agency, which contributes to the protection of critical national assets through a systemic approach oriented towards the prevention, management, and mitigation of cyber risks.

Thus, it is paramount not only to adopt measures, tools, and controls that can contribute to making the digital ecosystem safer and more resilient, but also to maintain an updated and coherent regulatory framework.

1115. The Agency is particularly focused on strengthening cybersecurity and resilience of those components that are most relevant to the State's stability, as mandated by the relevant cyber regulations such as those relating to the *National Security* Perimeter for Cyber and to the NIS and NIS 2 Directives.

1116. Indeed, in order to ensure cyber resilience, it is particularly important to guarantee that especially the most sensitive players use digital networks and systems that are secure and resistant to computer intrusions, as verified by the Agency's units devoted to technological screening.

1117. Concerning the application of the *Perimeter* norms, the Agency conducted several meetings with the entities subject to its rules, whose list underwent some variations throughout the year, reaching a total of 118 entities. Moreover, the ACN contributed to revise the rules for the notification of cyber incidents, extending the scope of assets subject to mandatory notifications in case of incident. This is aimed to improve the security provided by the Perimeter, to have a more thorough situational awareness, and to reduce the risk of cyberattacks, as they can often spread throughout the digital surface of a given entity.

1118. The Agency is also supporting the national process to transpose the NIS 2 Directive into domestic legislation, which is due by the 17th of October 2024. The ACN contributed to drafting the relevant articles of the law providing for criteria to determine the inclusion of public entities within the category of Public Administration (both at the national and local level), to confirm the role of ACN and of CSIRT Italia for the application of the Directive, to introduce the necessary modifications to the legal system to allow the transposition of the newly introduced European rules on coordinated vulnerability disclosure (CVD), and to review the sanctions and surveillance framework. Furthermore, the Agency conducted tailored meetings with entities that will fall within the scope of the revised Directive.

1119. The construction of a *secure digital ecosystem* also requires the adoption of *common standards* to guarantee the resilience of the technical solutions adopted and users' trust in the correct protection of their information assets. This is the primary function of the certification processes that concern the products and services that compose the fabric of modern complex digital systems. The Agency's role in this sector is quite extensive, as the National cybersecurity certification authority for various national, European, and international standards.

1120. The Italian scheme to evaluate and certify ICT products and services, which has been in force for over 20 years, provides the Agency's involvement in its capacity as Cybersecurity Certification Body ('Organismo di certificazione della sicurezza informatica', OCSI). As such, during 2023 the Agency issued:

i. 12 cybersecurity certifications based on the Common Criteria standard and further certification processes are still underway (14 as of the end of the year);
ii. 3 conformity assessments for qualified digital signature/seal based on the eIDAS Regulation.

1121. The national scheme will soon be replaced by European certification schemes, as provided for in the *Cybersecurity Act*, which aims to overcome the current fragmentation of the European internal market concerning cybersecurity certificates. Such common schemes will initially focus on certifications for the Common Criteria standard (EUCC), for cloud services (EUCS), and for 5G networks (EU5G).

1122. Technological screening of ICT solutions for subjects included in the National Security Perimeter for Cyber is a key task for the Agency, within which the National Assessment and Certification Centre ('Centro di valutazione e certificazione nazionale', CVCN) operates.

The Centre receives the communications by entities included in the Perimeter regarding their intention to use certain ICT components within their networks, information systems, and IT services which are essential for State functions or services and whose malfunctioning, interruption, or improper use might endanger national security. To fulfil this role, the CVCN has been involved with numerous proceedings, both in the phase of preliminary assessments and, when deemed necessary, with the execution of tests to verify the correct implementation of security functions as well as penetration tests. The CVCN worked to increase the efficiency of both kinds of proceedings, managing to reduce the time needed for the assessments by about 30%.

1123. In 2023, the screening conducted by CVCN allowed the identification of numerous vulnerabilities. These include 38 *zero-day* vulnerabilities, 22 of which have been considered 'high-level' or even 'critical level', for which the Agency underwent a responsible disclosure process.

1124. The ACN has also been involved in monitoring the activation of the *Assessment Centres* ('Centri di valutazione') of the Ministry of Defence and of the Ministry of the Interior. It also worked to facilitate the accreditation process of external laboratories tasked with assisting the Agency, namely *Accredited Testing Laboratories* ('Laboratori accreditati di prova'), which aid CVCN's activities, and Security Assessment Laboratories ('Laboratori di valutazione della sicurezza'), in support of OCSI.

Finally, the CAN launched an internal unit dedicated to inspections and assessments, tasked also with monitoring the high standards employed by the aforementioned laboratories.

In addition, the Agency has been involved in the processes relating to public sector cloud transition, in activities connected to the exercise of special powers (so-called *Golden Power*), and in fostering the use of cryptography as a cybersecurity tool.

1125. In particular, the ACN has given a significant contribution to the complex process of transitioning Public Administration's data and services to the cloud, as foreseen by the *Italian Cloud Strategy*, which charged the Agency with some of the responsibilities previously held by the Agency for Digital Italy.

1126. During 2023 the ACN has been involved, on the one hand, in further specifying the regulatory framework that Public Administrations should follow during the so-called transition period and, on the other hand, in responding to the hundreds of qualification requests received by private cloud service and digital infrastructure operators.

It has also followed closely the EU negotiation to draft a certification scheme for cloud services (the aforementioned EUCS), whose rules will have to be harmonized with national ones.

1127. Furthermore, concerning the exercise of the so-called *Golden Power*, the ACN has given its contribution to national procedures for operations falling within the scope of the relevant regulation: namely, those relating both to 5G networks (and in the future to other technologies such as cloud services) and to all other assets covered by the special powers' provisions. As such, the Agency has been involved in evaluating all notifications regarding 5G technologies and about 30% of the 'traditional' (i.e., non 5G) notifications.

1128. The Agency strives to remain at the forefront of technological innovation, with particular regard to those critical for cybersecurity, such as artificial intelligence and cryptography.

Beyond following the latest research in the field of post-quantum computing and its results for resistant encryption, the ACN published the first three documents of a series dedicated to 'Guidelines for cryptographic functions' that provide technical details and recommendations regarding cryptographic algorithms and related parameters, which should be adopted from the early stages of designing networks, applications, and services.

1129. The first document of the series, which has been jointly published with the Italian Data Protection Authority, aims to fill the serious gaps in terms of IT security in the field of *password storage*, as such archives are often breached due to various types of cyberattacks, making their encryption even more critical.

The other two documents pertain to the related fields of hash functions and message authentication codes, cryptographic solutions to strengthen data integrity, and authentication.[244]

§5. National Recovery and Resilience Plan

1130. Cybersecurity is also front and centre among the objectives of the *National Recovery and Resilience Plan* ('Piano nazionale di ripresa e resilienza', PNRR) which devotes considerable attention to improving the State's cybersecurity posture, within the context of the reforms needed to further digitize Italy.

1131. The Agency is responsible for the implementation of Investment 1.5 'Cybersecurity' of Mission 1, Component 1, Axis 1 of the PNRR, managed by the Department for Digital Transformation of the Presidency of the Council of Ministers. With an allocation of EUR 623 million, the investment's aim is to strengthen the national digital ecosystem and the services to manage cyber threats, as well as to support the initial functioning of the Agency.

1132. The investment's *three pillars* focus on strengthening:

i. the cyber capabilities of the Public Administration to secure data and services for citizens;
ii. cyber resilience capabilities across the State by fostering synergies and interconnection of means to monitor, share information, and respond to cyber events;
iii. national technology scrutiny and certification capabilities in order to assess and certify ICT goods, systems, and services, as part of the activation of the CVCN at ACN.

1133. Within these lines, specific projects have been dedicated to developing and raising national technological autonomy, by putting security and resilience in cyberspace as the foundation of the digital transformation of the Public Administration, as well as of the private sector and, more generally, of Italy.

---

244. *See* at https://www.garanteprivacy.it/home/docweb/-/docweb-display/docweb/9962240.

1134. Regarding the first pillar, dedicated to strengthening the cyber capabilities of the Public Administration, the Agency is supporting numerous entities in assessing and bolstering their cyber maturity level. In particular, in 2023 the ACN followed the evolution of the instruments launched the previous year, both in terms of cyber defence agreements signed with several Public Administrations and of Public Calls to appropriate dedicated funds to specific targets, such as central or local public entities.

1135. It also published a further Public Call with a total budget of EUR 15 million dedicated to supporting projects to raise the level of cyber maturity of several central Public Administrations with respect to the:

i. analysis of the cyber posture and plan for its improvement;
ii. improvement of processes and organization in cybersecurity management;
iii. support to personnel's awareness.

1136. Taken together, the activities funded by the Public Calls in this respect allowed to assess the cybersecurity posture maturity of the various concerned Public Administrations in 6 different areas of intervention:

i. governances and processes;
ii. cyber risk and operational continuity management;
iii. security incident management and response;
iv. logical access and digital identity management;
v. cybersecurity training and awareness;
vi. network, data, and application security.

1137. Each of these areas can be evaluated with a score from 0 (incomplete) to 5 (optimized). The concerned Public Administration can thus visualize through the dedicated graph how to improve the level of their cyber posture maturity, highlighting the current status (as-is maturity) and the progress to be made, both in the short term (quick-win maturity) and in the long term (target maturity).

1138. For what concerns the second pillar, thanks to the funding provided by the PNRR, the Agency is working on strengthening the national capabilities to prevent and face cyber threats, in particular by activating three crucial cyber services. These comprise a nation-level HyperSOC, which will gather information coming from the ACN as well as from relevant private SOCs in order to give a more accurate picture of the threat at hand.

1139. The HyperSOC will rely on a High Performance Computing (HPC) platform to manage the high amount of data. The other two national cyber services are a network of regional CSIRTs, which will support the work of CSIRT Italia by providing more accurate information regarding cyber threats detected at the local level, and a network of Information Sharing and Analysis Centres (ISAC), with a central hub to be instituted within ACN (ISAC Italia), and a series of sectoral ISACs to facilitate the diffusion of information and recommendations throughout the country.

1140. Finally, the Agency is building on the capacities to assess and certify ICT goods, systems, and services established within the Agency's CVCN, with a view to expand the network of laboratories for technological assessment and screening.

These laboratories will be associated to CVCN and cooperate with it in verifying the cybersecurity standards of solutions to be employed within the National Security Perimeter for Cyber. In this respect, the ACN is engaged – as mentioned – in supporting the Ministry of Defence and of the Interior in the activation of their Assessment centres and in supporting the development and operations of Accredited Testing Laboratories (including also through the disbursement of resources made available in 2022 through Public Call 5/2022).

So far, all the milestones and targets set for December 2022 have been met, while the activities aimed at meeting the ones previewed by December 2024 are in progress.

§6. International Cooperation

1141. Considering the intrinsically cross-border nature of cybersecurity risks, the ACN attaches considerable importance to the international dimension of its activities. The Agency is gradually raising its international profile, extending its bilateral network, deepening its participation in policy and technical dialogues at the EU level, and contributing to several multilateral initiatives. Throughout this, the Agency coordinates closely with the Ministry of Foreign Affairs and International Cooperation and aims to support Italy's broader policy priorities, with a particular attention to the most strategic regions.

1142. Bilaterally, the ACN has held several high-level meetings with the representatives of foreign counterparts from various key partners, with a particular focus on European, like-minded, and priority States for the Italian foreign policy objectives.

A particularly relevant mission has been conducted in the United States, where the Agency's Director General could exchange views with the US Deputy National Security Advisor and with the Director of the Cybersecurity and Infrastructure Security Agency (CISA).

1143. High-level meetings with foreign counterparts proved instrumental also to negotiate bilateral agreements, like the one signed with the Tunisian cybersecurity agency ('Agence Nationale de la Cybersécurité', ANCS), the first bilateral agreement ever reached by the ACN.

1144. At the European level, the Agency has been involved in a variety of settings, from a policy as well as a technical point of view. In particular, it participated in the Horizontal Working Party on Cyber Issues, which supports the EU Council on policy and legal developments, such as those relating the Cyber Resilience Act, Cyber Solidarity Act, and the Artificial Intelligence Act.

1145. The ACN has also been an active participant in a number of ENISA initiatives, taking part in the meetings of the Management Board and of the Network of Liaison Officers as well as in the working groups dedicated to the EU Cybersecurity Index and to National Cybersecurity Strategies. Furthermore, the ACN's representatives take part in the activities of EU cyber cooperation frameworks with a prevalent technical component, such as the NIS Cooperation Group, the CSIRTs Network, and the European Cybersecurity Certification Group.

1146. The CAN is also the National Coordination Centre (NCC), thus forming part of the network of the European Cybersecurity Industrial, Technology and Research Competence Centre, which manages funding programmes dedicated to cybersecurity investment and innovation.

1147. The NCC is thus responsible to coordinate national applications for the appropriation of such funds in the framework of the Digital Europe Programme and Horizon Europe Programme. During 2023, some of the priorities included the launch of a project to support the NCC operation and a cross-border project to strengthen the European network of Security Operation Centres (with support from the DEP budget of, respectively, EUR 2 million and EUR 24 million).

1148. Finally, at the multilateral level, the ACN guaranteed its participation in several cybersecurity-related fora, both in multilateral institutions such as the United Nations, NATO, and OSCE as well as in intergovernmental dialogues such as the G20 and G7. Particular attention has been given to the Italian participation in ad hoc initiatives supported by like-minded States. One important example in this respect is the participation in the Counter-Ransomware Initiative engaging in its third Summit (Washington, 31 October–1 November 2023) and in the joint declaration subscribed by the fifty members of the Initiative, committing the public administrations of adhering States not to pay ransoms to cybercriminals as well as to give mutual assistance in case of ransomware attacks against vital sectors. The Agency also adhered to the 'Guidelines for secure AI systems development' published by the UK National Cyber Security Centre and by the US Cybersecurity and Infrastructure Security Agency following the Bletchley Park Summit (1–2 November 2023). Together with the twenty-three agencies from eighteen States that subscribed the document, the ACN supports the adoption of high security standards by AI systems providers not only in the development phase, but throughout the whole life cycle of the system.

§7. Research and Innovation, Training, Awareness

1149. A further indispensable step in the ACN's strategy to face cybersecurity challenges concerns the need to equip Public Administrations, businesses, and citizens with an adequate capacity to best seize the opportunities offered by technological evolutions.

In this respect, the entrepreneurial sector and the research world are called upon to play a leading role, indispensable for strengthening the Italian digital ecosystem and producing safe innovation. Equally essential is the contribution of the university and school system as a whole, which will train not only the cybersecurity professionals of tomorrow, but also citizens to be better informed about cyber risks and therefore more capable of coping with them. This is an all-round effort whose results will only be fully appreciable in the long term, which ACN considers a priority in the process of strengthening national cyber defences.

1150. Indeed, strengthening the country's innovation ecosystem represents a national priority in many respects: for its importance in producing better cybersecurity products and services, in keeping a positive feedback loop between research and entrepreneurship, and in fostering national and European strategic autonomy. With this in mind, the ACN in 2023 launched a strategic programme called Cyber Innovation Network (CIN) with the aim of supporting innovative enterprises and to make the most of research results.

1151. In this first stage, the Agency published a public notice to select qualified operators such as startup incubators or accelerators with specific experience on cybersecurity. Through this selection, nineteen programmes proposed by sixteen operators were identified and 6 of them will initially be offered the possibility to sign an agreement with the ACN to give financial support to startups with a high innovative and scalability potential working on emerging technologies (especially data science, AI, robotics, Internet of things, blockchain, quantum computing, encryption).

1152. The support will amount to EUR 50,000 per startup for those seeking validation of their innovative solution, and to EUR 150,000 per startup in cases of development and scale-up of the validated solution and entrepreneurial project.

1153. In addition to supporting entrepreneurship, it is crucial to bolster the capability to produce authentically innovative ideas as well as to strengthen the network of public and private actors engaging in cutting-edge research.

That is why the Agency partnered with the Ministry of University and Research to publish the Cybersecurity Research and Innovation Agenda 2023–2026, that identifies the priority research topics in the cybersecurity field to be carried out in the coming years.

1154. The Agenda lists six thematic areas, each one presenting sub-areas and priority topics: (1) data security and privacy; (2) cybersecurity threat management; (3) software and platform security; (4) digital infrastructure security; (5) societal aspects; (6) governance aspects.

1155. The document will need to be periodically updated to guarantee that the identified topics remain consistent with the fast-paced technological evolution taking place in the field of cybersecurity.

The Agency has been able to rely on the qualified advice of its Technical-Scientific Committee that assists it in better cooperating with the university and research system and the business sector, as well as in supporting public-private cybersecurity initiatives.

1156. A solid digital ecosystem also requires adequately trained professionals, capable of covering the expanding needs of the cybersecurity job market. The Agency is thus working to reduce the still significant lack of cybersecurity experts at all levels, both technical and otherwise, because specific capabilities are needed not just for engineers and other IT security professionals, but also for those with management and decision-making responsibilities.

1157. With this in mind, the ACN is supporting multiple training programs aimed at the various educational levels, starting from primary school. Dedicated support in the form of scholarships were granted, starting the academic year 2024–2025, to students who attend post-diploma technical training courses called ITS Academy and to university students attending courses on cybersecurity.

At the university level, the Agency is also collaborating with the first national doctoral programme in cybersecurity, launched in 2023 at the IMT School for Advanced Studies Lucca, and it will work with the Ministry of University and Research to identify thirty university research projects, granting a scholarship to a PhD student for each project.

1158. Beyond training the cybersecurity professionals of tomorrow, the ACN recognizes the importance of expanding current employees' abilities and bridging skill gaps, particularly for those working in the public sector. That is why it signed an agreement with the National School of Administration ('Scuola nazionale dell'amministrazione', SNA) that paves the way for various training initiatives to benefit public employees.

1159. In addition to that, the Agency signed a total of 13 agreements during 2023 with different counterparts, which often include provisions to support training and awareness regarding cybersecurity issues.

1160. Further agreements have been signed with the two chambers of the Italian Parliament (the Chamber of Deputies and the Senate of the Republic) but significant work has also been conducted to implement agreements signed in the previous years.

Some examples include the agreement with the Bank of Italy and other important financial entities, which allowed the launch of an information campaign dedicated to the financial sector, as well as the agreement with Confindustria and Generali, that paved the way for drafting the Cyber Index PMI, a report dedicated to assessing the level of cybersecurity awareness and risk-management capacity of small and medium enterprises (SMEs). Raising the cybersecurity awareness of SMEs is also the aim of a project launched in 2023 in cooperation with the Department for Information and Publishing of the Presidency of the Council of Ministers, that will produce an information campaign aimed at SMEs' holders and workers as well as to their ICT providers.

1161. Awareness of the multiple risks stemming from cyberspace represents a key task to strengthen our resistance and resilience to cyber threats and this effort needs to encompass the whole civil society. ACN developed a cybersecurity awareness programme that will aid the planning of medium- and long-term initiatives and campaigns to sensitize the wider population and specific target groups.

In this view, the EU cybersecurity month (October) represents a central tool to spread awareness and in 2023 the ACN partnered with ENISA to launch a communication campaign (composed of a mini-website, short videos, and infographics) regarding the social engineering threat and how to recognize it.

§8. Implementing the National Cybersecurity Strategy 2022–2026

1162. Since the launch of the National Cybersecurity Strategy 2022–2026 in May 2022, the Agency has been engaged in monitoring its implementation and in facilitating the accomplishment of its ambitious targets. The Strategy aims to address a wide variety of challenges, ranging from strengthening resilience in the digital transition of the national economic system, to achieving strategic autonomy in the cyber dimension, anticipating the evolution of cyber threats, managing cyber crises and countering online disinformation.

1163. The Strategy, with its Implementation Plan, provides a roadmap identifying 82 concrete measures to be implemented in order to achieve the three main goals of protection, response, and development, along with the enabling factors of cooperation and cybersecurity training and awareness.

1164. Achieving that requires the contribution of the whole national fabric, from public authorities to the private sector, from civil society to academia.

1165. The ACN is responsible for directing, coordinating, and monitoring the progress of all the interventions planned in the Strategy's Implementation Plan and following the indicators detailed in the Operational Manual. To that end, the ACN is also tasked with allocating the funds made available through the Budget Law for the year 2023 (namely, the Fund for the implementation of the National Cybersecurity Strategy and the Fund for the management of cybersecurity) to the different administrations responsible for each single intervention.

1166. In addition to those dedicated funds, the various entities involved can also rely on other sources to finance the implementation of the Strategy, including proper funds of the Administrations as well as those from the PNRR.

1167. The monitoring conducted by the Agency in 2023 concerned 30 so-called quick-win measures, involving 11 Public Administrations in addition to the ACN. It allowed to track the progress on 166 interventions pertaining to the different goals of the Strategy). The Agency ensured the highest standard of effectiveness, timeliness, and transparency, thanks also to a constant coordination with the actors involved and to a detailed project, results, and financial monitoring model.

§9. The Role of ACN in Law 28 June 2024, No. 90

1168. On 2 July 2024, the Cybersecurity Law was published in the Official Gazette, containing 'Provisions on strengthening national cybersecurity and cybercrimes' (Law No. 90 or 'Cybersecurity Law'), which came into force on 17 July 2024.

The aim of the provision, in brief, is to strengthen the cybersecurity of the public administration and other specifically identified entities through:

i. more stringent obligations for reporting cyber incidents;
ii. the need to take swift action in the event of vulnerabilities reported by the Agency for National Cybersecurity; and
iii. the establishment of a cybersecurity structure.[245]

1169. The following are required to comply with the law: the central public administrations identified pursuant to Article 1(3) of Law No. 196/2009; the regions and autonomous provinces of Trento and Bolzano; metropolitan cities; municipalities with a population of over 100,000 inhabitants and, in any case, regional capitals; urban public transport companies with a catchment area of no less than 100,000 inhabitants and extra-urban public transport companies operating within metropolitan cities; local health companies; in-house companies providing IT services, transport services and the collection, disposal or treatment of urban, domestic or industrial waste water.

Some provisions of the Cybersecurity Act also apply to those who are already subject to the NIS1 Directive (and those who will be subject to the NIS2 Directive, which must be transposed by 17 October 2024); those subject to compliance with the regulations on the national cyber security perimeter set out in Law 133/2019; undertakings providing public communications networks or publicly accessible electronic communications services within the meaning of Article 40(3) of Legislative Decree 259/2003.

1170. The regulation provides for two different timelines for the preliminary reporting phase and the subsequent notification phase. The reporting of incidents must be carried out within a maximum of 24 (twenty-four) hours from the moment of becoming aware of them, while within the following 72 (seventy-two) hours

245. *See* https://www.rplt.it/nuova-legge-cybersicurezza/.

(again from the moment of becoming aware of them) notification must be made complete with all the available information, following the procedures available on ACN's institutional website.

1171. The objective of the Cybersecurity Law is therefore to equate the provisions that will be transposed with the NIS 2 Directive also to public administrations and in-house companies. The timeframes of 24 and 72 hours identified, in fact, coincide with those envisaged by the NIS 2 Directive (Article 23, paragraph 4, EU Directive 2022/2555) in that it is envisaged that without unjustified delay, and in any case within 24 hours, an 'early warning' of the event is given and that within the following 72 hours the incident is notified, providing all the necessary additional information.

1172. In the case of vulnerabilities reported by ACN, the addressees potentially exposed shall take the remedial actions indicated by ACN itself, without delay and in any case no later than 15 days from the notification, except for the imposition of sanctions.

1173. The sanctions will be applied in the event of failure or delay in adopting the decisive actions unless the subject promptly communicates to ACN the requirements of a technical-administrative nature that prevent their adoption or entail their postponement beyond the indicated deadline.

1174. In the event of non-compliance with this obligation, ACN will send a notice to the operator, advising that repeated non-compliance over a period of five years will result in the application of an administrative fine ranging from a minimum of EUR 25,000 to a maximum of EUR 125,000.

1175. The law then prescribes the establishment of a cybersecurity structure to deal, among other things, with activities such as the development of information security policies and procedures, the drafting and updating of a policy plan for the security of data, systems, and infrastructures, and the continuous monitoring and assessment of threats.

Within this structure there must be a cyber security contact person, identified on the basis of specific and proven professionalism and expertise in the field of cyber security, whose name must be communicated to ACN.

This contact person shall also act as the administration's single point of contact with ACN. State bodies in charge of the prevention, detection and prosecution of crimes, the protection of public order and security, the defence and military security of the State and the security intelligence agencies, as well as those subject to the NIS Directive and the legislation on the national cyber security perimeter, to whom the obligations provided for in the reference standards continue to apply, are not required to set up the above-mentioned structure.

1176. The law stipulates that public contracts for IT goods and services must comply with specific cybersecurity requirements, defined through a decree of the Presidency of the Council of Ministers, to be adopted within 120 days from the date of entry into force of the Cybersecurity Law, upon proposal of ACN. This is with the aim of reducing the risk of vulnerabilities and ensuring the protection of critical digital infrastructures.

1177. Other obligations introduced by the Cybersecurity Law include verifying that computer and electronic communication programs and applications in use, which employ cryptographic solutions, comply with the encryption guidelines and password storage guidelines adopted by ACN and the Garante per la protezione dei dati personali (available here https://www.garanteprivacy.it/web/guest/home/docweb/-/docweb-display/docweb/9962384) and do not contain known vulnerabilities.

1178. The Cybersecurity Law toughens the penalties for certain cybercrimes (such as abusive access to computer systems, dissemination of malware) and introduces new criminal offences, such as so-called cyber extortion, with the aim of stemming not only the growing spread of ransomware-type cyberattacks, but also the rampant ransom payments demanded by criminal organizations.

1179. Some amendments were also made to Legislative Decree No. 231/2001, expanding the list of predicate offences in the area of the administrative liability of entities and companies – also adding cyber extortion here – and tightening, in some cases, the pecuniary sanctions or interdictory sanctions against the entity (such as, for example, disqualification from exercising the activity, suspension or revocation of authorizations, licences or concessions functional to the commission of the offence, etc.).

1180. All entities provided for in Article 1, paragraph 1 of Law No. 90 of 28 June 2024 'Provisions on strengthening national cybersecurity and cybercrime' are required to notify the Agency of the appointment of the Cybersecurity Contact Person.

The communication to ACN (Article 8(2)) is made by sending a PEC to ACN's certified e-mail address(acn@pec.acn.gov.it) and must contain the appointment of the cybersecurity contact person (drafted in free form) digitally signed by the legal representative of the subject, or by a person delegated by him/her (in the latter case, also attach the proxy) and the cybersecurity contact person *form*, completed and signed by the cybersecurity contact person.

Chapter 2. General Obligations and Transposition of the NIS and NIS 2 Directive

1181. At the European Union level, the subject of cybersecurity was initially regulated by EU Directive (EU) 2016/1148 of 6 July 2016, which measures for a common high level of security of networks and information systems in the Union (so-called NIS Directive, Network and Information Security) in order to achieve a high level of network and information systems in the national context, contributing to a common level of security in the European Union.[246]

1182. The directive was transposed into Italian law by Legislative Decree No. 65 of 18 May 2018 (so-called NIS legislative decree), which dictates the internal legislative framework of the measures to be adopted for the security of networks and information systems and identifies the competent entities to implement the obligations under the NIS Directive.

1183. The rules introduced in 2016 were updated by Directive (EU) 2022/2555 of 14 December 2022 (so-called NIS 2 Directive), which replaces the framework in this regard, in order to take into account an increasing digitization of the internal market and an evolving landscape of cybersecurity threats.

The update of the directive also aims to eliminate the wide divergences between the Member States that have implemented the security and incident reporting obligations, as well as in supervision and enforcement obligations laid down in the NIS Directive in significantly different at national level, with a potentially detrimental effect on the functioning of the internal market.

1184. In particular, the NIS 2 directive establishes minimum standards and mechanisms for cooperation between the competent authorities of each Member State, updating the list of sectors and activities subject to the obligations in and providing for remedies and sanctions to ensure their enforcement.

1185. The Directive, in particular:

i. establishes obligations for Member States to adopt a national cybersecurity strategy, designate competent national authorities single points of contact and CSIRTs;
ii. requires Member States to establish obligations to manage and report cybersecurity risks for entities listed as essential actors in Annex I and as important actors in Annex II;
iii. requires Member States to establish obligations for sharing of cybersecurity information.

---

246. *See* I. Forgione, 'Il ruolo strategico dell'agenzia nazionale per la cybersecurity nel contesto del sistema di sicurezza nazionale: organizzazione e funzioni, tra regolazione europea e interna', in 'Diritto Amministrativo', fasc. 4, 2022, p. 1113; F. Casarosa, G. Comandè, 'Aspettando la NIS2: ovvero il diritto privato della cybersecurity', in 'Diritto dell'informazione e dell'informatica', fasc. 1, 2024, p. 29.

1186. As regards the main new features, the NIS 2 directive extends the scope of application, on the one hand, by including public central administration (leaving discretion to the Member States to include local authorities according to their institutional set-up), small and micro-enterprises (only if they operate in key sectors for society) and regardless of size, providers of public electronic communication public electronic communication services and publicly accessible electronic communication networks public, and on the other hand, significantly increasing the areas of application.

1187. Furthermore, whereas under the previous NIS Directive, the responsibility for determining which entities met the criteria to be considered operators of essential services was the responsibility of the Member States, the new directive NIS 2 introduces the size threshold rule. This means that all medium-sized and large entities operating in the sectors or providing services covered by the directive should fall within its scope. application.

1188. The new regime excludes from its application entities operating in areas such as national security, public security or defence, law enforcement, including law enforcement, including the prevention, investigation, detection and prosecution of crimes. Parliaments and central banks are also excluded.

1189. Furthermore, the NIS 2 directive provides for the establishment of a European network of cyber crisis liaison organizations EU-CyCLONe, aimed at supporting the coordinated management of large-scale cybersecurity incidents.

1190. Directive (EU) 2022/2555 makes some amendments to Regulation (EU) No 910/2014, known as the eIDAS (electronic Identification Authentication and Signature), which provides a common regulatory basis for secure electronic interactions between citizens, businesses and public administrations and enhances the security and effectiveness of electronic services and e-commerce transactions in the European Union.

1191. In particular, this regulation: establishes the conditions under which Member States recognize electronic identification means of natural and legal persons covered by a notified electronic identification scheme another Member State's electronic identification scheme; lays down the rules on trust services, in particular for electronic transactions; establishes a legal framework for electronic signatures, electronic seals, time stamps electronic documents, certified electronic delivery services and website authentication certificate services.

1192. Pursuant to Legislative Decree No. 65/2018 (Article 7), as amended by Decree-Law No. 82/2021, the National Cybersecurity Agency has been designated as the national NIS competent authority for the sectors and sub-sectors referred to in Annex II and for the services referred to in Annex III2.

1193. The following are designated as sector authorities (a) the Ministry of Economic Development, for the sector digital infrastructure digital services; (b) the

Ministry of Sustainable Infrastructure and Mobility, for the sector transport, air, rail, water and road sub-sectors; (c) the Ministry of Economy and Finance, for the banking sector and for the financial market infrastructure sector, in cooperation with the sector supervisory authorities, the Bank of Italy and Consob, according to (d) the Ministry of Health, for health care activities provided by operators employed or commissioned by the same Ministry or contracted with the same, and the Regions and Autonomous Provinces of Trento and of Bolzano, directly or through the health authorities territorially competent, for health care activities provided by operators authorized and accredited by the Regions or the Autonomous Provinces in their respective territorial areas of competence; (e) the Ministry of Ecological Transition for the energy sector, subsectors electricity, gas and oil; (f) the Ministry for Ecological Transition and the Regions and Provinces Autonomous Provinces of Trento and Bolzano, directly or through the Authorities territorially competent authorities, regarding the supply and distribution of drinking water.

1194. The status of 'competent NIS authority' (originally assigned to individual ministries according to the areas of competence) was centralized in the National Cybersecurity Agency by Decree-Law No. 82/2021. The individual ministries are designated as sector authorities (energy and transport sectors, banking sector, financial market infrastructure, health sector, supply and distribution of drinking water, digital infrastructure).

1195. Implementing Article 10 of the NIS 2 Directive, confirm the provisions of the aforementioned Legislative Decree No. 65/2018 on the establishment of the CSIRT Italy, as well as extend the provisions of the same decree by providing for collaboration between all public structures (CERTs) involved in the event of cyber security malicious events (letter e).

1196. Already currently, Legislative Decree 85/2018 implementing the NIS Directive, provides that at the Agency operates the CSIRT-Computer Emergency Response Team Italian, with a contingent of 30 people and the allocation of specific financial resources, to which are assigned the functions of the national CERT (previously at the Ministry for Economic Development) and the CERT- PA (previously at the Agency for Digital Italy-AGID).

1197. The CSIRT is defined by Directive 2016/1148 as a 'cyber security incident response team cyber security incident response team', which each Member State is required to designate with the task of dealing with incidents and risks according to a defined procedure.

1198. Article 10 of the new NIS 2 directive confirms the designation by each Member State of one or more CSIRTs, also within a competent authority.

CSIRTs must comply with the requirements set out in the directive and are responsible for incident management according to a well-defined procedure. Member States must ensure that each CSIRT has an adequate, secure and resilient appropriate, secure and resilient information and communication infrastructure through which through which information can be exchanged with key and important and other relevant stakeholders. They must also ensure the effective, efficient and secure collaboration of their CSIRTs to provide a transitional regime for entities already subject to the regulation of Legislative Decree No. 65/2018, transposing Directive (EU) 2016/1148, in order to better apply the provisions provided for by the NIS2 directive; during the referendum, the need was made explicit to ensure appropriate deadlines for adaptation (letter f).

1199. In this regard, it is recalled that Legislative Decree No. 65/2018 defines the obligations incumbent on operators of essential services and providers of digital services with reference to the security of the network and information systems they use in the context of the services identified in Annex III. Operators of essential services, for the purposes of the measure, are public or private entities of the types included in the list in Annex II (energy and transport sectors, banking sector, financial market infrastructure, health sector, supply and distribution of drinking water, digital infrastructure), identified by the competent NIS authorities.

Chapter 3. Sector-Specific Obligations

§1. The Framework

1200. Italy has implemented various sector-specific cybersecurity regulations to protect critical industries, such as healthcare, public administration, finance, and banking.

These regulations are often in line with broader European directives and are enforced by national authorities.

1201. Concerning Healthcare Sector, GDPR (General Data Protection Regulation), while not Italy-specific, is crucial in the healthcare sector. It sets strict guidelines on how personal and sensitive data, including health information, should be handled, stored, and transmitted.

National Cybersecurity Perimeter ('Perimetro di Sicurezza Nazionale Cibernetica'), introduced by Law Decree No. 105/2019, extends to critical sectors, including healthcare. It mandates that essential service operators in the health sector adopt robust cybersecurity measures to safeguard critical infrastructure. The Italian Data Protection Authority has issued specific guidelines for data processing in the healthcare sector, emphasizing the need for strong encryption, secure access controls, and regular risk assessments.

1202. Concerning the public Sector, the National Cybersecurity Framework, based on the National Institute of Standards and Technology (NIST) guidelines, provides a set of best practices and standards for public sector organizations in Italy. It focuses on identifying, protecting, detecting, responding to, and recovering from cyber incidents. AgID has issued various guidelines to ensure the security of digital public services. These guidelines cover areas such as secure software development, cloud security, and the protection of critical infrastructures within the public sector. Several legislative decrees transposes the European NIS and NIS 2 Directive into Italian law, imposing specific cybersecurity requirements on public sector entities considered essential service operators.

1203. Concerning finance and banking sector, D.lgs. No. 231/2001 addresses the administrative liability of companies, including those in the financial sector, and requires the adoption of adequate security measures to prevent cybercrimes. The Bank of Italy has issued various guidelines and circulars that financial institutions must adhere to. These guidelines focus on areas such as IT risk management, business continuity, and incident reporting.

1204. Critical Infrastructure (including public utilities, transportation, energy), are covered by the National Cybersecurity Perimeter ('Perimetro di Sicurezza Nazionale Cibernetica'). This law, as mentioned earlier, covers not only healthcare but also other critical infrastructure sectors like transportation, energy, and public utilities. It mandates operators of essential services to adopt stringent cybersecurity measures.

§2. DECREE 231

1205. Legislative Decree No. 231 of June 8, 2001, (often referred to simply as 'Decree 231') introduced in Italy a framework for the administrative liability of companies and other entities.[247]

This decree significantly changed the landscape of corporate liability by introducing the concept that companies and other entities can be held liable for certain criminal offenses committed by individuals in their organization. Here are the main legal issues and points concerning company responsibilities under Decree 231.

1206. Decree 231 applies to all legal entities, including corporations, associations, foundations, and other entities with legal personality, as well as to entities without legal personality (e.g., partnerships). Public entities are generally excluded unless they engage in commercial activities.

The decree outlines specific categories of crimes that can trigger corporate liability. These include, but are not limited to, corruption, fraud, money laundering, environmental crimes, occupational health and safety violations, and cybercrimes.

1207. The liability of a company is triggered when certain crimes (called predicate offenses) are committed in its interest or to its advantage by individuals in managerial positions or by individuals under their direction and supervision.

A company can be directly liable for crimes committed by individuals within the organization if those crimes are committed in the interest or to the advantage of the company. This includes crimes committed by: Senior management (e.g., directors, general managers). Subordinates if the crime occurs due to a lack of proper supervision or control by the company's management.

1208. Companies found liable under Decree 231 may face severe sanctions, including: Fines (calculated based on the severity of the offense). Disqualification from doing business (e.g., suspension of activities, exclusion from public tenders). Confiscation of assets or profits derived from the crime. Publication of the conviction.

1209. To avoid liability, companies can adopt and effectively implement an 'Organizational, Management, and Control Model' (MOG) that is designed to prevent the commission of crimes. If a company can prove that it has adopted such a model and that the crime occurred despite these measures, it can be exempt from liability.

---

247. *See* R. Caldarone, G. M. Garegnani, L. Troyer, 'Giurisprudenza e attualità in materia di diritto penale d'impresa - le novità introdotte dal d.lgs. 75/2020 alla normativa 231/2001 in attuazione della 'direttiva pif'', in 'Rivista dei Dottori Commercialisti', fasc. 4, 2020, p. 608; D. Galletti, 'I modelli organizzativi nel d.lgs. n. 231 del 2001: le implicazioni per la corporate governance', in 'Giurisprudenza commerciale', fasc. 1, 2006, p. 126.

The MOG must include: Identification of activities where crimes might be committed; Procedures to prevent these crimes; A code of ethics and disciplinary measures; A supervisory body (Organismo di Vigilanza or OdV) responsible for monitoring and updating the model.

1210. The OdV is an independent body within the organization that ensures compliance with the MOG. The effectiveness of the OdV and the MOG in practice is crucial for the company's defense against liability.

1211. Both the individual perpetrator and the company can be prosecuted in parallel. The company's liability does not absolve the individual of personal criminal liability.

Cases under Decree 231 are handled by criminal courts, and the proceedings are governed by the Italian Code of Criminal Procedure.

Companies have the right to defend themselves during proceedings, including presenting evidence that an effective MOG was in place or that the crime was committed by an individual acting solely in their interest without any benefit to the company.

1212. Like individuals, companies are presumed innocent until proven guilty, and the burden of proof lies with the prosecution.

Decree 231 can apply to crimes committed abroad if the company is headquartered in Italy and the offense is recognized as a crime under Italian law, with certain conditions.

The list of predicate offenses under Decree 231 has been continuously updated since its introduction, reflecting changes in the criminal landscape and the evolving nature of corporate crime. For example, recent updates have included cybercrimes and environmental crimes.

§3. The Implementation of the DORA Regulation

1213. The Digital Operational Resilience Act (DORA) is a European Union regulation that aims to ensure the operational resilience of the financial sector against digital risks.

It was adopted by the European Parliament in November 2022 and is a key component of the EU's broader Digital Finance Strategy. DORA is designed to establish a harmonized framework across the EU for managing and mitigating cyber risks in the financial sector. Here are the main principles of DORA:

1214. DORA applies to a broad range of financial entities, including banks, insurance companies, investment firms, payment institutions, crypto-asset service providers, and financial market infrastructures. It also covers third-party ICT (Information and Communication Technology) service providers, such as cloud service providers, that offer services to these financial entities.

1215. The regulation addresses all aspects of digital operational resilience, encompassing not just cybersecurity but also the ability to withstand, respond to, and recover from all types of ICT-related disruptions and threats.

1216. Financial entities are required to implement a comprehensive ICT risk management framework. This includes identifying, assessing, and managing ICT risks to ensure the continuity of operations and the security of data.

1217. Clear governance arrangements must be established, with the involvement of senior management in overseeing ICT risk management. Responsibilities for ICT risk management must be well-defined within the organization.

1218. DORA mandates that financial entities report significant ICT-related incidents to their competent authorities. The regulation sets out specific criteria for what constitutes a 'significant' incident, including its impact on the availability, integrity, and confidentiality of data, and the potential for financial loss or customer harm.

1219. Incidents must be reported within tight timelines, usually within 24 hours of detection, with subsequent updates as more information becomes available.

1220. Financial entities are required to conduct regular testing of their ICT systems to ensure resilience. This includes vulnerability assessments, penetration testing, and scenario-based testing.

For significant financial entities, DORA mandates the use of Threat-Led Penetration Testing TLPT, where simulated attacks are conducted under controlled conditions to identify potential weaknesses in the ICT systems.

1221. DORA imposes strict requirements on financial entities when outsourcing ICT services to third-party providers. This includes conducting due diligence, ongoing monitoring, and ensuring that third-party providers meet the required standards of digital operational resilience.

DORA introduces a specific regime for critical third-party providers, such as major cloud service providers. These providers will be subject to direct oversight by European Supervisory Authorities (ESAs).

1222. DORA encourages financial entities to share information related to cyber threats, vulnerabilities, and incidents within the sector. This is aimed at improving the collective resilience of the financial sector against digital threats.

1223. For financial groups, DORA requires a consolidated approach to ICT risk management. This means that group-level entities must ensure that their subsidiaries and affiliates also comply with DORA's requirements.

1224. Competent authorities in each EU member state are given powers to supervise compliance with DORA. This includes the ability to conduct inspections, request information, and impose sanctions for non-compliance.

1225. Financial entities that fail to comply with DORA can face significant penalties, including fines and other corrective measures.

Chapter 4. Liability and Remedies

§1. Introduction

1226. In Italy, the legal framework for liability and remedies in cybersecurity is shaped by a combination of European Union regulations, national laws, and sector-specific guidelines.

This framework addresses the responsibilities of organizations in preventing cyber incidents, the consequences of failing to do so, and the remedies available to affected parties.

§2. Cybersecurity in Data Protection and Privacy Laws

1227. GDPR (General Data Protection Regulation), as an EU regulation directly applicable in Italy, imposes strict obligations on organizations to protect personal data. This includes implementing appropriate technical and organizational measures to ensure data security.

Under the GDPR, organizations can be held liable for data breaches that result from inadequate cybersecurity measures. Liability extends to both data controllers (who determine the purpose and means of processing data) and data processors (who process data on behalf of controllers).

Individuals whose data has been compromised have the right to seek compensation for material or non-material damage resulting from the breach. This can include financial loss, emotional distress, and damage to reputation.

The GDPR allows for substantial fines for non-compliance, which can reach up to EUR 20 million or 4% of the company's annual global turnover, whichever is higher.

1228. Decree 231 establishes the administrative liability of companies for certain criminal offenses, including cybercrimes, committed by their employees or representatives. Companies can be held liable if crimes are committed to benefit the organization. Sanctions for companies under Decree 231 include fines, disqualification from certain activities, confiscation of assets, and publication of the conviction. These sanctions are intended to incentivize companies to adopt robust compliance programs, including cybersecurity measures.

1229. Digital Operational Resilience Act (DORA) imposes specific cybersecurity obligations on financial institutions. It includes provisions for managing ICT risks, incident reporting, and oversight of third-party service providers.

Financial institutions can face penalties for failing to comply with DORA, including fines and restrictions on their activities. Additionally, they may be held liable for damages caused to customers or other stakeholders due to cybersecurity breaches.

1230. Italy's Law Decree No. 105/2019, also known as the National Cybersecurity Perimeter, requires operators of essential services, including those in the public sector and critical infrastructure, to implement stringent cybersecurity measures.

Entities within the National Cybersecurity Perimeter that fail to comply with cybersecurity obligations can face sanctions, including fines and other administrative penalties.

Affected parties can seek compensation for damages resulting from cybersecurity incidents, though specific remedies depend on the contractual and regulatory context.

1231. Italy's Penal Code criminalizes various cyber offenses, including unauthorized access to computer systems, data interference, system interference, and the distribution of malware.

Individuals and organizations can be held criminally liable for committing or facilitating cybercrimes. Penalties can include imprisonment, fines, and seizure of assets.

If a cybercrime is committed to benefit an organization, the company itself can also be held liable under Decree 231.

1232. Concerning Civil Liability, under the Italian Civil Code, organizations can be held liable for damages caused by their negligence, including insufficient cybersecurity measures that lead to a data breach or cyber incident.

Victims of cyber incidents can file a civil lawsuit seeking compensation for damages. This may include direct financial losses, loss of opportunity, and compensation for non-material harm such as distress or reputational damage.

1233. Italy's data protection authority is responsible for enforcing GDPR compliance and can impose fines and other corrective measures for data protection violations.

Sector-specific regulators, such as the Bank of Italy for financial institutions, oversee compliance with cybersecurity regulations and can impose penalties for non-compliance.

1234. Victims of cybersecurity incidents can bring claims before civil courts to seek compensation for damages. Courts can award damages, issue injunctions to prevent further harm, and order other forms of relief.

Prosecutors can bring criminal charges against individuals and organizations involved in cybercrimes, leading to criminal penalties if convicted.

§3. Some Interesting Case Law

1235. According to Court Rovigo, section I, 10/07/2023, No. 603, Poste Italiane performs a dangerous activity pursuant to Article 2050 of the Italian Civil Code.

The activity carried out by Poste Italiane, in so far as it also relates to the computer processing of personal data, is to be considered dangerous due to the ever more frequent computer frauds (so-called phishing) aimed at fraudulently obtaining such data for the performance of unlawful operations, mostly aimed at accessing the personal data of the account holder in order to transfer sums from his current account to that of third parties.

1236. According to Court of Cassation, Civil section I, 13/03/2023, No. 7214, there can be no doubt of the decisively careless and negligent behaviour of the injured party, who had typed in his personal codes (probably requested from him by means of a fraudulent e-mail), thus enabling the unknown fraudster to subsequently use them, to make a bank transfer from the injured party's account (excluding, in the present case, the restitution of the sums withdrawn from a current account by means of an online bank transfer, given that the responsibility was to be borne by the injured party who had recklessly provided his personal codes, probably due to phishing activity).

1237. According to Court of Arezzo, 08/04/2020, No. 272, the bank that has not adapted to the security system approved by the Bank of Italy must return what has been stolen.

On the subject of phishing by connection to home – banking, the bank that has not adapted to the security system considered appropriate at the time by the Bank of Italy must return what was unlawfully taken from the current account. (In the case in point, a bank transfer of EUR 5,000.00 had been made which had not been ordered by the customer and the bank's security system for transfers did not provide for a password in addition to the access password and dispositive operations were notified to customers by e-mail and not by sms messages, which are more immediate and read more frequently than e-mail).

1238. According to Court of Parma, section I, 06/09/2018, No. 1268, in the event of unlawful transfers made to online current accounts, by means of fraudulent conduct aimed at stealing protection codes and embezzling sums of money (so-called phishing), it is up to the Bank to provide proof of the proper functioning of its system and, therefore, of the traceability of the transaction to the account holder who disowned it, in application of the well-established principle on the division of the burden of proof in matters of contractual liability. The credit institution is bound to a diligence that can be assessed taking into account the model of the professional operator, such as the shrewd banker (*bonus nummarius*); moreover, the correct operation of the banking service by means of telematic connection – which corresponds to an interest of the bank itself – is fully part of the business risk, with the consequence that the bank bears an objective or semi-objective liability, from which it can be exempted only by proving, at least by way of presumption, that the transactions contested by the customer are attributable to him.

1239. According to Court of Milan, section VI, 04/12/2014, in the performance of obligations inherent in the exercise of a professional activity, diligence must be assessed with regard to the nature of the activity exercised, pursuant to Article 1176(2) of the Italian Civil Code. In particular, in the contractual relationship of home banking, the bank has the capacity of a qualified contractor, who, not unaware of the methods of fraud by means of phishing long known in the sector, is obliged to adapt to the development of new security systems.

Part VI. Cybercrime

Chapter 1. Application of International and Regional Agreements

§1. Introduction: The Actual Italian Legal Framework

1240. The picture of the cybercrimes discipline in Italy is very interesting, having steadily evolved over the last 30 years.

T*hree regulatory measures*, in particular, have shaped the framework, trying to adapt the rules to the technological evolution: the first ever regulation in 1993 (Law No. 547), a subsequent amendment in 2008 (with Law No. 48), which included some changes required by international conventions, and the very recent Law No. 90 of June 2024, which combined cybercrimes and cybersecurity in the reform.

1241. The progressive emergence of forms of cybercrime in the early Seventies of the last century, made it clear to both European and Italian legislators that the digital world could not be regulated with the same tools elaborated for the analogical world, especially in the field of criminal law, characterized by a high degree of specificity in defining cases.[248]

Furthermore, with the occurrence of the first electronic computer breaches, it became necessary to distinguish between computer crimes *in a strict sense* – referred to as 'computer crimes' – and computer-related crimes *in a broad sense*, which are crimes connected with the use of computers.[249]

In the first category, it is possible to ascribe those crimes where computers (or telecommunication systems) are, for all intents and purposes, the 'victims' of the criminal action. The second category encompasses crimes committed using an IT device or where the computer plays an *ancillary role* to the main conduct (for example, consider cases of sexual exploitation of minors with the digitalization of images and videos and their subsequent diffusion through telematic channels).

1242. In Europe, a strong impulse to regulate these phenomena was offered by the Council of Europe, in particular with Recommendation 89 (9) of 13 September 1989 entitled 'Sur la criminalité en relation avec lor ordinateur'.

---

248. *See, generally*, A. Cadoppi, S. Canestrari, A. Manna (eds), 'Cybercrime' (UTET, Milan, 2019).
249. For an overview of computer crimes in the digital society, *see* C. Frediani, 'Cybercrime' (Hoepli, Milan, 2019).

The Recommendation contains *two lists of crimes* that the States adhering to the Council of Europe can consider, and possibly include, in their penal system: a 'minimum' list, containing offenses deemed essential due to the progressive technological progress and an 'optional' list containing other offenses for which Member States have to carry out more coherent work with respect to their existing criminal system.

1243. The following were included in the 'minimum' list:

i. computer fraud, meaning access, alteration or deletion of data or computer programs, or any other interference in computer processing which influences the result, and which for this reason determines an economic or material damage to another person, carried out with the intention of obtaining an illegitimate economic advantage for oneself, or for others;
ii. computer falsification: entry, alteration or deletion of data or computer programs or any other interference in computer processing, carried out with methods or conditions such as to constitute, according to national law, a crime of forgery if the facts themselves were committed in the regards of the traditional objects of this type of infringement;
iii. damage to data or computer programs: illegal damage, deterioration or cancellation of data or computer programs;
iv. cyber sabotage: entry, alteration or deletion of data or computer programs, or interference in computer systems, with the intention of hindering the functioning of an information system or a telecommunications system;
v. unauthorized access: access without rights to a computer system or network by violating the security rules;
vi. unauthorized interception: interception without right and through technical means of communications sent, originating or existing within a computer system or network;
vii. unauthorized duplication of a protected computer program: reproduction, distribution or communication to the public, without right, of a computer program protected by law;
viii. unauthorized reproduction of a topography: reproduction without right of a topography, protected by law, of a semiconductor product, or commercial exploitation or importation for this purpose, without having the right, of a topography or a semiconductor product manufactured with the help of this topography.

1244. The 'optional' list, however, included the following cases:

i. alteration of data or computer programs by those who had no right to intervene on them;
ii. cyber espionage, indicated as the obtaining, through illegitimate means such as unauthorized disclosure, transfer or use without right or other legal justification, of a commercial or industrial secret, with the intention of causing an economic prejudice to those having the right to secrecy or to obtain, for himself or for others, an illegal economic advantage;

iii. unauthorized use of a computer, that is the use without right of a system or a computer network carried out stressing a significant risk of causing a prejudice to the person who has the right to use the system, or to harm the system or its functioning, or in this way causing injury to the person who has the right to use the system or causing damage to the system or to its operation;
iv. unauthorized use of a protected computer program, i.e., the use without right of a program protected by law or reproduced without rights, with the intention of obtaining an illegal economic advantage for oneself or others, or to cause prejudice to the holder of this rights.

1245. The norms relating to the so-called computer crimes have been established, in Italy, after the need both to recover the pace compared to European Countries already with such legislation in force and to organize a defence against the growing phenomenon of cybercrime. The new legislation has followed the aforementioned directions of the Council of Europe and also benefited from the legislative experience gained in other countries.

These demands led the Minister of Justice of the time, the Hon Prof. Giuliano Vassalli, to appoint in January 1989 a commission composed of judges, academics and IT experts, to whom he entrusted the task to draw up a scheme to amend the relevant norms of the Criminal Code to fight cybercrime.

The Law of 23 December 1993, No. 547, entitled 'Amendments and Additions to the Rules of the Criminal Code and the Code of Criminal Procedure on Cybercrime', is an outcome of the work of the Commission. This first computer crimes law of 1993 was emended in 2008 with Law No. 48 of 2008 ('Ratification and Execution of the Council of Europe Convention on Cybercrime, done at Budapest on November 23, 2001, and Rules for the Adaptation of Domestic Law').

1246. The Italian legislator, in amending the Criminal Code and the Code of Criminal Procedure, had to make several legislative policy considerations.

The choice was between, on the one hand, introducing new criminal offences or, on the other hand, amending existing criminal offences in the codes that could be related to cybercrimes, adapting them to cover new cases.

The following year the legislature's attention was devoted to traditional computer crimes.

In the mid-years of last decade, reforms were introduced to regulate the sexual exploitation of minors and the dissemination of child pornography on the internet, while in more recent years the Italian legislature has focused on digital investigations and how best to manage the source of evidence in electronic form.

1247. Alongside legislative measures specifically aimed at regulating computer crimes, other laws were also enacted that, although originally designed for different sectors, address offences closely linked to the computer world.

The most striking example is Regulation (EU) 2016/679 on the protection of natural persons with regards to the processing of personal data and on the free movement of such data (General Data Protection Regulation or GDPR), implemented by L.D. No. 101/2018, which replaced parts of the 2003 Privacy Code.

The GDPR addresses the unlawful processing of data, that can be carried out effectively using computers. Additionally, certain crimes under Italian law considered 'classic' or 'traditional' (such as defamation or harassment) have increasingly been classified also as cybercrimes, since cases involving computers or cell phones now outnumber those committed physically.

§2. The Law No. 547 of 1993

1248. The Law of 1993, No. 547, is considered the cornerstone of the Italian system with regards to the offences related to new technologies, on top of other legislative initiatives (such as, for example, D.Lgs.. No. 518/92 concerning protection of computer programs), in which additional cases of crime committed by computer and electronic instruments are identified.

The subject has suffered profound changes following the law of 18 March 2008 No. 48, which authorized the ratification of the Convention on Cybercrime of the Council of Europe that Italy signed among the firsts far back as of 2001.

The aim of the Convention was essentially to harmonize the offences provided by internal laws and to provide the signatory states with a legislation for the effective conducting investigations and contrasting cybercrimes.

A second change was made, in 2024, with Law 28 June 2024, No. 90.

1249. Italian Law No. 48/2008 is composed of fourteen articles divided into four Chapters, with Chapter II and Chapter III being the most relevant, which led on the one hand to the integration of the existing Criminal Code and the Code of Criminal Procedure, and on the other hand to the introduction of new types of offences.

1250. The Italian legislator, in intervening on cybercrimes topics, had to make legislative policy choices.

From one perspective, the legislator had to choose whether to create *new* criminal offenses or to adapt and modify existing crimes that could in any way be associated with computer crimes.

Law No. 547/1993 has followed both directions: it has introduced new types of crimes and integrated existing provisions.

A second criminal policy choice involved deciding between modifying the Criminal Code, possibly by introducing a new head or title, or enacting a law that would integrate existing items into our system.

The second solution was considered preferable.

1251. The new rules introduced by Law 547/1993 contain some important statements on the legal nature of various elements of the IT world.

Between these:

i. the computer is also a new telecommunications medium;

ii. the most characteristic element of computers is not so much its physical component (the so-called hardware), but the set of data recorded in its memories (the data) and the algorithms that allow its processing and use for specific tasks (the software);
iii. the computer represents in all respects an offshoot of the individual, used to produce, receive and process information. To violate this personal 'space' is to violate the privacy of the individual;
iv. computer crimes, due to the importance of the values they affect, constitute a highly dangerous form of crime that it would have been unreasonable to leave unpunished.

1252. Law No. 547/93, therefore, integrated the Penal Code by inserting new articles, such as Article 615-*ter* on unauthorized access to a computer or electronic system, Article 615-*quater* related to the unauthorized possession or distribution of access codes to a computer or electronic system, Article 615-*quinquies* on the distribution of viruses and Article 640-*ter* on computer fraud.

However, the impact of the Law was not only supplementary but also extensive, affecting existing articles such as Article 392 of the Criminal Italian Penal Code relating to the arbitrary exercise of one's rights with violence against things or Article 420 Italian Penal Code concerning attacks on public utility facilities.

1253. Although law No. 547/1993 is not the only one to provide for hypotheses of crime related to new technologies, it still remains one of the *cornerstones* of our system in the field of cybercrime. Also other legislative interventions, such as the Law of 6 February 2006, No. 38 (Provisions on the fight against the sexual exploitation of children and child pornography also through the Internet) and the Law of 29 May 2017, No. 17 (Provisions for the protection of minors for the prevention and contrast of the phenomenon of cyberbullying), have contributed to identifying further hypotheses of illicit committed through IT and telematic tools.

In addition, Decree Law No. 93 of 14 August 2013 amended paragraph 2 of Article 612-*bis* of the Criminal Code, which regulates the crime of stalking, providing for an aggravated penalty if the crime is committed through computer or telematic tools.

Most recently, Law No. 69 of 19 July 2019 has introduced the crime of *revenge porn* in Article 612-*ter* Italian Penal Code.

1254. The publication in the Official Gazette of Law No. 90 of 28 June 2024 on 'Provisions on strengthening national cybersecurity and cybercrimes' brought several changes to the actual framework (the law entered into force on 17 July 2024).

The norm aims at introducing and harmonizing a very wide and varied range of cybersecurity-related topics: from governance to incident reporting obligations, from cybersecurity requirements in public contracts to preclusions for hiring certain types of professionals from the world of public cybersecurity and national security, from additions to L.D. of 8 June regulation 231 (Legislative Decree No. 231/2001 No. 231 on administrative the liability of legal entities) to the wide-ranging novelty on cybercrimes.

Among the new features are amendments to the Criminal Code aimed at tightening the sanctioning response for certain offences.

§3. The Evolution of the Concept of Computer Crime in Italy

1255. It is hard to succeed in giving a precise and exhaustive definition of 'crimine informatico' (computer crime) or, more correctly according to the Italian penal taxonomy, 'delitto informatico' (informatic delict).[250]

This difficulty is due to the many varied procedures through which it is possible to perform an action that can be considered a 'computer crime', the role that the information instrument can vest, and lastly, the technological evolution that renders outdated and inadequate every definition that refers to the instrument with which or on which the criminal conduct is performed.

It is often tempting to define 'computer crime' in the simplistic way, as any behaviour defined and punished by the Italian Penal Code or related special legislation where a computer or online (telematic) instrument is the object, subject or means of the crime. However, this definition is incorrect.

1256. The expression 'computer crime' has been borrowed in the Italian juridical taxonomy from Anglo-American law, to identify a range of unlawful phenomena related to computer sciences and activities, but this terminology has brought along the characteristics of Anglo-Saxon law that has the advantage of a practical approach to problems.

For this reason, the notion of 'computer crime' does not apply to delimit and frame the positive law provisions existing in the Italian juridical system.[251]

In substance, behaviours that could in abstraction be qualified as 'computer crimes' are identified by the use, in particular forms, of computers and/or online (telematic) instruments to perform actions qualified as unlawful by the juridical system. These behaviours can be classified neither by *genus* nor *species*; however, certain elements can help in correctly framing the problem.

1257. First, the computer crime has to concern a computer; it is preferable to assume the widest notion possible of 'computer' in order to include both the variable program computers and the so-called dedicated, namely, both those in which the program is inserted by means of software and those in which such insertion is pre-established by means of firmware.

---

250. Frequent use by the doctrine of the expression 'crimine informatico' comes from the translation of the expression 'computer crime' of clear Anglo-Saxon origin.

251. *See amplius* G. Amato-V.S. Destito-G. Dezzani-C. Santoriello, 'I reati informatici' (CEDAM, Padova, 2010); R. Borruso-G. Buonomo-G. Corasaniti-G. D'Aietti, 'Profili penali dell'informatica' (Giuffrè, Milano, 1994); L. Lupària (ed.), 'Sistema penale e criminalità informatica' (Giuffrè, Milano, 2009); P. Galdieri, 'Teoria e pratica nell'interpretazione del reato informatico' (Giuffrè, Milano, 1997); C. Pecorella, 'Diritto penale dell'informatica' (CEDAM, Padova, 2006); G. Pica, 'Diritto penale delle tecnologie informatiche' (UTET, Torino, 1999); L. Picotti, 'Il diritto penale dell'informatica nell'epoca di internet' (CEDAM, Padova, 2004); G. Ziccardi-P. Perri 'Tecnologia e Diritto' (Giuffré, Milano, 2017).

1258. Moreover, four conditions are required:

i. that it is an electronic instrument;
ii. that it functions 'by means of program';
iii. that the elaborated signals are digital and not analogue; and
iv. that such elaboration is performed on the basis of Boolean logic.

1259. Furthermore, in order to comprehend the concept of 'computer crime' in its entirety, it is necessary to consider the general notions of informatics and telematics:[252] by 'informatics' we mean 'the science that studies information and, more specifically, the elaboration of data and their automated processing through electronic processors'; by 'telematics', instead, 'the discipline that studies the technical and scientific aspects of the integration between telecommunication and electronic processing; the long-range managing of computer systems by means of employment of telecommunication networks; the entirety of services of computer nature or origin that can be supplied and used through a telecommunication network'.[253]

1260. It is therefore possible to distinguish two fundamental categories, now clearly identified by statute, into which computer crimes are divided:

1. those crimes perpetrated with the aid of computer instruments and programs, when the processor is the instrumental means through which the criminal behaviour is performed;
2. those crimes perpetrated against computer instruments or programs, when the target of the crime is a computer or telecommunication system and the data, information or programs it contains.

In an attempt to draw a first conclusion, it is possible to state that a 'magic formula' capable of including every possible meaning of the notion of 'computer crime' does not exist, but there are various definitions, all apt to define the concept of 'computer crime', not individually exhaustive.

1261. The main ones can be identified in the following:

i. computer crimes are crimes perpetrated through the use of a computer;
ii. computer crime is every 'illegal, dishonest or unauthorized' behaviour 'that concerns the automated data processing or transmission';[254]

---

252. An eminent doctrine, indeed, observes that 'the interpretative problem is caused by the fact that the expression the legislator used, 'computer or telecommunication system', doesn't define a physically existing and identified good . . ., but expresses an abstract concept we have to fill with the notions that reality offers us' *see* G. Pica, *supra.*, pp. 22 ss.
253. *See* entries 'Informatica' and 'Telematica' in VV.AA., 'Dizionario della lingua italiana' (Garzanti Linguistica, Milano, 2004).
254. This definition was formulated by the OECD Commission of experts, Paris, 1993.

iii. computer crime is any act or fact against penal provisions, in which a computer has been involved as object of the fact, as mean or as symbol'.

1262. A sufficiently exhaustive definition, however, can be identified in the following formulation that identifies the computer crime in the wrongdoing in which a processing system or a part of it vests one of the next roles: object, namely including the distribution or manipulation of the processor, or of the data or the programs it contains and the related support instruments; subject, when what happens in relation to the processor is not illegal in itself but is needed to perform crimes of other kind (for example, frauds or sabotages). Practically a processing system, and what is produced by the processor, is used as a means to perform frauds, sabotages, falsifications.

1263. Despite the apparent completeness, however, not even this definition is apt to include all the multiformity that is intrinsic in the notion of computer crime.

Up to the present day, therefore, we have a series of definitions that integrate and complete each other, but we lack a definition that succeeds in including in a single concept what can be considered a computer crime pursuant to the Italian penal law.

§4. Characteristics of Computer Crimes According to Italian Law

1264. Computer crimes are characterized by actions targeting goods of relevant value. The action can be physical, when the object of the criminal behaviour is the hardware; or logic, when the crime focuses on data, information and programs.

For instance, consider the computerized management of personal data by professional firms or health services.

1265. The volume of online transactions grows exponentially each day, making it a common practice to purchase goods and services from home by filling out web forms with debit card data, along with all the associated risks and potential problems.

The lack of proper security policies faces the challenge of the proverbial inventiveness of perpetrators who, benefiting from a relevant degree of impunity due to difficulties such as the identification of the *locus commissi delicti*, conducting cross-border investigations and the assessment of facts, are often able to succeed in performing various potentially criminal actions without facing any consequence.

1266. A further aspect is the reluctance of victims, particularly banks, to report the suffered damages.

This reluctance stems from the popular belief that the publicity of the crime will cause them more disadvantages than advantages, due to the customers' loss of esteem and trust, resulting in further economic damage that outweighs the initial loss. Moreover, it is often difficult to adequately prove facts, which poses the risk of banks being accused of defamation.

This results in what is known as the dark-number effect, namely the uncertainty in the quantification of computer crimes, which is also fuelled by the belief that a trial might end in the acquittal of the defendant or with a lenient punishment.

1267. In the *genus* of computer crimes identified beforehand, many *species* are identifiable. Usually, computer crimes are divided according to the discerning criteria of perpetration procedures and the criteria of the purpose of the criminal action.

1268. For this purpose, three different categories can be identified:

i. the first includes thoroughly heterogeneous cases: in some circumstances the profit of the author consists in the accumulation of considerable sums; in others, the perpetrator acts with the only purpose, for example, of not paying phone bills, by deviating charges on someone else's account;
ii. the second category includes crimes where the criminal action aims at destroying or damaging totally or partially hardware and/or software. These include cases where the perpetrators, by diffusing specific programs created ad hoc to damage systems, are able to destroy software and render the hardware unusable;
iii. the third category includes those crimes whose pursued aim is to cause physical damage to individuals, society or goods.

§5. Law No. 547 of 23 December 1993 and Law No. 48/2008: Inspiring Criteria

1269. In 2008 Italy ratified the Convention on Cybercrime, signed in Budapest (23 November 2001) with Law No. 48 of 18 March 2008.

This Law modified several parts of Statute 547/9 and contains the new crime of 'computer fraud perpetrated by the entity providing electronic signature certification services' (Article 640-*quinquies* of the Italian Penal Code): 'the person who provides services for the certification of electronic signature, who, in order to secure for himself or others an unfair advantage or to cause harm to others, violates the obligations required by law to issue a qualified certificate, shall be punished with imprisonment up to three years and a fine ranging from EUR 51 to EUR 1.032'.

1270. New is also the punishment of the distribution of equipment, devices, or software aimed at damaging or disrupting a computer or electronic system (Article 615-*quinquies* of the Italian Penal Code): 'whoever, in order to unlawfully damage a computer system or electronic communication, information, data or programs contained in or relevant to it or to encourage disruption, total or partial alteration of its operation, obtains, produces, reproduces, imports, disseminates, communicates, delivers or otherwise makes available to other equipment, devices or computer programs, shall be punished with imprisonment up to two years and a fine of up to EUR 10,329)'.

1271. Important are also some modifications to Article 635-*bis*, concerning damage of information, data and computer programs (unless the act constitutes a serious crime, anyone who destroys, reduces, cancels, alters or deletes information, data or computer programs of another person shall be punished, upon complaint of the victim, by imprisonment from six months to three years. If the act is committed with violence to the person or with abuse of its role as operator of the system, the punishment shall be imprisonment from one to four years).

1272. The new Article 635-*quater*, concerning damage to computer or telecommunications, dispose that, unless the act constitutes a more serious crime, anyone, by the conduct referred to in Article 635-*bis*, or through the introduction or transmission of data, information or programs, destroys, damages, makes – in whole or in part – useless telecommunications systems or seriously hinders the operation shall be punished with imprisonment from one to five years. If the act is committed with violence to the person or with abuse of its role as operator of the system, the punishment shall be increased.

1273. Article 635-*ter*, concerning damage of information, data and programs used by governments or other public body or any public utility, dispose that, unless the act constitutes a more serious crime, whoever commits a fact intended to destroy, damage, delete, alter or delete information, data or computer programs used by governments or other public body or relevant, or of public utility, shall be punished with imprisonment from one to four years.

If from the action follows the destruction, damage, deletion, alteration or suppression of information, data or computer programs, the punishment shall be imprisonment from three to eight years.

If the act is committed with violence to the person or with abuse of its role as operator of the system, the punishment shall be increased.

Similar discipline regulates also the damage to computer or telematic systems of public utility or the serious obstruction of their operation. Indeed, one of the main objectives of the Budapest Convention is to facilitate cooperation between the various Member States.

1274. The Convention is, in fact, the first international treaty on criminal offences committed via the Internet and on other computer networks, and deals in particular with copyright infringement, computer fraud, child pornography and network security breaches.

It also contains a series of appropriate measures and procedures, such as the search for computer network systems and the interception of data.

1275. Its main objective, set out in the preamble, is to pursue a common penal policy for the protection of society against cybercrime, especially by adopting appropriate legislation and promoting international cooperation.

1276. In particular, what the Convention wants to achieve is a minimum target of protection of legal assets offended by cybercrimes and a common minimum essential level of strategies to combat these offences, especially due to their generally transnational nature, which involves clearly the need for harmonization of the relative legislation of contrast in the various legal systems.

Increasing importance is also being acquired by the Additional Protocols to the Convention, which are intended to deal with specific areas of cybercrime where there is a need for ad hoc standardization.

1277. The first protocol concerned xenophobia and racism conveyed through telematic channels (opened for signature in Strasbourg on 28 January 2003); the second protocol, on enhanced co-operation and disclosure of electronic evidence (approved on 28 May 2021 and edited on 13 October 2021), aims to strengthen the cooperation tools between states, taking into account the growing dissemination of distributed technologies such as cloud computing, to be able to identify, collect and analyse the digital proof source also from a cross-border perspective.

1278. The Convention opens with some important definitions, which are used to outline the perimeter within which the subsequent rules will operate.

First of all, it is necessary to define what is meant by an IT system, a concept that is apparently easy to identify but that, for example, in our system has often requested clarifications from the Italian Court of Cassation.

1279. The computer system is to be understood as any equipment or group of interconnected or connected devices, one or more of which, based on a program, perform automatic data processing. The necessary coexistence of a hardware component and a software component is then reiterated, which will be able to perform the most varied operations on the data, always falling within the definition of 'computer system'.

1280. The definition of computer data is also interesting, identified as any presentation of facts, information or concepts in a form likely to be used in a computerized system, including a program capable of allowing a computerized system to perform a function and that of service provider, which indicates: '1. any public or private entity that provides users of its services with the possibility of communicating through an IT system; 2. any other entity that processes or stores computer data on behalf of such communication service or for users of such service'.

Finally, the last given definition is that of data transmission, which means 'any computerized information relating to a communication through an information system that forms a part in the communication chain, indicating the origin of the communication, the destination, the path, the time, date, size, duration or type of service'.

1281. With regard to the definitions referred to above, the Cassation reaffirmed that 'Art. 1 of the Budapest Convention of 23 November 2001, implemented in Italy with Law No. 48 of 2008, with the definition 'computer system' identifies any equipment or group of interconnected or connected devices, one or more of which, based on a program, perform automatic data processing; with the definition 'computer data' the same article identifies any presentation of facts, information or concepts in a form likely to be used in a computerized system, including a program capable of allowing a computerized system to perform a function; and with the definition 'data transmission' it identifies any computerized information relating to a communication through an information system that forms a part in the communication chain, indicating the origin of the communication, the destination, the path, the time, the date, the size, duration or type of service.

Precisely in consideration of the aforementioned characteristics, which according to the Treaty identify the essential elements of computer crimes, debit or credit cards, identified by a magnetic stripe or a chip (both elements suitable for storing and transmitting computer data), constitute a genuine computer system, capable of processing data, making them operational, when they connect to the POS equipment, allowing authorized access to the Banks financial information system.

1282. With regard to the substantive law measures, Chapter 2 of the Convention contains a series of crimes that can be divided into the following categories:

i. crimes against confidentiality, integrity and availability of data and IT systems (offences of illegal access fall into this category to a computerized or telematic system, offences of abusive interception, crimes against the integrity of data, crimes against the integrity of computer systems and abuse of instruments aimed at committing the crimes listed up to this point or subtracting passwords and access codes for identification in computer systems);
ii. computer crimes in the strict sense (so-called computer-related offences, i.e., computer forgery and computer fraud);
iii. crimes related to content (so-called content-related offence, essentially all crimes related to child pornography); and
iv. crimes against intellectual property and related rights, which recall the need to provide for criminal sanctions in the event of copyright infringement, in accordance with the decision taken under the Paris Act of 24 July 1971, which revised the Berne Convention for the protection of literary and artistic works. According to the Convention, these crimes must be punished with penalties that are 'effective, proportionate and dissuasive, including the deprivation of personal freedom'.

In compliance with both the principles and the detail of the cases contained in the Convention, Law No. 48/2008 has profoundly modified some provisions of the Italian Penal Code and the Code of Criminal Procedure.

1283. In particular, as regards the criminal cases, Article 491-*bis* of the Criminal Code concerning the falsification of a public electronic document with probative value and Article 495-*bis* related Italian Penal Code relative to the false declaration or attestation to the certifier of electronic signature on the identity or personal qualities of oneself or others.

1284. Article 615-*quinqies* c.p., relating to the dissemination of equipment, devices or computer programs aimed at damaging or interrupting an IT or electronic system and the entire regulations relating to IT damage are profoundly modified.

In fact, in addition to the replacement of Article 635-*bis* that, in its new version, concerns the damage to information, data and computer programs, three new cases are added which are 635-*ter* c.p.(Damage to information, data and computer programs used by the State or by another public body or in any case of public utility), 635-*quater* Italian Penal Code. (Damage to computer or telecommunications systems) and 635-*quinquies* (Damage to computer or telematic systems of public utility).

1285. The catalogue of the cases relating to computer fraud is also expanded, where a new article is inserted, namely the 640-*quinquies* of the Criminal Code concerning the computer fraud of the subject who provides electronic signature certification services.

1286. Finally, Article 420 Italian Criminal Code, in its new version punishes 'Anyone committing an act aimed at damaging or destroying public utility facilities, unless the fact constitutes a more serious offense, with imprisonment from one to four years.'

Chapter 2. Specific Computer Crimes

§1. 'Computer Violence' on Goods

1287. Article 1 of Statute No. 547/93 inserts after paragraph 2 of Article 392 of the Italian Penal Code (titled 'arbitrary exert of one's reasons'), a paragraph where the legal notion of 'violence on goods' is broadened, by its extension from traditional facts of offence, transformation or destination change to a series of behaviours that directly deal with computer programs or with the functioning of computer or telecommunication systems.

The newly formulated Article 392 allows conviction of any person who, in an attempt to assert an alleged right and having the option to apply to the Court, decides instead to take arbitrarily the law into their own hands.

Part of the doctrine has already stressed the fact that, under the technical profile, it is not useful, but rather dangerous, to operate on the already controversial 'general' notion of 'violence on goods' by broadening it further to include alterations, modifications or partial deletions, or even the mere 'impediment or disturbance' of the functioning of a computer or telecommunication system.[255]

1288. A wide range of cases has imposed the broadening of the expression 'violence on goods', since often hardware and mostly software houses have performed unlawful manumissions of the computer systems (partial mutilations, alteration of the normal system functioning) they supplied to customers, claiming rights on the derived software and therefore exercising a form of self-protection that the penal law forbids. However, according to doctrine, it is necessary to further distinguish situations in which the crime defined by Article 392 of the Penal Code and the crime of damage defined by Article 635 of the Italian Penal Code could be both configured. Namely, when violence against goods aimed at asserting an alleged right is accompanied by damage, an extensive interpretation of the notion of 'goods or chattels' is applied and the hypothesis of concurrence of these crimes is considered.

In the cited doctrine's perspective, it is possible to configure the concurrence of the crime of computer damaging and the crime of diffusion of virus-programs (or similar) defined by Article 615-*quinquies* of the Italian Penal Code.

The crime defined by Article 392, involving violence on goods, does not apply in cases where the alteration of a system is performed against the system user to coerce them into a subordinate position, compelling them to take or refrain from certain actions to achieve the full restoration of the system.

The modality of 'violence on goods' with reference to the configuration of the arbitrary exercise of one's reasons, therefore, can develop in many forms, and the

255. F. Borriello, 'Il ritorno all'origine nei rapporti fra l'esercizio arbitrario delle proprie ragioni e l'estorsione (Nota a Cass. pen., sez. II, 4 dicembre 2013, n. 51433, F.)' in 'Riv. Neldiritto', 2014; S. Braschi, 'La natura dei reati di ragion fattasi e il loro rapporto con la fattispecie di estorsione: alcuni chiarimenti dalle Sezioni Unite' in 'Dir. Pen. e Proc', 2021, p. 314; A. Laurino, 'Estorsione, ragion fattasi ed intensità della violenza nella giurisprudenza della suprema corte', in 'Cassazione penale', 2012.

crime can be performed, nevertheless, also through a conduct that dips into the functionality of a computer or telecommunication system even if it does not physically alter the program.

Article 5 of Law of 18 March 2008 No. 48, considerably extends the list of incriminating cases concerning data corruption, in addition to amending Article 635-*bis* of the Criminal Code with respect to the original wording introduced by Article 9 of the Law 23 December 1993, No. 547. In addition to updating the current crime-definition of 'corruption of data' (Article 635-*bis*, 'corruption of information, data and software': anyone who destroys, reduces, cancels, alters or deletes information, data or computer programs of another person shall be punished, upon complaint of the victim, by imprisonment from six months to three years), there was the introduction of three new criminal cases.

The first one, Article 635-*ter*, introduces the crime of 'corruption of information, data and programs used by governments or other public body': whoever commits a fact intended to destroy, damage, delete or alter information, data or computer programs used by governments or other public body, or of public utility, is punished with imprisonment from one to four years.

The second one, Article 635-*quater*, introduces the crime of 'damage to computer or telematic systems': anyone who, by the conduct referred to in Article 635-*bis*, or through the introduction or transmission of data, information or programs, destroys, damages, makes, in whole or in part, useless a telecommunications systems or seriously hinders the operation, shall be punished with imprisonment from one to five years. The last one, Article 635-*quinquies*, introduces the crime of 'damage to public utility telecommunication systems': if the act referred to in Article 635-*quater* is intended to destroy, damage, render, in whole or in part, useless computer or telecommunications systems of public utility, the punishment shall be imprisonment from one to four years. With Law No. 48/2008, the standard is much changed and what was contained in a single case has been divided into four different scenarios with varied rules, some of which also cover the possibility of damage to systems of public utilities actually included in the crime of attack on the facilities for public use.

1289. The actual text of 635-*bis* of the Criminal Code, after the 2024 reform, is the following: 'article 635-*bis* (Damage to computer information, data and programs) – Unless the act constitutes a more serious offence, anyone who destroys, deteriorates, deletes, alters or suppresses information, data or computer programmes of others shall be punished, upon complaint by the offended person, by imprisonment of from two to six years. The penalty is imprisonment for three to eight years: (1) if the offence is committed by a public official or by a person in charge of a public service, with abuse of power or with violation of the duties related to the function or service, or by a person exercising, also abusively, the profession of private investigator, or with abuse of the quality of system operator; (2) if the offender uses threats or violence to commit the offence or is manifestly armed'.

1290. The actual text of 635-*ter* of the Criminal Code, after the 2024 reform, is the following: 'article 635-*ter* (Damage to public information, data and computer programs or of public interest) – Unless the fact constitutes a more serious offence, whoever commits an act aimed at destroying, deteriorating, deleting, altering or suppressing computer information, data or programmes of military interest or relating to public order or public safety or health or civil protection or in any case of public interest, shall be punished by imprisonment of from two to six years. The penalty is imprisonment for three to eight years: (1) if the offence is committed by a public official or by a person in charge of a public service, with abuse of power or with violation of the duties related to the function or service, or by a person who exercises, also abusively, the profession of private investigator, or with abuse of the quality of system operator; (2) if the offender uses threats or violence to commit the offence, or is manifestly armed; (3) if the act results in the destruction, deterioration, deletion, alteration or suppression of information or in the removal, even by reproduction or transmission, or in the inaccessibility to the lawful owner of the data or computer programmes.

The penalty shall be imprisonment for four to twelve years when any of the circumstances set out in paragraphs 1) and 2) of the second subparagraph concur with any of the circumstances set out in paragraph 3'.

1291. The actual text of 635-*quarter* of the Criminal Code, after the 2024 reform, is the following: 'article 635-*quater* (Damage to computer or telecommunication systems). – Unless the act constitutes a more serious offence, whoever, by means of the conduct referred to in article 635-*bis*, or through the introduction or transmission of data, information or programmes, destroys, damages, renders wholly or partially unusable another person's computer or telecommunication system or seriously obstructs its operation, shall be punished by imprisonment of from two to six years. The penalty is imprisonment for a term of three to eight years: (1) if the offence is committed by a public official or by a person in charge of a public service, with abuse of power or in breach of the duties inherent in the function or service, or by a person exercising, also abusively, the profession of private investigator, or with abuse of the quality of system operator; (2) if the offender uses threats or violence to commit the offence or is manifestly armed.'

1292. The actual text of 635-*quinquies* of the Criminal Code, after the 2024 reform, is the following: 'article 635-*quinquies* (Damage to computer or telecommunication systems of public interest) – Unless the act constitutes a more serious offence, any person who, by means of the conduct referred to in article 635-*bis* or by introducing or transmitting data, information or programs, commits acts aimed at destroying, damaging or rendering useless, in whole or in part, computer or telecommunication systems of public interest or at seriously obstructing their operation shall be punished by imprisonment from two to six years. The penalty shall be imprisonment for three to eight years: (1) if the offence is committed by a public official or by a person in charge of a public service, with abuse of power or in breach of the duties related to the function or service, or by a person exercising, also abusively, the profession of private investigator, or with abuse of the quality of system operator (2) if the offender uses threats or violence to commit the act, or is manifestly armed; (3) if the act results in the destruction, deterioration, deletion, alteration or suppression of information, data or computer programmes. The penalty shall be imprisonment for four to twelve years when any of the circumstances referred to in subsections 1) and 2) of the second paragraph concur with any of the circumstances referred to in subsection 3'.

§2. ATTACKS TO PUBLIC-INTEREST SYSTEMS

1293. Considering the fundamental role played by public-interest systems in social organization, the legislature has decided, by means of Article 2 of Statute 547/93, to amend Article 420 of the Penal Code, in order to extend its scope to include acts performed to damage 'public interest computer or telecommunication systems'.

The material objects of the conduct are the 'technical systems'. The main characteristic of this crime is represented by the 'public interest' of the systems that are the object of the crime, and consequentially of the data stored and the programs used in them.

Without any doubt, it is the great number of users served by the system that determines the 'publicity' of the interest: in the notion of public interest we cannot therefore include neither the system that serves an apartment block, due to the limited number of users, nor the computer system of a firm, which is covered instead by Article 635-*bis* of the Penal Code (damage of computer or telecommunication systems). The local road exchange is identifiable as public because even if it serves a limited number of wired users in the area, it does not restrict the possibility of use by anyone who wants to communicate with these users.

The indispensable aspect that allows a system to be regarded as a public-interest system is the indefinability of the number and type of potential users of the service. The systems that are instituted for the benefit of society, and are therefore of public interest, include, for example, all telecommunications systems, electronic control and monitoring systems for environmental protection, power production and switching plants and electronic and video-telematic systems for the control of moving vehicles.

1294. According to Court of Florence, 27 January 1986, the offence of assault on public utility equipment can be committed by anyone who, by means of several actions carried out as part of the same criminal plan, tampers with the magnetic disks of a university data processing system, causing damage and alterations such as to prevent or in any case make it rather difficult to access and use the information contained therein.

Acts generically classifiable as 'sabotage' of a data-processing system are those magnetic alterations that make it impossible to access and use the information stored on discs, so that they are in practice destroyed, even if the damage caused to the media is to be considered *repairable.*

In the present case, although it was ascertained that the intentional causation, through the use of magnets, of numerous alterations and tampering with disks in use at the data processing centre of a university, the defendant was acquitted of the charge under Article 420 of the Criminal Code, first part and paragraph, for lack of evidence of the commission of the act on his part.

§3. Computer Forgery

1295. Article 3 of Statute No. 547/93 has introduced the case of the so-called computer forgery by adding the specific provision of Article 491-*bis* of the Italian Penal Code that concerns computer records: 'if any of the forgeries defined in this chapter regards a public or private computer record with probative value, the same provisions of this chapter that concern public records apply'.

In the same article there was the full definition, in the penal field, of what the legislature considered a 'computer record', that had to be read as 'any computer support that contains data or information that have probative value or programs that are specifically destined to process them'.

This definition, however, caused a wide debate about the perplexities it caused since it would have been much easier to identify the record with the data itself, unbundling it from its support, than with the physical support that contains it. By hooking the computer record to a material entity (more specifically, with the support that contains it), the legislature had left unsolved all those problems that derive from the impossibility of distinguishing originals from copies in the digital world, leaving the statute to deal with the task of defining which computer supports have to be used in order to give probative value to the computer record. This definition was removed in 2016.

1296. The expression that has interested the doctrine[256] the most, of course, is that of the 'probative value' that the article under analysis recognizes to the computer record: it has to be intersected with the various definitions and distinctions already existing on the traditional notion of 'record', in order to reach an exclusively penal settling of the concept contained in the provision under analysis. It is necessary to exclude, a priori, that a definition among the ones preceding the enforcement of Statute No. 547/93 could contain the elements needed to answer the difficulties of interpretation that the provision poses. It will then be necessary to proceed from other formulations, like those elaborated by jurisprudence about the telex and the telefax.

Therefore, having seen that the definition of the record cited by the provision is quite complex, the legislature has, at last, assigned a penal protection to those records to which a probative value is recognized according to other statutory provisions. Among them, there are: acts recorded on an optical support; Public Administration acts; administrative acts performed by means of a computer and regulated by special provisions; and public acts or private records apparently subscribed by the author, even if through a computer reproduction.

---

256. R. Borgogno 'Documento tradizionale e documento informatico, in Le falsità documentali' (a cura di Ramacci, Padova, 2001, p. 73); R. Borgogno 'Documenti informatici, in Trattato di diritto penale, Parte speciale, Reati contro la fede pubblica' (a cura di Ramacci, X, Milano, 2013); F. Crimi, 'Falso (delitti di)', in 'Dig. d. pen.', Torino, 2008, Agg. IV, p. 293; G. Pecorella, 'Diritto penale dell'informatica', Milano, 2006; L. Picotti, 'Reati informatici', in 'Enc. giur. Treccani', Roma, 1999, Agg., VIII, 1; C. Sarzana di S. Ippolito, 'Informatica, Internet e diritto penale', Milano, 2009.

1297. According to Court of Cassation, Criminal section V, 14 July 2023, Decision No. 33285, the *conduct* of a person who enters data relating to *examinations that were never taken* into a university's digital system constitutes the offence of forgery of a public computer document.

The crime of falsifying a public electronic document is committed when data relating to examinations that were never taken are entered in a university digital system which has an auxiliary function with respect to the paper archive, i.e., a potentially and provisionally probative function (a case in which the statute of limitations was in any case upheld).

With regard to forgery of documents, Article 491-*bis* of the Criminal Code addresses cases of document forgery involving Italian Penal both the hypothesis in which the computer system is supported by paper evidence and when it is entirely substituted for such evidence. In both cases, the provision encompasses two distinct articulations of the criminal offence, i.e., where the forgery directly concerns data and information endowed, in itself, with probative relevance and where it concerns programmatic contexts specifically intended to process data and information, as prescribed by the last part of the provision.

1298. Court of Cassation, Criminal section II, of 30 September 2022, with Decision No. 1851, stated that if the forgery constitutes an artifice to commit fraud there is material concurrence between the crime of forgery and that of *computer fraud.*

There is material concurrence, not operating absorption, between the crime of forgery under Article 491-*bis* of the Italian Penal Code and that of computer fraud, in the event that the forgery constitutes an *artifice* for committing the fraud, since the hypothesis of the complex offence does not apply, for the configurability of which it is not sufficient that the particular modalities of realization of the typical fact determine an occasional convergence of several rules and, therefore, a concurrence of offences, but it is necessary that it is the law that provides for an offence as a constituent element or aggravating circumstance of another offence.

1299. Finally, according to Court of Cassation, Criminal section VI of 18 April 2003, No. 31720, the conduct of a *public employee* who, in the capacity of the person responsible for the management of the computer archives of a public authority, deliberately enters false data into the electronic processors of the archive or modifies existing data in relation to acts or documents recorded therein, constitutes the offence of ideological or material falsity in public acts.

§4. Unauthorized Access to a Computer or Telecommunication System

1300. Article 4 of Statute No. 547/93 inserted, in the Italian Penal Code, Article 615-*ter*, regarding *unauthorized access* to a computer or telecommunication system.

This provision is placed in Title XII of Chapter I of the Italian Penal Code that regards all acts that damage or endanger fundamental rights of the individual, namely life, physical integrity, honour and both moral and personal freedoms. It is placed, as highlighted in the report of the Ministerial Commission on the bill, among the crimes against domicile inviolability, because the computer or telecommunication systems, the violation of which is punished, are an expansion of the area of respect related to the interested subject, guaranteed by Article 14 of the Constitution and, in its more essential and traditional aspects, by the penal protection of Articles 614 and 615 of the Italian Penal Code.

The report justifies the placement of the provision among the crimes against domicile inviolability by stating the existence of a new concept of domicile, namely the computer domicile.

Article 615-*ter* provides two well-distinguished criminal scenarios: (a) the act of 'the subject that abusively breaks into a computer or telecommunication system protected by security measures'; (b) the act of 'the subject that remains into a computer or telecommunication system protected by security measures against the expressed or tacit will of the subject that has the right to exclude him'.

1301. The conduct of 'breaking in' the computer system consists in the access to the system performed by using its same technology. Part of the doctrine[257] has highlighted how the expression is excessively generalist and could therefore include any kind of conduct through which the agent enters the system. But it is clear that, even if the agent performs physical acts to approach the system (for example by forcing the entrances to the place where it is kept), nevertheless the final act of 'introduction' required by the case in point in Article 615-*ter* can only be performed by means of the same computer technologies. This is, therefore, a 'computer break-in' that will occur through the use of hardware and software components.

1302. The problem of what the legislation means when referring to 'a computer or telecommunication system' is tightly connected with the qualification of the conduct required by the provision. It is questionable whether this expression 'has to be interpreted as equipment fitted with structuring and complexity levels superior to those of a personal computer'.

In the computer science field, 'system' has always been considered a complex whole of hardware and software elements. In the juridical field, therefore, 'system' will be considered a whole of interconnected elements (for example, an electronic processor, some input and output units connected to it and the software represented by the applicative programs used on that specific processor) that interact in a coordinated way, in order to obtain certain results for which the system has been created.

'Telecommunication system', instead, is considered a defined term to mean systems that apply the telecommunication principles and technologies and allow users to perform any kind of long-distance communication.

257. L. D. Cerqua, 'Accesso abusivo e frode informatica: l'orientamento della Cassazione', in 'Dir. e prat. Società', 2000, 16, p. 53; S. Civardi, 'La distinzione fra accesso abusivo a sistema informatico e abuso dei dati acquisiti', in 'Il diritto dell'informazione e dell'informatica', 2009, 1, p. 60; L. Picotti, 'Sistematica dei reati informatici, tecniche di formulazione legislativa e beni giuridici tutelati', in 'Il diritto penale dell'informatica nell'epoca di Internet' (Padova, 2004).

1303. The conduct of 'breaking in' cited by the provision under analysis appears to be, on the logical side, always and necessarily distinct from the conduct of 'remaining inside', since it appears obvious that it is impossible to 'remain inside' the system if one has not got in. Anyway, the double law provision is not at all useless, since there are frequent cases of lawful introduction in a system (allowed by its proprietor), followed by a permanence that is unlawful because it is operated out of line and in contrast with the agreements concluded with the proprietor of the system, or because it exceeds the borders of the access authorization. The conduct of 'remaining' in the computer system appears therefore to be provided precisely to punish those cases in which the introduction is lawful, as it is performed with the consent or the authorization of the proprietor, but the access to the system becomes unlawful during its duration (for example, due to the end of the time-course of allowed access).

1304. The text of Article 615-*ter* of the Italian Penal Code contains jointly both the adverbs 'abusively' and the parenthesis 'against the expressed or tacit will of the subject that has the right to exclude him'.

At the first reading of the provision the adverb 'abusively' appears related to the conduct of 'breaking in', while the parenthesis concerning the will of the proprietor appears related to the second conduct, the so-called permanence, in the computer or telecommunication system.

However, neither of the expressions refers with certainty to a conduct, with the automatic exclusion of the other. The repetition is due, presumably, to the desire to explicitly connote both the crime conducts with the requirement of the lack of the proprietor's authorization. It is more adequate, therefore, to use the adverb 'abusively' to qualify the introduction as an unauthorized act and therefore unlawful since the beginning, while to use the parenthesis 'against the expressed or tacit will of the subject that has the right to exclude him' to refer to the intervened unlawfulness of the 'permanence' conduct, which is autonomously defined to include in the provision the unlawful fact of unauthorized 'permanence' of the agent in the system after his lawful introduction.

1305. The case under analysis restricts its scope only to cases of access to a computer or telecommunication system 'protected by security measures'.

Through this formulation, the legislature has intentionally subordinated the effectiveness of the provision to the circumstance that the proprietor of the computer or telecommunication system has provided some means of protection in order to make clear that the access and the permanence in the system are reserved only to authorized subjects by the proprietor himself. These means of protection, in the legislature's intention, can be represented by more or less effective means, so that it is the requirement of the expression of the proprietor's will that prevails, rather than that of the real effectiveness of the rejection of unauthorized subjects. The provision cites 'security measures' (plural form), and a simple keyword or an access code cannot be considered 'security measures'; these have to be something more complex than a simple 'password'. The existence of a means of protection (even if, in substance, it is scarcely effective) has the mere function of rendering explicit and unequivocal the presence of a prohibition to access to the computer system.

1306. Another question of interpretation that the provision poses regards the specification of the moment in which the access can be considered performed, that is the introduction into the system. For this purpose, we have to clarify the boundary beyond which the unauthorized access can be considered as performed, namely when the subject has effectively accessed the system, and before which there is only an 'access attempt'. With reference to this matter, the provision on 'security measures' as characteristics of the material object of the conduct allows to suppose that the 'introduction' the legislation refers to is identifiable with the moment in which the subject has abusively (that is, without the authorization of the system's proprietor) and therefore unlawfully exceeded the hardware and/or software data protection barriers. This is the moment in which the subject effectively enters the system without authorization, intentionally bypassing the protections and therefore clearly showing his intention to unlawfully access the system.

The crime will occur only when the agent manages to elude the protection and access the data contained in the system. The effective knowledge on behalf of the subject of a part or of the whole data stored in the system he breaks into is not necessary since the provision does not require it.

1307. However, to commit the crime, it is required that the subject bypasses or cheats the protection measures and penetrates protected areas of the system. In every case in which the subject tries to bypass protections (for example, by attempting to type the required password many times) but does not succeed, it is instead possible to assess the 'attempt' (provided there is the dissent of the system's proprietor, as the word 'abusively' points out). The attempt hypothesis is disciplined by Article 56 of the Criminal Code.

There is not even an 'attempt' in those cases in which the subject connects long-distance or accesses from nearby a computer system belonging to another subject, but does not attempt to bypass the existing security measures: these cases are not acts aimed at the violation of the protection, and therefore the privacy, of the system, as the subject may have connected to the system still ignoring that the access to data is protected. The mere connection action is not included in the hypothesis of effective abusive intrusion.

1308. In case of 'physical' protection measures external to the computer system (for example, security doors that preclude the entrance to the room the system is in), or even placed in the hardware (for example, the security key of nearly every table computer, which does not allow to turn it on, use the keyboard or use other hardware components), a different approach applies. The mere bypassing of external barriers (doors, alarms that protect where the computer is kept) cannot be qualified as 'unequivocally aimed' to violate the computer system, so that even the possibility to assess the crime of 'attempted unauthorized access' is ruled out: general provisions on damaging, domicile violation or others will still be applicable.

1309. Article 615-*ter* of the Penal Code provides from two to ten years of imprisonment, and the unauthorized access is not any more a crime indictable as a result of personal prosecution but an indictable offence, if it is performed by a public officer or by a subject responsible for a public service, by abuse of his powers or infringement of the duties related to the function or service; by anyone who exercises even abusively the profession of private investigator; through the abuse of the quality of system operator (paragraph 2, No. 2),); by performing violence on goods or persons; or if the culprit is evidently carrying weapons; if the destruction or damage of the system or the total or partial interruption of its functioning derive from the fact; or if the destruction or damage of data, information or programs the system contains derive from the fact.

These are cases that can all be qualified as 'special effect' cases: three distinct and aggravated hypotheses that relate to the subjective profile (qualities of the subject who performs the crime), to the modalities of the action and to the deriving consequences.

1310. The following is the *final text* of Article 615-*ter* after the reform of June 2024: Article 615-*ter* (Unauthorized access to a computer or telecommunication system) – 'Whoever unlawfully enters a computer or telecommunication system protected by security measures or remains there against the express or tacit will of those who have the right to exclude him, shall be punished by imprisonment of up to three years.

The penalty shall be imprisonment for a term of between two and ten years: (1) if the offence is committed by a public official or by a person in charge of a public service, with abuse of power or with violation of the duties inherent in the function or service, or by a person who also abusively exercises the profession of private detective, or with abuse of the quality of system operator; (2) if, in order to commit the offence, the offender uses threats or violence against property or persons, or is manifestly armed; (3) if the act results in the destruction of or damage to the system or the total or partial interruption of its operation, or in the destruction of or damage to or removal, also by means of reproduction or transmission, or in the inaccessibility to the owner of the data, information or programs contained therein.

If the facts referred to in the first and second paragraphs concern computer or telecommunications systems of military interest or relating to public order or public security or health or civil protection or in any case of public interest, the penalty shall be, respectively, imprisonment for a term of three to ten years and four to twelve years.

In the case provided for in the first paragraph, the offence is punishable on the injured party's behalf; in other cases, the offence is prosecuted ex officio'.

1311. According to Court of Cassation, Criminal section V of 29 November 2023, Decision No. 1161, a *public official* who accesses the P.R.A. database to provide third parties with information that can be acquired only after payment is guilty of unauthorized access to the computer system. The crime of unauthorized access to a computer system, aggravated pursuant to paragraph 3 of Article 615-*ter* of the Criminal Code, constitutes the conduct of a public official who, without infringing the regulatory and organizational provisions of his office, accesses the data bank of the public motor vehicle register (P.R.A.) in order to provide third parties with information that can only be acquired upon payment of a fee.

In its grounds, the Court pointed out that the regulatory expression 'system of public interest' does not include only the 'critical infrastructures of the State', but also those activities which, although not concerning data of a confidential nature, are functional to the pursuit of a general interest of public relevance.

1312. According to Court of Cassation, Criminal section V of 22 February 2023, Decision No. 27900, the abusive access to a computer system contested in relation to the so-called dropbox postulates that the owner of the space must be identified.

On the subject of unauthorized access to a computer or telematic system, the case referred to in Article 615-*ter*, paragraph 1, of the Criminal Code, contested in relation to the so-called dropbox filing space, requires the identification of the person who owns the space and the relative *ius excludendi alios* to access the aforesaid application. It's a case in which the Court annulled with referral the decision, deeming it necessary to verify whether the so-called dropbox folder was the *exclusive property* of the defendants, who had created it and temporarily made it available to the company for which they worked, or belonged to the aforesaid company, given that only in the latter case could their access to change the account, through the change of the telematic address, carried out after the termination of the employment relationship, be considered abusive.

1313. Court of Cassation, Criminal section V, 30 January 2023, with Decision No. 17551, stated that the *police officer* who accesses the inter-force database in violation of internal procedures and for merely exploratory purposes commits an offence.

In relation to Article 615-*ter* of the Criminal Code, Article 9 of Law No. 121 of 1 April 1981 and Article 9 of Presidential Decree No. 378 of 3 May 1982, access to the inter-force database carried out in breach of the internal authorization procedures laid down for the judicial police office, as well as with a merely exploratory purpose, in the absence of even a qualified suspicion suitable to stimulate the initiative activity of the judicial police in order to obtain cognitive data, is to be considered *abusive*, which alone can permit the proportionate and justified interference in the processing of the private individual's personal data.

In the present case, the offence was recognized against a Carabinieri marshal who was charged with having abusively accessed, in the absence of reasons of service, the inter-force database by carrying out direct and detailed queries against seven colleagues, nine well-known protagonists from the world of entertainment, and three journalist bloggers.

1314. According to Court of Cassation, Criminal section V of 15 November 2022, Decision No. 46076, an *aggravating circumstance* is constituted in the case of changing the password for access to the e-mail box. On the subject of unauthorized access to a computer or telematic system, the aggravating circumstance referred to in Article 615-*ter*, paragraph 2, No. 3, can be established in the case of changing the access password to the electronic mail box and the credentials for retrieving it, resulting in the alteration of an essential component of the computer system that makes it temporarily unable to function.

1315. According to Court of Turin, of 1 September 2022, Decision No. 1461, regarding the crime of abusive access to a computer system, the integration of the crime is determined by the objective profile of both access to and retention in the system. Such Italian Penal Code objective profile of access to and detention in the computer system by a person who essentially cannot be considered authorized to access and remain in the system must be considered relevant, and this occurs both when the agent violates the limits resulting from the set of prescriptions issued by the owner of the system (prescriptions contained in internal organizational provisions in company practices or in clauses of individual employment contracts), or when he carries out operations of a nature that is ontologically different from those for which he is responsible and in relation to which access was permitted to him.

1316. Court of Cassation, Criminal section V, 24 January 2022, with Decision No. 7775, stated that a person who is only authorized to operate on the system for executive tasks is also qualified as a system operator.

For the purposes of the integration of the aggravating circumstance of abuse of the quality of system operator, such qualification is held not only by the holder of decision-making powers over the management of the contents or the configuration of the system, but also by the person who, even if destined to carry out merely executive tasks, is in any event authorized to operate on the system, modifying its contents or structure.

1317. According to Court of Cassation, Criminal section V, 30 April 2021, Decision No. 25683, unauthorized access to a computer system is integrated even if the access is carried out for reasons other than those for which it is authorized. The offence referred to in Article 615-*ter* of the Italian Penal Code is committed not only when the requirement of authorization to access to the databases is not met – the perpetrator, although abstractly authorized to access them, is not actually authorized to consult the databases of the computer system (hypothesis of 'absence of power') – but also when access is carried out for reasons unrelated to those for which the power is conferred on him (hypothesis of 'misuse of power', which presupposes the existence of the power to access the computer system).

1318. According to Court of Cassation, Criminal section V of 15 February 2021, Decision No. 15899, unauthorized access to a computer system is the conduct of a person who breaks into the tax drawer using modified passwords.

The conduct of a person who, through the use of modified 'passwords' and against the owner's will, breaks into someone else's 'tax drawer', a virtual space in the taxpayer's exclusive computer system of the Agenzia delle Entrate (Italian Revenue Agency), which falls within the notion of computer domicile, constitutes the offence of abusive access to a computer system.

In its reasoning, the Court stated that the previous authorization to access issued by the owner due to family or emotional ties and then revoked by means of conclusive behaviour is not relevant.

1319. According to Court of Cassation, Criminal section V of 19 February 2020, Decision No. 17360, the offence of abusive access to an information system can be concurrent with that of computer fraud. The offence of unauthorized access to an information system may be concurrent with that of *computer fraud*, the legal assets protected and the penalized conduct being different, since the former protects the so-called *computer domicile* under the profile of the 'ius excludendi alios', also in relation to the methods regulating the access of any authorized persons, while the second covers and penalizes the alteration of data stored in the system for the purpose of obtaining unfair profit.

In the case in point, the conduct specifically charged to the defendant was that of having proceeded, in conspiracy with an unknown person, to open, with his own identity documents, postal current accounts into which, shortly afterwards, sums withdrawn from current accounts or poste-pay cards of other persons flowed.

1320. According to Court of Cassation, Criminal section V of 15 July 2019, Decision No. 37339, the conduct of a person who enters the SICP with his credentials in order to provide information on investigations constitutes an offence of unauthorized entry into a computer system.

It constitutes the crime of unauthorized entry into a computer system, aggravated pursuant to Article 615-*ter*, paragraph 2, No. 1, of the Criminal Code by virtue of his capacity as a person in charge of a public service, the conduct of a driver and clerk, formally assigned to the general registry office of the public prosecutor's office, who, with his credentials, enters the SICP (Criminal Investigation Information System) of the investigating office in order to provide information relating to proceedings under investigation – which cannot be shown to third parties.

§5. Unauthorized Possession of Access Codes

1321. The activity described and punished by Article 615-*quater* of the Italian Penal Code, consisting of the possession and diffusion of computer systems' access codes, according to some scholars,[258] is one of the behaviours that are prodromal to the crime defined by Article 615-*ter* of the Italian Penal Code, namely the unauthorized access to computer systems.

It is not infrequent for an 'attacker' to acquire access codes before performing the computer intrusion, in order to penetrate the system in the least time possible and, as well, to arouse the least suspects possible. The qualifying element of the case in point consists of specific malice that, in the formulation of the provision, is contained in the expression 'to gain a profit for oneself or for others, or to cause a damage to others'. This excludes someone who lawfully communicates an access password to a third party. Due to this reason, many scholars[259] consider this provision indissolubly tied to the provision contained in Article 615-*ter* (unauthorized access), since it aims to prevent those unauthorized accesses that occur not by means of software modifications, but through an unauthorized 'impersonation' of a subject that has the adequate credentials to access to the system.

---

258. G. Fiandaca, E. Musco 'Diritto penale – parte speciale' (Zanichelli, Modena, 2023, p. 248).
259. G. F. D'Aietti 'La tutela dei programmi e dei sistemi informatici' (in Borruso, Buonomo, Corasaniti, D'Aietti 'Profili penali dell'informatica' Milano, 1994); G. Pecorella, 'sub art. 615-*quater*', in 'Comm. Dolcini, Marinucci sub art. 615-*quater*'; G. Pica 'Diritto penale delle tecnologie informatiche' (UTET, Torino, 1997).

The unlawful conducts that the provision prohibits are: to abusively acquire access codes or other means adequate (including biometrical credentials) to access a computer or telecommunication system protected by security measures; to diffuse, communicate or deliver to third parties, by any mean, access unlawfully detained credentials; to 'supply information or instructions adequate' to violate a computer or telecommunication system protected by security measures.

1322. The actual text of the Article, after the 2024 reform, is the following: 'article 615-*quater* (Unauthorized possession, dissemination and installation of equipment, codes and other means of access to computer or telecommunication systems) – Whoever, in order to procure for himself/herself or for others an advantage or to cause damage to others, unlawfully obtains, possesses, produces, reproduces, disseminates, imports, communicates, delivers, otherwise makes available to others or installs apparatus, tools, parts of apparatus or tools codes, passwords or other means of access to a computer or telecommunications system protected by security measures, or in any case provides indications or instructions suitable for that purpose, shall be punished with imprisonment of up to two years and a fine of up to EUR 5.164.

The punishment shall be imprisonment of from two to six years when any of the circumstances referred to in Article 615-*ter*, second paragraph, number 1) apply.

The penalty shall be imprisonment for a term of between three and eight years when the offence relates to the computer or telecommunications systems referred to in Article 615-*ter*, third paragraph.

1323. According to Court of Cassation, Criminal section II of 14 January 2019, Decision No. 21987, the offences referred to in Articles 615-*ter* and 615-*quater* of the Italian Penal Coode cannot be concurrent. The latter, in fact, constitutes a necessary *antecedent* of the former, since the two criminal offences are closely connected, by protecting the same legal asset, i.e., the 'computerized domicile', passing from less invasive conduct to more invasive conduct, which necessarily presupposes the former.

1324. According to Court of Cassation, Criminal section II of 3 October 2013, Decision No. 47021, the conduct of a person who receives credit card codes illegally downloaded from the computer system by a third party and inserts them into cloned credit cards then used to withdraw cash through the ATM system constitutes the offence of unlawful possession and dissemination of access codes to computer and telematic services (Article 615-*quater* of the Criminal Code) and not that of receiving stolen goods.

1325. According to Court of Cassation, Criminal section II of 17 February 2004, Decision No. 5688, the offence of unlawful possession and dissemination of access codes to computer or telematic services referred to in Article 615-*quater* of the Code can be integrated by a person who unlawfully obtains the serial number of a cellular telephone apparatus belonging to another person, since through the corresponding modification of the code of a further apparatus (so-called cloning) it is possible to establish an unlawful connection to the mobile telephony network, which constitutes a protected telematic system, also with reference to the banks concerning the external data of communications, managed by means of computer technology. It follows that the conscious purchase for profit of a mobile phone set up to access the telephony network by means of the codes of another ('cloned') user constitutes the offence of receiving stolen goods, of which the offence under Article 615-*quater* of the Italian Penal Code constitutes a predicate offence.

1326. According to Court of Cassation, Criminal section II of 17 January 2003, Decision No. 36288, the conduct consisting in the activation of a 'cloned' mobile phone on a number registered in the name of another user falls within the scope of the offence referred to in Article 615-*quater* of the Criminal Code (unauthorized possession and dissemination of access codes to computer or telematic systems), since it is only possible if the agent has abusively obtained the so-called serial, i.e., the reserved number which, combined with the user number, allows connection with the mobile telephony network, which constitutes a telematic system not only because of its function of transmitting communications but also because of its function of storing and processing by computer technology data outside the conversations.

§6. Diffusion of Computer Viruses

1327. Article 4 of Statute No. 547/93 has introduced a new crime, defined by Article 615-*quinquies* and titled as 'Diffusion of programs, equipment and devices aimed to damage or block a computer system'.

This provision was not present in the text written by the Commission, but it was added later by the legislative office. The authors of the definitive text considered necessary to specifically repress the behaviour of the subject that diffuses the so-called computer viruses.

The conduct of the crime consists in 'diffusing, communicating or delivering' to anyone, regardless of the reasons, a software self-made or made by others that has the characteristic, as an effect or an aim, of damaging a computer or telecommunication system or part of it (data, programs, information, etc.).

1328. The legislature has used three words that, from an etymological point of view, partially overlap to fully encompass every form of distribution and circulation of harmful programs. The concept of 'diffusion' has to be interpreted and considered according to the computer technologies through which noxious programs circulate. Therefore, it appears mostly related to the diffusion modalities of noxious programs through online (telecommunication) networks that allow the communication between different and distant computers and therefore allow the transfer between them not only of data and information but also of viruses. These, as stated, are created to diffuse themselves automatically, with the consequence of a progressive broadening of the infection, as in an epidemic. On this point, scholars stated that the concept of diffusion includes also the actions of material introduction of copies of virus-programs into computer systems, regardless of the fact that the action is performed surreptitiously, fraudulently or with violence or otherwise openly.[260]

1329. The text of Article 615-*quinquies* c.p.,. however, was profoundly renewed as a result of Law 18 March 2008 No. 48, since the Legislator made a broad expansion of the categories of the relevant conducts, this way including in the offence all the activities that may endanger the integrity and security of a system.

The new wording of the norm, however, did not solve some problems of interpretation and application nature, already reported about the letter of the old Article 615-*quinquies*, nor fully reflects the provisions of the European Convention on Cybercrime to which it should be inspired.

Article 6 of the Convention, entitled «Misuse of devices» provided the rule for national legislators by which 'each Party shall adopt such legislative and other measures as may be necessary to establish as criminal offences under its domestic law, when committed intentionally and without right: (a) the production, sale, procurement for use, import, distribution or otherwise making available of (i) a device, including a computer program, designed or adapted primarily for the purpose of committing any of the offences established in accordance with the above Articles 2 through 5; (ii) a computer password, access code, or similar data by which the whole or any part of a computer system is capable of being accessed, with intent that it be used for the purpose of committing any of the offences established in Articles 2 through 5; and (b) the possession of an item referred to in paragraphs ()(i) or (ii) above, with intent that it is used for the purpose of committing any of the offences established in Articles 2 through 5. A party may require by law that a number of such items be possessed before criminal liability attaches. This article shall not be interpreted as imposing criminal liability where the production, sale, procurement for use, import, distribution or otherwise making available or possession referred to in paragraph 1 of this article is not for the purpose of committing an offence established in accordance with Articles 2 through 5 of this Convention, such as for the authorized testing or protection of a computer system. Each Party may reserve the right not to apply paragraph 1 of this article, provided that the reservation does not concern the sale, distribution or otherwise making available of the items referred to in paragraph 1 (a)(ii) of this article'.

1330. Considering that the provision was already present, to some extent, in our system, the present norm consists in an expansion of the offence, especially in relation to the provision of new conducts related to the production, sale, supply for use, distribution or usability of equipment that can allow illegal access to a computer system, an illegal interception, an attack to the integrity of data or of a system, given that the previous wording was limited only to 'programs', to be intended as software.

---

260. *See*, generally, G. Pica, 'Diritto penale delle tecnologie informatiche' (UTET, Torino, 1999).

It is mainly paragraph (a)(i) of Article 6 of the Convention concerning the issue under consideration, since paragraph (a)(ii) is better referred to the case contemplated in Article 615-*quater* c.p., related to the illegal detention or dissemination of access codes to computer or telecommunication systems, whose discipline has been already briefly explained above.

The second paragraph of Article 6 of the Convention helps to find an answer to the interpretational doubts always at the centre of the scholars' discussions, as it leaves the option to the signatory Member States not to consider as criminal conducts the activities which, even following the criminal pattern, are not made in order to accomplish a crime. The doubts concerning the lawful use of programs or devices which could be identified as harmful are finally over, since the new wording of Article 615-*quinquies* detects only the specific intent to cause damage or disrupt a computer or telecommunication system, also clearly explained in Article 6, paragraph 2, mentioned above. This article expressly provides among the lawful hypothesis, *inter alia*, the 'authorized test' or 'the protection of a computer system', thereby recalling just the assumptions the scholars feared to be conducted to the crime, on the basis of which a technician in his duties could have been found punishable under the old wording of Article 615-*quinquies*.

From a crime of generic intent, therefore, the Italian legislator switches to a crime of specific intent, being no longer sufficient – for the integration of the offence – the awareness and willingness of the dissemination, communication or delivery of the program, together with the knowledge of the technical characteristics and its harming potential.

1331. In 2024, Article 615-*quinquies* was repealed.

However, we have chosen to retain the description and the most important case law of one of the most notable computer crimes in the national criminal context.

1332. According to Court of Appeal Bologna, section II of 17 March 2008, the conduct of altering a computer program exists when such program is manipulated in a way that it performs actions not intended by the user, or when its operating parameters are changed, even according to options and possibilities provided for in the program itself, against the will of the user, and it falls within the case punished by Article 615-*quinquies* of the Italian Penal Code.

The aggravating circumstances referred to in Article 615-*ter* of the Italian Penal Code do not apply when the user's system programs, despite the installation of the virus, remain perfectly operational, as before, with the same characteristics of use and purposes, without any change of data, environment, interaction, program, and the worm merely uses the web browsing application Explorer and Outlook e-mail applications, as well as the data in the e-mail address book, covertly.

1333. According to Court of Bologna of 21 July 2005, Decision No. 1823, the dissemination of a program having the purpose and effect of altering certain telematic functions of computer systems constitutes the offence referred to in Article 615-*quinquies* of the Criminal Code.. The concurrence of the offence of 'dissemination of programs intended to damage or disrupt a computer system' with that of 'unlawful access to a computer or telecommunications system' is considered to exist from the analysis of the subjective element, i.e., from the fact that the intent of the latter derives from the intent of the former.

For the purposes of the existence of the psychological element of the offence under Article 615-*quinquies* of the Criminal Code, consisting in the dissemination of programs (in this case, the Vierika program) designed to alter some of the telematic functions of computer systems, it is considered sufficient that there is an established intention by the perpetrator to disseminate the program with awareness of its effects, as the rule does not require that the purpose of the action be the destruction or damage of the computer system.

§7. Electronic Mail

1334. Article 5 of Statute No. 547/93 also amends Article 616 of the Italian Penal Code (regarding the violation, subtraction and suppression of correspondence) by including in the general notion of 'correspondence' communication that occurs through telecommunication or computer means (such as e-mail or instant messaging programs like Skype), or any form of long-distance communication.

The general case in point provided by Article 616 of the Italian Penal Code is therefore unvaried. The provision provides various hypotheses of crimes that damage other subjects' correspondence, all indictable as a result of personal prosecution and consisting of the action of acquiring knowledge of the content of closed correspondence not addressed to the agent; the subtraction or diversion of a closed or open correspondence not addressed to the agent, in order to acquire knowledge or let others acquire knowledge of the content; the destruction or suppression, total or partial, of other subjects' correspondence.

The second paragraph regards the hypothesis of the agent revealing the content of correspondence, totally or partly, without good cause.

1335. The only innovation brought by Statute No. 547/93, therefore, consists of an extension of the case in point, however severely criticized due to its total indeterminateness, that causes many interpretation issues and a difficulty to adapt to new technologies (for example, the reference to 'any other form of distant-range communication').

Another problematic aspect, besides the terminological indeterminateness, concerns the effective operability of Article 616 of the Italian Penal Code, with reference to online (telematic) correspondence that occurs directly, namely through a self-owned mail server, or is mediated, by using a mail server generally supplied by providers. According to commentators,[261] it would be more appropriate, given the realities of computer science, to address correspondence violations under Article 617-quarter rather than Article 616 of the Italian Penal Code.

---

261. G. Pecorella 'Dieci anni di giurisprudenza sui reati informatici: i principali problemi interpretativi sollevati dalle nuove disposizioni', in Cocco (a cura di) 'Interpretazione e precedente giudiziale in diritto penale' (CEDAM, Padova, 2005, p. 241); G. Corasaniti 'La tutela della comunicazione informatica e telematica', in Borruso, Buonomo, Corasaniti, D'Aietti 'Profili penali dell'informatica' (Giuffrè, Milano, 1994, p. 111).

1336. Lastly, additional problems have arisen regarding the concurrence of crimes, given that the extension of Article 616 applies to every 'provision in this section' and therefore also to cases provided by Article 618 (Revelation of the content of correspondence), 619 (Correspondence violation, subtraction and suppression performed by a subject in charge of mail, telegraph and telephone services) and 620 (Revelation of the content of correspondence performed by a subject in charge of mail, telegraph and telephone services) of the Italian Penal Code.

The reference to Articles 619 and 620 of the Italian Penal Code is considered merely theoretical, since the particular subjective quality of the agent seems, in concrete, to render them less easily applicable, provided an exception for further developments that the public postal service will undergo under the profile of telematic communications. Since 2018 those offences can be prosecuted upon complaint of the injured person.

1337. In conclusion, the interpretative issues related to Article 616 of the Italian Penal Code derive from the ambiguous boundaries inherent in computer and telecommunication technologies. Clear distinctions, such as those between 'open' and 'closed' correspondence or between 'written' correspondence and 'oral phone communication', have lost their relevance, as these forms are now incorporated and merged in the various communication modalities enabled by new technologies.

1338. According to Court of Cassation, Criminal section V of 24 October 2022, Decision No. 46063 regarding the disclosure of another person's correspondence, the offence of harm, which constitutes an objective condition for the punishability of the crime, is supplemented by any harm or danger of legally appreciable harm. This includes non-pecuniary harm, resulting from the injury of goods that are subject to economic evaluation.

In the case in point, an employee of a company, having gained unauthorized access to the computer system of the office, accessed the e-mail box of the managing director, thus gaining knowledge of information and data relating to disciplinary charges issued and to be issued against a colleague, to whom he disclosed what he had unlawfully learnt.

1339. According to Court of Cassation, Criminal section V of 29 September 2020, Decision No. 30735, the husband who produces his wife's emails in court does not commit a crime.

A husband who, using the keylogger computer program installed on his computer years before by mutual agreement with his wife to control their minor daughter, intercepts his wife's electronic correspondence in order to produce it in a personal separation judgment, is not guilty of any of the offences referred to in Articles 616, 617-*bis* and 617-*quater* of the Criminal Code.. The offences punished by Articles 616 and 617-*quater* of the Criminal Code have operational scopes that are clearly defined by the different configuration of the material object of the conduct. While Article 617-*quater* of the Criminal Code – which punishes the interception, obstruction or interruption of computer or telematic communications – refers the term 'correspondence' to communication at its dynamic stage, i.e., during transmission, Article 616 of the Criminal Code – titled violation, abduction and suppression of correspondence – typifies the conduct referring to communication from a static point of view, i.e., the thought that has already been communicated and fixed on a physical support.

1340. According to Court of Cassation, Criminal section V of 25 March 2019, Decision No. 18284, in the case of unauthorized access to an electronic mailbox protected by a 'password', the crime of unauthorized access to a computer system can be committed *concurrently* with the crime of violation of correspondence, in relation to the acquisition of the contents of the 'mails' stored in the archive, and with the crime of damaging computer data, in the case where the unauthorized modification of the access credentials results in the owner's inability to use the mailbox.

1341. According to Court of Appeal ('d'Appello'Turin, Labour Section of 27 March 2017, Decision No. 138, the circumstance that the company PC used by the plaintiff for work reasons (was) a company asset does not in any way authorize to analyse the contents of the hard disk and to acquire the Skype chats stored in the personal account because it harms a worker, blatantly violating the secrecy of his correspondence (including computer or telematic correspondence, as per Article 616 of the Italian Penal Code).

1342. According to Court of Cassation, Criminal section V of 2 February 2017, Decision No. 12603, accessing the content of e-mails from the addressee concerns the 'static' profile of the communication, and is therefore punishable under Article 616 of the Italian Penal Code and not under Article 617, which, on the other hand, concerns the 'dynamic' profile of the communication itself.

1343. According to Court of Cassation, Criminal section V of 11 December 2007, Decision No. 47096, given that computer or telematic correspondence can be considered 'closed' only in respect of persons who are not authorized to access the computer systems for sending and/or receiving individual messages, the offence of breach of correspondence does not exist where the hierarchical superior, legitimized by a company practice to use the passwords set up to protect computers and correspondence, accesses the employee's professional e-mail.

§8. Communication Interceptions

1344. Some articles inserted by Statute No. 547/93 specifically refer to telematic communications, such as Article 617-*quater* (interception, prevention or unlawful interruption of computer or telematic communications) and Article 617-*quinquies* (installation of devices apt to intercept, prevent or interrupt computer or telematic communications) of the Italian Penal Code.

It is necessary to immediately stress the legislation terminological inadequacy that indifferently refers to 'computer and telematic' communications, as communication performed by means of computer technologies can only be telematic.

The main characteristic of the conduct necessary to substantiate the crime is fraudulence.

1345. With reference to the object of the protection, doctrine[262] has highlighted how the structure of the cases introduced by Articles 617-*quater*, 617-*quinquies* and 617-*sexies* of the Italian Penal Code exceeds the scope of the protection of personal confidentiality and identifies a new kind of juridical good: 'the security of the computer or telematic system', which consists of the genuineness (authenticity of the content) and confidentiality (knowledge or possible knowledge of information only by authorized subjects) of communications.

The crime requires personal prosecution, while the following aggravated circumstances are indictable offences: if the act is performed against a computer or telecommunication system used by the State or other public organizations or by enterprises that exercise public services or public-interest services; if the act is performed by a public officer or by a subject responsible for a public service, by abuse of his powers or infringement of the duties related to the function or service, or through the abuse of the quality of system operator; if the act is performed by anyone who exercises even abusively the profession of private investigator.

1346. Article 617-*quinquies* of the Penal Code punishes the installation of devices designed to intercept, prevent or interrupt computer or telematic communications, mirroring the structure of Article 617-*bis* (installation of devices apt to intercept or prevent telegraphic or telephonic communications or conversations). This leads to the observation that the absolute structural identity of the case provided by Article 617-*quinquies* in comparison with that of Article 617-*bis* already providing for the interception of telegraphic or telephonic communications or conversations, with a mere distinction in the types of communication intercepted or to intercept, suggest that the insertion of this new provision is unnecessary. Instead, it could have been included as a new paragraph in the pre-existing Article 617-*bis* Italian, thereby avoiding the further proliferation of provisions.

1347. The actual texts of the two articles, after the 2024 reform, are the following:

> article 617-quarter (Unlawful interception, obstruction or interruption of computer or telematic communications) - Whoever fraudulently intercepts communications relating to a computer or telematic system or between several systems, or prevents or interrupts them, shall be punished by imprisonment of from one year and six months to five years.

---

262. F. Mantovani 'Diritto penale. Parte speciale II' (Wolters Kluwer, Alphen aan den Rijn, 2022).

Unless the act constitutes a more serious offence, the same punishment shall apply to any person who discloses, by any means of information to the public, in whole or in part, the contents of the communications referred to in the first paragraph.

The offences referred to in the first and second paragraphs shall be punishable upon complaint of the injured person. However, proceedings shall be brought ex officio, and the penalty shall be imprisonment for a term of between four and ten years if the act is committed:

(1) to the detriment of any of the computer or telecommunication systems indicated in article 615-ter, third paragraph;
(2) to the detriment of a public official in the course of or by reason of his duties or by a public official or a person in charge of a public service3), with abuse of powers or in breach of the duties inherent in the function or service, or by a person exercising, also abusively, the profession of private investigator, or with abuse of the quality of system operator.

'Article 617-*quinquies* (Illegal possession, dissemination and installation of equipment and other means of intercepting, impeding or interrupting computer or telematic communications) – Whoever, except in cases permitted by law, in order to intercept communications relating to a computer or telecommunications system or between several systems, or to prevent or interrupt them, obtains, holds, produces, reproduces, disseminates, imports, communicates, delivers otherwise makes available to others or installs equipment, programs, codes, passwords or other means capable of intercepting, preventing or interrupting communications relating to a computer or telecommunications system or between several systems, shall be punished by imprisonment of from one to four years.

When any of the circumstances referred to in Article 617-*quater*, fourth paragraph, number 2) apply, the penalty shall be imprisonment for a term of between two and six years.

If any of the circumstances referred to in Article 617-*quater*, fourth paragraph, number 1) apply, the penalty shall be imprisonment for a term of three to eight years.

1348. According to Court of Cassation, Criminal section V of 23 January 2023, Decision No. 17814, on the subject of the installation of equipment capable of intercepting, preventing or interrupting computer or telematic communications, the aggravating circumstance set forth in the combined provisions of Articles 617-*quinquies*, paragraph 2, and 617-*quater*, paragraph 4, No. 1, of the Italian Criminal Code, exists in case of affixing, at the ATM of a credit institution, of a device (so-called skimmer) aimed at intercepting data communications, given that the banking activity of collecting savings constitutes, pursuant to Article 359, paragraph 2, of the Criminal Code a service of public necessity. Although it is of a private nature, since it is exercised in the form of an enterprise by private persons such as credit institutions, it corresponds to a public interest and its exercise is subject to authorization and control by the competent administrative authorities.

1349. According to Court of Florence, Labour Section 21 December 2021, decision No. 885, private chat messages are equated with private correspondence and disclosure is punishable under Article 617 of the Criminal Code.

Since they are intended to reach a circle of specific persons through the use of a tool that has the characteristics of confidentiality of communication, the messages in *private chat* must be considered in the same way as private correspondence, closed and inviolable, so there is a contrary interest in the disclosure, even negligent, of facts and news; with the result that, not only are the legal requirements lacking to identify any defamatory conduct, but also the need to ensure the protection of freedom and secrecy of the communications themselves under Article 15 of the Constitution and Article 617 of the Criminal Code, which preclude their access to outsiders and their disclosure and use in any form whatsoever, save for exceptions based on a reasoned act of the judicial authority, with the guarantees established by law.

1350. According to Court of Cassation, Criminal section V of 26 November 2021, decision No. 1834, the installation of apparatus or instruments or parts thereof for the purpose of intercepting or preventing communications constitutes an offence.

The crime envisaged by Article 617-*bis* of the Criminal Code constitutes the installation of apparatus or instruments or parts of them functional to intercepting or preventing communications, conversations, or any other remote transmission of sounds, images or other data, even if the same, apart from the hypothesis of their absolute unsuitability, have not functioned or have not been activated.

1351. According to Court of Cassation, Criminal section V of 9 October 2020, Decision No. 869, the formal concurrence between the offence of unlawful interception, obstruction or interruption of computer communications and the offence of computer fraud is possible, in view of the diversity of the legal assets protected and of the sanctioned conduct, since the former protects the freedom and secrecy of telematic communications, whereas the latter protects the regular operation of computer systems and the confidentiality of the data contained therein, the alteration of which is contemplated for the purpose of obtaining an unfair profit. The case related to a computer fraud carried out through the unlawful interruption of the telematic and computer communications of a 'new slot' machine in order to modify downwards the winning percentages managed by the electronic card, thus profiting from the tampering of the 'software'.

1352. According to Court of Cassation, Criminal section V of 18 March 2019, Decision No. 15071, in the event of the installation inside a mobile phone of spy-software capable of intercepting its telephone communications, the possible existence of consent to intrusion, inferable from the inert conduct of the owner of the mobile phone concerned by the software, and as to the absence of an actual impairment of the freedom of communications of the addressee of the intrusive conduct, are irrelevant, because they refer to a situation – the interception of telephone communications – which represents a post-factum with respect to the time when the offence was committed, coinciding with the installation of the software.

1353. According to Court Milan, section IV of 1 October 2018, No. 8862, the crime of falsification or alteration of computer or telematic communications is not integrated when, to be altered, is a Facebook page of a conversation between two people without varying the published message (with the potential integration of the crime of defamation only).

In the case in point, the agent altered the content of a conversation between two subjects attributing racist statements to one of them and once the print of the altered conversation was created he spread it to several people, to damage and discredit work colleagues.

1354. According to Court of Cassation, Criminal section VI of 16 May 2018, Decision No. 39279, the installation of equipment designed to prevent communications constitutes an offence only if it is intended to prevent communications between persons other than the agent.

The offence of installation of equipment designed to intercept or prevent communications or conversations provided for in Article 617-*bis* of the Italian Penal Code only occurs if the installation is aimed at intercepting or preventing communications between persons other than the agent, so the offence does not occur if the 'telephone jammer' device, i.e., a frequency jammer used to prevent mobile telephones from receiving or transmitting radio waves, is installed to prevent the interception of communications that also concern the person installing the device. The incriminating provision, in fact, penalizes anyone who installs equipment aimed at intercepting or preventing conversations 'of others'. Moreover, this conclusion is confirmed by the placement of the incriminating provision – which 'anticipates' the threshold of punishability of Article 617 of the Criminal Code – in the group of 'offences against the inviolability of secrets', which are obviously such if they do not, directly or indirectly, involve the agent.

§9. FALSIFICATION

1355. Article 617-*sexies* introduces the crime of falsification, alteration or suppression of the content of telematic communications, therefore accomplishing, as with reference to Article 617-*quinquies*, a duplication of the case provided by Article 617-*ter* of the Italian Penal Code (falsification, alteration or suppression of the content of telegraphic or telephonic communications or conversations).

The actual text, after the 2024 reform, is the following:

> Article 617-sexies (Falsification, alteration or suppression of the content of computer or telematic communications) - Whoever, in order to procure for himself/herself or for others an advantage or to cause damage to others, falsely forms or alters or suppresses, in whole or in part, the content, even occasionally intercepted, of any of the communications relating to a computer or telecommunication system or between several systems, shall be punished, if he/she makes use of them or allows others to make use of them, with imprisonment from one to four years.

> The penalty shall be imprisonment for a term of three to eight years in the cases provided for in the fourth paragraph of article 617-quater.
> In the case provided for in the first paragraph, the offence shall be punishable upon complaint of the offended person.

The provision considers various forms of communication damaging, represented by falsity, alteration and suppression of the content and, from 2018, requires the injured person's complaint.

The concept of 'falsity' includes all those activities aimed to undermine the authenticity of the communication; the word 'alteration', instead, refers to those activities aimed to modify the content of the communication, therefore rendering it non-conforming to the original; lastly, the word 'suppression' designates those activities that have an impact on the existence of the communication itself.

1356. Some categories of communication shall be ruled out from the examined provision: among these, correspondence (protected by Article 616 of the Italian Penal Code), generic data or information and communications or conversations intervened between persons (already protected by Article 617-*ter*).

These distinctions, however, risk becoming meaningless, as it is not easy to exclude 'generic data and information', since every telematic communication consists of data or information; likewise, interpretative problems are aroused with reference both to communications between persons (for example, chat or instant messaging services) or to correspondence (since, in absence of specific provisions, telematic correspondence can well be assimilated into the traditional one).

1357. According to Court of Nola of 12 January 2023, Decision No. 1946, the offence of falsification, alteration or suppression of communications requires generic intent. The offence referred to in Article 617-*ter* and 617-*sexies* of the Criminal Code consists in intercepting, interrupting or impeding the communications of a computer or telecommunication system or between different systems. For this offence from a subjective point of view, the generic intent of the mere knowledge and will to engage in such conduct is required.

1358. As seen above, according to Court Milan sez. IV of 1 October 2018, No. 8862, the crime of falsification or alteration of computer or telematic communications is not integrated when, to be altered, is a Facebook page of a conversation between two people without varying the published message (with the potential integration of the crime of defamation only).

In the case in point, the agent altered the content of a conversation between two subjects attributing racist statements to one of them and once the print of the altered conversation was created he spread it to several people, to damage and discredit work colleagues..

1359. According to Court of Cassation, Criminal section V of 29 May 2017, decision No. 39768, the conduct of a person who falsifies the notification of the reading of an e-mail constitutes the offence of falsification of the content of computer communications.

The criminal offence referred to in Article 617-*sexies* of the Italian Criminal Code is a special type of forgery offence that is characterized by the specific intent to procure, to oneself or to others, an advantage, not necessarily financial, or to cause damage to others, as well as by the particular nature of the material object, consisting of the content of communications relating to a computer or telematic system or between several systems.

In this case, the Court of Cassation recognized the existence of the offence 'de quo' in relation to the falsification of the notification of the reading of an e-mail summons for a competitive procedure organized by a local authority.

§10. Damaging

1360. Article 9 of Statute No. 547/93 has introduced a new crime by inserting Article 635-*bis*, titled 'Damaging of Computer or Telecommunication Systems', in the Italian Penal Code.

The actual text, after the 2024 reform, is the following: 'Article 635-*bis* (Damage to computer information, data and programs). – Unless the act constitutes a more serious offence, anyone who destroys, deteriorates, deletes, alters or suppresses information, data or computer programs of others shall be punished, upon complaint of the offended person, by imprisonment of from two to six years.

The penalty is imprisonment for a term of three to eight years:

1. if the offence is committed by a public official or by a person in charge of a public service, with abuse of power or with violation of the duties inherent in the function or service, or by a person exercising, also abusively, the profession of private investigator, or with abuse of the quality of system operator;
2. if the offender uses threats or violence to commit the offence or is manifestly armed'.

The crime is included among the crimes against property, where 'property' has to be considered the complex of active and passive judicial relationships, susceptible of economic evaluation, that belong to a person.

Damaging is a classic case of a crime against property, so that the legislature decided, in 1993, to insert the specific provision of damaging against computer structures immediately after Article 635 of the Italian Penal Code and with the same conditions as the traditional case of damaging.

1361. The unlawful conduct provided by the new case in point is centred on the actions of destroying, deteriorating or rendering a computer or telecommunication system – or the programs, information and data stored within – partially or entirely unusable. The terms 'destroying' and 'deteriorating' have a precise meaning, that is 'to cause the destruction or the deterioration of the good that is object of the action.' Therefore the damage can be performed through both an omission and act.

1362. Moreover, the plurality of words used by the legislation to describe damaging conducts is not intended to render strictly the specific modality of the action but to point out every type of damage that can be caused to the good. Due to this reason, the provision contains words that are almost identical: 'to destroy' means to undo the thing, causing, namely, its total annihilation so that it is absolutely unusable for the function it had been destined to; 'to deteriorate' means to wreck something so that its instrumental function is impaired or, anyway, its value is considerably diminished (for example, to deteriorate a keyboard by breaking some keys);'to render unusable' means to modify the thing so that it is not any more, temporarily or definitively, adequate for its intended use (for example, to remove the monitor of a computer).

1363. Consequently, with reference to hardware, namely the physical computer considered in its totality (complex of electric, electronic, optical, magnetic and mechanic components), 'destruction' will be any action that causes the loss of the original functional identity of the good, while 'deterioration' will be every kind of wear that renders its functioning unreliable, but the restoration of which is possible with the substitution of the single damaged component. This hypothetical possibility to repair the damage is exactly the distinctive characteristic of 'deterioration' in comparison with 'destruction'.

The conduct of 'rendering unusable' appears to be added to the conduct of total destruction or deterioration of the whole, while it maintains its own autonomy with reference to the cases of damaging single system components, that do not endanger its reuse, upon substitution of the damaged component.

1364. The subjective element required to assess the crime is specific malice, namely the conscience and will to destroy, deteriorate, dissipate or render totally or partially unusable computer or telecommunication systems that belong to others, besides programs, information and data belonging to others as well. The specific purpose of causing damage to others or to obtain a profit from the damaging is not required.

1365. Lastly, the psychological element of the damaging crime is identified in the conscience and will to damage, and motives or purposes due to which the crime is performed are not relevant. Even if the act takes place without the direct purpose of causing damage, but as a means to achieve a different purpose, there can be liability. The psychological moment of malice includes the awareness of the act and that the damaged thing belongs to someone else.

Damage is probably the offence who has suffered the greatest distortion following the entry into force of Law No. 48/08. From a single offence brought by Article 9 of Law No. 547/93, by which Article 635-*bis* of the Italian Penal Code was introduced with the title 'Damage to computer or telecommunication systems', there are now a variety of offences and, consequently, of articles in the Criminal Code.

Articles ranging from 635-*bis* to 635-*quinquies* can be defined as the regulatory set of rules on the crime of damage. These articles identify different types of damage, also according to the provisions of the Convention on Cybercrime, which in Articles 4 and 5 differentiates the conducts of 'damaging, deletion, deterioration, alteration or suppression of computer data without right' from those of 'serious hindering without right of the functioning of a computer system by inputting, transmitting, damaging, deleting, deteriorating, altering or suppressing computer data'.

The aggravating circumstances as well have been completely rearranged, first by removing the reference to the aggravating circumstances of the general crime of damage and also by providing two more aggravating circumstances for all crimes consisting in damage with violence to the person or threat and in performing the fact of abusing the quality of the operator of the system.

1366. 'System operator' is at least vague, since it does not identify any technical qualification of normative origin.

In the world of computer jobs, there are four 'typical' ranges of qualifications, divided in growing order of importance (under the profile of both technical and professional background and of responsibility): operators, programmers, system analysts, analysts, defined as follows.

'Operator' is the subject who is appointed to input, output, computer start (bootstrap) or halt operations and to operate the console in order to check the regularity of its functioning, by manually performing, in case of need, operations of disk, tape, printout, upload or download.

'Programmer' is the subject who has the task of writing in sequence the instructions (instructions that have to be written in a specific language that the computer can understand and that are organized in the most compact and rational way possible) necessary to accomplish the algorithm on which the program is based.

> ' – Systems analyst' is the subject who has the task of studying and improving computers' operative systems (the so-called base software).

'Analyst' is the subject who has the task of discovering and/or inventing and adjusting algorithms.

1367. Since all these four computer technicians operate on a computer and therefore, if they wanted to, they could more easily sabotage its software and hardware, they all seem to be included in the category of 'system operators' provided by the legislation with reference to computer crimes' aggravating circumstances.

Therefore, the function of the aggravating circumstance is exclusively to punish more severely those subjects who infringe the ban on the conduct by abusing their own personal and particular knowledge: the provision, however, does not refer to a general and abstract technical knowledge that the subjects has, even if highly sophisticated, but rather to the effective possibility to operate, in their capacity as persons for any reason in charge, on the specific violated system, about which the operator has a series of information that privileges him in performing the damaging (for example, the knowledge of access password, the structure of various and possible access sills and the organization of stored data).

Article 635-*bis* now concerns only to information, data and software, and not also computer or telecommunication systems, which are included in a specific norm. Compared to the old formulation, the Legislator has better specified the conducts, providing for destruction, damage, deletion and alteration.

The non-aggravated offence can be prosecuted upon complaint of the offended, while in the old formulation to the entire offence was punishable ex officio.

The two aggravating circumstances under which the crime can be prosecuted ex officio concern: (i) the conducts committed with violence to person or threat and (ii) the abuse of the quality of system operator.

It is evident that the Legislator has entrusted the protection of interests of private character to Article 635-*bis* which, not surprisingly, can be prosecuted upon complaint of the offended, except in the case of aggravating circumstances, while the protection of public data is entrusted to Article 635-*ter*, which, given the greater sensitivity of the data of public utility, can be prosecuted ex officio. It is to be noted, finally, that the Legislator punishes the 'fact directed to destroy, damage, delete, [...]' and not the 'destruction', 'deterioration', 'cancellation', etc., with a patent widening of the punishable conducts. They can be found, in fact, also in the case of no actual damage or deletion of data, even only for having performed an action that was likely to produce this effect.

The last issue concerns the identification of a system of 'public utility' included in Article 635-*quater*. These systems can be identified in all systems and equipment designed to meet the needs of public interest, irrespectively of their public or private property.

1368. According to Court of Cassation, Criminal section V of 8 January 2020, Decision No. 4470, the destruction of external video surveillance cameras also constitutes an offence of damaging computer media.

For the purposes of the configurability of the offence referred to in Article 635-*quater* of the Criminal Code, 'computer or telematic systems', the material object of the conduct of damage, must be understood to mean a complex of devices interconnected or connected with peripheral units or external devices ('hardware' components) by means of the installation of a 'software' containing the instructions and procedures that enable the equipment to function and perform the activities for which it has been programmed.

A case involving the destruction, in order to perpetrate a theft, of two external video cameras in the access area of a nursing home, was recognized by the Court as peripheral components of a video-surveillance 'computer system', inasmuch as they were tools for shooting and transmitting images and data to central units for recording and storage.

1369. According to Court of Cassation, Criminal section V of 25 March 2019, Decision No. 18284, in the case of unauthorized access to an electronic mailbox protected by a 'password', the crime of unauthorized access to a computer system can be committed concurrently with the crime of violation of correspondence, in relation to the acquisition of the contents of the 'mails' stored in the archive, and with the crime of damaging computer data, in the event that the unauthorized modification of the access credentials results in the inability of the mailbox to be used by the owner.

In the event of unauthorized access to an electronic mailbox protected by a password, the offence referred to in Article 615-*ter* of the Italian Criminal Code is concurrent with the offence of breach of correspondence in relation to the acquisition of the contents of the e-mails stored in the archive and with the offence of damaging computer data, referred to in Articles 635-*bis* et seq. of the Criminal Code, in the event that the unauthorized modification of access credentials results in the owner's mailbox being rendered unusable.

1370. According to Court of Cassation, Criminal section II of 1 December 2016, Decision No. 54715, the offence of computer fraud differs from the offence of damaging computer data, referred to in Article 635-*bis* et seq. of the Italian Penal Code, because, in the former, the computer system continues to function, albeit in an altered manner with respect to the programmed one, whereas in the latter, the material element consists of merely damaging the computer or telematic system, and, therefore, of a conduct aimed at preventing the system from functioning.

1371. According to Court of Cassation, Criminal section II of 29 April 2016, Decision No. 38331, the employee who deletes from his company mail messages intended for the employer does not commit the crime of damaging computer data.

In particular, an employee who deletes messages of a professional nature intended for the employer, which were received on the mailbox reserved for him within the company computer system, does not commit the offence of damaging computer information, data and programs.

1372. According to Court of Cassation, Criminal section II of 14 December 2011, Decision No. 9870, the material object of the offence of damaging a computer system is the complex of interconnected or interlinked equipment, in which one or more of them carries out the automatic processing of data by means of a program (in the case in point, the video surveillance system of a judicial office, consisting of video recording equipment and a component dedicated to the processing of images and their storage, was qualified as a computer system).

1373. According to Court of Cassation, Criminal section V of 18 November 2011, Decision No. 8555, the offence referred to in Article 635-*bis* of the Italian Penal Code can be recognized in the event of the deletion of files from a computer system both when the deletion is temporary, by moving the files to the recycle bin, and when the deletion is final, with the subsequent emptying of the recycle bin, since it is irrelevant that even in the latter case the deleted files can be recovered through a complex technical procedure that requires the use of special application systems and presupposes specific knowledge in the field of information technology. The offence of computer damage, in fact, must be considered to be integrated by the tampering with and alteration of the state of the computer, which can only be remedied with posthumous recovery intervention, which, in any case, would not restore the original configuration of the work environment.

§11. Computer Fraud

1374. The criminal hypothesis contained in Article 640-*ter* of the Italian Penal Code (computer fraud) has always aroused discussions in doctrine, since the enforcement of the statute, because the ambiguity of the word 'fraud' has caused many problems for interpreters, who would have probably preferred the more appropriate denomination of 'computer guile'. However, this does not mean that, in trying to identify the lowest common denominator of the various fraud hypotheses, this can be recognized only in the objective deceptive adequateness of the action, while the agent's subjective purposes, the psychological situation of the passive subject and the effective modality of action represent occasional variables that the legislature introduced online with the type of crimes to indict.

Likewise for 'computer frauds', even in absence of any reference to leading someone astray, to artifices and to swindles, 'an objective deceptive adequateness of the action can be verified, since this is performed through the manipulation of computer systems, by altering and guiding their functioning according to logics that are consistent with the agent's intentions of unlawful profit but different from those wanted by the lawful proprietor and/or user of the system, and unbeknown to them'.

By coordinating the character highlighted with reference to the interpretation of the word 'fraud' with the other basic requisite of the provision, namely by coordinating the unjust profit with the damage to others (where, according to the most consolidated rulings, 'profit' has to be considered any kind of advantage, also of a non-economic nature, and therefore even any kind of impoverishment of the victim's property, while 'unjust' refers to an achieved profit that consists of an advantage that does not belong to the agent), it is possible to include all the activities for which these stand as a cause in the case in point of Article 640-*ter*. The doctrine states, indeed, that if the operation of the agent of the fraud is performed by altering the managing software of someone else's system, or the data contained in it, the subsisting crime will be of arbitrary exert of one's reasons by violence on goods, that, according to Article 392, paragraph 3 of the Italian Penal Code, is integrated by any manipulation of data software. Clearly, if this activity is aimed to voluntarily cause an impoverishment of the victim's property with consequent further pressure to accept conditions imposed by the producer, a violation of Article 640-*ter* also occurs.

1375. According to Court of Cassation, Criminal section II of 13 March 2024, Decision No. 13559, the notion of digital identity does not presuppose a validation procedure adopted by the P.A.

The notion of 'digital identity' cannot be limited solely to the validation procedures of the P.A. (Spid; CIE; digital signature) but also extends to the private sector, and in particular to the consumer credit sector. The will of the legislator (Decree-Law No. 93/2013) that introduced the aggravating circumstance, in fact, is precisely to expand trust in online tools and in the meantime to limit computer fraud. What is relevant is that the stolen access 'keys' serve to identify (with numbers, letters, etc.) in an 'exclusive and unambiguous manner a specific person'. The notion of 'digital identity', which integrates the aggravating circumstance referred to in Article 640-*ter*, paragraph 3, does not presuppose a validation procedure adopted by the Public Administration, but also applies in the case of use of access credentials to computer systems managed by private persons. Thus, even granted that the concept of digital identity requires 'a more exact definition as a result of doctrinal and jurisprudential elaboration', nevertheless 'there is no doubt that the defence argument that claims to limit digital identity to validation procedures adopted by the Public Administration (SPID, CIE, digital signature), duly certified, excluding access procedures through credentials to computer systems managed by private parties such as home banking services or online sales platforms, is without legal foundation'. According to the Court, having used, without authorization, the electronic key belonging to the account holder (which produces the code to carry out the transfer operation through a multi-channel banking system, thus unduly diverting sums of money), integrates the contested aggravating circumstance and presupposes, however, upstream, an unauthorized use of the account access credentials inherent in the person of its holder.

1376. According to Court of Cassation, Criminal section II of 14 February 2024, Decision No. 8793, the person who makes his current account available to the perpetrators of the offence is liable as an accomplice to the offence of computer fraud.

In particular, the defendant is liable for complicity pursuant to Article 110 of the Criminal Code in the predicate offence referred to in Article 640-*ter* and not also for money laundering.

1377. According to Court of Cassation, Criminal section II of 19 December 2023, Decision No. 2346, the conduct of manipulating computer systems for the allocation in authorized points of sale of national lottery tickets, aimed at identifying the winning tickets, to purchase them and collect the prizes established for winning, constitutes the crime of computer fraud. (In its grounds, the Court stated that the offence of aggravated fraud for the obtainment of public funds cannot be committed, since the element of inducing the taxpayer into error, who is required to pay the prize set for the winnings on the sole basis of the presentation of the winning ticket, is lacking).

1378. According to Court of Naples, section IV of 27 February 2023, Decision No. 2118, it is computer fraud to break into a bank's system and into someone's current account to purchase for goods of various kinds.

Computer fraud, for which the objective and subjective prerequisites are met, is constituted by the conduct of persons who, in the absence of title and authorization, break into the bank's system using codes and arrange for transfers from the offended person's account to purchase goods of various kinds.

1379. According to Court of Cassation, Criminal section II of 9 February 2023, Decision No. 13713, the conduct of a person who, with cloned cards, accesses the computer systems of service stations to abusively withdraws fuel, constitutes the crime of computer fraud.

The conduct of a person who, using previously cloned fuel supply cards, accesses the computer systems set up at the relevant facilities and subsequently abusively withdraws fuel, constitutes the offence of computer fraud, and not that of undue use of payment cards as per Article 55(9) of Legislative Decree No. 231 of 21 November 2001. (In its grounds, the Court specified that the specializing element of the offence referred to in Article 640-*ter* of the Criminal Code, represented by the fraudulent use of the computer system, constitutes an absorbing prerequisite with respect to the generic undue use of cloned payment cards, governed by Article 55(9) of Legislative Decree No. 231/2007).

1380. According to Court of Cassation, Criminal section II of 14 September 2021, Decision No. 47302, replacing the authentic card of a 'slot machine' with a 'cloned' card integrates the crime of computer fraud.

The crime of computer fraud, and not that of aggravated fraud to the detriment of the State, is constituted by the replacement of the authentic card of electronic devices for the game of entertainment ('slot machines') with the introduction of a 'cloned' card, so as to prevent the communication to the financial administration of the data of the actual bets, involving the activation of a different program by altering the operation of the computer system of the device.

1381. According to Court of Cassation, Criminal section V of 19 February 2020, Decision No. 17360, the crime of abusive access to an information system can be concurrent with that of computer fraud.

The offence of unauthorized access to an information system may be concurrent with that of computer fraud, the legal assets protected and the penalized conduct being different, since the former protects the so-called computer domicile under the profile of the 'ius excludendi alios', also in relation to the methods regulating the access of any authorized persons, while the second contemplates and sanctions the alteration of data stored in the system for the purpose of obtaining unfair profit (in the case in point, the conduct specifically charged to the defendant was that of having proceeded, in conspiracy with an unknown person, to open, with his own identity documents, postal current accounts into which, shortly afterwards, sums withdrawn from current accounts or poste-pay cards of other persons flowed).

1382. According to Court of Cassation, Criminal section II of 5 February 2020, Decision No. 10354, the crime of computer fraud differs from fraud in that the fraudulent activity involves the computer system and not the person.

The offence of computer fraud referred to in Article 640-*ter* of the Criminal Code has the same structure and the same constituent elements of fraud, from which it differs only because the agent's fraudulent activity does not involve the person, whose induction into error is lacking, but rather the computer system pertaining to the latter through its manipulation, so that, like fraud, it is completed at the time and in the place where the agent obtains the unfair profit with correlative financial damage to others. (In its grounds, the Court stated that the manipulation of the computer system, as a 'special' and typified mode of expression of the fraudulent conduct required to constitute 'simple' fraud, does not exhaust and perfect the offence which, therefore, is consummated at the time when the profit is obtained).

Chapter 3. Traditional Crimes in a Digital Context

§1. Cyberbullying

1383. The procedure of formal *warning* against the author of a conduct is now applied also against the crime of cyberbullying, introduced in 2017 by Law 29 May 2017, Decision No. 71.

This law contains the definition of cyberbullying as 'any form of pressure, aggression, harassment, blackmail, injury, denigration, defamation, identity theft, alteration, illicit acquisition, manipulation, unlawful processing of personal data to the detriment of minors, carried out electronically, and the dissemination of online content also concerning one or more members of the minor's family, whose intentional and predominant purpose is that of isolating a minor or a group of minors by carrying out a serious abuse, a harmful attack, or their ridicule'.[263]

1384. The victim of cyberbullying, who is at least fourteen years of age, and the parents or those responsible for the minor, can submit a request to the data controller or operator of the website or social media platform to obscure, remove or block any personal data of the child that has been disseminated on the Internet.

If the request is not fulfilled within 48 hours, the interested party can contact the Privacy Authority, which will intervene directly within the following 48 hours.

Additionally, all measures provided by Criminal Law can be activated, for example in the cases of insults (Article 594 of the Italian Penal Law), defamation (Article 595), threat (Article 612).

1385. On 27 January 2014, the Democratic Party MP Elena Ferrara presented in the Senate the bill 'Provisions for the protection of minors for the prevention and contrast of the phenomenon of cyberbullying', designed to guarantee young and very young people a more secure and responsible digital experience.

The draft law S. 1261 was approved by unanimous vote on 20 May 2015 and was then transmitted to the Chamber for the continuation of the parliamentary procedure.

Senator Ferrara herself had directly experienced the tragedy of one of her students, Carolina Picchio, who committed suicide at the age of fourteen on the night between 4 and 5 January 2013, after a video showing her drunk at a party was published on the Facebook platform.

In the video, several boys took advantage of Carolina's state of unconsciousness due to alcohol and abused her by simulating sexual acts and humiliating her with obscene proposals.

The images, in addition to being widespread among the girl's acquaintances, were also published online, leading to a series of insults and mockery that caused the 14-year-old profound shame and distress, ultimately pushing her to take her own life.

---

263. *See, generally*, M. Orofino, F.G. Pizzetti (eds) '*Privacy, minori e* cyberbullismo' (Giappichelli, Turin, 2018).

1386. The episode marked the starting point for the initiation of the procedure for the approval of an ad hoc Italian law for the repression of the phenomenon of electronic bullying.

Thus, after a very troubled parliamentary process, which lasted three years, the Law of 29 May 2017 Decision No. 71 was published in the Official Gazette on 3 June 2017 and entered into force on 18 June 2017.

1387. The first paragraph of Article 1 states that 'The objective is to counter the phenomenon of cyberbullying in all its manifestations, with preventive actions and with a strategy of attention, protection and education towards the children involved, both in the position of victims, and in that of responsible of illegal activities, ensuring the implementation of the interventions without distinction of age within the educational institutions.'

It therefore appears evident that the intent of the law is strongly linked to awareness raising and explicitly aimed at protecting minors.

1388. Moreover, for the first time, a legislative definition of cyberbullying was granted in the Italian Code, consisting of 'Any form of pressure, aggression, harassment, blackmail, insult, denigration, defamation, identity theft, alteration, illegal acquisition, manipulation, unlawful processing of personal data to the detriment of minors, carried out electronically, as well as the dissemination of content online also concerning one or more components of the child's family whose intentional and predominant purpose is to isolate a minor or a group of minors by implementing a serious abuse, a malicious attack, or their ridicule.'

1389. However, this definition is not homogeneous, as it combines de facto conducts (pressures, assaults, blackmail, identity theft) with legislative conducts (harassment, defamation, unlawful processing of personal data), some of which have been the subject of a decriminalization package in 2016, with the consequence that the law contains current crimes and decriminalized conducts.

1390. It is also interesting to note that the object of the discipline has been limited to cyberbullying, and no longer extended to bullying *tout court*: a small contradiction that sooner or later will have to be resolved, as it would seem inappropriate to leave all those unlawful acts excluded from the law performed daily by minors vis-à-vis other minors within the school walls or in places where children meet without the help of technology.

1391. Another aspect to be emphasized is the fact that the listing of the conducts carried out by the Legislator, far from being exhaustive, runs the risk of limiting the scope of the provision. There is indeed a shared opinion in doctrine on the need to introduce a final clause, such as 'unless the fact constitutes a more serious crime'.

1392. In Article 2, the provision provides that each victim of cyberbullying at the age of fourteen, as well as the parents and those responsible for the child, may present to the data controller or website operator a request to obscure, remove or block the personal data of the child spread on the Web and perceived as harmful.

When it is not possible to identify the data controller or the operator of the site or the social network, or when the latter, contacted by the interested party, has not taken steps to adopt the injunctive and prescriptive measures within 48 hours, it is possible to contact, upon notification or complaint, the Privacy Authority, which intervenes directly within the next 48 hours.

For the purposes of the law, any provider of information society services is included in the definition of website operator, with the exception of the provider of simple transport services (mere conduit), temporary storage (caching) and storage of information (hosting).

1393. Article 3 also provides for the establishment of a technical table for the prevention and contrast of cyberbullying, without burdens for public finance, since no type of emolument is given to the subjects participating in the work.

The coordination of the technical table is entrusted to the Ministry of Education, University and Research, which must draw up an integrated action plan, in compliance with European directives on the subject, and set up a data collection system aimed at monitoring the evolution of the phenomenon.

1394. Information and prevention initiatives for citizens must also be established, with the primary involvement of the socio-educational structures present in the area in synergy with the schools.

The Prime Minister, in collaboration with the Ministry of Education and the Communications Regulatory Authority, is entrusted with the task of activating periodic prevention and awareness campaigns on the main media.

1395. Article 4 sets guidelines for prevention and contrast in the school environment, also through the collaboration of the Postal Police and local associations.

1396. In particular, it is envisaged that in each institution a *referent* will be identified among the teachers with the task of coordinating the initiatives against cyberbullying, promoting an active role of students and former students in peer education activities, guaranteeing adequate training of the personnel education and providing support and rehabilitation measures for the children involved.

1397. Article 5 entrusts to the head teacher the task to promptly inform, unless the fact constitutes a crime, the families of the involved children and, if necessary, summon all the interested parties to adopt assistance measures in favour of the victim and sanctions and rehabilitation courses for the author.

1398. Article 6 is dedicated to the support measures provided for the activities of the Postal and Communications Police, which are also assigned annual reporting obligations to the technical table on the results of the law enforcement activity.

1399. Finally, Article 7 extends the warning procedure provided for by Article 612-*bis* of the Criminal Code for the crime of stalking: through this measure, as long as the victim has not made a complaint or presented a complaint for the crimes of insult, defamation, threat or unlawful processing of personal data committed through the Internet, the Questore, assuming information (if necessary) from the investigative bodies and hearing the informed persons on the facts, in the presence of at least one parent or other subject exercising parental authority, can summon the over-14-year-old minor responsible for cyberbullying acts, admonishing him/her orally about his/her conduct and urging him/her to restore a lawful behaviour.

1400. The warning request can be presented at any police office and must contain a detailed description of the facts, of the persons in any way involved and any attachments proving the above.

In this way, the Legislator wanted to make the children responsible while keeping them outside the penal circuit, with a provision that is fully consistent with the basic approach of the law, which aims to counter the phenomenon of cyberbullying with more educational than repressive actions.

1401. Law No. 70 of 17 May 2024, titled 'Provisions and delegation to the Government on the prevention and combating of bullying and cyberbullying' introduces, in Article 1, some amendments related to the previous Law No. 71/2017. In particular, it extends the scope of the legislation to include the phenomenon of bullying, as well as cyberbullying, giving it an express definition and qualifying it as 'repeated aggression or harassment, by an individual person or a group of persons, against a minor or a group of minors , suitable to provoke feelings of anxiety, fear, isolation or marginalization, through harassing acts or behavior, physical or psychological pressure or violence, incitement to suicide or self-harm, threats or blackmail, theft or damage, insult or mockery'.

1402. Article 2 then provides for several important innovations with regard to the measures of the Juvenile Court: specifically, it is established that measures with re-educational and restorative purposes may be activated for those minors responsible for aggressive conducts or conducts detrimental to the dignity of others, under the direction and control of social services and with the involvement of parents or those exercising parental responsibility. Such re-educational paths may include the performance of volunteer activities, participation in theater or creative writing workshops, the performance of sports or artistic activities or other activities suitable for stimulating feelings of respect for others in the minor, so as to enable the establishment of healthy and positive relational dynamics among peers.

1403. Article 3 delegates the government to adopt, within twelve months from the Law's entry into force, one or more legislative decrees aiming at, among other things, strengthening the service for assisting victims of acts of bullying and cyberbullying through the free, 24-hour public number 'Emergency Childhood 114,' and at having the National Institute of Statistics conduct a survey every two years to monitor the phenomena's trends.

Finally, the new Law, in Article 4, introduces the national 'Day of Respect', setting its anniversary on January 20, as a time for reflection and raising awareness on combating physical and psychological violence and against all forms of discrimination.

1404. According, to the Court of Sulmona of 9 April 2018, the parental liability is integrated in case of dissemination of photographs by minors containing a nude image of a peer without the consent of the concerned person. If minors disseminate, using telematic means (WhatsApp, Facebook, etc.), photographs containing the nude image of a girl of the same age and such dissemination takes place without the consent of the interested party, the parents of the authors of such dissemination must be held civilly liable, pursuant to Article 2048(1) of the Italian Civil Code, since *culpa in vigilando* and *in educando* can be ascribed to them. Parental liability can only be excluded, pursuant to paragraph 3 of Article 2048 of the Italian Civil Code, if the parents can prove that they were unable to prevent the act, meaning that they fully fulfilled their duty to educate their child by fostering adequate critical thinking and discernment skills.

The circumstance that, at the time of the commission of the offence, the photograph in question had already been circulated within the community to which the person photographed belonged to and that this was due, *inter alia*, to the uninhibited conduct of the person himself, mitigates the civil liability, but does not exclude it, since the person portrayed, and his parents, suffered non-pecuniary damage consisting in the impairment of a number of constitutionally protected interests, including the right to privacy, reputation, honour, image and the inviolability of correspondence.

§2. Stalking and Cyberstalking

1405. The crime of stalking was introduced in Italy by Law No. 38/2009 and is governed by Article 612-*bis* of the Criminal Code.

Cyberstalking is an harassment of a persecutory nature carried out mainly, or exclusively, with the aid of computer or telematic means and connected to electronic communication systems.

This particular case derives from the more general crime of stalking, governed by Article 612-*bis* of the Criminal Code, introduced in 2009 and titled 'Persecutory Acts'.

1406. The legislative decree 14 August 2013 No. 93, then, added in the second paragraph the aggravating circumstance of the 'fact being committed through computer or telematic tools', flanking it with that of the crime committed against a subject linked to the perpetrator of the crime by a previous affective relationship.

In spite of its name, the typical behaviour of the cyberstalker does not, however, commit a so-called computer crime but, as also happens for other crimes with free conduct, a criminal activity through the use of computer systems.

This offence can be counted among the crimes against *individual freedom* of people and against the particular aspect of their mental freedom; it has a residual nature because it does not apply in cases where the conduct assumes the features of a more serious crime.

It is not, therefore, a criminal hypothesis in its own right, but only a way in which a typical type of crime can come into being.

1407. In order to have cyberstalking, an harassment by sending a simple e-mail or the use of common messaging services will not be enough, but it will be necessary to complete a real 'cyberstalking', meaning the amplification of the harmful message and the annoying communication through the computer tool.

It should not – in short – be criminalized the means by which one acts, confusing it with the purpose since, indeed, the casuistry does not report cases of stalkers who do not also use the electronic means to carry out their criminal conduct.

1408. According to the case provided for by the second paragraph of Article 612-*bis* of the Italian Criminal Code, therefore, there is an amplification of the method of attack, using 'the IT or telematic tool' for the purpose of aggravating the harmful event.

The reason for this, which is also at the origin of the expectation of the aggravating by the Legislator, is inherent in the nature of the attack and in the greater extent of its consequences.

In recent years, in fact, there has been an exponential growth of the phenomenon, partly due to the increasing use and familiarity of electronic instruments and, in part, to the extreme ease, economy and speed of the medium, which make it a particularly palatable and pernicious weapon, if used for criminal purposes.

1409. As a consequence and corollary, this type of computer and telematic aggression can cause the victim far greater damage and extended to its sphere of relations than any other traditional means, precisely because of the diffusion and widespread use of the web and its platforms in the public, by now certainly for the individual the 'social formations where his personality takes place' (*see* Article 2 of the Italian Constitution) of greater diffusivity and visibility, albeit digital.

Consider, for example, the theft of credentials of the offended person, unauthorized access to his web pages, the possibility of introducing, in hypothesis, offensive or threatening phrases or images, such as to create damage that goes far beyond mere embarrassment, to get even the control of an entire computer system owned by the persecuted.

Add to this the frequent anonymity of the cyberstalker, which can be hidden behind the computer screen (for example, by creating false profiles in a chat room, a newsgroup, a social network, etc.), which makes it difficult to identify the offender and secure the sources of evidence to reach his sentence.[264]

---

264. *See*, C. Parodi 'Stalking e tutela penale: le novità introdotte nel sistema giuridico dalla l. 38/2009' (Giuffrè, Milano, 2009); G. Ziccardi, P. Perri 'Tecnologia e Diritto' (Giuffré, Milano, 2017).

1410. According to the article, anyone who repeatedly, by any means, threatens or harasses someone in such a way to inflict serious psychological harm, determines a justifiable fear for their personal safety or that of someone close to them or significantly affects their way of life, shall be punished, upon complaint of the victim, by imprisonment from one year to six years and six months.

The text of the article literally states that 'Unless the act constitutes a more serious crime, anyone who, with repeated conduct, threatens or harasses someone in such a way to cause a serious and continuing state of anxiety or fear, or to give rise to a justifiable fear for the safety of self or a close relative or person bound by the same loving relationship, and force himself to alter their habits of life, is punished with imprisonment from one year to six years and six months'.

1411. The crime is punishable upon complaint of the victim. The deadline for filing the complaint is six months and can only be remitted in the course of criminal proceedings. The complaint is irrevocable if the act was committed with repeated threats, as it is stated by paragraph 2, Article 612 of the Criminal Code. It is possible, however, to proceed ex officio if the offence is committed against a minor, a pregnant woman or a disabled person and when the fact is connected with another offence for which it is possible to proceed ex officio.

1412. The penalty is increased if the crime is committed by a spouse legally separated or divorced, or by a person who has been linked to emotional relationship to the victim.

The penalty is increased by up to half if the offence is committed against a minor, a pregnant woman or a disabled person, or by an armed person or a person who claims to be someone else.

1413. This crime includes not only the simple phone calls but also the use of SMS, MMS and e-mails.

The legal interests protected by this Law are, first of all, the moral freedom and the freedom of individual self-determination. Furthermore, that criminal conduct could affect the constitutionally guaranteed human good health. This Law represents a concrete response to the growing and worrying phenomenon linked to the commission of crimes of sexual violence perpetrated primarily against women.

This thorny issue of prevention and repression of crimes against the person has been previously, and in more than one occasion, discussed in the Italian Parliament.

1414. Before filing a formal complaint for the offence referred to in Article 612-*bis* of the Italian Penal Code, the victim may present the facts to a public security authority asking a formal *warning* against the author of the conduct.

Moreover, in line with these provisions, Law No. 38/2009 has introduced a new coercive measure which consists in banning the possibility to stay close to the places frequented by the victim. With the provision of the 'prohibition of approaching', the Court requires the offender not to approach certain places usually frequented by the victim, or to maintain a certain distance from such sites or the victim.

If there are additional requirements for protection, the Court may order the offender not to approach certain places usually frequented by close relatives of the victim or by persons living with or otherwise related to this affective relationship or to maintain a certain distance from such places or by such persons.

The Court may also prohibit the offender from communicating by any means (electronic means included) with the person.

1415. As already anticipated, Article 612-*bis* of the Italian Penal Code is aimed at repressing those behaviours that, in the most varied forms, are characterized by their persecutory character.

These include, by way of example, not only simple phone calls and stalking, but also the 'distorted' use of SMS, MMS and e-mails, and associated behaviours such as, sending and subscribing services not requested in favour of the victim, or the termination of utilities, and even voice calls, with or without a reply.

The typical nature of the conduct punished by the law is now well-defined in the light of numerous and prevalent interpretative guidelines.

There is certainly a pluralistic offence, since the legal right immediately protected is, first and foremost, psychic freedom, as can be deduced from the systematic placement of the norm and, second, the physical safety and life of the passive subject, given the plurality of behaviours described and obtainable from the literal scope of Article 612-*bis* Italian Penal Code.

1416. Physical violence is only a posthumous eventuality and is not necessary for the completion of the crime, which is characterized instead by: an atypical behaviour (i.e., not typed, in the sense that the offensive conduct can consist in any behaviour suitable to carry out the case), committed with threatening or harassing acts, frequent and repeated, such as to cause 'a lasting and serious state of anxiety or fear' in the attacked party, or from 'generating a well-founded fear' for his safety or that of a next relative or other person who is emotionally connected, or likely to cause an alteration of the victim's lifestyle.

1417. Therefore, it is a habitual crime and an event, characterized by reiteration, for which the identification of its most precise contours may be referred to the consolidated jurisprudence on mistreatment.

The action is, therefore, unique, although composed of several pipelines connected by a link of habituality and permanence and whose protraction is appreciably over time.

Therefore, there must be more homogeneous and continuous, repeated and frequent behaviours, aimed at the realization of the harmful event.

Therefore, for example, a telephone call per year will not be sufficient, although repeated every year, in this case lacking the connotation of the frequency such as to integrate a 'habitual vexatious conduct' (*see* Court of Cassation, Criminal section VI, decision No. 166250/1984), although not necessarily continuous, but also interspersed with moments of calm (*see* Court of Cassation, Criminal section VI, decision No. 183553/1989).

1418. The existence of the homogeneity, repetitiveness and frequency of the persecutory acts is, however, subject to the discretionary evaluation of the judge, with reference to the concrete case. And this is how, in a recent past, there are more contradictory judgments, which make the jurisprudence of merit (even of legitimacy) particularly wavering.

Article 612-*bis* of the Italian Penal Code, in the second paragraph, states: 'The punishment is increased if the offense is committed by the spouse, even separated or divorced, or by a person who is or has been linked by an affective relationship to the injured party or if the offense is committed through computer or electronic means'.

1419. As already mentioned above, a few years after the creation of the incriminating rule (Article 612-*bis*, introduced in 2009), the Legislator in 2013 decided to intervene to modify the original text, introducing a specific aggravating circumstance, which can be called 'cyberstalking'.

As already mentioned if, on the one hand, even the use of SMS, as well as the pounding sending of e-mails, may fall within the *latu sensu* channel of this possible form of externalization, on the other hand, these modes are more properly referable to the 'classic' ways of commission of the crime, well known since an age before the introduction of Law No. 11/2009.

In fact, only the medium with which the typical conduct is expressed changes, but in reality it always remains the same (for example, threat carried out with Skype or with voice MMS, rather than with the traditional landline connected to the common telephone line).

1420. The 'cyberstalking' and the related harassment, so that they can be said to be implemented by a real cyberstalker, will rather be those realized through the theft of digital identity, the activity of anti-forensics, or the distorted use of social networks, or – in general – through the 'creative' use of IT means (in the most rigorous technical sense) to cause damage, embarrassment and, hence, anxiety and fear in the victim.

1421. There is now a case history both in the public prosecutor's offices and in the prefectures and police headquarters, of real cases of 'cyberstalking'; commons are, for example, cases of victims who, due to targeted attacks, were forced to cancel their profile on social networks.

In the eyes of the operators, the 'fact committed through computer or telematic tools' is not represented by the simple e-mail or by the use of various messaging services, such as WhatsApp, or other.

As mentioned above, the *ratio* is not to criminalize the computer-telematic means (neutral in itself), but to verify the existence or not of the aggravating circumstance, verifying if the conduct was perpetrated by computer or telematic amplification of the harmful message.

Not the simple e-mail, therefore, if directed *ad personam*, so to speak but, for example, a massive, periodic and automatic sending of numerous e-mails can configure the aggravating circumstance here under consideration.

What matters is, therefore, the use of the medium for the purpose, in order to realize an amplification of the attack, as such capable of causing more offence and damage to the target of the cyberstalker.

1422. According to Court of Milan, section V of 2 March 2018, Decision No. 2568, the offence of cyberstalking is not a different offence from the offence of stalking but has a different modality of manifestation and falls within the conduct of cyber violence.

In the case, there was a charge of several acts of stalking including those carried out through Facebook and by means of telephone messages, but in view of the lack of evidence of the other acts and the lack of logic and coherence of the statements made by the offended person on the latter facts, the judge considered that only the offence of cyberstalking existed, in view of the documentary production of numerous messages, approximately 500 a day, with threatening and defamatory content, so much so that the offended person left the house in which she was staying to spend a few nights in her friend's house, causing her lasting psychological distress.

1423. According to Court of Cassation, Criminal section V of 14 October 2021, Decision No. 323, persecutory acts are committed by those who create social profiles falsely attributable to the victim from which sexual propositions from unknown third parties derive.

Such conduct constitutes the crime of persecutory acts, provided that the perpetrator acts in the awareness of the suitability of the habitual conduct to produce one of the events alternatively envisaged by the incriminating provision.

1424. According to Court of Cassation, Criminal section V of 31 March 2021, Decision No. 19363, the crime of persecutory acts can also be committed through computer or telematic communication tools.

The offence of persecutory acts may also be committed by means of computer or telematic means of communication. In such a case, there must be petulance or intimidating effect as well as the knowability of the vexatious message, which is to be taken for granted when the message is sent to the addressee's 'profile' or is published on a profile that is widely accessible, without prejudice to the relevance of the telematic threat even when the offended person may become aware of it through other persons, in a context from which the agent's intention to produce the intimidating effect may be inferred.

It is not so much the means by which the communication is disseminated that determines whether the offence under Article 612-*bis* of the Italian Penal Code has been committed, but rather the content of the communication itself. The content must constitute a concretely vexatious conduct to the detriment of the offended person, involving harassment or threatening and causing one of the typical events; this is especially relevant following Law No. 199 of 15 October 2013, which introduced the aggravating circumstance of the act committed by means of computer or telematic tools.

1425. According to Court of Milan, section V of 6 November 2018, Decision No. 12404, a person who sends numerous text messages to his ex-partner by lurking under her home and creating false profiles on adult websites with the woman's data is guilty of stalking.

It therefore constitutes the offence of stalking to send numerous text messages to one's ex-partner and cohabiting partner by lurking under the house and creating false profiles on adult Internet sites with the woman's data, inserting her photos and posting erotic advertisements.

1426. According to Court of Cassation, section V of 28 November 2017, Decision No. 57764, disparaging messages on Facebook can constitute stalking.

Messages or video clips posted on social networks can integrate the objective element of the crime of stalking and the harmful attitude of such conduct is not so much that of forcing the victim to be offended or threatened by telematic means, as that of spreading highly damaging data, true or false, on the internet.

1427. According to Court Milan section, section V of 20 January 2017, Decision No. 11748, the severe persistent state of anxiety is realized by stress that alters the psychic balance.

On the subject of persecutory acts, the severe persistent state of anxiety is realized by a stress that modifies the psychic balance.

In the case, the defendant's harassing and threatening behaviour, which had lasted for several months, had created anxiety in the victim given the serious threats sent by e-mail and partly committed by the publication on Internet sites of photos showing the victim naked.

1428. According to Court of Cassation, Criminal section V of 14 July 2014, Decision No. 46510, on the subject of the crime of persecutory acts, proof of the occurrence of the offence, i.e., of the offended person's causation of a serious and enduring state of anxiety or fear, must be anchored to symptomatic elements of such psychological disturbance that can be derived: from the victim's own statements; from her behaviour as a consequence of the agent's conduct; and, lastly, by taking into account the persecutor's conduct.

In the case in point, the obsessive nature of the defendant's conduct had been revealed by the threatening and insulting letters, the numerous telephone calls, the stalking, the continuous verbal and physical harassment and the sending of text messages and messages via the Internet delivered to the offended person, who had to change her lifestyle and lived in a state of anxiety and fear.

1429. According to Court of Cassation, Criminal section V of 9 June 2022, Decision No. 26456, *indirect harassment* is also relevant for the crime of persecutory acts.

For the purposes of the configurability of the typical conduct envisaged by Article 612-*bis* of the Criminal Code, indirect' harassment is also relevant, in the sense that even harassing or threatening communications directed to recipients other than the offended person, but linked to the latter by a qualified relationship of proximity, may be relevant, where the agent acts in the reasonable belief that the victim will be informed and in the awareness of the suitability of his habitual conduct to produce one of the events alternatively envisaged by the incriminating provision.

1430. According to Court of Cassation, Criminal section V of 31 March 2021, Decision No. 19363, the offence of stalking can also be committed by means of messages and communications disseminated through social media (in this case, Facebook), as stated by paragraph 2 of Article 612-*bis* of the Criminal Code, where an aggravated penalty is provided for when the offence is committed 'by means of computer or telematic tools'. Rather, for the purposes of the configurability of the offence, it is necessary, on the one hand, to verify, in fact, the character and intimidating effect of the posted writings, and, on the other hand, to verify the manner in which the messages were disseminated. With regard to the latter profile, it must be borne in mind that, in the case of Facebook (but also of other similar virtual communities), communications can be made either by sending them to the addressee's 'profile' or by posting them on the addressee's own 'profile'. In the first case, there is a direct invasion of another person's private sphere, which is relevant for the purposes of the configurability of the offence, not unlike what occurs with communications by telephone or with SMS or WhatsApp messages. In the second case, in order to be able to recognize the offence, the profile's accessibility to third parties must be verified, which is certainly taken for granted – even when direct access to the offended person's 'profile' does not result – when it is widely accessible, so that the victim can become aware of it through others.

1431. According to Court of Cassation, Criminal section V of 3 November 2020, Decision No. 34512, the publication of 'mocking' posts on a public Facebook profile does not constitute the crime of stalking.

In order to constitute the offence under Article 612-*bis* of the Criminal Code, a state of anxiety generated by invasive communications in the private sphere such as, for example, telephone text messages or WhatsApp messages addressed directly to the 'victim' must be triggered. Since, in the case at hand, the requirement of the inevitable invasiveness connected with sending private messages is lacking and falling within the limits of the legitimate freedom of manifestation of thought and the right to criticism, the publication is legitimate.

The publication of ironic news on Facebook is not likely to generate the state of anxiety of direct communications such as those on WhatsApp.

1432. According to Court of Milan, prel. investigation office of 31 October 2016, Decision No. 2918, stalking is committed by anyone who repeatedly contacts his ex-girlfriend with implicit references to the relationship that has taken place and to the possible disclosure of personal information.

Therefore, the offence of stalking is constituted by repeatedly contacting, at the end of a brief relationship, the ex-girlfriend via numerous text messages and WhatsApp messages and writing multiple messages via Instagram making implicit reference to the relationship that had taken place and to the possible disclosure of personal information, while also contacting the current boyfriend of the offended person telling him that he had interesting things to talk about.

§3. Online Grooming

1433. The introduction of the crime of soliciting minors responds to the need to fulfil the obligations that Italy has assumed by signing the Lanzarote Convention of 2007, ratified and implemented with Law No. 172 of 2012.

The Convention, in fact, required the signatory States to adopt the necessary measures to prevent any form of sexual exploitation and abuse against children and, to this end, required the introduction of new crimes, including soliciting minors.

In particular, Article 23 of the Lanzarote Convention has obliged the States to adopt specific legislative measures to render unlawful the conduct of those who, in order to perform sexual acts with minors or to produce child pornography material, propose to a minor a meeting through the use of communication and information technologies, on condition that the proposal is followed by material documents referable to said meeting.

The purpose of the offence is to anticipate the threshold of punishment before the actual meeting between the victim and the groomer, in order to protect the child but, at the same time, aims to ensure compliance with the principle of offensiveness by ensuring that criminal repression intervenes only when the agent's criminal intentions have assumed a concrete dimension through the actual organization of the encounter with the victim.

The objective pursued by Article 23 is to contain the phenomenon of the so-called child grooming, that is, the solicitation of the child on the Internet by means of psychological manipulation techniques such as to vitiate the will of the victim and create a relationship of trust for the purposes of abuse.

1434. In Italy, the ratification and implementation of Article 23 of the Convention took place with the approval of Law No. 172/2012 and the introduction of Article 609-*undecies* of the Criminal Code which punishes anyone who, for the purpose of committing one or more crimes related to the exploitation or sexual abuse of minors, lures a minor of sixteen years old, unless the fact constitutes a more serious crime.

The legislative provision, in order to eliminate the risk of indeterminacy of the case, was completed with an explicit definition of solicitation, understood as any act aimed at gaining the trust of the child through artifices, flattery or threats put in place also through the use of technologies.

In comparing Article 609-*undecies* of the Criminal Code and Article 23 of the Convention, it is immediately evident the fact that the Italian Legislator has disregarded the European guidelines and has elaborated an offence of autonomous solicitation different from that traced in the European offices.

1435. In terms of the objective element, Article 23 of the Convention places the threshold of punishment of child grooming at an advanced stage, that is at the moment in which the groomer has already performed executive acts aimed at meeting with the minor.

On the contrary, in Article 609-*undecies* any reference to the 'meeting proposal' and to the presence of 'material acts attributable to it' disappears, and those expressions are replaced by a generic reference to the 'soliciting' conduct that goes beyond any appointment proposed to the minor.

Consequently, the Italian Legislator has provided for a drastic retreat of the punishment threshold, as it punishes the facts of solicitation not only when there are no executive acts aimed at organizing the meeting with the minor but also when there has been no proposal for meeting: in essence, child grooming is punished already in the construction phase of the relationship of trust with the child, when the perpetrator acts for the purpose of committing one of the sexual crimes indicated by the law.

1436. Under a second profile, the Italian Legislator has included in the field of application of Article 609-*undecies* also facts committed against infants and children, despite the Lanzarote Convention refers to minors who are unable to express a valid consent in sexual matters and, therefore, in our system, to children under the age of fourteen.

The extension of the punishment to the case of subjects between the ages of fourteen and sixteen creates misunderstandings, above all in the cases in which the adherent, even if resorting to artifices and flattery, pursues the purpose of carrying out consensual sexual acts with the fifteen-year-old minor and therefore pursues legitimate and extraneous aims to the specific intent described by Article 609-*undecies*.

Finally, unlike the provisions of the Lanzarote Convention, which described solicitation as a conduct committed essentially via the Internet or other means of communication, Article 609-*undecies* punishes any form of child grooming by merely identifying the use of technologies as one of the possible typical methods of conduct.

1437. In this way, the scope of application of the standard has been further extended, based on the consideration that an enticement behaviour that occurs offline has the same offensive scope as an online conduct and is equally detrimental to the freedom of self-determination and the psychophysical integrity of the minor.

The case in point envisaged by the Italian Legislator is configured, therefore, as a crime of so-called indirect danger, since the criminal repression is anticipated for preparatory conduct of crimes that remain confined to the subjective sphere of the offender and for which no acts suitable and unambiguously directed to their commission have yet been realized. Consequently, a punishable attempt of the offences pursued by the agent, capable of absorbing the negative value of the facts of enticement, cannot be configured.

1438. The repression of crimes of indirect danger has raised wide debates in doctrine[265] about the compatibility with the constitutional principles of offensiveness and proportion. Therefore, in order to recover a minimum threshold of offensiveness,

265. B. Romano 'Reati contro la persona, III. Reati contro la libertà individuale' (Giuffré, Milano, 2015).

it is essential to carry out a punctual screening of the concrete suitability of the conduct to achieve the aim pursued by the agent and a rigorous assessment of the specific intent, in relation to which it is necessary that soul and mind of the offender is reflected in the concrete acts put in place.

1439. Article 609-*undecies*, in fact, configures the solicitation of minors as a specific crime. The Italian Legislator has chosen to include in the subject of specific intent all the cases put in place to protect the individual personality of children.

Consequently, for there to be a criminally relevant enticement, it is necessary that the offender acts to commit the crimes of reduction or maintenance in slavery, child prostitution, child pornography, sexual violence, sexual acts with a minor, corruption of a minor or group sexual violence.

1440. The harmful value configured by the incriminating rule does not focus only on the basic ground of enticement, but also on the teleological relationship between the latter and the illicit aim pursued.

The enticement conduct, therefore, constitutes the means for the attainment of the crime object of the specific intent, and, only where this instrumental connection exists, the basic fact of solicitation can be said to be typical and criminally relevant.

These considerations require the judge to carry out a rigorous assessment of the suitability of the conduct to achieve the specific purpose pursued by the agent through the examination of objective elements capable of revealing to an external observer the purpose pursued by the giver, not being able to apply the case in point when the real intent of the groomer remains completely uncertain.

As regards the methods of execution of the crime, Article 609-*undecies* requires that the perpetrator performs any act aimed at gaining the child's trust through artifices, flattery or threats.

1441. These methods constitute an essential element of the typical fact and must necessarily exist for the purposes of the integration of the criminal offence, which is therefore configured as a restricted offence. In the event that the conduct does not include the modus describedi in the rule, it will not be sufficient to supplement the details of the crime.

The artifices, the enticements and the threats have in common the fact of being three mechanisms to which the recruiter can resort to exert a strong psychological leverage on the victim and to obtain his artificial cooperation, annulling the defence capacity and the freedom of self-determination of the minor.

In particular, the artifice can be defined as a simulation, dissimulation, a deceitful and lying device capable of deceiving the victim and attracting her into the criminal plot devised by the offender.

1442. The concept of flattery, however, evokes conducts consisting in adulating, falsely gratifying, turning fake and excessive attention to win the sympathy and benevolence of someone to induce the receiver to a certain behaviour.

Finally, the Legislator has foreseen that solicitation can take place through threats and, that is, through the prospect of a future and unjust evil, whose verification depends on the will of the agent, and which presents itself suitable to generate a fear in the passive subject.

1443. According to Court of Cassation, Criminal section III of 7 July 2022, Decision No. 33257, any enticement by which the agent attempts to lure the child into his or her will constitutes flattery capable of winning the child's trust.

In the case in point, there was an agent who, by means of several WhatsApp messages, invited the twelve-year-old victim, to whom he had addressed words of appreciation, to send him photos or videos of himself or other minors containing child pornography, promising him the possibility of easy profits.

For the purposes of the configurability of the offence referred to in Article 600-*ter*, paragraph 4, of the Criminal Code, the proof of the conduct of the transfer to others of the pornographic material produced using minors under the age of eighteen years is correctly argued by enhancing the factual circumstance of the discovery of the aforementioned material in the computer folder called 'Sent' of the defendant's mobile phone, because this constitutes an element capable of demonstrating beyond reasonable doubt that the material was sent to other users.

For the purposes of the configurability of the offence of solicitation of minors (Article 609-*undecies* of the Criminal Code), from an objective point of view, the 'flattery' taken into consideration by the provision, envisaged as an alternative to 'artifices', does not imply deception, but may also consist in a simple 'enticement'. ; this is also because, in common linguistic usage, by 'flattery' is meant any enticement, made up of flattering phrases, friendly words, promises, outwardly benevolent acts, feigned attentions, which can be understood as 'flattery', by which an attempt is made to lure someone to our will, to win his confidence with the aim of inducing him to do something to our advantage. While, from the point of view of the intent of the offence, the purpose (among others) of committing the offence referred to in Article 600-*quater* of the Criminal Code, i.e., of procuring pornographic material made using minors under the age of eighteen, can also be configured in the case where such material was made by the minor himself.

1444. According to Court of Cassation, Criminal section III of 12 March 2021, Decision No. 23931, among the criminal behaviours for which Article 609-*undecies* of the Criminal Code provides an advanced form of protection, there is also the crime under Articles 600-*ter* and 600-*quater*.

In the case in point, the defendant had a twelve-year-old girl send him photographs of her intimate parts through WhatsApp.

1445. According to Court of Milan section office for preliminary investigations of 16 April 2019, Decision No. 1208, it is an offence of solicitation of minors to act by means of contacts via the internet and via WhatsApp with a minor of fourteen years of age, engaging in conversations of a sexual nature through an internet site and using artifices and flattery aimed at gaining her trust, including that of making her believe she is sixteen years old and that she is interested in having a romantic relationship, in order to obtain pornographic material and threatening her with sexual intercourse.

1446. According to Court of La Spezia section office for preliminary investigations of 30 June 2016, Decision No. 971, the offence of solicitation of minors is integrated if a person urges a minor to send erotic photos. It is an offence of solicitation of minors (Article 609-*undecies*) to convince a girl of fifteen years of age with blandishments, compliments and finally threats to send erotic photos via WhatsApp.

§4. Revenge Porn

1447. Revenge porn crime was introduced in Italy by Article 10 paragraph 1 of Law No. 69/2019 (the so-called Red Code), aimed at protecting victims of domestic and gender-based violence and is governed by Article 612-*ter* of the Criminal Code.

Revenge porn consists of the dissemination of pornographic or sexually explicit images for the purpose of vengeful purpose (e.g., to 'punish' the ex-partner who has decided to end a loving relationship), or to publicly denigrate, bully, and harass the person depicted.

It is therefore a phenomenon that can have psychological, social and even material effects on the lives of its victims.

1448. The conduct constituting the crime includes:

- sending, delivering, transferring, publishing and disseminating images or videos of a sexual nature, after created or taken such images or videos;
- sending, delivering, transferring, publishing and disseminating images or videos of a sexual nature, after having received them through other means. This conduct may be committed by a person other than the one who first disseminated the images and videos.

1449. The Legislator's intention is to counter the so-called virality of images.[266] Revenge porn requires that:

- the conduct is carried out without the consent of the persons depicted in the images and videos;
- the images and videos have sexually explicit content: the legislator has not provided a definition of 'sexually explicit content', leaving the definition of the content to case law;
- the images and videos are taken in a private and confidential context.

---

266. G. M. Caletti '*Revenge porn'. Prime considerazioni in vista dell'introduzione dell'art. 612-ter c.p.: una fattispecie 'esemplare', ma davvero efficace?*' in 'www.penalecontemporaneo.it', 2019.

1450. The crime is punishable upon complaint of the victim. The deadline for filing a complaint is six months and can only be remitted in the course of criminal proceedings.

The same punishment applies to anyone who, having received or acquired the images or videos, sends, delivers, transfers, publishes or disseminates them without the consent of the persons portrayed for the purpose of causing them harm.

The offense provides two aggravated circumstances: whether the crime is committed by a legally separated or divorced spouse, or by a person who has been linked by emotional relationship to the victim or through computer or telematic means; if the acts are committed against a person in a condition of physical or mental inferiority or against a pregnant woman. In this case, the crime is punishable ex officio.

1451. Revenge porn can be committed by anyone and is an offence of 'mere conduct', since it is perfected by the commission of the criminal act. The Data Protection Authority ('Garante per la protezione dei dati personali') plays a significant role in contrasting it, as determined by Article 144-*bis* of the Privacy Code:

1. Anyone, including minors over the age of fourteen, who has reasonable grounds to believe that sexually explicit images or videos concerning them, intended to remain private, may be sent, delivered, transferred, published, or disseminated without their consent in violation of article 612-ter of the Penal Code, may report or file a complaint with the Authority. The Authority, within forty-eight hours of receiving the request, shall proceed in accordance with article 58 of Regulation (EU) 2016/679 and articles 143 and 144.
2. When the images or videos involve minors, the request to the Authority may also be made by the parents or those exercising parental responsibility or guardianship.
3. For the purposes referred to in paragraph 1, the transmission to the Authority of sexually explicit images or videos concerning third parties, carried out by the concerned person, does not constitute the crime referred to in article 612-ter of the Penal Code.
4. Digital platform operators who receive the measures referred to in paragraph 1 shall retain the material subject to the report for evidentiary purposes only and in the terms indicated by the Authority, even within the same measures, that are suitable to prevent the direct identification of the concerned persons, for twelve months from the receipt of the measure itself.
5. The Authority, by its own measure, may regulate specific methods for conducting the procedures referred to in paragraph 1 and the measures to prevent the direct identification of the concerned persons referred to in the same paragraph.
6. Providers of audiovisual content sharing services, wherever established, that provide services accessible in Italy, shall promptly indicate to the Authority or publish on their website a contact to which the measures adopted pursuant to paragraph 1 can be communicated. In the event of non-compliance with the obligation referred to in the previous sentence, the

Authority shall warn the service provider to comply within thirty days. In case of non-compliance with the warning, the administrative pecuniary sanction referred to in article 83, paragraph 4, of the Regulation shall apply.

7. When the Authority, following the report referred to in paragraph 1, becomes aware of the commission of the crime referred to in article 612-ter of the Penal Code, even in attempted form, in the case of a crime subject to public prosecution, it shall forward the received report and the acquired documentation to the Public Prosecutor.

1452. According to Court of Pescara of 11 April 2024, Decision No. 304 the mere exhibition of pornographic photos made in such a way as to emotionally involve the offended person and compromise his or her sexual freedom constitutes the offence referred to in Article 609-*quinquies* of the Criminal Code.

Even the mere exhibition of pornographic photographs made in such a way as to emotionally involve the offended person and compromise his or her sexual freedom can constitute the objective element of the offence referred to in Article 609-*quinquies* of the Criminal Code (prior to the 2019 reform).

There is no doubt as to the materiality of the fact in the event that the photo depicting the genital organ was sent, accompanied by clear invitations of a sexual nature to the minor aimed at inducing her to perform sexual acts; by exhibition is to be understood not only direct exhibition, but also exhibition on social networks (in this case, WhatsApp): in fact, the crime in question also includes conduct carried out by means of telematic communication, since the physical presence of the active and passive subject is not necessary.

1453. According to Court of Cassation, Criminal section V of 5 March 2024, Decision No. 25516, whoever transmits to third parties videos acquired on a dating site with restricted access is responsible for unlawful dissemination of sexually explicit images.

The conduct of a person who, having received or in any case acquired visual material published on a 'web' dating site with access restricted to members only, transmits it to third parties without the consent of the depicted person, constitutes the offence of unlawful dissemination of sexually explicit images or videos, since such right, by virtue of the consent expressed by the latter at the time of opening the 'account', is restricted to members only of the virtual community to which the material was originally sent and solely within it.

1454. According to Court of Cassation, Criminal section V of 1 March 2024, Decision No. 24379, from the wording of Article 612-*ter* of the Criminal Code emerges that the perpetrator of the dissemination of sexually explicit material can only be the person who made the material himself or the person who took it away. In fact, the provision states that 'unless the act constitutes a more serious offence, anyone who, after having made or stolen them, sends, delivers, assigns, publishes or disseminates images or videos with sexually explicit content, intended to remain private, without the consent of the persons represented'. In the case, the Court annulled the decision that had rejected the request for the release of computer material containing the incriminated content; the applicant, having extracted a copy of the recordings of criminal proceedings against him, had come into possession of a recording showing two persons consummating sexual intercourse. The suspect had transferred said recording onto his mobile phone and onto a pen-drive; both the mobile phone and the said pen-drive had been subject to probationary seizure as they were considered to have been used to commit the offence referred to in Article 612-*ter* of the Criminal Code.

1455. According to Court of La Spezia, sec. prel. investigations of 27 February 2024, Decision No. 66, revenge porn is integrated even if the photo of an erogenous zone is spread.

For the purposes of the configurability of the crime envisaged by Article 612-*ter* of the Criminal Code, i.e., the unlawful dissemination of sexually explicit images or videos, the dissemination does not necessarily have to concern images or videos depicting sexual acts or genital organs but may concern close-ups of other erogenous parts of the body, in conditions and contexts such as to evoke their sexuality.

1456. According to Court of Cassation, Criminal section V of 23 February 2024, Decision No. 19201, Article 612-*ter* of the Criminal Code punishes, in paragraph 1, the conduct of anyone who, after having made or taken them, sends, delivers, assigns, publishes or disseminates images or videos with sexually explicit content, intended to remain private, without the consent of the represented persons. Therefore, what characterizes the unlawful conduct is that the offended, whose most intimate sphere, constituting interest protected by the offence, is violated, has not given consent to the disclosure of their sexual images to persons other than those with whom he has taken the images or video with sexually explicit content. The circumstance that the victim consented to being portrayed or filmed in the video that is subsequently disclosed is of no relevance for the offence to be committed, provided, of course, that the consent does not also concern that disclosure.

Article 612-*ter* of the Criminal Code punishes two offences that are identical in terms of conduct (sending, delivery, transfer, publication or dissemination without the consent of the persons depicted) and material object (images or videos with sexually explicit content intended to remain private), but differ in terms of premise (in the first case, having made or taken away, in the second case, having received or in any case acquired the images or videos) and purpose (irrelevant, in the first case, being in the presence of a case of general intent; essential, in the second, the 'purpose of causing harm' to the victim being the object of the specific intent).

1457. According to Court of Turin of 29 September 2023, Decision No. 1520, the son who posts a sexually explicit video of his mother on Facebook commits revenge porn.

The offence of revenge porn, as referred to in Article 612-*ter* of the Criminal Code, is committed when a son comes into possession of a video with sexually explicit contents, intended to remain private, portraying his mother and her new partner, and publicly disseminates it on Facebook, with the awareness and intention of damaging the dignity and private life of the victim, and accompanies the post with clear defamatory and offensive phrases.

1458. According to Court of Cassation, Criminal section V of 29 March 2023, Decision No. 32602, revenge porn also exists in case of online diffusion of contents depicting a person in underwear.

The 'sexually explicit' content, to which Article 612-*ter* of the Criminal Code refers, cannot be only identified with the reproduction of sexual intercourse (or self-eroticism), or even of organs belonging to the sexual-reproductive apparatus in the scientific sense. This means that the sexuality of a person, who is the victim of the offence, can be evoked in a manifest manner even if only through the depiction of 'erogenous' parts of his body other than their genitals, which are nevertheless capable of evoking, due to the context and the concrete conditions in which they are portrayed, the sexual instinct (the conviction for revenge porn was upheld for the man who had disseminated online videos and photos showing a person simply in underwear and not engaged in explicit sexual acts).

1459. According to Court of Cassation, Criminal section V of 22 February 2023, Decision No. 14927, the disclosure of sexually explicit images or videos may also concern erogenous parts of the body in such a condition as to evoke sexuality.

For the purposes of the configurability of the offence of unlawful dissemination of sexually explicit images or videos, the dissemination may concern not only images or videos depicting sexual acts or genital organs, but also other erogenous parts of the human body in conditions and contexts likely to evoke sexuality.

The offence of unlawful dissemination of sexually explicit images or videos, which is an instantaneous offence, is committed at the time of the first transmission to a recipient, regardless of the relationship existing between that recipient and the portrayed person.

In the case, the Court held correct the conviction of the defendant who, without the victim's consent, had sent images portraying his 'ex' lover in sexually explicit situations only to the latter's family members, who were interested in not feeding their subsequent dissemination to third parties.

§5. Online Defamation

1460. The crime of defamation is regulated by Article 595 of the Criminal Code, which punishes 'whoever, outside the cases indicated in the previous article, by communicating with several persons, offends the reputation of others'.

The requirements for the crime to be integrated are: the offense to the reputation of others, which is to be understood as an injury to the personal, moral, social and professional qualities of an individual; communication with several persons, which may also take place at different times, with intervals of varying length, and may occur either orally or in writing.

1461. According to authoritative jurisprudence, the fitness to injure a person's image, honour or decorum must be assessed in the specific case, based on the context in which the offense took place, the personalities of the offended and offender, and the social conscience. In other words, what matters is the offensive significance of the used expressions, and not so much the words themselves.

With reference to the second requirement, it has been clarified that it is necessary for the perpetrator of defamation to communicate with at least two people, but in such a way that the news will certainly come to the knowledge of others.

1462. For the integration of the crime of defamation, it is not necessary that the victim be precisely identified, but it is sufficient that he or she be identifiable, even by exclusion and deduction. It is however required that the defamer be aware that he/she is uttering (or writing) an injurious sentence to another person's reputation and that he/she is moved by the intention that the disparaging sentence should come to the knowledge of more than one person.

The criminal conduct may also consist of omissions, as long as the criminal intent can be demonstrated.

1463. In any case, to be relevant under the aforementioned rule, the conduct must be illegitimate, that is, not justified by the fulfilment of a legal obligation, nor by the exercise of a subjective right or legitimate interest, nor, again, by the consent of the person who should be offended or affected by it.

1464. The Italian Legislature then provided for a series of aggravating circumstances, the presence of which determine the increase of the penalty. These are, in particular, the following: the offended has been attributed a specific fact, suitable to make the offense against the victim's reputation more credible; the offense was caused by means of the press, advertisement or public act, since they are media that greatly amplify the defamatory message; the offense has been caused to a political, administrative, judicial body, its representation or an authority constituted in a college, the vilification of institutions being considered even more serious.

1465. So, when the defamatory message is transmitted through social networks, blogs, Internet sites or other telematic channels, the hypothesis referred to in the second point is met and the penalty is increased. The damaging scope of such conduct, in fact, is considered amplified, due to the ability of the technological medium to reach an indeterminate number of subjects in a significantly short time.

1466. This newer form of online defamation entails some problems with reference to the identification of the perpetrator. According to constant case law, in fact, the defamatory comment cannot be attributed to a person only as the owner of the account from which the comment itself was posted, since the account may have been unlawfully misappropriated by others. On the contrary, it is deemed necessary for the investigating authorities to locate the IP address so that they can locate the line from which the defamatory content was posted and verify that it can be traced back to the suspected individual.

1467. As seen, defamation requires that the injury to another's reputation occurs in the absence of the offended person. A different circumstance occurs when, on the contrary, the offended person is present (even if only virtually): in such a case, the crime of insult, governed by Article 549 of the Criminal Code, is committed.

1468. According to Court of Ferrara of 24 May 2024, Decision No. 432, the publication of intimate photos of the offended person on an erotic photo forum, without consent, constitutes the offence of defamation.

The offence of defamation by means of the press is committed when a person who receives intimate photos from the offended person by virtue of the relationship existing between them publishes them on a forum in which amateur erotic photos were published and subsequently circulated on Facebook, with the clear intention of damaging the victim's reputation, easily identifiable by the tattoos on his body.

1469. According to Court Lecce, section I of 9 May 2024, Decision No. 1374, the publication of a post with a defamatory content is assisted by the subjective element of the offence of defamation due to the intention of the expression whose damaging value is known.

The defamatory scope of a 'post' in which the defendant defines the public authorities, including the mayor of the municipality, as 'mafiosi' is evident, and this offence acquires an even greater defamatory charge since it refers not to an ordinary citizen, but to the mayor and to the entire town administered by him. The subjective element of the offence exists on the basis of the intention to communicate the expression (whose damaging value is known) to several persons, without the need for proof of the existence of an *animus diffamandi.*

1470. According to Court of Cassation, Labour section of 6 May 2024, Decision No. 12142, the publication on Facebook of an offensive comment against the employer constitutes cause for dismissal.

On the subject of disciplinary dismissal, the dissemination on Facebook of an offensive comment against the employer's company constitutes just cause for termination of employment, insofar as it is capable of damaging the bond of trust in the employment relationship, and since it constitutes defamatory conduct, due to the aptitude of the medium used to guarantee the circulation of the message among an indeterminate group of persons. In this case, in fact, the interpersonal relationship, precisely because of the medium used, is extended and enlarged to an indeterminate group of individuals, thus increasing the diffusive scope of the comment within this group and making it appreciable by numerical composition.

1471. According to Court of Cassation, Civil section III of 4 March 2024, Decision No. 5701, the existence of defamation must be excluded in case of several communications addressed on the private Facebook channel to a single addressee.

In the hypothesis of communication to a single person, the objective element of the offence, integrated by the diffusivity of the disparaging conduct, exists only in the hypothesis that the agent expresses the will or engages in conduct such as to cause the further dissemination of the defamatory content through the addressee, the intrinsic characteristics of the communication tool used not being sufficient to consider the sender's implicit acceptance of the risk of dissemination.

In the case in point, the Supreme Court upheld the contested sentence that had excluded the existence of the offence in the presence of several communications, but all addressed, on the private Facebook channel, to a single addressee, since it could not be presumed that the messages sent through social networks on private mail channels were, per se, intended for dissemination to other persons.

1472. According to Court of Ferrara of 23 February 2024, Decision No. 1659, aggravated defamation is the conscious diffusion on Facebook of sentences damaging other people's reputation.

The liability of the suspect for the offence of aggravated defamation perpetrated by means of the Facebook platform is established by virtue of the great diffusivity that the message offending the dignity and reputation of the public prosecutor may have for having been made public on a social platform, in the full awareness of the subject agent of uttering sentences damaging the dignity of others.

1473. According to Court of Cassation, Criminal section V of 23 January 2024, Decision No. 17141, the offence of defamation is committed when the message can be read by more than one person, even if the offended person is among them.

In the case in point, the defendant had used a photo of his ex-girlfriend on his WhatsApp profile, the dissemination of the offensive message being evident, as the man's WhatsApp profile was accessible to at least all the users of the social network whose contact was included in his phone book.

1474. According to Court of Udine of 20 November 2023, Decision No. 2196, the dissemination of defamatory phrases on websites or social networks is capable of constituting defamation due to the possibility of reaching an indeterminate number of people.

The dissemination via a website or social network of phrases offensive to another person's reputation is capable of constituting the offence of aggravated defamation, pursuant to Article 595(3) of the Criminal Code, given the undoubted public nature of such means of dissemination, which by their very nature and function are capable of reaching an indeterminate plurality of users enabled to connect to the web network; it follows from the nature of the offence of defamation as an eventual offence that it must be deemed to have been committed at the time and place where third parties perceive the defamatory expressions following the activation of the web connection.

1475. According to Court of Turin of 29 September 2023, Decision No. 1520, the son who posts a sexually explicit video of his mother on Facebook commits revenge porn.

The offence of revenge porn, as referred to in Article 612-*ter* of the Criminal Code, is committed when a son who, having come into possession of a video with sexually explicit contents, intended to remain private, portraying his mother and her new partner, publicly disseminates it on the Facebook platform, with the awareness and intention of damaging the dignity and private life of the father, accompanying the post with clear defamatory and offensive phrases.

1476. According to Court of Cassino of 28 August 2023, Decision No. 1006, the publication on a website of erotic videos without the consent of the person filmed therein, constitutes the offence of defamation.

The conduct of publishing on a website (in this case, on Facebook, with the insertion of the 'tag' to the profile of the offended persons) erotic videos depicting a person in pornographic postures, without his consent to the publication, constitutes the offence of defamation.

1477. According to Court of Catanzaro, section II of 23 August 2023, Decision No. 1363, defamatory Facebook post constitutes aggravated defamation.

Defamation by means of Facebook *peacefully falls* within the case of aggravated defamation pursuant to Article 595, paragraph 3 of the Italian Penal Code, given that the publication of the news on an Internet site constitutes a means of dissemination on a par with the press, all the more so if the post is published without any restriction of privacy, which presupposes the use of the contents by a potentially indeterminate group of persons. Therefore, the need to balance the right to criticism with the right to honour and reputation also applies in the particular case of defamation through the publication of news on Facebook.

1478. According to Court of Cassation, Civil section III of 18 August 2023, Decision No. 24818, the 'blogger' who fails to remove from his site writings with disparaging content is liable even if such content consists in the work of others.

On the subject of defamation, the blogger is liable for the crime in the aggravated form, pursuant to paragraph 3 of Article 595 of the Italian Penal Code, in terms of the offence caused by any other means of publicity, for the disparaging writings published on his own site by third parties when, having become aware of them, he does not promptly remove them, given that such conduct amounts to the conscious sharing of the content damaging to the reputation of others and allows the further dissemination of the defamatory comments.

1479. According to Court of Cosenza, section II of 3 August 2023, Decision No. 1367, the PEC is presumed to be of strictly personal use of the addressee and the possibility that the confidentiality of electronic mail may be violated because it is shared with other subjects does not mean that the PEC becomes a vehicle of publicity. In essence, the CEM message is not physiologically usable by an indistinct audience of subjects, and therefore the configurability of the offence of defamation through a CEM message must be excluded.

1480. According to Court of Cassation, Criminal section V of 14 July 2023, Decision No. 38755, the technical ascertainment of the ownership of the IP from which defamatory messages are sent is not necessary if the social profile is attributable to the defendant.

For the purposes of establishing liability for the offence of defamation, the technical verification of the ownership of the IP address from which the offensive messages were sent is not necessary, provided that the Facebook profile can be attributed to the defendant on the basis of logical elements that can be deduced from the convergence of multiple and precise circumstantial data such as the motive, the subject matter of the forum on which the messages are published, the relationship between the parties, the origin of the post from the defendant's virtual notice board using his nickname.

1481. According to Court of Cassation, Criminal section V of 27 June 2023, Decision No. 38144, the offence of defamation by e-mail requires proof that the message has been 'downloaded', i.e., transferred to the address user's device.

The offence of defamation is an event offence, which is committed at the time and place where third parties other than the agent and the offended person perceive the offensive expression. In order to identify that place, where the offence is committed electronically through the transmission to several recipients of an e-mail message, it is worth noting that e-mail is a communication directed to a predefined and exclusive recipient (even when several are the persons to whom it is addressed), to whom it is delivered electronically at the adopting server, by connecting to which, by means of its own device and using personal access keys, the latter can take knowledge of it. In this regard, proof of the actual delivery of the message is therefore required, whether it is the consequence of an automatic operation set up by the addressee or of dedicated access to the server. In other words, proof that the message has been 'downloaded' (i.e., transferred to the address user's device) is sufficient, while the actual reading can be presumed, unless there is proof to the contrary. According to the Court, the jurisdiction of the proceeding judge had been correctly identified because such proof had been achieved at least with regard to two of the addressees of the message, a sufficient condition for considering the place of commission of the offence to be the place where the receipt of the message had taken place.

1482. According to Court of Cassation, Criminal section V of 23 May 2023, Decision No. 31179, sending e-mails with defamatory content to individual reserved e-mail boxes does not constitute the aggravating circumstance of press offences.

On the subject of defamation, the sending of an e-mail with defamatory content to individual reserved e-mail boxes does not constitute the aggravating circumstance of offences caused in the press or by other means of publicity, since it does not entail any automatic dissemination to an indefinite number of subjects. In its grounds, the Court stated that the computerized instrument used to transmit the communication cannot be confused with its diffusion.

1483. According to Court of Cassation, Criminal section I of 19 May 2023, Decision No. 37618, dissemination of offensive message in WhatsApp chat does not constitute the aggravating circumstance of the use of a 'means of publicity'.

On the subject of military defamation, the dissemination of an offensive message in a chat of the 'WhatsApp' application does not constitute the aggravating circumstance of the use of a 'means of publicity', since it is a communication tool intended for a limited number of persons and lacking the necessary offensiveness.

§6. 'Detention Of' or 'Access To' Child Pornography

1484. The crime of detention of or access to child pornography is regulated by Article 600-*quater* of the Italian Penal Code, which punishes 'whoever (...) knowingly procures or possesses pornographic material made using minors under the age of eighteen years'. The penalty is imprisonment of up to three years or a fine of up to EUR 1,549.

1485. According to Article 600-*ter*, 'pornographic material' means any photographic or cinematographic representation involving the participation of a minor in scenes or contexts of a sexual nature, with the exclusion of the relevance of the mere depiction of nudity without relevance to the sexual sphere. This notion includes any type of depiction that depicts not only a minor's genitals, but also intimate parts of the minor, such as breasts or buttocks, as they are otherwise aimed at satisfying the lust of the holder in violation of the minor's sexual freedom.

1486. Evidence that the images or videos actually reproduce minors can also be inferred merely from the physical features of the portrayed adolescents and from the retrieval of the files from Internet sites whose URL address evokes the minor's age or has a name referable to children or child pornography content.

1487. The conduct of 'procuring' refers to the procuring of the material in any way put in place and delineates an instantaneous crime; that of 'possessing', on the other hand, requires the exercise of actual possession and configures a permanent offense that continues for as long as the availability of the material remains with the agent. The Supreme Court clarified that the two conducts do not integrate two different offenses, but two different ways of committing the same crime and, therefore, cannot be concurrent with each other if they concern the same material.[267]

1488. It was, likewise, held that integrating the crime under consideration is the ascertained possession of child pornography files subsequently deleted from the accessible memory of the operating system since the fact that they have been deleted determines only the cessation of the permanence of the crime and not, instead, the total exclusion of the same.[268]

1489. With regard to the use of minors referred to in Article 600-*quater* of the Italian Penal Code, the Supreme Court specified that this prerequisite does not exist

---

267. *See* Criminal Cassation, United Sections, Judgment No. 51815, 31 May 2018; Criminal Cassation, s. III, Judgment No. 38211, 25 May 2017.
268. *See* Criminal Cassation, s. III, Judgment No. 11044, 7 Apr. 2016.

in case the images or videos relate to the private sexual life of a minor who has reached the age of sexual consent, in the context of a relationship that, having assessed the circumstances of the concrete case, is not characterized by conditioning arising from the position of the author.[269]

1490. The rule under consideration then provides an aggravating circumstance for the case in which the material possessed is of 'large quantity': this hypothesis exists when a 'very large, relevant or consistent' number of child pornographic images are available, capable of concretely contributing to increasing the reference market.[270]

1491. As of 2021, a criminal offence is envisaged to punish those who carry out the conduct through the use of the Internet or other networks or means of communication. Thus, with this provision, the mere viewing of images of minors online, accomplished by knowingly accessing child pornography sites, even without the material being downloaded to one's computer device, has been incriminated. This is a subsidiary offense that applies outside cases in which the agent possesses or obtains child pornography. The adverb 'intentionally' requires full awareness, intent and foresight of each element of the conduct and the case in order for the crime to be integrated. The phrase 'without justifiable reason', on the other hand, implicitly provides for the exculpation of those who, for example, access sites containing child pornography for purposes of criminal investigation.

1492. Again with reference to the profile of the agent's awareness, the Supreme Court also ruled that the crime of possession or access to child pornography subsists even in the case of possession of temporary Internet files, which are obtained through visits made by the user to sites containing child pornography, remaining stored for an appreciable period of time in the corresponding folder and resulting, therefore, to all intents and purposes, held by the user. This, of course, always provided that the holder had knowledge of the existence of files acquired in the course of browsing.

1493. In 2006, Article 600-*quater*.1 of the Italian Penal Code was introduced to punish virtual child pornography, i.e., that having as its object virtual images made using images of minors or parts thereof. So, the crimes of child pornography and possession of child pornography material are also considered to be integrated if the images of minors are made with 'graphic processing techniques not associated in whole or in part with real situations, the quality of representation of which makes non-real situations appear as real'.

1494. According to Court of Appeal Lecce of 6 February 2024, Decision No. 1863, the aggravating circumstance of the large quantity of pornographic material is integrated with the possession of at least *a hundred images*.

---

269. *See* Criminal Cassation, United Sections, Judgment No. 39005, 28 Oct. 2021.
270. *See* Criminal Cassation, s. III, Judgment No. 17211, 31 Mar. 2011.

The configurability of the aggravating circumstance of the 'large quantity' in the crime of possession of child pornographic content requires the judge to take into account not only the number of computer supports held, a circumstantial fact in itself, but also the number of images, to be considered an objective unit of measurement, that each of them contains. The aggravating circumstance in question can be committed in the event of the possession of at least one hundred child pornographic images.

1495. According to Court of Cassation, Criminal section III of 18 October 2023, Decision No. 47187, even erotic drawings and illustrations depicting minors constitute the offence of possession of child pornographic material.

The offence of possession of child pornographic material is committed not only when there is a real reproduction of a minor in a situation of pornographic physicality, but also when there are drawings, paintings and anything else that is capable of giving the viewer the idea that the object of the pornographic representation is a minor. In the case in point, it was a matter of comic strips and illustrations of erotic tales depicting minors engaged in incestuous acts or other sexual activities.

1496. According to Court of Cassation, Criminal section III of 4 April 2023, Decision No. 36572, the availability of files with child pornographic content on the 'cloud storage' of Telegram group chats constitutes criminally relevant detention.

The availability of 'files' with child pornographic content stored on the 'cloud storage' of a group 'chat' in the 'Telegram' space, accessible, by means of their credentials, by any member of the group who has knowingly taken part in it, constitutes criminally relevant possession pursuant to Article 600-*quater*, paragraph 1, of the Italian Penal Code.

1497. According to Court of Cassation, Criminal section III of 19 January 2023, Decision No. 4212, the offence of possession of child pornographic material can also be committed in case of availability of files accessible through a virtual archive that can be consulted without restrictions.

The concept of possession of child pornographic material, as referred to in Article 600-*quater* of the Criminal Code, includes not only the availability of child pornographic files permanently stored in a computer device in the material possession of the holder but also the availability of files accessible, without limits of time and place, through access to a virtual archive, consultable, without restrictions, with exclusive authentication credentials or in any case known to the user.

1498. According to Court of Cassation, Criminal section III of 12 May 2022, Decision No. 44659, the large quantity of child pornographic material present on the computer leads to the belief that their downloading took place voluntarily.

The presence of a large amount of pornographic and child pornographic material on the two electronic devices leads without any uncertainty to believe that their downloading and, even more, their storage (also taking into account the amount of 'memory' occupied by such files) on the electronic devices cannot have taken place in the absence of a conscious choice of the owner of the devices themselves (confirmed, in this case, the conviction of the defendant in relation to the commission of the offence referred to in Article 600-*quater*, paragraph 2, of the Criminal Code).

1499. According to Court of Cassation Criminal sect. III of 19 November 2021, Decision No. 3275, the conviction for possession of child pornography is confirmed against a defendant whose home was found a hard disk with traces of child pornography files deleted from the computer before the installation of a well-known application for the secure deletion of data 'CCleaner'. From that circumstance, the appeal judges had reasonably inferred that the defendant had decided to use that sophisticated application precisely in order to prevent the trace of certain files that he held, used and then deleted from remaining.

1500. According to Court of Cassation Criminal section III of 7 April 2021, Decision No. 18153, on the subject of possession of child pornographic material, the aggravating circumstance of the use of means to prevent the identification of the access data to telematic networks, as referred to in Article 602-*ter*, paragraph 9, of the Criminal Code, can be established in the event the agent takes any action aimed at preventing his identification, by eluding the normal methods of recognition, starting from those relating to physical access to the computer to those of insertion in the network itself. In the case in point, the defendant had 'downloaded' child pornographic images from the web, by accessing a special link with the TOR system, which allowed surfing on child pornographic sites without showing his IP address.

1501. According to Court of Cassation, Criminal section III of 3 March 2021, Decision No. 24644, for the offence of possession of child pornographic material, the fact that the images have been deleted is not relevant.

For the purposes of the configurability of the offence of possession of child pornographic material, the fact that the images acquired are not immediately usable by the agent because they have been deleted or voluntarily set aside in parts that are no longer easily accessible in the electronic memory of the computer instruments is not relevant.

1502. According to Court of Cassation Criminal section III of 8 October 2020, Decision No. 32166, on the subject of possession of child pornographic material, the aggravating circumstance of the use of means designed to prevent the identification of the access data to telematic networks, as referred to in Article 602-*ter*, ninth paragraph, of the Italian Criminal Code, may be committed if the agent carries out any action aimed at preventing his identification, eluding the normal methods of recognition, starting from those relating to physical access to the computer up to those of insertion in the network itself.

In the case, the defendant had used a computer and a 'client' access not attributable to him as belonging to another person, also using different telematic identities – so-called nicknames – to operate on the 'peer-to-peer' file sharing platform called 'Gigatribe'.

1503. According to the Court of Appeal Rome sez. III of 6 May 2019, Decision No. 6055, the offence of possession of child pornography, pursuant to Article 600-*quater* of the Italian Criminal Code, includes both the conduct of 'procuring' the material in question, implying any means of procuring it, including by telematic means, and the conduct of 'disposing', which implies a broader concept of possession.

The subjective element of the offence is the direct intent, i.e., the will to procure or possess child pornographic material originating from the exploitation of minors. In the case in question, the Court of Appeal confirmed the conviction against the defendant, who did not deny the fact that he had surfed the Internet in search of child pornographic images, downloading them and storing them in 231 files, but recalculating the sentence, as the aggravating circumstance referred to in paragraph 3 of the provision 'of the large quantity of images' was found to be non-existent.

1504. According to Court of Cassation, Criminal section III of 10 April 2019, Decision No. 25558, following the legislative amendments referred to in Law No. 38 of 2006, the offence referred to in Article 600-*quater* of the Criminal Code (possession of pornographic material) may occur with two forms of conduct: procuring and possessing.

The two forms in which the offence may occur, even if they appear to be alternatives, nevertheless have a common element which is the possession, albeit momentary, of child pornography by the person who procures it; they are not two different offences, but two different ways of perpetrating the same offence and therefore the two forms of conduct cannot be combined.

1505. According to Court of Cassation, Criminal Section III of 27 September 2018, Decision No. 1647, the offence referred to in Article 600-*quater*, paragraph 3, of the criminal code is committed when the person posts pornographic photos depicting minors on a freely accessible site or when he propagates them by means of the Internet, sending them to a group or a discussion list from which anyone can download them, whereas the lighter offence referred to in Article 600-*quater*, paragraph 4, of the Criminal Code when the agent sends the photos to a specific person, attaching them to an e-mail message or via the recipient's Facebook profile, in such a way that only the latter has the possibility of downloading them.

§7. Deepfake

1506. Deepfakes are photos, videos, and audio created by special artificial intelligence software, called 'deep learning', which, starting from real content (images and audio), can modify or recreate, in an extremely realistic way, the features and movements of a face or body and faithfully imitate a given voice.

Deepfake technologies, developed as an aid to cinematic special effects, were initially very expensive and uncommon but, in recent times, apps and software have emerged that allow even highly sophisticated deepfakes to be created, using an ordinary smartphone. The prevalence of deepfakes has, as a result, greatly increased, and with it the associated risks.

That carried out with deepfakes is a particularly serious form of identity theft: people who appear in a deepfake without their knowledge, in fact, not only suffer a loss of control over their image, but are also deprived of control over their ideas and thoughts, which can be misrepresented based on the false speech and behaviour they express in the videos. They may, moreover, be depicted in places or contexts or with people they have never been with or would never be with, or in situations that might appear compromising.

1507. In essence, then, a deepfake can reconstruct contexts and situations that never actually occurred and, if this is not intended by those involved, can pose a serious threat to people's privacy and dignity.

In particular, the use of deepfakes can contribute to the phenomenon of cyberbullying: deepfake videos, in fact, can be created ad hoc to carry out real acts of cyberbullying, which mainly have young people as victims. A deepfake can be made to denigrate, mock, and discredit the people involved or, even, to blackmail them, making financial or other demands in exchange for not spreading the video (or for its deletion, if it has already been spread).

1508. Similarly, deepfakes may involve politicians or opinion leaders, with the aim of influencing public opinion. Deepfake videos may, for example, be shown or sent to voters who sympathize with a particular political figure, depicting him or her performing unlawful actions or being in unseemly situations, in order to discredit him or her and influence opinion or voting. In this way, deepfakes can, therefore, contribute to the spread of fake news and disinformation.

1509. Again, and more generally, deepfakes are employed in various areas of cybercrime. Deepfake videos or audio-messages created by malicious actors can be sent to our colleagues, friends, or relatives to invite them to click on links or open attachments to messages that expose PCs, smartphones, or other devices and systems to dangerous intrusions, or to convince them to provide, by deceiving their trust, sensitive information and data. Finally, today, many digital systems (home automation, voice assistants, smartphones, as well as some banking or health care systems) use voice and facial biometrics as an authentication system for access: video and audio deepfake messages could be used to deceive such systems.

1510. In particular types of deepfakes, known as deepnudes, then, the faces of unsuspecting people can be 'grafted', using special software, onto the bodies of other subjects, whether naked, in discreet poses, compromising situations, or even in pornographic contexts. It is also possible to take images of clothed bodies and 'undress' them, reconstructing what the body would look like under clothing and creating highly realistic images.

1511. Again, this phenomenon initially involved celebrities for the purpose of discrediting or blackmailing them. In recent times, however, the risk has also come to involve ordinary people, who can become the object of psychologically and socially very damaging actions.

1512. The deepnude content thus produced, in fact, can be used in the context of revenge porn, consisting of the online sharing, for the purpose of blackmail, denigration or revenge, by former partners, lovers or rejected suitors, of photos and videos with sexual or pornographic content.

1513. They can, likewise, also be used, without the full knowledge of the individuals depicted in the images, to fuel the practice of sexting (i.e., the exchange and dissemination of nude images), illegal pornography, and child pornography.

Finally, they can be exploited for extortion purposes: the reference here is to sextortion, i.e., the development of extortionary conduct in which sexually explicit multimedia content is used to extort utilities under threat of their online dissemination.

1514. It is clear, then, that artificially made images disseminated on the web could have the same effect as real ones on the reputation and dignity of the person portrayed, with the difference, however, that for real ones, the legal system provides effective legal protection. Just think of Article 612-*ter* of the Criminal Code, which regulates the unlawful dissemination of sexually explicit images or videos.

Such protection does not seem, however, to apply to artificially created images as well, although the offense to the protected legal asset might turn out to be the same. In fact, the principle of legality of criminal law – according to which no one can be punished for an act that is not provided for by law as a crime – entails, among other things, the prohibition of analogy.

1515. A different argument can be made, however, in the case where the crime concerns images depicting minors, as the Criminal Code provides for a specific crime of 'virtual pornography' in Article 600-*quater* 1: in fact, the crimes of child pornography and possession of child pornographic material are also considered to be integrated in the case where the images of minors are made with 'graphic processing techniques not associated in whole or in part with real situations, the quality of representation of which makes non-real situations appear to be true'.

1516. In 2021, a bill was submitted on a parliamentary initiative to introduce Article 612-*quater* of the Criminal Code to provide for a new criminal offence consisting of the dissemination of artificially manipulated images of real people, through the use of technological tools or artificial intelligence systems, for the purpose of obtaining nude representations of them, suitable for misleading.

1517. The proposed legislation contemplates four alternative ways of integrating the crime, which can be carried out by anyone who 'sends, gives, publishes and disseminates' the images, which therefore may not even coincide with the author of the manipulation. The penalty, unless the act constitutes a more serious crime, is imprisonment from two to seven years and a fine from EUR 6,000 to EUR 16,000.

The second paragraph, then, regulates the aggravating circumstances: in particular, the punishment is increased if the acts are committed by the spouse, even if separated or divorced, or by a person who is or has been linked by affectionate relationship to the offended person or if the acts are committed through computer or telematic tools.

Currently, however, the examined proposal has not yet been converted into law.

§8. Hate Speech

1518. In Italy, the regulation of hate speech, including homophobic speech and online antisemitism, is covered by various legal provisions and has been shaped by both national and European Union law.

Article 3 of the Italian Constitution (1948) guarantees equality before the law without distinction of sex, race, language, religion, political opinions, or personal and social conditions. This provision is a cornerstone in the fight against discrimination, including hate speech.

Article 21 of the Constitution guarantees freedom of expression. However, this right is not absolute and is subject to limitations, especially when it conflicts with other constitutional rights, such as the right to dignity or equality.

1519. Concerning criminal Code Provisions, Legge Mancino (Mancino Law – Law No. 205 of 1993 is one of the key legal instruments addressing hate speech in Italy.

It criminalizes acts of incitement to violence, hatred, or discrimination on racial, ethnic, national, or religious grounds. The law also penalizes the dissemination of ideas based on racial superiority or hatred, including the use of symbols or gestures related to racist ideologies, such as the Nazi salute.

1520. Article 604-*bis* of the Italian Penal Code, amended by the Mancino Law, specifically prohibits the incitement to discrimination or violence on the grounds of race, ethnicity, nationality, or religion.

Article 604-*ter* provides for aggravated penalties if crimes are committed with the purpose of discrimination or with hatred on the grounds mentioned above.

1521. Anti-Discrimination Law Legge Reale (Law No. 654 of 1975) originally transposed the International Convention on the 'Elimination of all forms of racial discrimination' into Italian law. It was later amended by the Mancino Law to include provisions against hate speech.

1522. Concerning homophobic speech, while there is no specific law exclusively addressing homophobia in the same way as racial or ethnic discrimination, homophobic speech can be prosecuted under the general provisions of the Penal Code, particularly where it overlaps with incitement to hatred or violence.

1523. In recent years, there has been significant debate around the so-called Zan Bill (DDL Zan), which sought to expand the existing anti-discrimination laws to include discrimination based on sexual orientation and gender identity. However, this bill was not passed into law due to political opposition and procedural blocks in the Senate.

1524. Antisemitism speech is treated under the broader context of hate speech against religious groups. The provisions under the Mancino Law apply to antisemitic acts, and the Italian legal system has historically been active in prosecuting Holocaust denial and similar offenses.

In 2016, Italy introduced a law specifically criminalizing Holocaust denial (Law No. 115 of 2016), making it an aggravating factor for the offense of spreading ideas based on racial or ethnic hatred.

1525. From an international point of view, concerning Framework Decision 2008/913/JHA, Italy, as an EU member, is required to comply with the EU's Framework Decision on combating certain forms and expressions of racism and xenophobia by means of criminal law. This decision mandates member states to criminalize public incitement to violence or hatred based on race, colour, religion, descent, or national or ethnic origin.

1526. According to Rome Court ('Tribunale') of 3 December 2022, the operator of a social media platform has an obligation to remove content based on racial or ethnic hatred and to suspend the account of the user who posted it

In the event of the publication within a social media platform of content characterized by hate speech based on race or ethnicity and of symbols representing or praising an organization that incites hatred or incites violence, according to the contractual conditions governing the service, the platform operator may suspend or permanently disable the user's access to his or her personal account. Such content not only violates the contractual conditions but is unlawful under the entire national and European regulatory system, and the platform operator, once it becomes aware of it, has a legal duty to remove it.

1527. Rome Court of Law of 23 February 2020 decided on hate speech and online hate behaviour in an important political case.

Freedom of manifestation of thought does not include hostile and discriminatory speech based on intolerance (prohibited at various levels by domestic and supranational law). The obligations imposed by supranational law require that control be exercised, and this obligation is also imposed, within certain limits, on social networks such as Facebook.

Facebook's terms of use prohibit content that can be construed as hate speech, which takes the form of a direct attack on people on the basis of aspects such as race, ethnicity, nationality of origin, religion, sexual orientation, caste, sex, gender or gender identity, and disability or serious illness, because it creates an environment of intimidation and exclusion and, in some cases, can promote real violence.

On the basis of the aforementioned internal and supranational regulations and their constant application in case law, and the Code of Conduct signed with the European Commission and the terms of use, Facebook has the right to terminate the contract with users who as administrators manage the pages of the various branches of the Forza Nuova organization; Facebook has a legal duty to terminate the contracts, since it is clear that the reference to the ideals of fascism in numerous public initiatives and public demonstrations qualifies Forza Nuova as a hate organization, i.e., an association of at least three people organized with a name, sign or symbol and which carries out an ideology, statements or physical actions against individuals on the basis of characteristics such as race, religious belief, nationality, ethnicity, gender, sex, sexual orientation, serious illness or disability.

1528. According to Court of Cassation Criminal section V of 15 May 2013, Decision No. 25870, the aggravating circumstance of the purpose of discrimination or of ethnic, national, racial or religious hatred is integrated when the action relates, in the current meaning, to the manifest prejudice of the inferiority of a race, since it is not necessary that the incriminated conduct is intended or, at least, potentially capable of making the reprehensible sentiment or, therefore, of arousing it, perceptible to the outside world, in any case, the danger of discriminatory behaviour or emulative acts, also because this would have the unreasonable consequence of excluding the aggravating circumstance in question in all cases where the damaging action took place in the absence of third persons. In the case, the Court confirmed the aggravating circumstance in question for the insults addressed to a Nigerian boy by some of his classmates.

1529. According to Court of Cassation Criminal section V of 26 October 2022, Decision No. 3417, the aggravating circumstance of the purpose of discrimination or ethnic, racial or religious hatred is configurable not only when the action, due to its intrinsic characteristics and to the context in which it takes place, is intentionally aimed at making perceivable to the outside world and at arousing in others similar feelings of hatred and in any case at giving rise, in the future or in the immediate future to the concrete danger of discriminatory behaviour, but also when it relates, in the current meaning, to a manifest prejudice of inferiority of a single race, the subjective motion of the agent not being relevant. In the case, the aggravating circumstance was recognized with respect to the offence of defamation committed by the defendant in relation to an expression, with which he had unduly attributed to the offended person the unworthiness of being a member of the assembly of Italian citizens, evoking an alleged inferiority in light of his African origins and the colour of his skin.

1530. According to Court of Cassation, Criminal section I of 6 December 2021, Decision No. 4534, the like on antisemitic posts published on social networks is a serious indication of the crime of incitement to racial hatred. The like, in fact, not only demonstrates, crossed with other evidence, adherence to the virtual Nazi-fascist group, but also contributes to the greater dissemination of a message, already in itself capable of reaching an indeterminate number of people. This was said by the Court of Cassation, rejecting the appeal against a precautionary measure ordered by the Gip, for the crime of incitement to racial hatred, a crime contested mainly based on the social activity of the suspect, who interacted with a neo-Nazi virtual community, whose main purpose was propaganda and incitement to racial hatred.

The judges emphasized the way in which social networks, and Facebook in particular, work, centred on an algorithm that considers likes relevant and assigns a higher value to posts that receive more comments.

1531. According to Court of Cassation, Criminal section I of 19 November 2021, Decision No. 3808, the distribution of leaflets in the public street extolling the superiority of the white race integrates the crime of propaganda of ideas based on racial hatred.

It is an offence to propagandize ideas based on racial or ethnic superiority or hatred, as well as on the denial of the Shoah, to distribute leaflets and posters in the public street extolling the superiority of the white race against the presence of Judaism in Europe, inspired by National Socialism and the denial of the Jewish Holocaust, since the justification of the right to the free expression of thought cannot be invoked in the dissemination of negationist or 'revisionist' assertions totally detached from the criticism and historical analysis of facts definitively ascertained and documented by the international community.

1532. According to Court of Cassation, Criminal section V of 7 May 2019, Decision No. 32862, for the purposes of the configurability of the offence provided for in Article 3, paragraph 1, letter a), first part, of Law No. 654, as amended, 'propaganda of ideas' consists in the dissemination of opinions aimed at influencing the behaviour or psychology of a wide public and gathering adhesions; 'racial or ethnic hatred' is integrated by a feeling capable of determining the concrete danger of discriminatory behaviour, and not by any feeling of generic antipathy, intolerance or rejection ascribable to reasons relating to race, nationality or religion; 'discrimination on racial grounds' is that based on the personal quality of the subject, and not – instead – on his behaviour. Applying this principle, the Court reclassified under the provision indicated the conduct of the applicant, an MEP who, in the context of a radio broadcast, had commented on the meeting between the President of the Chamber of Deputies and representatives of the Sinti and Roma communities, attributing to the latter 'a certain technological culture of burglarizing the lodgings of honest people' and a tendency to aversion to work, and justifying as 'a Pavlovian reflex dictated by centuries of experience' the instinct 'to put your hand in your wallet pocket to prevent them from taking it away'.

1533. According to Court of Cassation, Criminal section V of 2 November 2017, decision no. 7859, the aggravating circumstance of the purpose of racial discrimination is configurable even if the discriminatory message is spread on Facebook.

The aggravating circumstance of the purpose of discrimination or ethnic, racial or religious hatred is configurable not only when the action, due to its intrinsic characteristics and the context in which it takes place, is intentionally aimed at making it perceivable externally and arousing in others similar feelings of hatred and in any case at giving rise, in the future or in the immediate future, to the concrete danger of discriminatory behaviour but also when it relates, in the current meaning, to a manifest prejudice of inferiority of a single race.

The case related to the offence of aggravated defamation by means of a message published on Facebook in which the defendant invited the offended person, of African ethnicity, to return to the 'jungle'.

1534. According to Court of Rome, section VI of 12 November 2013, Decision No. 18931, stating Holocaust denier theses in an aseptic manner, without using terms indicative of the superiority of the Aryan people and without expressing hatred towards the Jewish people does not constitute the offence of spreading or propagating ideas based on racial superiority or hatred (Article 3, paragraph 1, letter a) L. 654/1975).

In the present case, an art history teacher had expounded Holocaust denialist theses with a pupil outside class hours, and in a subsequent class council meeting with two colleagues.

§9. Substitution of Person

1535. The traditional crime of substitution of person, not designed for a digital age, has made a comeback in recent years thanks to the use of e-mail and, above all, social networks and profiles.

1536. According to Trento Court of Appeal of 6 May 2024, Decision No. 58, the negotiation was carried out on WhatsApp, following an advertisement on a website for the sale of goods, in which the defendant gave false personal details and, by means of deception and artifice, captured the victim's trust by convincing him to give money, constitutes the offences of substitution of person and fraud. Whereas the mere failure to deliver a good offered for sale does not constitute a 'quid pluris', represented by the malicious conduct of the agent, as well as by facts and circumstances capable of determining in the victim a reasonable reliance on the apparent honesty of the active subject's intentions and on the actual delivery of the good itself.

1537. According to Court of Vicenza of 7 March 2024, Decision No. 244, the use of a false identity for the publication of an advertisement on the Internet is substitution of person.

The offence of substitution of person shall be committed by anyone who, using a false name, places an advertisement on an Internet platform for the rental of a holiday property and enters into negotiations with the offended person. It must be declared that there is no need to proceed with the offence of fraud in case of failure to file a complaint.

1538. According to Court of Cassation, Criminal section V of 20 September 2022, Decision No. 41801, the hypothesis of substitution of person exists in the conduct of a person who creates a false profile on a social network using the references of the offended person.

The conduct of a person who creates a false profile on a social network using the offended person's references, thereby misleading those who communicated with him through the chat and causing them to disturb or harass the victim.

In the case in point, it had emerged that the defendant had used a mobile telephone number available to him so the judges had logically considered that the creation of the false profile was the work of the defendant.

1539. According to Court of Cassation, Criminal section V of 14 October 2021, Decision No. 323, the offence of substitution of person is committed by those who create and use social profiles using the personal data of another person.

The conduct of a person who creates and uses 'social profiles' and 'Internet accounts' by using the personal data of another person, in order to make the latter responsible for the connections made on the network, integrates the crime.

1540. According to Court of Pescara of 12 February 2021, No. 2246, the creation of a false profile on a social dating platform, by means of which one engages in conversations of a sexual nature, passing oneself off as the person whose identity has been stolen, communicating with several people by disseminating information and photos detrimental to the person's reputation, constitutes the offences of substitution of person and defamation by means of publicity.

1541. According to Court of Cassation Criminal section V of 5 February 2021, Decision No. 12062, a person who creates a social profile using the image of a different and unaware subject constitutes the crime of person substitution.

The conduct of a person who creates and uses a profile on a social network abusively using the image of a different (and unaware) subject, insofar as it is suitable for the representation of a digital identity not corresponding to the subject who uses it, constitutes the offence of substitution of person.

1542. According to Court of Cassation, Criminal section V of 13 July 2020, Decision No. 25215, a person who creates and uses sim cards with personal data of a different, unaware subject commits the offence of substitution of person.

The conduct of a person who creates and uses a 'sim-card' using the personal data of another person, unaware of the fact, with the aim of making the attribution of the connections made on the network fall on the latter, thus disguising their personal use, constitutes the offence.

The case related to the use of a plurality of 'sim cards', abusively registered in the name of unaware third parties, in order to carry out, in their name, 'on-line' movements on current accounts, for the reversal of the funds transferred therein.

1543. According to Court of Cassation Criminal section V of 6 July 2020, decision No. 22049, the creation of a profile on a social network using the image of another person constitutes the offence referred to in Article 494 of the Criminal Code.

The conduct consisting in the creation of a profile on a social network with the abusive use of the image of a totally unaware person constitutes the offence of substitution of person, since in this way a digital identity is represented that does not correspond to the person using the profile.

In the present case, the Supreme Court declared inadmissible the appeal of the defendant, convicted for the offences referred to in Articles 494 and 595 of the Criminal Code, for having created false Facebook profiles represented by caricature photos of the offended person and having damaged the reputation of the same through the Internet, pointing out that, for the purposes of the configurability of the crime of substitution of person, the illegitimate substitution of one's own person for the person of another is sufficient, with the consequent irrelevance of the fact that a caricature image of the offended person was disclosed, the latter circumstance being relevant for the purposes of the integration of the crime of defamation.

1544. According to Court of Cassation Criminal section II of 2 July 2020, No. 23760, whoever enters in the home banking system using the identification codes of another unaware person commits substitution of person.

The conduct of a person who enters the operating system of a home banking service by using the personal identification codes of another unaware person, in order to obtain an unfair profit to the detriment of the owner of the identity abusively used, by means of money transfer operations, constitutes the offence of substitution of person pursuant to Article 494 of the Criminal Code.

The case related to a computer fraud to the detriment of the holder of a postal bank card, committed prior to the introduction of the third paragraph of Article 640-*ter* of the Criminal Code, in which the Court held exempt from censure the judgment that had found the formal concurrence of the offences referred to in Articles 640-*ter* and 494 of the Criminal Code.

1545. According to Court of Cassation Criminal section V of 19 November 2019, Decision No. 652, the act of creating a false social profile, attributing oneself the identity of another person, if it is isolated, is to be considered of minor entity.

For the purposes of the configurability of the offence of substitution of person pursuant to Article 494 of the Criminal Code through the establishment of a social profile in the name of another person, the sending of a post is not enough to consider the offensiveness of the fact on the presumed breadth of the dissemination on the internet. This was said by the Court of Cassation, considering the fact of creating a false social profile, thus attributing oneself the identity of another person, to be of minor importance if the fact is isolated. For the judges of legitimacy, if committed only once, the fact may not be punishable based on Article 131-*bis* of the Criminal Code, which introduced precisely a particular cause of exclusion of punishability when the conduct as a whole is considered minor.

1546. According to Court of Cassation Criminal section V of 22 June 2018, Decision No. 42572, the conduct of a person who, using the personal data of another person, creates a false account on the eBay website constitutes substitution of person.

The offence of substitution of person (Article 494 of the Criminal Code) constitutes the conduct of a person who creates and uses an account and a mailbox or registers on an e-commerce site using the personal data of a different unaware person, with the aim of causing the latter to be responsible for the non-fulfilment of the obligations resulting from the purchase of goods by participating in online auctions or other contractual tools.

1547. According to Court of Cassation Criminal section V of 23 March 2018, Decision No. 20485, through the IP address it is possible to identify the associated electronic device but not the user, whose identification requires further investigation.

Through the IP (Internet Protocol) address, it is possible to objectively identify the associated electronic device, while the identification of the operator who used that device requires further investigations, of a technical or logical nature. In the case, the Court, considered correctly motivated the identification of the defendant as the author of the offences, through the exploitation of the fact that he had turned out to be the exclusive user of the personal computer connected to the IP address, in the absence of elements that could lead to believe the use by third parties of the home network, protected by a password.

In matters of computer crimes, the ascertainment of the IP address of the device is sufficient, even in the absence of further technical investigations, for the conviction for abusive access and substitution of person of the person who accesses the Facebook profile of a third party. This was established by the Court of Cassation, which rejected the defendant's appeal, considering it unnecessary to carry out further technical investigations necessary to overcome the limits in the association between the Internet Protocol detected and the user/owner of the system. For the Court, therefore, the IP address is sufficient, consisting of a numerical code that uniquely identifies a device – host – connected to a computer network that uses the Internet Protocol as its network protocol.

Chapter 4. Criminal Procedural Aspects

§1. Criminal Procedure and New Technologies in Italy (and Some General Principles)

I. Introduction

1548. The relationship between new technologies and *criminal procedural law* has been developing, in Italy, since the mid-1990s, when the first criminal cases related to the new legislation on computer crimes, Law Bo. 574 of 1993[271] (later amended in 2008), began to emerge.[272]

This legislation, in addition to introducing computer crimes (and thus initiating criminal proceedings in this regard), also amended some provisions of the Code of Criminal Procedure to better regulate the collection of digital evidence sources and their production in Court.[273]

1549. The first cases that were discussed before Italian jurisprudence concerned the *repeatability* or *non-repeatability* of certain activities performed on computer systems, the best ways to *intercept* computer and telematic communications and the limits to be respected, the correct way to make a *copy-image* of devices and data (without seizing and blocking the entire system), the use of particularly *invasive tools* in investigations (such as computer 'capturers' or trojans) and, in more recent times, the nature of communications via WhatsApp.[274]

1550. A lively debate has also arisen in recent years with regard to the problem of *data retention*, the use of *hacking tools* by law enforcement agencies, the use of *anti-forensic* tools by criminals (such as encryption) and the handling of data in new social networks and secure messaging systems.[275]

1551. In this Chapter, we will briefly address all these issues, starting with substantive and procedural law and enriching the exposition with the most interesting *case law* that has occurred in Italy in recent years.

1552. A first, general principle was stated by the Court of Cassation, section V of 23 March 2022, Decision No. 15648, declaring that the prosecutor may retain the full copy of the digital data *only* for the time necessary to select the information having evidentiary function.

---

271. *See* the full official text, in Italian, at https://www.normattiva.it/uri-res/N2Ls?urn:nir:stato:legge:1993-12-23;547.
272. *See*, G. Vaciago '*Digital evidence. I mezzi di ricerca della prova digitale nel procedimento penale e le garanzie* dell'indagato' (Giappichelli, Torino, 2012).
273. *See*, M. Iaselli '*Investigazioni* digitali' (Giuffrè, Milano, 2020).
274. *See*, S. Aterno, F. Cajani, G. Costabile, D. Curtotti (eds) '*Cyber forensics e indagini digitali. Manuale tecnico-giuridico e casi* pratici' (Giappichelli, Torino, 2021).
275. *See*, G. Ziccardi, L. Lupária '*Investigazione penale e tecnologia informatica.* L'accertamento del reato tra progresso scientifico e garanzie fondamentali' (Giuffrè, Milano, 2007).

According to the judges, on the subject of evidence, the judicial authority, in order to examine a large mass of information whose contents are potentially relevant to the investigation, may order a seizure with *very extensive contents*, providing, however, in accordance with the principles of *proportionality* and *adequacy*, the *immediate return* of the items subjected to constraint as soon as the time reasonably necessary for the investigations has elapsed.

So that, in the event of failure to timely return, the interested party may submit the relevant application and assert its reasons, if necessary, including through the remedies offered by the system.

This is particularly relevant in the case of seizure of computer equipment, copy of the seized equipment and return of the computer equipment, in the sense that, once the equipment has been returned, the public prosecutor may retain the full copy of the equipment only for the time strictly necessary to select, among the multiplicity of information contained therein, only what fulfils the evidentiary function underlying the seizure and, once the selection operations have been completed, he must return the copy to the rightful claimants.

1553. A second interpretation was stated by Court of Cassation, Criminal Section, section VI of 20 December 2018, Decision No. 15838, about the mentioned 'unrepeatable' technical assessments and analysis.

According to the judges, the notion of 'ascertainment' in hypothesis 'unrepeatable' (Article 360 of the Code of Criminal Procedure) does not include activities that result in the ascertainment or collection of materials pertinent to the crime or its evidence, which are exhausted in simple 'findings', but only activities that result in the study and critical elaboration of such findings, which can be defined as 'unrepeatable' if they are *no longer reproducible* in the hearing except with the definitive loss of the evidentiary information or its genuineness.

As a result, the taking of gunpowder, the enhancement and subsequent extraction of fingerprints, the *extraction of copies of files from a computer*, the activity of extrapolating frames from a video medium, are some examples.

From these premises, the Court ruled out the applicability of the rules on unrepeatable technical investigations pursuant to Article 360 of the Code of Criminal Procedure in relation to the activity of *extracting* films and images taken from a video surveillance system, arguing that the files reproducing the video recordings made by the video surveillance system should instead be considered as 'documents', which can be acquired in the trial according to the rules laid down in Article 234 of the Code of Criminal Procedure.

1554. According to Court of Cassation, Criminal section, section I of 10 June 2021, No. 38909, the extraction of data stored on the memory of a mobile phone *does not constitute* an irrepealable technical assessment.

In the written words of the judges, the extraction of data stored in a computer medium, such as the memory of a mobile phone, *does not constitute* a non-repeatable technical assessment, not even after the entry into force of Law No. 48

of 18 March 2008,[276] which only introduced the obligation to adopt acquisition methods suitable for guaranteeing the conformity of the computer data acquired with the original data, with the result that neither the failure to adopt such methods nor, upstream, the failure of the parties to discuss the matter entail the impossibility to use the acquired evidentiary results, without prejudice to the need to assess, in concrete terms, the existence of any alterations to the original data and the correspondence with them of the extracted data.

1555. In the decision of the Court of Cassation, Criminal section V of 4 December 2017, No. 5175, the judges stated that the *printing* of the insulting post is sufficient to prove defamation.

Law No. 48 of 2008 (Ratification of the Budapest Convention on Cybercrime) does not introduce *any legal proof requirement*, limiting itself to requiring the adoption of technical measures and procedures suitable to ensure the preservation of the original computer data and the conformity and immutability of the extracted copies to avoid the risk of alteration, *without* however imposing *typified procedures.*

It follows that the judge may assess them according to his *own free conviction* (this was a case concerning the publication of an insulting post on Facebook).

1556. The Italian Criminal Procedure Code was amended during the last twenty-five years, in order to facilitate the work of investigators and procedural mechanisms in case of events related to computer crimes.

In particular, the examined topics were that of telecommunication interception, acquiring the correct source of digital evidence and law enforcement, or covert, in telecommunication environments (with particular reference to cases of child pornography).

The changes, however, have not been many. Traditional institutions in the Code are often adapted without difficulty to the new technological framework.

1557. The first changes date back to 1993. The Commission appointed to modify the Criminal Code in order to include those crimes that have, as their object or means, an electronic processor, has also dealt with some provisions of the Criminal Procedure Code, in particular, for what concerns the interception of information or telematic communications. It has proposed, through Articles 11, 12 and 13 of Law No. 547/93, the insertion of Article 266-*bis* in the Criminal Procedure Code ('Interception of Computer and Telematic Communications') and the modification of Article 268 (relating to the execution of interception operations).

This choice was justified, by the bill's accompanying report, with the 'exigency to prepare more adequate forms of penal protection against the so-called computer criminality … jointly with the proposal to reassess the substantial cases in point of the Criminal Code'.

1558. It is useful to immediately observe that the provision contained in Article 266-*bis* allows the interception of the flow of communication between computer and

---

276. *See* https://www.normattiva.it/uri-res/N2Ls?urn:nir:stato:legge:2008;48.

telecommunication systems in all those cases in which the proceeding's object is the assessment of crimes performed by employing computer or telematic technologies.

On the object of the examined provision, doctrine and jurisprudence[277] agree that 'telematic flows' has to be identified with the collection, by means of computer or telematic instruments, of restricted communications or correspondences.

The strict hypothesis in which the interception of conversations or communications is allowed is the same provided by Article 266 of the Criminal Procedure Code and refers in particular to proceedings that regard unintentional crimes for which the punishment provided is life imprisonment or imprisonment five years over the maximum, determined according to Article 4, that include: (i) crimes against Public Administration for which the punishment provided is imprisonment not less than a maximum of five years, determined according to Article 4; (ii) crimes concerning drugs or psychotropic substances; (iii) crimes concerning weapons or explosive substances; (iv) crimes of contraband; (v) crimes of insult, threat, usury, abusive financial activity, harassment or disturbance of persons through a telephone; (vi) crimes provided by Article 600-*ter* (child pornography); (vii) ordinances relating to crimes performed through the use of computer or telematic technologies.

1559. The interception of flows, even if regards a computer or telematics communication, is subject to the general regulation provided by Article 266 of the Criminal Procedure Code with reference to its admissibility; therefore, the public prosecutor has to request the judge for preparatory investigations to authorize the disposition of interception operations, except in urgent cases in which the public prosecutor can dispose of the interception through a motivated ordinance that has to be validated within 48 hours from its issuance.

The length of interception operations cannot exceed 15 days, renewable by the judge for another 15 days.

1560. Regarding Article 268 of the Code of Criminal Procedure, Statute 547/93 has provided the inclusion of the possibility to perform interceptions through systems belonging to private parties that cannot deny their disposability.

The implementation of the 2001 Council of Europe Convention on Cybercrime (Budapest Convention on Cybercrime) was completed through Law No. 48 of 18 March 2008. Changes also affected the Code of Criminal Procedure.

From the words used, it is clear that, for the first time, there is a legislator's attention to the techniques of computer forensic to search for digital evidence.

1561. Where the inspections cover digital traces, under Article 244 as amended, any technical operation in relation to computer systems or telecommunications must adopt technical measures aimed at ensuring the preservation of the original data and prevent the alteration.

During the search, as amended by Article 247, where there are grounds to believe that data, information, software or other evidence relevant to the offence are in a

277. L. Marafioti, 'Digital evidence e processo penale', in 'Cass. pen.', n. 12/2011, 2011, p. 4509B; V. Plantamura, 'La tutela penale delle comunicazioni informatiche e telematiche', in 'Dir. inform.', fasc. 6/2006, 2006, p. 847. For jurisprudence *see* below.

computer system or computer, even if protected by security measures, the investigator must adopt technical measures aimed at ensuring the preservation of the original data and prevent tampering.

The amended Article 352 authorizes law enforcement officers, adopting technical measures for the conservation and to prevent the alteration, to search the computer systems or computer, even if protected when there is reason to believe that there are hidden data, information, computer programs or traces still relevant to the offence that might be deleted or missing.

The judicial police officers shall, also, adopt technical measures or provide prescriptions necessary to ensure preservation and prevent tampering and access, and provide, where possible, the bit-stream image copy to appropriate supports, through a procedure that ensures compliance of the original copy and its immutability.

1562. Law No. 48 of 18 March 2008 introduced in the Italian Code of Criminal Procedure some important rules on inspection and searching activities of computers or telecommunication networks.

The extreme volatility of the electronic data, in fact, has forced the Legislator of the Budapest Convention and, consequently, the Italian one, to indicate specific modalities to ensure a proper preservation of the data integrity, thereby fully incorporating computer forensics in the Italian Criminal Procedure Code.

II. Articles of the Code of Criminal Procedure of Interest

1563. More than 15 years ago there was the publication in the Official Journal of Law No. 48/2008, a provision through which the legislature has established and recognized, *inter alia*, the usefulness of computerized investigations and the acquisition of digital evidence in criminal proceedings.

The regulation in question, in its effectiveness, a law transposing the well-known Budapest Convention, has among other things and as far as it is of specific interest here, reformulated several articles of the Code of Criminal Procedure dedicated to the means of obtaining evidence.

1564. Through this reformulation, the legislator made a very precise choice: rather than regulating in detail the operational methods of intervention on computer data, it established the need to adopt 'technical measures aimed at ensuring the preservation of the original data and preventing their alteration' (Articles 244, paragraph 2, 247, paragraph 1-*bis*, as well as 352, paragraph l-*bis*, 354, paragraph 2, of the Code of Criminal Procedure); but it has also provided that the data must be processed using a procedure that ensures 'the conformity of the data acquired with the original data and their immutability' (Articles 254-*bis* and, again, 354, paragraph 2, of the Code of Criminal Procedure).

1565. The protection of integrity and authenticity represents the objective, the goal, which must guide the activity of all those actors/subjects that interact with digital data from the first contact with the latter.

The preservation of data therefore unites inspections, searches, and all seizures of computer data at service providers. In a nutshell, the judicial police in charge of carrying out searches and seizures commonly referred to as 'computer' seizures, must adopt technical measures aimed at ensuring the preservation of the original data and preventing their alteration.

1566. The assumption, 'technical measures aimed at ensuring the preservation of the original data and preventing their alteration', is thus summarized and translated into the fact that the judicial police, who first come into contact with digital evidence, will have to take particular care to not to disperse the data, not alter them in any way, ensure their integrity, genuineness and preservation. Law No. 90/2024 amended Article 240 of the Criminal Code on seizure: 'In the case of a conviction, the judge may order the seizure of items that were used or intended to commit the crime, as well as items that are the product or profit of the crime. Seizure is always ordered:

1) of items that constitute the price of the crime;
   1-bis) of goods and computer or telecommunication tools that have been, in whole or in part, used for committing the crimes referred to in articles 615-ter, 615-quater, 615-quinquies, 617-bis, 617-ter, 617-quater, 617-quinquies, 617-sexies, 635-bis, 635-ter, 635-quater, 635-quinquies, 640, second paragraph, number 2-ter), 640-ter, and 640-quinquies, as well as of goods that constitute the profit or product of the crime or sums of money, goods, or other utilities that the perpetrator has at their disposal for a value corresponding to such profit or product, if it is not possible to carry out the seizure of the direct profit or product;
2) of items whose manufacture, use, carrying, possession, or sale constitutes a crime, even if no conviction has been pronounced.

The provisions of the first part and numbers 1 and 1-*bis* of the previous paragraph do not apply if the item or good or the computer or telecommunication tool belongs to a person unrelated to the crime. The provision of number 1-*bis* of the previous paragraph also applies in case of application of the penalty upon request of the parties pursuant to Article 444 of the Code of Criminal Procedure.

The provision of number 2 does not apply if the item belongs to a person unrelated to the crime and its manufacture, use, carrying, possession, or sale can be permitted through administrative authorization'.

1567. The Supreme Court of Cassation in judgment No. 12094/2020, confirmed that the methods of acquisition consisting in the extraction of a forensic copy and the subsequent selection of data by means of keywords, temporal selection and comparison of digests, are to be considered legitimate, proportional and guarantors of a balance between the investigative purposes and the procedural protections provided for, principles that were also affirmed shortly thereafter in another judgment No. 13165/2020.

1568. In the latter case, in addition to affirming the legitimacy and proportionality of the already described methodology, the Court went further in examining the *proportionality* of the measure adopted and the *operational limits* in the acquisition of computer material.

Specifically, the Court, in recognizing the balance between the purposes of investigation and the need of protection, also required adequate evaluations under the quantitative, qualitative and temporal profile of the proportionality of the adopted measure.

1569. According to Court of Cassation, Criminal section VI of 15 February 2024, No. 17312, the prosecutor's decree must set out *the reasons* why it is necessary to order an extensive and all-encompassing seizure.

In particular, in case of evidentiary seizure of computer or telematic devices, in consideration of their technical characteristics (including smartphones), of their memory and storage capacity of a heterogeneous mass of data (messages, photos, e-mails) pertaining to the personal sphere of the owner, in order to allow an adequate assessment of the 'proportionality' of the measure both in the genetic and in the subsequent enforcement phase, it is necessary for the Public Prosecutor to illustrate in the evidentiary seizure decree: (i) the reasons why it is necessary to order an extensive and all-inclusive seizure or, alternatively, the specific information to be searched; (ii) the criteria that must govern the selection of the computer material stored in the device, justifying, also, the possible temporal perimeter of the data of interest in terms significantly different from the temporal perimeter of the provisional indictment; (iii) the timeframe within which such selection will be made with consequent restitution also of the computer copy of the non-relevant data.

1570. The Criminal Court of Cassation, section V of 10 January 2024, Decision No. 13018, stated that the *time limit* within which one may request a review against the prosecutor's search order runs from the date of apprehension of the computer material.

On the subject of evidentiary seizure having as its object computer or telematic devices, the *ten-day time limit* within which the concerned person may apply for a review against the prosecutor's search and seizure decree runs from the date of apprehension of the computer material, including both the hardware and the computer data contained therein, *not from the restitution* to the person entitled of the 'computer container', subsequent to the execution of the full forensic copy, nor from the restitution of the computer data deemed irrelevant, following the extrapolation of the relevant ones, fulfilments that simply determine as many sequential reductions of the objective scope of the original seizure.

In the case in point, in which the apprehension of the computer material and the notification of the seizure order coincided in time, the Court specified that the party may provide evidence that its interest in challenging the order arose only after the concrete enucleation of the data considered to be of investigative relevance, with the consequent identification of the dies a quo for bringing a review on the date on which it was officially notified of the 'reduced' material actually seized.

1571. Regarding the important topic of the *full copy* of computer data subject to seizure, Court of Cassation section VI of 22 September 2020, Decision No. 34265 stated that, according to the principles of proportionality and reasonableness, although it is possible to proceed to the evidentiary seizure of computer or telematic devices, proceeding to the creation of a *clone-copy* of the hard disk conforming to the original, so as to allow the return of the device, it is not however legitimate to retain the whole of the data seized beyond the time necessary to select, among the multiplicity of information collected and contained in the copy, only those pertinent to the crime for which one is proceeding.

Otherwise, in fact, there would be an elusion and an emptying of the scope of Article 253(1) of the Code of Criminal Procedure, which legitimizes the probative seizure only of those things 'necessary' for the ascertainment of the facts.

It follows that the Public Prosecutor, not being able to retain the full copy of the data seized except for the time strictly necessary for their selection, is required to set up an adequate organization to carry out such selection *in the shortest time possible*, especially where the data have been seized from persons unconnected with the offence for which proceedings are being prosecuted, since he must then, immediately after the selection, return the full copy of the data to the rightful claimants.

III. Data Retention

1572. In 2021, in Italy, a lively debate was (re)ignited on the issue of data retention, i.e., the retention time of communication data by telephone companies and providers.

The Garante for data protection, in particular, has asked the government several times for a reform of the discipline: the provision of *seventy-two months* of retention of citizens' information would appear to be contrary, in the interpretation of the Authority, both to the principles derived from the provisions of the European Union and to the idea of minimizing processing, even when carried out for purposes of justice.

1573. From a strictly regulatory point of view, reference is made, in particular, to the storage of both telephone and telematic traffic data as regulated in Article 132 of the Personal Data Protection Code (also known as the Privacy Code, Legislative Decree No 196 of 30 June 2003)[278] and in Article 24 of Law No. 167 of 20 November 2017.[279]

1574. The aforementioned Article 132 provided, in particular, for shorter deadlines: 'without prejudice to the provisions of Article 123(2), data relating to telephone traffic shall be retained by the provider for twenty-four months from the date of communication, for the purposes of investigating and prosecuting offences,

278. *See* https://www.garanteprivacy.it/codice.
279. *See* https://www.gazzettaufficiale.it/eli/id/2017/11/27/17G00180/sg.

while, for the same purposes, data relating to telematic traffic, excluding in any case the contents of communications, shall be retained by the provider for twelve months from the date of communication.

Data relating to unanswered calls temporarily processed by providers of publicly available electronic communications services or of a public communications network shall be retained for thirty days.

Within the retention period imposed by law, if there are sufficient indications of offences for which the law prescribes a penalty of life imprisonment or imprisonment of not less than a maximum of three years, determined in accordance with Article 4 of the Code of Criminal Procedure, and of offences of threatening and harassing or disturbing persons by means of a telephone when the threat, harassment or nuisance is serious, where it is relevant to the ascertainment of the facts, the data is acquired subject to authorization issued by the judge by reasoned decree, at the request of the Public Prosecutor or at the request of the defence counsel of the accused, the person under investigation, the injured party and other private parties'.

1575. Note how Article 24 has significantly lengthened the time:

> 1. With the implementation of article 20 of Directive (EU) 2017/541 of the European Parliament and of the Council of 15 March 2017 on combating terrorism and replacing Council Framework Decision 2002/475/JHA, in order to ensure effective investigative tools in view of the extraordinary needs to combat terrorism, including international terrorism, for the purposes of the investigation and prosecution of the offences referred to in articles 51(3-quater) and 407(2)(a) of the Code of Criminal Procedure, the retention period for telephone and telematic traffic data as well as data relating to unanswered calls, referred to in article 4-bis(1) and (2) of Decree-Law no. 7, converted, with amendments, by Law no. 43 of 17 April 2015, is set at seventy-two months, by way of derogation from the provisions of article 132, paragraphs 1 and 1-bis, of the Personal Data Protection Code, referred to in Legislative Decree no. 196 of 30 June 2003.

1576. The controversy that arose concerned several important aspects.

There is, first of all, an implicit criticism that the Public Prosecutor who directs the investigations should not be the one to 'authorize' themselves to access the data stored by operators, but that this should be decided by a third party to ensure an impartial control on the appropriateness of such access.

In addition to the problem of the reasoned decree of the Public Prosecutor under Italian law, there is, however, also the problem of the retention time of traffic data.

1577. In particular, the Court of Justice had repeatedly recalled the need for a strict principle of *proportionality* in balancing data protection and public security requirements, especially when the retention measures affect all citizens in an undifferentiated manner and without providing, moreover, sufficient guarantees to prevent abuse.

The expansion of retention periods in 2017, from 24 months for telephone traffic, 12 months for telematic traffic and 30 days for unanswered calls, to 72 months (six years) for all types of traffic, has radically worsened the picture.

The motivation is said to be the fight against terrorism, which requires the establishment of increasingly effective investigative tools.

1578. The Garante demanded, therefore, a constructive and corrective intervention in two directions.

The first is to subordinate the acquisition of data to the self-appointment of the G.I.P. or of an administrative authority, i.e., a third party that would initiate an ad hoc procedure and verify the grounds.

In case of urgency, the action of the public prosecutor should still be verified and validated *ex post*.

The second envisages a precise differentiation of the types of traffic – in particular telephone and telematic – and the need for the stricter application of the principle of proportionality, thus lowering retention periods.

1579. An interesting, recent decision of Court of Cassation, Criminal section VI of 9 March 2023, No. 15422, debated about the results of so-called electronic GPS tracking data and their use by the judicial authorities without the need for authorization.

According to the judges, the localization of movements by means of a GPS satellite tracking system (so-called *electronic tailing*) is an atypical means of searching for evidence that does not imply a massive accumulation of sensitive data by the service provider, so that the relevant findings can be used without the need for authorization by the judicial authority, since the provisions of Article 132, paragraph 3, legislative Decree No. 196 of 30 June 2003, as amended, do not apply on printouts, nor do the principles affirmed by the judgment of the EU Court of Justice, Grand Sect, 5 April 2022, case C-140/2020, concerning the compatibility of 'data retention' with directives 2002/58/Ce and 2009/136/Ce, on the processing of personal data and the protection of privacy in the communications sector.

1580. A decision of Court of Cassation, Criminal section II of 10 December 2019, No. 5741, dealt with the *compatibility* with European law of the Italian regulation of traffic data retention. According to the judges, on the subject of the acquisition of data contained in telephone printouts, the Italian rules on the retention of traffic data – so-called data retention – set out in Article 132 of Legislative Decree No. 196 of 30 June 2003, *is compatible* with Directives No. 2002/58/Ce and 2006/24/Ce on the protection of 'privacy', as interpreted by the case law of the Court of Justice of the European Union (Grand Chamber, 8 April 2014, C-293/12 and C-594/12; Grand Chamber, 21 December 2016, C-203/15 and C-698/15), since the exemption established by the rule to the confidentiality of communications is provided for a limited period of time, has as its exclusive objective the investigation and prosecution of offences and is subject to the issuance of a measure by a judicial authority.

The case related to the crime of criminal conspiracy aimed at committing crimes against property in which access to telephone traffic data was deemed lawful following a decree of the public prosecutor, with acquisition made within two years of the communication to the supplier.

IV. Wiretapping

1581. Also in the Italian legal framework, the term 'wiretapping' ('intercettazioni') is generally used to indicate the direct and secret listening and recording of communications, usually by means of mechanical or electronic instruments.[280]

Several constitutional principles revolve around the issue of wiretapping, such as the procedural need to obtain evidence while simultaneously respecting fundamental human rights, i.e., the protection of *privacy*.

In particular, the secrecy of communication is enshrined in Article 15 of the Italian Constitution.[281]

1582. Wiretapping activities constitute a typical activity that finds its natural place in preliminary investigations, especially within the Code of Criminal Procedure, in Articles 266 to 271.

The legislator has provided that wiretapping is only admissible according to *specific limits*: the first concerns the initiation, mainly carried out by the Public Prosecutor; the second relates to control, which concerns the Judge for Preliminary Investigations (GIP).[282]

1583. The prerequisites for wiretapping are set out in Article 267 of the Code of Criminal Procedure, which provides that authorization for operations shall be granted by the G.I.P. by motivated decree, at the request of the Public Prosecutor, if the following two conditions are met: (i) the presence of serious criminal evidence, and (ii) the absolute indispensability of wiretapping for the continuation of the investigation.

A further hypothesis for the use of wiretapping is set out in Article 295 of the Code of Criminal Procedure, when it is necessary to facilitate the search of a fugitive.

1584. Article 266 of the Code of Criminal Procedure defines the objective limits of admissibility of wiretapping, *listing exhaustively* the offences for which this means of searching evidence is allowed: non-culpable offences for which the penalty is life imprisonment or imprisonment for a maximum of more than five years; offences against public administration for which the penalty is imprisonment of not

---

280. *See* D. Scarpino, '*Intercettazioni e delitti di 'criminalità organizzata' tra vecchi problemi e nuove* soluzioni', in 'Cassazione Penale', fasc. 5, 2024, p. 1657.

281. *See* F. N. Ricotta, '*Questioni sull'utilizzo della backdoor a scopo di* investigazione', in 'Cassazione Penale', fasc.7-8, 2022, p. 2836.

282. *See* F. Centorame, '*Le indagini tecnologiche ad alto potenziale intrusivo fra esigenze di accertamento e sacrale inviolabilità dei diritti della* persona', in '*Rivista Italiana di Diritto e Procedura* Penale', fasc. 2, 2021, p. 499.

less than a maximum of five years; offences concerning narcotic drugs or psychotropic substances; offences concerning weapons and explosives, offences of smuggling; offences of insult, threat, usury, abusive financial activity, abuse of privileged information, market manipulation, harassment or disturbance of persons by means of telephone; offences under Article 600-*ter*, third paragraph, of the Criminal Code.

1585. The legislation provides for a maximum period for the duration of wiretapping operations of 15 days, with three possible subsequent extensions up to a maximum limit of 75 days if the conditions for ordering wiretapping continue to be met.

Once this term has expired, the Public Prosecutor has the power to request extensions not exceeding a period of 15 days, if such extensions may allow the acquisition of elements fundamental to the investigation of the offence being prosecuted.

1586. Wiretapping can be divided into three different types: telephone, environmental and telematic.

Telephone wiretapping consist of tapping the conversation that takes place at a distance between two persons, by means of telephone equipment. Despite the evolution of technology, they are still the most widespread today. In order to proceed, it is necessary for the auxiliaries of the Public Prosecutor's Office to ask the telephone operators to compulsorily fulfil the requests made by the Judicial Authority through the use of appropriate technological and organizational facilities. The telephone operators intercept, then duplicate the telephone lines, in a manner that is completely transparent to the user, without him being aware that he is being intercepted. The latter are sent to the Telephone Interception Centre – C.I.T. of the Public Prosecutor's Office from which the request originated. Recordings of intercepted telephone calls are protected with encryption systems so that they are unreadable by persons or computers that do not have the key to decipher their contents. The downside of wiretapping lies in the advancement of technology, as with modern smartphones, traditional calls have become less exploited in favour of those made via the Internet (e.g., WhatsApp voice calls), which are not intercepted by tapping the telephone line.

Environmental eavesdropping refers to the recording of what can be heard within a given location. There are several types of equipment used to carry out this type of eavesdropping, e.g., audio and/or video bugging devices (bugs); micro-recorders; directional laser microphones, for listening to conversations through windows and walls; GPS detectors with possible audio bugs attached. The downside of environmental eavesdropping is mainly backgrounding noise, such as traffic, radio, other people's voices, the use of machinery and various instruments, which very often degrade the quality of audio. As a result, files are enhanced, trying, where possible, to attenuate unnecessary sounds and raise voices of interest.

Internet wiretapping consists of intercepting what is exchanged via the Internet and computer media. This type of eavesdropping can be carried out by acquiring data packets in transit over a network. It can be set up to capture data that is transmitted or received by a user or groups of users. Basic techniques make it possible to acquire data packets while they are in transit from the transmitting device to the receiving one, or by means of spy software installed on the victim's devices, which in turn transmit the data of interest to the eavesdropping station to the unsuspecting user.[283]

1587. In the latter type of interception, spy software must be installed inside the computer devices to be monitored.

Spy software, whether installed on fixed devices such as PCs or on mobile devices such as smartphones or tablets, are special applications that allow to control how the device is used and what information it generates or receives.

Often, internal vulnerabilities in the operating system are exploited to install it, as the spy software needs administrator privileges to be able to record and monitor events that occur. When the spy software is installed, through access to a dedicated portal, the user is able to monitor the contents obtained practically in real time.

1588. The use of spy software on computer devices is permitted only when the clues as to the criminal activity of the suspect are serious and well-founded; in fact, it is up to the judge to determine the place and duration of the interceptions.

It is specified that they are used for serious offences and, in addition, their application has been extended to offences against the public administration committed by public officials, thus specifying exactly the offences for which spy software is to be used in interceptions: mafia-type criminal conspiracy; offences of a terrorist nature; non-culpable offences for which life imprisonment and a sentence of not less than five years is provided for; offences against the Public Administration for which a term of imprisonment of not less than five years is provided for; offences involving psychotropic and narcotic substances, weapons and explosive substances; smuggling offences; insult, usury, market manipulation, abuse of privileged information, harassment and disturbance of persons by telephone; pornography and child pornography offences.

1589. According to Court of Cassation, Criminal section VI of 26 October 2023, No. 44154, the foreign acquisition of *encrypted messaging* on the 'SKY-ECC' platform is not computer data that can be used pursuant to Article 234-*bis* of the Code of Criminal Procedure.

For the judges, on the subject of the European Investigation Order, the subject of the acquisition abroad of encrypted messaging on the 'SKY-ECC' platform does not constitute usable computer data within the meaning of Article 234-*bis* of the Code of Criminal Procedure, so that, in such a case, the acquisition activity, if concerning communications occurred in the 'static' phase, must be framed under the provisions on search and seizure and, in particular, under Article 254-*bis* of the Code of Criminal Procedure, while if concerning communications occurred in the 'dynamic' phase, it must be framed under the provisions of Articles 266 et seq. of the Code of Criminal Procedure on the subject of telephone calls.

283. *See* F. N. Ricotta, '*Obblighi di collaborazione con l'autorità giudiziaria nella decrittazioone dei dispositivi informatici e privilegio contro l'auto*-incriminazione', in 'Cassazione Penale', fasc. 2, 2022, p. 880.

1590. According to Court of Cassation, Criminal section V of 30 May 2017, Decision No. 48370, there are *several limits* in wiretapping and computer capturing.

The use of the computer interceptor cannot be deemed to be excluded for those present in places of private residence where the criminal activity is taking place and must be deemed to be permitted for the execution of wiretapping, pursuant to Article 266-*bis* of the Code of Criminal Procedure.

It is the appellant's duty to specify, in accordance with the principle of specificity of the appeals, which of the data captured by means of a Trojan horse may be considered to be affected by the sanction of *unusability* and to clarify their impact on the overall body of evidence already assessed, so that it may be inferred that they are decisive with reference to the contested measure.

The interception of communications between persons present by means of the installation of a computer capturing device which follows the movements in space of the user of an electronic device (smartphone, tablet, portable PC), is permitted only in proceedings for organized crime offences without the need for prior identification and indication of such places and regardless of the demonstration that they are the site of ongoing criminal activity.

This activity refers, therefore, exclusively to present persons, with the result that the use of this capturing tool is considered legitimate for persons present in the places of private residence where the criminal activity is taking place, but does not exclude other forms of wiretapping, including those pursuant to Article 266-*bis* of the Code of Criminal Procedure, which are not characterized by the dual requirement of being both communicative and between persons present.

On the subject of computer communications, as provided for and regulated by Article 266-*bis* of the Code of Criminal Procedure, the use of computer interceptors (so-called trojans) that are transmitted on the electronic devices (personal computers, tablets, smartphones, etc.) of the subject to be controlled must be considered lawful, with the consequent usability of the results of the flow of intercepted communications, regardless of the place where such devices are located from time to time.

V. The Italian Supreme Court's Guidelines on Computer Seizures

1591. In Decision No. 34625 of 22 September 2020, the Court of Cassation discussed the issue of the operating methods and limits of the probative seizure of computer and telematic material.

In particular, the judges of legitimacy affirmed that, if the seizure is carried out through the 'physical' ablation of the memories, first of all it is necessary to create a *complete copy* of the content of the seized equipment, functional to the restitution of the latter to its legitimate owner.[284]

---

284. *See* among others, on this issue, M. Pittiruti, '*Dalla Corte di cassazione un vademecum sulle acquisizioni probatorie informatiche e un monito contro i sequestri digitali* omnibus', in 'Sistema Penale', 2021, https://www.sistemapenale.it/it/scheda/cass-sez-vi-sent-22-settembre-2020-dep-2-dicembre-2020-n-34265-pres-di-stefano-rel-silvestri.

1592. Subsequently, the full copy thus obtained must be subjected to *analysis* in order to select the information content relevant to the offence for which proceedings are being prosecuted.

At the end of this selection, the integral copy must be *returned* to the rightful owners, since it is not relevant, per se, as something pertinent to the crime, since it is 'a set of indistinct and magmatic data'.[285]

1593. Therefore, the Public Prosecutor may retain the full copy only for the *time strictly necessary* for the selection operation, since he/she must, consequently, make adequate arrangements to carry out this activity in the shortest possible time.

1594. Reading this topical decision, is evident that the issue of copying seized digital data and returning the 'containers' of such data is crucial.[286]

According to the judges, the impact of so-called digital evidence on criminal proceedings has imposed a *rethinking of conceptual models* and the traditional *investigative approach*, precisely because of the particular nature of computer data.

1595. On this topic, it has been explained how the computer document exists regardless of the physical support on which it is embedded (hard disk, pen drive, CD or other suitable instrument); this type of document can be transferred from one support to another and is, for this reason, particularly fragile since the computer data can be altered either by its author or by other persons.

1596. Moreover, one must consider that computer systems contain an innumerable amount of data.

The latter can be of a different nature and circulate easily within the system and can be duplicated on several media.

The heterogeneous nature of the data contained in a computer system means that during computer investigations, 'sensitive' or 'supersensitive' information, i.e., relating to the private and intimate sphere of the suspect, may also be acquired.

1597. As seen before, in order to guarantee the integrity and genuineness of computer data, Law No. 48 of 18 March 2008 intervened by amending the rules on the means of obtaining evidence.

With regard to inspections (Article 244(2) of the Criminal Procedure Code) and searches (Article 247(1-*bis*) of the Criminal Procedure Code) of computer or telematic systems, the adoption of technical measures aimed at ensuring the preservation of the original data and preventing their alteration is prescribed.

1598. In particular, Article 354, paragraph 2, of the Code of Criminal Procedure, in regulating urgent investigations by the judicial police, provides for the adoption of *technical measures* necessary to ensure the preservation of and prevent

---

285. *See* M. Pisati, '*Full collection of data e diritto di* difesa', in 'Rivista Italiana di Diritto e Procedura Penale', fasc.4, 2019, p. 2239.

286. *See* S. Aterno, '*Le investigazioni informatiche e l'acquisizione della prova* digitale', in 'Giur. Merito', fasc. 4, 2013, p. 0955.

the alteration of access to computer systems, also establishing that, where possible, the same police should take care of their immediate duplication on suitable supports, by means of a procedure that ensures the conformity of the copy to the original and its immutability.

1599. A similar reference to the need to make a copy is contained in Article 254-*bis* of the Criminal Procedure Code with reference to the *seizure* of computer data from service providers.

The most appropriate procedure to guarantee the integrity of data consists, as is well known, in the creation of a *clone copy* of the hard disk that conforms to the original, which is made unmodifiable by means of special procedures.

In concrete terms, except in cases where it is necessary to carry out the immediate analysis during the inspection, the seizure of the computer device may precede the search activity, which will then take place in the laboratory and is usually aimed at acquiring the digital data and forming the so-called forensic copy.

1600. In particular, the computer data can be subject to seizure irrespective of the media where it is embedded.

And yet, once the so-called original copy has been created, it is not relevant in itself as something pertinent to the offence since it contains a set of indistinct and magmatic data with respect to which no selective function has been performed in order to verify the link of instrumentality between res, offence and probative need.

1601. The so-called *integral copy* contains all the data included in the container (pc., tablet, telephone), but does not at all satisfy the need to place under seizure only the digital material that is relevant to the offence for which proceedings are being conducted and that performs a necessary evidentiary function.

It follows, as has been specified by the Court of Cassation, that the so-called full copy constitutes only a copy – which allows the return of the container.[287]

1602. The full copy makes it possible to do, after the seizure, what should naturally have been done before, i.e., the verification of which, among the data contained in the container, are those relevant to the crime.

The so-called integral copy is a servant copy, a 'means' copy and not an 'end' copy.

It follows that, once the container has been returned, the Public Prosecutor may retain the integral copy only for the time strictly necessary to select, among the multiplicity of the information contained therein, those which really perform the probative function underlying the seizure.

The selection of the relevant res requires the return of the full copy, the retention of which would otherwise result in a *circumvention* and emptying of the scope of Article 253(1) of the Code of Criminal Procedure, which consents the probative seizure only of those things that are 'necessary' for the ascertainment of the facts.

287. *See* Court of Cassation, s. VI of 4 Mar. 2020, n. 13156.

1603. It follows that the Public Prosecutor: (i) cannot withhold the so-called full copy of the seized data except for the time strictly necessary for their selection; (ii) is required to set up an adequate means to carry out the selection in question in the shortest time possible, especially in the case in which the data have been seized from persons unconnected with the offence for which proceedings are being conducted; (iii) once the selection operations have been completed, the so-called full copy must be returned to the rightful claimants.

1604. According to this decision,[288] the review court did not correctly apply the principles indicated.

The Court, even though it had been asked specific questions relating to the relevance of the seized items and to the proportionality of the means of searching the evidence, did not explain: (i) why, in the face of isolated payments to the Open Foundation by extraneous third parties, an omnivorous and invasive seizure of an undifferentiated series of personal data should be considered legitimate in relation to the offence for which proceedings were being conducted (not in relation to other possible offences, to which no reference was made); (ii) why, in the present case, the possibility of ascertaining the existence of the relevance nexus had to be conformed in a contractual manner in relation to third parties? (iii) why it was quantitatively and qualitatively necessary to carry out the ablation in concrete abatement carried out in relation to the present appellants? (iv) what were the reasons why that documentation was considered relevant in relation to the evidentiary requirements indicated? (v) how could it be consistent with the principles of appropriateness and proportionality for a seizure following which the full copy of the data had to be brought to the attention of the judicial police for preliminary examination? (vi) why that full copy should not be returned? (vii) what was the function of that preliminary examination by the judicial police if the selection of the relevant material was to be carried out by means of a consultation, in which the parties would be heard.

1605. The seizure, which is the subject of the order under appeal, is structurally asymmetrical with respect to the criminal offence in respect of which proceedings were being conducted, to the fact being investigated, to the role that the present applicants would have played in that fact, to its subject-matter; a seizure ends up assuming, on a quantitative and qualitative level, an impermissible exploratory function, aimed at the possible acquisition, direct or indirect, of other criminal offence information.

1606. These are fundamental issues that in themselves empty of value – also in a prospective sense – the framework of reference and absorb the other issues raised; it follows that the contested order and the search and seizure order of 20 November 2019 must be annulled without referral with restitution to the rightful owners of the seized items and without withholding a copy of the data.

---

288. Court of Cassation, s. VI of 4 Mar. 2020, n. 13156.

VI. WhatsApp Communications, Instant Messaging and Digital Forensics in Italy

1607. In digital forensics, particularly within the context of criminal procedures, WhatsApp and instant messaging presents several critical issues.

These challenges are often related to the nature of the platform, the encryption protocols it employs, and the legal implications of accessing and using data retrieved from the app.[289]

1608. WhatsApp uses end-to-end encryption, meaning that messages are encrypted on the sender's device and only decrypted on the recipient's device.

This encryption makes it extremely difficult for investigators to intercept and read messages in transit.

Law enforcement and forensic experts must rely on physical access to the devices or cooperation from the service provider, which may have limitations based on jurisdictional laws and privacy concerns.[290]

1609. Regarding data collection and preservation, ensuring that data collected from WhatsApp is preserved in a forensically sound manner is critical.

WhatsApp data, including messages, media files, and metadata, can be volatile, and improper handling can lead to data corruption or loss.

Investigators must use specialized tools and follow strict protocols to ensure that WhatsApp data is collected and preserved without altering its integrity, making it admissible in court.[291]

1610. Concerning authentication and integrity, establishing the authenticity and integrity of WhatsApp messages as evidence is crucial.

The risk of message manipulation, spoofing, or the use of fake accounts complicates this process.

Investigators need to provide clear proof that the data presented is unaltered and accurately represents the communication between parties involved. This often requires corroborating WhatsApp data with other evidence.

1611. Gaining legal access to WhatsApp data can be difficult, especially when dealing with cross-border investigations. Service providers may be unwilling or unable to provide access to encrypted data without violating privacy laws.

Law enforcement agencies must navigate complex legal frameworks, including obtaining appropriate warrants and working with international legal bodies, to access relevant data.

---

289. *See* O. Mazza, '*Critica delle prove atipiche nella deriva* giurisprudenziale', in 'Diritto di Difesa', fasc.1, 2022, p. 59.

290. *See* A. Capone, '*Intercettazioni e Costituzione: problemi vecchi e* nuovi', in 'Cassazione Penale', fasc.3, 2017, p. 1263.

291. *See* R. Orlandi, '*Usi investigativi dei cosiddetti captatori informatici. Criticità e inadeguatezza di una recente* riforma', in 'Rivista Italiana di Diritto e Procedura Penale', fasc. 2, 2018, p. 538; *see, also*, W. Nocerino, '*Il captatore informatico: un giano bifronte. Prassi operative vs. risvolti* giuridici', in 'Cassazione Penale', fasc. 2, 2020, p. 824.

1612. Also attribution is critical, and it could be difficult to proof that a specific individual sent or received a message on WhatsApp due to the possibility of device sharing or spoofing.

Establishing clear attribution requires linking the account and the device to the individual, which may involve additional forensic evidence such as fingerprints on the device, other linked accounts, or circumstantial evidence.

1613. While the content of WhatsApp messages is encrypted, metadata such as timestamps, message delivery status, and contacts can still be accessible. However, the interpretation of such metadata can be complex.

Forensic experts need to accurately interpret metadata to reconstruct communication timelines and establish connections between suspects, which requires specialized knowledge and tools.

1614. WhatsApp data can be backed up to third-party services like Google Drive or iCloud. These backups may not be encrypted in the same way as the data on the device but accessing them raises privacy concerns and may require different legal procedures.

Investigators must consider these backups as potential evidence sources, but they must also ensure that the retrieval of such data complies with relevant legal standards.

1615. Modern smartphones often have sophisticated locking mechanisms, including biometric locks, which can prevent access to WhatsApp data.

Forensic experts may need to employ advanced techniques to bypass these security features, which can be time-consuming and legally contentious.

1616. WhatsApp is used across various platforms (iOS, Android, Windows, etc.), each with its own data storage and security mechanisms, complicating the forensic process.

Forensic experts need to be familiar with the nuances of different operating systems and how they handle WhatsApp data to ensure comprehensive evidence collection.

1617. Even if WhatsApp data is retrieved and analysed, its admissibility in court can be challenged by how the data was collected, preserved, and interpreted.

Ensuring that the forensic process follows legal standards is essential for the evidence to be admissible. This involves documentation of the chain of custody, adherence to legal protocols, and expert testimony to explain the findings.

1618. A number of very recent case law rulings have concerned communications via WhatsApp in Italy: this is a very topical issue, in which case law is adapting, not without difficulty, to the new forms of communication, trying to embed them in traditional procedural legal categories.

1619. In the decision of Court of Cassation, section II of 15 May 2024, No. 25549, the debate involved the acquisition of WhatsApp messages in accordance with the forms provided for by Article 254 of the Code of Criminal Procedure for the seizure of correspondence.

According to the Court, on the subject of evidence, e-mail messages, 'WhatsApp' messages and text messages stored in the memory of an electronic device retain the legal nature of correspondence even after they have been received by the addressee, so that their acquisition must take place in accordance with the forms provided by Article 254 of the Code of Criminal Procedure for the seizure of correspondence, unless, due to the passage of time or other cause, they lose all topicality in relation to the interest of confidentiality, becoming a mere 'historical' document.

It was a case in which the Court held that there had been no breach of the provisions of Article 254 of the Code of Criminal Procedure on the ground that the judicial police had merely seized the mobile telephone, whereas access to the contents of the correspondence had been granted subsequently by the public prosecutor with his consultant.

1620. In conclusion, on the subject of evidence, e-mails, messages and text messages stored in the memory of an electronic device retain the nature of correspondence even after they have been received by the addressee and they have lost all relevance in relation to the interest in its confidentiality, becoming a mere 'historical' document, so that – until such time – their acquisition must take place in accordance with the forms provided by Article 254 of the Code of Criminal Procedure for the seizure of correspondence.

1621. A second, interesting case (Trento Court of Appeal of 6 of May 2024, No. 58), regarded the use of a false name in a WhatsApp negotiation following an ad on a site, causing fraud and substitution of person.

According to the judges, the negotiation carried out following an advertisement on a website for the sale of a good, in which the defendant gave false personal details and, by means of deception and artifice, captured the victim's trust by persuading him to give money, constitutes the offences of substitution of person and fraud.

Whereas the mere failure to deliver a good offered for sale does not constitute a 'quid pluris', represented by the malicious conduct of the agent, as well as by facts and circumstances capable of causing the victim to reasonably rely on the apparent honesty of the intentions of the active party and on the actual delivery of the good itself.

1622. A third case (Court of Naples section I of 22 March 2024, No. 3236) was related to the probative value of the conversation made via WhatsApp. According to the Court, conversations and text messages extracted from the telephone user are devoid of probative value if they are produced by mere 'Word' transcription and devoid of the computer supports in which the conversations are contained.

The need to deposit the support lies in the fact that this allows the reliability of the evidence itself to be 'checked' by direct examination of the support in order to verify with certainty both the authorship of the recordings and the reliability of what they document.

Given that it is not always possible to deposit the original device (for reasons related to the privacy of the contents, unavailability of the hardware, damage, loss, etc.) and given that the concept of 'original' no longer exists in the digital sphere, since the forensic copy of a device has the same probative value as the device, it is possible to assess the deposit of the forensic copy of the recording device (digital recorder, smartphone, camera, etc.) so as to confer the legal value of computer and documentary evidence to its contents (recordings, films, SMS messages, etc.).

1623. In an important case decided by the Italian Constitutional Court (of 27 July 2023, No. 170), it was established that the notion of correspondence encompasses any communication of thought between individuals also through technological means.

Correspondence, according to the Court, is a broadly inclusive concept, capable of embracing any communication of human thought (ideas, intentions, feelings, data, news) between two or more specific persons, implemented in a manner different from face-to-face conversation and regardless of the characteristics of the technical means used for the purpose of transmitting thought, including any instrument that technological evolution makes available for interpersonal communication purposes, including electronic and computerized ones.

1624. In the decision of the Criminal Cassation section VI of 28 June 2023, No. 38678, the debate was related to the legitimate acquisition by mere photographic reproduction of WhatsApp messages and text messages stored in the phone memory. According to the Court, the messages and text messages stored in the memory of a mobile phone have the nature of documents pursuant to Article 234 of the Code of Criminal Procedure, so that their acquisition by mere photographic reproduction is lawful, since neither the rules on wiretapping nor those relating to the acquisition of correspondence pursuant to Article 254 of the Code of Criminal Procedure are applicable: in fact, we are not in the presence of the capture of a flow of communications in progress, but of the mere ex post documentation of such flows.

1625. The Rome Labour Court of 30 May 2023, No. 5561, stated that WhatsApp messages form full evidence of facts and things represented, if the person against whom they were produced does not disavow their conformity. According to the Court, WhatsApp messages can be included in mechanical representations produced on paper to which the provision of Article 2712 of the Civil Code is applicable, which provides that '...every mechanical representation of facts and things forms full evidence of the facts and things represented, if the person against whom they have been produced does not disavow their conformity ...'.

In the present case, which concerned a case in which the appellant employee had challenged her dismissal on the grounds that the facts on which the dismissal was based were manifestly unfounded, the court hearing the case, in upholding the appeal, held that the dispute brought by the respondent employer had been brought out of time, outside the preclusion period sanctioned by Article 416 of the Code of Civil Procedure so that the aforementioned messages had to be considered as uncontested.

1626. Also According to Criminal Cassation section III of 25 November 2015, No. 928, the rules laid down in Article 254 of the Code of Criminal Procedure concerning the seizure of correspondence are not applicable, but rather those laid down in Article 234 of the same code, concerning documents, with reference to messages and text messages found in a mobile phone subject to seizure, since these texts, not being the direct object of the seizure, do not even fall within the concept of 'correspondence', the notion of which implies a dispatch activity in progress or in any case initiated by the sender by delivery to third parties for delivery.

1627. According to Criminal Cassation, section III of 26 April 2017, No. 38681, messages sent by the defendant via WhatsApp and Facebook to a minor constitute documents originating from the defendant. By document originating from the defendant is meant, pursuant to Article 237 of the Code of Criminal Procedure, the document of which the defendant is the author, i.e., that which specifically concerns his person, even if not signed by him, even if seized from others or produced by others.

In this case, the Court considered correct the acquisition by the trial judge of messages sent through social networks and Facebook by the defendant to a minor, and made available by her to the judicial police at the time of the filing of the complaint.

1628. According to Criminal Cassation, Section V of 19 June 2017, No. 49016, relating to the evidentiary relevance of WhatsApp conversations in digital forensics, the judges stated that the recording of conversations that took place on the computer channel, although it constitutes a form of memorization of a historical fact that can certainly be legitimately used for evidentiary purposes, since it is documentary evidence, must be acquired in the correct manner for the purposes of the trial, as it is not possible to disregard the acquisition of the same telematic or figurative support containing the aforementioned recording in order to verify with certainty both the authorship of the recordings and the reliability of what is documented by them.

1629. The decision of Criminal Cassation section V, 21 November 2017, No. 1822, stated that computer data contained in the mobile phone, SMS or WhatsApp messages, do not fall within the concept of correspondence.

The computer data acquired from the memory of a telephone in use by the person under investigation (text messages, messages, e-mail messages 'downloaded' and/or stored in the memory of the mobile phone) have the nature of documents within the meaning of Article 234 of the Code of Criminal Procedure. The relevant acquisition activity is not subject either to the discipline dictated by Article 254 of the Code of Criminal Procedure for correspondence, since SMS texts do not fall within the concept of 'correspondence', the notion of which implies a dispatch activity in progress or in any case initiated by the sender by means of delivery to a third party for delivery, nor to the rules on wiretapping.

1630. An interesting civil law case is stated in Civil cassation, section VI of 13 May 2021, No. 12794, about the quality of evidence of computer reproductions of conversations via SMS, email or WhatsApp messages.

On the subject of the probative efficacy of computer reproductions pursuant to Article 2712 of the Civil Code, the disavowal of such reproductions capable of causing them to lose their quality of evidence, degrading them to simple presumptions, must be not only timely, being subject to precise procedural preclusions, but also clear, circumstantial and explicit, and must take the form of the allegation of elements attesting the non-correspondence between factual reality and the reproduced reality.

In order for computer reproductions of a chat to lose the quality of evidence in a trial, a 'clear, circumstantial and explicit' disavowal is required, which must take the form of 'the allegation of elements attesting the non-correspondence between factual reality and reproduced reality'. Therefore, mere references, made by the appellant, to his own defence writings in which he declared that what was represented by the computer reproductions did not correspond to the reality of the facts described therein, are ineffective. This was clarified by the Court of Cassation, thus confirming the importance of computer reproductions of conversations by text message or e-mail. The case at hand concerned an extramarital affair engaged in by the appellant to whom the judges of merit had charged the separation.

1631. Concerning Telegram, Criminal Cassation section II of 7 February 2023, No. 20193 stated that evidence acquired after admission to the abridged procedure in the absence of cross-examination is unusable.

The purpose of terrorism was ascertained by the judges on the basis of a note from the police headquarters informing them of the instruction disseminated by Isis to all affiliates or would-be affiliates to delete texts and contacts from Telegram. Nothing appeared on the defendant's Telegram other than the trace of the deletion of messages and contacts. From this, the Court of Appeal had derived the proof of the terrorist purpose for which the defendant had allegedly frequented sites demonstrating the creation and use of war material, downloading their contents and saving them according to precise and technical cataloguing. Moreover, the same Court had emphasized the Italian defendant's intention to move to Saudi Arabia in order to prove the terrorist purpose of his online information activity. The Court of Cassation annulled the conviction, with referral to the merits phase, due to the flaw in the acquisition of the questor's note, which, according to the judges, had provided a further and decisive element of proof of the second purpose (the terrorist one) necessary to integrate the crime provided for by Article 270-*quinquies* of the Criminal Code.

In fact, the note had been acquired after admission to the abridged procedure and was included in the trial file, but in the absence of cross-examination. It was therefore unusable evidence and now the referring judge will have to prove the existence of the purpose of committing terrorist acts on the basis of the only usable elements that were ritually entered in the trial.

1632. Lastly, Civil cassation, sec. un. of 27 April 2023, No. 11197 discussed about a disciplinary proceeding against magistrates and the use of WhatsApp messages and text messages. According to the judges, in the matter of disciplinary proceedings against magistrates, in support of such usability, of messages and text messages stored in the memory of a mobile phone, it has been repeatedly reiterated that the same, have the nature of documents within the meaning of Article 234 of the Code of Criminal Procedure, and as such can be legitimately acquired by simple photographic reproduction, as neither the regulations on wiretapping nor those on the acquisition of correspondence (Article 254 of the Code of Criminal Procedure) apply in this matter.

In the case, the fact that the material support on which the messages were stored was not acquired is of no relevance whatsoever, since, for the purpose of verifying their origin, the certification of their conformity to the original, which emerges from the transfusion of the same in the reports of the Public Prosecutor and of the President of the Court, which, moreover, as far as it appears, were also included among the relevant addressees, since they were messages circulated through the chat in which all the magistrates of the Office took part, must be considered sufficient.

VII. The Italian Legislative Reform on Trojans

1633. There is a very lively *debate* going on in Italy on the topic of trojan horses ('captatori informatici') used by law enforcement during certain investigations.

The debate originated between 2016 and 2017, following an important decision by the Court of Cassation, United Sections ('Scurato' decision, No. 26889/2016) and a legislative reform ('Orlando Reform', Law 23 June 2017, No. 103)[292] that placed this investigative tool at the attention of scholars.

In 2019, the Law No. 3 of 31 January 2019[293] returned to the subject further, extending the possibility of using trojan horses to *corruption cases*.

1634. The framework is, to date, very *confused*.

On the one hand, the Italian Legislator has formally recognized the possibility of using trojan horses during certain types of investigations, but on the other it has not yet been issued a *technical regulation* that governs the computerized precautions to be taken while using tools that may be harmful for the rights of the suspect.

1635. 1645 One of the parts of the Italian Criminal Procedural Code which was significantly amended by the Law of 23 June 2017, No. 103, starting the implementation of the so-called Orlando Reform, is the one that deals with the regulation of interceptions, a change that was further detailed in the expected Legislative Decree 216/2017.[294]

---

292. *See* https://www.normattiva.it/uri-res/N2Ls?urn:nir:stato:legge:2017-06-23;103.
293. *See* https://www.normattiva.it/uri-res/N2Ls?urn:nir:stato:legge:2019-01-09;3.
294. *See* https://www.normattiva.it/uri-res/N2Ls?urn:nir:stato:decreto.legislativo:2017-12-29;216~art6-com2.

The novel concerned both the 'traditional' wiretapping and those made through the most recent technological tools, referred to as 'trojan horses' or 'data collectors'.

1636. The importance of the 'Orlando Reform' manifests itself, in this attempt to clarify the picture, from a double aspect.

On the one hand, the use of trojan horses entered in the Italian legal system as an investigative tool usable and admitted (within certain limits).

On the other hand, the substantial equivalence between software absolutely *sui generis* for the capturing of any type of data, and a 'simple' instrument for interceptions, despite the intrinsic complexity of trojans, is difficult to admit.

The explicit provision of an obligation, for the Government, to regulate the interception of communications or conversations between present persons by placing trojan horses in portable electronic devices has immediately focused the attention of the interpreters and operators towards the two aspects that most have been criticized in the text of the sentence of the United Sections:

i. the possibility of using the trojan also in private places, and
ii. the possibility of using it even in the absence of the assumption of the commission of the crime.

1637. It was decided, then, to specify that the activation of the microphone can only take place as a result of a specific command sent remotely, and not only with the insertion of the computer sensor, in compliance with the limits established by the judge's authorization decree, and that the registration audio must be initiated by the Judicial Police or by the appointed personnel, on the indication of the operating Judicial Police, who will be required to indicate the start and end time of the recordings, according to circumstances to be attested in the report describing the procedures for carrying out the operations.

1638. The parameters that seem, then, to design the new framework are connected to a constant control by the Judicial Police, to the fact that it will not be possible to have an indiscriminate collection of information in places of private dwelling, limiting the use to cases only in the which in those places a criminal activity is taking place, and to an increase in motivation imposed on the Judge of the Preliminary Investigations in the drafting of the authorization decree: for the first time it is envisaged that such a decree must indicate the reasons for which this specific method of interception is necessary for the carrying out the investigations.

1639. The 'transfer' of the registrations is then regulated, providing that the same must be carried out only to the server of the Prosecutor's Office, so as to guarantee the originality and integrity of the registrations.

1640. A further innovation is that, at the end of the registration, the trojan will have to be *deactivated* and made permanently unusable on the indication of the Judicial Police personnel operating in the specific context.

Only specific computer programs can be used that comply with technical requirements established by (a future) ministerial decree.

1641. At the same time, the power of the Public Prosecutor to use such an instrument in cases of urgency is limited, and the results of the information collected by the collector can be used for trial purposes only of the crimes covered by the authorization provision and may be used in different procedures provided that they are indispensable for ascertaining the crimes referred to in Article 380 of the Criminal Procedure Code.

1642. Protection against the invasive capacity of the sensor would then be guaranteed by the fact that the results of interceptions that have occasionally involved subjects unrelated to the facts for which they are proceeding cannot be known in any way.

If this framework is analysed with a Legal Informatics approach, the principle that most seems to worry the Legislator, and that clearly transpires, is the desire to achieve a *good balance* between the use of innovative tools and the limitation of circulation of data which, inevitably, are acquired without directly involving the suspects and are detrimental to the privacy of the people.

There is almost a sort of 'awareness' that the sensor is 'genetically' designed to intercept any type of information in any context and with reference to all the people in the vicinity of the device or who come into contact and communicate with that computer tool. Without any possibility of distinction.

1643. It should be noted that, despite technical doubts (and awaiting a technical specification), Articles 4, 6 and 7 of Legislative Decree No. 216, however, try to draw an organic picture, addressing the main problems.

Article 266 paragraph 2 of the Code of Criminal Procedure, for example, has been modified indicating that 'in the same cases the interception of communications between present individuals is allowed, which can also be performed through the insertion of a computer sensor on a portable electronic device'.

Therefore, only the interceptions seem to be governed by means of a computer sensor of conversations 'between present' on 'mobile' devices, which are, however, as was said above, only one of the many possible uses of the sensor.

1644. The sensors are inserted in the genus of interceptions between present persons, so they are always allowed in places other than a private residence, while if they are to be carried out in places of private residence they can be authorized by the Judge for crimes other than those indicated by the Code only if they exist justified reason to believe that criminal activity is taking place there (for organized crime offences such interception is always allowed, and therefore even if it takes place in domiciliary places regardless of whether criminal activity is taking place there, and for the crimes of public officials against the Public Administration punished with imprisonment of no less than a maximum of five years, when there is reason to believe that criminal activity is taking place there).

1645. A series of conditions connected to the authorization decrees is, instead, inserted in Article 267 of the Code of Criminal Procedure, requiring that in the case of use of an IT trojan for interceptions on portable devices the authorization decree must indicate the reasons that make this method necessary for the conduct of the investigations and, if there are crimes other than those referred to in Article 51, paragraphs 3-*bis* and 3-*quater*, the places and time, even indirectly determined, in relation to which the activation of the microphone is allowed.

In summary, a further motivational effort is required to justify the use of such an instrument.

Article 268 then modified the methods of conducting interceptions, for which it is possible to make use of suitable persons for the start-up and termination of registrations (therefore: technicians of private companies who manage services interception).

1646. The intercepted communications are transferred exclusively to the plants of the Public Prosecutor's Office, and the data acquired during the operations preliminary to the insertion of the computer sensor on the portable electronic device and the data acquired outside the time and place limits indicated cannot be used in the authorization decree (this last aspect is not easy to understand, and will certainly be better clarified by the Legislator or by the Ministry later on).

1647. As can be seen, the legislative decree did not 'insist' very much on the technical side, limiting itself to a nod to the 'targeted' use of the sensor ('place' and 'time', and a sort of 'switch') for activation and deactivation), on the security that must have the flow of data generated by the sensor (which should reach directly the servers of the Prosecutor) and on the possibility of using 'external' specialized technicians to perform such delicate operations.

The framework will be completed (hopefully) by a technical specification, but it was useful to highlight the most debated Legal Informatics aspects in Italy on this point.

Selected Bibliography

A. Maritati, *Conoscere la Costituzione italiana. Un percorso guidato*, Laterza, 2019.

S. Loffredi, *La Costituzione degli animali. La nascita della Costituzione italiana spiegata ai bambini*, Piemme, 2020.

A. Barbera, *La Costituzione della Repubblica italiana*, Giuffrè, 2016.

V. Cocozza, *Percorsi ricostruttivi per la lettura della Costituzione italiana*, Giappichelli, 2016.

V. Franceschelli, 'Convergenza' (Giuffrè, Milano, 2009).

F. Bassan, 'Diritto delle comunicazioni elettroniche' (Giuffrè, Milano, 2010).

W. D'Avanzo, 'E-government e società del controllo. Il lato oscuro del mondo digitale', Rubbettino, Soveria Mannelli, 2023.

L. Tivelli e S. Masini, 'Un nuovo modo di governare, Fazi, 2002.

A. Rocchi, Nuovi modelli organizzativi nella pubblica amministrazione', Rubbettino, Soveria Mannelli, 2015.

M. Iaselli, 'L'e-procurement', Liguori, Napoli, 2005.

F. Cafiero and A. Lisi, 16 Mar. 2022, 'Codice dell'amministrazione digitale, cos'è e quali sono i punti principali da conoscere', at https://www.agendadigitale.eu/documenti/codice-dellamministrazione-digitale-cose-e-quali-sono-i-punti-principali-da-conoscere/.

G. Manca, 'Breve storia della PA digitale: la genesi e l'evoluzione del Codice dell'Amministrazione Digitale', 6 Jul. 2020, at https://www.agendadigitale.eu/cittadinanza-digitale/breve-storia-della-pa-digitale-la-genesi-e-levoluzione-del-codice-dellamministrazione-digitale/.

S. Patti, 'Le condizioni generali di contratto' (Cedam, Padova, 1996).

L. Nissolino, 'Le clausole abusive nei contratti', 'Il Sole 24 Ore', 2004.

F. Mosconi, C. Campiglio, 'Diritto internazionale privato e processuale' (Utet, Milano, 2022).

S. Armellini, B. Barel, 'Diritto internazionale privato' (Giuffrè, Milano, 2022).

D. Carreau, F. Marrella, 'Diritto internazionale' (Giuffrè, Milano, 2023).

A. Gioia, 'Diritto internazionale' (Giuffrè, Milano, 2022).

A. Tanzi, 'Introduzione al Diritto Internazionale Contemporaneo' (Cedam, Padova, 2023).

M. Lamicela, 'Pratiche commerciali scorrette e rimedi: nuove strategie di private enforcement tra restituzioni e risarcimento' (Giappichelli, Torino, 2024).

Selected Bibliography

G. De Cristofaro (ed.), 'Pratiche commerciali scorrette e codice del consumo: il recepimento della direttiva 2005/29/Ce nel diritto italiano (decreti legislativi nn. 145 e 146 del 2 agosto 2007)' (Giappichelli, Torino, 2008).

M. De Benedetto, 'L'autorità garante della concorrenza e del mercato: organizzazione, poteri, funzioni' (Il Mulino, Bologna, 2000).

G. Colangelo, 'Big Data, piattaforme digitali e antitrust', in 'Mercato, concorrenza, regole', vol. 54 (3), 2016, pp. 425-460.

U. Minneci, G. Greco, L. Ammannati, A. Canepa, 'Algoritmi, Big Data, Piattaforme Digitali – E-Book: La regolazione dei mercati in trasformazione' (Giappichelli, Torino, 2021).

M. Hindman, 'The internet trap : how the digital economy builds monopolies and undermines democracy' (Princeton University Press, Princeton, 2018).

V. Cuffaro, R. D'Orazio, V. Ricciuto, 'I dati personali nel diritto europeo' (Giappichelli, Torino, 2019).

V. Ricciuto, 'Lo scambio di dati con i contenuti e i servizi digitali: una nuova modalità di contrarre?', in 'European Journal of Privacy Law & Technologies', fasc. 1, 2023, pp. 20-33.

M. Sebastiani, 'L'evoluzione dei mercati e la sorte della regolazione dell'accesso nei settori a rete', in 'Economia dei Servizi', fasc. 3, 2010, pp. 471-496.

D. Sorace, 'La desiderabile indipendenza della regolazione dei servizi di interesse economico generale', in 'Mercato, Concorrenza, Regole', fasc. 2, 2003, pp. 337-354.

C.E. Cazzato, S. De Luca, 'Zero rating: tra regolazione e concorrenza. Una prima analisi', in 'Mercato, Concorrenza, Regole', Vol. 57 (3), 2017, pp. 527-546.

P. Lupi, A. Perrucci, 'Quanti giorni in un mese?', in 'Mercato, Concorrenza, Regole', Vol. 59 (2), 2018, pp. 247-268.

G.B. Ramello, F. Silva, A. Nicita (eds), 'La nuova televisione: Economia, mercato, regole' (Il Mulino, Bologna, 2009).

F. Bassan, E. Tosi (eds), 'Diritto degli audiovisivi: commento a nuovo Testo Unico dei servizi di media audiovisivi e radiofonici come modificato dal D. lgs. 15 marzo 2010, n. 44' (Giuffrè, Milano, 2012).

M. Maggiore (eds.), 'Il commercio elettronico: Digital Markets act, Digital Services act e altre dimensioni giuridiche' (Giappichelli, Torino, 2024).

G.B. Ramello, F. Silva, A. Nicita (eds), 'La nuova televisione: Economia, mercato, regole' (Il Mulino, Bologna, 2009).

F. Bassan, E. Tosi (ed.), 'Diritto degli audiovisivi: commento a nuovo Testo Unico dei servizi di media audiovisivi e radiofonici come modificato dal D. lgs. 15 marzo 2010, n. 44' (Giuffrè, Milano, 2012).

S. Lavagnini, 'The Italian implementation of Article 17 of Directive 2019/790: complaints, appeals and the new powers of AGCOM', in 'Journal of intellectual property law & practice', Vol. 17 (5), 2022, pp. 443-449.

S. Parisi, 'Right words, right actions? Il regolamento AGCOM contro l'hate speech nei mass media e la libertà di espressione', in 'Quaderni costituzionali', 2019, pp. 687-690.

A. Preto, B. Carotti, 'Review of Independent Authorities: the Agcom Case', in 'Rivista trimestrale di diritto pubblico', fasc. 1, 2016, pp. 123-154.

R. Mosca, '14 years of AGCOM, what has changed in the Italian TLC since 1998, in L'industria: rivista di economia e politica industriale', Vol. 33 (3), 2012, pp. 429-460.
L. Casini, "Il nastro dei sogni'? Il diritto (pubblico) del cinema e dell'audiovisivo', in 'Aedon', fasc. 3, 2017.
A. Fraternale, 'I contratti a distanza' (Giuffrè, Milano, 2002).
F. Bravo, 'I contratti a distanza nel codice del consumo e nella direttiva 2011/83/UE: verso un codice europeo del consumo' (Giuffrè, Milano, 2013).
M. P. Pignalosa, 'Contratti a distanza e recesso del consumatore' (Giuffrè, Milano, 2016).
G. Pedrazzi, 'Le clausole vessatorie nei contratti telematici con i consumatori', in E. Tosi (ed.), 'La tutela dei consumatori in Internet e nel commercio elettronico' (Giuffrè, Milano, 2012).
G. Finocchiaro, 'Il perfezionamento del contratto on line: opportunità e criticità', in 'Diritto comunitario e degli scambi internazionali', fasc. 1, 2018, pp. 187-202.
G. Ziccardi, 'Crittografia e Diritto' (Giappichelli, Torino, 2003).
C. Giustozzi, A. Monti, E. Zimuel, 'Segreti, spie, codici cifrati' (Apogeo, Milano, 1999).
C. Gallotti, 'Sicurezza delle informazioni' (StreetLib, Lecce, 2022).
D. Baliani, 'Il regime comunitario dei controlli sulle esportazioni di beni a doppio uso', in 'Il Diritto dell'Unione Euroeepa', fasc. 2, 2002, p. 265.
F. Gaspari, 'Recenti sviluppi in materia di regolazione multilivello del commercio di armi: problemi e prospettive', in 'Rivista Italiana di Diritto Pubblico Comunitario', fasc. 2, 2015, p. 423.
F. Minazzi, 'Il codice dell'amministrazione digitale riformato', Giuffrè, Milano, 2017.
G. Vitrani, R. Arcella, 'Il codice dell'amministrazione digitale', Giuffrè, Milano, 2024.
F. Trojani, 'Il nuovo codice dell'amministrazione digitale', Maggioli Editore, Rimini, 2016.
L. Zorloni, 'Come funziona la prima simulazione di voto elettronico in Italia', at https://www.wired.it/article/voto-elettronico-simulazione-ministero-interno-13-14-dicembre/.
R. Scarfato, 'Voto digitale: una soluzione contro l'astensionismo?' at https://www.agendadigitale.eu/cultura-digitale/voto-digitale-una-soluzione-contro-lastensionismo/.
G. Rigobello, 'Questioni digitali e analogiche: la 'digital democracy' nuovamente alla prova della Corte Suprema del Kenya', in 'Diritto dell'Informazione e dell'Informatica' (Il), fasc.2, 1 Apr. 2023, pag. 363.
M. Cian, 'L'intervento e il voto elettronici nelle assemblee di s.p.a.', in Riv. soc., fasc.6, 2011, pag. 1065.
L. Trucco, 'Il voto elettronico nella prospettiva italiana e comparata', in Dir. informatica, fasc.1, 2011, pag. 47.
P. Costanzo, 'Quale partecipazione politica attraverso le nuove tecnologie comunicative in Italia', in Dir. informatica, fasc. 1, 2011, pag. 19.
G. Gometz, 'Democrazia elettronica. Teoria e tecniche', Edizioni ETS, 2017.

F. Orazi and M. Socci, 'Il grillismo. Tra democrazia elettronica e movimento personale', Carocci, Roma, 2014.
D. Pitteri, 'Democrazia elettronica', Laterza, Bari-Roma, 2007, and G. Fioriglio, 'Democrazia elettronica. Presupposti e strumenti', CEDAM, Padova, 2017.
V. E. Vertua, 'La fatturazione elettronica' (Giuffrè, Milano, 2019).
N. Santangelo, 'Guida alla fatturazione elettronica tra privati' (Maggioli Editore, Rimini, 2019).
M. Zavani, P. Di Toma, 'L'innovazione nei processi amministrativi delle PMI. Opportunità e vincoli della fatturazione elettronica' (Franco Angeli, Milano, 2013).
R. Battaglini, M.T. Giordano (eds), 'Blockchain e smart contract: funzionamento, profili giuridici e internazionali, applicazioni pratiche' (Giuffrè, Milano, 2019).
E. Carloni (ed.), 'Codice dell'amministrazione digitale: commento a D.lgs. 7 marzo 2005 n. 82' (Maggioli, Santarcangelo di Romagna, 2005),
R. Arcella, G. Vitrani, 'Il codice dell'amministrazione digitale: disciplina e applicazioni' (Giuffrè, Milano, 2024).
M. Vincenti, M. Sala, 'Manuale di diritto di internet' (La Tribuna, Piacenza, 2003).
C. Leanza, 'L'identità personale nell'era telematica: l'identità digitale', in 'Il diritto di famiglia e delle persone', fasc. 4, 2023.
B. Brunelli, 'Le notificazioni civili nella riforma Cartabia', in 'Rivista trimestrale di diritto e procedura civile', fasc. 1, 2024.
F. Annunziata, 'Il recepimento di MiFID II: uno sguardo di insieme tra continuità e discontinuità', in 'Rivista delle Società', fasc. 4, 2018.
F. Della Negra, 'MiFID II and private law: enforcing UE conduct of business rules' (Hart, Oxford, 2019).
F. Della Negra, 'I rimedi per la violazione di regole di condotta MIFID II: una riflessione di diritto UE', in 'Banca, Borsa, Titoli di Credito', fasc. 5, 2020.
M. Tola, 'Valute virtuali e frode alla legge', in 'Banca, Borsa, Titoli di Credito', fasc. 6, 2023.
G. Corasaniti, 'Prove digitali e interventi giudiziari sulla rete nel percorso della giurisprudenza di legittimità', in 'Diritto dell'informazione e dell'informatica', fasc. 3, 2011.
M. Daniele, 'La formazione digitale delle prove dichiarative: l'esame a distanza tra regole interne e diritto sovranazionale' (Giappichelli, Torino, 2012).
S. Aterno, 'Le investigazioni informatiche e l'acquisizione della prova', in 'Giurisprudenza di merito', fasc. 4, 2013.
M. Rocchi, 'Le prove digitali nel processo civile: profili giuridici e informatico-forensi' (Pacini giuridica, Pisa, 2021).
G. Rognetta, 'L'archiviazione ottica dei documenti: profili giuridici della conservazione digitale dei documenti' (Giuffrè, Milano, 2003).
F. Ruggieri, 'Novità. il protocollo 16 alla cedu in vigore dal 1° agosto 2018. la proposta per l'ordine europeo di conservazione o di produzione della prova digitale', in 'Cassazione Penale', fasc. 7, 2018.
C. Dalia, 'Sanzioni e rimedi individuali 'effettivi' per il consumatore in caso di pratiche commerciali scorrette: le novità introdotte dalla direttiva 2161/2019/UE', in 'Rivista di diritto industriale', fasc. 6, 2020.

L. Guffanti Pesenti, 'Pratiche commerciali scorrette e rimedi nuovi. La difficile trasposizione dell'art. 3, co. 1, N. 5), dir. 2019/2161/UE', in 'Europa e diritto privato', fasc. 4, 2021.

A. Purpura, 'Private enforcement delle pratiche commerciali scorrette: il nuovo comma 15-*bis* dell'art. 27 c. cons', in 'Europa e diritto privato', fasc. 4, 2023.

R. Palma, 'Agro-ecologia e indicazioni geografiche tra magia e razionalità nel diritto dell'UE e dell'OMC: 'reinventare' le designazioni d'origine per preservare l'economia rurale, il patrimonio culturale e l'ambiente', in 'Rivista di Diritto Industriale', fasc. 6, 2017.

M. Imbrenda, 'Filiera agroalimentare e pratiche commerciali sleali', in 'Europa e diritto privato', fasc. 4, 2019.

G. Spoto, 'Le filiere agroalimentari e i divieti di pratiche commerciali sleali', in 'Europa e diritto privato', fasc. 1, 2022.

A. Sardini, 'La 'product liability' e il commercio elettronico', in 'Il diritto dell'informazione e dell'informatica', fasc. 1, 2021.

A. Manganelli, 'Piattaforme digitali e social network, fra pluralità degli ordinamenti, pluralismo informativo e potere di mercato', in 'Giurisprudenza Costituzionale', fasc. 2, 2023, p. 883.

V. Falce, 'Piattaforme ed ecosistemi digitali. Scelte pro-concorrenziali', in 'Rivista di Diritto Industriale', fasc. 4-5-6, 2022, p. 172.

A. Alù, 'La responsabilità dei motori di ricerca: quale regime applicabile?', in 'Diritto di Famiglia e delle Persone' (Il), fasc. 1, 2021, p. 338.

R. Panetta, 'Il ruolo dell'Internet Service Provider e i profili di responsabilità civile', in 'Responsabilità Civile e Previdenza', fasc. 3, 2019, p. 1017.

R. Petruso, 'Responsabilità degli intermediari di Internet e nuovi obblighi di conformazione: robo-takedown, policy of termination, noice and take steps', in 'Europa e Diritto Privato', fasc. 2, 2017, p. 451.

G. Mirabile, 'Le tendenze evolutive della giurisprudenza riguardo alla nozione di attività pericolosa', in 'Responsabilità Civile e Previdenza', fasc. 2, 2018, p. 454.

M. De Cata, 'La responsabilità civile dell'Internet service provider'(Giuffrè, Milano, 2010).

E. Apa, O. Pollicino, 'Modeling the liability of internet service providers: Google vs. Vivi down. A constitutional perspective' (EGEA, Milano, 2013).

R. D'Arrigo, 'Recenti sviluppi in tema di responsabilità degli Internet Services Providers'(Giuffrè, Milano, 2012).

M. Iaselli, 'Responsabilità del provider: la Cassazione detta rilevanti principi di diritto', at https://www.altalex.com/documents/news/2019/03/20/diritto-d-autore-responsabilita-dell-hosting-provider.

R. Panetta, 'Il ruolo dell'internet service provider e i profili di responsabilità civile', in 'Responsabilità civile e previdenza', fasc. 3, 2019, p. 1017.

L. C. Ubertazzi, 'Commentario breve alle leggi su proprietà intellettuale e concorrenza' (Cedam, Padova, 2019).

S. Lavagni, 'Regolamento Agcom sul diritto d'autore: novità e problemi', 2024, at https://www.agendadigitale.eu/mercati-digitali/nuovo-regolamento-agcom-sul-diritto-dautore-novita-e-problemi/.

G. Morretta e L. Brandoli 'Condotta contraffattiva: porta aperta ai danni punitivi', in 'Il Diritto industriale', fasc. 4, 2021.

G. Ghidini, E. Arezzo, 'Il software fra brevetto e diritto d'autore. primi appunti sulla proposta di direttiva comunitaria sulle «invenzioni attuate per mezzo di elaboratori elettronici»', in 'Rivista di diritto industriale', fasc. 1, 2005, p. 46.
V. Falce, 'La disciplina comunitaria sulle banche dati. Un bilancio a dieci anni dall'adozione', in 'Rivista di diritto industriale', fasc. 6, 2006, p. 227.
V. Falce, 'L''insostenibile leggerezza' delle regole sulle banche dati nell'unione dell'innovazione', in 'Rivista di diritto industriale', fasc. 4, 2018, p. 337.
C. Sganga, 'Ventisei anni di Direttiva Database alla prova della nuova Strategia Europea per i Dati: evoluzioni giurisprudenziali e percorsi di riforma', in 'Diritto dell'informazione e dell'informatica', fasc. 3, 2022, p. 651.
M. W. Monterossi, 'Estrazione e (ri)utilizzo di informazioni digitali all'interno della rete internet. il fenomeno del c.d. web scraping?', in 'Diritto dell'informazione dell'informatica', fasc. 2, 2020, p. 327.
T. F. Giupponi, 'Il governo nazionale della cybersicurezza', in 'Quaderni costituzionali', fasc. 2, 2024, p. 277.
I. Forgione, 'Il ruolo strategico dell'agenzia nazionale per la cybersecurity nel contesto del sistema di sicurezza nazionale: organizzazione e funzioni, tra regolazione europea e interna', in 'Diritto Amministrativo', fasc. 4, 2022, p. 1113.
F. Casarosa, G. Comandè, 'Aspettando la NIS2: ovvero il diritto privato della cybersecurity', in 'Diritto dell'informazione e dell'informatica', fasc. 1, 2024, p. 29.
R. Caldarone, G. M. Garegnani, L. Troyer, 'Giurisprudenza e attualità in materia di diritto penale d'impresa - le novità introdotte dal d.lgs. 75/2020 alla normativa 231/2001 in attuazione della 'direttiva pif'', in 'Rivista dei Dottori Commercialisti', fasc. 4, 2020, p. 608.
D. Galletti, 'I modelli organizzativi nel d.lgs. n. 231 del 2001: le implicazioni per la corporate governance', in 'Giurisprudenza commerciale', fasc. 1, 2006, p. 126.
A. Cadoppi, S. Canestrari, A. Manna (eds), 'Cybercrime' (UTET, Milan, 2019).
C. Frediani, 'Cybercrime' (Hoepli, Milan, 2019).
G. Amato-V.S. Destito-G. Dezzani-C. Santoriello, 'I reati informatici' (CEDAM, Padova, 2010).
R. Borruso-G. Buonomo-G. Corasaniti-G. D'Aietti, 'Profili penali dell'informatica' (Giuffrè, Milano, 1994).
L. Lupària (ed.), 'Sistema penale e criminalità informatica' (Giuffrè, Milano, 2009).
P. Galdieri, 'Teoria e pratica nell'interpretazione del reato informatico' (Giuffrè, Milano, 1997).
C. Pecorella, 'Diritto penale dell'informatica' (CEDAM, Padova, 2006).
G. Ziccardi-P. Perri 'Tecnologia e Diritto' (Giuffré, Milano, 2017).
F. Borriello, 'Il ritorno all'origine nei rapporti fra l'esercizio arbitrario delle proprie ragioni e l'estorsione (Nota a Cass. pen., sez. II, 4 dicembre 2013, n. 51433, F.)' in 'Riv. Neldiritto', 2014.
S. Braschi, 'La natura dei reati di ragion fattasi e il loro rapporto con la fattispecie di estorsione: alcuni chiarimenti dalle Sezioni Unite' in 'Dir. Pen. e Proc', 2021, p. 314.
A. Laurino, 'Estorsione, ragion fattasi ed intensità della violenza nella giurisprudenza della suprema corte', in 'Cassazione penale', 2012.
R. Borgogno 'Documento tradizionale e documento informatico, in Le falsità documentali' (a cura di Ramacci, Padova, 2001, p. 73).

R. Borgogno 'Documenti informatici, in Trattato di diritto penale, Parte speciale, Reati contro la fede pubblica' (a cura di Ramacci, X, Milano, 2013).
F. Crimi, 'Falso (delitti di)', in 'Dig. d. pen.', Torino, 2008, Agg. IV, p. 293.
G. Pecorella, 'Diritto penale dell'informatica', Milano, 2006.
L. Picotti, 'Reati informatici', in 'Enc. giur. Treccani', Roma, 1999, Agg., VIII, 1.
C. Sarzana di S. Ippolito, 'Informatica, Internet e diritto penale', Milano, 2009.
L. D. Cerqua, 'Accesso abusivo e frode informatica: l'orientamento della Cassazione', in 'Dir. e prat. Società', 2000, 16, p. 53.
S. Civardi, 'La distinzione fra accesso abusivo a sistema informatico e abuso dei dati acquisiti', in 'Il diritto dell'informazione e dell'informatica', 2009, 1, p. 60.
L. Picotti, 'Sistematica dei reati informatici, tecniche di formulazione legislativa e beni giuridici tutelati', in 'Il diritto penale dell'informatica nell'epoca di Internet' (Padova, 2004).
G. Fiandaca, E. Musco 'Diritto penale – parte speciale' (Zanichelli, Modena, 2023, p. 248).
G. F. D'Aietti 'La tutela dei programmi e dei sistemi informatici' (in Borruso, Buonomo, Corasaniti, D'Aietti 'Profili penali dell'informatica' Milano, 1994).
G. Pecorella, 'sub art. 615-*quater'*, in 'Comm. Dolcini, Marinucci sub art. 615-*quater'*.
G. Pica, 'Diritto penale delle tecnologie informatiche' (UTET, Torino, 1999).
G. Pecorella 'Dieci anni di giurisprudenza sui reati informatici: i principali problemi interpretativi sollevati dalle nuove disposizioni', in Cocco (a cura di) 'Interpretazione e precedente giudiziale in diritto penale' (CEDAM, Padova, 2005, p. 241)
G. Corasaniti 'La tutela della comunicazione informatica e telematica', in Borruso, Buonomo, Corasaniti, D'Aietti 'Profili penali dell'informatica' (Giuffrè, Milano, 1994, p. 111).
F. Mantovani 'Diritto penale. Parte speciale II' (Wolters Kluwer, Alphen aan den Rijn, 2022).
M. Orofino, F.G. Pizzetti (eds) '*Privacy, minori e* cyberbullismo' (Giappichelli, Turin, 2018).
C. Parodi 'Stalking e tutela penale: le novità introdotte nel sistema giuridico dalla l. 38/2009' (Giuffrè, Milano, 2009).
G. Ziccardi, P. Perri 'Tecnologia e Diritto' (Giuffré, Milano, 2017).
B. Romano 'Reati contro la persona, III. Reati contro la libertà individuale' (Giuffré, Milano, 2015).
G. M. Caletti '*Revenge porn'. Prime considerazioni in vista dell'introduzione dell'art. 612-ter c.p.: una fattispecie 'esemplare', ma davvero efficace?*' in ' www.penalecontemporaneo.it', 2019.
G. Vaciago '*Digital evidence. I mezzi di ricerca della prova digitale nel procedimento penale e le garanzie* dell'indagato' (Giappichelli, Torino, 2012).
M. Iaselli '*Investigazioni* digitali' (Giuffrè, Milano, 2020).
S. Aterno, F. Cajani, G. Costabile, D. Curtotti (eds) '*Cyber forensics e indagini digitali. Manuale tecnico-giuridico e casi* pratici' (Giappichelli, Torino, 2021).
G. Ziccardi, L. Lupária '*Investigazione penale e tecnologia informatica.* L'accertamento del reato tra progresso scientifico e garanzie fondamentali' (Giuffrè, Milano, 2007).

Selected Bibliography

L. Marafioti, 'Digital evidence e processo penale', in 'Cass. pen.', n. 12/2011, 2011, p. 4509B.

V. Plantamura, 'La tutela penale delle comunicazioni informatiche e telematiche', in 'Dir. inform.', fasc. 6/2006, 2006, p. 847.

D. Scarpino, '*Intercettazioni e delitti di 'criminalità organizzata' tra vecchi problemi e nuove* soluzioni', in 'Cassazione Penale', fasc. 5, 2024, p. 1657.

F. N. Ricotta, '*Questioni sull'utilizzo della backdoor a scopo di* investigazione', in 'Cassazione Penale', fasc.7-8, 2022, p. 2836.

F. Centorame, '*Le indagini tecnologiche ad alto potenziale intrusivo fra esigenze di accertamento e sacrale inviolabilità dei diritti della* persona', in '*Rivista Italiana di Diritto e Procedura* Penale', fasc. 2, 2021, p. 499.

F. N. Ricotta, '*Obblighi di collaborazione con l'autorità giudiziaria nella decrittazioone dei dispositivi informatici e privilegio contro l'auto-*incriminazione', in 'Cassazione Penale', fasc. 2, 2022, p. 880.

M. Pittiruti, '*Dalla Corte di cassazione un vademecum sulle acquisizioni probatorie informatiche e un monito contro i sequestri digitali* omnibus', in 'Sistema Penale', 2021, https://www.sistemapenale.it/it/scheda/cass-sez-vi-sent-22-settembre-2020-dep-2-dicembre-2020-n-34265-pres-di-stefano-rel-silvestri.

M. Pisati, '*Full collection of data e diritto di* difesa', in 'Rivista Italiana di Diritto e Procedura Penale', fasc.4, 2019, p. 2239.

S. Aterno, '*Le investigazioni informatiche e l'acquisizione della prova* digitale', in 'Giur. Merito', fasc. 4, 2013, p. 0955.

O. Mazza, '*Critica delle prove atipiche nella deriva* giurisprudenziale', in 'Diritto di Difesa', fasc.1, 2022, p. 59.

A. Capone, '*Intercettazioni e Costituzione: problemi vecchi e* nuovi', in 'Cassazione Penale', fasc.3, 2017, p. 1263.

R. Orlandi, '*Usi investigativi dei cosiddetti captatori informatici. Criticità e inadeguatezza di una recente* riforma', in 'Rivista Italiana di Diritto e Procedura Penale', fasc. 2, 2018, p. 538.

W. Nocerino, '*Il captatore informatico: un giano bifronte. Prassi operative vs. risvolti* giuridici', in 'Cassazione Penale', fasc. 2, 2020, p. 824.

Index

The numbers here refer to paragraph numbers.

www.ingramcontent.com/pod-product-compliance
Ingram Content Group UK Ltd.
Pitfield, Milton Keynes, MK11 3LW, UK
UKHW020130290926
15471UKWH00003B/404

9 789403 528793